SOLUTIONS TO CASES IN MANAGEMENT ACCOUNTING AND BUSINESS FINANCE

Published in 2007 by
The Institute of Chartered Accountants in Ireland
CA House, Pembroke Road
Ballsbridge, DUBLIN 4

Designed and typeset by Compuscript, Shannon, Ireland
Printed by Four Print, Dublin, Ireland

ISBN-13   978-0-903854 26 9

SOLUTIONS TO CASES IN MANAGEMENT ACCOUNTING AND BUSINESS FINANCE

Edited by Noel Hyndman and Donal McKillop

The Institute of Chartered Accountants in Ireland
Dublin

Preface to Solutions and Contents

These solutions have been prepared by the author(s) and offer indicative, rather than definitive, answers to the cases. They are provided in order to support lecturers as they use the cases in a classroom/lecture application. As appropriate, they contain, among other things, computations for quantitative requirements, discussions of qualitative factors and recommended courses of action. Many are presented in report or memorandum form, as demanded by the author(s) in the case requirements. As they use the material, lecturers may develop alternative approaches for some of the cases. If this is so, they are invited to submit such ideas to the editors by email (n.hyndman@qub. ac.uk or dg.mckillop@qub.ac.uk) so that they may be considered in any future edition.

The solutions are numbered as per the case book, with the solutions to the management accounting cases being presented first (section A), followed by the solutions to the cases in business finance (section B).

Section A: Cases in Management Accounting

Section B: Cases in Business Finance

SECTION A

SOLUTIONS TO CASES IN MANAGEMENT ACCOUNTING

Case 1

Solution to Malvern Limited

Ciaran Connolly, Queen's University Belfast

Question 1

a) Raw Materials Budget (kgs)

	June (kgs)	July (kgs)	August (kgs)	September (kgs)
Opening stock	100	85	50	26
Purchases	150	160	150	140
	250	245	200	166
Production (1½ kgs per unit)	(165)	(195)	(174)	(135)
Closing stock	85	50	26	31*

Finished Goods Budget (Towing mechanisms)

	June	July	August	September
Opening stock	110	100	105	106
Production	110	130	116	90
	220	230	221	196
Sales	(120)	(125)	(115)	(100)
Closing stock	100	105	106	96**

b) Sales Budget

	June	July	August	September	Total
	€	€	€	€	€
Sales (€300 each)	36,000	37,500	34,500	30,000	138,000

Production Cost Budget

	June (110)	July (130)	August (116)	September (90)	Total
	€	€	€	€	€
Material (€40 × 1½ kgs)	6,600	7,800	6,960	5,400	26,760
Wages & var. o/hs (€70)	7,700	9,100	8,120	6,300	31,220
	14,300	16,900	15,080	11,700	57,980

Closing Stock at 30th September 2XX6

| Raw materials | *31 kgs @ €40 | = €1,240 |
| Towing mechanisms | **96 towing mechanisms @ €110 | = €10,560 |

Debtors at 30th September 2XX6

	€
August sales	34,500
September sales	30,000
	64,500

Creditors at 30th September 2XX6

| September purchases (140 × €40) | €5,600 |

c) Cash Budget

	June €	July €	August €	September €
Receipts:				
Debentures		150,000		
Sales (W1)	5,900	13,100	36,000	37,500
Total receipts	5,900	163,100	36,000	37,500
Payments:				
Machinery		130,000		
Raw materials (W2)	3,400	6,000	6,400	6,000
Wages & var. overheads (W3)	7,700	9,100	8,120	6,300
Fixed overheads	3,500	3,500	3,500	3,500
Total payments	14,600	148,600	18,020	15,800
Net cash flow	(8,700)	14,500	17,980	21,700
Balance b/f	(17,250)	(25,950)	(11,450)	6,530
Balance c/f	(25,950)	(11,450)	6,530	28,230

Workings:

1. Sales
- April – debtors of €5,900 (Appendix 1 of case study) are received two months later in June.
- May – debtors of €13,100 (Appendix 1 of case study) are received two months later in July.
- June – credit sales of €36,000 (see sales budget) are received in August.
- July – credit sales of €37,500 (see sales budget) are received in September.

2. *Raw material purchases*
   - May – credit purchases of €3,400 (Appendix 1 of case study) are paid for one month later in June.
   - June – credit purchases of €6,000 (€40 × 150 kgs) are paid for one month later in July.
   - July – credit purchases of €6,400 (€40 × 160 kgs) are paid in August.
   - August – credit purchases of €6,000 (€40 × 150 kgs) are actually paid in September.

3. *Wages and variable overheads*
   - These vary with production and there is no delay involved in payment (see production cost budget).

Question 2

MEMORANDUM

FROM: A. Adviser
TO: Tony
RE: Budgetary Control

The budgeting information that you have prepared has proved most useful in the recent past as an aid to planning and for negotiations with our lenders. However, we can make further use of this information by using it as a means of controlling actual activities. We can record the actual activities and compare this with the planned activities. If we discover any differences between the two we can undertake an investigation to discover why actual activities are not as planned and take remedial action where necessary.

In order to identify those responsible for the variances, the information must be reported in responsibility-centre format. Therefore I suggest you analyse the monthly budget figures into the following responsibility centres: stores, production, selling and distribution and administration. Each report should only include those revenues and costs for which the manager is responsible. A possible layout for the monthly departmental reports might be:

	Monthly Values			Cumulative Values		
	Actual	Budget	Variance	Actual	Budget	Variance
Department:	€	€	€	€	€	€
Cost line						

Where appropriate, each report should include non-financial information, such as number of units produced, to support the financial data.

Within 10 days of each period end, forward the reports on stores and production to Fred and the other two directly to me. This timing is very important as it ensures that corrective action can be taken, where necessary, as soon as possible. Fred may be reluctant to use the information at first. He may feel that you are 'spying' on him and, because he has coped up to now without this information, he may question why it has suddenly become necessary. You should explain to him that the reports are designed to help him control his areas of responsibility and that they show him the financial consequences of his operational decisions. Emphasise that he has nothing to fear from the reports and that they will form the basis of discussions between us on a regular basis in the future.

In instigating the new system, you must be prepared to change and adapt the reports as our knowledge of the business improves. Be prepared to amend the reports on the basis of the users' comments and in the light of their changing needs.

Question 3

The newly purchased machinery will be delivered and installed in June 2XX6 and paid for the following month. The purchase price of €130,000 appears to have been met through the debenture issue of €150,000, with the additional €20,000 possibly being to cover installation and commissioning costs and initial working capital requirements. The additional investment of €30,000 is not to purchase machinery to replace the newly acquired plant, but to enhance its capabilities, thus enabling Malvern Limited to expand its potential market. The following points should be borne in mind.

Effect on Existing Production Requirements

With 30% spare capacity, the additional production should not pose any difficulties unless demand outstrips total production capacity. However, it may not be possible to utilise full capacity, so careful production scheduling may be required. In addition, Malvern Limited may have existing contractual commitments and therefore may have to schedule additional orders to avoid disruption. Examining production schedules and records may determine the nature and extent of the spare capacity. Maintenance records may be of little use because the machinery is new.

Staffing

Current labour may be insufficient to produce the new towing mechanisms, and the cost of hiring additional labour will reduce the profitability of entering the new market. Examining standard cost data for current production and wage records compared with manufactured output should give an indication of labour requirements.

Expertise

The company must have the expertise to produce the new towing mechanisms and be able to provide adequate customer support to new customers. Repeat orders might not be forthcoming. Consultation of personnel records and discussion with Fred, the factory supervisor, should indicate the expertise of current staff and the availability of suitable temporary staff. Although, this point may be irrelevant if the new towing machines are substantially the same as those currently produced.

Furthermore, if the company is to continue to grow in the medium to long term and maintain its position within the industry, plans need to be put in place for suitable research and development activities. This expertise and creativity may have been lost following the departure of Bill Malvern and may lead to problems in the future.

Purchase Consideration

The purchase price of the new machinery will have to be met and so availability of finance will have to be investigated. While Kate has arranged an overdraft facility of

€30,000, this is not a sensible way of financing the investment. Leasing may be an alternative, or perhaps the land, which appears to be undervalued, could be used as security. Longer term finance requirements could be met through the development or sale of the unused land.

Benefit to the Company

Even if the investment is an enhancement of existing productive capacity, the benefits to the company should be compared with the cost to determine the net benefit to the firm. For such a small amount, simple payback may suffice. However, expected future benefits, in the form of incremental revenues less incremental cost, will need to be determined. Kate should make trade enquires about how much she will be able to charge for the new towing mechanisms and the likely size and frequency of orders. The cost of direct materials and labour, as well as variable production overheads will need to be estimated, perhaps by Tony using existing cost records. Tony will need to bear in mind that use would be made of existing spare capacity and so care will need to be taken to ensure that only relevant costs of production are included.

New Market

Entering new markets is risky, but utilisation of existing spare capacity reduces the risk to the company's current operations. Kate will need to investigate the proposed new market, perhaps by talking with managers of companies currently in the field. This might be through local trade contacts or professional contacts. An alternative to entering the market as a new competitor would be to determine whether any current manufacturers of the 'new' towing mechanism had excess demand, and so were looking to find someone to subcontract the work to. This would give Kate an assured outlet for the extra production without the need to secure new customers, although there would be a lower price to balance against the increased convenience and security.

Fred the Supervisor

Fred's resistance to change could make things very difficult as far as the production of new items was concerned. It will be important that key members of staff support the changes and feel part of the decision making process.

Question 4

Budgeted Profit and Loss Account for the
Four Months to 30th September 2XX6

	€	€
Sales (per sales budget)		138,000
Cost of sales:		
Opening stock of finished goods (per 31/5/x6 balance sheet)	12,100	
Production costs (per production budget)	57,980	
	70,080	
Closing stock of finished goods (see closing stock calculation)	(10,560)	(59,520)
Gross profit		78,480
Expenses:		
Fixed costs (€3,500 × 4)	14,000	
Depreciation (€500 + €16,000 + €5,500)	22,000	(36,000)
Operating profit		42,480
Accrued debenture interest (€150,000 × 10% 3/12 months)		(3,750)
Retained profit for the year		38,730
Retained profit brought forward (per 31/5/x6 balance sheet)		56,450
Retained profit carried forward		95,180

Budgeted Balance Sheet as at 30th September 2XX6

	€	€	€
Fixed Assets	Cost	Acc. Depn.	NBV
Land and buildings	120,000	(20,500)	99,500
Machinery (incl. additions €130,000)	180,000	(60,000)	120,000
Vehicles	52,000	(21,500)	30,500
	352,000	(102,000)	250,000
Current Assets			
Raw materials (see closing stock calculation)		1,240	
Finished goods (see closing stock calculation)		10,560	
Debtors (see debtors calculation)		64,500	
Bank (see cash budget closing balance)		28,230	
		104,530	
Creditors: amounts falling due within 1 year			
Trade creditors (see creditor calculation)		(5,600)	
Accrued debenture interest (see P & L)		(3,750)	95,180
			345,180
Creditors: amounts falling due after more than 1 year			
10% debentures			(150,000)
			195,180
Capital and Reserves			
Ordinary share capital			100,000
Profit and loss account			95,180
			195,180

Case 2

Solution to Quoile Industries

Noel Hyndman, Queen's University Belfast

Internal Memorandum

Topic: Issues Facing Quoile Industries

To: Crawford Bell, Chairman, Quoile Industries
From: Sonia O'Hare, Finance Director, Quoile Industries
Date: XXXX

1. Introduction

Further to your communication of xx/xx/xx, I present the memorandum requested dealing with the issues that you have raised. It contains:

(a) An analysis of the current budgeting and standard costing system as used by Quoile Industries identifying eight major weaknesses, explanations of the possible consequences of these, and recommendations for improvement. As requested, this is presented in tabular format.
(b) Calculations of the market size and market share variances with respect to the FB2008 flatbed trailer, together with comments on their interpretation.
(c) Calculations as to profitability and breakeven with respect to the possible acquisition of a forklift truck manufacturer, and a suggestion as to the possible course of action that should be pursued by Quoile Industries in this regard.

Should you wish to discuss the matters raised in this memorandum, I am more than happy to discuss them with you on your return from the Ukraine.

2. The Current Budgeting and Standard Costing System: Weaknesses, Consequences and Recommendations

As requested, Table 1 contains an analysis of the current budgeting and standard costing system (including the bonus system for sales staff) and outlines major weaknesses, consequences of such weaknesses and recommendations for improvement.

Table 1 – Major Weaknesses, Consequences and Recommendations*

Weakness	Consequences	Recommendations
(a) Lack of strategic planning. This was discontinued several years ago because of difficulties in predicting the external environment.	Shorter term plans (such as budgets) should align with a well developed strategic plan that considers, among other things, key objectives of major stakeholders, the external environment which the company faces and the internal strengths and weaknesses of Quoile. A lack of strategic planning makes budgeting difficult. In addition, it makes it problematical to decide on the appropriateness of strategic possibilities (such as the decision to acquire a forklift manufacturing company).	Need to reintroduce strategic planning in order to provide direction to Quoile Industries and to provide a benchmark against which to evaluate strategic choices.
(b) There is a lack of appropriate analysis of discretionary cost budgets (such as advertising, training and research and development). In addition, cuts in these budgets are being considered on an arbitrary basis.	It is possible that significant expenditure may be incurred that is contributing little to the organisation. Conversely, in an attempt to meet short-term budget objectives (such as profit or cash flow), insufficient expenditure may occur in key areas, possibly resulting in an inability to meet long-term objectives. Given the company's desire to be at the leading edge of technological development, major reductions in research and development budgets may have an exceptionally deleterious impact.	Postpone the proposed reductions in these budgets. Consider the use of zero-base budgeting, or at least a review of expenditures in these areas.
(c) The only personnel involved in budget preparation are three directors. Other personnel, who are expected to achieve the budget, are not consulted.	Budgets may be unrealistic because much information that could be useful is not available. There may also be a lack of commitment by middle managers to the budget targets because of their non-involvement in the budget-setting process.	Much greater participation should be facilitated. Possibly consider the establishment of a budget committee with the key departments having representation.
(d) Budget preparation commences only two months before the commencement of the budget period.	This is too late to commence a comprehensive budget process and may result in unrealistic budgets being set and a lack of proper co-ordination.	Need to commence the process much earlier. Should begin with the identification of the key budget factor (appears to be sales in Quoile at present, but there is limited evidence that it should be).

(e)	The budget appears to be largely sales driven but hard information on sales forecasts appear not to be collected and used. The budgets for sales volumes and sales prices are derived on the basis of the judgement of the sales director.	This will affect the accuracy of the control information produced, particularly with respect to sales. If the budget is inappropriate, then control is weakened. The sales budget has a major impact on all cost budgets.	Need to acquire better 'hard' sales information as a basis for better budgeting. Market information (in home market and export market) should be obtained.
(f)	The sales director, who is a major player in developing the budget, benefits from the sales team achieving the sales budget through the bonus system. The sales budget is viewed by many company personnel as being 'soft'.	The perception, or perhaps reality, of the sales budget being 'soft' undermines the legitimacy of the budget targets and may cause resentment from non-sales employees. In addition, it may result in an easily achievable sales target that results in underperformance by sales staff.	Given his much wider responsibilities, the sales director should be rewarded on the basis of overall company profit rather than merely achievement of sales targets. In addition, steps should be taken to ensure that sales budgets are realistic and stretching (see previous point).
(g)	To reward the entire sales team on the basis of achievement of the sales budget may be inappropriate.	Given that many sales staff work independently of one another, such a team bonus system is unlikely to provide the correct motivational stimulus. In addition, it may encourage 'free riders'. Overall, the present bonus system may result in lower total sales.	Individual sales targets should be established for members of the sales team and these used for bonus purposes.
(h)	Bonuses are paid to sales staff once a year.	The lag between effort and reward may be too long to provide the most effective stimulus for sales staff.	Bonuses should be awarded each month on the basis of monthly sales against target.
(i)	Standard cost information is not developed in a scientific way. As a result standard costs may be inaccurate.	Poor standards lead to poor control and, given that the standards are used as a basis for budgeting, they also result in inaccurate budgets.	Need to review standard costs in order to make them more realistic and better instruments for control. More scientific investigation is required for the technical standards required. More hard information for cost standards is also required.
(j)	Variance information, although reported, is not acted upon.	The lack of reaction to reported variances undermines the usefulness of the standard costing system (and weakens control procedures within the company). For example, if major adverse cost variances are reported and no corrective action undertaken, then significant excess expenditure would be incurred by the company. It is likely that the existence of inaccurate cost standards has influenced the behaviour of managers.	Once the standard costs have been revised to make them more accurate, managers should be required to provide explanations (and action plans, if necessary) for significant variances for which they are responsible.

*Note: only eight are requested in the memorandum but 10 are included for teaching and learning purposes.

3. *FB2008: Market Size and Market Share Variances*

The market size and market share variances for FB2008 flatbed trailer are (shown in Appendix 1) are summarised here:

Market size variance = **€5,250,000 (F)**
Market share variance = **€3,750,000 (A)**

Comments relating to these are:

(a) Due to the fact that the size of the market for flatbed trailers was larger than anticipated (62,500 rather than 45,000), Quoile's contribution should have been €5.25 million higher (the market size variance) from FB2008. This would have been the case if Quoile's market share had been 10% (as budgeted).

(b) However, Quoile only achieved 8% of the market for flatbed trailers (rather than 10%). This resulted in a loss of possible contribution of €3.75 million (the market share variance), reflecting a reduction of 2% in the company's market share (1,250 fewer units at a standard margin of €3,000 per unit).

(c) The claim by the sales director that the sales team is doing well in terms of market share with respect to the FB2008 is erroneous.

4. *Possible Acquisition of a Forklift Truck Manufacturer*

As you are aware, the production director is keen to engage in the strategic acquisition of a forklift truck manufacturer. Two possible acquisition candidates (both in North America) have been identified: Boucher Forklifts, based in Ottawa in Canada (which produces the Carleton); and Jackson Engineering, based in Tallahassee in the USA (which produces the Wakulla). An evaluation of these mutually exclusive options is given below.

(a) Expected Profitability of Boucher and Jackson Proposals

Appendix 2 presents detailed calculations of the expected profitability of each of the options. The calculations are based on the expected sales prices, costs and sales volumes made available. Some of the key features of the analysis can be summarised as follows:

	Boucher Forklifts – Carleton	Jackson Engineering – Wakulla
Expected annual profit in local currency	C$19,896 k	US$17,025 k
Expected annual profit in €s	€14,211 k	€13,620 k
Lowest possible profit in local currency	-C$3,000 k	US$350 k
Lowest possible profit in €s	-€2,143 k	€280 k
Highest possible profit in local currency	C$30,920 k	US$29,350 k
Highest possible profit in €s	€22,086 k	€23,480 k

Comments:

- The total expected profit is higher with Boucher (€14,211 k compared to €13,620 k).
- However there is a 5% chance that a loss will be made with Boucher; there is no possibility of a loss with Jackson.
- The worst possible outcomes are a loss of €2,143 k with Boucher (probability 5%) compared with a profit of €280 k with Jackson (probability 5%).
- The best possible outcomes are €22,086 k (probability 35%) with Boucher compared with €23,480 k with Jackson (probability 5%).

(b) Return on Investment and Payback for the Two Options

Appendix 3 presents detailed calculations of the expected return on investment (ROI) and payback of the Boucher and Jackson options. The key figures produced are:

	Boucher Forklifts Carleton	Jackson Engineering Wakulla
Total investment €s k	114,286	84,000
Return on investment	12.4%	16.2%
Payback (years)	8.04	6.17

In producing these calculations, the following assumptions were made:

- Profit equals cash flow.
- The year one profit and investment figures will continue at these levels in future years.
- From a payback perspective, the annual cash inflows will occur evenly throughout the year.

Comments on the ROI and payback:

- The investment required for the Boucher is over 35% higher (€114,286 k compared with €84,000 k).
- Because of this, even though the expected profit of Jackson is lower, the ROI for Jackson is 3.8% higher at 16.2%.
- Similarly, given the much more substantial investment required for Boucher, the payback from Jackson is somewhat shorter at just over six years.

(c) Breakeven Sales Relating to the Boucher and Jackson Options

Detailed calculations of the breakeven points for each option are shown in Appendix 4. These illustrate that the breakeven points for the two options are:

	Boucher Forklifts Carleton	Jackson Engineering Wakulla
Breakeven sales units	10,708	9,903
Breakeven sales in value (local currency) :		
• Boucher (C$ k)	149,906	
• Jackson (US$ k)	111,414	
Breakeven sales (€s k)	107,075	89,131

Comments:

- The contribution per unit is higher with Boucher (€3,028 compared with €2,900).
- However, the fixed costs relating to Boucher are higher (in excess of €32 million compared with less than €29 million).
- Overall, this results in a higher breakeven point (in both sales value and units) for Boucher.

(d) Recommendation on Course of Action

The following issues would need to be considered when deciding on whether or not to pursue the acquisition of a forklift truck manufacturer:

- The extent to which the numbers provided in the above analysis could be relied upon would need to be investigated further.
- The return on investment is 16.2% with Jackson and 12.4% with Boucher. This should be compared with the risk-free rate of perhaps 5% to indicate the extent of the risk premium. Given the riskiness of the venture, being an overseas acquisition in an area where Quoile has no previous expertise, a risk premium of about 11% may be inadequate.
- The payback period for Jackson is just over six years compared with over eight for Boucher. This should be compared with any cut-off that Quoile uses for the evaluation of capital projects.
- The breakeven points with both projects are relatively low considering the range of possible sales volumes that could be achieved.
- Management's attitude to risk needs to be weighed up. Jackson appears less risky as it makes a profit at all anticipated sales levels. In addition, Jackson offers the greatest possible outcome if 18,000 units are sold.
- The availability of finance would have to be established. Obviously the acquisition of Boucher would require substantially more finance.

- Both of the acquisition targets are relatively young companies. Any potential sales growth should be brought into the analysis.
- If these products could be sold profitably to Quoile's existing customers then substantial additional profits could be made. More detailed investigation of this should be undertaken.
- Whether or not this is an appropriate strategic direction for Quoile is unclear. More consideration of strategy should be undertaken (see above points relating to the budgeting system).
- Given that each of these options has foreign exchange implications, an analysis of potential foreign exchange risk should be undertaken.
- Does management at Quoile have sufficient time and expertise to manage and/ or oversee an acquisition?
- Will a commitment to either acquisition target lock away management's capacity to deal with other, possibly more appropriate, options that could arise in the near future?
- The extent to which Quoile can rely on the management of either of the acquisition targets would have to be established.
- The tax implications of an overseas subsidiary would need to be considered.
- Quoile has no experience in the manufacture of forklift trucks.

Recommendation:
Of the two identified options, Jackson is preferable (higher return on investment, lower payback, lower breakeven sales, less investment required. less risky). However, I believe such a decision should be deferred for now because:

- No strategy for Quoile Industries has been developed and agreed.
- This is a high risk course of action given that Quoile has limited knowledge of manufacturing (or managing the manufacture of) forklifts.
- The potential returns are insufficient to warrant the level of risk.
- While the acquisition of a forklift manufacturer is favoured by the production director, no other key personnel appear to have been involved in the decision to date.
- The available information on which to base such a key decision needs to be more thoroughly investigated and established; and
- A more sophisticated financial analysis (using discounted cash flow techniques and cost of capital figures) should be undertaken before a decision is made.

Appendix 1
Market Size and Market Share for Previous Year for Product FB2008

Actual sales in units = Sales price variance in total/Sales price variance per unit

= €2,500,000 (F)/€500 (F)

= 5,000 units

Sales volume variance (units) = Sales volume variance (€s)/Standard margin per unit (€s)

= €1,500,000/€3,000

= 500 units

Budgeted sales (units) = Actual sales in units − Sales volume variance in units

= 4,500

Actual sales = 8% actual market (i.e. 8% = 5,000 units)

Therefore actual industry sales volume = 5,000/.08

= 62,500 units

Budgeted sales = 10% market
Therefore budgeted market size (units) = 45,000 (i.e. 4,500/.10)

Market size variance = Budgeted market share % × (Actual industry sales volume − Bud individual sales volume)

× standard margin per unit.

= 10% × (62,500 − 45,000) × €3,000

= €5,250,000 (F)

Market share variance = (Actual market share % − Budgeted market share %) × Actual industry sales volume ×

standard margin per unit.

= (8% − 10%) × 62,500 × €3,000

= €3,750,000 (A)

Appendix 2
Expected Profitability of the Two Options

Boucher Forklifts – Carleton

	Cont/unit C$	T. Cont C$ k	FCs C$ k	Profit C$ k	Prob	EV C$ k
10,000	4,240	42,400	45,400	−3,000	0.05	−150
12,000	4,240	50,880	45,400	5,480	0.15	822
14,000	4,240	59,360	45,400	13,960	0.20	2,792
16,000	4,240	67,840	45,400	22,440	0.25	5,610
18,000	4,240	76,320	45,400	30,920	0.35	10,822
					C$ k	19,896
					€s k	14,211

Jackson Engineering –Wakulla

	Cont/unit US$	T. Cont US$ k	FCs US$ k	Profit US$ k	Prob	EV US$ k
10,000	3,625	36,250	35,900	350	0.05	18
12,000	3,625	43,500	35,900	7,600	0.10	760
14,000	3,625	50,750	35,900	14,850	0.40	5,940
16,000	3,625	58,000	35,900	22,100	0.40	8,840
18,000	3,625	65,250	35,900	29,350	0.05	1,468
					US$ k	17,025
					€s k	13,620

Appendix 3
Return on Investment and Payback of the Two Options

	Boucher Forklifts Carleton C$ k	Jackson Engineering Wakulla US$ k
Anticipated cost of investment:		
Consideration	140,000	80,000
Further investment in new technology	20,000	25,000
Total investment required in local currency	160,000	105,000
Exchange rate per €	1.40	1.25
Total investment €s k	**114,286**	**84,000**
Expected profitability (€s k)	14,211	13,620
Return on investment	**12.4%**	**16.2%**
Payback (years)	**8.04**	**6.17**

Appendix 4
Breakeven Calculations Relating to the Options

	Boucher Forklifts Carleton	Jackson Engineering Wakulla
	C$	US$
Variable costs (per unit):		
Production	8,500	7,000
Selling	1,260	625
Total	**9,760**	**7,625**
Selling price	14,000	11,250
Contribution per unit	**4,240**	**3,625**
	C$ k	**US$ k**
Fixed costs (total):		
Production	27,800	25,800
Selling	7,200	3,000
Administation	10,400	7,100
Total	**45,400**	**35,900**
Breakeven sales units	10,708	9,903
Breakeven sales in value (local currency) :		
Boucher (C$ k)	149,906	
Jackson (US$ k)		111,414
Breakeven sales (€s k)	107,075	89,131

Case 3

Solution to Toffer Group plc

Ciaran Connolly, Queen's University Belfast

Question 1

For decision making, only future costs and revenues are relevant. Past costs are gone (sunk) and should be ignored, although there may be psychological influences to the contrary. Marginal costing, because it concentrates on variable costs, is more in line with decision-making theory. This is not to say that fixed costs are not relevant; they can be manageably variable, i.e. to the individual company a general manager's salary is a fixed cost but to James Grant in the future such a cost is manageably variable.

Question 2

Marginal costing allows a greater degree of flexibility to a decision maker, particularly for short-term strategies. It may be that James Grant is looking for short-term improvement to justify investment, or the concentration on volume output, or the switching of production between plants, all of which are more easily accomplished on a marginal approach. In the longer term, however, all costs must be accounted for and contributions must be sufficient to cover every fixed cost.

Question 3

There are a number of possible alternatives:

a) The hi-low approach (or variations upon it) which, by comparing the highest and lowest levels of activity isolates the variable element. For example:

Hours of activity	Overhead
	€
Lowest 3,000	6,000
Highest 9,000	13,200

A step of 6,000 hours gives an increase in overhead of €7,200, therefore €7,200/6,000 = €1.20 per hour, i.e. the variable element.

At the 3,000 level of activity, variable cost is €3,600 (€1.20 × 3,000) so fixed cost must be €2,400 (€6,000 – €3,600). At 9,000 hours, V.C. = €10,800 and F.C. = €2,400.

b)   Scatter graph techniques (lines of the best fit).

c)   Method of the least squares.

Question 4

Contribution per hour, Department Y the constraining factor:

Product	Alpha	Beta	Gamma
Contribution	€30	€55	€64
Hours in Department Y	6 hours	8 hours	10 hours
Contribution per hour	€5.00	€6.875	€6.40

Question 5

This may be achieved by maximising profit in the short term, and subject to employment and redundancy legislation. The maximum profit could be achieved by producing products in the order of their highest contribution factor per unit of limiting factor (Alpha, Beta and Gamma).

Hours available in Department Y:

6 hours × 5,000	=	30,000
8 hours × 2,000	=	16,000
10 hours × 3,000	=	30,000
		76,000

The available hours are allocated to the products in the order of their contribution per hour. The maximum demand for Beta and Gamma is 4,000 units of each. The remaining hours are allocated to Alpha. Maximum profit is therefore:

		Hours		€
Beta	4,000 × 8	32,000 × €6.875	=	220,000
Gamma	4,000 × 10	40,000 × €6.40	=	256,000
				72,000
Alpha	Balance	4,000 × €5.00	=	20,000
		76,000		496,000
Fixed overhead				152,000
Profit				344,000
Extra profit over original budget				44,000

Question 6

Redundancy in Departments X and Z:

Produce	Units
Alpha (See note)	666
Beta	4,000
Gamma	4,000

Note: 666 units of Alpha are to be manufactured, i.e., 4,000 hours in Department Y at 6 hours per unit.

Product	Original hrs		Max. profit hrs		Reduction in hrs
Department X:					
Alpha	5,000 × 30	150,000	666 × 30	19,980	
Beta	2,000 × 15	30,000	4,000 × 15	60,000	
Gamma	3,000 × 32	96,000	4,000 × 32	128,000	
		276,000		207,980	68,020
Department Z:					
Alpha	5,000 × 15	75,000	666 × 15	9,990	
Beta	2,000 × 8	16,000	4,000 × 8	32,000	
Gamma	3,000 × 32	96,000	4,000 × 32	128,000	
		187,000		169,990	17,010

Then redundancy, Department X:	68,020 / 1,920	=	35 employees
Department Z:	17,010 / 1,920	=	9 employees

Question 7

Bebe:

Financial statement for last year in marginal form:

	No. of units	Per unit (€)	€'000
Sales	8,000	1,000	8,000
MC of sales:			
Variable cost of product	12,000	500	6,000
Less stock	(4,000)	500	2,000
			4,000
Contribution			4,000
Fixed costs:			
Production		2,880	
Selling		1,200	4,080
Loss			80

Note:

Per Appendix 3, profit under an absorption approach is €880,000. Under marginal costing, there is a loss of €80,000, resulting in a total difference of €960,000. This is explained as follows:

Stock values per machine, €740 (absorption) and €500 (marginal).

Therefore, €240 × 4,000 units stock = €960,000.

Question 8

(a)   Absorption costing principles

	No. of units	Per unit (€)	€'000
Sales	12,000	1,000	12,000
Production cost:			
Variable cost	12,000	500	6,000
Fixed cost	12,000	240	2,880
		740	8,880
Stocks:			
Opening	4,000	2,960	
Closing	4,000	2,960	
			-
			8,880
Factory profit			3,120
Selling etc.			1,200
Net profit			1,920

(b)   Marginal costing principles

	No. of units	Per unit (€)	€'000
Sales	12,000	1,000	12,000
Cost of sales:			
Variable cost	12,000	500	6,000
O/stock & C/stock	4,000		
			-
Contribution			6,000
Fixed costs (€2,880 + €1,200)			4,080
Net profit			1,920

See how, when production and sales are the same, profit is €1,920,000 under either system of accounting. Profit differences arise where there are changes in the level of stocks.

Question 9

(a)   Absorption costing principles

	No. of units	Per unit (€)	€'000
Sales	16,000	1,000	16,000
Production cost:			
Opening stock	4,000	740	2,960
Variable cost	12,000	500	6,000
Fixed cost	12,000	240	2,880
			11,840
Factory profit			4,160
Selling etc.			1,200
Net profit			2,960

(b)   Marginal costing principles

	No. of units	Per unit (€)	€'000
Sales	16,000	1,000	16,000
Cost of sales:			
Opening stock	4,000	500	2,000
Variable cost	12,000	500	6,000
Contribution			8,000
Fixed costs (€2,880 + €1,200)			4,080
Net profit			3,920

When sales exceed production, the marginal system reports higher profits (profit difference is stock movement × €240 = €960,000).

Question 10

	Absorption €'000s	Marginal €'000s
Last year	880	(80)
This year	1,920	1,920
Next year	2,960	3,920
Total over three years	5,760	5,760

The total over the three-year cycle is the same, yet the individual years may differ. Decisions are based on reported profits, and therefore policy in Bebe would most likely be different if a loss had been reported as opposed to the profit.

Question 11

In support of absorption costing:

- Modern manufacturing techniques result in highly specialised machinery, e.g. robots, without which there would be no production. This fixed cost in the form of depreciation is the core cost of production and must therefore be included in the valuation of stock.
- The 'matching' principle of accounting is satisfied, i.e. costs and revenues are matched in the same period. In seasonal trades this avoids the phenomena of fictitious profits and losses occurring.
- Profit trends are directly related to production activity, therefore the figures generated by the system can more easily be used to monitor and control day to day affairs.
- There are inherent dangers with the marginal approach. The temptation to obtain orders or retain products on low contribution margins can lead to over-trading, or a final profit that cannot be justified on the level of investment.

In support of marginal costing:

- It allows much greater flexibility to a decision maker, who can see more easily what are the consequences of changing volumes of production or regulating sales demand through pricing. This advantage is very necessary in highly competitive situations, particularly perhaps during a recession.
- It avoids the very arbitrary apportionment of company fixed costs, which at all times can result in misleading profit reports upon which decisions may be based.
- Under/over absorption of overheads can be largely avoided, i.e. where production levels vary widely from a 'normal capacity' level this can give rise to strange accounting.
- Some would argue that a fair proportion of company fixed cost (rates, salaries, depreciation etc.) are incurred in relation to time. Within a period they cannot be avoided no matter what level of output is achieved, and therefore it follows the 'prudence' concept to write off such costs in the period to which they relate and not anticipate profit. Profit flow and cash flow are also more fairly matched.

Question 12

The need to consider both quantitative and qualitative factors.
Budgets can be useful for:

- Co-ordination of departments;
- Communication between managers;
- Control;
- Making planning happen, etc.

Need to identify and forecast the budgeting information required:

- Limiting factors, e.g. sales demand;
- Costs - direct and indirect;
- Cost behaviour - variable and fixed;
- Cost centres, e.g. different department and administration etc.;
- Allocation and apportionment bases;
- Stock levels.

Also, it could be useful to set up a budget committee and involve departmental heads in the budget construction. This participation may encourage more realistic forecasts and may lead to greater motivation to achieve targets.

Not only are quantitative aspects important i.e. the motivations, aspirations, capabilities, and reactions of individual people also need to be considered.

Specific examples of behavioural issues might be as follows:

- How will managers react to budgets? Probably not favourably unless they are introduced with their support and co-operation;
- Managers may also need convincing of the potential benefits. Some may prefer being 'told' what they need to achieve, rather than being involved;
- Budgets may cause resentment and 'dysfunctional' behaviour if they are not designed and implemented carefully.

Reference may be made to Hopwood (1976) *Accountancy and Human Behaviour* e.g. budget-constrained style, profit-conscious style and non-accounting style. Other points include:

- Evaluation of managers performance could be discussed;
- The aim is to alter the behaviour of individuals by encouraging them to act in the best interests of the organisation as a whole;
- Budget pressure may lead to tension, feelings of failure and a focus on weaknesses rather than positive aspects of work;
- Setting budget targets may increase motivation. The level of difficulty needs careful consideration as too high a level may de-motivate, being perceived as too difficult;
- The educational role of the accountant may also be mentioned.

Question 13

Machinery bought 10 years ago is a 'sunk' cost and of no consequence. If the machinery had a saleable value then this income would be of benefit if the work were transferred elsewhere. Of course, the theory must be modified in real situations where there are psychological and political consequences. For example the accounts would disclose a loss on sale of €25,000, and this coupled with perhaps highly emotional industrial relations might be unacceptable.

Question 14

The decision should be based on relevant costs:

	1,000 Navigators €
Direct material	32,500
Direct labour	40,000
Indirect labour	10,000
Power	1,500
Maintenance	1,000
Sundries	500
Insurance	75
Electricity	675
Canteen & welfare	1,250 **
	87,500

Cost from Turpin Limited is also €87.50/unit (€85 + €2.50 shipping etc.).

** The relevant canteen and welfare cost is obtained using the proportion of directly attributable labour costs (€40,000 + €10,000) compared with total labour for the department (€105,000 + €35,000).

Therefore, $\dfrac{€50,000 \times €3,500}{€140,000} = €1,250$

Question 15

Clearly the figures are finely balanced. There would seem to be no advantage in transferring the work to Turpin Limited. Note, however, if the figures for the Navigator component had been based on full cost, i.e. including some portion of fixed overhead, as opposed to relevant cost, substantial savings would have seemed possible. Such figures are in danger of being 'politically' manipulated, the fixed overhead again, for example, such fixed costs are not relevant to the decision. However, a transfer of work away from the department will reduce its capability of recovering these costs on the remaining output, and therefore expose the employees to further schemes to achieve 'greater efficiency'.

Ian's view on morale is valid; also important are trade unions' attitudes and redundancy costs. It is well known, however, that multinational companies can appear justifiably to move work amongst their divisions on 'transfer prices' which at times seem strangely artificial.

Case 4

Solution to Castlegrove Enterprises
Tom Kennedy, University of Limerick

Pedagogical Objectives

The case is intended to make students aware of the difficulty in determining the most appropriate costing systems to use in organisations and the application of those systems in different situations. The case content has the potential to cover all three elements of management accounting; namely full costing, differential costing and responsibility accounting.

Required:

To prepare a draft set of guidelines and briefing notes on how McGuire might structure her presentation to the Castlegrove senior management team. Your response should deal with the overall concerns expressed by Maloney and the specific issues arising from the new product decision.

Report from the management consultant to Mary McGuire, Castlegrove Accounting Manager.

Presentation Objective

The overall aim of your presentation should be to convince the Castlegrove senior management team of the potential contribution that the management accounting function can make to strategic development and its operational implementation. It should facilitate an inclusive discussion on how to address the substantive issues raised by Maloney and, specifically, in regard to the projected performance of the 'Pulse' project. The presentation should be pitched at a level suitable for a non-accounting audience. It should result in an understanding of the context and the language that accountants use to communicate economic information on a regular basis.

Presentation Structure

In order to achieve your objective, I suggest that you use the following structure or an appropriate variation. I, also, attach some background notes in the Appendix that your colleagues might find useful.

(i)   Overview of the management accounting framework.
(ii)   Overview of the different costing system choices facing organisations, with particular reference to Castlegrove`s situation.
(iii) Presentation of a revised variable costing income statement for 2XX6 and 2XX7.
(iv)   Presentation of an absorption costing income statement for 2XX6 and 2XX7.
(v)   Explanation of the difference between the operating income statements.
(vi)   Key issues to be addressed by the Castlegrove senior management team in reviewing the projected performance of the 'Pulse' new product line.

I advise you to prepare your presentation slides from the attached supporting material and edit, as appropriate, to suit your specific audience, style and the time available. I have prepared the supporting material, based on our discussions and the information you gave me. I, also, reviewed the Castlegrove audit file. Based on your experience to date, I emphasise that your task is not likely to be achieved at a once-off event. I see it as part of a long-term and on-going educational process.

Executive Summary

Castlegrove should continue to use its job costing system to determine the cost of its products. It should present its operating income statements under both absorption and variable costing formats. Absorption costing is required in order to satisfy statutory and regulatory requirements. Variable costing is a fundamental component of the managerial decision-making process and you should exploit the capability you have acquired in classifying costs between fixed and variable. Consequently, the reliability and relevance characteristics of good accounting information are delivered and this underpins the integrity of non-routine decision making at Castlegrove. This should mitigate against dysfunction behaviour and motivate all management to seek the more efficient use of resources and agree optimal performance levels.

The application of variable costing can, also, help to highlight the phenomenon of 'unintended consequences' through inventory building caused by absorption costing. The 'Pulse' project provides some evidence of how this could happen and this aspect of the project needs to be addressed, as a matter of urgency. Specifically, the appropriate balance between the production and sales volumes projected for 'Pulse' needs to be reviewed in order to protect its viability and the overall Castlegrove business performance. Revised operating income statements should then be prepared and regularly updated to reflect performance.

Castlegrove should continue to use the normal costing valuation method in order to incorporate some element of pre-determination. The choice of the practical capacity denominator is appropriate for its financial reporting, product costing and pricing requirements. Some thought should be given to replacing volume with transaction-based drivers in order to better identify the underlying causes of its overhead. The above scenario at Castlegrove is consistent with the notion that there are 'different systems for different purposes'.

Finally, in addition to operating both cost classification systems to varying degrees, Castlegrove could develop its own balanced scorecard set of performance measures in order to reduce the emphasis on financial measures. This would widen the scope of performance evaluation and, if properly implemented, could encourage behaviour that is consistent with the organisations strategy.

Supporting Material

(i) Overview of the management accounting framework

Definition

There are many different definitions of management accounting. As a compromise, one could adopt the normative definition put forward by Wilson and Chua (1993) 'managerial accounting encompasses techniques and processes that are intended to provide financial and non-financial information to people within the organisation to make better decisions and, thereby, achieve organisational control and enhance effectiveness'.

Relationship with Financial Accounting

- Optional versus mandatory
- Internal focus largely versus external
- Future versus the past
- Disaggregated versus aggregated
- Subjective versus objective

Primary Functions of Management Accounting

- Inventory valuation/profit determination (full costing – scorekeeping)
- Decision-making (differential costing – problem solving)
- Operational control and performance measurement (responsibility accounting – attention directing)

Scope of Management Accounting

Management accounting is important in its ramifications and social impact and is not just a collection of techniques. It can range from social/behavioural to closed/prescriptive/rational. The challenge today is 'how to put the management back into management accounting', (Otley, 2001, British Accounting Review, 33, 243–261).

Changing Role of Management Accountant

- From functional to holistic
- From what to why and how
- From inward looking to outward looking
- From backward looking to forward looking
- From accountant to information manager
- From country based to global
- From slave to technology to master of technology
- From closed department overhead role to integrated specialist

(ii) Overview of the different costing system choices facing organisations, with particular reference to Castlegrove's situation

Objective of a costing system: To record, classify, trace and assign costs for inventory valuation/profit determination, decision-making and performance measurement purposes.

There are three substantive questions that organisations need to address before deciding on the appropriate costing system(s) to use

(a) What costing system to use in order to assign costs to products or services?
(b) What cost classifications to make?
(c) What valuation method to adopt?

(a) What costing system to use?

Job costing and process costing are the <u>principal systems</u> that determine the cost of products or services through the <u>assignment of costs to the cost object</u> (product or service). In practice, hybrid systems can be used for different parts of the operation. The choice of system should reflect the underlying operations of the business, provide information that is useful for financial reporting and decision-making and be subject to a cost/benefit test.

Specific to Castlegrove
Castlegrove currently uses a job costing system, because of the product-oriented layout of its plant and the relative uniqueness of its individual product lines and customers. Some consideration could be given to using activity-based costing, as the cost profile of the plant has changed in recent years, due to automation. However, like any commodity, its installation should be subject to a cost/benefit test. This is unlikely to be positive at this time.

Process costing is not appropriate, because Castlegrove does not mass-produce homogeneous products. I understand some consideration has been given to changing the plant layout to a more functional model, due to the overlap in the material specifications for some of the products and in order to maximise machine utilisation. This may result in the introduction of a process costing system to that part of the plant in the future.

(b) What cost classifications to make?

Variable costing, absorption costing and throughput costing systems primarily describe the <u>cost classifications</u> or <u>types of cost</u> included in inventory. These classifications are <u>direct material, direct labour, variable or fixed overhead</u>. The absorption costing format includes all four cost classification elements, variable costing includes direct material, direct labour and variable overhead and throughput costing only includes direct material. These systems or formats can all be used with job, process or hybrid costing systems. The manner in which an organisation can operate these systems is quite flexible. Surveys of company practice show that up to 30% of companies use them as standalone, with many others extracting the relevant variable cost data from their absorption costing system.

Specific to Castlegrove

Castlegrove currently uses an absorption costing system to value its inventory. This 'full costing' approach is in compliance with regulatory accounting standards and is the current basis used by Castlegrove for performance measurement, both internally and externally. This means that the fixed manufacturing overhead element of product cost, associated with 'Pulse', is recorded on Castlegrove`s balance sheet as an asset and only expensed when the product is sold.

Castlegrove currently uses a variable costing presentation format to inform its decision-making process. It extracts the relevant information from the absorption costing system, as it does not have the resources or the need to operate two standalone systems. This is the appropriate basis to use in assessing the likely impact of non-routine decisions, such as whether it should manufacture 'Pulse'. This format means that the fixed manufacturing overhead element of product cost associated with 'Pulse' is expensed in the period in which it is incurred and is not recorded on Castlegrove`s balance sheet as an asset. This decision-relevant approach seeks to identify the quantitative differential costs and revenues associated with a decision. It does not reflect the qualitative factors, which should always be considered before the final decision is made.

(c) What valuation method to adopt?

Actual costing, normal costing, and standard costing describe the <u>valuation method</u> than can be used by the job or process costing systems. This reflects the timeframe and the degree of sophistication used to prepare the income statements. An actual costing system records costs historically. Normal costing involves some element of pre-determination by incorporating a budgeted indirect or manufacturing overhead rate. Standard costing incorporates 'carefully' set standards for all inputs and facilitates comparison with the outputs. All three systems can be used in conjunction with the absorption costing, variable costing or throughput costing cost classification processes.

Specific to Castlegrove

Castlegrove currently uses a normal costing system. This allows it to accumulate its product costs by recording the direct manufacturing (material & labour) costs by product line and adding the appropriate level of indirect costs using a predetermined overhead rate by product line. It operates this in conjunction with a budgeting system that is organised by responsibility centre. This process involves estimating the overhead for the year, allocating it and re-allocating it to the production cost centres and classifying it into fixed and variable. It then selects the appropriate absorption base and the activity level in order to compute the pre-determined overhead rate by product line.

Castlegrove currently uses allocation bases such as floor area, book value of equipment, number of employees and the value of material to allocate overhead that it cannot trace directly to its cost centres. It then uses an agreed formula to re-allocate the approximate benefit received by the production departments resulting from the administration and engineering support departments. I understand, this formula has been the subject of intense debate at the annual budget meetings and is likely to continue to be a contentious issue.

Castlegrove currently uses volume (number of units) as the absorption base, primarily because of its size and the nature of its product lines. As it grows and develops new products, it could consider alternatives such as machine hours, labour hours and percentage of material costs. As its product variety and level of automation increases, it may need to look at a more sophisticated way of determining the underlying 'drivers' of its overhead by using activity-based costing.

Castlegrove currently uses the practical capacity denominator level, as it is required for financial and tax reporting purposes. This recognises the fact that capacity usually takes time to build up and that some reasonable level of excess is sustainable in the early stages of any product life cycle. This denominator level identifies the cost of idle/excess capacity and, in effect, treats it as a planning variance. It is important that the performance evaluation process takes that into account and holds management accountable for the operational aspect over which they have control. In practice, this is impossible to achieve because of the natural interdependencies that exist in most organisations. A working compromise that could be discussed is 'to hold managers accountable for the performance areas that you want them to pay attention to' (Merchant, 1998), even if they have less than full control.

By using the practical capacity denominator level, management should be able to make a better-informed and more sustainable long-term pricing decision. This is particularly important in a new and/or highly competitive market, where a company should not seek to recover too large a burden of fixed manufacturing overhead at the outset or recover the cost of its idle capacity too quickly. If it attempts to do this, by using the master-budget level denominator, it may fall well short of achieving its immediate sales targets. This can lead to the company becoming more un-competitive, losing more market share and being effectively in a sales volume 'downward spiral'.

(iii) Revised variable costing income statement for 2XX6 and 2XX7

The revised variable costing statements, in Appendix 1, provide useful information for managerial decision-making. They supplement the information presented to the board in October 2XX5 and show that 'Pulse' is generating a very acceptable level of 'contribution' at €22 per unit. They confirm that the expected profit-volume ratio is well in excess of the company target of 20%, at 26% (€22/€85). They, also, confirm the break-even level of sales at approximately 4,109 units (€90,400/€22) and the very acceptable anticipated margin of safety of 25% (1,391/5,500) in 2XX6 and 37% (2,391/6,500) in 2XX7. Based on this information, the board was right to approve the 'Pulse' project. It is projected to contribute €30,600 and €52,600 to operating income in 2XX6 and 2XX7, respectively. This should act as a stimulus to the commercialisation of the other new product ideas under investigation.

(iv) Absorption costing income statement for 2XX6 and 2XX7

As Castlegrove must prepare an absorption costing income statement for financial and tax reporting, the anticipated performance of 'Pulse' is presented, using that method, in Appendix 2. This shows that the projected operating income for 2XX6 and 2XX7 is €39,600 and €64,600 respectively. Appendix 2 shows the 'full' cost for 'Pulse' and that it is well capable of paying its 'fair share' of overhead. This positive outcome is evidenced by the projected gross margin of 22% and the increase in operating income from 8% in 2XX6 to 12% in 2XX7.

However, caution needs to be exercised in interpreting the operating income increase from 2XX6 to 2XX7. This increase has the potential to give a misleading impression, as it is partly driven by the choice of capacity denominator and inventory valuation methodology. This aspect is addressed under the next heading.

(v) Explanation of the difference between the operating income statements

In identifying the difference between the operating income statements, it is useful to summarise them by (a) year and (b) by format.

(a) Difference by year

As the variable costing statements reflect the impact of sales only, this results in the 1,000 additional sales units in 2XX7 adding €22,000 to the operating income, as shown in Appendix 3. This means that Castlegrove's operating income for 2XX7 gets the 'full contribution' effect of the additional 1,000 sales units, as it is projected to be operating well above the breakeven point that year.

As the absorption costing statements reflect the impact of both sales and production volumes, this results in the additional 1,000 sales units in 2XX7, combined with the comparative stock increase of 500 units (sales +1,000/production + 1,500), adding €25,000 to the bottom line, as shown in Appendix 3. This means that the Castlegrove operating income statement in 2XX7 is getting the benefit of deferring an additional €3,000 of fixed manufacturing overhead allocated to the 500 'Pulse' units at €6 per unit.

(b) Difference by format

As the variable costing statements treat fixed manufacturing overhead as a period cost, the €60,000 budgeted fixed manufacturing overhead is written off in both years. In contrast, the absorption costing statements treat fixed manufacturing overhead as part of product cost and assign the amount associated with the units still in inventory. This means that the €9,000 (1,500 units × €6) assigned to inventory in 2XX6 and the €12,000 (2,000 × €6) assigned to inventory in 2XX7 account for the difference between the projected operating income statement under the different formats. In effect, €51,000 (€33,000 + €18,000) of the fixed manufacturing overhead will be expensed in 2XX6 and €48,000 (€39,000 + €9,000) in 2XX7 under absorption costing versus €60,000 under variable costing in both years.

(vi) Key issues to be addressed by senior management in reviewing the projected performance of the 'pulse' product line

The projected positive results, prepared by you for the first two years of the project, confirm its strong viability. This is also the case, if one extrapolates the data for another three years, as I have done in the attached Appendices 5, 6 and 7. Based on your cost data and incorporating the stated assumptions about production and sales volume, the 'Pulse' project is projected to increase operating income significantly each year, under both formats.

However, the projected operating income statements mask a potential significant problem in regard to the appropriate balance that is sustainable between production and sales volume, particularly with the launch of a new product. A small variation that is well managed and part of an integrated sales and production strategy, is to be expected and is sustainable. However, Appendix 4 presents a situation, which is worrying at this early stage.

Appendix 4 shows a continuous and significant stock build-up that peaks at the end of 2XX8. As a result, Castlegrove would need to be able to finance a stock valuation that rises to approximately €300,000. This is a significant figure for Castlegrove, based on its previous history and I suggest it needs to be reviewed, as a matter of urgency. The following profile maybe a useful way to generate some serious discussion, so that agreement can be reached now on the appropriate action, rather than later in crisis mode.

> Year-end stock level 2XX6: 1,500 units or about 12 weeks 2XX7 anticipated sales
> Year-end stock level 2XX7: 3,500 units or about 24 weeks 2XX8 anticipated sales
> Year-end stock level 2XX8: 4,525 units or about 27 weeks 2XX9 anticipated sales
> Year-end stock level 2XX9: 4,429 units or about 23 weeks 2X10 anticipated sales

The above profile is completely at variance with the sales strategy articulated by Jones and reflects the need to ensure that the individual goals of the sales and production managers are synchronised in the best interests of Castlegrove The problem could be further exacerbated by Holmes's personal anxiety to increase plant capacity utilisation further in the short-term. As the projected income statements, do not properly reflect this underlying trend, there is a real danger that a significant write-off of unsaleable stock may have to take place at a later date or plant capacity for 'Pulse' may have to be retired for a prolonged period, with obvious consequences.

Alternatively, this situation could lead to undue pressure being placed on Jones to deliver more sales, even if it means pushing distributors and wholesalers beyond comfortable stocking levels. This manifestation of serious dysfunctional behaviour needs to be tackled by the managing director and the board, if necessary, in order to protect the underlying viability of 'Pulse' and Castlegrove's business, in general. The following questions would be a good basis to start the discussion with:

- What strategy is Castlegrove pursuing, in regard to 'Pulse'? Is it one of cost leadership, product differentiation or some combination of both?
- Can sales volume be boosted by pursuing a more aggressive pricing and/or marketing strategy?
- What is the logic in building up such high levels of inventory, when the vast majority of sales are anticipated to be made to order?
- Should production be more closely matched with sales projections, even if it means 'retiring' some of the skilled operatives and running the plant at a lower capacity level? What are the cost implications of these alternatives?
- Can some of the plant capacity be used for some other productive internal purposes or outsourced?
- Is there any potential for productivity and expenditure improvements?
- Is this the time to incorporate a carrying charge for inventory in order to reflect its financing cost?

The outcome of this review process should be reflected in a revision of the projected revised operating income statements. These should then become the basis of the performance evaluation process and be subject to revision in the usual way.

Brief summary of the merits of variable and absorption costing systems

Absorption Costing

- Consistent with financial and tax reporting requirements
- Does not understate the importance of fixed costs
- Fixed costs are assigned to the product rather than to the passage of time
- Avoids fictitious losses being reported for businesses with a high degree of seasonality
- Theoretically superior to variable costing, because of the application of the revenue production concept

Variable Costing

- Provides more useful information for decision-making and has a more user friendly format

- Removes from profit the effect of stock changes
- If used as a basis for performance reward system, can help to prevent the unnecessary build up of inventory or 'cherry picking' products with high fixed manufacturing overhead absorption rates
- Avoids fixed costs being capitalised in unsaleable stocks

Different capacity options available and their possible application

Possible Capacity Levels	Possible Applications (Not Definitive)
Theoretical	Academic
Normal	Product Costing/Capacity Management and Pricing
Practical	Financial Statements/Regulatory Requirements
	Product Costing/Capacity Management and Pricing
Master-Budget	Performance Evaluation

Appendix 1
Projected Operating Income Statement for 'Pulse'

Revised Variable (Relevance) Costing Statement

Period: 12 months ended	Dec 2XX6		Dec 2XX7	
	Unit €	Gross €	Unit €	Gross €
Revenue	85	467,500	85	552,500
Variable Costs				
Variable Manufacturing				
Direct Material	5	27,500	5	32,500
Direct Labour	25	137,500	25	162,500
Variable Manufacturing overhead	30	165,000	30	195,000
Variable Cost of Goods Sold	60	330,000	60	390,000
Variable Non-Manufacturing overhead	3	16,500	3	19,500
Total Variable Costs	63	346,500	63	409,500
Contribution Margin	22	121,000	22	143,000
Fixed Costs				
Fixed Manufacturing overhead		60,000		60,000
Fixed Non-Manufacturing overhead		30,400		30,400
Total Fixed Costs		90,400		90,400
Operating Income		30,600		52,600
Note				
Sales (units)		5,500		6,500
Production (units)		7,000		8,500
Breakeven level of sales (units)		4,109		4,109
Profit-volume ratio		26%		26%
Margin of safety		25%		37%

Appendix 2
Projected Operating Income Statement for 'Pulse'

Absorption Costing Statement

Period: 12 months ended	Dec 2XX6			Dec 2XX7		
	Unit €	Gross €	%	Unit €	Gross €	%
Revenue	85	467,500		85	552,500	
Cost of Goods Sold						
Variable Manufacturing						
Direct Material	5	27,500		5	32,500	
Direct Labour	25	137,500		25	162,500	
Variable Manufacturing overhead	30	165,000		30	195,000	
Fixed Manufacturing overhead absorbed	6	33,000		6	39,000	
Cost of Goods Sold	66	363,000		66	429,000	
Gross Margin	19	104,500	22	19	123,500	22
Production Volume Variance	3.27	18,000	*	1.38	9,000	*
Adjusted Gross Margin	15.73	86,500	19	17.62	114,500	21
Operating Costs						
Variable Non-Manufacturing overhead	3.00	16,500		3.00	19,500	
Fixed Non-Manufacturing overhead	5.53	30,400		4.68	30,400	
Total Operating Costs	8.53	46,900		7.68	49,900	
Operating Income	7.20	39,600	8	9.94	64,600	12

Note 1

Stock Input/Output Matrix (units)	2XX6	2XX7	Difference
Opening	0	1,500	1,500
Production	7,000	8,500	1,500
Less Sales	5,500	6,500	1,000
Closing	1,500	3,500	2,000
Stock Movement	**1,500**	**2,000**	**500**

Note 2

Production-Volume Variance	2XX6	2XX7
Practical Capacity Denominator Level (units)	10,000	10,000
Actual Production (units)	7,000	8,500
Under/Over Recovery (units)	3,000	1,500
Fixed Manufacturing Overhead Rate per Unit €	6.0*	6.0*
Production-Volume Variance €	18,000	9,000

*€60,000/10,000 units

Appendix 3
Difference in Operating Income Between the Two Statements

Operating Income	Dec 2XX6	Dec 2XX7	Difference
Variable (Relevance) Costing	30,600	52,600	−22,000*4
Absorption Costing	39,600	64,600	−25,000*3
Difference	**−9,000*1**	**−12,000*2**	

*1 1,500 (Stock Increase) Units at €6 fixed mnfg o/head p.u.

*2 2,000 (Stock Increase) Units at €6 fixed mnfg.o/head p.u.

*3 1,000 (More Sales) Units at €19 (gross margin) p.u. + PVV €9k - Var NMF o/head 1,000 Units at €3 p.u.

*4 1,000 (More Sales) Units at €22 contribution p.u.

Fixed Manufacturing overhead Reconciliation	€ Dec 2XX6	€ Dec 2XX7
Fixed Manufacturing overhead absorbed	33,000	39,000
Add Production Volume Variance	18,000	9,000
Add Profit Difference (Absorption v Variable)	9,000	12,000
= Budgeted Fixed Manufacturing Overhead	60,000	60,000

Appendix 4
Projected Stock Input/Output Matrix (units)

Details	2XX6	2XX7	2XX8	2XX9	2X10	Summary
Opening	0	1,500	3,500	4,525	4,429	0
Production	7,000	8,500	8,500	8,500	8,500	41,000
Less Sales	5,500	6,500	7,475	8,596	9,885	37,956
Closing	1,500	3,500	4,525	4,429	3,044	3,044
Stock Movement	1,500	2,000	1,025	−96	−1,385	3,044
Stock Valuation (p.u.)	€66	€66	€66	€66	€66	
Stock Valuation (gross)	€99,000	€231,000	€298,650	€292,314	€200,904	

Appendix 5
Absorption Costing Statement

Period: 12 months ended	Dec 2XX6			Dec 2XX7			Dec 2XX8			Dec 2XX9			Dec 2X10		
	Unit €	Gross €	%	Unit €	Gross €	%	Unit €	Gross €	%	Unit €	Gross €	%	Unit €	Gross €	%
Revenue	85	467,500		85	552,500		85	635,375		85	730,660		85	840,225	
Cost of Goods Sold															
Variable Manufacturing															
Direct Material	5	27,500		5	32,500		5	37,375		5	42,980		5	49,425	
Direct Labour	25	137,500		25	162,500		25	186,875		25	214,900		25	247,125	
Variable Manufacturing overhead	30	165,000		30	195,000		30	224,250		30	257,880		30	296,550	
Fixed Manufacturing overhead absorbed	6	33,000		6	39,000		6	44,850		6	51,576		6	59,310	
Cost of Goods Sold	66	363,000		66	429,000		66	493,350		66	567,336		66	652,410	
Gross Margin	19	104,500	22	19	123,500	22	19	142,025	22	19	163,324	22	19	187,815	22
Production Volume Variance	3.27	18,000	*	1.38	9,000	*	1.20	9,000	*	1.05	9,000	*	0.91	9,000	*
Adjusted Gross Margin	15.73	86,500	19	17.62	114,500	21	17.80	133,025	21	17.95	154,324	21	18.09	178,815	21
Operating Costs															
Variable Non-Manufacturing overhead	3	16,500		3	19,500		3	22,425		3	25,788		3	29,655	
Fixed Non-Manufacturing overhead	5.53	30,400		4.68	30,400		4.07	30,400		3.54	30,400		3.08	30,400	
Total Operating Costs	8.53	46,900		7.68	49,900		7.07	52,825		6.54	56,188		6.08	60,055	
Operating Income	7.20	39,600	8	9.94	64,600	12	10.73	80,200	13	11.41	98,136	13	12.01	118,760	14

Note 1

Stock Input/Output Matrix (units)

	2XX6	2XX7	2XX8	2XX9	2X10
Opening	0	1,500	3,500	4,525	4,429
Production	7,000	8,500	8,500	8,500	8,500
Less Sales	5,500	6,500	7,475	8,596	9,885
Closing	1,500	3,500	4,525	4,429	3,044
Stock Movement	1,500	2,000	1,025	−96	−1,385
Stock Valuation €	99,000	231,000	298,650	292,314	200,904

Note 2

Production-Volume Variance Calculation

	2XX6	2XX7	2XX8	2XX9	2X10
Practical Capacity Denominator Level (units)	10,000	10,000	10,000	10,000	10,000
Actual Production (units)	7,000	8,500	8,500	8,500	8,500
Under/Over Recovery (units)	3,000	1,500	1,500	1,500	1,500
Fixed Manufacturing Overhead Rate per unit €	6 *	6 *	6 *	6 *	6 *
Production-Volume Variance €	18,000 *	9,000 *	9,000 *	9,000 *	9,000 *

*€60,000/10,000 units

Appendix 6
Revised Variable (Relevance) Costing Statement

Period: 12 months ended	Dec 2XX6		Dec 2XX7		Dec 2XX8		Dec 2XX9		Dec 2X10	
	Unit	Gross	Unit	Gross	Unit	Gross	Unit	Gross	Unit	Gross
	€	€	€	€	€	€	€	€	€	€
Revenue	85	467,500	85	552,500	85	635,375	85	730,660	85	840,225
Variable Costs										
Variable Manufacturing										
Direct Material	5	27,500	5	32,500	5	37,375	5	42,980	5	49,425
Direct Labour	25	137,500	25	162,500	25	186,875	25	214,900	25	247,125
Variable Manufacturing overhead	30	165,000	30	195,000	30	224,250	30	257,880	30	296,550
Variable Cost of Goods Sold	60	330,000	60	390,000	60	448,500	60	515,760	60	593,100
Variable Non-Manufacturing overhead	3	16,500	3	19,500	3	22,425	3	25,788	3	29,655
Total Variable Costs	63	346,500	63	409,500	63	470,925	63	541,548	63	622,755
Contribution Margin	22	121,000	22	143,000	22	164,450	22	189,112	22	217,470
Fixed Costs										
Fixed manufacturing overhead		60,000		60,000		60,000		60,000		60,000
Fixed non-manufacturing overhead		30,400		30,400		30,400		30,400		30,400
Total Fixed Costs		90,400		90,400		90,400		90,400		90,400
Operating Income		30,600		52,600		74,050		98,712		127,070

Note Period: 12 months ended	Dec 2XX6	Dec 2XX7	Dec 2XX8	Dec 2XX9	Dec 2X10
Sales (units)	5,500	6,500	7,475	8,596	9,885
Production (units)	7,000	8,500	8,500	8,500	8,500
Breakeven level of Sales (units)	4,109	4,109	4,109	4,109	4,109
Profit-volume ratio	26%	26%	26%	26%	26%
Margin of safety	25%	37%	45%	52%	58%

Appendix 7
Difference in Operating Income between the two statements

Operating Income	€ Dec 2XX6	€ Dec 2XX7	€ Dec 2XX8	€ Dec 2XX9	€ Dec 2X10
Variable (Relevance) Costing	30,600	52,600	74,050	98,712	127,070
Absorption Costing	39,600	64,600	80,200	98,136	118,760
Difference	−9,000	−12,000	−6,150	576	8,310
Stock Difference	1,500	2,000	1,025	−96	−1,385
Fixed Manufacturing overhead p.u €6					

Fixed Manufacturing overhead Reconciliation	€ Dec 2XX6	€ Dec 2XX7	€ Dec 2XX8	€ Dec 2XX9	€ Dec 2X10
Fixed Manufacturing overhead absorbed	33,000	39,000	44,850	51,576	59,310
Add Production Volume Variance	18,000	9,000	9,000	9,000	9,000
Add Profit Difference (Absorption v Variable)	9,000	12,000	6,150	−576	−8,310
= Budgeted Fixed Manufacturing Overhead	60,000	60,000	60,000	60,000	60,000

Case 5

Solution to Spektrik plc

Falconer Mitchell, University of Edinburgh

Question 1

Computation of alternative target costs for Product 107.

a) Single target cost applying throughout product life cycle

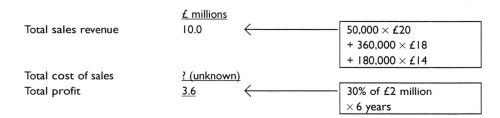

	£ millions
Total sales revenue	10.0
Total cost of sales	? (unknown)
Total profit	3.6

50,000 × £20
+ 360,000 × £18
+ 180,000 × £14

30% of £2 million
× 6 years

Therefore:

Cost of sales = £6.4 million
Target cost = £10.85 per unit (£6.4 million ÷ 590,000 units)

b) Dynamic target cost applying at different stages in the product life cycle.

	Introduction £ millions	Maturity £ millions	Decline £ millions	Total £ millions
Sales revenue	1.0	6.48	2.52	10.0
Cost of sales	0.55	4.68	1.17	6.4
Profit (Note 1)	0.45	1.8	1.35	3.6

Note 1

Required profit computation	30% × £2m × ¾ yr	30% × £2m × 3 yrs	30% × £2m × 2¼ yrs
Target cost	£11.00 (£0.55m ÷ 50,000)	£13.00 (£4.68m ÷ 360,000)	£6.50 (£1.17m ÷ 180,000)

Question 2

The static target cost of £10.85 has the advantages of clarity and simplicity but it does not reflect the dynamics of the life cycle where cost advantages can be gained through scale economies and through continuous (or Kaizen) cost reduction efforts.

The dynamic set of target costs does address this issue in part by establishing a different target for each stage of the life cycle. However the use of the required rate of return as a constant has resulted in the peculiarity of the target cost rising during maturity (when price has fallen and when economies of scale should be obtained). Moreover the target cost falls extensively in the decline stage and the achievement of such a stiff target would be difficult. Thus the dynamic approach followed in this way would not generate product cost targets which encourage a steady cost reduction pattern. An alternative dynamic approach which overcomes this difficulty is presented in 4 below.

Question 3

Setting a target cost is only the first stage in achieving cost control and reduction. A set of supportive mechanisms should be put in place to help in realising cost control. Some suggestions are listed below

(a) Communicate the target to designers so that they become conscious of cost issues. This can be aided by incentive or reward schemes based on target achievement. In addition product cost information should be available in a form which ensures product design engineers are aware of how their design actions influence product cost. For example, activity based costing may help here by giving visibility to the multiple cost drivers (and cost driver rates) which determine overhead cost levels.

(b) Give ownership of and responsibility for cost target achievement to a multi-disciplinary team which has an involvement throughout the product life cycle.

(c) Adopt cost reduction tools. In Japan these include employee suggestion, value analysis, close supplier relationships and cost tables designed to quickly discover the cost implications of designer options.

Question 4

Some suggestions for improving target costing in Spektrik plc are as follows

(a) Make cost reduction a continuous activity which will not cease even if a target is achieved.

(b) Include personnel from the purchasing function in the team.

(c) Consider the investment figure used in the determination of the cost target. Should the initial investment be used rather than the investment occurring at each life cycle stage. This may change due to depreciation and varying needs for working capital.

(d) Use the overall sales margin percentage of 36% to determine the target costs.

	Introduction £ millions	Maturity £ millions	Decline £ millions	Total £ millions
Sales	1.0	6.48	2.52	10.0
Cost of sales	0.64	4.1472	1.6128	6.4
Profit				
(36% of sales)	0.36	2.3328	0.9072	3.6
Target cost	**£12.80** (£0.64m ÷ 50,000)	**£11.52** (£4.1472 ÷ 360,000)	**£8.96** (£1.6128 ÷ 180,000)	

This results in a pattern of product cost targets which achieve the overall return on investment requirement and also show a steady downward progression consistent with continuous cost reduction efforts.

Case 6

Solution to the Castleward Cycle Company

Noel Hyndman, Queen's University Belfast

<u>REPORT ON ISSUES FACED BY THE CASTLEWARD CYCLE COMPANY</u>

Prepared by: J Milkins

Consultant

For: Central Management of the
Down Industries Group

1. Terms of Reference

Further to our discussions of xx/xx/xx, I present the report requested. With respect to the Tollymore Tourer department of CCC, it contains an analysis and discussion of the transfer pricing system being used, together with comments on other related issues. In the case of the Donard Trekker department within CCC, it contains calculations of variances for the most recent month (together with possible reasons for them), comments on how standards should be set and the extent to which present standards are realistic, and questions that could be asked of Brian Thompson, CCC's chief executive, regarding the pilot standard costing system. In addition, it comments on the performance evaluation system as presently used in DIG and the advisability of using non-financial measures. The calculations included in the report are based on figures which have been supplied by Brian Thompson via your office and which I have not verified.

2. Recommendations

(a) The transfer pricing system should be changed to one based on variable cost plus a lump sum.
(b) Replacement cost, rather than historic cost, should be used to value assets.
(c) The possible cancellation of expenditure on research and development and training should be considered on the basis of its long-term impact.
(d) A detailed analysis of the potential contribution of standard costing to management within divisions and departments should be conducted. This could draw on the experiences to date in the DT department.
(e) A wider basis of performance evaluation should be introduced, with non-financial measures (possibly based on a balance scorecard perspective) utilised.
(f) The practice of rewarding managers solely on the basis of return on investment (ROI) should be discontinued.

3. Issues Relating to the Tollymore Tourer Department

(a)   Existing ROI calculations

Both CCC and EEE are evaluated using the single measure of ROI. This is calculated using profit before interest and tax as the numerator and net book value (using historic cost) as the denominator. The budget figures for the TT department within CCC, and the department within EEE responsible for the manufacture of the cycle frame used by CCC in the manufacture of the TT, are shown in Appendix 1 (using a transfer price of €80 for the cycle frame). These show ROIs of:

- EEE (that department within EEE responsible for the production of the cycle frame for CCC) 54.3%
- CCC (TT department) 5%

On the basis of these figures, it would appear that the relevant department of EEE is doing extremely well. ROI is significantly higher than the TT department within CCC, and way above the target of 15%. Conversely the TT department figure gives rise to concern.

(b)   Discussion of the ROIs

As far as possible, a system of performance appraisal should: promote goal congruence; encourage long-run views; and provide a fair basis for comparison between divisions. The ROI figures produced are misleading for a number of reasons:

(i)   The transfer pricing system is inappropriate. Goods are transferred from EEE at 'market price' even though there is no market for the units being transferred from EEE at €80.

(ii)   Assets are valued at NBV based on historic cost. This will tend to overstate the ROI of divisions with old assets and possibly provide a disincentive to managers to make new investments in capital assets (even though investments should not be made with regard to impact on ROI). Given the comparatively new assets in the Donard Trekker department of CCC, such a valuation base will show up its financial performance in a relatively disadvantageous light (when compared with EEE).

(c)   Changes in Transfer Pricing System and Financial Performance Measurement System

(i)   A more appropriate transfer price might be one based on the opportunity cost of making the transfer. Because EEE has spare capacity at present and can meet CCC's demands without affecting its own external sales, this would be reflected by using the variable cost as the basis for the transfer, i.e. €40. This would produce ROI figures as shown in Appendix 2 of:

- EEE (that department within EEE responsible for the production of the cycle frame for CCC) 14.3%
- CCC (TT department) 40%

(ii)   A problem with such a transfer price is that EEE would enjoy no benefit from the transfer even though the company makes significant profits from the ultimate sale. This would undermine any evaluation of the contribution of the EEE to the overall company performance, and would not be accepted by EEE without central intervention (thus undermining autonomy). In the circumstances, it is recommended that variable cost plus a lump sum is used as the basis for the transfer price. This would reduce resentment in EEE. Given that the TT department of CCC is budgeted to use approximately 40% (35K frames of a total output of 85K) of the budgeted output of the EEE department responsible for producing the cycle frame, perhaps the lump sum should be 40% of the its budgeted fixed costs (transfer price of €40 plus a lump sum of €600K). Such a transfer price would produce ROI figures as shown in Appendix 3 of:

- EEE (that department within EEE responsible for the production of the cycle frame for CCC) 31.4%
- CCC (TT department) 25%

(iii) No adjustment has been made to the basis of the valuation of the assets in this calculation as no information was available. A valuation of fixed assets based on the concept of replacement cost would be more useful as it reflects the economic value of the assets and therefore makes ROI figures more comparable.

(iv) With respect to the financial performance measurement system generally, the company should consider using residual income (or economic value added) as an alternate to ROI for measuring financial performance. Such measures would provide less incentive for managers to hold on to old, inefficient assets when it was not in DIG's best interests. However, it should be understood that such a switch does make comparability between division's more difficult (residual income and economic value added being monetary measures that do not automatically take account of size differences).

(d)   Other Issues

(i) The cancellation of research and development expenditure may be short sighted. Such a course of action is encouraged by a focus on short-term ROI, although it may be against the best long-term interests of the company. The ability of CCC to develop both new products and innovations relating to existing products (important in terms of maintaining and enhancing competitive position) may be undermined by such action. A full investigation of this should be conducted.

(ii) Similarly, cutbacks on training may improve ROI in the short term but, in the medium to long term, leave CCC with difficulties regarding the skill sets of its employees. An investigation of the impact of such a change should be undertaken with this in mind.

(iii) Bonus payments based solely on ROI may cause dysfunctional consequences (as suggested above) in order to boost short-term performance at the expense of the long-term health of the division and company. They may also discourage necessary capital investment by motivating managers to hold on to old, inefficient assets. This practice should be discontinued.

4. Issues Relating to the Donard Trekker Department

(a)   Material, labour and overhead variances for the last period

As requested, variances for material, labour and overhead have been calculated (see Appendix 4 for detailed calculations). These are:

Material A	
Direct material price	€6,000 (F)
Direct material usage	€3,240 (A)
Material B	
Direct material price	€3,400 (A)
Direct material usage	€4,500 (A)
Grade × labour	
Direct labour rate	€118 (A)
Direct labour efficiency	€68 (F)
Grade Y labour	
Direct labour rate	€0
Direct labour efficiency	€675 (A)
Total overhead cost variance	€265 (A)
Total of variances	**€6,130 (A)**

(b) Reasons for Variances

Possible reasons for the particular variances are:

DM Price	• Efficient purchasing (material A); inefficient purchasing (material B) • Inappropriate standards being set without proper forecasting • Lower quality material than standard being purchased (material A); higher quality material being purchased than standard (material B) • Unpredictable external price movements that are not controllable
DM Usage	• Optimistic (and unrealistic) standards being set for usage with both materials • Poor physical controls • Mixing too much material for fear of running out of mixed material • Poor quality materials
DL Rate	• Unrealistic standard (grade X) • Using higher grade workers than standard thus costing more (grade X) • Overtime being worked (higher rate paid) • Unpredictable external rate movements because of skills shortages in the market that are unpredictable and not controllable (grade X)
DL Efficiency	• Optimistic standard (grade Y) • Slow/inefficient workers (grade Y) • Perhaps slowdown caused by poor quality materials or equipment
Overhead variance	• Poor predictions • Poor negotiations in terms of main items of expenditure • Poor control (and inefficient use) of supplies and services that make up overhead

The variances themselves would have to be investigated to identify the causes. In addition, decisions would have to be taken whether they arise because of factors that can be controlled and whether the benefits of investigation and correction justify the costs of investigation and correction.

(c) Accuracy of Present Standard, Setting of Standards and Questions That Could be Asked Regarding the Pilot System

(i)   Overall, the variances calculated amount to just over €6,000 (see a above). These represent approximately five per cent above the standard cost of the production of the month (standard cost of 430 carbon fibre frames is €128,334). While this is not huge, if corrective action is not taken (assuming the standard is an appropriate benchmark), it may encourage a drift from the standard which could gain momentum if it is perceived by employees that standards are not important.

(ii) From the information provided it is not possible to be very specific about how the standards have been set. However, for the standard to be useful for planning and controlling, as well as motivating staff, it must be well set so that it provides an acceptable and realistic benchmark against which to judge actual performance.

(iii) Overall, the standard cost should be developed by reference to each major item of cost (direct materials, direct labour, and variable overhead and fixed overhead). In particular with respect to materials and labour, well developed technical standards (for example, what materials and how much of each material, and what grades of labour and what time for each grade) as well as accurate cost predictions based on good available information (for example, cost per kg. for future material acquisitions) are necessary. It is not clear what sort of analysis has been undertaken with respect to the pilot study relating to the carbon fibre frames.

Questions that should be asked include:

- To what extent was there detailed investigation of the amount of material/ labour required for a frame? Were there studies of methods of production? Were there studies of options for use of labour? Were time and motion studies carried out?
- How were the cost standards set? Were current prices used? Were forecasts for the next year used? What information was accessed to do this?
- Who was involved in setting the standard? At present, it seems that the influence of Hurst and Little is dominant. Who 'owns' the standard?
- From a motivation point of view, what level of performance has been included in the standard? Is the standard stretching but achievable? What evidence is there of this?
- What feedback is provided from the system and how is this used? Who gets the information? What discussions take place?

5. Comments on Advisability of Using Non-financial Measures in Performance Evaluation within DIG

(a) Comment on the evaluation of the divisions within the DIG

At present the company evaluates the performance of divisions on the basis of ROI. While this may lead to managers making decisions that are in the best interests of the company, too much emphasis on ROI in the short term (especially when reinforced by related bonus payments) may take away from the important determinants of success in the long term. It has been argued by some management writers that financial measures are 'lagged' indicators of past good decisions, whilst other non-financial measures of performance are 'lead' indicators of future success. It should be recognised that there are potential dysfunctional consequences of too much focus on financial measures such as ROI (see 3 (d) above).

(b) Comment on the evaluation of the Donard Trekker department

Within the Down Trekker department, a pilot standard costing system has been introduced in order to facilitate planning and control. However, it is clear that control of productivity and cost are not the key reasons for the success of the Down Trekker (as perceived by Thompson). While productivity objectives, and the control of cost, may influence the bottom line, too much focus on these issues may take away from the important long-term determinants of success. Therefore a wider performance framework may be required that links the overall strategy of the department, the division and the group to the targets that are set for operational management (and become the focus of control). This should include important financial and non-financial measures.

(c) Specific suggestions:

(i)   DIG should consider whether the calculation of the key financial measure used to evaluate divisional performance (ROI) should be amended (for example, regarding the basis of valuation of assets) or replaced. Other measures of financial performance (such as residual income or economic value added) might offer more to the DIG.

(ii) The company should develop targets and measures of actual performance in relation to key results areas possibly related to innovation, quality and meeting customers needs.

(iii) Such targets and measures should be integrated into the planning and control system in the organisation.

(iv) The balanced scorecard might be considered as a useful basis for developing such measures and targets. The four perspectives of financial, customers, internal business processes, and learning and growth may be utilised by the

DIG (and its divisions and departments) to give direction to managers. Cost-benefit issues need to be considered regarding any decision with respect to the balanced scorecard (and off-the-shelf solutions offered by consultants should be treated with caution).

(v)   Developed targets and measures (both financial and non-financial) should be integrated into any bonus payment scheme to replace the sole reliance on ROI related bonuses.

(vi) A detailed analysis of the potential contribution of standard costing to management within divisions and departments should be conducted. This could draw on the experiences to date in the DT department. Consideration should be given to the possible dysfunctional consequences of too much focus on standard costing variances in certain situations. It is possible, should standard costing be deemed appropriate to aspects of the DIG operations, that a much looser form of standard costing, and a more flexible approach to interpreting variances, should be used than that represented in traditional management accounting textbooks.

Appendix 1
Calculation of Present Rates of Return

Budgeted return on investment
With TP €80:

	EEE Division (appropriate department) €000s	CCC Division (TT department) €000s
Sales Revenue		
External sales	4,000	4,200
Internal transfers	2,800	—
	6,800	4,200
Variable Costs:		
Own	3,400	700
Transfers	—	2,800
	3,400	3,500
Contribution	3,400	700
Fixed costs	1,500	500
Profit	1,900	200
ROI	54.3%	5%

Appendix 2
Calculation of ROIs with TP of €40

With TP €40 (= Variable cost):

	EEE Division (appropriate department) €000s	CCC Division (TT department) €000s
Sales Revenue:		
External sales	4,000	4,200
Internal transfers	1,400	
	5,400	4,200
Variable Costs:		
Own	3,400	700
Transfers	—	1,400
	3,400	2,100
Contribution	2,000	2,100
Fixed costs	1,500	500
Profit	500	1,600
ROI	14.3%	40%

Appendix 3
Calculation of ROIs with TP of €40 plus a lump sum of £600K

With TP €40 (= Variable cost):

	EEE Division (appropriate department) €000s	CCC Division (TT department) €000s
Sales Revenue:		
External sales	4,000	4,200
Internal transfers	2,000	
	6,0000	4,200
Variable Costs:		
Own	3,400	700
Transfers	—	1,400
	3,400	2,100
Contribution	2,600	2,100
Fixed costs	1,500	1,100
Profit	1,100	1,000
ROI	31.4%	25%

Appendix 4
Variance Calculations (DT department of CCC)

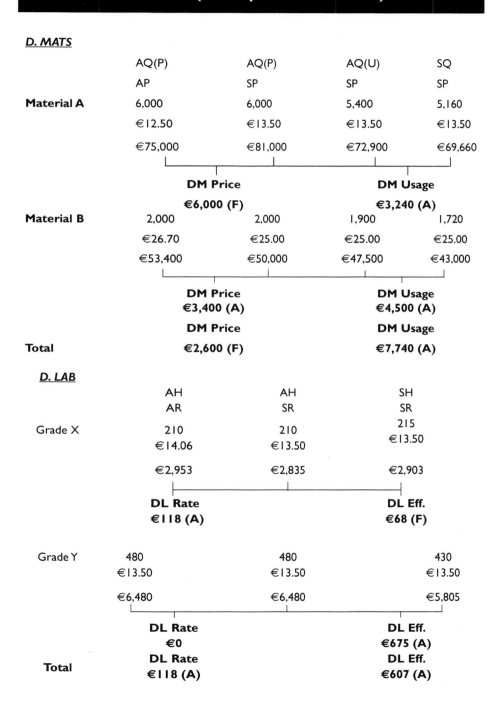

D. MATS

	AQ(P) AP	AQ(P) SP	AQ(U) SP	SQ SP
Material A	6,000	6,000	5,400	5,160
	€12.50	€13.50	€13.50	€13.50
	€75,000	€81,000	€72,900	€69,660

DM Price   **DM Usage**
€6,000 (F)   **€3,240 (A)**

Material B	2,000	2,000	1,900	1,720
	€26.70	€25.00	€25.00	€25.00
	€53,400	€50,000	€47,500	€43,000

DM Price   **DM Usage**
€3,400 (A)   **€4,500 (A)**

DM Price   **DM Usage**
Total   **€2,600 (F)**   **€7,740 (A)**

D. LAB

	AH AR	AH SR	SH SR
Grade X	210	210	215
	€14.06	€13.50	€13.50
	€2,953	€2,835	€2,903

DL Rate   **DL Eff.**
€118 (A)   **€68 (F)**

Grade Y	480	480	430
	€13.50	€13.50	€13.50
	€6,480	€6,480	€5,805

DL Rate   **DL Eff.**
€0   **€675 (A)**

DL Rate   **DL Eff.**
Total   **€118 (A)**   **€607 (A)**

Overhead

Note: Because of the way the information is given, there are a few reasonable approaches to dealing with the information.

One possible approach is:

Total Overhead	
Budget (Flexible):	
Fixed Overhead	€4,374
Variable Overhead (€6.48 × 430)	€2,786
Total Flexible Budget	€7,160
Actual Overhead Cost	€7,425
Overhead Cost Variance	**€265 (A)**

Case 7

Solution to Drumview Limited

Ciaran Connolly, Queen's University Belfast

Question 1

(a)

	Fixed Budget	Flexed Budget	Actual	Variance
Sales units:				
Standard	1,300	1,000	1,000	
Deluxe	1,500	1,700	1,700	
Sales revenue:	€	€	€	€
Standard	(1,300 × 150) 195,000	(1,000 × 150) 150,000	(1,000 × 140) 140,000	10,000A
Deluxe	(1,500 × 400) 600,000	(1,700 × 400) 680,000	(1,700 × 420) 714,000	34,000F
Total revenue	795,000	830,000	854,000	24,000F
Materials:				
Hardwood	(1,300 × 30) 39,000	(1,000 × 30) 30,000	(1,400 × 28) 39,200	9,200A
Pine	(13,500 × 10) 135,000	(15,300 × 10) 153,000	(15,500 × 13) 201,500	48,500A
Fabric	(2,800 × 10) 28,000	(2,700 × 10) 27,000	(2,700 × 6) 16,200	10,800F
Labour	(11,400 × 8) 91,200	(11,500 × 8) 92,000	(12,000 × 10) 120,000	28,000A
Packaging	(2,800 × 15) 42,000	(2,700 × 15) 40,500	(2,800 × 15.20) 42,560	2,060A
Variable o/hs	(11,400 × 6) 68,400	(11,500 × 6) 69,000	72,000	3,000A
Total VC	403,600	411,500	491,460	79,960A
Contribution	391,400	418,500	362,540	55,960A
Fixed costs	70,000	70,000	80,000	10,000A
Profit	321,400	348,500	282,540	65,960A

Reconciliation of Budgeted and Actual Profits:

	€	€
Budgeted profit		321,400
Sales margin volume variance – standard (W1)	15,900A	
Sales margin volume variance – deluxe (W1)	43,000F	
Sales margin Price variance – standard (W1)	10,000A	
Sales margin Price variance – deluxe (W1)	34,000F	51,100F
Manufacturing variances (W2)		79,960A
Fixed cost variance (W3F)		10,000A
Actual profit		282,540

Workings:

1. Sales Variances

	Standard		Deluxe	
		€		€
Margin volume:				
AQ × SM	1,000 × (150 − 97)	53,000	1,700 × (400 − 185)	365,500
SQ × SM	1,300 × (150 − 97)	68,900	1,500 × (400 − 185)	322,500
		15,900A		43,000F
Margin price:				
AQ × AM	1,000 × (140 − 97)	43,000	1,700 × (420 − 185)	399,500
AQ × SM	1,000 × (150 − 97)	53,000	1,700 × (400 − 185)	365,500
		10,000A		34,000F

2. Summary of Manufacturing Variances

		€	€
Hardwood (W3Ai)	Usage	12,000A	
	Price	2,800F	9,200A
Pine (W3Aii)	Usage	2,000A	
	Price	46,500A	48,500A
Fabric (W3B)	Usage	0	
	Price	10,800F	10,800F
Labour (W3C)	Efficiency	4,000A	
	Rate	24,000A	28,000A
Packaging (W3D)	Usage	1,500A	
	Price	560A	2,060A
Variable overhead (W3E)	Efficiency	3,000A	
	Rate	0	3,000A
Total manufacturing variances			79,960A

3. Manufacturing Variances Workings:
A. Materials
i) Hardwood

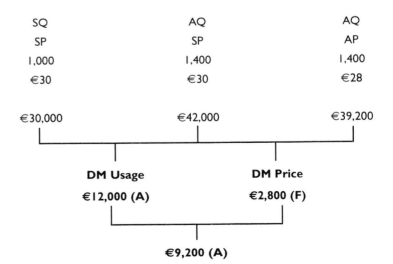

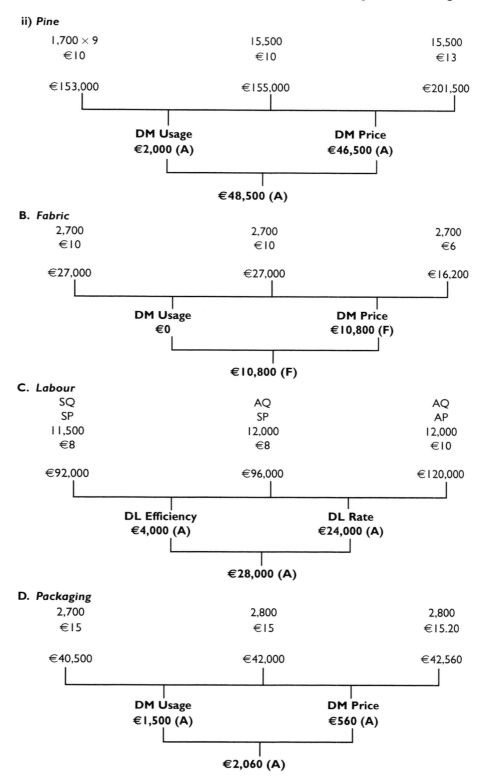

ii) *Pine*

1,700 × 9	15,500	15,500
€10	€10	€13
€153,000	€155,000	€201,500

DM Usage €2,000 (A)   **DM Price** €46,500 (A)

€48,500 (A)

B. *Fabric*

2,700	2,700	2,700
€10	€10	€6
€27,000	€27,000	€16,200

DM Usage €0   **DM Price** €10,800 (F)

€10,800 (F)

C. *Labour*

SQ	AQ	AQ
SP	SP	AP
11,500	12,000	12,000
€8	€8	€10
€92,000	€96,000	€120,000

DL Efficiency €4,000 (A)   **DL Rate** €24,000 (A)

€28,000 (A)

D. *Packaging*

2,700	2,800	2,800
€15	€15	€15.20
€40,500	€42,000	€42,560

DM Usage €1,500 (A)   **DM Price** €560 (A)

€2,060 (A)

E. *Variable overheads*

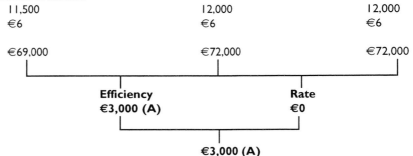

```
    11,500                    12,000                    12,000
    €6                        €6                        €6

    €69,000                   €72,000                   €72,000
    |                         |                         |
    |_____|_____|
              Efficiency                 Rate
              €3,000 (A)                  €0
                   |                       |
                   |_____|
                              |
                         €3,000 (A)
```

F. *Fixed overheads*

Actual €80,000 − Budget €70,000 = €10,000
(Standard marginal costing system, fixed overhead volume variance not required.)

(b) Possible causes for the variances calculated might include:

Hardwood

Adverse usage variance €12,000

- Purchase of cheaper quality wood making it more difficult to use and leading to more waste;
- Inefficient cutting leading to higher wastage and/or scrap;
- Incorrect standard.

Favourable price variance €2,800

- Purchase of lower grade material than planned for (see adverse usage variance);
- Suppliers have not imposed a planned price increase;
- Negotiation of better purchase discounts;
- Competitive action by rival suppliers causing price reduction;
- Incorrect standard.

Pine

Adverse usage variance €2,000

- Purchase of cheaper quality wood making it more difficult to use and leading to more waste;
- Inefficient cutting leading to higher wastage and/or scrap;
- Incorrect standard.

Adverse price variance €46,500

- Unforeseen supplier price increase;
- Failure to take advantage of purchase discounts;
- Incorrect standard.

Fabric

Nil usage variance

- Usage in line with standard (but does not necessarily mean standard is appropriate).

Favourable price variance €10,800

- Purchase of lower grade material than planned for (but not necessarily supported by usage variance);
- Suppliers have not imposed a planned price increase;
- Negotiation of better purchase discounts;
- Competitive action by rival suppliers causing price reduction;
- Incorrect standard.

Labour

Adverse efficiency variance €4,000

- Workers less efficient than planned due to being less motivated, using poorer quality equipment or materials;
- Workers working more slowly due to problems with hardwood and pine (see variances above);
- Discontent over having to package goods;
- Lack of training;
- Incorrect standard.

Adverse rate variance €24,000

- Use of higher-skilled workers on higher rates of pay;
- Wage increase implemented not planned for;
- Recruitment of new staff on higher rates of pay;
- Incorrect standard.

Packaging

Adverse usage variance €1,500

- Labour discontent at having to pack goods (see labour efficiency variance);
- Purchase of cheaper quality packing (i.e. arising from bulk purchase) making it more difficult to use and leading to more waste;
- Inefficient cutting leading to higher wastage and/or scrap;
- Incorrect standard.

Adverse price variance €560

- Unforeseen supplier price increase;
- Failure to take advantage of purchase discounts;
- Incorrect standard.

Variable Overheads

Adverse efficiency variance €3,000

* Driven by adverse labour variances.

Nil rate variance

* Rate in line with standard (but does not necessarily mean standard is appropriate).

Question 2
(a)

Students should be familiar with some strategic analysis tools. They may attempt a PEST Analysis, a SWOT analysis or use McKinsey's 7-S framework (staff, strategy, shared values, systems, style, skills and structures). Students may also use other appropriate models of which they may be aware.

Some students, however, may not use any of these, but may instead discuss the pertinent issues. Generally, students should identify that Drumview Limited operates in a competitive, and possibly global, environment and therefore not only needs to take account of, and deal with, issues specific to the country in which it operates, but also be aware of the threat posed from foreign competitors.

Given that Drumview Limited operates in a very competitive market, price is likely to be largely outside their control. Consequently, in order to maintain or increase profitability, the company must control costs. It is not important that students get the issues under the right headings, but rather that they identify them as important. For example:

EXTERNAL:

Political Influences

* Possible threat of industrial action by 'unhappy' skilled workers;
* General demand for minimum wage.

Economic Influences

* Growing economy and threat of cheaper foreign competition.

Technological Influences

* Operations appear to be largely labour intensive and therefore there could be a threat from cheaper mass produced goods;
* However, perhaps this is an opportunity for the company to target customers that place greater emphasis on traditionally made high-quality goods.

Sociological Influences

* Moves towards higher minimum wage.

INTERNAL:

Staff

- Company has three departmental mangers, a management accountant and a chairman. Operatives are possibly dissatisfied and underpaid, though, and are expressing this through dysfunctional behaviour (e.g. with respect to packaging).

Systems

- Production and information systems seem to be professional, although budgetary control systems are only now being developed and possibly more work needs to be done in order to gain the support of all the departmental managers. The recent buying problems suggest there are communication problems.

Skills

- It is difficult to assess if the operatives are skilled;
- Accounting skills are evident.

Strategy

- Different pricing strategies for the two models.

Style

- Attempting to introduce a more participative style of management, but suffering a number of teething problems. Departmental managers appear to need more experience with this new approach. Control is apparently exercised via accounting information.

Structure

- Hierarchical, but still fairly flat, structure appears evident, and seems appropriate for the size of the organisation.

Shared Values

- Christopher appears to be trying to encourage shared values, but obviously needs more time;
- Some evidence of dysfunctional behaviour, or at best poor communication. For example, recent bulk buying decisions.

(b)

The Management Accountant would need to consider:

- Likely minimum wage levels;
- Rates which would currently satisfy the operatives;
- Future raw material costs in the light of minimum wage and growing economy;
- Short term impact of not meeting production and/or sales targets;

- Potential for a sales price increase;
- Potential for reducing fixed costs;
- Potential for greater efficiency in production via technology and motivation.

(Students may offer a variety of other examples.)

Possible sources (internal and external) of information include:

- Market research;
- Opinion gathering;
- Accounting system;
- Formal channels (e.g. official documents, newspapers, various media sources);
- Informal channels (e.g. networks of acquaintances, gossip).

(Students may offer a variety of other sources.)

Question 3

(a)

Basic standards represent constant standards that are left unchanged over long periods. They provide a basis for comparison with actual costs over several years and enable efficiency trends to be established.

Ideal standards represent the minimum costs that are possible under the most efficient operating conditions.

Attainable standards represent the costs incurred under efficient operating conditions, allowing for normal wastage, machine breakdowns and lost time.

Basic standards are rarely used. The management accountant could use ideal standards as representing goals to be aimed at, rather than targets to be achieved, since the fact that such standards are unlikely to be achieved, this would have a negative effect on employee motivation. The management accountant could use attainable standards as the basis for budgetary planning and control, as their achievement could be motivating and lead to economies.

(b)

Budgetary planning and control helps a company to achieve its strategic objectives over a budget period, and calls for:

- preparing plans for future activity;
- implementing those plans;
- monitoring actual performance;
- comparing actual performance with plan;
- taking action to correct any differences.

In formulating the budget for Drumview Limited, the management accountant will need to bear in mind the strategic objectives of the company. In large organisations, a Budget Committee would have responsibility for developing and co-ordinating budgets. However, this would not seem to be appropriate for Drumview Limited. The Management Accountant will need to:

- make forecasts of key factors, such as expected changes in raw material costs, in order to prepare realistic budgets;
- identify the principal budget factor, which is usually sales;
- prepare feasible quantity budgets for sales, finished goods, production, raw materials, and so on. This will require extensive consultation with the other departmental managers if the budget is to be accepted by them. Some of the departmental managers have suggested that the budget needs to be changed;
- prepare financial budgets from the quantity budgets, including a cash budget, and co-ordinate and review these budgets for consistency;
- prepare a master budget, i.e. a budgeted profit and loss account and balance sheet, for the individual budgets, showing overall planned performance for the budget period;
- agree the budgets with Christopher and the departmental managers.

The Management Accountant may considering developing a Budget Manual, which is a collection of instructions governing responsibilities, procedures, forms and records regarding the preparation and use of the required budgetary data, and offers guidance and information about the budgetary process.

Students could also discuss the difference between fixed and flexible budgets:

- A fixed budget is prepared from estimated sales and production volumes and is not adjusted if actual volumes are different in a control period;
- A flexible budget is a fixed budget which has been flexed for a different level of activity than expected, and can be used at the end of a control period to provide control information about performance at the actual activity level in that period.

Case 8

Solution to Elveron Limited

Barbara Flood and Bernard Pierce, Dublin City University

REPORT

To: David Ledger, General Manager, Truck Division, Elveron
From: Jane Smith, Consultant
Re: Control issues in the Truck Division, Elveron
Date: 11th April 2XX6

Introduction

This report has been prepared at your request and in the context of your instructions as outlined at our meeting on 5th April 2XX6. The report is based solely on the information you supplied to me and has been prepared to meet the deadline you set.

The remainder of the report is structured as follows. Section 1 addresses your concerns regarding the budgetary control system of Elveron and the flaws embodied in the performance report issued to you regarding the Truck Division. The second section provides a reconciliation of the budgeted and actual gross profit for the Truck Division in the first quarter of 2XX6, showing cost and revenue variances in as much detail as the information supplied allowed and the subsequent commentary highlights potential reasons for the variances. Section 3 addresses your concerns regarding labour standards while Section 4 highlights a number of factors associated with the potential changes to the remuneration scheme for production workers.

I hope the report meets your needs. If you have any queries, please do not hesitate to contact me. Finally, I look forward to working with you again in the future.

Section 1

(a) Budgetary control system

In my view, there are a number of problems with the budgetary control system operated by Elveron in the first quarter of 2XX6:

Firstly, it appears that a ***new budgetary control system*** has been introduced in Elveron as a result of the purchase of the company by Cooper Inc. The control system introduced is in line with the control system operated by Cooper Inc in all its subsidiaries around the world. While a common system has considerable merits for the group as a whole, it is important to ensure that any new system is adapted **to take account of the particular context**. In this situation, it appears that Todd Lyman and his senior management team have paid little attention to the way that Elveron was run before Cooper Inc took over. The new budgetary control system of Elveron encourages considerable focus on budgetary targets, whereas it appears that Tom Bridge had used budgets in a non-accounting style. Additionally, it is good practice to acknowledge **cultural differences**, whereas Cooper Inc and Todd Lyman have attempted to introduce a new system in Ireland without any obvious investigation about whether that system needs adaptation for cultural variation compared to when it was introduced elsewhere.

Additionally, when introducing a new system, it is important to **involve participants** and ensure that they are well informed regarding the changes. There is typically a need to allay the fears of staff regarding the changes and to clearly outline the implications for them. While it must be acknowledged that David Ledger was not present when Cooper Inc took over in November 2XX5, when he returned he was **not made aware of the new budgetary control system** and how it would impact on his new role.

Given that an objective of control systems is to enhance organisational effectiveness through goal congruence, it is very surprising that David Ledger was **not involved in the planning and budgeting activities** for 2XX6. He is responsible for the operation of the Truck Division, yet he was not made aware of the targets and budgets set. While David was perhaps away during the budget setting period, it would be expected that he would be informed of the budget on taking up his role. Indeed, as David settled into the job and had a chance to reflect on the budget, a process of budget revision may have been appropriate to enable him feel involved and responsible for the activities.

Similarly, it is not appropriate that he was **not aware of the form of performance review** that would take place on a quarterly basis. Not knowing that there was a formal budget in place, he did not expect to have a review of actual financial performance to budget at the quarter end. He was only made aware of the review when it was sent to him via email. Given that David is only settling into his job during a very turbulent time for the company, the impersonal, authoritarian style of communication has frustrated David and is likely to de-motivate him. A more personal, team-oriented, consultative style of review would have been more appropriate at that point of time.

Problems with the **form and content of the performance report** include:

- While the variance in the actual volume of activity compared to the budgeted level is detailed on the report, the budget has not been flexed to enable a meaningful comparison to actual results.
- The report is too aggregated and does not provide detail of the elements of each revenue/cost category, which might enable the manager focus on problem areas.

- The report does not distinguish between revenues/costs that are controllable by the manager and those that are not and thus the manger will be frustrated to be held responsible for cost overspends which were not under his control, e.g. HQ costs.
- The tone of the introduction to the report is critical, authoritarian and does not attempt to acknowledge the efforts of the manager in his first period in charge. This is de-motivating. Additionally the tone and content of the introduction is threatening, as it indicates that job losses might arise as a result of the poor performance.
- The report is wholly financial and quantitative in nature and is heavily focused on profit measures. There is no use made of non-financial performance measures which may assist in developing a more rounded view of performance in the quarter.
- The report does not provide any context to the financial performance of the division. No overview of how the sector has performed or Cooper Inc generally has performed is provided.
- The report requires a written reply from the manager. It does not provide the opportunity to meet and discuss in a positive, team-oriented manner either the review process or the actual performance.

(b) *Recommendations regarding the performance report*

In light of the above problems, I would recommend the following changes be made to the performance report issued by the senior management to the Truck Division.

1. It must be acknowledged that the typical objective of performance reports is to evaluate organisational effectiveness or, in other words, to determine if the division has achieved its short term goals in the light of its long-term strategy. Thus, I recommend that the performance report should set the context of the review by reiterating the key goals and objectives of the division. This should be done in a narrative form and not only expressed in terms of the static budget numbers.
2. Effective control systems motivate managers and encourage goal congruence and thus performance reports must assist these objectives. I recommend that the report for the Truck Division be written in a more encouraging and supportive way. The language should encourage a sense of shared understanding and effort and it should attempt to praise as well as offering constructive criticism. In the period under review, it would have been much more effective if the report had acknowledged that David had only started in his role as general manager of the division and that the company was going through an unsettling period as a result of the change in ownership.
3. Within the numerical part of the report, I recommend that a flexed budget be included to enable comparison of the actual data to meaningful budget data. In this way, an actual revenue/cost can be compared to the budgeted amount for the equivalent volume.
4. Greater analysis of the financial data should be provided. For example, as there is concern over labour cost, if the labour figure was split between the

three types of production labour, potential problems with one grade might be exposed.

5. Cost/revenue items which are not controllable by the divisional manager should be separated from the controllable items and his performance should be reviewed relative to the controllable items only. He cannot affect the incurrence of items like central Elveron costs or Cooper Inc HQ costs, yet those items have been included in the operational profit measure for which David has then been criticised.

6. The report should capture some non-financial measures of performance which would give a more rounded view of performance, e.g. orders delivered on time to customers. The non-financial measures should be aligned to the strategic objectives of the division and the company.

7. Rather than simply requiring the manager to provide a written response to the performance report, it may lead to better goal congruence if the divisional manager met Todd Lyman and the senior management team and the performance of the division could then be discussed in a more holistic way.

Section 2

(a) Reconciliation of actual and budgeted gross profit

<u>Note</u>: The calculation of all variances included in the reconciliation is shown in detail in Appendix 1 to this report.

Truck Division, Quarter 1, 2XX6
Reconciliation of budgeted gross profit to actual gross profit

		€	€
Budgeted (static) gross profit			143,500
Variances:			
Sales price		8,500A	
Market size variance		14,350F	
Market share		16,400F	
Materials price		1,105F	
Materials efficiency:	X	10,200A	
	Y	10,200A	
Labour rate:	I	796F	
	II	816F	
	III	900F	
Labour mix		3,437A	
Labour yield		13,790A	
Overhead spending		1,947A	
Overhead efficiency		10,548A	
PVV		15,000F	
Rounding		<u>5F</u>	<u>9,250A</u>
Actual gross profit			**134,250**

(b) *Commentary on the reconciliation statement*

As is evident from the reconciliation above, the actual gross profit achieved in the division was lower than that expected in the static budget by €9,250. That total variance masks a range of variances, some of which are positive and others negative.

Firstly, it must be acknowledged that the activities of the division outstripped budget levels by over 21%, as sales and production levels grew from 70,000 units to 85,000 units. There are two aspects to the sales growth. In the first instance, the market for truck components grew in Europe by 10% which led to the positive market size variance outlined in the reconciliation statement. The second aspect relates to the fact that not only did the truck division of Elveron maintain its share as the market grew, it actually increased its market share, resulting in the positive market share variance indicated. The increasing market share from 20% to 21.078% most likely reflects the strong efforts made by the sales team to generate volume growth. Additionally, it is likely that some volume growth has been achieved from dropping the selling price from the budgeted €6 per unit to €5.90 per unit. It is possible the reduction in sales price was decided upon by the sales team as part of a growth strategy or it may have simply been a reaction to changes in the external market in terms of customers' price demands or competitors' pricing strategies.

In examining the materials variances, it is clear that a favourable price variance has been incurred. Due to the inadequacy of the purchase record-keeping, that variance cannot be analysed between the two materials used in making the component. It is possible that the favourable price variance has arisen due to the change in suppliers. As materials are now acquired from companies supplying the Cooper Inc group globally, it is feasible that Elveron availed of price discounts which it had not previously expected. Additionally, it is possible that the company is buying in bigger quantities than planned and obtained bulk discounts. In terms of material efficiency, it appears that the division has performed poorly with adverse variances of €10,200 arising with regard to both materials. There is a range of potential reasons for this adverse variance. Firstly, it is possible that the material supplied by the new suppliers are not of the quality expected and so there is increased wastage of material within the manufacturing process. Secondly, as the employees were shifted around in their activities, it is possible that they were not appropriately trained for some of the tasks they completed and so wastage of materials arose. Thirdly, any difficulties that may have arisen with regard to production technology/equipment may have adversely affected materials usage.

With regard to labour, it is clear that a saving of 10% was achieved concerning the wage rates of each grade. While this is positive from the company's perspective in terms of cost savings, it must be monitored in light of its behavioural affect on the employees. It must be considered that the reduced wage rate may affect employee efficiency and may be a factor in explaining the poor labour yield as demonstrated by the adverse labour yield variance. Another factor which should be investigated regarding labour is the appropriateness and effectiveness of moving employees around between tasks. In the first instance, this may result in inappropriately trained staff completing tasks which could hinder efficiency both within the labour task itself and with regard to material usage as already indicated. Additionally, when the reallocation results in employees of the higher grade completing tasks that could be done by a lower paid grade, an increase in costs occurs. As is evident from the mix variances calculated in the period under review, less work was done by the lowest grade workers and more was done by the higher paid workers which resulted in an adverse mix variance. Additionally, there is little doubt that there is poor morale among the work force since the sale of the company to Cooper Inc., and the impact of this poor morale must be considered in evaluating the labour efficiency variances.

It appears that there has been good control over overhead spending as the adverse variance is less than €2,000. The adverse variable overhead efficiency variance which amounts to €10,548 is connected to the labour inefficiency as labour time is the basis of variable overhead absorption. The favourable production volume variance (PVV) regarding fixed overhead arises because the predetermined rate for fixed overhead absorption was based on the static budget activity level of 70,000 units which was exceeded in the period by over 21%.

In reviewing performance in the context of a standard costing system, the extent to which variances arise due to inaccurate standards must always be considered. Save for the labour standards considered in the subsequent section of this report, no information has been provided regarding either how standards have been set or the accuracy of those standards.

Section 3
(a) Labour standards

(i) Potential impact of inaccurate labour standards in the Truck Division:

- Inaccurate standards, which require a level of efficiency which is impossible or exceptionally difficulty for workers to achieve, may have a demotivating impact on workers and may lead to reduced work effort or carelessness resulting in increased inefficiency.
- The review of performance based on the inaccurate standards will be misguided, inappropriate and is likely to lead to negative behavioural consequences for all involved, workers and managers alike.
- The inaccurate labour standards have resulted in large adverse labour efficiency variances which will attract the attention of senior management unnecessarily. Consequently, other serious issues in the business may not get the attention they deserve.
- Inappropriate decisions may be made as a result of reviewing variances which are based on inaccurate standards. In the case of the Truck Division, the inaccurate labour standards which have resulted in large adverse labour efficiency variances may cause the senior management team to unnecessarily seek changes in the remuneration scheme of workers or indeed to design a redundancy scheme to alter perceived inefficiencies.

Setting standards

The objective in setting standards is to aid the planning process of the division and to provide an appropriate benchmark against which actual performance can be reviewed in order to assist in the control activities of the division. To determine the accuracy of the revised labour standards proposed by David:

- Conduct a technical engineering review of the labour element of the production process to determine if the time taken by the various grades of labour is appropriate. It would be worth investigating the impact of altering the mix of labour grades used. Any changes in the manufacturing process should be considered and the implication of variation in materials quality should be evaluated.
- Rates of pay should be checked with the HR department and likely changes due to national pay agreements or other events should be taken on board.
- If possible, the labour standards for the Truck Division should be benchmarked against those of other similar companies.
- Feedback from the workers concerning the revised standards should be obtained in order to check the reasonableness of the standards and to determine the extent of motivation which they provide.

(b) *Planning and operating variances*

Truck Division, Quarter 1, 2XX6
Reconciliation of budgeted labour cost to actual labour cost

Note: The calculation of all variances included in the reconciliation is shown in detail in Appendix 2 to this report.

	€	€
Budgeted labour cost (static)		89,250
Variances:		
Labour rate -		
Planning variance	2,512F	
Operating variance	Nil	
Labour efficiency -		
Planning variance	15,729A	
Operating variance	1,500A	
Labour volume variance	19,125A	
Rounding	4F	33,838A
Actual labour cost		123,088

As a result of the calculation of revision variances, in the form of planning and operating labour rate and efficiency variances, it is clear that a significant portion of the previously calculated labour variances as shown in Section 2 of this report, was caused by the inappropriateness of the standards. If the operational variances above are reviewed, it can be seen that there is no rate variance and a relatively minor efficiency variance. Consequently, the performance of the division and its manager and workers can be more appropriately evaluated.

Section 4

(a) Comparison of the two schemes

The table below provides a comparison of the wages that would be earned by John Murphy at the different activity levels under the existing time-based scheme and both of the suggested incentive schemes. All workings are shown in Appendix 3 to this report.

	1,000 units	1,250 units	1,300 units	1,600 units
Wages earned:				
Time-based	€470.40	€646.80	N/a	N/a
Piece-rate	€360	€450	€468	€576
Differential piece-rate	€340	€425	€507	€720

The preference of each employee is likely to differ and will be affected by factors such as: risk preferences, personal and work related goals, amount of work effort currently expended, amount of overtime currently worked etc.

However, examining the differing schemes, and assuming that the general concerns of workers will relate to safeguarding their current earnings, it would seem likely that they would rather stay with their existing scheme. The time-based scheme is not output-related and it guarantees a minimum wage of €470.40 per week which is considerably higher than wound be earned under the incentive schemes at the lower activities levels. To earn equivalent or higher wages under the incentive schemes, significant increases in activity compared to the current level would be required. Additionally, the existing scheme offers the possibility of over-time pay which is attractive in terms of boosting earnings.

(b) Potential benefits and drawbacks of new scheme

From the organisation's perspective the issues to be considered in the context of moving from a time-based remuneration scheme to an incentive scheme are:

- To consider the impact on the quality of work that will be completed. Is it possible that the workers will complete the work to a lower standard in order to boost their output and hence their wages? It will be important to have appropriate quality control checks in place.
- To consider whether the assumed increases in efficiency are feasible. Todd Lyman appears to think that workers are currently slacking and thus have the capacity to increase output. He hopes the incentive scheme will provide the motivation for increased efficiency, but if workers will be unable to earn a 'fair' wage under the new scheme, they will be dissatisfied and demotivated. Are there other changes required in the division in terms of equipment, technology or training that would be required to enable the achievement of the expected efficiency gains?

- How will staff react to the proposed scheme?

  If the objective of the scheme is to boost output, then worker support will be required. Negotiation may be needed to achieve worker buy-in and/or it may be useful to provide a trial period of operation with a meaningful review process in order to solicit support. It is possible that Todd sees the introduction of the incentive scheme as an opportunity to separate the workers between those that are anxious to work hard and those that are not. By incurring a financial penalty for low levels of work, it may be that Todd perceives that the less motivated workers may resign or might be targeted for redundancy.

- Industry practices

  It would be worth establishing the nature of the remuneration schemes used in other companies in the industry. In so doing, lessons learnt elsewhere could be incorporated into the Elveron system. Additionally, information concerning practices in the local area would be useful, as it would enable the company to increase its competitive advantage in the labour market.

- Cost

  The company needs to consider the cost of introducing and operating the new system. A holistic analysis of benefits versus costs must be conducted.

Appendix 1
Calculation of variances

Favourable variances are labelled 'F', whereas adverse variances are labelled 'A'.

Sales price variance $(AP - SP) \times AQ$

$(5.90 - 6) \times 85,000$ = 8,500A

Working:
AP = €501,500/85,000 units = €5.90

Market size variance (Budgeted market share % $\times$ (Actual Ind sales – Budgeted Ind sales) $\times$ SGP

$20\% \times (385,000 - 350,000) \times 2.05$ = 14,350F

Workings:
Budgeted industry volume for the quarter = 70,000/20% = 350,000
Actual industry volume = 350,000 × 110% = 385,000

Market share variance $(Actual\ market\ share\ \% - Budgeted\ market\ share\ \%) \times Actual\ Ind\ sales \times SGP$

$(22.078\% - 20\%) \times 385,000 \times 2.05$ = 16,401F

Working:
Actual market share %: 85,000/385,000 = 22.078%

Materials price variance $AQ \times (AP - SP)$

€78,795 − [(11,050 × 4) + (5,950 × 6)] = 1,105F

Workings:
Actual quantity used X: 1,000 + 13,000 − 2,950 = 11,050
Actual quantity used Y: 1,000 + 6,500 − 1,550 = 5,950

Materials usage variance $(AQ - SQ) \times SP$

X: (11,050 − 8,500) × 4	=	10,200A
Y: (5,950 − 4,250) × 6	=	10,200A
		20,400A

Workings:
Standard quantity X: 85,000 × 0.1kg = 8,500
Standard quantity Y: 85,000 × 0.05kg = 4,250

Labour rate variance $(AR - SR) \times AH$

Grade I: (9.80 − 10) × 3,980	=	796F
Grade II: (11.76 - 12) × 3,400	=	816F
Grade III:(14.70 − 15) × 3,000	=	900F
		2,512F

Labour mix variance *(AH in std mix proportions – AH)* × SR

Grade I: (4,791 –3,980) × 10	=	8,110F
Grade II: (3,194 – 3,400) × 12	=	2,472A
Grade III: (2,395 – 3,000) × 15	=	9,075A
		3,437A

Workings:
Total actual hours: 3,980 +3,400 +3,000 = 10,380
Actual hours in standard mix proportions:
I: 10,380 × 3mins/6.5mins = 4,791
II: 10,380 × 2mins/6.5mins = 3,194
III: 10,380 × 1.5mins/6.5mins = 2,395

Labour yield variance *(AY – SY from actual input)* × SR for standard mix

(85,000 – 95,815) × 1.275	=	13,790A

Working:
SY from actual input: 10,380hours × 60 mins/6.5mins = 95,815 units

Overhead spending variance *[fixed and variable]*

165,367 – [(10,380 × 9) + 70,000]	=	1,947A

Working:
Budget amount for fixed overhead: 70,000 units × €1 per unit = 70,000

Overhead efficiency variance *[variable] (AH – SH)* × SR

(10,380 – 9,208) × 9	=	10,548A

Working:
SH Grade I: 85,000 × 3mins/60 = 4,250
SH Grade II 85,000 × 2mins/60 = 2,833
SH Grade III: 85,000 × 1.5mins /60 = 2,125
Total = 9,208

PVV [fixed] Budgeted – Absorbed

70,000 – (85,000 × 1)	=	15,000F

Appendix 2
Planning and Operating Variances

There is a variety of approaches to the calculation of planning and operating variances. Approaches other than that set out below are acceptable.

Labour price variances

Planning variance (RSR − SR) × AH

Grade I: (9.80 − 10) × 3,980	=	796F
Grade II: (11.76 − 12) × 3,400	=	816F
Grade III: (14.70 − 15) × 3,000	=	900F
		2,512F

Operating variance (AR − RSR) × AH

All actual rates equalled revised standard rates, thus there is a NIL operating price variance.

Labour efficiency variances

Planning variance (RSH − SH) × SR

Grade I: (4,037.50 − 4,250) × 10	=	2,125F
Grade II: (3,258.33 − 2,833) × 12	=	5,104A
Grade III: (2,975 − 2,125) × 15	=	12,750A
		15,729A

Workings:

RSH Grade I: 85,000 × 2.85mins/60 = 4,037.50
RSH Grade II: 85,000 × 2.3mins/60 = 3,258.33
RSH Grade III: 85,000 × 2.1mins/60 = 2,975
SH Grade I: 85,000 × 3mins/60 = 4,250
SH Grade II: 85,000 × 2mins/60 = 2,833
SH Grade III: 85,000 × 1.5mins/60 = 2,125

Operating variance (AH − RSH) × SR

Grade I: (3,980 − 4,037.50) × 10	=	575F
Grade II: (3,400 − 3,258.33) × 12	=	1,700A
Grade III: (3,000 − 2,975) × 15	=	375A
		1,500A

Labour volume variance (AQ − BQ) × Std labour cost per unit
(85,000 − 70,000) × €1.275   =   19,125A

Appendix 3
Remuneration Schemes

I. Time based scheme

Weekly basic wage: 40 hours × €11.76	=	€470.40

Assumption: Overtime hours are calculated relative to actual efficiency rather than standard efficiency

Total actual hours worked for Grade II labour	=	3,400
Actual output	=	85,000 units
Actual Grade II labour time per unit	=	2.4 minutes

Actual time to manufacture:

1,000 units × 2.4 minutes = 40 hours No overtime required.

1,300 units × 2.4 minutes = 52 hours Not possible. 50 hours max = 1,250 units

Cost of labour for 1,000 units	=	€470.40
Cost of labour 1,250 units = (50 × €11.76) + (10 × 11.76 × 50%)	=	€646.80

2. Piece rate

Cost of labour for 1,000 units = 1000 × €0.36	=	€360
Cost of labour for 1,250 units = 1,250 × €0.36	=	€450
Cost of labour for 1,300 units = 1,300 × €0.36	=	€468
Cost of labour for 1,600 units = 1,600 × €0.36	=	€576

3. Differential piece rate

Cost of labour for 1,000 units = 1000 × €0.34	=	€340
Cost of labour for 1,250 units = 1,250 × €0.34	=	€425
Cost of labour for 1,300 units = 1,300 × €0.39	=	€507
Cost of labour for 1,600 units = 1,600 × €0.45	=	€720

Case 9

Solution to Autoparts SA

Tony Brabazon and Tony O'Dea, University College Dublin

Question 1

		Varin	Yatese
		€	€
ROCE	(900/2800 = 32.14%)	30,000	
	(1400/6600 = 21.2%)		Nil
Bonus Pool		90,000	200,000
Total		120,000	200,000

If the revaluation is put through, there are affects on both the asset base and the reported profit figures.

Current net assets		2,800,000	6,600,000
Asset adjustment	(Buildings)	500,000	2,000,000
	(Machinery)	(20,000)	(200,000)
	(Debtors)	(105,000)	(130,000)
		3,175,000	8,270,000
Current profit figures:		900,000	1,400,000
Add back depreciation		35,000	200,000
Deduct adjusted depreciation		118,000	580,000
		817,000	1,020,000
ROCE on adjusted values:		25.7%	12.3%

Both ROCEs fall but Varin still exceeds the 22% cut-off.

	Varin	Yatese
	€	€
ROCE	30,000	
		Nil
Bonus Pool	81,700	200,000
Total	111,700	200,000

Question 2

A wide variety of solutions could be acceptable. The quality and flow of the argument is the critical factor. Points raised could include:

General comments

Compensation systems attempt to achieve several (sometimes conflicting) objectives:

1. Assist goal congruence
2. Be easy to administer
3. Be perceived as 'fair'
4. Balance incentives between short term and long term (strategic considerations)
5. Balance risk
   Of worker: e.g. if incentive agreement imposes much uncontrollable risk on the employee could => significant risk premium will be sought (employee is most likely risk adverse)
   To firm: e.g. risk of major payout.
6. Attract and retain high quality staff

It is notable that the existing bonus scheme does not have a long term component and that the bonus to be paid is determined solely by financial factors. This could motivate the manager to take a short run perspective in decision making. Strategic and non-financial factors relating to customer satisfaction and internal process efficiency are missing (e.g. customer retention rate, on-time delivery %, breakages, complaints).

It is also noticeable that the compensation system of each manager is solely linked to the performance of their division. There is no linkage to 'group' performance. This would not encourage intra-divisional co-operation although it is not clear from the scenario details whether significant intra-group trading does take place.

The answer should consider the potential benefits and shortcomings of a bonus pool system:

No lower or upper cut-off, deferred payment acts as golden handcuff but weakens link between performance and reward, avoids 'hard-threshold' problem.

General comments would be expected on ROCE measure, its advantages and potential disadvantages. The solution should also recalculate the ROCE for each division based on the revalued asset figures.

Solution should note that bonus payments are substantial relative to the basic management salaries.

Question 3

Allocating general group administration costs makes the CEO of each subsidiary aware that these costs exist and must be covered by the individual subsidiaries for the company as a whole to be profitable. However, the CEOs of each subsidiary may feel that they are being asked to bear a share of costs over which they have no control. Care must be taken to ensure that overheads are not allocated on an arbitrary basis between the divisions as this would create cross-subsidisation.

The greater the portion of a manager's salary which is linked to the profit figure, the greater is the potential for conflict. Heavy reliance on pay for short-term performance will increase the potential for dysfunctional behaviour.

A distinction can be drawn between the evaluation of the manager and the evaluation of the division. A strong argument can be made for not including uncontrollable costs when evaluating managerial performance but for including them when evaluating the performance of the division.

Question 4

A wide variety of answers could be valid.

The key requirements are that the solution must demonstrate how the proposed system will overcome the shortcomings of the current scheme.

In general, better designed compensation systems attempt to achieve these objectives by taking a segmented approach and consist of three major components, a base salary, short term incentives and long term incentives. It is expected that the proposed schemes will contain all three components. Good answers may also discuss intrinsic vs extrinsic rewards. The proposed scheme should also take into account the strategic position of each subsidiary. Will the new scheme encourage entrepreneurial behaviour on the part of management of Yatese?

Case 10

Solution to IXL Limited

Joan Ballantine, Queen's University Belfast

REPORT ON THE FINANCIAL ACCEPTABILITY OF THE SAP ERP AUTOMOTIVE SUPPLIER PACKAGE

Prepared by the Financial Controller
IXL Limited

REPORT ON THE FINANCIAL ACCEPTABILITY OF THE SAP ERP AUTOMOTIVE SUPPLIER PACKAGE

Executive Summary

- The attached financial analysis indicates that the ERP/JIT project is financially viable in terms of all three criteria used, namely Return on Investment (ROI), Net Present Value (NPV) and Payback.
- The ROI of the project initially yields 20% in year one and this rises to an astonishing 469% in year five. With the exception of the first year, the ROI more than exceeds the company's target return of 22%.
- The ERP/JIT project yields a positive NPV of €7,952,059 when discounted at the company's cost of capital of 8% which indicates that the project should be accepted;
- The undiscounted payback of the project is two years and two months which is a relatively short period of time within which the initial investment is paid back. When the time value of money is taken into account, the payback period increases to two years and five months.
- The attached financial analysis does not take account of a number of important factors, namely taxation, inflation and risk. Before a final decision is made it is important that these factors are accounted for in the financial analysis.
- The ERP/JIT project is expected to generate additional sales volume. However, this is likely to exacerbate the problems currently experiencing by the Dublin site in terms of managing accounts receivable. This report has highlighted a number of issues which should be addressed by the Dublin site to help alleviate this problem.

Main Report

Terms of Reference

Further to your request, please find attached my report on the financial acceptability of the ERP/JIT system within the Dublin site. The report contains a financial analysis of the project using a number of criteria: return on investment; net present value and payback. As requested, I have also considered a number of additional issues, including the incorporation of risk, inflation and taxation, and have outlined how the financial analysis presented might be adjusted to take these into account. Before making a final decision regarding the ERP/JIT project, these issues should be incorporated fully into the financial analysis. Additionally, a number of qualitative issues should also be considered.

This report addresses two further issues. First, it outlines the problems associated with using ROI and considers how the alternative methods of appraisal applied here, namely net present value and payback, help alleviate these problems. Secondly, the report outlines what actions need to be taken by the Dublin site to ensure effective management of accounts receivable which has been identified as a potential problem area given the increased sales volumes which are expected to flow through following the implementation of the ERP/JIT system.

Recommendations to Management

1. Financial Analysis of the ERP/JIT Project

The financial analysis of the ERP/JIT project has been carried out using a number of criteria: return on investment, net present value and payback (additionally internal rate of return could be calculated). In carrying out the analysis a number of assumptions have been made:

- The costs incurred to date of €50,000 for employing specialists to determine cost/revenue estimates are sunk and therefore irrelevant to the investment decision;
- The additional fixed operating overheads of €100,000 charged to the Dublin site are irrelevant as they will be incurred irrespective of whether the project is accepted or not;
- Taxation and inflation have been ignored.

(a) ROI

The calculation of ROI is presented in Appendix 1. The ROI has been calculated for all five years of the project. ROI has been calculated using average annual profits (net cash flows after adjusting for depreciation) divided by average investment (opening plus closing investment divided by two). The ROI for the first year of the project is 20% which just falls short of the current requirement of 22%. However, for all remaining years of the project, the ROI obtained more than exceeds the company's target. On the basis of ROI then the company should accept the project with the proviso that the target is not quite met in the first year of the project.

(b) Net Present Value

The NPV of the project has also been calculated, details of which can be found in Appendix 3 (Appendix 2 provides details of the calculation of contribution per unit which is used in Appendix 3). The NPV alleviates some of the potential problems of ROI (see later) by taking into account the time value of money (i.e. money received in the future is worth less than that received today). In order to calculate NPV we use the company's cost of capital of 8%. When the cash flows are discounted using 8%, the project yields a positive NPV of €7,952,059. On the basis of this financial analysis, the NPV indicates that the ERP/JIT project should be accepted.

(c) Payback

The payback, both discounted and otherwise, of the ERP/JIT project has also been calculated. Payback is one of the most frequently used methods of appraisal in practice and is defined as the length of time that is required for a stream of cash flows from an investment to equal the original cash outlay required for the investment. Payback alleviates some of the problems of ROI by using cash flows and, in the case of discounted payback, taking account of the time value of money. The payback of the current project is two years and two months which is a relatively short period of time. This suggests that our initial investment is paid back fairly quickly. However, if we take into account the time value of money, the payback increases to two years and five months. This still represents a fairly short period within which the initial investment is recouped by the ERP/JIT project.

(d) Qualitative Issues

On the basis of the financial appraisal of the ERP/JIT project, IXL Limited would be advised to proceed with the project as it will enhance the company's long-term value. However, before a final decision is made, there are a number of qualitative issues which need to be considered. First, is the project in line with the long term strategy of the company? Secondly, has IXL Limited got the expertise internally to implement the ERP/JIT project or will external help be required? If external support is required, how will this impact on the costs of the project? Thirdly, how reliable are the estimates of costs and benefits which are used to determine the ROI, NPV and Payback calculations?

2. Discussion of ROI and its appropriateness as an appraisal technique

Historically capital investment decisions have been made by IXL Limited on the basis of Return on Investment (ROI) which is currently set at a level of 22%. Whilst ROI is a widely used technique of investment appraisal it suffers a number of limitations which limits its usefulness. Each of these will be discussed below.

(i)   ROI can lead managers to make sub-optimal investment and divestment decisions, that is, decisions which are not in the best interests of the company;

(ii) ROI is based on the measurement of profits as opposed to techniques such as NPV and IRR which are based on cash flows. Profit measures invariably suffer from the inclusion of non-cash items such as depreciation and amortisation and are affected by accounting policy choice;

(iii) ROI is a relative accounting ratio and therefore fails to reflect the absolute size of an investment;

(iv) ROI fails to take into account the time value of money;

(v)   ROI can encourage managers to adopt a short-term perspective to decision making;

(vi) No standard measure of investment and profit exist for calculating ROI. As a result huge variations can arise when calculating ROI based on for example, opening values of investment as opposed to average or closing values, the use of historical asset costs as opposed to revalued amounts or replacement costs.

The use of NPV as an alternative method of appraisal alleviates many of the problems of ROI. It does this in a number of ways:

(i)   It adopts a long-term perspective by selecting projects that increase shareholder value;

(ii) NPV uses cash flows not profits;

(iii) NPV takes account of the time value of money;

(iv) NPV is an absolute measure.

3. Incorporation of Risk

Risk is an important element which should be considered when appraising capital projects. For example, it is entirely feasible that acceptance of a profitable but highly risky investment proposal may increase the perceived riskiness of the total business and result in a reduction in the long-term value of the firm.

Risk is defined as the set of unique consequences for a given decision which can be assigned probabilities. In the context of investment decisions, risk refers to the variability in the capital project's expected cash flows. There are two ways of dealing with risk in relation to capital projects. The first method aims to incorporate the investor's perception of the risk of the project within the NPV formula. It does this by adjusting the discount rate by a risk premium. The higher the perceived riskiness of a project, the greater the risk premium which should be added to the discount rate used to discount cash flows. The second method of dealing with risk aims to describe the riskiness of a given project. This can be done, for example, by carrying out sensitivity analysis which aims to identify the factors or variables that are potentially risk sensitive. Sensitivity analysis aims to provide the decision maker with answers to a whole range of 'what if' question. For example, what would the NPV be if sales volumes were 10% lower than expected or variable costs increased by 5% per annum?

The ERP/JIT project should be assessed for risk. If the project is considered to have a higher than average level of risk, then a risk premium should be added to the discount rate before the net cash flows are discounted. This would have the effect of increasing the discount rate which in turn would reduce the NPV. Sensitivity analysis should also be performed by adjusting some of the key variables. These are likely to include sales volumes, the cost savings from holding stock and the initial investment in the ERP system. Sensitivity analysis can be carried out by adjusting the key variables one at a time or alternatively by adjusting a number of variables simultaneously.

4. Treatment of Taxation and Inflation

The exclusion of taxation from a NPV calculation is likely to either overstate the value of a capital project or understate it where generous capital allowances are relevant. For these reasons, taxation is generally taken into account in arriving at the NPV of a capital project.

The tax implications of the ERP/JIT project would be accounted for as follows:

(i)   the taxation payable is first calculated by adjusting the accounting profit for non-allowable expenses such as depreciation;
(ii) if capital allowances exist (which is likely to be the case for the production machinery), these are also deducted from accounting profits;
(iii) the corporation tax payable is arrived at by multiplying the taxable profits arrived at after adjusting for (i) and (ii) above by the current corporation tax rate;
(iv) the tax payable is then included as a cash outflows in the year to which it relates.

Inflation can be ignored where all cash inflows and outflows are affected by the same inflation rate. If this is the case for the ERP/JIT project then real cash flows (i.e. unadjusted for inflation) can be discounted by the real discount rate. In practice, however, different elements of cash flow will be affected by different inflation rates. For example, cash outflows related to material costs might rise by 2% during a particular period whereas cash inflows related to sales revenue might rise by 3% during the same period. In this situation, inflation cannot be ignored. Rather individual cash flows need to be adjusted by their respective inflation rates to produce nominal cash flows which should then be discounted by a nominal (i.e. money) discount rate. A further complication arises when both taxation and inflation are present and need to be accounted for in the investment appraisal. Since capital allowances are not affected by inflation (i.e. they are based on nominal values), cash flows are required to be adjusted for inflation (i.e. nominal cash flows) and discounted using a nominal (i.e. money) rate.

The effect of inflation on the ERP/JIT project should be assessed before a final decision is taken. It should also be noted that we are not told if the current cost of capital of 8% represents a real or nominal discount. This would also need to be clarified.

5. Management of Accounts Receivable

As you are aware the Dublin site have in the past found it difficult to effectively manage their accounts receivable. The implementation of the ERP system provides the Dublin site with a timely point at which to assess its management of accounts receivable. There are a number of issues which the management of the Dublin site should pay particular attention to at this point in time. These include the following:

(i)   Custom and practice within the industry – the Dublin site should have regard to what is considered to be normal practice within the industrial sector in which it operates. For example, it should attempt to understand what is normal practice with respect to credit periods, the operation of cash settlement discounts and the likely or acceptable level of bad debts. The Dublin site needs to compare normal practice with its own current practice to ascertain if it is giving sufficient credit terms to attract new customers. Alternatively, it may be offering very generous cash settlement discounts which are detrimental to the company as a whole.

(ii) Credit rating procedures – having determined basic credit terms, the Dublin site needs to set up procedures aimed at identifying those customers whom it is willing to offer credit to. This involves an assessment of the likelihood of the potential customer defaulting on the debt. A wide range of sources of information can be used to assess the credit worthiness of potential customers, including bank and trade references and the use of credit agencies.

(iii) An effective credit management system should also be set up to ensure that as far as practicable all credit customers adhere to the terms of credit which were offered to them. In the case of the Dublin site, this would involve: ensuring that new customers have been given adequate credit checks; ensuring that invoices are generated and dispatched to the customer as soon as possible after the goods have been delivered; ensuring that customers are monitored in terms of their adherence to credit terms; setting up effective debt collection procedures to ensure for example, that statements are set out at the end of accounting periods, reminder letters are sent to customers who fail to make payment on time and that appropriate action is taken to deal with customers who are in default of their debt.

Appendix 1
Calculation of ROI

Year	1	2	3	4	5
Net Cash Flows	3,020,000	3,772,500	4,150,625	4,295,406	4,362,877
Less Depreciation:					
Production Machinery	1,200,000	1,200,000	1,200,000	1,200,000	1,200,000
Software	500,000	500,000	500,000	0	0
Average Annual Profits	1,320,000	2,072,500	2,450,625	3,095,406	3,162,877
Average Investment					
Investment at beginning of year	7,500,000	5,800,000	4,100,000	2,400,000	1,200,000
Depreciation	1,700,000	1,700,000	1,700,000	1,200,000	1,200,000
Investment at end of year	5,800,000	4,100,000	2,400,000	1,200,000	150,000
Average Investment	6,650,000	4,950,000	3,250,000	1,800,000	675,000
ROI	**20%**	**42%**	**75%**	**172%**	**469%**

Appendix 2
Calculation of contribution per component

	€	€
Selling Price		380
Direct Labour	107	
Direct Materials	85	
Variables Manufacturing Overheads	50	
Variables selling and distribution costs	30	272
Contribution per unit		108

Appendix 3
Calculation of Net Present Value

Relevant Cash Flows

Year	0	1	2	3	4	5
Outflows						
Investment in ERP System	1,500,000					
Investment in Production Machinery	6,000,000					
Fixed Manufacturing Costs		900,000	900,000	1,150,000	1,150,000	900,000
Fixed Selling & Distribution Costs		250,000	250,000	375,000	460,000	375,000
Opportunity Cost of Rental		400,000	200,000			
Total Cash Outflows	**7,500,000**	**1,550,000**	**1,350,000**	**1,525,000**	**1,610,000**	**1,275,000**
Inflows						
Cost savings from stock holding		250,000	262,500	275,625	289,406	303,877
Contribution		4,320,000	4,860,000	5,400,000	5,616,000	5,184,000
Resale of production machinery						150,000
Total Cash Inflows		**4,570,000**	**5,122,500**	**5,675,625**	**5,905,406**	**5,637,877**
Net Cash Flows	**(7,500,000)**	**3,020,000**	**3,772,500**	**4,150,625**	**4,295,406**	**4,362,877**
8% NPV Factors	1	0.9259	0.8573	0.7938	0.7350	0.6806
NPV	(7,500,000)	2,796,296	3,234,311	3,294,900	3,157,252	2,969,300
Overall NPV	**7,952,059**					

Payback		2 year 2 months
Discounted Payback		2 years 5 months

Lennon Department Store Limited

Bernard Pierce and Barbara Flood, Dublin City University

REPORT ON PROJECTED INCOME FOR YEAR ENDING 31ST DECEMBER 2XX7, PROPOSALS FOR REVISION OF ALLOCATION OF STORE FLOOR SPACE AND RELATED STRATEGIC ISSUES

Lennon Department Store Limited

Report on projected income for year ending 31st December 2XX7, proposals for revision of allocation of store floor space and related strategic issues

Introduction

This report addresses a number of issues recently raised by the Board. Financial projections are presented for year ending 31st December 2XX7, together with a commentary on those projections. Detailed analysis and commentary are presented regarding two proposals for revisions to the allocation of store floor space. The report also addresses longer term strategic issues.

Projected Profit Statement

The projected profit statement is shown in Appendix 1. Calculations are based on assumptions regarding cost and revenue behaviour patterns which the company has been using in the preparation of financial projections. Although these assumptions have been confirmed as being valid for the projected level of activity, it is important to point out that it would be inappropriate to apply them to other proposed levels of activity and care should be exercised in interpreting the resulting projections. In particular, the projections facilitate only limited assessment of the projected performance and do not provide a useful basis for assessing strategic options of the type currently under consideration.

Projected turnover is €607m, generating a projected gross profit of €177m, or 29%. Gross profit margins vary from 40% for hardware down to 25% for supermarkets, while the average concessions commission is 20%. These figures should be benchmarked against industry statistics and any shortfall should be fully investigated. There may be a need to review company policy in areas such as pricing, purchasing, discounts and store layout. The rationale behind floor space allocation also needs to be carefully examined.

Projected net profit of €2.37m represents 0.4% of turnover. Again, this should be benchmarked against industry norms. The figures shown for Product Group Profit are not reliable for comparison purposes across product groups, across different store sizes or with external benchmarks. This is because the information on which the projections are based does not permit an analysis of payroll and overhead costs between fixed and variable components. Fixed costs, by their nature, do not change within a specified range of activity and it is therefore necessary that such costs be identified and removed from the analysis before any attempt is made to draw comparisons in situations of varying activity levels. Therefore, while the overall accuracy of the estimates has been confirmed for the given level of activity, the figures do not provide a reliable basis either for assessing projected performance or evaluating alternatives.

In order to complete a full evaluation of the projected net profit figure, it would be necessary to obtain a complete analysis of payroll and overhead figures, analysed by product group and store category where appropriate. Some further analysis of cost behaviour patterns is included in later sections of the report, based on additional details provided by the consultants.

Depreciation and Head Office costs combined amount to €17.5m. While it is appropriate that these costs should be allocated to stores, it is important to recognise the arbitrary nature of such allocations and the fact that these costs are not controlled at store level. Accordingly, there is a need to conduct an evaluation of these costs using appropriate benchmarks and to carry out a review of related decision making and control procedures at Head Office.

Proposal 1

Proposal 1 involves the possibility of discontinuing the supermarket business and devoting the space currently occupied by supermarkets to increasing the space available for group 1 business. Clearly, this proposal only affects category A stores and the analysis is therefore confined to the five stores in this category. References to the analysis below all relate to Appendix 2.

Schedule 1 shows the current projections for category A stores, generating a combined Product Group Profit of €6,526,860. Schedule 2 repeats these projections, using the additional information provided by the consultants to analyse payroll and overheads between fixed and variable components. This information forms the basis of contribution calculations shown in Schedule 3. Those calculations show that if current sales levels could be maintained, then closing the supermarkets and transferring the additional 30,000 sq. ft. per store to hardware would increase combined category A stores profits by 24% to €8,122,360.

However, it is expected that closing the supermarkets may result in some reduction in footfall, although there is some uncertainty regarding what the impact of this will be. Schedule 3 shows that if proposal 1 is implemented, then the combined category A stores profit could vary between €5.76m and €7.83m. These projections are based on management's estimates varying from a possible decrease of 1% in projected turnover (probability 15%) to a decrease of 3% (probability 60%) or in a worst case scenario, to a decrease of 8% (probability 25%). The projections indicate that there is a 25% chance that implementation of proposal 1 will result in a lower profit than is currently projected. If this occurs, then Category A store profits will fall €764,558 below current projections, thereby reducing overall projected company net profit of €2,374,557 by 32%.

The range of possible profits for the combined category A stores, taking into account the uncertainty regarding footfall, is shown in Schedule 4. Expected value of profits represents an average of the likely outcomes, weighted according to probability of occurrence. Although this analysis seems to suggest that the overall outcome will be an increase in combined Category A stores profits of €430,221 or 6.6%, it is important to point out that the expected value is a term used for a notional average and does not represent a likely out-turn. The analysis is totally dependent on estimates of footfall and on the subjective probabilities of those estimates materialising.

Because of the difficulties in predicting how the proposed action would affect footfall, the directors have requested a calculation of what could be termed a 'breakeven' footfall, i.e., what level of footfall would be required after implementing proposal 1 in order to maintain the existing level of combined category A store profits? The analysis shows that as long as any reduction in category A store sales is less than 5.4% of current projected turnover, the implementation of proposal 1 would result in an increase in profits. If turnover drops below this level, it will result in decreased profits (Schedule 5).

In making a decision in relation to proposal 1, Management may wish to consider closely the estimates that form the basis of the analysis. In particular, estimates of drop in footfall, probabilities, and cost and revenue functions clearly have a major impact on the projected outcome. Management's attitude to risk is also an important consideration. Given such a low company net profit margin, it may be considered too risky to implement a proposal with a 25% likelihood of reducing profits further.

A further consideration relates to the allocation of space to product groups that would arise from implementation of proposal 1. Half of the entire space in a category A store would then be allocated to hardware. While hardware is clearly a profitable line of business and is successful in all store categories, management should consider whether this is an appropriate long-term strategic emphasis. Current estimates of the anticipated impact on footfall seem to be based on the likely drop in customer traffic due to the fact that the stores will no longer incorporate a supermarket. Any adverse effect on the company's image could result in a further reduction in footfall. For example, would category A stores be viewed as predominantly hardware and DIY stores by some customers and would this have a negative impact on demand for ladies', men's and children's clothing? Would it compromise possible opportunities for profitable concession arrangements? Is it in keeping with the kind of image and reputation that management wish to build for the company? It is also questionable as to whether sales performance in hardware can be maintained in terms of sales per sq. ft., in circumstances where such a large proportion of the store is allocated to one product group. Some additional fixed costs and capital investment may also be necessary in those circumstances.

Proposal 2

Proposal 2 requires that floor space in every store be allocated to product groups in a way that maximises the company's annual profits, subject to 25% of the space in every store being devoted to concessions and a maximum of 25,000 sq. ft. being allocated to any one product group. A further requirement is that a minimum of 10% of space in each store will be allocated to each product group, except that category B stores will not have supermarkets, and category C stores will only have hardware and concessions. An evaluation of this proposal is presented below, based on analyses shown in Appendix 3.

Schedule 1 shows a calculation of the contribution margin per sq. ft., which is an appropriate basis for establishing the optimum space allocation. Contribution is calculated based on Gross Profit less variable payroll and overhead costs. Accepting the assumptions regarding sales per sq. ft. as valid, the driver of turnover (and contribution) in any product group is therefore the number of sq. ft. allocated to that product group. The key to optimising space allocation with a view to maximising profits is therefore to identify the product group that generates the highest contribution for every sq. ft. of floor space allocated to that product group.

Using this criterion, hardware is clearly the most attractive product group in all store categories. Supermarkets represent the next most profitable group for A stores, while Ladies is the next most profitable for B stores.

Based on these rankings and recognising the various conditions that have been set, the optimum space allocation is set out in Schedule 2. For example, for Category A stores, concessions are allocated 25% of space or 22,500 sq. ft. and all other product groups are allocated 10% of space or 9,000 sq. ft. Remaining space is allocated 16,000 sq. ft. to hardware and 6,500 sq. ft. to supermarkets, thereby allocating a total of 25,000 sq. ft. to hardware and 15,500 sq. ft. to supermarkets. The revised allocations show a turnover figure for the company of €566m, representing a 7% reduction on the original projected turnover. Despite this, the revised projections show an increase of 5.1% in total contribution and an increase of €3.7m or 156% in overall net profit. These increases reflect the fact that the revised plan prioritises those product groups that generate the highest contribution (and therefore net profit) per sq. ft. of floor space.

Cost and revenue estimates need to be carefully examined before making a final decision on proposal 2. For example, will there be a need for increased fixed costs where there is a very large increase in floor allocation? Are the concession estimates realistic, especially for C stores where there are no existing concessions? Will it be possible to secure concessions for small stores? As for proposal 1, are GP estimates realistic, especially where a significant increase or decrease in floor allocation and sales are predicted and suppliers' terms and conditions may be affected?

Before proceeding with a decision on proposal 2, Management should consider longer term strategic issues such as those set out below. A fundamental issue concerns the long-term vision for the company and the possible tension between a desire to carry a broad range of product groups on the one hand, and the need to generate an acceptable level of profits and cash flow on the other, in order to finance growth and expansion, and secure the company's long-term future.

Longer Term Strategic Issues

Management may wish to consider a number of issues regarding longer term strategic planning.

The view expressed by Deirdre Lennon is to some extent supported by the analysis. Appendix 3, Schedule 1 shows that, for every product group, the rate of contribution earned per sq. ft. of floor space is higher in the larger stores. The growth strategy pursued by the company has therefore had some success, but it may not be appropriate to pursue this for all stores, given that local conditions regarding population patterns, level of competition, etc. need to be considered for each individual store.

The policy regarding allocation of floor space needs to be carefully considered. The analysis has shown that profitability can be improved by re-allocating space to product groups that yield the highest return, in terms of sales less all variable costs, per sq. ft. of floor space. This may present some options for enhancing profitability and cash flow, thereby providing an improved return to the shareholders and potential for growth and re-investment. However, this needs to be carefully managed in order to ensure consistency with the long-term vision for the company and its image and reputation among its customers. If it is desired to maintain the original Lennon policy of carrying the full range of products, then this clearly places constraints on allocation of floor space.

The policy of allocating the same space to product groups in stores of equal size also needs to be re-considered. As the number of stores has expanded over the years, local conditions are likely to show wide variations, despite the fact that the areas chosen for store location have similar characteristics. It may be appropriate to allow for some flexibility in terms of space allocation in individual stores in response to local conditions. Again, this will need to be done in the context of overall guidelines which will need to be developed in order to maintain consistent long term strategic focus.

Decision making in the company is highly centralised. Consideration needs to be given to allowing an appropriate amount of decentralised decision making, particularly where quick decisions are needed in response to local competition. If implemented, this needs to be done in the context of appropriate guidelines and suitably tailored control and information systems in order to ensure appropriate levels of coordination and control are maintained. Linked to this is the possibility of introducing some form of incentive scheme for local management. This would need to be based on a suitable set of performance indicators, both financial and non-financial, that reflect the company's key priorities. Suitably tailored and accompanied by appropriate information and control systems, these measures could provide enhanced motivation and job satisfaction for managers, help improve company performance, and develop management potential.

Profitability for product groups varies widely. Hardware is clearly very profitable in all stores. Supermarkets also appear to be highly profitable and have a positive effect on footfall in stores where they are located. Children's wear is the least profitable product, irrespective of store size. This needs to be investigated and perhaps the policy of stocking children's wear needs to be re-considered. Concessions also appear less profitable than most other product groups, in all three types of stores. This needs to be examined, particularly in the context of the requirement put forward in proposal 2, whereby 25% of floor space in the revised allocations will be allocated to concessions. For example, the allocation of 25% of C stores to concessions, as envisaged in proposal 2, would result in lost contribution of €1.64m for the combined C stores. The company should conduct a detailed examination of its use of concessions, including the rate of commission charged compared to industry norms, the likely impact of concessions on the company's own sales and the possibility of fixed cost savings in the longer term if use of concessions is increased.

Conclusion

The scope of this report is restricted by the information made available and confined to the two specific proposals put forward. Given the range of activities and the complexities of the company's operating environment, a more comprehensive analysis would be necessary in order to provide a sound basis on which to determine future strategic direction.

MCF Consultants
November 2XX6

Appendix 1
Projected Profit Statement Y/E 31st December 2XX7

	Group 1A Hardware	Group 2A Ladies	Category A (5) 90,000 sq. ft.					TOTAL A
			Group 3A Mens	Group 4A Childrens	Group 5A Concessions	Group 6A Supermarkets		
Sq. Ft.	15,000	10,000	7,500	7,500	20,000	30,000		90,000
Sales/sq. ft.	500	450	425	400	600	1,000		
VAT rate	1.21	1.21	1.21	1.1	1.21	1.08		
Excl.VAT	413.22	371.90	351.24	363.64	495.87	925.93		
Sales per store	6,198,347	3,719,008	2,634,298	2,727,273	9,917,355	27,777,778		52,974,059
No. Stores	5	5	5	5	5	5		5
Total Sales	30,991,736	18,595,041	13,171,488	13,636,364	49,586,777	138,888,889		264,870,294
GP Margin	0.4	0.35	0.34	0.3	0.2	0.25		
Gross Profit	12,396,694	6,508,264	4,478,306	4,090,909	9,917,355	34,722,222		72,113,751
Payroll %	0.13	0.15	0.14	0.15	0	0.15		
Payroll	4,028,926	2,789,256	1,844,008	2,045,455	0	20,833,333		31,540,978
Overhead %	0.16	0.16	0.16	0.16	0.16	0.1		
Overheads	4,958,678	2,975,207	2,107,438	2,181,818	7,933,884	13,888,889		34,045,914
Prod Group Profit	3,409,091	743,802	526,860	-136,364	1,983,471	0		6,526,860
Depreciation (Note 1)								2,142,857
Category Profit (Note 2)								4,384,002
Head Office								4,361,084
Net Profit								22,918

Note 1.   €15,000,000 ÷ 7

Note 2.   €10,000,000 × 43.61%

Category B (12) 50,000 sq. ft.

	Group 1B Hardware	Group 2B Ladies	Group 3B Mens	Group 4B Childrens	Group 5B Concessions	TOTAL B
Sq. Ft.	10,000	7,500	5,000	5,000	22,500	50,000
Sales/sq. ft.	500	450	425	400	600	
VAT rate	1.21	1.21	1.21	1.1	1.21	
Excl.VAT	413.22	371.90	351.24	363.64	495.87	
Sales per store	4,132,231	2,789,256	1,756,198	1,818,182	11,157,025	21,652,893
No. Stores	12	12	12	12	12	12
Total Sales	49,586,777	33,471,074	21,074,380	21,818,182	133,884,298	259,834,711
GP Margin	0.4	0.35	0.34	0.3	0.2	
Gross Profit	19,834,711	11,714,876	7,165,289	6,545,455	26,776,860	72,037,190
Payroll %	0.13	0.15	0.14	0.15	0	
Payroll	6,446,281	5,020,661	2,950,413	3,272,727	0	17,690,083
Overhead %	0.18	0.18	0.18	0.18	0.18	
Overheads	8,925,620	6,024,793	3,793,388	3,927,273	24,099,174	46,770,248
Prod Group Profit	4,462,810	669,421	421,488	-654,545	2,677,686	7,576,860
Depreciation	(Note 3)					3,771,429
Category Profit						3,805,431
Head Office	(Note 4)					4,278,174
Net Profit						-472,743

Note 3. €26,400,000 ÷ 7

Note 4. €10,000,000 × 42.78%

Category C (8) 25,000 sq. ft.

		Group 1C Hardware	COMPANY
Sq. Ft.		25,000	
Sales/sq. ft.		500	
VAT rate		1.21	
Excl. VAT		413.22	
Sales per store		10,330,579	
No. Stores		8	
Total Sales		82,644,628	607,349,633
GP Margin		0.4	
Gross Profit		33,057,851	177,208,792
Payroll %		0.13	
Payroll		10,743,802	59,974,862
Overhead %		0.2	
Overheads		16,528,926	97,345,087
Prod Group Profit		5,785,124	19,888,843
Depreciation	(Note 5)	1,600,000	7,514,286
Category Profit		4,185,124	12,374,557
Head Office	(Note 6)	1,360,742	10,000,000
Net Profit		2,824,382	**2,374,557**

Note 5.	€11,200,000 ÷ 7
Note 6.	€10,000,000 × 13.61%

Appendix 2
Proposal 1
Schedule 1 – Current Projections

	Group 1A Hardware	Group 2A Ladies	Group 3A Mens	Group 4A Childrens	Group 5A Concessions	Group 6A Supermarkets	TOTAL A
				Category A (5) 90,000 sq. ft.			
Sq. Ft.	15,000	10,000	7,500	7,500	20,000	30,000	90,000
Sales/sq. ft.	500	450	425	400	600	1000	
VAT rate	1.21	1.21	1.21	1.1	1.21	1.08	
Excl.VAT	413.22	371.90	351.24	363.64	495.87	925.93	
Sales per store	6,198,347	3,719,008	2,634,298	2,727,273	9,917,355	27,777.778	52,974,059
No. Stores	5	5	5	5	5	5	5
Total Sales	30,991,736	18,595,041	13,171,488	13,636,364	49,586,777	138,888,889	264,870,294
GP Margin	0.4	0.35	0.34	0.3	0.2	0.25	
Gross Profit	12,396,694	6,508,264	4,478,306	4,090,909	9,917,355	34,722,222	72,113,751
Payroll %	0.13	0.15	0.14	0.15	0	0.15	
Payroll	4,028,926	2,789,256	1,844,008	2,045,455	0	20,833,333	31,540,978
Overhead %	0.16	0.16	0.16	0.16	0.16	0.1	
Overheads	4,958,678	2,975,207	2,107,438	2,181,818	7,933,884	13,888,889	34,045,914
Prod Group Profit	3,409,091	743,802	526,860	-136,364	1,983,471	0	**6,526,860**

Schedule 2 – Current Projections showing Analysis of Payroll and Overheads

	Group 1A Hardware	Group 2A Ladies	Group 3A Mens	Group 4A Childrens	Group 5A Concessions	Group 6A Supermarkets	TOTAL A
Sq. Ft.	15,000	10,000	7,500	7,500	20,000	30,000	90,000
Sales/sq. ft.	500	450	425	400	600	1000	
VAT rate	1.21	1.21	1.21	1.1	1.21	1.08	
Excl.VAT	413.22	371.90	351.24	363.64	495.87	925.93	
Sales per store	6,198,347	3,719,008	2,634,298	2,727,273	9,917,355	27,777,778	52,974,059
No. Stores	5	5	5	5	5	5	5
Total Sales	30,991,736	18,595,041	13,171,488	13,636,364	49,586,777	138,888,889	264,870,294
GP Margin	0.4	0.35	0.34	0.3	0.2	0.25	
Gross Profit	12,396,694	6,508,264	4,478,306	4,090,909	9,917,355	34,722,222	72,113,751
Fixed Payroll %	0.3	0.3	0.3	0.3		0.3	
Fixed Payroll	1,208,678	836,777	553,202	613,636	0	6,250,000	9,462,293
Payroll %	0.13	0.15	0.14	0.15	0	0.15	
Variable Payroll	2,820,248	1,952,479	1,290,806	1,431,818	0	14,583,333	22,078,685
Total Payroll	4,028,926	2,789,256	1,844,008	2,045,455	0	20,833,333	31,540,978
V Payroll/Sales	0.09	0.11	0.10	0.11	0	0.11	
Fixed Overhead %	0.35	0.35	0.35	0.35	0.35	0.35	
Fixed Overhead	1,735,537	1,041,322	737,603	763,636	2,776,860	4,861,111	11,916,070
Overhead %	0.16	0.16	0.16	0.16	0.16	0.1	
Variable Overheads	3,223,140	1,933,884	1,369,835	1,418,182	5,157,025	9,027,778	22,129,844
Total Overheads	4,958,678	2,975,207	2,107,438	2,181,818	7,933,884	13,888,889	34,045,914
V Overhead/Sales	0.10	0.10	0.10	0.10	0.10	0.07	
Prod Group Profit	3,409,091	743,802	526,860	-136,364	1,983,471	0	6,526,860

Schedule 3 – Assuming Current Sales Level

	Group 1A	Group 2A	Group 3A	Group 4A	Group 5A	TOTAL A
	Hardware	Ladies	Mens	Childrens	Concessions	
Sq. Ft.	45,000	10,000	7,500	7,500	20,000	90,000
Sales/sq. ft.	500	450	425	400	600	
VAT rate	1.21	1.21	1.21	1.1	1.21	
Excl. VAT	413.22	371.90	351.24	363.64	495.87	
Sales per Store	18,595,041	3,719,008	2,634,298	2,727,273	9,917,355	37,592,975
No. Stores	5	5	5	5	5	5
Total Sales	92,975,207	18,595,041	13,171,488	13,636,364	49,586,777	187,964,876
GP Margin	0.4	0.35	0.34	0.3	0.2	
Gross Profit	37,190,083	6,508,264	4,478,306	4,090,909	9,917,355	62,184,917
V Payroll/Sales	0.09	0.11	0.10	0.11	0	
V Payroll	8,460,744	1,952,479	1,290,806	1,431,818	0	
V Overhead/Sales	0.10	0.10	0.10	0.10	0.10	
V Overhead	9,669,421	1,933,884	1,369,835	1,418,182	5,157,025	
Total V Cost	18,130,165	3,886,364	2,660,640	2,850,000	5,157,025	32,684,194
Contribution	19,059,917	2,621,901	1,817,665	1,240,909	4,760,331	29,500,723
Fixed Payroll						9,462,293
Fixed Overhead						11,916,070
Total F Cost						21,378,363
Prod Group Profit						8,122,360

Category A (5) 90,000 sq. ft. (header spanning Group 1A–Group 5A)

Assuming 8% Decrease

Contribution						27,140,665
Total F Cost						21,378,363
Prod Group Profit						5,762,302

Assuming 3% Decrease

Contribution						28,615,701
Total F Cost						21,378,363
Prod Group Profit						7,237,338

Assuming 1% Decrease

Contribution						29,205,716
Total F Cost						21,378,363
Prod Group Profit						7,827,353

Schedule 4 – Expected Value of Profits

Sales	Profit	Probability	EV
8% Decrease	5,762,302	0.25	1,440,576
3% Decrease	7,237,338	0.6	4,342,403
1%Decrease	7,827,353	0.15	1,174,103
Total EV of Profit			6,957,081

Schedule 5 – 'Breakeven' Decrease in Sales

Current Profit	6,526,860
Fixed Costs	21,378,363
Current Contribution	27,905,223
Proposal 1 at 100%	29,500,723
B/E Sales	0.945
B/E Decrease	0.054

Assuming 5.4% Decrease

Contribution	27,905,223
Total Fixed Cost	21,378,363
Prod Group Profit	6,526,860

Appendix 3
Proposal 2
Schedule 1 – Contribution per sq. ft. based on current projections

	Group 1A Hardware	Group 2A Ladies	Category A (5) 90,000 sq. ft.		Group 5A Concessions	Group 6A Supermarkets	TOTAL A
			Group 3A Mens	Group 4A Childrens			
Sq. Ft.	15,000	10,000	7,500	7,500	20,000	30,000	90,000
Sales/sq. ft.	500	450	425	400	600	1,000	
VAT rate	1.21	1.21	1.21	1.1	1.21	1.08	
Excl. VAT	413.22	371.90	351.24	363.64	495.87	925.93	
Sales per Store	6,198,347	3,719,008	2,634,298	2,727,273	9,917,355	27,777,778	52,974,059
No. Stores	5	5	5	5	5	5	5
Total Sales	30,991,736	18,595,041	13,171,488	13,636,364	49,586,777	138,888,889	264,870,294
GP Margin	0.4	0.35	0.34	0.3	0.2	0.25	
Gross Profit	12,396,694	6,508,264	4,478,306	4,090,909	9,917,355	34,722,222	72,113,751
Payroll/Sales	0.13	0.15	0.14	0.15	0	0.15	
Total Payroll	4,028,926	2,789,256	1,844,008	2,045,455	0	20,833,333	31,540,978
Fixed Payroll %	0.3	0.3	0.3	0.3	0	0.3	
Fixed Payroll	1,208,678	836,777	553,202	613,636	0	6,250,000	9,462,293
Variable Payroll	2,820,248	1,952,479	1,290,806	1,431,818	0	14,583,333	22,078,685
Overhead/Sales	0.16	0.16	0.16	0.16	0.16	0.10	
Total Overheads	4,958,678	2,975,207	2,107,438	2,181,818	7,933,884	13,888,889	34,045,914
Fixed Overhead %	0.35	0.35	0.35	0.35	0.35	0.35	
Fixed Overhead	1,735,537	1,041,322	737,603	763,636	2,776,860	4,861,111	11,916,070
Variable Overhead	3,223,140	1,933,884	1,369,835	1,418,182	5,157,025	9,027,778	22,129,844
Prod Group Profit	3,409,091	743,802	526,860	-136,364	1,983,471	0	6,526,860
Fixed Payroll	1,208,678	836,777	553,202	613,636	0	6,250,000	9,462,293
Fixed Overhead	1,735,537	1,041,322	737,603	763,636	2,776,860	4,861,111	11,916,070
Prod Group CM	6,353,306	2,621,901	1,817,665	1,240,909	4,760,331	11,111,111	27,905,223
Sq. ft. per store	15,000	10,000	7,500	7,500	20,000	30,000	90,000
Stores	5	5	5	5	5	5	
Total sq. ft.	75,000	50,000	37,500	37,500	100,000	150,000	450,000
CM per sq. ft.	84.71	52.44	48.47	33.09	47.60	74.07	62.01
Ranking	1	3	4	6	5	2	

Category B (12) 50,000 sq. ft.

	Group 1B Hardware	Group 2B Ladies	Group 3B Mens	Group 4B Childrens	Group 5B Concessions	TOTAL B
Sq. Ft.	10,000	7,500	5,000	5,000	22,500	50,000
Sales/sq. ft.	500	450	425	400	600	
VAT rate	1.21	1.21	1.21	1.1	1.21	
Excl.VAT	413.22	371.90	351.24	363.64	495.87	
Sales per Store	4,132,231	2,789,256	1,756,198	1,818,182	11,157,025	21,652,893
No. Stores	12	12	12	12	12	12
Total Sales	49,586,777	33,471,074	21,074,380	21,818,182	133,884,298	259,834,711
GP Margin	0.4	0.35	0.34	0.3	0.2	
Gross Profit	19,834,711	11,714,876	7,165,289	6,545,455	26,776,860	72,037,190
Payroll/Sales	0.13	0.15	0.14	0.15	0	
Total Payroll	6,446,281	5,020,661	2,950,413	3,272,727	0	17,690,083
Fixed Payroll %	0.3	0.3	0.3	0.3	0	
Fixed Payroll	1,933,884	1,506,198	885,124	981,818	0	5,307,025
Variable Payroll	4,512,397	3,514,463	2,065,289	2,290,909	0	12,383,058
Overhead/Sales	0.18	0.18	0.18	0.18	0.18	
Total Overheads	8,925,620	6,024,793	3,793,388	3,927,273	24,099,174	46,770,248
Fixed Overhead %	0.35	0.35	0.35	0.35	0.35	
Fixed Overhead	3,123,967	2,108,678	1,327,686	1,374,545	8,434,711	16,369,587
Variable Overhead	5,801,653	3,916,116	2,465,702	2,552,727	15,664,463	30,400,661
Prod Group Profit	4,462,810	669,421	421,488	−654,545	2,677,686	7,576,860
Fixed Payroll	1,933,884	1,506,198	885,124	981,818	0	5,307,025
Fixed Overhead	3,123,967	2,108,678	1,327,686	1,374,545	8,434,711	16,369,587
Prod Group CM	9,520,661	4,284,298	2,634,298	1,701,818	11,112,397	29,253,471
Sq. ft. per store	10,000	7,500	5,000	5,000	22,500	50,000
Stores	12	12	12	12	12	12
Total sq. ft.	120,000	90,000	60,000	60,000	270,000	600,000
CM per sq. ft.	79.34	47.60	43.90	28.36	41.16	48.76
Ranking	1	2	3	5	4	

Category C (8) 25,000 sq. ft.

	Group 1C Hardware	COMPANY
Sq. Ft.	25,000	
Sales/sq. ft.	500	
VAT rate	1.21	
Excl. VAT	413.22	
Sales per Store	10,330,579	
No. Stores	8	
Total Sales	82,644,628	607,349,633
GP Margin	0.4	
Gross Profit	33,057,851	177,208,792
Payroll/Sales	0.13	
Total Payroll	10,743,802	59,974,862
Fixed Payroll %	0.3	
Fixed Payroll	3,223,140	17,992,459
Variable Payroll	7,520,661	41,982,404
Overhead/Sales	0.2	
Total Overheads	16,528,926	97,345,087
Fixed Overhead %	0.35	
Fixed Overhead	5,785,124	34,070,781
Variable Overhead	10,743,802	63,274,307
Prod Group Profit	5,785,124	19,888,843
Fixed Payroll	3,223,140	17,992,459
Fixed Overhead	5,785,124	34,070,781
Prod Group CM	14,793,388	71,952,082
Sq. ft. per store	25,000	
Stores	8	
Total sq. ft.	200,000	1,250,000
CM per sq. ft.	73.97	57.56

Schedule 2 – Profit Projection Based on Optimum Space Allocation

Category A (5) 90,000 sq. ft.

	Group 1A Hardware	Group 2A Ladies	Group 3A Mens	Group 4A Childrens	Group 5A Concessions	Group 6A Supermarkets	TOTAL A
Sq. Ft.	25,000	9,000	9,000	9,000	22,500	15,500	90,000
Sales/sq. ft.	500	450	425	400	600	1000	
VAT rate	1.21	1.21	1.21	1.1	1.21	1.08	
Excl.VAT	413.22	371.90	351.24	363.64	495.87	925.93	
Sales per Store	10,330,579	3,347,107	3,161,157	3,272,727	11,157,025	14,351,852	45,620,447
No. of stores	5	5	5	5	5	5	5
Total Sales	51,652,893	16,735,537	15,805,785	16,363,636	55,785,124	71,759,259	228,102,234
GP Margin	0.4	0.35	0.34	0.3	0.2	0.25	
Gross Profit	20,661,157	5,857,438	5,373,967	4,909,091	11,157,025	17,939,815	65,898,493
V Payroll/Sales	0.091	0.105	0.098	0.105	0	0.105	
V Payroll	4,700,413	1,757,231	1,548,967	1,718,182	0	7,534,722	17,259,516
V Overhead/Sales	0.10	0.10	0.10	0.10	0.10	0.07	
V Overhead	5,371,901	1,740,496	1,643,802	1,701,818	5,801,653	4,664,352	20,924,021
Contribution	10,588,843	2,359,711	2,181,198	1,489,091	5,355,372	5,740,741	27,714,956
Fixed Payroll							9,462,293
Fixed Overhead							11,916,070
Depreciation							2,142,857
Store Fixed Cost							23,521,220
Store net profit							**4,193,735**

	Group 1B Hardware	Group 2B Ladies	Group 3B Mens	Group 4B Childrens	Group 5B Concessions	TOTAL B

Category B (12) 50,000 sq. ft.

	Group 1B Hardware	Group 2B Ladies	Group 3B Mens	Group 4B Childrens	Group 5B Concessions	TOTAL B
Sq. Ft.	22,500	5,000	5,000	5,000	12,500	50,000
Sales/sq. ft.	500	450	425	400	600	
VAT rate	1.21	1.21	1.21	1.1	1.21	
Excl. VAT	413.22	371.90	351.24	363.64	495.87	
Sales per Store	9,297,521	1,859,504	1,756,198	1,818,182	6,198,347	20,929,752
No. of stores	12	12	12	12	12	12
Total Sales	111,570,248	22,314,050	21,074,380	21,818,182	74,380,165	251,157,025
GP Margin	0.4	0.35	0.34	0.3	0.2	
Gross Profit	44,628,099	7,809,917	7,165,289	6,545,455	14,876,033	81,024,793
V Payroll/Sales	0.091	0.105	0.098	0.105	0	
V Payroll	10,152,893	2,342,975	2,065,289	2,290,909	0	16,852,066
V Overhead/Sales	0.12	0.12	0.12	0.12	0.12	
V Overhead	13,053,719	2,610,744	2,465,702	2,552,727	8,702,479	29,385,372
Contribution	21,421,488	2,856,198	2,634,298	1,701,818	6,173,554	34,787,355
Fixed Payroll						5,307,025
Fixed Overhead						16,369,587
Depreciation						3,771,429
Store Fixed Cost						25,448,040
Store net profit						**9,339,315**

Category C (8) 25,000 sq. ft.

	Group 1C Hardware	Group 5C Concessions	TOTAL C	COMPANY
Sq. Ft.	18,750	6,250	25,000	
Sales/sq. ft.	500	600		
VAT rate	1.21	1.21		
Excl. VAT	413.22	495.87		
Sales per Store	7,747,934	3,099,174	10,847,107	
No. of stores	8	8	8	
Total Sales	61,983,471	24,793,388	86,776,860	566,036,119
GP Margin	0.4	0.2		
Gross Profit	24,793,388	4,958,678	29,752,066	176,675,352
V Payroll/Sales	0.091	0		
V Payroll	5,640,496	0	5,640,496	39,752,078
V Overhead/Sales	0.13	0.12		
V Overhead	8,057,851	2,900,826	10,958,678	61,268,071
Contribution	11,095,041	2,057,851	13,152,893	75,655,204
Fixed Payroll			3,223,140	
Fixed Overhead			5,785,124	
Depreciation			1,600,000	
Store Fixed Cost			10,608,264	59,577,525
Store net profit			2,544,628	16,077,679
Head Office				10,000,000
Company Net Profit				**6,077,679**

Case 12

Solution to Top Flite plc.

Joan Ballantine, Queen's University Belfast

REPORT ON THE PERFORMANCE OF THE BELFAST DIVISION USING ROI AND ALTERNATIVE PERFORMANCE MEASURES

Prepared by the Financial Controller
Belfast Division, Top Flite plc.

Executive Summary

- The ROI of the Belfast Division has increased from 2XX1 to 2XX5. However, the division was unable to achieve the target ROI of 6% set by the board of directors, Top Flite plc for the years 2XX1 and 2XX2. From 2XX3, performance has improved with the Belfast Division consistently achieving its target ROI.

- The consistent increase in ROI reported is 'artificial', caused primarily as a result of a declining asset base.

- The use of a controllable figure for calculating the ROI of the Belfast Division shows a much higher return achieved in excess of the Division's target than that using a non-controllable figure between 2XX1 and 2XX5.

- The controllable residual income of the Belfast Division is positive over the period 2XX1-2XX5 which indicates that the Belfast Division makes a healthy positive contribution towards Top Flite plc.

- The three independent capital projects are assessed using ROI, residual income and NPV. The results suggest that Project C should be accepted since this is the only project to generate a positive NPV and a positive residual income over the life of the project.

- The analysis of the capital projects serves to illustrate the dysfunctional consequences of using ROI as the primary method of evaluating divisional performance, particularly when a short-term perspective is adopted. The use of a long-term residual income measure illustrates that there is a greater likelihood that divisional managers will be encouraged, when acting in their best interests, to make decisions which are in the best interests of the company (i.e. those that produce positive NPVs).

- A number of issues which need to be considered by our division prior to getting involved in the design and implementation of a multi-dimensional performance measurement system such as the balanced scorecard have been identified. These include preparing the division for change; obtaining buy in at all levels of the division; creating an open forum for discussion and debate; ensuring sufficient resources, both financial and time, are devoted to the project and the need to develop a detailed plan of the process required to facilitate the balanced scorecard project.

Main Report

Terms of Reference

Further to your request, please find attached my report which addresses a number of issues relating to the current debate on performance measurement which is taking place within Top Flite plc.

The first part reports on the historical performance of the Belfast Division using the existing ROI measure together with any issues this raises. The second section of the report measures divisional performance using a controllable figure for both ROI and residual income. The rationale for using a controllable figure for both calculations is outlined before going on to discuss the performance of the division based on the numbers presented. The third section of the report evaluates the viability of the three significant capital investment proposals which have been submitted for consideration to the finance director of the Belfast Division. The evaluation takes both a short and long-term divisional perspective in addition to considering the proposals from Top Flite's perspective. The fourth section of the report will outline the balanced scorecard concept generally and explain how it can be used as a strategic management system within the Belfast Division. Finally, the report outlines the key issues that the Belfast Division would need to consider in advance of getting involved in the design and implementation of a multi-dimensional performance measurement system such as the balanced scorecard.

Main Report

1. Historical Performance of the Belfast Division using ROI

Table one, Appendix 1, outlines the historical performance of the Belfast Division using the exiting ROI measure. The results clearly show that ROI is increasing year on year. However, the division was unable to achieve the target ROI of 6% set by the board of directors, Top Flite plc for the years 2XX1 and 2XX2. From 2XX3, performance has improved with the Belfast Division consistently achieving its target ROI.

A closer examination of the figures in Table 1 reveals that whilst the ROI has been increasing the absolute profit of the company has been declining since 2XX3. It is also the case that the asset base of the company has been reducing since 2XX3. The combined effect of a reduction in absolute profits and a decline in invested capital results in an increasing ROI. On the face of it, the steady increase in ROI would over time suggest an improvement in managerial performance within the Belfast Division. However, the economic reality is somewhat different.

Currently the Belfast Division calculates ROI on the basis of invested capital after deducting depreciation. The consistent increase in ROI reported here is an 'artificial' one caused primarily as a result of a declining asset base. In effect, the increasing ROI masks a deteriorating situation with respect to profits within the division. This is clearly an issue which needs to be addressed by the Belfast Division. It would also suggest that the management of Top Flite plc needs to consider more carefully the denominator used in the ROI calculation. There are a number of ways of valuing fixed assets within an ROI calculation: original cost, net book value, economic cost or replacement cost. If the original cost is used this will understate the true return achieved and not motivate managers. The use of written down values, on the other hand, will overstate the ROI. The theoretically correct solution to the problem is to value assets at their economic costs, that is the present value of future net cash inflows. However, this may present serious practical difficulties. An alternative solution would be to value assets at their replacement cost which would provide a reasonable approximation of what would be obtained using a net present value approach.

2. Performance of the Belfast Division using controllable ROI and residual income

Table 2, Appendix 1 shows the ROI and residual income, based on a controllable figure, for the years 2XX1 to 2XX5 for the Belfast Division. The ROI and residual income are calculated using controllable profits and invested capital.

Discussion of controllable profits and invested capital

The controllable profits of the Belfast Division are calculated as follows:

Divisional revenues minus controllable costs of the division

The divisional profit historically reported by the Belfast Division is arrived at after deducting central overheads which are charged to the divisions of Top Elite plc on the basis of the divisions' ability to bear such costs. Since 2XX0, the Belfast Division has consistently been charged central overheads equal to 4% of its invested capital. In order to calculate ROI and residual income on a controllable basis, we therefore need to add back the central overheads charged by the head office to the profit of the Belfast Division (see Table 2, Appendix 1). The use of a controllable profit figure is essential when calculating both ROI and residual income since it measures how divisional managers have used the resources under their direct control. Any arbitrary overhead allocations from the head office function are excluded from the calculation since divisional mangers have no control over such costs. It should also be noted that the figure of invested capital used for calculating both controllable ROI and controllable residual income is assumed to be a controllable one.

Controllable ROI

The use of a controllable figure for calculating the ROI of the Belfast Division shows that the controllable ROI is much higher than that achieved using the existing ROI measure. In all years the controllable ROI (measured after adding back central overheads of 4% which relate to services provided to the Belfast Division) is much higher than the target return of 6%. If the board of directors of Top Flite plc decide to now use a controllable figure when calculating ROI within the company, it is likely that the target ROI for the Belfast Division will increase somewhat from the existing 6%. In light of the proposed changes to ROI, the directors of the Belfast division will also need to consider setting individual targets for divisional managers which reflect the costs under their control.

Controllable Residual Income

Controllable residual income is calculated after adding back central overheads of 4% which relate to services provided to the Belfast Division. The controllable residual income of the Belfast Division is positive over the period 2XX1-2XX5 which indicates that the Belfast Division makes a healthy positive contribution towards Top Flite plc.

3. Evaluation of the capital projects

An evaluation of the three capital projects currently being assessed by the finance director is provided in Appendix 2 using the decision criteria ROI and residual income. A third measure, Net Present Value (NPV) has been used to assess each project from a corporate, Top Flite plc, perspective.

A summary of the performance of each of the three projects is provided in Appendix 3. These will be considered next. However, it should be borne in mind that the evaluation is set within the context of the existing divisional target ROI of 6% and that this might alter as a result of Top Flite plc adopting a controllable figure when assessing both ROI and residual income.

Project A

Project A yields a short-term (i.e. one year perspective) positive ROI which is in excess of the division's target ROI of 6%. If the finance director adopts a short-term perspective, and assuming that divisional managers continue to be rewarded on the basis of ROI, then project A will be selected since it generates a positive ROI in excess of the division's ROI target and a positive residual income in year one. However, if we examine project A from a longer-term perspective, that is over the lifetime of the project, it is seen to yield an overall negative -8.96% ROI which does not meet the division's target ROI of 6%. Therefore the project is likely to be rejected by the finance director. If we examine the residual income generated by project A, a positive residual income of €3.2 million is achieved in the short-term while over the lifetime of the project a negative residual income of –€4.75 million is achieved. Project A serves to illustrate the conflicting results achieved when using both ROI and residual income both in the short and long-term. Adopting a company perspective, investment decisions ought to be made on the basis of NPV. In the case of project A, the NPV is –€15.76 million which suggests that the project should be rejected from a corporate perspective. Whilst the NPV result is consistent with the longer-term ROI and residual income result achieved, it is contrary to the short-term results achieved using both measures.

Project B

Project B yields a short-term positive ROI of 6.25% which exceeds the division's target ROI of 6%. Therefore adopting a short-term perspective, project B would be accepted. The short-term result of ROI is consistent with the longer-term perspective of ROI for project B, with an average of 10.73% achieved over the life-time of the project. Therefore, if the finance director adopts either a short or long-term perspective, project B would be accepted on the basis of ROI alone. If we compare this with the residual income measure, project B yields a small negligible residual income of €0.2 million in the short term and a zero residual income in the longer term. Project B also serves to illustrate the conflicting results achieved when using both ROI and residual income. Adopting a company perspective, project B yields a negative NPV of –€537,000 which concurs with the residual income measure suggesting that the project should not be accepted.

Project C

Project C yields a short-term positive ROI of only 2.5% which does not exceed the division's target ROI of 6%. Based on this the finance director might be inclined to reject project C. However, adopting a longer-term perspective the project is seen to generate an ROI of 22.5% which suggests that it is a worthwhile project over the long-term. If we compare this result with the residual income result we see that project C generates a short-term negative residual income of –€2.8 million and a long-term positive residual income of €2.5 million. The longer-term residual income result is consistent with the NPV result of €7.27 million which suggests that the project is worthwhile from the company's perspective and should therefore be accepted.

The above discussion serves to illustrate the dysfunctional consequences of using ROI as the primary method of evaluating divisional performance, particularly when a short-term perspective is adopted. The use of a residual income measure serves to illustrate that there is a greater likelihood that divisional managers will be encouraged, when acting in their best interests, to make decisions which are in the best interests of the company. However, this is only the case when divisional managers adopt a long-term perspective. Project C should be accepted since this is the only project to generate a positive NPV and a positive residual income over the life of the project.

4. The Balanced Scorecard: a strategic management system

The balanced scorecard is a performance management *system* that enables organisations to clarify their vision and strategy and translate them into action. It's authors, Robert Kaplan and David Norton, suggest that organisational performance needs to be viewed from four alternative perspectives which seek to provide answers to a number of questions (see figure below): the customer perspective – how do customers see us?; the internal business process perspective – what must we excel at?; the learning and growth perspective – how can we continue to improve and create value?; and finally, the financial perspective – how do we look to shareholders?

The Balanced Scorecard

Since the early work of Kaplan and Norton (1993), the concept of the balanced scorecard has been developed as a strategic management system. According to Kaplan and Norton (1996), the balanced scorecard can be implemented as a strategic management system by developing four key processes, that separately and in combination, contribute towards linking long-term strategic objectives with short term actions. The four key processes are as follows:

1. Translating the organisation's/division's vision and strategy into specific strategic objectives. This entails defining the vision and strategy as an integrated set of objectives and measures that are agreed upon by senior management and which describe the long-term drivers of success of an organisation.
2. Communicating and linking strategic objectives and measures – this requires managers to communicate the strategy throughout the organisation and to link it to divisional, departmental and individual objectives. The balanced scorecard provides a means by which managers can ensure that the long-term strategy and divisional, departmental and individual objectives are aligned.
3. Business planning, setting targets and aligning strategic initiatives – this entails setting balanced scorecard measures which are used as the basis for allocating resources and setting priorities to help the organisation achieve its strategic objectives.
4. Feedback and learning – this entails evaluating strategy in the light of performance in the four perspectives of the balanced scorecard and making changes to the strategy where necessary.

5. Key issues to be considered prior to designing and implementing a multi-dimensional performance measurement system such as the balanced scorecard.

There are a number of issues which need to be considered by our division prior to getting involved in the design and implementation of a multi-dimensional performance measurement system such as the balanced scorecard. Some of these are discussed below:

(i)   Prepare the division for change – the implementation of the balanced scorecard in most cases represents a substantial change management programme which must be managed appropriately. One key aspect of successful change management requires that adequate communication and education is undertaken throughout the organisation concerning the objectives of the performance measurement system, the likely impact on working practices and the process of development including likely timescales. Communication at the early stages may take various forms including for example, newsletters, the divisional intranet site and workshops.

(ii) Get 'buy-in' at all levels of the division – implementing the balanced scorecard is likely to result in a significant change in the way employees view their job. Thus it is important to ensure that employees at all levels, from senior executives to those on the factory floor buy-in to the concept of the balanced scorecard.

(iii) Ensure sufficient resources, both financial and time, are devoted to the design, development and implementation of the balanced scorecard project. This will entail obtaining sufficient funding from the corporate of Top Flite plc. Since the development and implementation of a balanced scorecard is likely to take several months, we will need to ensure that any disruption to normal work procedures is taken into account and plans are put in place to minimise disruption.

(iv) The Belfast Division will need to develop a detailed plan of the process required to facilitate the design, development and implementation of the balanced scorecard. This process should recognise the involvement of relevant staff at a number of levels of the organisation.

(v)   We will also need to consider the information technology implications of implementing the balanced scorecard within our division.

(vi) We need to ensure that we create an open forum for discussion and debate concerning the balanced scorecard project within the Belfast Division. This will ensure that members are kept informed and will allay any fears that employees might have.

References

Kaplan R.S. and D.P. Norton (1993). 'Putting the Balanced Scorecard to Work', Harvard Business Review, September-October, pp. 134-147.

Kaplan, R.S. and D.P Norton (1996), 'Using the Balanced Scorecard as a Strategic Management System', Harvard Business Review, Jan-Feb, pp. 75-85.

Appendix 1
Table 1, Belfast Division: Top Flite plc
Calculation of ROI and Profit

	2XX1 €'m	2XX2 €'m	2XX3 €'m	2XX4 €'m	2XX5 €'m
Invested Capital	550	535	500	440	390
ROI	5.45%	5.98%	6.60%	6.82%	6.92%
Profit	30	32	33	30	27

Table 2
Belfast Division: Top Flite plc
Calculation of Controllable ROI and Residual Income

	2XX1 €million	2XX2 €million	2XX3 €million	2XX4 €million	2XX5 €million
Invested capital	550	535	500	440	390
ROI	5.45%	5.98%	6.60%	6.82%	6.92%
Profit	30	32	33	30	27
Residual income	−3	−0.1	3	3.6	3.6
Allocated overheads (4%)	22	21.4	20	17.6	15.6
Controllable profit	52	53.4	53	47.6	42.6
Controllable ROI	9.45%	9.98%	10.60%	10.82%	10.92%
R.I. charge (6%)	33	32.1	30	26.4	23.4
Controllable R.I.	19	21.3	23	21.2	19.2

Appendix 2
Project A

Project A	Year 0 €million	Year 1 €million	Year 2 €million	Year 3 €million	Year 4 €million
Net asset value at beginning of year		80	60	40	20
Net cash flow		28	15	15	15
Depreciation		20	20	20	20
Net profit		8	−5	−5	−5
Cost of capital	6%	4.80	3.60	2.40	1.20

(continued)

Appendix 2 (continued)

Residual income			3.20	-8.60	-7.40	-6.20
ROI			10.00%	-8.33%	-12.50%	-25.00%
Discount Factors			0.9434	0.8900	0.8396	0.7921
Present Value		-80	26	13	13	12
NPV		-15.76				

Project B

Project B	Year 0 €million	Year 1 €million	Year 2 €million	Year 3 €million	Year 4 €million
Net asset value at beginning of project		80	60	40	20
Net cash flow		25	18	22	27
Depreciation		20	20	20	20
Net profit		5	-2	2	7
Cost of capital	6%	4.80	3.60	2.40	1.20
Residual income		0.20	-5.60	-0.40	5.80
ROI		6.25%	-3.33%	5.00%	35.00%
Discount Factors		0.9434	0.8900	0.8396	0.7921
Present Value	-80	24	16	18	21
NPV	**-0.54**				

Project C

Project C	Year 0 €million	Year 1 €million	Year 2 €million	Year 3 €million	Year 4 €million
Net asset value at beginning of project		80	60	40	20
Net cash flow		22	20	25	35
Depreciation		20	20	20	20
Net profit		2	0	5	15
Cost of capital	6%	4.80	3.60	2.40	1.20
Residual income		-2.80	-3.60	2.60	13.80
ROI		2.50%	0.00%	12.50%	75.00%
Discount Factors		0.9434	0.8900	0.8396	0.7921
Present Value	-80	21	18	21	28
NPV	**7.27**				

Appendix 3
Summary of Project A, B and C

Decision Criteria		Year 1	Year 2	Year 3	Year 4	Average
ROI						
Project A		10.00%	−8.33%	−12.50%	−25.00%	−8.96%
Project B		6.25%	−3.33%	5.00%	35.00%	10.73%
Project C		2.50%	0.00%	12.50%	75.00%	22.50%
Residual income						
Project A		3.20	−8.60	−7.40	−6.20	−4.75
Project B		0.20	−5.60	−0.40	5.80	0
Project C		−2.80	−3.60	2.60	13.80	2.5
NPV						
Project A	€'m	−15.76				
Project B	€'m	−0.54				
Project C	€'m	7.27				

Case 13

Solution to Mississippi Inc.

Tony Brabazon and Tony O'Dea, University College Dublin

Question 1

Cost of distribution centre for next two months
First, work out the variable portion of the activity costs:
number of items (last month) = 400,000
number of orders (last month) = 200,000

Total costs of each activity:

	Volume	Cost driver rate (€)	Total (€)
Picking	400,000	1.25	500,000
Packing	400,000	0.25	100,000
Shipping	200,000	0.75	150,000
Transfer	200,000	0.50	100,000

Split fixed and variable components out:

	Total (€) – Fixed	Total VC	Volume	Var cost
Picking	500,000 – 400,000	100,000	400,000	0.25
Packing	100,000 – 80,000	20,000	400,000	0.05
Shipping	150,000 – 100,000	50,000	200,000	0.25
Transfer	100,000 – 80,000	20,000	200,000	0.10

Next two months:

	Month 1	Month 2
Sales volume + 30%	€13m	€16.9m
Av. Order value (€65)		
Number of orders	200,000	260,000
Items (*3)	600,000	780,000

Costs for next month:

	Fixed (€)	Activity	Var cost	Total (€)
Picking	400,000	600,000	0.25	550,000
Packing	80,000	600,000	0.05	110,000
Shipping	100,000	200,000	0.25	150,000
Transfer	80,000	200,000	0.10	100,000
				910,000

Costs for following month:

	Fixed (€) (+10%)	Activity	Var cost	Total (€)
Picking	440,000	780,000	0.25	635,000
Packing	88,000	780,000	0.05	127,000
Shipping	110,000	260,000	0.25	175,000
Transfer	88,000	260,000	0.10	114,000
				1,051,000

Question 2

Outsourcing option:

	Month 1	Month 2
Sales volume + 30%	€13m	€16.9m
Commission (8%)	€1,040,000	€1,352,000

Question 3

If outsourced: BEP = FC / CMR
                    = €4m / 12%
                    = €33.33m
(CMR = SP − VC = 100% − 80% − 8% = 12%)

Question 4

Examining the financial implications of the outsourcing option for the next two months, it can be seen that outsourcing is more expensive than maintaining the distribution activities in-house. Unless USP are prepared to reduce their 8% commission charge, there is no compelling financial reason to outsource.

Leaving aside the financial considerations, the outsourcing of the distribution centre's activities is a decision that should not be taken lightly. Maintaining high-levels of customer service are critical to ensuring Mississippi's continuing success. If USP were to let service levels slip, this could have a devastating impact on the business, as on-line retailing is critically dependent on customer trust. One possible mechanism to help insure that USP maintain high standards of customer care, is to negotiate a commission rate which is linked to agreed metrics of customer satisfaction.

Conversely, if USP have an established track record in running such distribution centres effectively; it may be low risk to outsource the activities to them. One side benefit of this is that it would allow Mississippi to concentrate on the marketing and IT sides of the business without having to devote management time to running the distribution centre.

Question 5

Balanced Scorecard	
Perspectives	**Scorecard Measures**
Financial	Sales growth
	Profit by product line
	Profit per customer
	Distribution centre costs
	Customer satisfaction
	Customer satisfaction index
	Customer retention rate
	Number of new customers
	Number of customer complaints
	Market share
Internal business processes	On-time deliveries to customers
	On-time deliveries from suppliers
	Delivery cycle time
	Productivity
	Number of stock-outs
	Quality defects
Learning and growth	Employee satisfaction index
	Employee turnover
	Employee suggestions
	Employee training
	Number of new products introduced

The four perspectives chosen consist of an integrated set of performance measures that are derived from the company's strategy. In the balanced scorecard developed above, there is a clear cause and effect linkage between each of the perspectives. To increase sales and profitability, it is necessary to retain existing customers and increase new customers. It is important that these customers are satisfied. Customers require speedy delivery of their orders in good condition and containing the correct items. Customers also require a wide range of products. Finally, to underpin all of the above, it is important that the workforce is highly motivated and properly trained.

Case 14

Solution to EasyONline

Tony Brabazon and Tony O'Dea, University College Dublin

Question 1

Monthly Sales

	Manchester (€)		London (€)
9a.m. – 6p.m. (12,000*1*€1)	12,000	(80,000*1*€1)	80,000
6p.m. – 9a.m. (28,000*2*€1)	56,000	(100,000*2*€1)	200,000
	68,000		280,000
Computer Usage = 60%			
=> 'Other Sales' = 40%	45,333		186,667
Total Sales	113,333		466,667

Question 2

Number of half-hour blocks to breakeven

	Manchester
Fixed Costs:	
Staff	10,000
Lease	20,000
Connection	15,000
General	5,000
	50,000

Next, work out the contribution margin per half-hour block of time:

Selling price per half hour block of computer time	€1.00
Add: 'other sales' per half hour (€1 / 60% * 40%)	0.66
Total sales	€1.66

Variable costs per half-hour block:	€
Staff	0.167
Computer rental (0.1*€1)	0.10
Other: Admin (0.05*€1.67)	0.083
Other: Costs of 'other revenue' (30%*€0.66)	0.198
	0.548

Therefore, contribution margin per half-hour is: €1.66 − €0.548 = €1.112, and the breakeven point is:

50,000 / 1.112 = 44,964 half-hour blocks per month.

(**Note:** Assume that all the costs of 'other sales' are variable => the contribution margin on these sales is also 30%)

Question 3

Current levels	Manchester (€)	London (€)
Sales	113,333	466,667
Less Variable Costs:		
Staff (10% of revenue)	11,333	46,667
P.C. leasing (10% of computer rev.)	6,800	28,000
Administration (5% all)	5,667	23,334
Costs of 'other revenue' (30% of 'other rev')	13,600	56,000
Total Contribution Margin	75,933	312,666
Less Fixed Costs:		
Staff (1/12)	10,000	10,000
Lease (1/12)	20,000	300,000
Connection	15,000	35,000
Administration	5,000	5,000
Profit (Loss)	**25,933**	**(37,334)**

Sales + 10%	Manchester (€)	London (€)
Sales	124,666	513,334
Less Variable Costs:		
Staff (10% of revenue)	12,467	51,333
P.C. leasing (10% of computer rev.)	7,480	30,800
Administration (5% all)	6,233	25,667
Costs of 'other revenue' (30% of 'other rev')	14,960	61,600
Total Contribution Margin	83,526	343,934
Less Fixed Costs:		
Staff (1/12)	10,000	10,000
Lease (1/12)	20,000	300,000
Connection	15,000	35,000
Administration	5,000	5,000
Profit (Loss)	**33,526**	**(6,066)**

Question 4

- Why might the chain's profitability have slipped?
- Set-up costs of new cafes may have impacted on profitability (marketing costs, slow ramp-up of customer demand, staff training etc.)
- Mix of cafes may have veered towards smaller cafes, in which it is harder to recover fixed costs

- There may be a change in usage patterns, even though total number of customers has not declined (staying on-line for less time)
- 'Other revenues' may have declined.

Question 5

Pricing strategy is a critical decision in any organisation as it impacts directly on sales volume, cash flows and profitability. While the current pricing strategy (flat rate pricing) is easy to implement and is easy for customers to understand, it fails to consider that different customers will place differing value on the product (internet access), and that the same customer will place differing value on the product at different times of the day.

Ideally, the optimal pricing strategy is to charge each customer the full value they receive from consuming the product (perfect price discrimination) but this is rarely possible as firms do not have complete information on their customers. A variant on this idea which is commonly seen in high-fixed cost industries such as power generation or indeed running an internet café, is to offer lower rates during off-peak. This can help reduce peak demand and therefore reduce the level of (expensive) capacity that the firm needs to invest in.

Variants on offering off-peak rates would be to offer additional services off-peak (for example, free coffee or reduced cost printing).

Case 15

Solution to Beara Bay Cheese

Margaret Healy, University College Cork

REPORT ON ISSUES FACING
BEARA BAY CHEESE

Prepared by: Andrew Healy
Healy O'Rourke Consulting

For: Jana Williams and Thom Williams
Beara Bay Cheese

1. Terms of reference

This report reviews the sales and marketing strategy of Beara Bay Cheese and considers the adequacy or otherwise of the existing management accounting system in informing such decisions. Following preliminary discussions as of xx/xx/xxxx, I now present the report requested. Costing and breakeven calculations generated for Beara Bay are presented and reviewed. The relevance and limitations of cost-volume-profit analysis to business decisions at Beara Bay Cheese is explained and the proposed implementation of an activity-based costing system is considered. The viability of expanding turnover via the outsourcing of sales activity to Thom is also considered, both from Thom's perspective and in light of its impact on the existing business. All calculations included in this report are based on figures supplied by Beara Bay Cheese and have not been independently verified.

2. Recommendations

(a)   The benefits of installing an extensive activity-based costing system for monitoring product costs are unlikely to justify the costs involved, particularly given that Beara Bay does not employ a full-time accounting professional.

(b)   Reliance on a single unit level overhead allocation base in the current costing system does not reflect the underlying economics of the sales process at Beara Bay Cheese. Careful consideration should be given to the periodic use of an ABC model for ad hoc studies, providing Beara Bay with greater insights into the factors driving the consumption of organisational resources.

(c)   Weighed average contribution rather than simple average contribution should be used in determining breakeven product volumes.

(d)   Thom's proposal offers a return greater than that currently available from all existing customer segments. It should therefore be taken up by Beara Bay.

3. Concerns regarding the existing management accounting system

Concerns regarding the existing management accounting system at Beara Bay Cheese are reflected in the perceived usefulness or otherwise of the resulting accounting information, in particular that regarding breakeven analysis and that regarding overhead allocation. Each of these aspects of the accounting information system is discussed in greater detail in the following paragraphs.

(a) Breakeven analysis

Breakeven or CVP analysis is a way of systematically evaluating the relationship between changes in activity and changes in sales revenues, expenses and net profits. This information is vital to the management of Beara Bay Cheese as it allows identification of the critical levels of sales such that no losses will occur in the short term. Extending the analysis to the longer term is complex and questionable, in that the relevant ranges assumed in the short term may no longer apply. Extending production at Beara Bay Cheese for example requires increments in fixed costs – e.g. additional sales-persons salary; acquisition of additional capacity once the current excess capacity is used up. In the longer term, volume will not be the only factor that impacts on total costs, total revenues and profits.

In situations involving more than one product breakeven calculations should be based on the weighted average unit contribution. The initial analysis did not differentiate between the contribution available from 1 kg of the CaiseBui cheese and 1 kg of the BearaBeag cheese, even though the latter offers a significantly higher level of contribution per unit. Recalculating the contribution per kilogram of cheese for each of the products individually recognises the differing levels of contribution of each product and allows the use of cost-volume-profit analysis to provide insights into the breakeven level of sales mix. Revised breakeven results for Beara Bay based on the business plan estimates provided for the current year (detailed analysis shown in Appendix 1) are as follows.

	CaiseBui	BearaBeag
Contribution per kg.	€8.12	€10.48
Breakeven sales volume	2,974 kg	4,107 kg

CVP analysis also has a number of other limitations:

(i)   All variables other than volume are assumed to remain constant; i.e. volume is the only factor assumed to affect fixed costs. However, as will be shown in the results of the ABC analysis presented later in this report, some of the causal factors for fixed costs are related to non-unit level activities. If there are significant changes in the levels of these activities, then the outcomes of the CVP analysis will be incorrect.

(ii) CVP analysis assumes that the levels of sales for each product will be in accordance with the sales mix as anticipated in the business plan. However if this initial assumption does not hold true (as the information supplied indicates is the case at Beara Bay Cheese), then the analysis must be viewed with caution.

(iii) Total costs and total revenue are assumed to be linear functions of output. CVP analysis assumed unit costs and selling price are constant – i.e. that the behaviour of sales and costs will remain constant despite increases or decreases in the level of sales.

(iv) Profits are calculated on a variable costing basis. It is assumed that the fixed costs incurred during the period are charged as an expense for that period only.

(v)   Complexity-related fixed costs are assumed to not change.

(b) Overhead allocation process

At Beara Bay overheads represent a substantial proportion of the total costs. When these overheads are traced back to their underlying causal factors, it can be seen that they are not primarily driven by volume, but are related instead to the complexity of the sales process and the unequal consumption of overhead resources by each customer grouping. Simply allocating overheads on a 'per kilo of cheese' sold basis does not reflect the differing selling activities and consequent costs involved in selling each kilogram. Reviewing the costs per customer using activity-based costing practices yields the following information (see appendix 2 for detailed calculations):

	Midleton market	Bantry market	Catering trade
Sales Revenues	59,330	21,470	153,100
Contribution	24,165	10,075	63,990
(as % of Revenues)	41%	47%	42%
Net Profit	€6,998	€3,659	€12,724
(as % of Revenues)	12%	17%	8%

Activity-based costing systems consider the activities undertaken in the production and sale of products to be the causal factor explaining overhead costs. Rather than simply allocate overheads to costs using a unit-level driver (e.g. kilo of cheese), activity-based costing systems instead seek to trace those costs to the underlying activities causing the costs to increment. ABC uses measures of activity rather than volume to trace indirect costs to the cost objects, thus recognising that:

- Costs may be related to batches of a product rather than units of that product, as is the instance of the €8,685 of overheads incurred for 'transactions' related activity.
- Costs may be related to one product or customer only, as is the case in relation to the €3,756 cost of rush orders to the catering trade.

ABC systems therefore use cause-and-effect allocation bases, unlike the existing absorption costing system at Beara Bay which relied on an arbitrary unit-level allocation – 'kilogram of cheese.'

(c) Implementing an ABC system

The current costing system at Beara Bay does not provide adequate information for distinguishing the most profitable customer segments available to the company – key information in relation to the decision scenario currently facing the organisation. Inaccuracies resulting from the inability of the absorption costing system to capture sufficiently the consumption of overhead resources by product or customer groupings distort reported costs.

Simple cost systems such as that in present use at Beara Bay are inexpensive to operate, making extensive use of arbitrary cost allocations but in turn providing lower levels of accuracy in circumstances such as that pertaining to Beara Bay. At Beara Bay, overheads are a large percentage of total costs (51% of actual costs in the current year). These overhead costs are not primarily driven by volume or some other unit-level driver, but are instead related to a variety of other transaction drivers, as was indicated in both the information supplied by Beara Bay and that underpinning the customer cost and profitability calculations provided in appendix 2 of this report.

Sophisticated costing systems such as ABC rely on cause-and-effect allocation mechanisms. They are more expensive to operate given the amount of information required to identify and operationalise such drivers; however this investment is often more than redeemed in terms of the higher levels of accuracy provided and low cost of errors. When considered vis-à-vis each other, products/customers do not consume organisational resources in similar proportions. More sophisticated cost information than that currently available is required therefore to capture this diversity and to more accurately assign overhead costs to products.

4. Feasibility of the proposal to expand sales

The proposal currently on offer to Beara Bay from Thom is reviewed in this section of the report. This review is conducted in respect of two perspectives: that of Thom (see (i) below) and that of Beara Bay Cheese (discussed in (ii) below).

(i)   For Thom's proposal to reach its target profit level of €2,500, the maximum he should pay for the cheese is €13.23 per kg (see appendix 3 for detailed calculations). In order to simply breakeven (assuming a purchase price of €13.23 per kg) Thom will need to sell 767 kg of cheese. This purchase price however is below that which Jana is prepared to accept the offer at.

(ii) Appendix 4 details the profits available to Beara Bay Cheese (based on the information provided) for each of the cheese purchase prices proposed. At €14 per kg., the proposal generates an expected return of 42% or €7,116. At the lower price of €13.23 per kg., the proposal offers an expected return of 39% or €6,192.

Rather than focus solely on the financial consequences of the proposal as outlined above, there are a number of other issues that also have a bearing on the proposal.

(i)   Lack of product availability seems to be the biggest factor preventing expansion of existing sales. Beara Bay Cheese products are popular in the marketplace, with demand exceeding supply. The agency proposal, even if it is only availed of in the shorter term, may allow Jana extra time to concentrate on expanding cheese production.

(ii) The return available from sales to Thom is far in excess of that available to Beara Bay via sales to existing customers. Jana may have strategic marketing reasons for continuing to serve the Midleton and Bantry farmers markets, but should also consider out-sourcing this activity to Thom.

(iii) The €10,000 charge for marketing consultancy services is adversely impacting on the profitability of the catering trade customer segment. The charge however is unlikely to be incurred in the future.

(iv) Beara Bay should consider the introduction of a charge for rush orders. Given existing demand and supply conditions in the marketplace, it is unlikely to adversely impact upon sales. Greater insights into the pattern of rush orders would also help determine if such orders occur randomly or are largely related to one or a few trade customers. Information regarding the catering trade customer segment currently groups all such customers as one homogenous entity.

Appendix 1
Breakeven Analysis, Based on Business Plan

	CaiseBui	BearaBeag
Net profit	12,600	34,160
Contribution	40,600	73,360
Overheads	**€28,000**	**€39,200**
At €5.60 per kg: - the number of kg's sold:	5,000	7,000
% of Sales mix	42%	58%
Contribution per kg	40,600 / 5,000 = **€8.12**	73,360 / 7,000 = **€10.48**

Weighted average contribution:

(42% * 8.12) + (58% * 10.48)   =   €9.49

Breakeven point:

€67,200 / €9.49   ≈   7081 kg

Of this breakeven volume:

CaiseBui	42%	≈	2,974 kg
BearaBeag	58%	≈	4,107 kg

Appendix 2
Analysis of Customer Profitability Using Activity-based Costing Practices
(Based on actual cost figures as supplied by Beara Bay Cheese)

	Midleton market	Bantry market	Catering trade
Sales:			
– CaiseBui	25,330	4,470	59,600
– BearaBeag	34,000	17,000	93,500
	59,330	21,470	153,100
Direct Costs:			
– Materials	13,270	4,930	34,400
– Labour	13,111	4,449	33,470
Production overheads	8,784	2,016	21,240
Contribution	**24,165**	**10,075**	**63,990**

(continued)

Appendix 2 (continued)

Market-related overheads:

— Packaging	1,850	650	4,750
— Travel mileage	3,120	416	22,753
— Advertising	633	633	10,000
— Product Promotions	1,606	647	—
— Rush orders	—	—	3,756
— Administration:			
• Market registration fee	250	100	—
• Book-keepers salary	3,805	1,377	9,818
• Transactions	5,903	2,593	189
	17,167	6,416	51,266
Net Profit	**€6,998**	**€3,659**	**€12,724**
(as % of Revenues)	12%	17%	8%

Appendix 3
Analysis of Thom's Proposal
(Based on actual cost figures as supplied by Beara Bay Cheese)

Costs of Thom's proposal: €'s

Registration Fee	300
Levy – insurance	100
Mileage (130 * 0.40 * 52)	2,704
Display stand & scales	520
Packaging costs	800
	€4,424

Anticipated sales revenue:

1,200 kg * €19.00 per kg   €22,800

Calculation of Contribution per unit:

1,200 units	=	(4424 + 2500) / contribution per unit
Contribution per unit	=	(4424 + 2500) / 1200 units
	=	€5.77
Sales Price €19.00 – Contribution €5.77	=	Cost: €13.23

Breakeven:

Fixed costs / Contribution per unit	=	4,424 / 5.77
	=	767 kg
OR		€14,568

Appendix 4
Net Profits from the Agency Proposal
(Based on actual cost figures as supplied by Beara Bay Cheese)

	At €14 per kg of cheese	At €13.23 per kg of cheese
Sales:	16,800	15,876
Direct Costs:		
– Materials	4,800	4,800
– Labour	3,960	3,960
Production overheads	864	864
Contribution	**7,176**	**6,252**
Market-related overheads:		
– Packaging	60	60
Net Profit	**€7,116**	**€6,192**
(as % of Revenues)	(42%)	(39%)

Case 16

Solution to Newtown Manufacturing Limited

Tom Kennedy, University of Limerick

Pedagogical Objective

The case is intended to make students aware of the circumstances in which more refined product costing models are appropriate in informing managerial decision-making in terms of product pricing and product profitability. It facilitates comparison between a traditional product costing model and the more contemporary ABC approach. The case content is categorised under the full costing element of managerial accounting.

Question 1: Prepare revised product-costing models for the components product group.

As there are real concerns that the current traditional costing system distorts the cost of product lines, it is appropriate to prepare revised models using methods which are deemed to be better able to represent the demands made by each product line on Newtown's resources.

The current practice of using a method, based on direct labour, is likely to provide biased product cost information and lead to significant cross-subsidisation. Direct labour, as a basis for assigning general overheads, is becoming increasingly irrelevant, as it generally bears no relationship to how they were incurred. Direct labour is being replaced by sophisticated machinery and becoming a much smaller component of total product cost. Therefore, a more appropriate measure that could better reflect the new technological environment is machine-hours. Appendix 1 presents the revised product line performance report for January-March 2XX6, using machine-hours as an allocation base.

In recognition of the fact that general overheads in the modern business environment are not homogeneous in terms of being primarily influenced by volume and in order to capture the increasing complexity of business activity, the ABC method could be used. This method is based on two basic principles, namely:

(a) that all costs (resources) are perceived as a result of the activities performed such as mould design/manufacture, manufacturing operations, quality inspection etc

(b) that all costs are first related to activities and then to cost objects, depending on how much each cost object draws on the activities.

Appendix 2 presents the revised product line performance report for January-March 2XX6, using the major activities and associated cost drivers identified as part of the pilot study and presented in Appendix 2 of the case.

Question 2: Comment on the outcome of the revised costing models.

The aim of the pilot study was to critically review the components product group cost structure and see if Newtown could or should revise its pricing policy. A review of Appendix 1 of the case study shows that Newtown is achieving a healthy mark-up on its costs of 18% versus a target of approximately 20%. However, the results are not consistent across the three product lines. Alpha is reporting a mark-up of 14%, Beta 21% and Gamma 18%. This suggests that Alpha is the product line that is underperforming, Beta is overperforming and Gamma is in a relatively strong position to address the competitive threat from the Malaysian supplier.

However, a traditional costing system, using direct labour hours as an allocation base has the potential to give unreliable product cost data and lead to significant product cross-subsidisation. This type of broad averaging or cost smoothing is an expected outcome of the system currently used by Newtown. Its consequences are particularly critical for companies who place great reliance on mark-up as a pricing basis and/or strategy. Therefore, 'more appropriate and refined' allocation methods such as machine hours and ABC should be used in order to better inform managerial decision-making.

Appendix 1 shows a revised product line performance report, using machine hours as the allocation base. This allocation base better reflects the greater complexity and automation associated with the individual product lines. It shows that both Alpha and Beta are overperforming at 25% and 23% respectively and that Gamma is only barely profitable with a mark-up of 3%.

Appendix 2 incorporates the results of the pilot study and shows a revised product line performance report, using ABC data as the allocation base. This methodology further reflects the greater complexity and automation associated with the individual product lines. It shows that Alpha is performing well with a mark-up of 20%, Beta is the jewel in the business at 34% and Gamma is not even covering its costs at a minus 2% mark-up.

These outcomes should come as a major surprise to the senior management team and are likely to be seriously challenged. Questions will be asked about the integrity and reliability of the process that gave rise to this information. Reference should be made to the principles underpinning the model and the input of the various parties in activity and cost driver identification. Some caution should be expressed as to the claims of absolute accuracy, but ultimately the debate should focus on what model best reflects the consumption of resources in the organisation. In effect, do the revised models better capture the underlying complexity and variety of tasks as identified by Appendix 2 (of the case) by product line and are they consistent with reasonable expectations. In other words, are they intuitively sound and rational? If so, management should, therefore, concentrate their efforts in using the 'new' information to make the appropriate decisions and continue their search for further refinement of the process.

Further, at a micro level, Appendix 2 presents powerful information in terms of resource usage, efficiency and the potential for greater economies by identifying a cost driver rate. For example, it shows the impact of Gamma using more moulds and having higher distribution and order processing costs relative to the other product lines. This information should focus the attention of individual managers for corrective action. Serious consideration needs to be given to initiating greater efficiencies in the areas clearly identified by the magnitude of the individual cost driver rates.

Appendix 3 and 4 present a comparison by product line and allocation base. They suggest that Newtown should look seriously at its pricing strategy for both Alpha and Beta with a view to generating more volume in both cases. This potential re-balancing of its product mix may offer some possibilities of protecting or improving its overall profitability while it is dealing with the specific Gamma product line competitive threat. In the absence of the pilot study and the insights gained by the activity analysis, management action would be likely to compound the current problem by making the wrong decision. Appendix 3 and 4 clearly show that Gamma is not operationally efficient and a knee-jerk reaction in reducing the price is not the solution. Newtown is typical of a lot of firms who place 'blind' faith in championing a product line that is strategically driven, technologically rich and resource intensive but cost poor relative to its other products.

In summary, the current traditional costing system appears to mask serious undercosting in the Gamma product line and some overcosting in both the Alpha and Beta product lines. Consequently, as currently manufactured and delivered, Newtown is not in a position to address the competitive threat to Gamma from the Malaysian supplier through price competitiveness. In the short-term, it may have to address the threat by focusing on the non-price attributes, such as functionality, reliability, service quality, flexibility, after-care service etc. This is due to the fact that it would take some time to implement the operational decisions identified by the activity identification exercise. Obviously, the option to do nothing is not sustainable, as the competitive threat is real and could be potentially very damaging. A combination of serious market re-evaluation of all product lines, better informed and more focussed operational action has to be undertaken with some urgency.

Question 3: Advise on whether Newtown should adopt ABC.

ABC has generally proved highly successful in firms that have implemented it. Product costs and profitability have been shown to be significantly different and overhead cost causality has been better understood. There is evidence to suggest that cost-driver measures can have strong motivational effects on those in contact with them (Jonez and Wright, 1987). With careful selection of cost-drivers, the dysfunctional consequences of ill-considered measurement systems could be reduced. Ultimately, the utility of ABC will be dependent on how well the system fits the circumstances of the organisation.

Adopting a fully customised ABC system would represent a significant strategic decision by Newtown and would require the full support of all management in order to be successful. The pilot project could be seen as a first step in improving the quality and integrity of the management information and should continue. The process could be further refined by critically reviewing the choice of activities and cost drivers on an on-going basis. It could be embellished by further classification of the cost categories and an attempt at constructing a cost hierarchy under four levels: unit, batch, product and facility. It could attempt to increase the degree of costs directly traceable to individual products or product lines. Attention should also be brought to bear on the direct costs and the need for ongoing competitiveness in these areas. The appropriate level of sophistication adopted would be subject to the cost/benefit test and the contingency theory perspective.

In effect, the process should be seen as a continual search for a greater understanding of the link between resource spending and consumption and confidence in the choice of activities and drivers. The financial analyst, Mick Dowd should continue to champion the process and engage with all the functional department heads and other relevant personnel. Newtown would benefit greatly from the deepening interaction between operational managers and accounting staff and the availability of relevant non-financial data.

In the short-to medium term, the process could be mapped and supported using excel. It is unlikely that the investment in technology and intellectual capital necessary for the installation of a fully customised system would be feasible at this time. The process could, in time, be expanded to include budgeting, cost modelling and performance measurement.

Finally, a refined costing model using machine hours or ABC is not a panacea for all the problems associated with the provision of costing information to management. Like any conventional system they are concerned with yesterday's costs. However, it is fair to suggest that a better understanding of the past is a prerequisite for enhancing the ability of management to better predict the future.

Question 4: Circumstances in which ABC would be most benefical.

Circumstances in which you would expect ABC to be most beneficial:

- high overhead costs that are not proportional to the unit volume of individual products;
- significant automation that has made it more difficult to assign overhead to products using the traditional approach;
- the production of a wide variety of products or services;
- profit margins that are difficult to explain; and
- hard-to-make (complex) products that show profits and easy-to-make products that show losses.

Key attributes of ABC:

- New technology/new way of thinking with potential to offer new insights (Friedman & Lyne, 1995);
- Evolutionary rather than revolutionary (Bromwich & Bhimani v Kaplan & Cooper);
- A more equitable allocation of overheads (determines underlying 'driver' of the activities);
- An ability to deal with a complex and opaque cost structure (range of measurement and calculative routines);
- An ability to integrate the non-accounting aspects – transaction costing (process of activity identification – minutiae of production process);
- Characteristics of diversity and enrichment versus conservatism and uniformity of traditional systems; and
- A control device – disciplinary technique, enabling 'managing of managers,' depersonalises act of control.

Essential features:

- Activity analysis;
- Enlarged concept of cost variability. Treat as many costs as is possible as variable;
- Flexibility;
- Compatibility with general process approach to organisations, i.e. business process engineering; and
- Diversity in use and wider application than a traditional volume based costing system.

Appendix 1
Components Group: Revised Product Line Performance Report
(Traditional Job Costing System using Machine Hours): January–March 2XX6

	Product Lines (Gross)				Rate per machine hour *1	Product Lines (Unit)		
	Alpha	Beta	Gamma	Total		Alpha	Beta	Gamma
	€	€	€	€	€	€	€	€
Sales Value	1,600,000	1,650,000	1,150,000	4,400,000		80.00	110.00	115.00
Direct Costs								
Direct Material	400,000	255,000	250,000	905,000		20.00	17.00	25.00
Direct Labour	220,000	225,000	135,000	580,000		11.00	15.00	13.50
Total Direct Costs	620,000	480,000	385,000	1,485,000		31.00	32.00	38.50
General Overhead								
Manufacturing	221,964	291,327	249,709	763,000	11.10	11.10	19.42	24.97
Engineering	82,327	108,055	92,618	283,000	4.12	4.12	7.20	9.26
Sales & Distribution	161,018	211,336	181,146	553,500	8.05	8.05	14.09	18.11
Administration*2	189,673	248,945	213,382	652,000	9.48	9.48	16.60	21.34
Total General Overhead	654,982	859,663	736,855	2,251,500	32.75	32.75	57.31	73.68
Total Product Cost per Traditional System (Machine Hours)				3,736,500		63.75	89.31	112.18
Profit by product line/unit	325,018	310,337	28,145	663,500	Mark-up 18%	16.25	20.69	2.82
(Before inventory adjustments)					Mark-up	25%	23%	3%
*1 Total machine hours	20,000	26,250	22,500	68,750				
*2 Includes contribution of €130,000 to corporate head office								
Volume (units)	20,000	15,000	10,000	45,000				

Appendix 2
Components Group: Revised Product Line Performance Report (ABC System): January–March 2XX6

	Product Lines (Gross)					Rate per	Unit Product Cost €		
	Alpha €	Beta €	Gamma €	Total €	Dept	Cost Driver €	Alpha €	Beta €	Gamma €
Sales Value	1,600,000	1,650,000	1,150,000	4,400,000			80.00	110.00	115.00
Direct Costs									
Direct Material	400,000	255,000	250,000	905,000			20.00	17.00	25.00
Direct Labour	220,000	225,000	135,000	580,000			11.00	15.00	13.50
Total Direct Costs	620,000	480,000	385,000	1,485,000			31.00	32.00	38.50
General Overhead									
Activities									
Mould design/manufacture	72,222	126,389	126,389	325,000	Manf	3,611.11	3.61	8.43	12.64
Manufacturing operations	67,782	88,964	76,254	233,000	Manf	3.39	3.39	5.93	7.63
Supervision of direct labour	41,739	46,957	31,304	120,000	Mnfg	2.09	2.09	3.13	3.13
Quality inspection	23,448	29,310	32,242	85,000	Mnfg	586.21	1.17	1.95	3.22
Plant engineering/utilities	66,105	41,316	49,579	157,000	Eng	5.51	3.31	2.75	4.96
Process and test engineering	47,547	42,792	35,661	126,000	Eng	2,377.36	2.38	2.85	3.57
Distribution	131,250	131,250	175,000	437,500	S/D	4,375.00	6.56	8.75	17.50
Sales & marketing expenses	29,455	30,375	21,170	81,000	S/D	810.00	1.47	2.03	2.12
Invoicing	10,938	13,125	10,937	35,000	S/D	437.50	0.55	0.88	1.09
Materials management	42,681	32,638	42,681	118,000	Adm	502.13	2.13	2.18	4.27
Procurement	57,459	36,630	35,911	130,000	Adm	1,300.00	2.87	2.44	3.59
Order processing	13,103	22,931	58,966	95,000	Adm	655.17	0.66	1.53	5.90
Customer administration	15,758	19,697	29,545	65,000	Adm	1,969.70	0.79	1.31	2.95
Information systems support	18,667	10,667	9,666	39,000	Adm	333.33	0.93	0.71	0.97
General administration	71,304	80,217	53,479	205,000	Adm	3.57	3.57	5.35	5.35
Total general overhead	709,458	753,258	788,784	2,251,500			35.48	50.22	78.89
Total product cost				3,736,500			66.48	82.22	117.39
per ABC system									
Profit by product line/unit	270,542	416,742	−23,784	663,500			13.52	27.78	−2.39
			Mark-up	18%			20%	34%	−2%

Data from ABC Process

		Product Lines				
		Alpha	Beta	Gamma	Total	Dept.
Activities	**Cost Drivers**	Cost Driver Volume				
1 Mould design/manufacture	no. of parts-square foot	20	35	35	90	Manf
2 Manufacturing operations	no. of machine hours	20,000	26,250	22,500	68,750	Manf
3 Supervision of direct labour	no. of direct labour hours	20,000	22,500	15,000	57,500	Mnfg
4 Quality inspection	no. units audited	40	50	55	145	Mnfg
5 Plant engineering/utilities	square feet	12,000	7,500	9,000	28,500	Eng
6 Process and test engineering	no. of eng. change revisions	20	18	15	53	Eng
7 Distribution	% traced directly to customers	30	30	40	100	S/D
8 Sales & marketing expenses	% of sales revenue	36	38	26	100	S/D
9 Invoicing	no. of invoices	25	30	25	80	S/D
10 Materials management	no. of stock transactions	85	65	85	235	Adm
11 Procurement	% of direct material	44	28	28	100	Adm
12 Order processing	no. of orders	20	35	90	145	Adm
13 Customer administration	no. of customers	8	10	15	33	Adm
14 Information systems support	no. of desktop units	56	32	29	117	Adm
15 General administration	no. of direct labour hours	20,000	22,500	15,000	57,500	Adm

Relevant Additional Data

	Product Lines			
	Alpha	Beta	Gamma	Total
		Cost Driver Volume		
Production volume (units)	20,000	15,000	10,000	45,000
Direct material (unit) €	20	17	25	
Direct material €	400,000	255,000	250,000	905,000
Direct material %	44	28	28	100
Machine hours (unit)	1.00	1.75	2.25	
Total machine hours	20,000	26,250	22,500	68,750
Direct labour hours (unit)	1.00	1.50	1.50	
Total direct labour hours	20,000	22,500	15,000	57,500
Direct labour rate per hour	11.00	10.00	9.00	
Direct labour hours €	220,000	225,000	135,000	580,000
Sales price (unit)	80.00	110.00	115.00	
Sales revenue €	1,600,000	1,650,000	1,150,000	4,400,000
Sales revenue %	36	38	26	100

Appendix 3
Components Group Product Profitability Comparison: Overview by Product Line

	Alpha			Beta			Gamma			Overall
Sales Value €	80.00	80.00	80.00	110.00	110.00	110.00	115.00	115.00	115.00	
	Allocation Base			Allocation Base			Allocation Base			
	DL	MH	ABC	DL	MH	ABC	DL	MH	ABC	
Direct Costs €										
Direct Material	20.00	20.00	20.00	17.00	17.00	17.00	25.00	25.00	25.00	
Direct Labour	11.00	11.00	11.00	15.00	15.00	15.00	13.50	13.50	13.50	
Total Direct Costs €	31.00	31.00	31.00	32.00	32.00	32.00	38.50	38.50	38.50	
General Overhead €										
Manufacturing	13.27	11.10	10.26	19.90	19.42	19.44	19.90	24.97	26.62	
Engineering	4.92	4.12	5.68	7.38	7.20	5.61	7.38	9.26	8.52	
Sales & Distribution	9.63	8.05	8.58	14.44	14.09	11.65	14.44	18.11	20.71	
Administration	11.34	9.48	10.96	17.01	16.60	13.52	17.01	21.34	23.04	
Total General Overhead €	39.16	32.75	35.48	58.73	57.31	50.22	58.73	73.68	78.89	
Total Product Cost €	70.16	63.75	66.48	90.73	89.31	82.22	97.23	112.18	117.39	
Profit by Product: Unit €	9.84	16.25	13.52	19.27	20.69	27.78	17.77	2.82	−2.39	
Profit by Product: Gross €	196,868	325,018	270,542	288,979	310,337	416,742	177,653	28,145	−23,784	663,500
Mark-up	14%	25%	20%	21%	23%	34%	18%	3%	−2%	18%
Production Volume (units)	20,000	20,000	20,000	15,000	15,000	15,000	10,000	10,000	10,000	45,000

Appendix 4
Components Group Product Profitability Comparison: Overview by Allocation Base

Labour Hours

Allocation Base	Alpha	Beta	Gamma	Total
Sales Value	80.00	110.00	115.00	
Direct Costs €	DL	DL	DL	
Direct Material	20.00	17.00	25.00	
Direct Labour	11.00	15.00	13.50	
Total Direct Costs €	31.00	32.00	38.50	
General Overhead €				
Manufacturing	13.27	19.90	19.90	
Engineering	4.92	7.38	7.38	
Sales & Distribution	9.63	14.44	14.44	
Administration	11.34	17.01	17.01	
Total General Overhead €	39.16	58.73	58.73	
Total Product Cost €	70.16	90.73	97.23	
Profit by Product: Unit €	9.84	19.27	17.77	
Profit by Product: Gross €	196,868	288,979	177,653	663,500
Mark-up	14%	21%	18%	18%
Production Volume (units)	20,000	15,000	10,000	

Machine Hours

Allocation Base	Alpha	Beta	Gamma	Total
Sales Value	80.00	110.00	115.00	
Direct Costs €	MH	MH	MH	
Direct Material	20.00	17.00	25.00	
Direct Labour	11.00	15.00	13.50	
Total Direct Costs €	31.00	32.00	38.50	
General Overhead €				
Manufacturing	11.10	19.42	24.97	
Engineering	4.12	7.20	9.26	
Sales & Distribution	8.05	14.09	18.11	
Administration	9.48	16.60	21.34	
Total General Overhead €	32.75	57.31	73.68	
Total Product Cost €	63.75	89.31	112.18	
Profit by Product: Unit €	16.25	20.69	2.82	
Profit by Product: Gross €	325,018	310,337	28,145	663,500
Mark-up	25%	23%	3%	18%
Production Volume (units)	20,000	15,000	10,000	

ABC

Allocation Base	Alpha	Beta	Gamma	Total
Sales Value	80.00	110.00	115.00	
Direct Costs €	ABC	ABC	ABC	
Direct Material	20.00	17.00	25.00	
Direct Labour	11.00	15.00	13.50	
Total Direct Costs €	31.00	32.00	38.50	
General Overhead €				
Manufacturing	10.26	19.44	26.62	
Engineering	5.68	5.61	8.52	
Sales & Distribution	8.58	11.65	20.71	
Administration	10.96	13.52	23.04	
Total General Overhead €	35.48	50.22	78.89	
Total Product Cost €	66.48	82.22	117.39	
Profit by Product: Unit €	13.52	27.78	-2.39	
Profit by Product: Gross €	270,542	416,742	-23,784	663,500
Mark-up	20%	34%	-2%	18%
Production Volume (units)	20,000	15,000	10,000	

Case 17

Solution to Smith Specialist Car Components

Noel Hyndman, Queen's University Belfast

REPORT ON ISSUES FACED BY SMITH SPECIALIST CAR COMPONENTS

Prepared by: N. Nixon
consultant

For: Tony Smith, Managing Director,
Smith Specialist Car Components

1. Terms of Reference

Further to your communication of xx/xx/xx, I present the report requested. It contains a calculation of product costs based on an ABC system, using Mae Brown's preliminary assumptions (as provided), together with an explanation of the differences in product costs compared to the existing costing system, comments on what this suggests in terms of product profitability and strategic direction of the company, and issues to be considered relating to the possible change of the costing system to one utilising an ABC approach. Furthermore, and as asked for, it contains a calculation of the target cost of an oil pump, using the existing costing system as a base, suggestions as to why this figure should be treated with caution and views on the potential contribution of a system of target costing to Smith. Finally, an evaluation of the possibility of replacing the machines in workstation AA13 is provided. The calculations included in the report are based on figures which you have supplied and which I have not verified.

2. Recommendations

(a) An investigation into the possibility of changing from the existing costing system to one based on ABC principles should be undertaken with urgency as the present unit cost and profit signals are misleading to management.

(b) Using Mae Brown's (chief accountant) early rough workings on ABC issues to recalculate product costs, it would appear that the product costs as presently calculated, and resulting prices, should be changed. In particular, the price of catalytic converters needs to be increased because the unit costs are much higher than presently indicated.

(c) Smith should continue to focus on the brake disc market as its main market; a profitable market in which it is price competitive and where it yields the greatest proportion of its revenues.

(d) On this basis of the existing costing system it would seem appropriate to manufacture and sell oil pumps. However, given concerns as to the accuracy of the costing system in tracing costs to the products that cause costs, a decision should be delayed until information from an improved costing system is available.

(e) Target costing, coupled with an improved costing system, should be utilised in informing the pricing decision with respect to all products.

(f) On the basis of the financial information provided, it appears that machines AA/2 and AA/4 should be replaced in workstation AA13 immediately. However, a consideration of the wider qualitative factors of this decision should be undertaken before this is finalised.

3. Product Profitability Issues

(a) Product Costs using ABC system

Using Mae Brown's (chief accountant) early rough workings, as provided by you, the costs of the three products have been restated on an ABC basis using budgeted volumes and the production overhead budget for the year as a base. ABC is a more sophisticated system than the present method of cost allocation used by Smith, and attempts to allocate individual 'pools' of cost to products based on a product's consumption of the factors that cause the cost to be incurred (cost drivers). In Mae's workings, five cost drivers were identified (direct labour hours, machine hours, machine set-ups, quality inspections and value of material used and purchased). The total number of these for each product is shown in Appendix 1 and, using these numbers, the allocation of production overhead costs (in their individual cost pools) to individual products is shown in Appendix 2. Finally, the direct costs (direct material and direct labour) of each product are added to give the unit cost of production for each product as follows (detail in Appendix 3):

	ABC Production Cost per Unit
Brake Disc	€175.25
Cam Shaft Kit	€169.33
Catalytic Converter	€1,323.04

(b) Differences in ABC Unit Cost and Existing Unit Costs

The differences between the ABC unit costs and those produced by the existing system (shown in Appendix 3) are summarised here:

	Brake Discs	Cam Shaft Kits	Catalytic Converters
Production cost per unit ABC	€175.25	€169.33	€1,323.04
Production cost per unit using existing system (direct labour hrs)	€252.00	€168.00	€600.00
Difference %	•30%	1%	121%

As can be seen there is a significant decrease in cost with respect to brake discs (a high volume, relatively simply produced product) and a massive increase in cost in the case of catalytic converters (a low volume, relatively complex product). Important comments relating to this are:

(i)   The change in cost is because the existing cost allocation system uses a single cost driver (direct labour hours) as the basis for allocating all production overheads to products and this loads brake discs with inappropriate levels of production overhead cost. Given that brake discs are responsible for just over 70% of all the direct labour hours worked, in total brake discs carry over 70% of production overhead.

(ii) However, according to Mae Brown's calculations, there appear to be other cost drivers which are responsible for significant amounts of production overhead. A number of these relate more to the complexity of the product, rather than the volume (for example, catalytic converter production is responsible for over 50% of all machines set-ups).

(iii) It has been argued, and Mae Brown appears to be concurring with this contention, that ABC provides more accurate cost allocation by more clearly allocating overhead costs to products based on the principle of cause and effect.

The fact that catalytic converters, although using relatively modest quantities of direct labour time, cause substantial overhead in relation to machine set-ups, quality inspections and handling of materials is not recognised in the existing cost allocation system.

(iv) Overall there is considerable product cost distortion, with brake discs being overcosted and catalytic converters being considerably undercosted.

(c) Comments on Product Profitability Report and its Strategic Significance

Product cost is foundational information in calculating product profitability and can have a considerable impact in decision making and control within the company. The change in product costs from Smith's existing system to an ABC system is seen in Appendix 3 and the resulting impact on product profitability demonstrated in Appendix 4. From Appendix 4 it is seen that the comparative unit gross margins between the two cost systems are as follows:

	Brake Discs	Cam Shaft Kits	Catalytic Converters
Gross margin as % of actual selling price (using ABC cost)	54%	41%	Ð10%
Gross margin as indicated by existing cost per unit	34%	41%	50%

Observations regarding these figures are:

(i)   The differences in the costing systems result in clearly different signals to management as to what action is appropriate. For example, with the existing system it appears that brake discs are underperforming in terms of the target margin (achieving only a 34% gross margin at current selling price). This may encourage management to reduce the focus of Smith's activities from its main product brake discs, which accounts for 60% of revenues, and switch attention to catalytic converters which show a margin of 50%. However, with the ABC system, signals are reversed, with brake discs appearing the most profitable and catalytic converters showing up as unprofitable.

(ii) It could be argued that the existing system of cost allocation is inaccurate in moving production overhead costs to the products that cause this cost because it is highly unlikely in the circumstances described that the cause of the all production overhead cost can be traced to a single cost driver (direct labour hours). Given this, information emanating from the existing costing system may be highly problematical in terms of decision making and control (although may be adequate for inventory valuation purposes related to external reporting).

(iii) The ABC costs may be more accurate, assuming that Mae Brown's draft workings on which the ABC costs are based are reasonable in identifying cause and effect relationships. Obviously, in the long run, if a system of ABC was to be developed for Smith for routine cost accumulation purposes, more detailed investigation into appropriate cost pools and cost drivers would have to be undertaken.

(iv) Recognising the above may explain the actions of competitors relating to the prices of brake discs and catalytic converters. Price competition in the market for brake discs may be caused by competitors using more accurate costing systems (possibly ABC systems) that indicate more realistic unit costs for the product and therefore they are willing to accept lower prices that Smith's original budgeted selling prices.

(v) The inaccurate costing system may also explain the reason why Smith has been able to raise the price of catalytic converters considerably above the budgeted selling price. Indeed, the fairly sizable favourable sales volume variance with respect to catalytic converters may be indicative of prices still significantly below the competition.

(vi) In terms of the cost of catalytic converters, the possibilities for reducing the number of machine set-ups, the number of quality inspections or the number/sensitivity/cost of direct material parts should be explored with product designers. The extensive use of activities relating to these result in a high unit cost and low profitability.

(vii) The price charged for catalytic converters should be increased. This should be done with reference to competitors' prices and a more accurate assessment of cost. Only after this has been done should a decision regarding the focus of Smith's future pattern of production and sales be undertaken.

(viii) No reduction of focus on the brake disc market should be undertaken.

(ix) Given the high unit profitability of brake discs (54% using ABC unit cost information), consideration should be given to reducing prices in order to expand volume. Overall, such action could improve Smith's total profitability.

4. Issues to be Considered by Smith in a Decision on Whether or not the Present Costing System Should be Changed to one Utilising ABC

A range of issues need to be considered by Smith regarding a decision to implement ABC. These include:

(a) The costs and benefits arising from the implementation needs to be considered. It is highly likely that there will be substantial costs incurred (including external consultancy, system design change and training costs) if ABC is implemented. Benefits are likely to be less visible and may take some time to emerge. As a result, top management support is vital in ensuring a successful implementation.

(b) ABC is most likely to be useful in situations: where there is intensive competition in the markets which a company services; non-volume related indirect costs form a large proportion of total costs; and a diverse range of products is produced, all consuming expensive support activities in varying proportions. Each of these conditions applies to Smith.

(c) Management should consider the extent to which the present cost system (utilising direct labour hours to absorb overhead into products) provides useful information that can help planning and control within Smith. From the analysis already conducted it appears that there are major problems in the present costing system (see cost information relating to catalytic converters) and improvement is necessary. This is particularly the case with respect to the strategic decisions relating to pricing and product emphasis, and is likely to be equally significant with respect to ongoing control issues.

(d)   If ABC is to be implemented, significant work in identifying appropriate cost pools and cost drivers needs to be undertaken.

(e)   Many non-production overheads may be capable of being assigned to products through cost pool/cost driver analysis. If this is done, more accurate cost information should result.

(f)   The extent to which one cost is appropriate for all variations within a product grouping should be considered. For example, if the variations in brake discs are major, with different brake discs consuming activities in different proportions, then more detailed separate cost calculations may be apt (at present one cost calculation is produced for all brake discs on the assumed basis that they are similar).

(g)   ABC type information can provide essential support for techniques such as target costing (see later) and life-cycle costing that may help to improve decision making within Smith.

(h)   It must be remembered that an ABC system is not a panacea for cost allocation problems. ABC information often suggests an inappropriate degree of variability that does not exist. In addition, it is highly likely that even where variability clearly does exist, relationships between cost pools and cost drivers will not follow a simple linear basis. In each of these cases, appropriate interpretation and use of ABC information may be difficult, particularly for the financially non-sophisticated manager.

5.   *Oil Pumps and Target Costing*
(a) Target Cost of an Oil Pump

At present Smith uses a cost-plus approach to setting prices, by calculating production cost per unit (after absorbing production overhead on the basis of a direct labour hour rate) and then adding a margin to ensure a gross profit margin of 40% on selling price (the equivalent of adding two-thirds to cost price to arrive at selling price). An alternative approach is target costing, which works in reverse of a cost-plus pricing approach, by, first of all, determining the price that customers would be prepared to pay for the product and then reducing this by a target profit margin. This gives the target cost and the aim is to ensure that the future cost will not exceed this. If, for example, a company, after considering a variety of design and production options, is unable to make the product for a cost equal or less than the target cost, then the company will not enter the market. With respect to Smith expanding the product range by producing oil pumps for the sports car market, the target cost of an oil pump (using the existing costing system) is €270 (see Appendix 5). The estimated cost to produce an oil pump (using the existing costing system that absorbs production overhead on the basis of direct labour hours) is

€250 (see Appendix 5). On this basis it would seem appropriate to manufacture and sell oil pumps.

(b) Concerns about the Target Cost for an Oil Pump

Possible concerns that Mae Brown may have regarding the calculated target and actual costs are:

(i)   Both the target cost and actual cost are inappropriate because the most significant cost element in each calculation is production overhead and this is absorbed into the cost unit based on direct labour hours which is an unsuitable cost driver for moving production costs into cost units.

(ii)   The lack of detailed analysis of costs and cost-drivers that are essential for calculating accurate unit costs has not been undertaken (see previous concerns relating to the existing costing system and ABC) and therefore costs calculated (both target and actual) are of questionable accuracy.

(iii) The fact that non-production costs are not included in the unit cost calculations undermines their usefulness (see previous ABC comments).

(c) Advantages of Target Costing

The advantages of target costing are:

(i)   It is much more realistic in terms of setting prices that the market is likely to pay, as it is based on market information rather than cost information. As a consequence of this, prices will be set that ensure profitability.

(ii)   Analysis of likely sales revenues and costs will take place in advance of production decisions, therefore products will not be produced that cannot be sold at a profit.

(iii) The process encourages a system of continuous improvement and cost reduction.

(iv)   A team approach is used in an attempt to achieve the target cost, thus encouraging joined-up thinking and a cross-departmental commitment to the objective of improving profitability.

(v)   The approach can be used at the design and planning stage, thus encouraging creative and innovative thinking by designers, engineers, and marketing and finance staff.

(vi)   It is particularly useful for the production and sales of products which are non-customised and sold in high volumes (as is the case with Smith's products).

6. Evaluation of the Possibility of Replacing the Machines in Workstation AA13

Two options of replacing the individual machines in workstation AA13 (machines AA/1, AA/2, AA/3 and AA/4) have been identified. Option 1 relates to the replacement of the four individual machines with individual equivalent energy efficient machines (option 1). Option 2 is the replacing of all the current machines with a single flexible multipurpose machine.

(a) Quantitative Analysis

(i) The original capital costs of the current machines are irrelevant in any quantitative analysis (these being sunk costs). The relevant benefits of any replacement decision are the savings in operating costs as a result of using the new energy efficient machines. All relevant costs and benefits of the two options have been discounted at Smith's cost of capital (8%) and the calculations, together with the resulting net present values, are shown in Appendix 6.

(ii) As can be seen the net present values of the two options are as follows:

- Option 1 (replacement of the four individual machines with individual equivalent energy efficient machines) – €60,015
- Option 2 (replacing of all the current machines with a single flexible multipurpose machine) – €233,130.

(iii) On the basis of these two options, it would be preferable to take option 2 as it provides the highest net present value.

(iv) However, a third option, that is a variation on option 1, could be analysed whereby only the individual machines where replacement would yield a positive net present value would be replaced with energy efficient machines (in this case machines AA/2 and AA/4 only). This would mean that where the case for the replacement of individual machines did not show a positive net present value, those machines would not be replaced. In this case (option 3), an overall net present value of €361,405 (see Appendix 7) can be achieved. On quantitative grounds, this option is optimal.

(b) Other Factors

Other factors that should also be considered before making a decision include:

(i) Risk. To what extent are the figures included in Appendices 6 and 7 firm numbers (e.g. capital cost, savings in annual running costs, economic life and cost of capital)? Possibly sensitivity analysis should be conducted.

(ii) The tax implications of the options could impact on the decision. These should be factored into the analysis.

(iii) To what extent will any changeover of machinery cause disruption to production and possibly loss of profit? In addition, there may be training costs associated with the acquisition of new machinery and this should be considered.

(iv) Will any changeover lead to redundancies? If so, these costs would need to be included in the analysis and the resulting impact on morale of staff taken into account.

(v) Is finance readily available to replace these machines? It should be noted that option 3 has a lower initial capital outlay (€725,000) than either of the other two options.

(vi) Are these new machines, possibly utilising unproven technology, as reliable as the existing machines? This is a risk factor.

(vii) Will it be possible to acquire new AA/2 and AA/4 machines (option 3) at the same prices as indicated if AA/1 and AA/3 machines are not acquired? If the same supplier has quoted on the basis of total replacement, it may require higher prices if only two new machines are purchased.

Appendix 1
Cost Driver by Product

	Brake Discs	Cam Shaft Kits	Catalytic Converters	Total
Direct labour hours	285,715	107,142	12,000	404,857
Machine hours	114,286	107,142	60,000	281,428
Number of machine set-ups	200	200	500	900
Number of quality inspections	100	150	300	550
Value of direct material used	€1,542,861	€1,178,562	€3,060,000	€5,781,423

Appendix 2
Allocation of Overhead to Products and Production Overhead Unit Cost Using ABC

	Overhead (cost pool)	Cost driver	Brake Discs	Cam Shaft Kits	Catalytic Converters	Total
Supervision of direct labour	€900,000					
Other labour related overhead	€738,816					
	€1,638,816	Number of direct labour hours	€1,156,542	€433,699	€48,575	€1,638,816
Machine depreciation	€2,400,000					
Machine running costs	€700,000					
	€3,100,000	Number of machine hours	€1,258,889	€1,180,196	€660,915	€3,100,000
Engineering set-up costs	€1,640,000	Number of machine set-ups	€364,444	€364,444	€911,112	€1,640,000
Quality inspection costs	€1,566,894	Number of quality inspections	€284,890	€427,335	€854,669	€1,566,894
Material receipt and handling costs	€4,200,000	Value of material used and purchased	€1,120,834	€856,184	€2,222,982	€4,200,000
		Total overhead	€4,185,599	€3,261,858	€4,698,253	€12,145,710
		Budgeted units of production	57,143	35,714	6,000	
Production overhead cost per unit using ABC			**€73.25**	**€91.33**	**€783.04**	

Appendix 3
Comparison of ABC Unit Cost and Existing System Unit Cost

	Brake Discs	Cam Shaft Kits	Catalytic Converters
Overhead cost per ABC (per Appendix 2)	€73.25	€91.33	€783.04
Direct material cost	€27.00	€33.00	€510.00
Direct labour cost	€75.00	€45.00	€30.00
Production cost per unit ABC	**€175.25**	**€169.33**	**€1,323.04**
Production cost per unit using existing system (direct labour hrs)	€252.00	€168.00	€600.00
Difference %	**•30%**	**1%**	**121%**

Appendix 4
Comparison of Gross Margins – ABC versus Existing Costing System

	Brake Discs	Cam Shaft Kits	Catalytic Converters
ABC production cost per unit	€175.25	€169.33	€1,323.04
Actual selling price	€380	€286	€1,200
Gross margin as % of actual selling price (using ABC cost)	54%	41%	−10%
Gross margin as indicated by existing cost per unit	34%	41%	50%

Appendix 5
Target Cost of Oil Pump Compared with Estimated Cost (using existing costing system)

Target cost of an oil pump:

Market price	€450
Less target gross margin (40%)	€180
Target cost	**€270**

Cost (using existing costing system):

Direct materials	€70
Direct labour (4 hours @ €15)	€60
Overhead (4 hours @ €30)	€120
Estimated cost	**€250**

Appendix 6
Net Present Value Calculations for Options 1 and 2 Relating to Replacing the Machines in Workstation AA13

Option 1

New machine:	Capital cost	Annual Savings	Discount Factor*	Net present value
Machine AA/1	€400,000	€50,000	4.623	Đ€168,850
Machine AA/2	€300,000	€110,000	4.623	€208,530
Machine AA/3	€225,000	€20,000	4.623	Đ€132,540
Machine AA/4	€425,000	€125,000	4.623	€152,875
		Overall net present value of Option 1		€60,015

Option 2

	Capital cost	Annual Savings	Discount Factor*	Net present value
Flexible multipurpose machine	€1,200,000	€310,000	4.623	€233,130

*Discounted at cumulative present value factor at 8% for six years (4.623)

Appendix 7
Net Present Value Calculation for Option 3 – Only Replace the Individual Machines That Show a Positive Net Present Value

Option 3

New machine:	Capital Cost	Annual Savings	Discount Factor*	Net present value
Machine AA/2	€300,000	€110,000	4.623	€208,530
Machine AA/4	€425,000	€125,000	4.623	€152,875
		Overall net present value of Option 3		€361,405

Solution to Halvey's Bakery

John Doran and Margaret Healy, University College Cork

REPORT ON PROPOSALS FOR EXPANSION AT HALVEY'S BAKERY

Prepared by: James O'Connell
O'Connell Consulting

For: Annie & Denis Halvey
Halvey's Bakery

1. Terms of Reference

This report considers the issues raised as of our discussions of xx/xx/xxxx. The report analyses the cost structure of the speciality breads proposal using absorption costing and activity-based costing (ABC). The impact that the choice of accounting method may have on this decision is considered. Issues arising from the outsourcing alternative are also raised. All calculations are based on information provided by Halvey's Bakery and have not been verified in the production of this report.

2. Recommendations

(a) Reconsideration of the current terms of the speciality breads proposal: the proposal generates favourable returns for only two of the three products included in the bundle if activity-based costing methods are used.

(b) Cross-subsidisation of the projected losses on the Sultana Pan should only be considered if the production and sale of all three products is maintained at contract levels.

(c) If production is to be maintained at the Macroom Bakehouse, greater consideration of production process efficiencies is needed and can be informed by the contents of the ABC analysis.

(d) Greater consideration of the longer term implications of the outsourcing option is needed. Halveys need to commission an in-depth study of the comparative return on investment offered from the various proposed uses of the existing bakehouse building.

3. Proposed Specialty Breads Initiative

(a) Costing Calculations

Costs have been produced for the specialty breads proposal under both the existing costing practices of the firm, and under ABC. Results are presented in Appendices 2 and 3. In summary the calculations show:

All amounts in cents	Harvest Loaf	Sultana Pan	Bagel Loaf
Production Cost (per loaf)			
-under existing costing practices	16.18	23.91	17.18
-under ABC	14.37	44.85	17.66
Target Selling Price	20.00	30.00	25.00
Budgeted Net Margin (per loaf)			
-under existing costing practices	3.82	6.09	7.82
-under ABC	5.63	(14.85)	7.34

The implications of the results above are twofold. The commercial implications of these cost estimates in discussed under (b) below. The critical impact that the choice of cost accounting regime may have on estimates of profitability and commercial viability generally is discussed in (c).

(b) Commercial implications of the Cost Estimates

On the basis of the ABC figures it would appear that the Harvest Loaf and the Bagel Loaf offer a return on sales of 28.1% and 29.4% respectively. However the Sultana Pan produces a loss on sales of 49.5%. On this basis the firm has a number of options if the proposal is to be pursued.

- Proceed with the production of the Harvest Loaf and Bagel Loaf but drop the proposed Sultana Loaf offering.
- Reprice the Sultana Loaf as a premium product. However this would have to be explored both with the retailer customers, and tested with end consumers to assess its viability.
- Customer pressure may require that all three products are supplied as a 'package' at close to the original prices. If so then the projected losses on the Sultana Pan should not necessarily be seen as a 'deal breaker'. Although the projected loss on this product is almost 50% of revenue, the low volumes projected would limit the damage to budgeted margin to around €89,000. This would leave a combined annual margin on the complete contract of €655,000. In effect the projected losses on the Sultana Pan could be cross subsidised by the other two products.
- This cross subsidy can only operate if production of all three products is maintained at or close to the budgeted levels. To rely on this the firm must ensure that contract negotiations focus on capping the volume of the loss making product supplied, and also guarantee minimum orders of the two more profitable products.
- The bakery should examine the possibility of reconfiguration of the business processes which drive the Sultana Pan cost up to 44.85 cent per unit. The ABC cost per unit working in appendix 2 indicates that the relative cost of this loaf is primarily increased at two stages of the production process, mixing and baking. The combination of longer baking time (50 minutes) and a smaller production run (15 units) accounts for the higher cost of this loaf. If the production lot size is driven by management policy then this should be reviewed. If it is driven by technical constraints then technological innovations should be explored to see if changes are possible, e.g. through larger ovens, revised material mix or temperature changes.

(c) Cost Effectiveness of the Product Costing Mechanism

The cost analysis above shows very different results depending on which costing mechanism is adopted. The main options open are those used in section (a) above:

- Continue using the existing system of absorbing overhead costs into product costs on the basis of the products direct labour cost component.
- Adopt a system of ABC. This would group indirect (overhead) costs into groups around activities. The costs of each of the activities would then be shared

amongst the products on the basis of each product's usage of a cost driver. The costs in each pool are assumed to be variable in proportion to the level of the driver activity rather than the quantity of output.

- A compromise between the two systems would be to continue to use absorption costing for financial accounting purposes but conduct occasional ABC exercises to monitor product costs for cost management purposes and whenever new product launches are being considered. The five cost pools used in this ABC exercise might also be reduced to four. The two smallest cost pools – 'Shaping / Proofing' and 'Mixing' – could be integrated as the cost drivers for each (the weight of materials and the number of loaves) are likely to be highly correlated.

The choice of mechanism is dependent on the trade-off between the benefits to be gained by the extra information and the costs of maintaining the system as the ABC system requires a greater analysis of costs into pools. This introduces increased record-keeping. The existing absorption costing basis may have been appropriate up to now because of the homogenous nature of the products in their impact on overhead costs. However the information in appendix 1 shows that this will not be the case for newer specialty breads.

In general, an ABC system is justified in cases where:

- Indirect costs are a higher proportion of total costs.
- There is increased competition, particularly if competitors are segmenting the market and concentrating on some product offerings. (You can survive with poor costing information and weak cost management if it is no worse than your competitors).
- A diverse range of products consume resources in differing proportions. (It is clear that some costs in the bakery are driven at batch level via the number of production runs or sales orders while others are volume related).
- There are clearly identifiable links between cost drivers and ABC cost pools.

4. The Outsourcing Option

The following issues need to be considered in evaluating this alternative.

- Savings in capital investment – The continued operation of the bakery will inevitably involve upgrading and reinvestment to support a wider product range. This will tie up the capital of the owners and their ability to raise funds for other commercial opportunities.
- Release of the site – Outsourcing will allow the site to realise its alternative use-value for apartment development which is well in excess of its current use-value.
- Reliability of volume estimates – Outsourcing contracts need to be constructed carefully to ensure that the outsourcing firm does not carry a residual risk should the requirements of the end customer change. In this case if the contract with the supermarkets is for fixed amounts then comparable clauses need to apply to the

outsourced supplier. If the supermarket will have the right to vary the quantity delivered then the outsourcing contract should allow for similar levels of variation. Management need to consider the possible losses that could be incurred through any lack of symmetry between both contracts.

- Management commitment required – Outsourcing will require less day to day management time and this may allow Noleen to pursue her interest in further new product development and media work.
- Core competency – The outsourcing of production in such a highly competitive market raises the inevitable risk of ultimately being by-passed through a direct relationship being forged between the supplier and the supermarket group. This is a larger risk for a commodity product such as bread. Halvey's must consider carefully what it would uniquely bring to this relationship. Will its competency in new product development, packaging and branding be sufficient to guarantee its position? To maintain the visibility of its branding Noleen should further develop her media profile as a food-writer and in television appearances. The future of the small Halvey bakery stores is also important in this context.
- Strategic Implications – Is outsourcing seen as an end in itself or as a growth opportunity which will release capital for the launch of another line of products? If it represents a growth opportunity, then a detailed programme and timeline should be developed for the integrated strategy.
- Price support in the long term – Reliance on one large customer will make the bakery very vulnerable to imposed price reductions when the term of the first supermarket contract expires. It may be that this contract should be seen as the first of several to diversify the customer base.
- Labour relations – The costs and management time involved in human resource management may fall as a consequence of outsourcing. However the redundancy process of staff will need to be handled carefully to minimise damage to the brand image and goodwill. Financial provision should also be made for severance payments as well as re-employment assistance. The case of staff who are unable to take up a voluntary severance package could be dealt with through their redeployment to the proposed expansion of the niche bakery shops.
- Availability of special skills – It should be recognised that outsourcing is not easily reversed particularly in a traditional craft industry. The decision to outsource will most likely be irreversible.

Appendix 1
Halvey's Bakery – Cost Driver Information

	Harvest Pan	Sultana Loaf	Bagel Loaf	Total
Budgeted sales price	€0.20	€0.30	€0.25	
Direct-material cost (per loaf)	€0.05	€0.09	€0.06	
Direct-labour cost (per loaf)	€0.03	€0.04	€0.03	
Projected units of output (loaves)	8,000,000	600,000	4,000,000	12,600,000
Production batch size (average)	100	15	50	
Sales order batch size (average)	50	15	50	
Weight of materials (grams per loaf)	400	450	300	
Baking time required (minutes per batch)	40	50	25	

From these above, can be further estimated:

	Harvest Pan	Sultana Loaf	Bagel Loaf	Total
Number of production runs	80,000	40,000	80,000	200,000
Number of sales orders	160,000	40,000	80,000	280,000
Total weight of materials used (kgs)	3,200,000	270,000	1,200,000	4,670,000
Total time required – mins (baking time × no. of production batches)	3,200,000	2,000,000	2,000,000	7,200,000

Appendix 2
Halvey's Bakery – Speciality Breads Costing – ABC Method

Cost pool – charged to product by driver	Harvest Pan	Sultana Loaf	Bagel Loaf	O/head Total
Direct-material cost	€400,000	€54,000	€240,000	€694,000
Direct-labour cost	240,000	24,000	120,000	384,000
Set-up	176,000	88,000	176,000	440,000
Mixing	83,597	7,054	31,349	122,000
Shaping and Proofing	50,794	3,810	25,397	80,000
Baking	113,333	70,833	70,833	255,000
Packing and Delivery	85,714	21,429	42,857	150,000
Total Budgeted Cost	**€1,149,439**	**€269,125**	**€706,436**	**€2,125,000**
Number of units	8,000,000	600,000	4,000,000	
Unit Cost	**€0.1437**	**€0.4485**	**€0.1766**	

Each bread type is charged with the (Product's share of absorption basis/Absorption basis) × Total O/h in this cost pool. Allocation bases are as follows:

Set-up	*number of production runs*
Mixing	*weight of materials*
Shaping and proofing	*number of loaves*
Baking	*time required*
Packing and delivery	*number of sales orders*

Cost per unit (in cents)	Harvest Pan	Sultana Loaf	Bagel Loaf
Direct-material cost	5.00	9.00	6.00
Direct-labour cost	3.00	4.00	3.00
Set-up	2.20	14.67	4.40
Mixing	1.04	1.18	0.78
Shaping and Proofing	0.63	0.63	0.63
Baking	1.42	11.81	1.77
Packing and Delivery	1.07	3.57	1.07
Total production cost per unit (cents)	14.37	44.85	17.66

	Harvest Pan	Sultana Loaf	Bagel Loaf	Total
Total budgeted revenue	€1,600,000	€180,000	€1,000,000	€2,780,000
Total budgeted cost	€1,149,439	€269,125	€706,436	€2,125,000
Budgeted Margin	450,561	(89,125)	293,564	655,000

Appendix 3
Halvey's Bakery – Speciality Breads Costing – Conventional Costing Method

Overhead cost-pools combined

Set-up	440,000
Mixing	122,000
Shaping and proofing	80,000
Baking	255,000
Packing and delivery	150,000
Total Overhead	1,047,000

Total Cost (except direct materials and labour) per euro spent on direct-labour:

Total O/H / Direct labour cost

$$= €1,047,000 / €384,000$$
$$= 272.7\% \text{ of direct-labour cost}$$

	Harvest Pan	Sultana Loaf	Bagel Loaf	Total
Direct-material cost per unit	5.00	9.00	6.00	
Direct-labour cost per unit	3.00	4.00	3.00	
Other production costs per unit (O/H)	8.18	10.91	8.18	
Total production cost per unit (cents)	16.18	23.91	17.18	
Number of units	8,000,000	600,000	4,000,000	
Total budgeted cost	€1,294,375	€143,438	€687,188	€2,125,000

Case 19

Solution to Chicken Pieces

Peter Clarke, University College Dublin

MEMORANDUM

To: Ray Fullam
From: A. Student
Re: Major issues faced by the company
Date: As per postmark

Further to our recent meeting, I have undertaken a preliminary assessment of the major issues currently facing the company and report my main findings below. Please appreciate that I had a limited amount of time and information available to prepare this memo for you, so that my recommendations and conclusions are, necessarily, tentative. However, I hope that they should highlight some important aspects that need your attention. I have structured my memo to coincide with some of the questions that you raised with me.

1. *Critical issues and performance measures*

There are several critical success factors that could be applied to your business but these should be developed in the context of overall company goals and strategy. A critical success factor represents a key area in which performance must excel if the company is to be successful and they will usually include reference to product quality, customer service and cost competitiveness. In turn, it is usual to highlight these areas to employees and management staff by way of related performance measures. Based on my quick assessment of your operations, it appears that critical success factors and related performance measures include the following:

Critical success factor	Performance measure
New customer acquisition	No. of new customers
	% sales to new customers
Overall customer satisfaction	Customer satisfaction index
Delivery on time	% of on-time deliveries (OTD)
Quality including overall hygiene	% rejects by customers
	No. of hygiene violations
Cost competitiveness	Cost per unit and relative price index
Innovation including new products	No. of new products introduced
	% sales from new products
Dispatch efficiency	Cost per unit shipped
Productivity	No. of chickens processed per employee

(Note: Students will only be expected to provide four critical success factors and related performance measures).

2. Apportionment of costs of jointing process

The apportionment of jointing costs can be done in a number of ways. I have prepared calculations on the basis of the physical number of units involved. This quick calculation gives a joint cost of 50c per unit as shown below:

Total joint costs to be apportioned		
Chickens (used)	35,000 chickens @ 60c each	21,000
Storage and other jointing costs (given)		70,000
Disposal costs (given)		14,000
		105,000

Product:	Units	%	Joint costs	Joint costs (per unit)
Breasts	70,000	33.3%	€35,000	50c
Wings & legs	140 ,000	66.7%	€70,000	50c
Total	210,000	100%	€105,000	

The main limitation of the physical output, i.e. units method of apportioning joint costs is that each joint product is assigned the same cost per unit. This method is not realistic in the context that all costs are incurred to create value. Thus, it would make much more sense to apportion costs in relation to their net realisable value.

3. Separate process accounts

I detail below my calculations regarding the cost of your three main processes i.e. jointing, breast fillets and finishing of wings/legs.

Jointing (of carcass) process account					
	Chickens	€		Chickens	€
Purchases	40,000	24,000	WIP (breasts)	35,000	35,000
Bank	N/a	70,000	WIP (wings/legs)		70,000
Bank (disposal)	N/a	14,000	Balance	5,000	3,000
	40,000	108,000		40,000	108,000

Work in progress account (Filleting of breasts)					
	Units	€		Units	€
Transferred in	70,000	35,000			
Conversion costs	N/a	32,500	T/f to COGS	70,000	67,500
	70,000	67,500		70,000	67,500

Work in progress account (Finishing of wings/legs)					
	Units	€		Units	€
Transferred in	140,000	70,000			
Conversion costs	N/a	31,000	T/f to COGS	140,000	101,000
	140,000	101,000		140,000	101,000

4. Overall cost/income statement

Based on the information provided to me, which I did not verify, the following is my summarised cost/income statement as requested.

Summarised profit and loss account for year...

	Breasts	Wings/legs	Total
No. of units sold	70,000	140,000	210,000
Sales revenue (see working below)	140,000	102,000	242,000
Less: Cost of goods sold:	(67,500)	(101,000)	(168,500)
= Gross profit margin	72,500	1,000	73,500
Selling, distribution and admin. costs			(85,000)
25K + 60K			
Net loss for year			(11,500)

Working: Schedule of Sales

	Buns	Mosssgo	Superdim	Total
Breasts (70,000)	€60,000	€38,000	€42,000	€140,000
Wings/legs (140,000)	€48,000	€36,000	€18,000	€102,000
	€108,000	€74,000	€60,000	€242,000

5. Breakeven point

A crucial target for any business is to reach, at least, its breakeven point. As detailed below, I estimated that the breakeven point is represented by sales of about €255,000 per annum. It should be noted that overall sales in the current year amounted to €242,000. Thus an overall increase in gross revenue of about 5% is required. This additional revenue can be generated either by selling more or at higher prices to existing customers, introducing new products and/or acquiring new customers.

Calculation of BEP (in €)
Summarised profit and loss account for year:

		€
Sales revenue		242,000
Less: Cost of goods sold:	168,500	
Selling and administration expenses	85,000	
Total costs	253,500	
Less: variable costs (chickens used)	(21,000)	(21,000)
Total fixed costs	232,500	
Contribution		221,000
Less: fixed costs		(232,500)
Net loss for year		(11,500)
Contribution/sales ratio		0.913
BEP (€)	€232,500/ .913	€255 K ®
Alternatively:		
Average selling price per unit	€242,000/210,000	€1.15
Less: Variable costs (€21,000/210,000)		(0.10)
Average unit contribution		€1.05
BEP (units)	€232,500/ 1.05 =	221,429 units
BEP (revenue)	221,429 × €1.15 =	€255 K ®

6. *Relevant costs of accepting special disposal offer*

Currently your company is paying €14,000 per annum to dispose of waste from your operations. This is an important issue due to the range of health and safety legislation which prevails, and also environmental concerns by the public at large.

By my provisional calculations, the proposal to 'sell' waste to the local pet food manufacturer is attractive in financial terms as detailed below as it reduces the company's overall costs to €5,000 – generating an overall cost saving of €9,000:

(i) Current disposal cost payable by company	(14,000)
(ii) Revenue from Pet Food manufacturer	3,000
Less: Additional storage costs	(8,000)
Estimated future cost of selling to Pet Food manufacturer	(5,000)

However, there are a number of other issues to be considered:

- Is the manufacturer reliable in terms of collection of waste and payment?
- The additional storage time (three weeks) on average may create additional problems e.g. smell and appearance.
- Such waste produce may be useful to delicatessens who are now using the carcasses to produce chicken stock for cooking purposes. Certainly, there is a demand for such 'waste.' Alternatively, the company could use the waste in order to expand its product range e.g. manufacture its own brand of pet food. Also, there is an increasing tendency to produce 'Mechanically Removed Meat' or MCM. As the term suggests, this meat is removed from the carcass by special machines and the produce is used to manufacture 'Chicken Nuggets' for human consumption – sold mainly through fast food outlets! However, a fuller analysis needs to be undertaken before a final decision is made.

In conclusion, I hope you find this memorandum of interest and benefit to you. Should you have any queries or require any additional information, please do not hesitate to contact me.

SECTION B

SOLUTIONS TO CASES IN BUSINESS FINANCE

Case 20

Solution to the Pottery Company Limited 1

Ann-Marie Ward, Queen's University Belfast

REPORT ON THE GROWTH STRATEGY AND WORKING CAPITAL POLICY OF POTTERY COMPANY LIMITED AT 2XX3 AND 2XX5

Prepared by: A. Candidate

For: The directors of PCL

1. Terms of Reference

This report has been prepared in response to the requirements outlined in the job application pack. The report explains working capital, the importance of managing working capital and costs associated with it. It also describes the differing types of working capital strategies that can be followed (highlighting which policy is suited to differing economic conditions) and recommends a strategy for PCL. PCL's performance, liquidity and working capital levels on 31st December 2XX3 are scrutinised and compared to 31st December 2XX5. The report makes some recommendations on how to improve the working capital position. The only change in the company over the two year period was the introduction of a growth strategy. This was pursued from 1st January 2XX4. This report reconsiders the initial growth strategy proposal (supplied by T. Brewster) and re-calculates it in light of the changes in working capital and any errors and omissions. The proposal is then re-evaluated on the assumption that the working capital policy of 2XX3 is maintained, the only exception being an assumption that the trade receivables policy can be changed to the industry norm. Fast-track corrective action is recommended to alleviate the liquidity problems of PCL.

2. Recommendations

(a) PCL has been overtrading for the past two years. To address the funding issues, PCL needs to obtain long term financing immediately. Based on the information provided, long-term debt of at least €20 million is required.

(b) The company should pursue a more neutral working capital policy. Funds tied up in working capital should be released as soon as possible. This will have an immediate positive impact on cash flow and on profitability. Over €32 million can be released from funds tied up in working capital. This combined with the long-term funding requirement outlined in (a) should leave the company in a net cash position.

(c) The agreement with the supplier of raw materials should be renegotiated to that in existence in 2XX3. There will be an initial cash outflow, though this will be offset by funds being released from the raw material inventory that is currently stored. The relationship with the supplier should improve resulting in a reduction in the price of the raw material inventory to that agreed in 2XX3. This will increase gross margins.

(d) Inventory levels are too high. Production should cease on a Saturday, until inventory levels reach 915,000 units. Thereafter, additional staff should be employed to maintain production levels. There is spare machine capacity and the increased demand is expected to be permanent.

(e) A new credit control member of staff should be recruited as soon as possible and the credit control department should focus on reducing bad debts to 1%.

They should also renegotiate the credit period allowed to 30 days in line with other companies in the same industry. This will not only improve cash flow but also reduce fixed costs and net income.

(f) A full business plan should be prepared for the bank manager outlining the corrective action that the directors are putting in place. Negotiations with the bank manager should focus on reducing the overdraft rate to 8%. This will result in improved cash flows and reduced fixed costs, resulting in increased net income.

(g) A finance director should be recruited as a matter of urgency. The finance director can prepare the business plan, evaluate and select the most appropriate form of long-term financing, provide a more detailed evaluation of the company's financial position and inform the directors on the benefits of having a dividend policy.

3. Working capital management and costs

(a) Working capital?

The net working capital of a business is simply defined as its current assets less its current liabilities. Current assets encapsulate all cash, near cash and assets that are likely to be realised as cash within a one year timeframe. The main categories are inventories (i.e. raw materials, work in progress and finished goods), trade receivables and prepaid expenses, investments, bank and cash. Current liabilities are all debts that are repayable within one year, or on demand. The main categories include trade payables, tax owing, dividends due, accrued expenses and loans payable within one year. The latter encapsulates short-term loans and the portion of long term loans that are payable within one year.

(b) The importance of working capital and associated costs

Holding appropriate levels of working capital is vital for the smooth running of a business. For example, without sufficient raw material inventory, production will be affected. Where insufficient finished goods are not held, the business runs the risk of losing sales. This is the reasoning behind the production director's (R. Gallagher) current inventory policy. However, holding inventories has costs. There are increased storage costs (i.e. heat and light, rent, rates, insurance, inventory personnel, etc), increased risk of obsolescence and theft and damage. In addition, there is a finance cost. Net working capital is usually an asset. All assets need to be financed. This has a cost. Therefore, any increase in working capital requirements (as in PCL's situation), leads to a direct increase in the funds required to finance it, resulting in an increase in costs. In PCL's case the growth in working capital has been financed by the overdraft, which attracts an interest rate of 15%.

Even if PCL had plenty of readily available funds to finance an additional working capital requirement, an opportunity cost would result, as the additional funds tied up could be used elsewhere to obtain a return. In this hypothetical scenario the cost of investment in working capital is the additional cash requirement by the company's cost of capital.

As mentioned, increases in the level of working capital leads to a demand for finance. If this is not correctly catered for, then it is likely that the company will have liquidity problems, as in PCL's case. Having sufficient liquidity is vital for a firm's survival. Most businesses have a daily cash requirement. For example: to pay wages when they fall due; to pay for expenses; and to pay suppliers for raw materials when due. If these requirements are not met then the supply of labour and materials cannot be guaranteed. Even a profitable company, like PCL, may fail if it does not have adequate cash flow to meet its liabilities as they fall due.

(c)   *Working capital management*
Managing working capital involves balancing the business working cycle requirements so that the smooth running of the business is not affected, whilst also maximising the return a business receives on its assets. It involves ensuring that sufficient liquid funds are available so there is no risk of insolvency, however, also ensuring that no funds are tied up unnecessarily, that could be earning a return elsewhere for the business.

(d)   *Working capital strategy*
The levels of working capital required, depend on the nature of the business. For example, a manufacturing company usually holds more inventory than a company in the service industry. In addition, the stability of demand for a company's products and changes to that demand impact on the levels of working capital that are required. For example, a business with unpredictable fluctuating demand would need to hold higher levels of inventory than one with constant demand, like PCL. In addition, as the quantity of output by a business increases, then the volume of working capital required will also increase.

The theoretical aim of good working capital management is to keep efficient levels of inventory, maintain efficient debt collection procedures and cash management and pay trade suppliers in sufficient time to minimise the supply cost, relative to the cost of expending resources, whilst maintaining good relations. However, the strategy adopted is also impacted on by management preferences, the availability of funds and the environment.

Three strategies are commonly discussed in the context of the economic environment. The strategies range along a continuum from aggressive, through neutral to conservative. An aggressive strategy results in a very efficient use of funds, whereas the other polar strategy – the conservative, is considered to result in an inefficient use of funds. Companies usually adopt a strategy along this continuum, shifting in tune with economic conditions.

Aggressive

When an aggressive strategy is adopted current assets are minimised. This working capital policy will result in a liquidity ratio of about 0.5:1. In this scenario, current liabilities are used to finance all of the current assets, and a portion of the non current assets. This is deemed to be a very efficient use of funds, with inventories minimised, trade receivables minimised and trade payable days maximised. Theoretically, this policy should result in high return on asset ratios. However, the policy is likely to lead to stock-outs. By only allowing very short credit terms, a company is also more likely to lose sales, hence contribution. Taking long credit terms will result in lost discounts and unhappy suppliers; this may impact on the price that the company has to pay for its supplies. It may even result in loss of supply. This policy will only be successful in a boom economy, wherein lost sales are easily replaced. In a stagnant or declining economy, sales and customers will be lost and are unlikely to be replaced by others. Hence, adopting this strategy would do much harm to the future of the business.

Neutral

When a neutral strategy is adopted a business will hold higher levels of current assets, compared to when an aggressive policy is adopted. Working capital levels usually reflect a liquidity ratio of about 2:1. In this scenario, current liabilities finance half of the current assets, with the remainder being financed by long term sources. All non-current assets are financed by long term sources. The higher levels of long term debt will result in higher interest costs. This higher asset base combined with increased costs, usually results in a lower return on assets, than that expected were an aggressive policy adopted. When the economy is stagnant, this policy allows a company to trade successfully, as it can hold some buffer inventory, to offer discounts for early payment and to pay suppliers in accordance with their agreement (these actions result in increased working capital costs when compared to an aggressive policy).

Conservative

When a conservative strategy is adopted a business will hold even higher levels of current assets, relative to the neutral strategy. The working capital levels usually result in a liquidity of over 3:1. In this instance the assets of the company are mostly financed by long term sources. The return on assets is expected to be low as the total asset base is greater, as are the costs. For instance, the yearly interest cost is greater due to the high level of long term finance and costs associated with holding higher levels of working capital are also greater. This policy is considered to be the least efficient in terms of the use of funds tied up. In terms of the economic environment, this policy is deemed to be least suited to a booming economy, where sales are guaranteed as the high costs associated with such a policy will result in high prices. It is regarded as most suitable in a declining economy, as this policy will maximise sales relative to the companies that pursue other policies, as there will be no stock-outs and long credit periods are allowed. In this economic environment suppliers usually push for quicker payment and this policy allows for their earlier repayment.

(e) *PCL policy suggestion*
PCL is a manufacturing company that produces, distributes and retails china, a luxury item. The economic environment in Ireland at this time can be regarded as in boom. However, the text book polarised aggressive policy should not be pursued, as the product's demand though influenced by the economy, is likely also to be affected by trends, marketing, production design, etc. The marketing campaign has been successful, though it should be noted that most of the new sales are abroad (5 million pieces), with the remaining growth being in internet sales, which might also be abroad. Therefore, even though the economy is booming, home sales of units in the traditional manner have remained steady at about three million units. Therefore a more neutral policy is recommended. (This recommendation might change if more detail is obtained on the source and pattern of the internet sales.)

4. *Evaluation of the performance, liquidity and working capital of PCL at 31st December 2XX3, compared to the current position (2XX5)*

(a) *PCL's performance, liquidity and working capital position in 2XX3*
In 2XX3 PCL sold six million units of china at an average price of €25.00. It made a gross profit of €30,000,000 (20% of the sales value) and a net profit of €7,500,000 (5% of the sales value). It had a liquidity ratio of 5.64:1, which may seem high, however, in this type of firm the level of trade payables is low, as the main cost associated with manufacturing the product is wages, which are paid monthly. More information would be required on the level of stock-outs etc, to determine if inventory levels are inefficient. PCL has some cash in its current account (€150,000), though has an overdraft of €3,750,000 on which it is charged 8%. The company is financed entirely by equity, and the total equity and reserves amount to €47.4 million. The equity holders earn a return on their investment of 15.8% (see Appendix 1: Table 1 for calculations).

Excepting cash, PCL's total working capital requirement at the 31st December 2XX3 is €28,000,000 (see Appendix 1: table 2). This costs approximately €2,240,000 in interest each year. The company does not hold any raw material inventory as it has a very good relationship with the supplier, who delivers each day's requirements before the factory opens. The supplier is paid on average 36.5 days after the goods are delivered (see Appendix 1: table 3). This agreement works as production is constant each day. There is little indication of any stock-outs in the past which have led to a disruption in production. PCL holds 450,000 units of finished goods at a value of €9 million. This represents 27.38 days of finished goods inventory (Appendix 1: table 3). There is little information on whether the company experiences stock-outs with this level. 27 days, for this type of good seems quite low, though is feasible so long as the distribution channels work efficiently. Customers take just under 50 days to pay their accounts, which is high when compared with the days allowed by other similar manufacturers as highlighted by B. Owen in the directors' meeting.

(b) *Working capital position in 2XX5*

In 2XX5 PCL sold 12.2 million units of china for €294,160,000. It made a gross profit of €44,124,000 (15% of the sales value) and a net profit of €2,941,600 (1% of the sales value). Though sales have virtually doubled, gross profit has not increased by the same amount, and net profit has fallen by €4,558,400. PCL has a liquidity ratio of 1.36:1. This low ratio is not considered an efficient use of working capital due to the nature of the current liabilities. These are predominately the bank overdraft €50,000,000 on which interest is now payable at 15% (Appendix 1: table 1). Overdrafts are repayable on demand and the lack of available cash suggests that PCL has serious liquidity problems. On the face of it, PCL is still equity financed, with the equity investment falling to €43.5 million. This is a result of losses made in the prior year, reducing retained earnings. The return made by the equity holders in the year has fallen to 6.76%.

Excluding cash, PCL's total working capital requirement at the 31st December 2XX5 is €72,000,000 (Appendix 1: table 2). This costs approximately €10,800,000 per year in interest. The company has started to hold three months of production requirements of the raw material (clay). This is a direct increase in the working capital requirements by €9,000,000. This is financed to an extent by the company extending the period of time it takes to pay the supplier to 103.4 days. The inventory of finished goods has increased to €33,350,000 representing 48.68 days. Trade receivables are received in 49.01 days, a small reduction (less than a day) when compared to the credit period taken in 2XX3 (Appendix 1: tables 2 and 3).

(c) *Evaluation of the change in the performance and liquidity of PCL from 31st December 2XX3 to 31st December 2XX5 (Appendix 1)*

Profitability

PCL's sales have increased by 96%, from €150 million to €294.16 million, over the two year period; however, expenditure has increased by higher margins. The cost of sales has increased from 80% to 85% of the average sales price. This is as a result of an increase in the variable costs, labour and material.

The level of fixed costs also increased. The result of these increases is a reduction in the gross margin obtained on each sale from 20% to 15% and a reduction in the net income percentage from 5% to 1%. The company does not seem to have invested in any major non-current assets, channelling its whole investment into working capital. The return on investment by the shareholders has fallen from 15.8% to 6.76% (Appendix 1: table 1). This reflects the reduction in profitability and the under-utilisation of assets.

Overtrading/liquidity

The weakening performance is due to the strategy that has been pursed in relation to managing the company's working capital. It would seem that the company has been 'overtrading'. The textbook symptoms of overtrading include:
- *Large increases in income* (PCL's income has increased by 96%);
- *Increases in current assets and sometimes non current assets.* It is even more problematic when the inventory and/or trade receivable days increase, as in PCL's case. This reflects the fact that inventory levels have increased at higher rates than sales levels.
- *Only a small increase in long term financing* (in PCL case the situation is worse than the theoretical symptoms, as their long term financing has actually deteriorated from €47.4 million to €43.5 million). PCL has financed its growth by lengthening the period of time it takes to pay its suppliers from 36.5 days in 2XX3 to 103.4 days in 2XX5 (Appendix 1: table 3) and by extending its bank overdraft. The net cash position has deteriorated from a negative balance of €3.6 million in 2XX3 to €50 million in 2XX5. The bank is obviously very concerned and the future of the company may be at risk.
- *Debt and liquidity ratios deteriorate.* PCL's liquidity ratio has fallen from 5.64:1 to 1.36:1 (Appendix 1: table 1). The company does not use long-term debt, however, seems to use the overdraft as though it is a permanent source of funds.

Working capital

The changes in working capital have lead to cost increases. There has been an increase in the funding requirements by €44 million, at an additional interest cost of €8.56 million (Appendix 1: table 2). In 2XX3 cash conversion cycle was 72.7 days; by 31st December 2XX5 this had increased to 95.8 days (Appendix 1: table 3).

In terms of the different working capital elements, there have been cost increases all round. Firstly, the new policy on holding three months of raw material clay increases costs. This inventory has to be stored, insured, managed by a store person, etc. In addition, if clay is exposed to air it will not be usable therefore it may be that there are additional costs due to damage.

The suppliers of the clay are being paid 67 days later than they were in 2XX3. This has resulted in the price of clay increasing from €2.50 to €3.00 per unit. In addition, it seems that the suppliers are not happy with the current credit period taken. I have to point out that they may stop supplying to PCL.

The inventory of finished goods held has increased by 21 days. This is also likely to result in increased insurance costs and store management costs. Having overcrowded stores is likely to increase the risk of breakages resulting in higher costs.

Though the trade receivable days have improved slightly, bad debts have increased to 1.5% in total, from 1%. This will result in additional costs to PCL. This is evaluated further in section 5.

(d) *Suggested working capital improvements*
A key problem facing the company is the financing of their working capital requirements (this is dealt with in section 7 of this report). In this section, the individual areas, inventories, payables and trade receivables are covered.

Inventories and payables

R. Gallagher highlights the fact that production would be affected if raw material inventories were not available, however, this scenario is unlikely to occur. Before 2XX3, the special relationship with the supplier, wherein he delivered the products each morning in advance of the factory opening, was successful, with no stock-outs occurring. I recommend that this agreement be reintroduced.

This will have an initial impact on PCL's cash flows as the company will have to pay the supplier any amounts outstanding in advance of 36.5 days. However, this will reduce the cost of the clay to €2.50 per unit, and the company will not have to order any units until the current inventory is used in production. Storage costs will also fall as no storage space is required for the clay. This should cause a reduction in fixed costs.

The inventory of finished goods held has also increased by 21 days. There is no evidence to suggest that the company was losing sales when inventory was held for 27 days. Therefore, I recommend that production is slowed until finished good inventory levels fall to an amount that is equivalent to 27 days (915,000 units – see Appendix 4). Thereafter this can be re-evaluated. It may even be possible to reduce this further. You have indicated that you do not wish to reduce staff levels; therefore I suggest that you slow down production by stopping production on a Saturday and running down inventories over a period of time. When inventories reach 915,000 units, other members of full-time production staff should be employed. This will ensure that no overtime rates are paid, which will help cash flow and profitability.

Trade receivables

In the pack provided by T. Brewster (Appendix 3), it states that other companies in the china industry are allowing 30 days credit and experience bad debts at a 1% level. B. Owen states that this policy could be adopted if another credit control member of staff were recruited. I recommend that this happens as soon as possible. Bad debts have increased by €2.9 million over the initial projected increase, directly impacting on profits and cash flows. In addition, reducing the debtor days from the current 49.01 days to 30 days will result in a large cash benefit (see Appendix 3).

5. Evaluation of the 2XX3 proposal for the growth and development of PCL

The proposal included in the pack (also reproduced in this report in Appendix 2) contains many errors and omissions. In all instances the errors or omissions served to overstate the potential profit. When the initial proposal is recalculated assuming that the actual working policy experienced over the two year period is pursued, an expected loss per year of €1.372 million results. Based on this re-calculation, it is likely that the growth strategy would not have been pursued. The main adjustments are summarised as follows:

(a) *Sales to distributor*

Sales were correctly valued at €23.00 per unit. However, the cost of sales was taken as 80% of this value. The actual cost of making a unit of china at this date was 80% of the average sales price, which was €25.00. In addition to this error, it was not prudent to hold the cost of sales percentage at this rate; given that R. Gallagher knew that the production staff would have to be paid overtime rates for working on a Saturday. A higher estimate should have been substituted. In addition, it is common practice to loose discounts, or be penalised, if suppliers are not paid within an agreed credit period. This also impacts on the cost of sales rate that should have been used. I have reworked the schedule using the actual rate experienced by the company (85%). Using this figure the expected contribution towards fixed costs has fallen from €23 million to €8.75 million.

(b) *Sales by internet*

In this instance an incorrect figure was used to represent sales and the cost of sales. As before, the cost of sales calculation was based on a percentage of the sales amount, not the average and the percentage applied was understated. The main error though was the failure to include the 10% discount on sales price for internet sales. This reduced the sales by €3.24 million from €32.4 million to €29.16 million. The adjusted net contribution towards specific fixed costs on the sales by internet has fallen from €6.48 million to €3.66 million.

(c) *Working capital costs*

The only cost included in the original schedule relating to working capital is an increase in the expected bad debts. This was estimated at 1% of the reported additional sales. A more prudent approach should have been adopted. B. Owen had concerns regarding the internet sales and felt that the company would be at more credit risk. There was little detail on the credit risk exposure that may have arisen by the expansion of sales by the distributor to other countries. A larger percentage, to reflect the expected increased risk should have been utilised in the calculations. I have used the actual rate observed. This has resulted in the estimated cost for bad debts increasing from €1.474 million to €2.912 million.

The initial expected costs did not include any value associated with financing the increase in working capital investment. Based on the actual working capital policy pursued, this cost amounts to €8.56 million (Appendix 1: table 2).

6. Re-evaluation of the initial growth strategy proposal assuming the working capital policy of 2XX3 does not change (with the exception of trade receivables which are assumed to follow industry norm terms)

Had a similar working capital policy to that followed in 2XX3 been adopted and the credit policy tightened, then the estimated growth proposal would show an estimated expected profit of about €15 million. The reworked growth proposal schedule is included in Appendix 3, table 2. The updated proposal is now explained.

The income amounts do not differ to the adjusted proposal, provided in Appendix 2, table 1. It is assumed that the cost of sales will not change as a percentage of the average sales price from the 2XX3 level (i.e. remains at 80%). New employees would be hired to produce the additional units (it is assumed that the machines have spare capacity) therefore there is no need for PCL to pay overtime rates. The agreement with the supplier would not change; hence the cost of materials remains constant. These measures result in an additional €7.75 million of contribution towards fixed costs.

It is assumed that the estimates for advertising, sales staff, credit control staff, internet staff and software development are realistic: hence, they are not changed. The industry norm credit policy is to allow 30 days credit. As this is the case, it is unlikely that PCL will suffer loss of sales if it adopts the same policy. By receiving the debts earlier, the potential for bad debts reduces. It is assumed that the industry norm of having bad debts of 1% is achievable. Based on this assumption an expected bad debt cost for each of the two differing growth streams can be calculated as 1% of the expected sales value (€1.15 million for sales through the distributor and €0.292 million for internet sales). This represents a cost saving of €1.47 million relative to the bad debts that were experienced. The cost of the additional credit control staff member is also included. Given the extent of change expected in the credit control procedures, this cost seems understated and may need to be reassessed by B. Owen.

Finally, in Appendix 3: table 1, the working capital requirements based on the policy in place in 2XX3 and the new credit policy suggests that €39.2 million in working capital is required. In 2XX3, the investment in working capital was €28 million; therefore the proposed growth strategy should include the cost of an additional €11.2 million of finance. This has been included at the 8% rate (cost: €0.9 million). This interest rate is a conservative estimate. I would recommend that a long-term source of funds be sourced. These are normally cheaper than short-term sources of funds.

If this working capital policy were to be introduced from now on, the company's profits should increase by about €16.85 million per year (€1.372 million plus €15.477 million). This estimate is based on the reworked growth proposal which has been calculated in light of information provided in the recruitment pack. If employed, I would have to undertake a very detailed analysis of the costs and income. I expect that this re-assessed schedule will change in light of a deeper investigation into costs.

7. Recommended immediate action to alleviate PCL's liquidity problem

At present €72 million is tied up in working capital, so changing to the policy proposed in this report will release about €32 million in cash over the next few months (see Appendix 3: table 1). This can be used to reduce the €50 million overdraft. The remaining overdraft deficit should be financed from long-term sources. PCL has not matched its asset investment with appropriate funding. The company is using its overdraft as a long-term source of finance which is not recommended.

Appendix I
Evaluation of working capital at 31st December 2XX5 compared to 31st December 2XX3

Table 1: Overall working capital investment, liquidity and performance indicators

	2XX5 €'000	2XX3 €'000
Liquidity ratio	Times	Times
2XX3: €29,650,000:€5,250,000		5.64:1
2XX5: €82,000,000:€60,000,000	1.36:1	
Net cash balances	€'000	€'000
Cash less overdraft	(50,000)	(3,600)
Gross margin		
2XX3: €30,000,000/€150,000,000		20%
2XX5: €44,124,000/€294,160,000	15%	
Net income percentage		
2XX3: €7,500,000/€150,000,000		5%
2XX5: €2,941,600/€294,160,000	1%	
Return on investment		
2XX3: €7,500,000/€47,400,000		15.8%
2XX5: €2,941,600/€43,500,000	6.76%	

Table 2: Actual monetary investment in working capital (excluding cash) at 31st December 2XX5 compared to 31st December 2XX3

	2XX5 €'000	2XX3 €'000
Inventories: Raw Materials (w1)	9,150	-
Finished goods (€42,500,000 – €9,150,000)	33,350	9,000
Trade receivables	39,500	20,500
Trade payables	(10,000)	(1,500)
Working capital requirement	**72,000**	**28,000**
Overdraft interest rate	15%	8%
Yearly cost of funds tied up in working capital	**10,800**	**2,240**

(w1) 3 months of the raw material (clay) is kept in store. This equates to 12% of the average sales price in 2XX5 (€25.00 × 12% = €3.00 per item produced). Sales are now 12.2 million units (six million plus the five million to the distributor and the 1.2 million in internet sales). It is assumed that these occur evenly over the year. Therefore three months inventory equates to 12,200,000 units × €3.00 × 3/12 = €9,150,000

Working capital funding requirement

There has been an increase in working capital requirements amounting to €72,000,000 – €28,000,000 = €44,000,000

Actual costs associated with the growth strategy

The increase in working capital investment will result in additional interest cost of €10,800,000 – €2,240,000 = €8,560,000 per year, relative to the 2XX3 position.

Table 3: Working capital cash conversion cycle

		2XX5	2XX3
		Days	Days
Raw materials			
None (JIT system)			–
90 days (this affects 12% of the product cost)	90 × 12%/85%	12.71	
Finished goods			
€9,000,000/120,000,000 × 365			
€33,350,000/(€294,160,000 – €44,124,000) × 365		48.68	27.38
Trade receivables			
€20,500,000/€150,000,000 × 365			
€39,500,000/€294,160,000 × 365		49.01	49.88
Trade payables			
€1,500,000/€15,000,000(w2) × 365 = 36.5 days			
(this affects 10% of the product cost)	(36.5) × 10%/80%		(4.56)
€10,000,000/€35,599,200 (w3) × 365 = 103.4 days			
(this affects 12% of the product cost)	(103.4) × 12%/85%	(14.60)	
Net cash conversion cycle		**95.8**	**72.7**

(w2) 6,000,000 units × €25.00 × 10% = €15,000,000 (yearly purchases of raw material)
(w3) €250,036,000 × 12%/85% = €35,299,200

Appendix 2
Actual Revenue and Cost Analysis Schedule Agreed by the Directors in 2XX3

Table 1: Actual Revenue and Cost Analysis Agreed by the Directors in 2XX3.

	Distributor €'000	Ireland €'000
Income (5,000,000 × €23.00)	115,000	
Income (1,200,000 × €27.00)		32,400
Cost of goods sold (€115,000,000 × 80%)	(92,000)	
(€32,400,000 × 80%)		(25,920)
Additional contribution before specific fixed costs	23,000	6,480
Advertising cost	(1,000)	(500)
Additional sales staff	(400)	
Additional internet staff		(300)
Additional credit control staff (€30,000 × 2)		(60)
Internet software costs		(50)
	21,600	5,570
Total net contribution from additional sales	27,170	
Bad debts (€115,000,000 + €32,400,000) × 1%	(1,474)	
Expected additional profit	25,696	

Table 2: Initial cost analysis revisited in light of current knowledge.

	Distributor €'000	Ireland €'000
Income (5,000,000 × €23.00)	115,000	
Income (1,200,000 × €27.00 × 90%)		29,160
Cost of goods sold (5,000,000 × €25.00 × 85%)	(106,250)	
(1,200,000 × €25.00 × 85%)		(25,500)
Additional contribution before specific fixed costs	8,750	3,660
Advertising cost	(1,000)	(500)
Additional sales staff	(400)	
Additional internet staff		(300)
Internet software costs		(50)
Additional credit control staff (€30,000 × 2)		(60)
Contribution after specific fixed costs	7,350	2,750

	€'000
Total net contribution from additional sales	10,100
Bad debts (w1)	(2,912)
Increased cost of funds tied up (see Appendix 1: table 2)	(8,560)
Expected additional losses	(1,372)

(w1) Bad debts
Company bad debts were traditionally 1% and amount to about €150,000,000 × 1% = €1,500,000
Now they have increased to 1.5% of total sales (€150,000,000 + €115,000,000 + €29,160,000) €294,160,000 × 1.5% = €4,412,400
Incremental bad debts is €4,412,400 − €1,500,000 = €2,912,400. This increase relates to the overall sales of the company and cannot be accurately apportioned to the two new sale sources.

Appendix 3

Table 1: Comparison of actual working capital in 2XX5 and balances based on the policy in 2XX3 (with the exception of trade receivables which are revised to the industry norm of 30 days)

	2XX5 Revised €'000	2XX5 Actual €'000	Difference €'000
Inventories: raw materials	–	9,150	9,150
Finished goods (915,000 (ap. 4) × €20)	18,300	33,350	15,050
Trade receivables (€294,160,000 × 99% × 30/365)	23,936	39,500	15,564
Trade payables (12,200,000 × €25 × 10% × 36.5/365)	(3,050)	(10,000)	(6,950)
Total	**39,186**	**72,000**	**32,814**
Overdraft interest rate	8%	15%	
Yearly cost of funds tied up in working capital	**3,135**	**10,800**	**7,665**

Table 2: Initial cost analysis revisited in light of revised working capital policy and cost estimations

	Distributor €'000	Ireland €'000
Income (5,000,000 × €23.00)	115,000	
Income (1,200,000 × €27.00 × 90%)		29,160
Cost of goods sold (5,000,000 × €25.00 × 80%)	(100,000)	
(1,200,000 × €25.00 × 80%)		(24,000)
Additional Contribution before fixed costs	**15,000**	**5,160**
Advertising cost	(1,000)	(500)
Additional sales staff	(400)	
Additional internet staff		(300)
Internet software costs		(50)
Additional credit control staff (€30,000 × 2)		(60)
Expected bad debts	(1,150)	(292)
Contribution after specific fixed costs	**12,450**	**3,958**

	€'000
Total net contribution from additional sales	**16,408**
Additional credit control staff focusing on reduction in debtor days	(36)
Interest cost on the financing of additional working capital[1]	(895)
Expected additional profits	**15,477**

1. Revised 2XX5 working capital level €39,186,000 less the 2XX3 balance €28,000,000 indicates an expected funding requirement of €11,186,000. This is assumed to incur an interest cost of 8% (€11,186,000 × 8%) = €894,880.

Appendix 4
Workings to Determine the Closing Levels of Finished Goods Inventory Assuming the 2XX3 Working Capital Policy is Maintained

	2XX5	2XX3
2XX3: Units €9,000,000/(€25.00 × 80%)		450,000
2XX3: Level 450,000/6,000,000		7.5%
2XX5: Level (should remain the same as in 2XX3)	7.5%	
2XX5: Units 12,200,000 × 7.5%	915,000	

Case 21

Solution to The Pottery Company Limited 2

Ann-Marie Ward, Queen's University Belfast

REPORT ON FINANCE AND LIQUIDITY ISSUES FACED BY THE POTTERY COMPANY LIMITED

Prepared by: Successful Candidate

For: The directors of PCL

Table of contents	Page number

1. Terms of Reference

This report focuses on liquidity and finance issues faced by Pottery Company Limited (PCL). It has been prepared in response to a request from T. Brewster, the managing director. The first part of the report (section 3) provides information on the benefits of having a finance function. Section 4 justifies the choice of long-term finance. In section 5 the expected net income earned for the six month period from April and September 2XX6 is detailed. Cash projections based for the same period are provided in section 6. Finally, other information that would assist the bank manager in determining whether to provide a long-term loan facility is provided in section 7.

2. Important summary points

Five slides detailing the key issues are included in appendix 3.

3. Benefits of recruiting a finance manager

A company's activities should be periodically evaluated in light of changes in the environment. In addition, to remain successful, directors should continually assess their strategies for the future development of the company. Having a finance manager is vital for successful decision making. Financial managers are primarily concerned with the management of finances within a company. This role normally involves obtaining funds for investment and investing those funds to maximise the value of the company. This normally involves evaluating various investment possibilities and choosing those that maximise profitability, so long as the investment is consistent with long-term sustainability. Decisions taken are not always straightforward and may even result in short-term profitable projects being sacrificed in the interest of long-term profitability. As part of this process the financial manager will collect information from all departments, i.e. production, marketing, sales, management accounting, etc.

Financial managers are concerned with three main types of decision, which are interlinked. These are now briefly outlined.

(b) *Investment decision-making*

Investment decisions involve either committing a company's funds to an internal investment, an external investment (takeovers) or disinvestment in a project (for example, the sale of part of the business). The growth strategy adopted by PCL over the past two years is an example of an internal investment. A finance manager can bring more companywide knowledge of potential costs to the decision-making process, including the cost of financing any investment. In addition, a finance manager is trained in the evaluation of investments and a more accurate financial proposal is likely to result.

(c) *Finance decisions*

The assets of all companies have to be financed. The main types of finance are equity or debt. Equity includes share capital and reserves and represents the owners' investment in a company. Debt can either be long-term or short-term liabilities. When a company grows, like PCL has, it will require additional funds from one of these sources. In PCL's case the growth was financed by the overdraft, a short-term liability. This resulted in a profitable company having serious liquidity problems. A main concern of a finance director is cash management and maintaining sufficient liquidity.

The growth achieved by PCL over the period 2XX3 to 2XX5 resulted in an increase in working capital requirements. This should be financed with long-term liabilities. A finance director would be aware of this from the outset, and would have been able to provide all directors with an evaluation of the various sources of funds available and their terms, including cost. The impact of this additional funding would be integrated into the investment decision and an assessment of the change of the capital structure on the financial risk of the company considered.

(d) *Dividend decisions*

The third key decision considered by a finance manager is the dividend policy adopted by a company. As you are aware, dividends are distributions made out of net income. In listed companies the policy adopted impacts on the share price of the company. As PCL is not a public listed company, this decision is not as important. However, dividends distributed reduce the level of internal funding that is available for investment, hence growth, and may also cause an immediate cash flow burden. When a dividend is distributed, additional financing may be required.

The negative impact on cash and growth of paying a dividend has to be balanced with the requirements of the shareholders who may be dependent on the yearly income from dividends. This is more pronounced in a private limited company as there is not a readily available market for the shareholders to sell the shares. More information would be required to evaluate this appropriately.

4. Funding issues

(a) PCL has been overtrading for the past two years. It has liquidity problems and is dependent on the bank for its survival. PCL is using the overdraft to fund its growth. The overdraft was €50 million in 2XX5. The company has not been managing the funding of its assets appropriately. Non-current assets and the permanent portion of working capital should be financed by long-term sources as was the case in 2XX3.

(b) Reliance on short-term funding such as an overdraft is a risky strategy as this type of finance is repayable on demand. The increased risk for the bank has resulted in interest cost increases, hence reduced profit margins.

(c) As a matter of urgency the company has to obtain new funding from a long-term source. The funds should be used immediately to reduce the overdraft. This will allow PCL to negotiate better short-term interest terms with the bank on the overdraft as the bank's risk-exposure is reduced.

(d) There are two main categories of long-term funding, either additional equity capital from shareholders, or long-term debt. The company is a limited company, is not listed on the stock market and is owned by a limited number of shareholders. Therefore, it is likely that obtaining additional funding from this source may be limited. If the current shareholders were willing to change the balance of control in the company, there is the possibility of floating the company on the stock exchange, to gain funding. However, this is costly, and the company's finances are not being managed appropriately at present, a factor which would negatively impact on the market price of the shares.

(e) Therefore, I recommend that the company seeks long-term debt. There are various types of long-term debt. Debt capital such as debentures or loan stock can be issued by the company on the stock market. Alternatively, a long-term loan can be sourced. Given that T. Brewster is meeting the bank manager in two months time and that corrective action has to be agreed on, or in place for this meeting given the severity of your liquidity position at present, I recommend that a long-term loan of a minimum of €20 million is sourced.

Increase is a tax deductible expense, reducing its real cost to the company. In addition, long-term debt can be obtained at cheaper rates than short-term debt. The rates usually depend on the credit rating and riskiness of the company. PCL is a long-established company that is experiencing liquidity problems, brought on by overtrading in the past two years. PCL is profitable. Indeed, with appropriate action the company can increase its profitability, by just managing its finances and working capital better. At this juncture I would recommend that the loan is taken for a period of 15 years, payable monthly, and should be secured on the non-current assets. Having security available for a loan will put PCL in a stronger position to negotiate a lower interest rate.

(f) The other main funding source is working capital. I recommended steps that will reduce the current levels of funds tied up in the working capital of the company to just under €40 million. The steps recommended at this initial stage should release funds of €32.8 million over the next few months (see appendix 1).

(g) If both of these measures are adopted then the company can increase its cash balances by approximately €52.8 million, leaving it in a net cash position within six months. If everything holds constant, the cash balances should increase monthly thereafter. However, it seems from the movement in non-current assets between 2XX3 and 2XX5 that there has not been much investment in capital over the past two years. Therefore a review of assets is recommended and it is likely that additional resources will be required in the near future.

5. *Expected net income statement for the six months ended 30th September 2XX6*

	April €'000	May €'000	June €'000	July €'000	August €'000	September €'000	Total €'000
Income							
Sales (W1)	24,513	24,513	24,513	24,513	24,513	24,515	147,080
Production cost of goods sold (W5)	21,330	21,147	21,025	20,852	20,577	20,445	125,376
Gross income	**3,183**	**3,366**	**3,488**	**3,661**	**3,936**	**4,070**	**21,704**
Expenses							
Fixed costs (W7)	2,240	2,240	2,240	2,240	2,240	2,240	13,440
Bad debts (W1)	306	245	245	245	245	245	1,531
Additional salaries (W2)	11	11	12	11	11	12	68
Depreciation (W7)	179	179	179	179	179	180	1,075
Interest on long-term loan (W8)	133	133	133	133	133	135	800
Interest on overdraft (section 6)	197	132	45	1	–	–	375
Total expenses	**3,066**	**2,940**	**2,854**	**2,809**	**2,808**	**2,812**	**17,289**
Net income	**117**	**426**	**634**	**852**	**1,128**	**1,258**	**4,415**

The workings for the above statement are included within Appendix 2.

In 2XX5 PCL made €2,941,600 in profits (see appendix 1 of the question). From the movement in the equity reserves (negative) it would seem that a loss was made in 2XX4. The profitability of the company will be improved when the recommendations are implemented. The average cost of goods being produced will fall from €21.25 per unit to €20.11 over the six month period (Appendix 2: W5). This will eventually fall to €20.00. The weighted average method was used to value raw material inventory issues; hence the fall in price from €3.00 to €2.50 will take longer to influence profitability. The overall drop in the cost of goods issued increases the level of gross margin made. In addition to this, the level of bad debts will fall, as will the yearly interest charge (see appendix 2: W7). Based on my calculations the company should generate profits of over €1 million each month (see August and September above).

Some key assumptions underlying the above net income statement are as follows.

(a)   When working capital is reduced, this will lead to a reduction in fixed costs as there should be lower storage costs i.e. insurance, rent, heat and light etc. This was not estimated due to information and time constraints.

(b)   The above schedule does not take into account taxation. Tax rates are not known at this stage.

(c) Sales remain constant over the period and the adjustment to the credit period will not impact on demand.

(d) There are no additions to non-current assets, and none are scrapped in the year.

(e) The long-term debt is obtained at 8% per year. The repayments occur on a monthly basis over the period of the loan (This is a conservative estimate as a lower rate to this is likely).

(f) The overdraft interest rate is negotiated to 8% and is charged monthly at 0.67% on the balance outstanding on the last day of the month.

(g) When PCL is in a net cash position, the funds will be invested to earn a return. At this stage the potential interest/investment income has not been anticipated.

6. Projected cash flows for six months to 30th September 2XX6

	April €'000	May €'000	June €'000	July €'000	August €'000	September €'000
Receipts						
Sales (W1)	24,145	27,813	30,320	24,268	24,268	24,268
Long-term debt	20,000	–	–	–	–	–
Total receipts	**44,145**	**27,813**	**30,320**	**24,268**	**24,268**	**24,268**
Payments						
Additional salaries (W2)	11	11	12	11	11	12
Wages (W5)	12,708	12,708	12,708	13,059	15,250	15,250
Direct variable overhead costs (W5)	2,118	2,118	2,118	2,176	2,542	2,542
Raw materials – clay (W6)	6,328	544	–	–	744	2,251
Fixed element costs (W7)	2,240	2,240	2,240	2,240	2,240	2,240
Long-term debt repayment (W8)	195	195	195	195	195	195
Dividend	–	–	–	–	–	500
Taxation	–	–	–	–	–	1,200
Total payments	**23,600**	**17,816**	**17,273**	**17,681**	**20,982**	**24,190**
Running bank balance						
Opening balance	(50,000)	(29,652)	(19,787)	(6,785)	(199)	3,087
Receipts less payments	20,545	9,997	13,047	6,587	3,286	78
Closing balance	**(29,455)**	**(19,655)**	**(6,740)**	**(198)**	**3,087**	**3,165**
Interest (0.67% per month)	197	132	45	1	–	–
Closing balance after interest	**(29,652)**	**(19,787)**	**(6,785)**	**(199)**	**3,087**	**3,165**

The workings for the above statement are included within Appendix 2.

Over the six month period the overdraft will be eliminated and the company will be in a net cash position. It is expected that this position will increase by about €1.5 million per month thereafter. Key assumptions and issues relating to the expected cash flows are as follows:

(a) Sales are expected to occur evenly over the year. When the new credit control policy is adopted on 1st April, it is assumed that it will be fully complied with by the end of the month. Therefore in April an average collection period of 40 days and an average in 1.25% of bad debts are expected. Thereafter the industry expected policy of allowing 30 days and incurring 1% of bad debts is assumed.

(b) The long-term debt will be used to reduce the bank overdraft immediately.

(c) Suppliers are paid a lump sum in April (€6.328 million) to reduce their account balances to 36.5 days. There will not be any purchases of clay until the clay inventory is used up.

(d) Production is slowed until the excess finished good inventories are reduced to 915,000 units. This results in PCL having to spend less on variable direct overhead costs and on wages and salaries as the factory is no longer operated on a Saturday.

(e) An overdraft interest rate of 8% will be negotiated.

(f) The overdraft interest rate applied at the end of the month is applied to the balance on that date (not a daily calculation as I do not have sufficient information to calculate this).

(g) There are no purchases or sales of non-current assets.

7. Information to be included in the business plan for the meeting with the bank manager

It is assumed that at the meeting T. Brewster will request long-term funding. I have recommended that PCL source €20 million debt repayable over 15 years in equal monthly instalments. In addition, I have recommended that T. Brewster negotiate the overdraft rate back to the original 8%.

(a) The business plan should state that PCL is requiring €20 million debt on 1st April 2XX6 to be repaid over the 15 years in equal monthly instalments. The €20 million should be justified (The €20 million plus the increase in working capital of €32 million represents the amount required to put the company in a net cash position).

(b) Having debt secured on non-current assets is an option which is likely to reduce the interest rate offered by the bank on the long-term debt. Therefore, the business plan should include a schedule of non-current assets. The bank will be particularly interested in buildings and land as these assets usually appreciate over time hence reducing the credit exposure even further. Indeed, a current market valuation for any property, or land held should be included as this is likely to improve the balance sheet of the company (I have assumed that the balance sheet is prepared based on historic cost principles).

(c) The business plan should state the purpose of the loan. In this instance the purpose is to reduce the bank overdraft. However, more detail is required as the bank will refuse to provide a loan if it just sees the transaction as a window dressing arrangement that transfers one type of debt into another. Therefore, you need to inform the bank manager of the reasons for the deterioration in liquidity and profitability over the past two years and outline the steps being taken to improve the liquidity and profitability of PCL.

(d) The section detailing the cause of the liquidity problems should highlight the fact that PCL's sales grew too quick, doubling in two years, with no attention being directed to the financing of this growth. Point out that the investment in working capital actually increased from €28 million to €72 million. This €44 million would have directly impacted on the overdraft over the two years. Highlight the fact that the lack of control over working capital caused an increase in the variable costs from 80% to 85% and also increased fixed costs.

(e) Include a section on the steps being taken to get the company back on track. Stress that the company was profitable and a net cash generator in 2XX3. Highlight that the growth proposal is in fact a worthy venture (see the net income statement), however, the failure to replace the finance director resulted in many of the costs increasing due to improper control over the working capital and financing of the company.

(f) List the improvements implemented already and those to be implemented: the recruitment of a qualified finance director (provide my profile and CV); the renegotiation with the clay supplier; the running down of clay inventory; the reduction in production until the finished goods inventory falls to the levels that were stored in 2XX3; the recruitment of production staff and how this will reduce the wages bill as there will be no overtime; the new credit control policy and how this will reduce bad debts and make more cash available.

(g) Include the projected monthly net income statement from section 4. I also recommend that net income projections for the coming 3 years based on an optimistic, most likely and pessimistic outcome be prepared. These could be included in the appendix and referred to.

(h) Include the projected monthly cash requirement from section 5. As in (g) I recommend that projections for the coming three years assuming three differing outcomes are included. We would need to discuss the non-current assets and whether there is a requirement to update equipment, etc. as this will impact on these projections.

(i) The bank is usually interested to know the portion of the investment being provided by equity holders relative to debt holders. Therefore, you should include the gearing ratio and highlight that the equity holders will have a net investment of more than double that of the bank (€43.5 million) compared to €20 million by the bank as of September 2XX6. Though included in the cash projections I would recommend that the €0.5 million dividend be waived in this year. The pattern of having a low constant dividend by the equity holders should be highlighted. If this policy is to remain, then the bank manager should be made aware of this. Any retained earnings not distributed to shareholders are equivalent to an equity contribution by them to the company each year. This has been substantial in the past.

(j)   We will need to discuss the strategic plan of the company and to include this in the business plan. Has the market been saturated or is there room for more growth? We should do a detailed analysis of the profitability of the differing types of sales and should even consider down-sizing if profit levels are not sufficient in any area.

Appendix 1

Table 1: Comparison of actual working capital in 2XX5 and balances based on the recommendations provided.

	2XX5 Revised	2XX5 Actual	Difference
	€'000	€'000	€'000
Inventories: raw materials	–	9,150	9,150
Finished goods (915,000[1] × €20)	18,300	33,350	15,050
Trade receivables (€294,160,000 × 99% × 30/365)	23,936	39,500	15,564
Trade payables (€120,200,000 × €2.50 × 36.5/365)	(3,050)	(10,000)	(6,950)
Total	**39,186**	**72,000**	**32,814**

Workings to determine the closing levels of finished goods inventory assuming the recommendations are implemented.

	2XX5	2XX3
2XX3: Units €9,000,000/ (€25.00 × 80%)		450,000
2XX3: Level 450,000/6,000,000		7.5%
2XX5: Level (should remain the same as in 2XX3)	7.5%	
2XX5: Units 12,200,000 × 7.5%	915,000	

Appendix 2

W1. Sales

Yearly sales are €294,160,000. Therefore monthly sales are €24,513,000 (rounded). Bad debts are currently running at 1.5%. It is assumed that bad debts will fall to 1% over the month of April. Therefore an average rate of 1.25% is assumed for this month.

	Feb €'000	Mar €'000	April €'000	May €'000	June €'000	July €'000	August €'000	Sept €'000
Sales	24,513	24,513	24,513	24,513	24,513	24,513	24,513	24,515
Bad debts	1.5%	1.5%	1.25%	1%	1%	1%	1%	1%
Bad debts	368	368	306	245	245	245	245	245
Expected cash	24,145	24,145	24,207	24,268	24,268	24,268	24,268	24,268
Debtor days	50	50	40	30	30	30	30	30
Cash-flows			(average)					
Within 30 days	–	14,487[1]	14,487	18,155[3]	24,268	24,268	24,268	24,268
Remainder			9,658[2]	9,658	6,052[4]			
Total receipts			24,145	27,813	30,320	24,268	24,268	24,268

1. €24,145,3000 × 30/50 = €14,487,000 (rounded)
2. €24,145,000 – €14,487,000 = €9,658,000
3. €24,207,000 × 30/40 = €18,155,000 (rounded)
4. €24,207,000 – €18,155,000 = €6,052,000

W2. Additional salaries

Credit control employee: Yearly salary €36,000/12 = €3,000 each month payable at the month end.
Finance director: Yearly salary €100,000/12 = €8,333 per month

W3. Production requirements

Key factors

It is assumed that from April the new measures will bring the wages cost back down to 60% of the average 2XX3 unit sales price (€25.00 × 60% = €15.00), and the material purchases back down to 10% of the average 2XX3 unit sales price (€2.50). The remainder of the variable costs 'direct overhead costs' is assumed to remain unchanged at 10% (€2.50 per unit cost).

From April procedures will be in place to bring trade payables days back to their original amount (36.5 days) and production will be slowed to bring finished goods inventory down to the original levels held as a percentage of the sales units. Additional full-time production staff will then be employed and there will no longer be a requirement to pay overtime.

The inventory of finished goods is currently – €33,350,000/ (€25.00 × 85%) = 1,569,412 units

Inventory levels before the business finance manager left in 2XX3 were €9,000,000/ (€25.00 × 80%) = 450,000 units

In each month there are 4 working weeks and at present 6 working days. Therefore the production per day is assumed to be (1,016,666[1]/24 = 42,361 units per day)

To reduce costs without affecting the labour supply, the company can operate a five-day week at full production until inventory levels decline to their original level before the business finance manager left.

Therefore production is 42,361 × 20 (5 × 4) = 847,222 units per month until the closing inventory of finished goods falls to 915,000 units (see appendix 1). Then proceed in normal fashion producing the monthly sales requirements of 1,016,666 units, though increase the permanent production staff to keep up with sales demand (it is assumed that there is sufficient machine capacity). This will keep the variable cost constant at 60%.

1. Yearly units 12,200,000 divided by 12 = 1,016,666 per month.

Production requirements schedule (Units)

	Feb Units	Mar Units	April Units	May Units	June Units	July Units	August Units	Sept Units
Opening inventory	1,569,412	1,569,412	1,569,412	1,399,968	1,230,524	1,061,080	915,000	915,000
Production	1,016,666	1,016,666	847,222	847,222	847,222	870,586[1]	1,016,666	1,016,666
Total available	2,586,078	2,586,078	2,416,634	2,247,190	2,077,746	1,931,666	1,931,666	1,931,666
Sales	1,016,666	1,016,666	1,016,666	1,016,666	1,016,666	1,016,666	1,016,666	1,016,666
Closing inventory	1,569,412	1,569,412	1,399,968	1,230,524	1,061,080	915,000	915,000	915,000

This was obtained by working back from the desired closing inventory of 915,000 units.

Production requirements schedule (Costs)

	Feb Units	Mar Units	April Units	May Units	June Units	July Units	August Units	Sept Units
Production in units	1,016,666	1,016,666	847,222	847,222	847,222	870,586	1,016,666	1,016,666
Wages rate	€15.75[1]	€15.75	€15.00[2]	€15.00	€15.00	€15.00	€15.00	€15.00
Material	€3.00[3]	€3.00	€2.50	€2.50	€2.50	€2.50	€2.50	€2.50
Variable overhead	€2.50	€2.50	€2.50	€2.50	€2.50	€2.50	€2.50	€2.50

1. €25.00 × 63% = €15.75
2. €25.00 × 60% = €15.00
3. €25.00 × 12% = €3.00

W4. Purchases of Raw materials

Before the business finance director left, he had negotiated a deal with the suppliers whereby he did not have to hold any raw material inventory (clay), as it was delivered each day. The suppliers are willing to go back to this arrangement so long as PCL starts to pay them according to the original timeframe. This will be agreed from April onwards.

Raw material requirements schedule

	Feb €'000	Mar €'000	April €'000	May €'000	June €'000	July €'000	August €'000	Sept €'000
Opening inventory	9,150	9,150	9,150	6,608	4,066	1,524	–	–
Purchases	3,050[1]	3,050	–	–	–	906	2,542	2,542
Total available	12,200	12,200	9,150	6,608	4,066	2,430	2,542	2,542
Production	3,050	3,050	2,542	2,542	2,542	2,430	2,542[2]	2,542
Closing inventory	9,150	9,150	6,608	4,066	1,524	–	–	–

[1] 1,016,667 units × .00 = €3,050,000
[2] 1,016,667 units × €2.50 = €2,541,665 (Rounded to €2,542,000)

Store of raw material movement schedule (first in – first out valuation method used)

	Units	Value	Issues
Opening inventory	3,050,000	€3.00 (€25.00 × 12%)	
April issue to production from stock	847,222	€3.00	€2,541,666
Inventory 1st May	2,202,778		
May issue to production from stock	847,222	€3.00	€2,541,666
Inventory 1st June	1,355,556		
June issue to production from stock	847,222	€3.00	€2,541,666
Inventory 1st July	508,334		
Require 870,586 units			
July issue to production from stock	508,334	€3.00	€1,525,002
Purchase the remainder (870,586 – 508,334)	362,252	€2.50 (€25.00 × 10%)	€905,630
Inventory 1st August	–		
August purchases	1,016,667	€2.50	
August issue to production from stock	1,016,667	€2.50	€2,541,667
Inventory 1st September			
September purchases	1,016,667	€2.50	
September issue to production from stock	1,016,667	€2.50	€2,541,667

W5. Cost of goods produced

Total cost of goods produced for stock valuation (see W3 and W4 for units produced and expense rates)

	Feb €'000	Mar €'000	April €'000	May €'000	June €'000	July €'000	August €'000	Sept €'000
Wages (cash flow)	16,012	16,012	12,708	12,708	12,708	13,059	15,250	15,250
Variable overhead (cash flow)	2,542	2,542	2,118	2,118	2,118	2,176	2,542	2,542
Material	3,050	3,050	2,542	2,542	2,542	2,430	2,541	2,541
Total cost of goods issued for sale	**21,604**	**21,604**	**17,368**	**17,368**	**17,368**	**17,665**	**20,333**	**20,333**

Costs released to the Income statement (weighted average method of inventory valuation)

	Feb €	Mar €	April €	May €	June €	July €	August €	Sept €
Opening inventory	33,350[1]	33,350	33,350	29,388	25,609	21,952	18,765	18,521
Production	21,604	21,604	17,368	17,368	17,368	17,665	20,333	20,333
Total available	**54,954**	**54,954**	**50,718**	**46,756**	**42,977**	**39,617**	**39,098**	**38,854**
Units sold	21,604	21,604	21,330[3]	21,147	21,025	20,852	20,577	20,445
Closing inventory	**33,350**	**33,350**	**29,388**	**25,609**	**21,952**	**18,765**	**18,521**	**18,409**
Average rate to cost units sold	€21.25	€21.25	€20.98[2]	€20.80	€20.68	€20.51	€20.24	€20.11

1. This is the €42,500,000 less the €9,150,000 raw material stock.
2. This represents the average value of the units available for sale, i.e. €50,718,000/2,416,634 = €20.98 (see production requirements schedule).
3. Therefore the expense released to the income statement is the number of units sold in the period 1,016,666 × €20.98 = €21,329,653 rounded to €21,330,000.

W6. Payment for raw materials
Raw material payments schedule

	Dec €'000	Jan €'000	Feb €'000	Mar €'000	April €'000	May €'000	June €'000	July €'000	August €'000	Sept €'000
Purchases (W4)	3,050	3,050	3,050	3,050	–	–	–	906	2,542	2,542
Within 30	–	888[1]	888	888	2,506[3]	–	–	–	744	2,088
Within 60			888	888	2,162	544	–	–	–	162
Within 90				888	1,274[2]					
Remainder					386					
Cash flow					6,328	544	–	–	744	2,250

Up to the end of March PCL has been taking 103 days credit. To get the cheaper price for new supplies PCL has to pay an amount to bring the credit days back down to their original 36.5 days (assume there are 30 days in each month).

1. 3,050,000 × 30/103 = 888,000 (rounded)
2. January's amount owing less what has already been paid, must be paid now as it is over 36.5 days old, to bring PCL back in line with the original 36.5 days policy (€3,050,000 - €888,000 - €888,000 = €1,274,000).
3. 3,050,000 × 30/36.5 = €2,506,000

W7. Fixed costs

At present fixed costs represents the difference between the net profit amount and the gross profit amount, which is (€44,124,000 – €2,941,600) = €41,182,400. This contains all fixed expenses that are chargeable to the Income Statement. However, some items do not involve cash flows (depreciation) and others will change i.e. it is assumed that the bank manager will be supportive and resort back to the original agreement of charging 8% per year, or 0.67% per month on the balance outstanding.

Schedule Adjusting Fixed Costs to Estimate Cash Flows

	€'000
Total fixed costs in 2XX5	41,182
Less depreciation[1]	(2,389)
Less bad debts[2]	(4,412)
Less interest (will change)[3]	(7,500)
Cash requirement	26,881

[1] Depreciation is being charged at 10% per annum using the reducing balance method. Therefore the depreciation charge in the prior year was €2,389,000, calculated as follows: €21,500,000/90% = €23,889,000 (Opening net book value in 2XX5 – rounded). Therefore the charge for the year is €23,889,000 × 10% = €2,389,000 (rounded). The depreciation charge estimated in this year is €21,500,000 × 10% = €2,150,000 for the year (€179,000 per month – rounded).

[2] Bad debts. Though these are removed from the receipts figure in the cash budget, in the Income Statement they are located within 'Administration costs' and not included in the 'Cost of Goods Sold'. In the prior year these amounted to 1.5% of the total actual sales figure €294,160,000 = €4,412,400.

[3] Interest. Current charge is €50,000,000 × 15% = €7,500,000

Therefore a monthly cash outflow of €2,240,000 is estimated (€26,881,000 divided by 12), in respect of all other fixed costs.

W8. Long term debt repayment.

This is a long term loan that is repayable over 15 years and is being charged 8% interest per year. Therefore the yearly repayments are × multiplied by 8.559 (15 year annuity @ 8%) = €20,000,000. × is therefore €2,336,721. The monthly repayment is estimated at €194,726 rounded to €195,000, (€2,336,721 divided by 12).

Six months interest on this loan in the first year is estimated at €20,000,000 × 8% = €1,600,000/2 = €800,000. The monthly interest estimate is €800,000/6 = €133,333.

Appendix 3

FINANCE FUNCTION

Aids successful strategic decision making

Main decision areas:

- -Investment
- -Financing
- -Dividend

PCL's liquidity and profitability problems would have been avoided if the growth strategy was properly financed

FUNDING ISSUES

Liquidity problems due to overtrading

Over-reliance on short-term funding

Factors affecting choice of funding:

-The equity holders are several local individuals, it is assumed that it would be difficult to get timely cash injections

-Listing is expensive and dilutes control

-Debt capital is not possible due to time constraints (issue is expensive)

-A long-term bank loan is a quick, tax deductible solution

EXPECTED NET INCOME

Expected to stabilise at €1.2 million to €1.3 million per month

Main causes of increase:

-The production cost of goods sold falls from 85% to 80% of the average sales price

-Bad debts fall from 1.5% to 1% of gross sales

-Interest charge falls (better working capital management will result in an influx of over €32 million in cash over the coming months)

There is a new long term debt interest charge

CASH FLOWS

Over the 6 months cash flows will improve from an overdraft of €50 million to a net cash position of €3 million. Net cash inflow will stabilise at €1.3 to €1.5 million per month

Main causes:
-Reduction in working capital levels releases about €32 million
-Sourcing long term debt of €20 million
-PCL is more profitable

May need to invest in non current assets

BUSINESS PLAN INFORMATION

Amount required

Term

Security (non current asset schedule)

Repayment schedule

Purpose, including:
-Reason for cash/profit deterioration
-Steps to improve position
-Finance director profile
-Projections (net income, cash flow
 and Balance sheet)
-PCL's future strategy

Case 22

Solution to Waterlife plc

Evarist Stoja, Queen's University Belfast

REPORT ON FINANCING DECISIONS CONCERNING WATERLIFE PLC

Prepared by: M. H.
Consultant

For: Board of Directors
Waterlife PLC

1. Terms of Reference

Further to our previous discussion on the financing matters concerning your company, I am pleased to offer my advice. This report includes a calculation and discussion of Waterlife actual capital structure and cost of capital along with remarks regarding other related matters. I have based my advice on the data and comments I was given by the senior management. The calculation of cost of capital and capital structure and the associated discussion relates to situations that your company had faced in the past, is facing now and/or may face in the future. Further, the calculation and discussion of these matters considers the underpinning theory as well as the practical issues.

2. General Recommendations for Future Reference

Although in practice it is very difficult to separate the financing decision and investment decision (as well as the dividend decision) as they are intrinsically linked, analysis of capital structure (and cost of capital) should start from the assumption that the two are separate.

Market imperfections should be assumed away. This will provide the management with a useful framework to initiate the analysis and understand the implications of capital structure and cost of capital on firm value.

Once a clear conclusion of the impact (or lack of impact of) capital structure on firm value has been established, the next step should be to 'bring into the picture' the elements which were assumed away. For example, analyse the impact of taxes, increased risk that comes with debt financing, type of assets that a firm employs, information asymmetry between the managers and investors and so on, on income and ultimately firm value.

Adjust the firm's capital structure while considering adjustment costs such as transactions costs and the lumpiness of security issues as well as the most likely movements of security markets in the foreseeable future.

3. Issues Relating to the Weighted Average Cost of Capital (WACC) of Waterlife

Cost of equity, and ultimately WACC are calculated employing the capital asset pricing model (CAPM). It is important to note that this model relies on many assumptions that do not always hold in practice and hence it is important to remember the model does not yield a precise estimate of cost of equity.

Although the market risk premium of 8% (see Appendix 1(a) for detailed calculations) is not particularly high, a beta of 1.5 is very high and Waterlife's stock can be classified as aggressive. What this means is that Waterlife's share price is very sensitive to the market movement. Nick is right to say that they are in a very sensitive industry. This implies that recoveries in the economy which will be accompanied by stock market buoyancy will lead to an even higher percentage increase in Waterlife's share price. Recessions of the economy however, which will be accompanied by stock market pessimism, will lead to even higher percentage decreases in the firm's share price. This is done through the effect that beta has on the cost of capital and ultimately share price.

In this case, the cost of equity is 16%. If the market risk premium increases by 2% this will lead to a 3% increase in cost of equity of Waterlife. The opposite is also true: a 2% decrease in market risk premium will lead to a 3% decrease in the cost of equity (see Appendix 1(b) for detailed calculations).

With a cost of equity of 16% and a cost of debt of 8%, accounting for the tax rate Waterlife's WACC is 14.36% (see Appendix 1(c)). This estimate is based on the following:

- Equity capital is estimated in market values rather than book values. The reason for this is that if capital structure matters, it impacts upon the market value of the firm and book value is of little help when valuing a firm.
- Equity capital includes retained earnings. Although, this source of funds is not originally contributed by shareholders, it belongs to them as they are the owners of the company and own everything that is left after the firm meets all of its obligations.
- Debt book value is the equivalent of market value as they are essentially the same thing as long as the firm is not in financial distress, which Waterlife is not.
- We exclude the short-term loan from the calculation of the proportion of debt on capital employed. This source of funds constitutes a relatively small part of the financing for Waterlife and is not very likely that it will make a large impact on the estimates of WACC. Further, we are more interested about long-term firm value. I do however, recognise that the decision to omit short-term loan is somewhat arbitrary. Short-term debt however has the potential to lead to bankruptcy and ultimately liquidation.

It is true that Waterlife's cost of capital is relatively high, due mainly to a high equity beta. With its current leverage ratio of 15.8%, its WACC is 14.4%. It may be possible to reduce the WACC by employing more debt provided it does not significantly increase financial distress risk (see example in Appendix 2).

From a theoretical viewpoint this would not be possible. As argued by Modigliani and Miller (1958) (MM) and cited by one of the directors, the cost of equity of a levered firm increases in proportion to the leverage ratio so that the WACC remains constant. This implies that no combination of debt and equity is better than any other. Analytically this is expressed as:

$$r_{equity} = r_{assets} + D / E(r_{assets} - r_{equity})$$

MM's analysis and conclusions relate to a 'perfect world' where there are no distortions and/or imperfections. They assume among other things that there are no taxes, borrowing rates are the same for all market participants and they can borrow as much as they like regardless of current debt levels. In this perfect world, the board director would be right and the junior finance manager would be wrong: changing the capital structure does not lead to changes in the cost of capital and the value of Waterlife would remain constant regardless of the debt level it employs. Therefore, the senior management/board of directors can ignore capital structure issues and concentrate exclusively on investment decisions such as expanding production capacity to serve a wider market.

This theory however, ignores many distortions of the real world, one of which is tax. The government allows Waterlife (and all of the other companies) to deduct interest expenses from the tax bill. In the Income Statement of Waterlife, this is shown by the fact that interest payable is paid before taxes and the tax bill is calculated as a percentage of earnings after interest payments. The deductibility of interest expense from the tax bill provides debt financing with a clear advantage over equity. Analytically, the weighed average cost of capital of Waterlife is:

$$WACC = r_{debt}(D/V)(1 - tax) + r_{equity}(E/V)$$

This equation clearly shows that by increasing the leverage ratio, Waterlife would be able to decrease the WACC and hence cash-flows are now discounted at a lower rate, creating some extra value for shareholders. Therefore, we may conclude that once we account for taxes that Waterlife pays, increases in the leverage ratio lead to decreases in WACC. Therefore, from this perspective the junior finance manager is right.

4. Issues Relating to the Negative Prospects of the Economy and the Impact upon Financing Commitments

Waterlife like other firms runs operational and financial risk. Operational risk, or otherwise known as business risk, refers to variability of operating income (or earnings before interest and tax – EBIT) due to adverse economic conditions. Financial risk refers to variability of earnings per share (EPS) due to debt financing. Debt financing increases uncertainty and hence risk of share returns. If EPS of Waterlife change, this will have a valuation impact upon its share price. If, for example, EPS decrease, this might make it difficult for Waterlife to maintain the same dividend payout ratio. Waterlife may be forced to reduce its dividend payments which most likely will lead to decreases in share price. While this is clearly undesirable and will lead to a decreased demand for Waterlife shares, shareholders cannot force Waterlife to pay any dividends until it recovers. Eventually Waterlife may recover and increase its dividend payments to the previous level. The point here is that while dishonouring equity, financing commitments will have an undesirable effect on share price and shareholders may be reluctant to contribute fresh equity capital, Waterlife will still be able to survive.

However, when adverse economic conditions lead to a lower EBIT than interest payments or generally when interest payments are just too high to be covered by EBIT then this would not just have a valuation impact (share price decrease in this case). Therefore, looking at the Income Statement, if EBIT is equal to or less than interest payable then the company is on the brink of financial distress or bankruptcy (see Appendix 3(a) for detailed calculations). If this situation persists and the company cannot find the extra cash needed to pay the interest, it will have to declare bankruptcy. In Appendix 2 (of question), this happens in the first 35% probability scenario: EBIT is €320,000, well below the €599,000 interest payable. If this occurs and Waterlife cannot find the extra €279,000 (suppose the €1,200,000 of Cash and Marketable Securities is tied up), it may have to declare bankruptcy. The ratios EBIT-to-interest payable normally should be above 2 for the company to be considered financially safe and often is as high as 5.

The losses suffered by different companies during bankruptcy are different and depend to a large extent on the tangible assets (the proportion of fixed-assets to total-assets) employed. In the case of Waterlife's this ratio is around 64% (see Appendix 3(b)). While this ratio is not particularly low, we know that other firms in the industry employ a higher level of tangible assets. Waterlife on the other hand, invests heavily on research and development and other intangible assets which have value only in Waterlife as a going concern. These intangible assets suffer great losses during bankruptcy and hence will reduce its value even further. Depending on the severity of the costs encountered and the length of time it remains insolvent, Waterlife might be forced into liquidation. From this perspective, although dishonouring financing commitments will have a valuation impact upon the share price, the inability of Waterlife to meet debt financing obligations is far more critical for its long-term survival. It may lead to bankruptcy, and if quick recovery is not possible, even liquidation.

5. Issues Relating to Statements in the Financial Press regarding Efficiency

It is true that other things equal, the higher the debt level, the more efficient the management. High interest payments encourage management to work harder to meet financing obligations. Low debt levels on the other hand, may lead to managers taking it easy and expand their perks with cash that should be paid back to shareholders. This will ultimately lead to an inefficient firm because managers do not have contractual obligations to pay out cash and may even invest it projects that yield a return below the cost of capital. This type of agency problem is studied by Jensen (1986) and he argues that it is particularly severe for mature firms with a widely dispersed-ownership structure where management owns few shares if at all.

But does this theory apply to Waterlife? I do not have any data to comment on the ownership dispersion of Waterlife. It is however a reasonably small firm with growth opportunities that are expected to generate a return above the cost of capital. Further, the EBIT-to-interest payable is under 2 in all 3 scenarios, classifying it as not safe financially. Additionally, Waterlife does not have the required asset structure (a significant proportion of tangible assets) to increase the debt level. However, even if it did have the required asset structure, increasing the leverage as a means to increase efficiency, particularly at this point in time when the prospects of the economy are not particularly optimistic, would be dangerous. If Waterlife has some financial slack, I think it would be better to save it for the future when quick access to debt financing might be essential for the company. I therefore agree with Nick who thinks that a fast-growing firm with not as many tangible assets as other firms in the industry as Waterlife should not increase its leverage ratio to preserve flexibility as well as avoid financial distress costs.

6. Issues Relating to the Equivalence of Cost of Capital Minimisation and Firm Value Maximisation

The discussion relating to this issue is somewhat theoretical and is based on the assumption that Modigliani and Miller's Proposition I does not hold. This proposition states that the capital structure of a firm is irrelevant to its market value. If this is the case, then it will not be possible to change the value of the firm by changing its capital structure.

However, this proposition is based on the assumption that investment and financing decisions are totally different and do not interact. Other implicit assumptions are: the capital markets are perfectly competitive and securities are infinitely divisible; information is costless and available to all market participants; there are no transaction and bankruptcy costs or taxes; all market participants are price takers; investors can borrow on the same terms as firms; firms can be classified into homogeneous risk classes.

Many of these assumptions clearly do not hold in the real world. Waterlife is paying taxes and it incurs transactions costs every time it raises capital from the securities markets. Further, if Waterlife cannot honour its debt financing commitments and bankruptcy occurs, this will not be costless. A large proportion of its asset value will be lost due to its particular structure (i.e. intangible assets). Hence, these violations (and others which I have not discussed for efficiency of presentation) of the assumptions upon which MM's Proposition I is based, seriously challenge Proposition I. Whenever one adjusts the MM assumptions to allow for the 'tax shield' effect (discussed in Section 3), the WACC of the firm declines as the proportion of debt financing increases. As the value of the firm is the present value of the future cash-flows attributable to it, this means that as gearing increases, so does the value of the firm. However, in practice, as the level of gearing increases, so does the probability of the company facing liquidation or bankruptcy. This potential future cost must also be included in determining the present value of the firm; hence, there is a trade-off when increasing the level of gearing in a firm between the benefits of the reduced future tax bills and the cost of potential default on its debt commitments. This results in WACC decreasing with gearing up to a point (as the benefits of the tax shield are outweighing the possible bankruptcy costs), before increasing again, as the probability of bankruptcy becomes higher (see Appendix 4 for a graphical depiction of this). If this theory holds, then firm value *can* be maximized by adjusting the capital structure so as to minimize WACC.

7. Issues Relating to Financing with Retained Earnings as the Most Preferred Source of Funds

Clearly Waterlife, like all the other firms has three main financing options: retained earnings, equity capital or debt capital. Retained earnings are an internal source of financing. Earnings that Waterlife has generated through trading have partly been paid to shareholders and partly been retained. Hence, access to this source of funds is transactions costs-free because they are already within the company.

If however, Waterlife decides to raise external capital in the form of debt and /or equity it will not just incur transactions costs. If it decides to raise debt, investors who do not have as much information about its future prospects and the probability of financial distress/bankruptcy, might worry that a higher debt-level might bring about bankruptcy and might only be willing to buy the new bonds at a discount to compensate them for these potential costs. If however, Waterlife decides to issue equity, investors might interpret this as a sign that senior management is not optimistic about the future and that current share price is overvalued and might again only be willing to buy the new shares at a discount. Hence, if Waterlife decides to finance the new project with retained earnings, it will not save only the transactions costs but also the signalling and information asymmetry costs. In this respect, retained earnings are the cheapest, quickest and most convenient form of financing and hence the most preferred one.

Joe is right to think that borrowing short-term and rolling it over could indeed constitute a form of long-term financing but this issue is important and requires particular attention. A large proportion of companies in practice appear to employ this technique to meet their financing needs. It is important however, to respect the Maturity-Matching principle: long-term (fixed) assets are financed with long-term finance and current assets are financed with short-term finance. Adopting the alternative approach where long-term (fixed) assets are funded with short-term finance is generally considered as aggressive and dangerous. Waterlife might not have started to receive a return from its investment in long-term assets by the time short-term debt payments are due. This will cause serious liquidity problems which are potentially as dangerous to Waterlife as defaulting on long-term debt finance and may lead to bankruptcy and ultimately liquidation.

8. Issues Relating to the Value of Waterlife adopting the Trade-off Theory of Capital Structure

The main advantage of debt is that interest payments are tax deductible. If the current debt level is permanent, then the tax shield will be worth €600,000. If however, Waterlife decides to increase its debt level to €7.3 million and roll it over on a permanent basis then the tax shield is worth 1,590,000 + 600,000 = €2,190,000 (see Appendix 4(a)).

However, this strategy is not riskless. Increasing the leverage ratio means increased probability of default on interest payments given the current economic situation.

In Appendix 2 (of question), we see that there is a 35% chance that Waterlife will not meet its interest obligations, in which case it will go bankrupt. If bankruptcy occurs, due to its particular asset structure, bankruptcy costs will be €5 million. Therefore, the ex-ante bankruptcy costs are €1.75 million. It would appear that by increasing its leverage ratio from 15.8% to 40.6%, Waterlife might increase its market value by €440,000. How does this come about? Taking the MM Proposition I as the starting point and allowing for taxes, probability of bankruptcy and costs incurred, the value of Waterlife will be (see Appendix 4(b) for a graphical representation):

$$V_{levered} = V_{unlevered} + Tax\ Shields - Possible\ Distress\ Costs$$

Therefore the value of Waterlife, if it increases leverage from the current debt level (€2 million) to €7.3 million will be:

$$V_l = 11,000,000 + 2,190,000 - 1,750,000 = 11,440,000$$

The implied tax is 30% and is calculated as €1,590,000 / €5,300,000 = 0.3

These calculations implicitly assume that the new debt level (€7.3 million) will be maintained for eternity and hence the tax shield will have a present value of €2.19 million. This is clearly a strong assumption. The tax rate might change in the future. For example, if it decreases to 25% then the tax shields will only be worth €1.825 million. Further, Waterlife might decide to reduce or even pay off all its debt in the future. Additionally, it is not certain that Waterlife will always be profitable and hence have income to shield from tax. If it makes losses, then the tax shields during this loss-making period will be gone for ever. Therefore, the tax shield value of €2,190,000 is risky and may turn out to be much lower.

While the benefits of increasing the debt level are risky, we also need to consider the costs that a higher debt level will bring and how likely these costs are. In the Appendix 2 (of question), it is shown that there is a 70% (35 + 35) chance that Waterlife will either not honour its debt commitments or will honour them with difficulty, and only a 30% chance that there will be something left for shareholders after interest and tax payments. These estimates are not very optimistic and we also need to allow for a margin of error. Once we allow for this possibility, then bankruptcy is more threatening to the market value of Waterlife because it lacks the required asset structure to increase leverage to such high levels. As already discussed, other firms in the industry can support the high leverage ratios with a large proportion of tangible (fixed) assets which retain most, if not all, of their value when sold should the company go bankrupt. If bankruptcy occurs, the intangible assets such as research and development, patents, know-how and staff training that Waterlife has been investing in, will have little if any value. Therefore, raising debt in these circumstances is a risky strategy for Waterlife.

9. Issues Relating to the reasons why Equity is Safer than Debt and Options to Make Debt Payments Safer

Nick is right to think that equity is the safer option. However, in reaching this conclusion he is taking the firm's perspective, not an investor's. From the investor's perspective, the fact that interest payments are guaranteed but dividend payments are not, makes debt the safer option. However, the fact that interest payments are guaranteed no matter what the level of operating income, and dividend payments are discretionary, makes debt a risky financing alternative, and equity a safer one from the firm's perspective.

At the moment, given the economic situation and current market coverage, it appears that bankruptcy is not just a hypothetic or a remote situation. There is a 35% chance that Waterlife will go bankrupt and a 35% chance that it will meet its obligations with difficulty. Therefore, issuing debt is a very risky strategy unless Waterlife expands and enters the national market. Currently, there are one million young people and this group is predicted to increase by 4% each year. Further, one in 100 of them is likely to get involved in these sports and spend on average €500. Therefore, if Waterlife covers this market, the extra stream of income for the next three years would be: €5,000,000; €5,200,000; €5,408,000.

With this stream of extra income, Waterlife can comfortably meet its existing and new debt obligations with substantial amounts of earnings to retain and/or pay out to shareholders. It must be noted however, that these estimates ignore competition, i.e. the fact that this market might already be served by other companies and hence the actual extra stream of income would be less. However, even if the extra stream of income is half of the forecasted one, interest payments will still be relatively safe.

10. Issues Relating to the Possible Reasons for the Share Price Decrease Subsequent to the Potential Share Issue

It is a well documented fact that share issues are accompanied with a share price decrease. While the potential share issue might lead to a weaker position of the existing shareholders (they will own a smaller proportion of Waterlife compared to their current holding proportion), it is unlikely that the share price decrease is due to this dilution effect. The share price decrease is more appropriately attributed to agency relationships and information asymmetry. An agency relationship occurs when there is separation of ownership and control. In this case Waterlife shareholders have delegated control over the firm to managers (agents) who have expertise in running the business. The separation of ownership and control may lead to agency costs. Managers (agents) are assumed to put their self-interest first rather than shareholders' and may at times make suboptimal decisions which increase their utility at the expense of shareholders. Shareholders recognise this possible outcome ex-ante and are only willing to buy the shares at a discount that they think is appropriate.

It is widely accepted that managers in general will know more about the company that they are running than outside investors. This situation is known as information asymmetry and affects more small companies than large ones. In this respect, I think that Waterlife suffers from a relatively serious asymmetric information problem which will become more evident when Waterlife goes to the capital markets. Investors could be unable to evaluate the fair value of the securities issue. Thus, the decision to issue debt or equity will be interpreted as a sign of what managers know/think about the future prospects of Waterlife. Investors know that if Waterlife cannot meet its debt obligations, it will land on serious trouble and managers will lose their jobs. Thus, if Waterlife decides to issue debt, then the market will interpret this as a sign of managerial optimism about the future. If however, Waterlife decides to issue equity, then the market will interpret this as a sign of pessimism. Management do not want to issue debt because they think that the earnings generated by the new project might not be enough to honour debt financing commitments with something left over for shareholders. Further, investors might also interpret this as a sign that management think the stock is overvalued and might try to 'cash in' on this situation. Hence, the announcement to issue equity will be accompanied by a share price decrease.

On balance, I think a debt issue is a dangerous financing strategy and unless Waterlife decides to enter the national market, it will most likely lead to financial distress. On the other hand, a share issue will induce a share price decrease. It will however, give Waterlife the safety it needs during this time of weak economic performance as well as preserve its financial flexibility. Therefore, I suggest that Waterlife issues 616,280 shares at €8.6 to raise €5.3 million required to finance the new project.

A few points that a manager should bear in mind when faced with a capital structure decision are:

- The tax rate – what is the marginal (not average) tax rate that the company pays? Will it have enough earnings in the future to shield it from tax by borrowing? Are there any less risky alternative ways, such as depreciation, to shield the income?
- Business and financial risk – what is the business risk of the company? How sensitive is the firm's income to variations in GDP? Are its sales more like those of a supermarket (stable throughout the business cycle) or like those of luxurious goods (very high during expansion periods and very low during recession periods)? How likely is financial distress and bankruptcy given the actual and future economic conditions?
- Asset structure – what type of assets does the company employ? Are they tangible, fixed assets such as land, buildings, machineries and equipment which maintain most of their value should the company sell them in the second-hand market or are they intangible assets such as patents, brand names, research and development which have value only in the firm as a going concern?
- Debt capacity – what is the actual level of debt and the maximum the firm can employ without leading to financial distress and a significant increase in probability or bankruptcy? How valuable is financial slack? Is it likely that the company will need external finance at short notice or financial slack will lead to a 'sleepy' management?

Appendix 1

(a)

Market Risk Premium $MRP = r_m - r_f = 12 - 4 = 8\%$

Equity Beta $\beta = \dfrac{Cov(r_m, r_w)}{Var(r_m)} = \dfrac{150}{10^2} = 1.5$

Cost of Equity $r_E = r_f + \beta(r_m - r_f) = r_m = r_f + \beta(MRP) = 4 + 1.5 * 8 = 16\%$

(b)

$$r_{EI} = 4 + 1.5 * 10 = 19\%$$
$$\Delta r_E = r_{EI} - r_E = 19 - 16 = 3\%$$

$$r_{E2} = 4 + 1.5 * 6 = 13\%$$
$$\Delta r_E = r_{E2} - r_E = 13 - 16 = -3\%$$

(c)

The formula for the Weighted Average Cost of Capital is:

$$WACC = r_D * \frac{D}{D + E} * (1 - Tax\ Rate) + r_E * \frac{E}{D + E}$$

Therefore, we need the proportions of debt and equity Waterlife employs in its capital structure as well as the tax rate.

There are several ways to compute the implied tax rate that Waterlife pays. The first one is to employ the following formula:

Tax Rate $TR = \dfrac{Tax\ Paid}{EBIT - Interest\ Paid} = \dfrac{2,700}{608,000 - 599,000} \times 100 = 30\%$

Where the numerator and denominator come from the Income Statement (Appendix 2)
Another way to calculate the implied tax rate paid by Waterlife is the following:
We know that *Value of Tax Shield = Tax Rate*Value of Debt.*

Therefore, Tax Rate $TR = \dfrac{Value\ of\ Tax\ Shield}{Value\ of\ Debt} = \dfrac{1,590,000}{5,300,000} = 30\%$

Now we can compute Waterlife's cost of capital:

$$WACC = 8 * \frac{2,000,000}{12,700,000} * (1 - 0.3) + 16 * \frac{10,700,000}{12,700,000} = 14.36\%$$

Appendix 2

The current leverage ratio is around 15.8%. Now, suppose this ratio increases to 25% without increasing Waterlife's financial distress/bankruptcy risk. Then we have:

$$WACC1 = 8 * 0.25 * 0.7 + 16 * 0.75 = 13.4\%$$

Therefore, a 58% increase in the leverage ratio leads to a 6.7% decrease in WACC.
Now suppose that the leverage ratio increases from 15.8% to 30% assuming again that this does not lead to an increase in financial distress/bankruptcy risk. Then we have:

$$WACC2 = 8 * 0.3 * 0.7 + 16 * 0.7 = 12.9\%$$

Therefore, a 90% increase in the leverage ratio leads to a 10.3% decrease in WACC. Thus, we may conclude that although Waterlife's WACC is not extremely sensitive to changes in the leverage ratio, it still decreases with increases in debt levels.

Appendix 3

(a)
A useful indicator of financial safety or distress is the Interest Coverage ratio given by the following formula:

$$Interest\ Coverage = \frac{EBIT}{Interest\ Paid}$$

This ratio measures the 'financial safety' of the firm i.e. to what extent can it cover the interest payments to its debt holders? A rule of thumb for this ratio is that firms should be concerned if this ratio falls below about 5.
For Waterlife, depending on the probability scenario we have the following estimates:

Scenario 1 (35% probability): $\frac{320,000}{599,000} = 0.54$

Scenario 2 (35% probability): $\frac{606,000}{599,000} = 1.02$

Scenario 3 (30% probability): $\frac{880,000}{599,000} = 1.47$

Therefore, Waterlife should be very worried as it is close to financial distress.

(b)
A useful indicator of tangibility of assets is the Tangibility of Assets ratio given by the following formula:

$$Tangibility\ of\ Assets = \frac{Fixed\ Assets}{Total\ Assets} = \frac{7,000,000}{11,000,000} = 63.6\%$$

We can also compute the Intangibility of Assets ratio as follows:

$$\frac{Total\ Assets - Fixed\ Assets}{Total\ Assets} = \frac{11,000,000 - 7,000,000}{11,000,000} = 36.6\%$$

By construction these two ratios have to add up to 1 (or 100%):
63.6 + 36.4 = 100%

Appendix 4

(a)

We can compute the Value of the Tax Shield to Waterlife employing the following formula:

Value of Tax Shield = Tax Rate*Value of Debt.

We computed the tax rate in Appendix 1 in the following way:

$$TR = \frac{Value\ of\ Tax\ Shield}{Value\ of\ Debt} = \frac{1,590,000}{5,300,000} = 30\%$$

Therefore, if the current level of debt is rolled over permanently, the financial benefit to Waterlife will be:

Value of Tax Shield =0.3*2,000,000=€600,000

If however, the debt level is increased to €7,300,000 then the value of the tax shields to Waterlife will be:

Value of Tax Shield = 0.3*7,300,000=€2,190,000

(b)

The Trade-off theory of Capital Structure can be represented graphically in the following way:

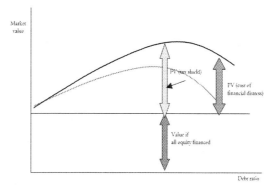

Case 23

Solution to Margin Limited

Derry Cotter, University College Cork

REPORT TO MARGARET DRUMM, MANAGING DIRECTOR, MARGIN LIMITED

Prepared by: Crimpson & Co.
Chartered Accountants

For: Managing Director, Margin Limited

Contents

1. Capital Investment Project

Margin Limited has a weighted average cost of capital (WACC) of 11% (see Appendix 1). This rate is used to evaluate the proposed capital project, which is similar to Margin Limited's existing portfolio of products.

The project has a net-present-value of €1.13 million (see Appendix 2). This means that the value of the equity shares of Margin Limited should increase by this amount if the project is undertaken. On this basis, I would recommend that Margin Limited should proceed with the project.

The project has a payback period of approximately three years, and an accounting rate of return (ARR) of 23% (see Appendix 3).

2. Takeover Bid

The equity share capital of Margin Limited is worth in the region of €8.5 million, based on an earnings valuation of the company (see Appendix 4). This is considerably more than its net asset value of €2.65 million. In order to obtain a selling price close to the upper level of this valuation range, Margin Limited shareholders may have to agree to at least part of the sales consideration being dependent on the achievement of agreed profit targets.

3. Foreign Exchange Risk

An exposure statement should be prepared for each foreign currency in which an entity has transactions. This statement identifies the level of exposure in each currency, thus enabling the entity to reduce or eliminate the identified risks, should they wish to do so.

A number of risk-management methods are available in respect of the currency risk associated with the purchase of materials from a US supplier. The alternatives, in respect of the recent purchase of goods for $500,000, are outlined in Appendix 5. A forward contract, the most cost effective alternative, would have guaranteed a fixed cost for the goods of €435,498.

Appendix 1
Weighted Average Cost of Capital

(i) Ordinary Shares

The cost of Margin Limited's ordinary share capital can be computed using the following model:

$$Ke = \frac{Div\ 1}{MV_0} \times 100 + G$$

MV_0 should be the current ex-div market price = €4 – 20c = €3.80

Div_1 = Current dividend × 1.1   = 20c × 1.1

$\quad$ = 22c

$\quad$ G = the dividend growth rate, i.e. 10%

$$Ke = \frac{.22}{3.80} \times 100 + 10\%$$

$$Ke = \quad 15.8\%$$

(ii) Preference Shares

$$Kp = \frac{Annual\ dividend}{MV_0} \times 100$$

$$Kp = \frac{.10}{1.50} \times 100$$

$$Kp = \quad 6.7\%$$

(iii) Debentures

The cost of redeemable debentures can be approximated by computing the cost of a similar coupon irredeemable debenture, + the average annual premium on redemption.

$$Kd = \frac{Annual\ interest\ (1-t)}{MV_0} \times 100 + (Average\ annual\ premium\ on\ redemption)$$

$$\frac{8\ (1-0.125)}{107}$$

$$Kd = \quad 8.5\ \%$$

The WACC of Margin Limited can be computed as follows:

Source	Market value €	Proportionate Mkt. Value	Cost	Proportionate Cost
Ord. shares	3.8 million	38%	15.8%	6%
Pref. shares	3 million	30%	6.7%	2%
Debentures	3.2 million	32%	8.5%	2.7%
Total	10 million	100%		10.7%

Margin Limited's WACC is approximately 11%

Appendix 2
Proposed Capital Project

A decision regarding Margin Limited's proposed new product can be made by estimating the product's future cash flows, and discounting these to present value, so as to compute the NPV.

	Cap. Equip.	Contrib.	Store Mgr. (N1)	Work. Cap. (N2)	Disc & Bad debts	Fixed O/Hs	Tax	Net Cash Flow	Disc. Factor @ 11%	DCF & NPV
	€'000	€'000	€'000	€'000	€'000	€'000	€'000	€'000		€'000
T_0	(2,000)			(361)				(2,361)	1	(2,361)
T_1		1,250	(32)		(45)	(100)		1,073	.901	967
T_2		1,250	(32)		(45)	(100)	(90.4)	982	.812	797
T_3		1,250	(32)		(45)	(100)	(90.4)	982	.731	718
T_4	200	1,250	(32)	361	(45)	(100)	(90.4)	1,543	.659	1,017
T_5							(15.4)	(15)	.594	(9)
								2,204		1,129

Schedule 1 – Taxation

	Profit	Interest	Cap Alls	Total taxable	Tax at 12.5%	Payable
	€'000	€'000	€'000	€'000	€'000	
Year 1	1,073	(50)	(300)	723	90.4	Year 2
Year 2	1,073	(50)	(300)	723	90.4	Year 3
Year 3	1,073	(50)	(300)	723	90.4	Year 4
Year 4	1,073	(50)	(900)	123	15.4	Year 5

Note 1: Store Manager Salary Cost

	€
20% probability of annual salary being €60,000	(€12,000)
80% probability of annual salary being €40,000	(€32,000)
80% probability of avoiding pension costs of €15,000	€12,000
Expected value of annual cost of stores manager	**(€32,000)**

Note 2: Working Capital

(a) Investment required in **stocks** (€2.5 million × 30% × 1/12) = €62,500

(b) Investment required in **debtors**:

	€
(i) No discount policy:	
Bad debts	(50,000)
Debtors:	
(€2.5 million − €50K) × 60/365 = 402,740	
Financing cost at 11%	(44,301)
(ii) Discount policy	
Total cost of no discount policy	(94,301)
Bad debts	(25,000)
Cash discount (€2.5 million × 2% × 40%)	(20,000)
Debtors:	
(€2.5 million − €25K) × 60/365 × 60% =	244,110
€2.5 million × 20/365 × 40% =	54,795
	298,905
Financing cost at 11%	(32,880)
Total cost of discount policy	(77,880)

The discount policy should be adopted, resulting in the following working capital costs:

	€
Stock	62,500
Debtors	298,905
	361,405
	=======

Conclusion:

The new product has a net present value of €1.13 million and should be undertaken.

Appendix 3
Payback Period and Accounting Rate of Return

(i) Payback period

The project's payback period can be calculated using the net cash-flow column in Appendix 2 above.
Investment @ T_0 = €2.36 million
This is recovered in three years. Thus, the payback period is approximately three years

(ii) Accounting rate of return

The total net cash flow in the table in Appendix 2 above amounts to €2.204 million. This equates to profit after tax on the project. Therefore the average annual profit after tax equals €2.204 million / 4 = €551,000.
The initial investment in the project is €2.36 million.
Therefore the ARR is (€551k / €2.36 million) × 100 = 23%

Appendix 4
Potential Takeover Bid

(a) Profit-based valuation

Margin Limited can be valued on an imputed market value basis, using a price/earnings ratio derived from Left-Right plc, a quoted company in the same industry.

Deriving a price/earnings ratio:
Left-Right share price = €5
Dividend per share of Left-Right 25c
Dividend cover = 2
Therefore, Left-Right has an EPS of 50c
Thus, Left-Right's P/E ratio is 10

Taking account of the lack of marketability of Margin Limited's shares, a discount of 20% could be applied to Left-Right's P/E ratio, giving a ratio for Margin Limited of 8.

Calculation of maintainable profit of Margin Limited:

	€'000
Profit after taxation	600
Add R&D savings	300
Rental income (net of tax @ 12.5%)	87.5
Rationalisation savings (net of tax @ 12.5%)	175
	1,162.5
P/E	8
Earnings valuation	9,300
Less once-off rationalisation costs	(800)
Earnings based valuation	8,500

(b) Asset valuation

	€'000
Balance sheet net assets of Margin Limited	8,800
Less:	
Goodwill	(1,000)
Long-term borrowings	(5,000)
Debtor insolvency	(400)
Write-off of inventory (including disposal costs)	(400)
	2,000
Add:	
Premium on valuation of buildings	400
Litigation proceeds	250
Asset based valuation	2,650

Appendix 5
Foreign Exchange Risk

The following foreign currency risk avoidance mechanisms could be employed by Margin Limited in respect of the recent purchase from its US supplier:

(i) Lead payment

Margin Limited could pay the US supplier on 1st August 2XX6. This would involve the following cost:

$$\frac{500,000}{1.1311} = €442,048$$

(ii) Forward market

Margin Limited could purchase $500,000 on the forward market on 1st August 2XX6. Computation of forward rate:

$$\text{Forward rate} = \text{Spot rate} \times \frac{(1 + 3 \text{ month interest rate on \$s})}{(1 + 3 \text{ month interest rate on €s})}$$

$$\text{Forward rate} = 1.1311 \times \frac{(1.01)}{(1.015)}$$

$$\text{Forward rate} = 1.1256$$

Therefore, the cost of a forward market transaction for Margin Limited will be:

$$\frac{500,000}{1.1256} = €442,208$$

(iii) Money market cover

A third way for Margin Limited to eliminate its foreign exchange risk is to arrange for money market cover:

On 1st August 2XX6, the company has a liability of $500,000, payable in three months.

On 1st August, Margin arranges a dollar deposit of $\frac{500,000}{1.005^{*}} = \$497,512$

* Based on the quarterly equivalent of an annual deposit interest rate of 2% (2% below base).

On 1st November, these funds will mature to give $500,000, which can be used to pay the supplier.

In order to put the $ funds on deposit on 1st August, Margin will have to purchase $497,512 at the spot exchange rate at that date. This involves the following cost:

$$\frac{497,512}{1.1311} = €439,848$$

Summary cost of alternative foreign exchange risk avoidance techniques:

	€
Lead payment cost	442,048 (payable on 1st August)
Forward market cost	444,208 (payable on 1st November)
Money market cost	439,848 (payable on 1st August)

So as to compare the alternatives on a comparable basis, the forward market cost should be discounted by 3 months to give its present value cost. As Margin Limited has an overdraft, it will avoid paying interest for 3 months @ 8% per annum if the forward market option is adopted. Thus the PV cost of the forward market alternative is as follows:

$$€444,208 / 1.02 = €435,498$$

Revised summary cost of alternative foreign exchange risk avoidance techniques restated on a PV cost basis.

	€
Lead payment cost	442,048
Forward market cost	435,498
Money market cost	439,848

The forward market alternative offers the most cost-effective means of avoiding the exchange risk in this transaction.

Case 24

Solution to DalCais Aer plc

Antoinette Flynn and Mairead Tracey, University of Limerick

Question 1

Declan's current debt ratio	=	all debt/total capital employed
	=	129/237.25
	=	54%

Declan's projected debt ratio	=	all debt/total capital employed
	=	(129 + 15)/252.25
	=	57%

(Technically, Declan should have included the current bank debt in the denominator as well as the numerator if he is treating it as a source of capital. This would have given him revised figures of 49% and 51%.)

Clara's current debt ratio	=	long term debt/total capital employed
	=	100/237.25
	=	42%

Clara's projected debt ratio	=	long-term debt/total capital employed
	=	(100 + 15)/252.25
	=	46%

Clara's return on investment of 20%, derived by dividing net-cash flow €3 million/€15 million initial investment = 20%. Inaccurate assessment of investment return, ARR is calculated as net profit/€15 million initial investment.

Clara's statement is correct: 'A current yield of 5% and with a tax break on the interest on borrowing, our real cost of borrowing is 4.38%' (see question 2(a)). However, contrary to Clara's suggestion, the cost of equity is not the same as the dividend yield (dividend/market price).

Question 2 (a)

Long-term capital is available to a firm from various sources, principally being debt and equity. Each source will have a different cost. The cost of equity capital is conventionally referred to as Ke and the cost of loan capital is conventionally referred to as Kd. Normally as holders of fixed interest/dividend securities are entitled to prior payment of their interest or dividends out of profits, Kd will be smaller than Ke. Both debt and equity contribute to long-term capital and therefore both Ke and Kd contribute to the cost of capital. Hence, cost-of-capital is a weighted average of the costs of equity and debt. Cost of capital to the firm as a whole is referred to as the weighted average cost of capital (WACC) being the average of Ke and Kd weighted based on the relative values of capital contributed by equity and debt.

After tax cost of debt

$$Kd = \frac{c(1-T)}{MV}$$

Where Kd is the after tax cost of debt, c is the coupon (interest) earned (paid) on each unit of debt, T is the current tax rate and MV is the market value of a unit of debt.

Note the current yield on debt is 5%, which is equal to coupon/market price. Therefore, the market price of debt is 100/price = .05, 100/.05 = €2,000.

$$Kd = \frac{100(1 - .125)}{2000}$$

$$= 4.375\%$$

Ke = Cost of Equity

Dividend Growth model

$$Ke = \frac{Div_0 (1 + g)}{MV} + g$$

Current price cum dividend is €15.90. The dividend this year is €9 million with ten million shares outstanding. Therefore, the dividend per share is 9/10 = 90 cent per share. The share price ex-dividend is €15.

$$Ke = \frac{0.90 (1+.075)}{15} + 0.075$$

$$Ke = 0.0645 + .075 = 13.95\%$$

CAPM

$$Ke = Rf + \beta(Rm - Rf)$$

Where Rf is the risk free rate of 4%, Rm minus Rf is the risk premium of 8% and the β beta is 1.25.

$$Ke = 4\% + 1.25(8\%) = \textbf{14\%}.$$

Market Value Weights

| Debentures: | 100,000,000/1000 = 100,000 units | MV | Weights |
| | 100,000 × 2000 | 200m | 57% |

Ordinary shares	10,000,000 outstanding		
	10 m × 15 (ex div)	150m	43%
		350m	100%

Element	Cost	Weight	WC
Debenture (After Tax)	4.375%	.571	2.50%
Equity	14%	.43	6.00%
		WACC	**8.50%**

Note: 8.50% is near Declan's figure of 9%.

(b)

The WACC assuming that DCA board of directors decide to borrow the investment funds required, via a term loan with comparable terms to existing debentures. New debt is a term loan of €15 million, with an interest rate of 10%.

After tax cost of new debt

$$Kd_{new} = c(1 - T) = 10(1 - .125) = 8.75\%$$

After tax cost of debt

$$Kd_{existing} = \frac{c(1 - T)}{MV}$$

$$Kd = \frac{100(1 - .125)}{2000}$$
$$= \textbf{4.375\%}$$

Ke = Cost of Equity

Dividend Growth model

$$Ke = \frac{Div_0 (1 + g) + g}{MV}$$

$$Ke = \frac{0.90 \ (1 + .075)}{15} + 0.075$$

$$Ke = .0.0645 + .075 = \mathbf{13.95\%}$$

CAPM

$$Ke = Rf + \beta(Rm - Rf)$$
$$Ke = 4\% + 1.25(8\%) = \mathbf{14\%.}$$

Market Value Weights

		MV	Weights
Debentures:	100,000,000/1000 = 100,000 units		
	100,000 × 2000	200m	54.8%
New debt	15,000,000	15m	4.1%
Ordinary shares	10,000,000 outstanding		
	10 m × 15 (ex div)	150m	41.1%
		365m	100%

Element	Cost	Weight	WC
Debenture (after Tax)	4.375%	.548	2.40
New debt (after tax)	8.75%	.041	0.36
Equity (CAPM)	14%	.411	5.75%
		WACC	**8.51%**

(c)

In this part, WACC assuming that DCA's board of directors decide to issue new stock to raise the investment funds required, and assuming that Declan's predictions of post-issue share price movement and expected net proceeds per share are accurate, is calculated.

The net proceeds from the issue are expected to be €10 per share. DCA needs to raise €15 million with the issue so the company should issue 1.5 million shares.

After tax cost of debt

$$Kd = \frac{c(1-T)}{MV}$$

$$Kd = \frac{100(1 - .125)}{2000}$$

$$= \mathbf{4.375\%}$$

Ke = Cost of Equity

For new shares issued, use the marginal cost of equity

$$Ke_{new} = \frac{Div_1}{\text{Net proceeds per share}} + g$$

$$Div_1 = (.90 \times 1.075) = .9675$$

$$Ke_{new} = \frac{.9675}{10} + 0.075$$

$$= \mathbf{17.18\%}$$

Existing Shares: Dividend Growth model

$$Ke_{existing} = \frac{Div_0 (1 + g)}{MV} + g$$

Assuming market price falls by 10%, 10% of 15 = €1.50. New price = €13.50

$$Ke = \frac{0.90 (1+.075)}{13.50} + 0.075$$

$$Ke = .0716666 + .075 = \mathbf{14.66666\%}$$

CAPM (unchanged)

$$Ke = Rf + \beta(Rm - Rf)$$

$$Ke = 4\% + 1.25(8\%) = \mathbf{14\%.}$$

Market Value Weights

		MV	Weights
Debentures:	100,000,000/1000 = 100,000 units		
	100,000 × 2000	200m	56.3%
New shares	1,500,000 at 13.50 each	20.25m	5.7%
Ordinary shares	10,000,000 outstanding		
	10 m × 13.5 (ex div)	135m	38.0%
		355.25m	100%

Element	Cost	Weight	WC
Debenture (after tax)	4.375%	.563	2.46
New equity	17.18%	.057	0.98
Equity (Dividend Model)	14.666666%	.380	5.58
		WACC	**9.02%**

Question 3 (a)

From the calculations in solutions 1 and 2, I recommend that DCA raise the necessary funds through a term loan, especially as the company is offered the same terms. The introduction of new debt results in a slight increase in the the company's WACC, but the increase is less than if the investment is funded with new equity. As can be seen from the introduction of new equity, the value of the company falls and the WACC rises to 9.02%. The gearing ratio is not excessive with the additional €15 million debt, irrespective of the definition of gearing used and when the total debt to capital employed is used, it approximates the industry target ratio. Therefore, financial distress is not a concern for DCA at the moment (especially if one employs the long-term debt: capital employed ratio).

Assuming that the company secures a term loan of €15 million, the present value of receiving €3m per annum for 15 years (using the adjusted WACC of 8.5%)

$$PV = C \times \left(\frac{1 - (1+r)^{-t}}{r} \right)$$

Present value of Ordinary Annuity
Where C is the annual receipt, r is the discount rate (WACC) and t is the time, 15 years.

$$PV = 3m \times \left(\frac{1 - (1+.085)^{-15}}{0.085} \right)$$

$$= 3m \times 8.3042366$$
$$= €24,912,710 \text{ (for an investment of €15,000,000)}$$

If the company decided to raise the investment funds through a stock issue, the present value of the investment would decrease and the overall wealth of the organisation would be lowered by €759,170, assuming a WACC of 9.02% is used in the calculations.

$$PV = 3m \times \left(\frac{1 - (1+.0902)^{-15}}{0.0902} \right)$$

$$= 3m \times 8.051180$$
$$= €24,153,540 \text{ (for an investment of €15,000,000)}$$

Overall, the company should opt for the investment and finance it with a term loan. It is acknowledged that new debt can increase a firm's value by reducing its taxes. This tax shield increases the value of the firm. It is often argued that leverage also reduces the agency costs arising between management and shareholders. Therefore, the new debt can be thought of as a type of control device for the shareholders of

DCA. As well as tax and agency benefits, increased debt brings with it some costs in the form of financial distress and financial slack. When firms such as DCA increase their reliance on debt, they also increase the likelihood of financial distress. Financial distress can be formal bankruptcy. However, financial distress may occur without bankruptcy. Depletion of financial slack incurs new debt increases well beyond traditional industry norms. Loss of financial slack can preclude strategic options if competitors increase capital spending or lower prices.

Question 3 (b)

As part of your report, elaborate on the significance of the following statement from Clara Sullivan, 'equity finance is usually the last resort for companies seeking investment funding, as it is the most expensive source', in relation to Modigliani and Miller's (1958) theory of capital structure.

Clara is referring to the pecking order theory of capital structure. The pecking order theory argument is that external financing transaction costs, especially those associated with the problem of adverse selection, create a dynamic environment in which firms have a preference, or pecking-order of preferred sources of financing, when all else is equal. Internally generated funds are the most preferred, new debt is next, debt-equity hybrids are next, and new equity is the least preferred source. Research has shown that stock sales announcements tend to drive stock prices down, indicating that investors think managers feel the stock price is overvalued if they attempt to sell equity. Likewise, the announcement of a debt issue has little or no affect upon equity prices. Therefore, businesses prefer to issue debt rather than equity if internally generated cash-flow is insufficient. Use of internally generated funds does not have the signalling effect, positively or negatively, that external funding does. If external funds must be raised, equity will be used reluctantly, reserved as the residual in the financing pecking order.

Under the pecking order theory there is no target debt/equity ratio because there are two kinds of equity: internally generated earnings retained and external stock sales. Internal equity is the first choice for financing ahead of debt, and finally, external equity funding. Profitable firms have sufficient internally generated capital to fund their high NPV investments. Hence, they are all equity funded or have low debt-equity ratios. Less profitable firms tend to issue more debt as they run out of internally generated funds quickly and turn to debt as the next source of funding in the pecking order.

Next, the student will discuss the Modigliani and Miller (MM) theory of capital structure irrelevance and comment on the assumptions of MM's theory and introduce the effects of financial distress and tax on the choice between debt and equity.

Three assumptions of Modigliani and Miller's (MM) theory of capital structure irrelevance

1. Perfect capital markets
2. Arbitrage
3. Homemade leverage

The assumptions of a perfect capital market are: perfect competition; all participants are price-takers, firms and investors can borrow and lend at the same interest rate, investors have equal access to all relevant information, there are no transaction costs, taxes or bankruptcy costs. A summary of the MM theory of capital structure irrelevance is as follows: investors can lever-up an investment in an unlevered firm by borrowing money and buying stock. Investors can unlever an investment in a levered firm by selling stock and lending money. Conclusion: investors can create their own payoff patterns, irrespective of the capital structure. In essence, Modigliani and Miller argue that the shareholders will require an increased return equivalent to that which they could earn by substituting personal leverage for corporate leverage. If the rate of return, which the company can generate on capital employed, is greater than Kd (cost of debt), a surplus arises.

Modigliani and Miller argue that the shareholders will demand this surplus as they are in a position to obtain it themselves by borrowing the same funds which the company has borrowed and investing their own funds plus borrowed funds in non-geared companies. In the latter case, their leverage would be the same as if they invested in the company, which had borrowed funds. However, they would receive themselves the surplus of return and capital employed over cost of borrowings. Since they would be in a position to do this themselves through personal leverage, they will not accept a rate of return from a geared company any less than the return they could achieve based on the same amount of personal gearing. Shareholders will tend to sell their shares in geared companies and buy shares in non-geared companies and therefore increase the Ke up to the level required by shareholders. The Modigliani and Miller approach rests largely on the assumption that this arbitrage process will be unimpeded.

2 of MM's Propositions

PROPOSITION I
The value of the firm is independent of its capital structure; the WACC is constant, regardless of the capital structure.

PROPOSITION II
A firm's cost of equity capital is a positive linear function of its capital structure; the cost of equity must increase, as leverage is increased, in order for the WACC to remain constant

MM depends on perfect capital markets and markets are generally well-functioning but not always perfect. Other factors that may affect the original MM propositions include: corporate taxes, costs of financial distress, agency costs, debt capacity, and personal taxes. When MM incorporates taxes, the implication is that firms will maximise their value by taking on maximum debt. However, empirical evidence suggests that firms take on only modest amounts of debt. This is due to financial distress. Financial distress occurs when a firm has difficulty meeting its financial obligations. Sometimes it leads to the 'ultimate distress' of bankruptcy. Investors are concerned that a levered firm may fall into financial distress. The value-of-firm is equal to the value of all equity-financed plus the present value of the tax shield, minus the present value of the costs of financial distress. The costs of financial distress depend on the probability of distress, the magnitude of costs encountered if distress occurs.

To conclude, Modigliani and Miller, under the arbitrage assumption, hold that a firm's cost of capital is unaffected by its capital structure. However, the arbitrage proposition is dependent upon many assumptions, which are questionable in the imperfect capital markets of real life. Furthermore, their proposition should be adjusted for taxes and extreme leverage. The overall affect of these adjustments is that the cost-of-capital does vary with capital structure and there is an optimum capital structure at which the cost-of-capital is minimised. Companies should therefore, strive to find their optimum capital structure mix. The theory is that there is an optimum debt/ratio that maximises market value, offsetting the benefits of the tax shield against the increasing costs of financial distress is called the trade-off theory. The support of the trade-off theory is evidenced by a wide variety of debt/equity ratios between industries and companies, but with some consistent with the trade-off theory and some operating inconsistently with the theory.

Question 3 (c)

As part of the report, critically discuss the different theoretical arguments that the CFO and the CEO allude to, in the following extracts from the case study: Declan recommended that 'this dividend increase would provide a tangible signal of management's confidence in the future of the company and would buoy up the issue' and Clara argues that 'if we increase the dividend, we will need to increase the amount of the stock issue; so we will just be paying the higher dividend out of the shareholders' own pockets'.

The position taken by the CFO, Declan Murphy, reflects two views; the information content of dividends (signalling potential) and the traditional view of dividend policy which assumes that investors would prefer dividends today rather than either dividends or capital gains at some future date. From the signalling perspective, the value of the firm is not increased by increased dividends; firm value increases only if management's increase in dividends signals the presence of high net present value (NPV) opportunities. In markets where there is little information, increased dividends portend increased future cash flows, where dividend policy is a form of communication to the market about future prospects. Just as dividend increases add to expectations of favourable future prospects, dividend cuts are assumed by the market to be a signal of bad news to come.

The traditional view of payments is based on the assumption that investors prefer a certain sum of cash today to an uncertain return in the future. The implications of this view for dividend policy are that companies should attempt to pay out as much in the form of current dividends as is consistent with the long-term objectives of the company. It is argued that, because investors dislike uncertainty, they will apply a rising discount rate to future returns. Thus, if current dividends are lowered in order to ensure high investment for the future, the value of the company will fall as future dividends will be discounted at an increasing rate over time. However, many believe that such views are based on a misconception of the nature of risk. It can be argued that there is no reason why risk need necessarily increase over time. Risk arises from the nature of the activities undertaken by the company and investors will normally demand a higher return from companies, which engage in high-risk ventures than companies, which engage in low-risk ventures. The level of risk associated with the activities of a company will already be reflected in the discount rates applied to investment projects when assessing future returns.

The opposing view of the CEO, Clara Sullivan, reflects the work of Miller and Modigliani (1961). MM demonstrated that, given certain restrictive assumptions, dividend policy is irrelevant. They show that dividends do not change shareholder wealth, only its location. MM argue that the value of a company will be determined by future earnings and the degree of risk associated with the company. The way in which earnings are divided between dividends and retentions is not important. The level of dividend will not influence share values providing the amounts retained are invested in similarly profitable projects. Any reduction in dividends will be compensated by an increase in capital gains. In the event that a shareholder requires cash, 'home-made dividends' may be created through selling a portion of the shares held. Thus, any differences in the consumption patterns of shareholders will be irrelevant. In short, if markets are efficient, dividend policy should not affect shareholder value. Assuming that a business' capital budgeting decision (accept all positive NPVs) and borrowing decisions have been made, it then becomes a choice as to how to raise equity capital: internally from earnings paying cash common dividends or financing externally from the sale of stock.

The arguments of MM concerning dividend irrelevance rest on a number of important assumptions, which include the absence of taxes and share transaction costs, and shareholders and managers having identical information concerning future investment opportunities. These assumptions do not hold in the real world and, as a result, the arguments put forward by MM are weakened. Differences in tax treatment between dividends and capital gains have led many investors to prefer capital gains. In addition, share transaction costs can be relatively high when small amounts are being dealt with. However, there are practical problems associated with the view that dividends should not be paid. The creation of 'home-made dividends' as a substitute for a company dividend policy, may be difficult due to problems which include the share transaction costs, the indivisibility of shares leading to investors being unable to sell precisely the amount of shares required, and the lack of marketability of shares in unlisted companies.

Further, companies tend to have long-run target payout ratios and focus on dividend changes, not absolute levels and dividend changes follow changes in the long-run, not short-run earnings. There is a reluctance to make dividend changes that may have to be reversed. A firm's dividend payout ratio affects its stock price; dividend payments operate as a signal to financial markets; dividend announcements provide information to financial markets, investors think that dividends are safer than retained earnings; investors are not indifferent between dividends and price appreciation; and stockholders are attracted to firms that have dividend policies that they like. In summary, a constant payout ratio implies that dividends will vary as earnings vary. Generally, companies tend to change dividends steadily in response to a sustainable increase in earnings. Cash dividends per year are more stable than earnings and future earnings prospects by managers are built into dividend policy. Higher earnings tend to follow higher dividends and lower earnings follow low dividends.

Overall, Declan is correct is his assumption that a dividend increase will act as a signal to the market. However, the market may not interpret this dividend increase in a positive light, as a long-term signal of increased firm wealth. Clara is also correct when she argues that using the proceeds of a stock issue to pay dividends is unreasonable. In this scenario, the shareholders may interpret the dividend increase (in conjunction with a stock issue) as a negative signal of the management's decision-making ability.

Case 25
Solution to Bradaun Limited
Ray Donnelly, University College Cork

I. *Criteria for Evaluation of the Project*

Introduction

The correct criterion for the project's evaluation can only be determined in the light of the objectives of Bradaun. It is normal to assume that Bradaun wishes to maximise shareholder wealth. It is clear that Ms. Pitt is mindful of the Board's attitude. It is not unreasonable to assume that the latter will be determined at least in part, by the shareholders to whom they must report on an annual basis. It may well be that the Board is interested in profits only insofar as they affect the share price. A point that should be made is that the reduction in overall ROR if this project is taken, is not necessarily a bad thing. The project analysis should not be confused by considering the profitability of independent existing projects.

Jack McBride is quite correct to use the Net Present Value (NPV) analysis. The main reason for using the NPV criterion is that its use is entirely consistent with the objective of maximising shareholder wealth. If a firm with a value of €100 million takes on a project with a NPV of €10 million it will then be worth $110 million. This should help keep the shareholders and the board happy. Also, any positive NPV project will eventually yield enhanced profits as its cash-flows come to be recognised by the accounting system. Thus, if the project truly has a positive NPV, profits *will* be enhanced.

Profits and the Rate of Return (ROR)

It is not appropriate to evaluate projects solely on profits. To do so ignores that capital has to be invested to earn the profits and this capital, which is provided by shareholders, is not costless. After all the shareholders could put their money into other investments which could yield a return. Capital clearly has an opportunity cost. This fact has not escaped Penny. Rather than just focusing on profits she has considered the accounting rate of return (ROR). This is simply the average annual profits, divided by the initial investment. It has the merit of taking some cognisance of the fact that profits or returns must in some way be related to the level of investment required to generate them. However, the ROR has weaknesses. First, it ignores the time value of money. That is, cash today is worth more than the same amount of cash in the future. Since the current project spans several years this is clearly a problem. Secondly, it is ambiguous with regard to the hurdle rate. That is, what is an acceptable ROR? If a firm wished to maximise its ROR it would simply invest in one project – that with the highest ROR. It is axiomatic that this may lead to sub-optimal decisions since many projects which may fall short of the maximum ROR will be acceptable. An alternative is to compare the ROR with the company's cost of capital. It will be demonstrated below, that with some further modification to take account of the time value of money, this may be a reasonable way of adjusting the ROR criterion. There is another problem with ROR in that its definition is ambiguous. If we are to reconcile it with NPV we have to be very specific regarding how we compute it.

Net Present Value

As well as being consistent with the objectives of the company the NPV approach has the following advantages:

- It recognises the cost of capital.
- It has a clear decision rule: accept projects with a NPV > 0 and if projects are mutually exclusive choose the one with the highest NPV.

It is clear that the NPV is the theoretically correct investment appraisal criterion for firms whose objective is to maximise value and hence owners' wealth. This is the crucial point; its advantages over other methods also include:

1. It recognises the time value of money – unlike ROR.
2. It is generally easy to use.
3. It can deal with multiple discount rates – unlike IRR or ROR.
4. It is not affected by differences of scale – unlike the profitability index, ROR or internal rate of return (IRR).
5. The discipline of estimating future cash-flows makes for better capital budgeting decisions.

However, the NPV cannot deal with strategic options without adaptation. When using NPV everything is not cut-and-dried as the calculations might lead one to expect. However, every complication that has been mentioned with regard to the use of the NPV can also be attributed to the ROR. Yet some of the problems with the ROR do not apply to the NPV. The latter is the most theoretically correct and versatile tool for the evaluation of investments.

NPV is difficult to use in later performance evaluation of managers – the ROR is easy to use (and misuse) in this regard. EVA® or residual income (RI) may be of use as an ex-post measure of whether managers are enhancing company value. This method adjusts accounting profits to be closer to economic profits (changes in value). In particular, it levies a charge for capital used against profits. It can be reconciled with the NPV criterion since the PV of RI is the same as the NPV of the cash-flows.

Summary

In summary, the NPV rule is consistent with the objectives of maximising share-holder wealth. It imposes a good discipline in project evaluation in that it forces management to carefully consider the future in order to quantify the cash-flows arising from a project. But, using the NPV rule will never be a substitute for good business analysis i.e. the manager must know his business. If someone cannot make informed estimates of future business conditions and their associated cash-flows all the sophisticated techniques in the world will not prevent them making incorrect choices.

2. Assessment of Jack's Analysis

Jack has applied the NPV criterion and was clearly correct to do so. The first step in computing the NPV is to determine the appropriate cash-flows of the project. All projects should be considered on an incremental basis. That is the project's cash flows are those of the firm with the project less those without the project. These cash-flows are then discounted at a cost of capital appropriate to their risk.

For our purposes here we can assume that Jack's forecasts of cash-flows cannot be improved on. By appearing to ignore cash-flows after year 5 Jack is implicitly assuming that these cash-flows provide a rate of return equal to the cost of capital and, thus, their NPV is zero. His assumption that the project will eventually only earn a return equal to the cost-of-capital is consistent with economic theory but we would have preferred a more detailed analysis here and discuss this in the context of the link between ROR and NPV below. We know that Jack has projected nominal cash-flows thus we must use a nominal discount-rate. If he had projected the cash-flows in real-terms we would have had to adjust the nominal discount-rate for inflation.

Jack's analysis is clear and for the most part correct. One of the major difficulties of using the NPV rule is the estimation of the appropriate cost-of-capital. (This difficulty is also a facet of the use of ROR). The correct discount rate is that which reflects the risk of the cash-flows that are being discounted. Jack has chosen the borrowing rate. This is not appropriate since it reflects the risk to a bank of lending money to Bradaun not the risk of the cash-flows from the new project. Furthermore, Bradaun should use the project's, not the company's, cost-of-capital. The Capital Asset Pricing Model (CAPM) provides a method of calculating the project's cost-of-capital. However, it is not clear that all the shareholders are well diversified. Therefore beta may not be the appropriate measure of risk for all the shareholders. A conflict may occur! The analysis in the following section details the computation of the correct discount rate for the project on the assumption that Bradaun's shareholders are well diversified.

3. Evaluation of the Project

The first step here is to compute the appropriate cost-of-capital. This will be the project's cost-of-capital. We estimate the project's cost-of-capital as the average cost-of-capital for the preserved fruit industry. The equity beta is 0.9. But this reflects both business and financial risk. The debt to equity ratio is 0.5 so debt-to-total value (D/V) is 0.33. Thus, letting E equal to equity value, if we make the standard assumption that the beta of debt is zero, the asset-beta is E/V*0.9 = 2/3*0.9 = 0.6. Applying the CAPM (E(Ri) = Rf + β(Rm – Rf)) gives 6 + 0.6(5) = 9%. The discounted Cash-Flows are computed in an Excel® spreadsheet and outlined in Appendix 1. The Cash-Flows are outlined exactly as per Jack's analysis in the question. The present value of the residual income is also computed. The project has a positive NPV at its cost of capital and should be taken since it will add to the value of the company and hence shareholder wealth.

We have included the Residual income calculation for the benefit of Sir Rex and the board. It is clear from Appendix 1 the present value of residual income is exactly the same as the NPV of the project. Residual Income (RI) is the net profit each year minus a capital charge. The capital charge is the book value of the project at the beginning of the year (BVt – 1) multiplied by the cost-of-capital. Thus, RI is a measure of the profitability of the project. RI has the advantage that it is a better ex-post measure of managerial performance than cash-flows.[1] An alternative way of computing RI is to compute the ROR as Earnings/BVt – 1 and RI then becomes (ROR – Cost-of-Capital)*BVt – 1. This is done in Appendix 2 and we observe that the residual income in each year is the same as in Appendix 1. Thus, assuming a positive opening-book value, if ROR is higher than the cost-of-capital, residual income will be positive. Through residual income we see that there is a clear link between a project's profitability and its NPV.

We also note that using the approach where RI is computed as (ROR – Cost of Capital)*BVt – 1 makes it more explicit why Jack used a five-year horizon for a project, which continues for far longer. He is suggesting that while the project will continue to be profitable from year 6 onwards the rate of profitability will only compensate for the opportunity cost-of-capital, so from year 6 onward the project does not add value to Bradaun. That is, ROR eventually declines to equal the cost-of-capital: presumably due to increased competition and, the RI falls to zero. This is consistent with economic theory pertaining to competition. See Appendix 5 for illustration.

We also notice that the average annual ROR is only 17.2%. Why then is a project with such a low rate of return desirable? Mainly because it has a lower risk that Bradaun's other business as evidenced by the lower beta. Thus, the expected rate-of-return or cost-of-capital is lower for this project than for other projects in the company.

On the basis of the figures presented, the project is viable since it adds value to the company. Consideration should also be given to the potential financing side-effects of the project.

4. Sensitivity Analysis and Computation of IRR

The figure of 9% for cost-of-capital is only an estimate of what the shareholders required rate of return is deemed to be. Estimating required rates of return is not

---

[1] However, RI does suffer from the same allocation problems as accounting profits.

a trivial matter and presents significant practical problems. Accordingly, there are two types of risk to take account of. First, the project's risk which pertains to the fact that the cash-flows may not be as expected. This type of risk can be taken account of by adjusting the discount rate. The second type of risk relates to the fact that the discount rate itself is only an estimate. Interest rates and risk premia are not constant over time. Thus one would be tempted to establish how sensitive the project's NPV is to different discount rates. It must be stressed that this is entirely different to a scenario analysis where cash-flows would be low and discount rates high for the pessimistic scenario and vice versa for the optimistic scenario. The latter may be preferable if one is especially worried about downside risk. However, some sensitivity analysis has been done with respect to the discount rate and this is outlined in Appendix 3. This analysis does not give any cause for concern. It is clear that the project will have a negative NPV at a cost of capital of 21% but it has a positive NPV if the discount rate is 20%. Accordingly, its IRR (the discount rate that makes NPV=0) is between 20% and 21%. It is actually 20.092% (see Appendix 4). Computing the margin between the IRR and the cost-of-capital is a shortcut method of establishing the sensitivity of a project to the discount rate (assuming the projected cash-flows are reasonably accurate). Bradaun needs to be confident that the cost-of-capital will not exceed 20% before proceeding. Since we estimate the projects cost-of-capital to be only 9% which is far less than its IRR there is a large margin for error in the computation of the discount rate. This sensitivity analysis confirms that the project is a good one from Bradaun's point of view.

5. Investment and Financing Decisions

The capital-structure aspects of the investment and their interaction with the investment itself need to be considered. Specifically, one needs to consider the impact of the project on the capital structure of the company. Note that one cannot attach a particular type of financing to a specific project. This is because a company needs a balance of debt and equity so to suggest that one project is financed by debt and another by equity is totally incorrect. What is relevant, however, is the impact that a project has on the company's debt capacity i.e. how does it affect the optimal capital structure. The project may allow some borrowing. It is clear that Bradaun is not geared at the moment so is not exploiting the tax advantages of borrowing. The new Spanish plant may well provide some collateral to borrow against and a 5-year loan might be considered. The tax shield provided by this loan would probably enhance the NPV of the project.

6. Cash Surplus

If a company does not have sufficient cash it has a problem. However, Penny seems to have a problem in that Bradaun has too much cash. It may be a problem for Penny but it should not be a problem for the shareholders. If Bradaun cannot invest in positive NPV projects it can return the cash to the shareholder either through a special dividend or a share repurchase. The problem from Penny's point of view is that a persistent excess of cash could be perceived stemming from a paucity of ideas on her part regarding what to do with this capital. After all, shareholders can put money in the bank themselves. They do not need Bradaun to do this for them. Also a company with a cash mountain may become a takeover target. This is a good scenario for the shareholders but not management. The former can expect to receive a premium for their stock in the company and the latter might expect to lose their employment.

7. Conflicts of Interest

The project here does not seem to be conglomerate diversification in that the technologies for canning seafood and fruit & vegetables should be similar. Thus, the project is probably not an opportunity that the shareholder's could replicate themselves. Note, also that while the CAPM would seem to suggest that conglomerate diversification is not in shareholders interests, this model is derived assuming perfect capital markets. Accordingly, it precludes the possibility of bankruptcy costs. Thus, some diversification at firm level may be of benefit to well-diversified shareholders if it reduces that probability of bankruptcy and the associated costs. However, as discussed above bankruptcy does not seem a likely scenario given the low financial risk of Bradaun.

There are also conflicts of interest between Penny who is an insider and the outside shareholders. The latter are only interested in maximising their wealth whereas Bradaun means more to Penny than a mere investment. Furthermore, she has all of her human capital tied up in Bradaun. If she has not diversified her financial assets she will have a very different perception of the risk of the project and beta will not be a good risk measure from her perspective.

Appendix 1
Calculation of NPV and PV of Residual Income

Time	0	1	2	3	4	5
Net cash-flows	−1,000.00	350.00	400.00	400.00	250.00	200.00
Depreciation (1000/5)		200.00	200.00	200.00	200.00	200.00
Profit		150.00	200.00	200.00	50.00	0.00
NPV of cash-flows @ 9%	273.74					
BVt − 1		1,000.00	800.00	600.00	400.00	200.00
Residual income		60.00	128.00	146.00	14.00	−18.00
ROR		0.15	0.25	0.33	0.13	0.00
NPV of RI @ 9%	273.74					
Average ROR per annum	0.17					
$(1 + R)^t$		1.09	1.19	1.30	1.41	1.54
DCF	−1,000.00	321.10	336.67	308.87	177.11	129.99
Cumulative DCF		−678.90	−342.23	−33.35	143.75	273.74
Discounted RI		55.05	107.74	112.74	9.92	−11.70
Cumulative Discounted RI		55.05	162.78	275.52	285.44	273.74

Appendix 2
Residual Income and Rate of Return

	1	2	3	4	5
Annual ROR	0.15	0.25	0.33333	0.125	0
Cost of Capital	0.09	0.09	0.09	0.09	0.09
ROR t − Cost of Capital	0.06	0.16	0.24333	0.035	−0.09
BVt − 1	1000	800	600	400	200
Residual Income	60	128	146	14	−18

The average annual ROR is 0.172

Appendix 3
Sensitivity Analysis

		1	2	3	4	5	Cost of Capital
Cash-Flows	−1,000	350.00	400.00	400.00	250.00	200.00	
$(1 + R)^t$		1.09	1.19	1.30	1.41	1.54	0.09
DCF	−1,000	321.10	336.67	308.87	177.11	129.99	
Cumulative DCF		−678.90	−342.23	−33.35	143.75	273.74	
Cash-Flows	−1,000	350.00	400.00	400.00	250.00	200.00	
$(1 + R)^t$		1.10	1.21	1.33	1.46	1.61	0.10
DCF	−1,000	318.18	330.58	300.53	170.75	124.18	
Cumulative DCF		−681.82	−351.24	−50.71	120.04	244.22	
Cash-Flows	−1,000	350.00	400.00	400.00	250.00	200.00	
$(1 + R)^t$		1.11	1.23	1.37	1.52	1.69	0.11
DCF	−1,000	315.32	324.65	292.48	164.68	118.69	
Cumulative DCF		−684.68	−360.04	−67.56	97.12	215.81	
Cash-Flows	−1,000	350.00	400.00	400.00	250.00	200.00	
$(1 + R)^t$		1.12	1.25	1.40	1.57	1.76	0.12
DCF	−1,000	312.50	318.88	284.71	158.88	113.49	
Cumulative DCF		−687.50	−368.62	−83.91	74.97	188.45	
Cash-Flows	−1,000	350.00	400.00	400.00	250.00	200.00	
$(1 + R)^t$		1.16	1.35	1.56	1.81	2.10	0.16
DCF	−1,000	301.72	297.27	256.26	138.07	95.22	
Cumulative DCF		−698.28	−401.01	−144.75	−6.67	88.55	
Cash-Flows	−1,000	350.00	400.00	400.00	250.00	200.00	
$(1 + R)^t$		1.20	1.44	1.73	2.07	2.49	0.20
DCF	−1,000	291.67	277.78	231.48	120.56	80.38	
Cumulative DCF		−708.33	−430.56	−199.07	−78.51	1.86	
Cash-Flows	−1,000	350.00	400.00	400.00	250.00	200.00	
$(1 + R)^t$		1.21	1.46	1.77	2.14	2.59	0.21
DCF	−1,000	289.26	273.21	225.79	116.63	77.11	
Cumulative DCF		−710.74	−437.54	−211.75	−95.12	−18.01	

Appendix 4
The IRR of 20.092% was computed using Excel ®. The NPV of the net cash flows discounted at the IRR are outlined below as a check

Net cash-flows	−1000	350.00	400.00	400.00	250.00	200.00	Discount rate
$(1 + R)^t$		1.20092	1.44	1.73	2.08	2.50	0.20092
DCF	−1000	291.44	277.35	230.95	120.19	80.07	
Cumulative DCF		−708.56	−431.21	−200.26	−80.07	0.00	

An alternative calculation of the IRR (not using Excel) would be to use linear interpolation.

1. Take a low discount-rate (to ensure a positive NPV): the NPV is 273.74 if the discount-rate is 9% as outlined above
2. Take a high discount-rate (to ensure a negative NPV) e.g. 25% − the NPV is −91.26 at this rate

Cash-flows	−1,000	350.00	400.00	400.00	250.00	200.00	
$(1 + R)^t$		1.25000	1.56	1.95	2.44	3.05	0.25000
DCF	−1,000	280.00	256.00	204.80	102.40	65.54	1.25000
Cumulative DCF		−720.00	−464.00	−259.20	−156.80	−91.26	

3. So for a 16% change in the discount-rate one gets a 365 change in NPV
4. For a 1% change one might expect a 365/16 = 22.8125 change assuming a linear relation between NPV and the discount-rate (the relation is actually curvilinear).
5. This suggests that a 4% drop in the discount-rate from 25% would give an NPV of approximately 0. Thus an initial guess at the IRR would be 21%.
6. Appendix 3 above shows that 21% is too high and 20% is too low. However, a 1% drop from 21% to 20% changes the NPV by 19.87. We only need to decrease NPV by 1.86 from that at 20% so we increase the discount-rate by 1.86/19.87 (0.09375) to get the IRR.

Cash-flows	−1,000	350.00	400.00	400.00	250.00	200.00	
$(1 + R)^t$		1.20094	1.44	1.73	2.08	2.50	0.20092
DCF	−1,000	291.44	277.34	230.94	120.19	80.06	1.20094
Cumulative DCF		−708.56	−431.22	−200.28	−80.09	−0.03	

This is close enough for our purposes.

Appendix 5

This appendix illustrates how a project (company) can be profitable and add nothing to value. Let us assume that after five years Bradaun needs to invest another €500 million to replace and update some equipment to keep the Spanish canning factories in operation for a further five years. The table below shows that the project continues to be profitable in each of years six to ten. However, the ROR is just equal to the cost of capital and RI is therefore zero. This means that the project just earns a fair rate of return and its NPV is zero. The interested student can also see that if the ROR is less than 9% but greater than 0% (say 5%) in each year a profitable project could actually cause the value of the company to decline.

Time	5	6	7	8	9	10
Cash-flows	−500.00	145.00	136.00	127.00	118.00	109.00
Depreciation (1000/5)		100.00	100.00	100.00	100.00	100.00
Profit		45.00	36.00	27.00	18.00	9.00
NPV of cash-flows @ 9%	0.00					
BV_{t-1}		500.00	400.00	300.00	200.00	100.00
ROI		0.09	0.09	0.09	0.09	0.09
Residual income		0.00	0.00	0.00	0.00	0.00
NPV of RI @ 9%	0.00					
$(1 + R)^t$		1.09	1.19	1.30	1.41	1.54
DCF	−500.00	133.03	114.47	98.07	83.59	70.84
Cumulative DCF		−366.97	−252.50	−154.44	−70.84	**0.00**
ROI		0.09	0.09	0.09	0.09	0.09
Cumulative ROI	0.45					
Average ROI per annum	0.09					
Discounted RI		0.00	0.00	0.00	0.00	0.00
Cumulative Discounted RI		0.00	0.00	0.00	0.00	0.00

Case 26

Solution to Blackwater Hotel Group plc

Peter Green, University of Ulster at Jordanstown

REPORT ON THE PROPOSED NEW LUXURY HOTEL IN BELFAST

Prepared by: A. Student
Management Consultant

For: Blackwater Hotel Group plc

1. Executive Summary/Recommendations

Further to our discussions of xx/xx/xx, I present the report requested. With respect to the financial viability of the proposed new luxury hotel group in the dockland area of Belfast, on the basis of the information that you have supplied to me, it would appear that whilst with 100% occupancy the investment is viable with a positive net present value of €14 million, on consideration of the occupancy rate required to 'breakeven', approximately 87%, this may be considered too high (see Appendix 1).

Of particular concern is the accuracy of the estimates made in the project evaluation, given both the long evaluation time horizon and the fact that the data supplied is based upon the popular seaside resort of Blackpool, using a fixed exchange rate. Whilst Belfast has certainly exhibited significant growth, both in infrastructure and tourism, it is highly unlikely that direct comparison with Blackpool is appropriate. Further, unless the UK government shortly agree to join a single European currency, foreign exchange risk is likely to exist.

I would conclude that the proposal should be rejected at this time, but further consideration should be made in the future as the hotels operations could change due to internal developments and external environmental factors. As a consequence, whilst additional independent analysis now is likely to be of limited use, it may be informative to perform sensitivity analysis to identify which input variables are the ones which cause most uncertainty in the evaluation of the breakeven occupancy rate.

2. Consideration of the accuracy of the analysis

2.1 Estimation of Revenues

There are a number of key factors to consider in the estimation of revenues. First, the hotel industry, particularly in seaside resorts upon which the data has been gathered for this analysis, is highly seasonal. Obviously, the summer months may be expected to attract the most tourists, although given the nature of weather conditions this may not be as big a factor for a hotel in Belfast as it would be for hotels located in a warmer climate. Second, and related to the first, is the need to reduce room charges to secure block bookings in 'off-peak' seasonal times. For example, Blackpool and other resorts are apparently successful in attracting conference bookings in autumn. Whether or not Belfast would attract such clienteles is uncertain, although Dublin has achieved some success in doing so.

Third, luxury hotels in particular, are influenced by the state of the economy. During periods of boom, with surplus residual income, luxury hotels generally may be expected to perform well. However, in recession, a luxury hotel located in an area with historically low disposal income may not perform as well as those located in a relatively affluent location. Whether or not the dockland area of Belfast should be considered affluent or not is open to interpretation.

Finally, the residual value of the hotel has been estimated at 50 million after tax. There are no supporting calculations, nor any indication as to how this figure has been derived. Given that you are proposing to purchase a 100 year leasehold, it is not clear whether the hotel would be sold as a going-concern, including or excluding the leasehold. This clearly is a matter of fundamental importance. As is, any restrictions as to how the leasehold could be utilised, for example, is it possible to sell the leasehold for further housing development in the area?

2.2 Estimation of costs

Similar to the above arguments, costs are also subject to inaccuracy. All of the calculations have been based upon average occupancy rates per room, and a standard gross-profit margin for each source of revenue. Whilst statistically it may be appropriate to calculate an average occupancy rate of 1.5, it cannot be guaranteed in advance that this figure will be achieved in practice, and gross profit margins may also vary in accordance with seasonality and the state of the economy. In addition, the cost estimates would appear somewhat 'ad hoc'. For example, no details of the way in which specific price level inflation might affect particular costs have been given and the cost models employed (the split between fixed and variable costs and the use of particular cost drivers) have not been clearly identified.

2.3 Estimation of the cost-of-capital

Appendix 2 outlines how the cost-of-capital may have been estimated.

In order to calculate the cost-of-equity, it would appear that the company have used the capital asset pricing model (CAPM). The CAPM produces a required return based upon the expected return of the market, expected project returns, the risk-free interest rate and the variability of project returns relative to the market return.

The CAPM is based upon a number of unrealistic assumptions, such as:

(i)   All investors hold well-diversified portfolios and have homogeneous expectations with regard to future share price performance.
(ii)   Return, risk and correlation can be evaluated over a single time period.
(iii) Risk is measured entirely by the variability of returns.
(iv)   There is a perfect capital market.

As many of these assumptions are unrealistic, it is not surprising that there are numerous examples of inaccurate predictions made by the CAPM (technically known as empirical regularities). For example, when it is applied to small companies, companies with low equity betas, certain days of the week or months of the year. Further, the only feasible way of estimating a company's beta factor or the market risk premium, is by examining historical data and making the assumption that the future will be the same as the past.

When applied to capital investment appraisal, which is the case here, the CAPM makes the additional assumption that companies make decisions on behalf of the shareholders only. This ignores the position of other stakeholders such as employees, who have different attitudes to risk because they find it more difficult to diversify their position than shareholders do.

The greatest practical problems with the use of the CAPM in capital investment decisions are:

(a) The beta factor represents the sensitivity of the company's shares to the risk of the economy. It is hard to estimate returns on projects under different economic environments, market returns under different economic environments and the probabilities of the various environments.

(b) The CAPM is a single period model. Few investment projects last for one year only and certainly not the one under consideration. To extend the use of the model to more than one time period would require both project performance relative to the market and the economic environment to be reasonably stable. This is highly unlikely over a 17 year period and historically beta factors are not stable through time.

(c) It may be difficult to determine the risk-free rate of return. Government debt (bonds) are usually considered risk free, however the return (yield) on these securities varies according to their term to maturity.

In performing the discounted cash-flow analysis in Appendix 1, the weighted average cost of capital (WACC) has been employed. The WACC can be used in investment appraisal if the following assumptions are made:

(i) The project is small relative to the overall size of the company.

(ii) The WACC reflects the company's long-term future capital structure, i.e. the cost of capital to be applied to the project evaluation should reflect the marginal cost of new capital. If this were not so, the current WACC would become irrelevant because eventually it would not relate to any actual cost of capital.

(iii) The project has the same degree of 'business risk' as the company currently has.

(iv) New investments must be financed by new sources of funds: retained earnings, new share issues, new loans and so on.

The arguments against using the WACC as the cost of capital for investment appraisal are largely based on criticisms of the assumptions outlined above. Specifically,

(i) The project is relatively large. The company's current market valuation (debt and equity) is approximately €203 million and the proposed investment is approximately €82 million (including working capital at the end of year two). On the basis of these figures the investment would appear to be relatively large.

(ii) New investments undertaken by a company might have different business risk characteristics from the company's existing operations. From the information provided, although the proposed investment is in the same industry as the company's current investments, the financial director does consider the construction of hotel in Belfast to be of a higher risk and consequently, the hotel has been appraised over a fifteen year operating time horizon, rather than their standard twenty year period. This method of dealing with the risk of the investment may be considered rather 'ad hoc', without any theoretical basis.

(iii) There is no information provided to indicate how the proposed investment is to be financed. However, as a general point, many companies raise floating rate debt as well as fixed-interest rate debt. Floating-rate debt is difficult to incorporate into a WACC computation, as the cost of this debt will fluctuate as market conditions vary.

Overall, the use of a required return of 12%, based upon the current weighted average cost of capital and the application of the capital asset pricing model to establish the cost of equity, is questionable.

3. Issues relating to the risk of the proposed investment

It is evident (as noted above) that the financial director perceives the proposed investment as having more risk than your current investments. Consequently, the analysis performed has been restricted to a 15 year operating time horizon. There are a number of ways in which risk can be formally incorporated within an appraisal. For example: applying a higher discount rate than the current weighted average cost of capital (see section 2.3); probability analysis; the application of certainty equivalents; simulation analysis; and sensitivity analysis. Given my recommendation not to proceed with this investment at this time, I feel that risk should be further investigated via sensitivity analysis.

Probably, the area of greatest concern with regard to the proposed investment is the accuracy of the estimates made in the project evaluation, given both the long evaluation time horizon and the fact that the data supplied is based upon the popular seaside resort of Blackpool. Essentially sensitivity analysis identifies which key input variables (for example average occupancy rates, gross profit margins, required return etc.) the decision to invest is most sensitive to, which can change by the least percentage before the net present value of the investment falls to zero. Further analysis can then be directed to these key input variables in order to determine the reliability of the estimates currently being employed.

Appendix I

Hotel cost			80,000,000	Tax allowable	50,000,000
	0.1	Year 0	8,000,000		5,000,000
	0.5	Year 1	40,000,000		25,000,000
	0.4	Year 2	32,000,000		20,000,000

Capital allowances		0.04	Straight line	
Corporation tax rate		0.3275	Payable in the year it arises	
Working capital	Year 2	2,000,000		
Hotel capacity		320	Bedrooms	
Average occupied		1.5	People per night	
Charge per night		140	Whether one or more people are in room	
Food and drink spend		60	Per person per day	
GPM on Food etc		0.5		
Other facilities		25	Per person per day	
GPM on other facilities		0.2		

Non-resident income	3,000,000	Food and drink
	1,000,000	Other facilities
Function room rental	1,000,000	Pre-tax contribution
Total Contribution	2,700,000	Pre-tax

Annual Expected Outlays

Staff	5,000,000	
Gas, etc	1,400,000	
Other	1,000,000	
Redecoration costs	12,000,000	Every five years allowable in the year incurred
Hotel evaluation period	15 years	Operating horizon
Residual value	50,000,000	After tax, excluding end of period refurbishment and release of working capital.
Number of days in the year	365	
All estimates at current prices		
Rate of inflation	0.04	per year
Nominal cost of capital	0.12	

Real Contribution per Room

Food per guest per day	30
Other per guest per day	5
	35
Per room	52.5
Room charge per day	140
Total	192.5
Less tax	−63.04
After tax	129.46
Per annum (365 days)	47,252

Annual Operating Cash Flows

Staff	−5,000,000
Services	−1,400,000
Maintenance	−1,000,000
	−7,400,000
Income from non–residents	2,700,000
Total	−4,700,000
Add tax relief	1,539,250
After tax	−3,160,750

Year	1	2	3	4	5	6	7	8	9
Rate of inflation	0.04	0.04	0.04	0.04	0.04	0.04	0.04	0.04	0.04
Nominal contribution per room per annum			53,152	55,278	57,489	59,788	62,180	64,667	67,254
DCF (12%)	0.89285	0.79719	0.71178	0.635518078	0.567426856	0.506631121	0.452349215	0.403883228	0.360610025
PV nominal contribution per room per annum			37,832	35,130	32,621	30,291	28,127	26,118	24,252
Nominal annual operating CF			-3,555,414	-3,697,630	-3,845,536	-3,999,357	-4,159,331	-4,325,705	-4,498,733
DCF (12%)	0.89285	0.79719	0.71178	0.635518078	0.567426856	0.506631121	0.452349215	0.403883228	0.360610025
PV annual operating cash flows			-2,530,673	-2,349,910.994	-2,182,060.209	-2,026,198.765	-1,881,470.282	-1,747,079.548	-1,622,288.151

Year	10	11	12	13	14	15	16	17
Rate of inflation	0.04	0.04	0.04	0.04	0.04	0.04	0.04	0.04
Nominal contribution per room per annum	69,944	72,742	75,651	78,677	81,824	85,097	88,501	92,041
DCF (12%)	0.321973237	0.287476104	0.256675093	0.22917419	0.204619813	0.18269626	0.163121662	0.145644341
PV nominal contribution per room per annum	22,520	20,911	19,418	18,031	16,743	15,547	14,436	13,405
Total PV nominal contribution per room								355,382
Nominal annual operating CF	-4,678,682	-4,865,829	-5,060,463	-5,262,881	-5,473,396	-5,692,332	-5,920,025	-6,156,826
DCF (12%)	0.321973237	0.287476104	0.256675093	0.22917419	0.204619813	0.18269626	0.163121662	0.145644341
PV annual operating cash flows	-1,506,410.426	-1,398,809.682	-1,298,894.704	-1,206,116.511	-1,119,965.332	-1,039,967.808	-965,684.3932	-896,706.9366
Total PV nominal annual operating cash flows								**-23,772,237.12**

Working Capital Investment

Year	0	1	2	3	4	5	6	7	8
Incremental			−2,000,000	−80,000	−83,200	−86,528	−89,989	−93,589	−97,332
DCF (12%)		0.89285714	0.79719387	0.71178024	0.63551807	0.56742685	0.50663112	0.45234921	0.40388322
PV working capital investment			−1,594,387.755	−56,942	−52,875	−49,098	−45,591	−42,335	−39,311
Redecoration costs									
Real cost	−12,000,000								
Less tax	3,930,000								
After tax	−8,070,000								
Nominal value redecoration cost								−10,619,569	
DCF (12%)		0.89285714	0.79719387		0.63551807	0.56742685	0.50663112	0.45234921	0.40388322
PV redecoration costs								−4,803,753.91	
Hotel construction and sale costs									
Construction cost	−8,000,000	−40,00,000	−32,000,000						
Allowable									
Capital allowance		−200,000	−1,200,000	−2,000,000	−2,000,000	−2,000,000	−2,000,000	−2,000,000	−2,000,000
Tax benefit		−65,500	−393,000	−655,000	−655,000	−655,000	−655,000	−655,000	−655,000
Net construction costs	−8,000,000	−40,065,500	−32,393,000	−655,000	−655,000	−655,000	−655,000	−655,000	−655,000
DCF (12%)	1	0.89285714	0.79719387	0.71178024	0.63551807	0.56742685	0.50663112	0.45234921	0.40388322
PV construction and sale	−8,000,000	−35,772,767.86	−25,823,501.28	−466,216.06	−416,264.34	−371,664.59	−331,843.38	−296,288.73	−264,543.51

Year	9	10	11	12	13	14	15	16	17
Incremental	-101,226	-105,275	-109,486	-113,865	-118,420	-123,156	-128,083	-133,206	3,463,352
DCF (12%)	0.36061002	0.32197323	0.28747610	0.25667509	0.2291741	0.20461981	0.18269626	0.16312166	0.14564434
PV working capital investment	-36,503	-33,896	-31,474	-29,226	-27,139	-23,400	-23,400	-21,729	504,418
Total PV working capital investment									-1,604,689.943
Redecoration costs									
Nominal value redecoration cost				-12,920,330					
DCF (12%)	0.36061002	0.32197323	0.28747610	0.25667509	0.2291741	0.20461981	0.18269626	0.16312166	0.14564434
PV redecoration costs				-3,316,326.905					
Total PV redecoration costs									-8,120,080.816
Hotel construction and sale costs									
Capital allowance	-2,000,000	-2,000,000	-2,000,000	-2,000,000	-2,000,000	-2,000,000	-2,000,000	-2,000,000	-2,000,000
Tax benefit	-655,000	-655,000	-655,000	-655,000	-655,000	-655,000	-655,000	-655,000	-655,000
Net construction costs	-655,000	-655,000	-655,000	-655,000	-655,000	-655,000	-655,000	-655,000	-655,000
After tax residual value									50,000,000
DCF (12%)	0.36061002	0.32197323	0.28747610	0.25667509	0.2291741	0.20461981	0.18269626	0.16312166	0.14564434
PV construction and sale	-236,199.56	-210,892.47	-188,296.84	-168,122.18	-150,109.09	-134,025.97	-119,666.05	-106,844.68	7,186,820.00
Total PV of hotel construction and sale costs									-65,870,426.64

Summary

Total PV nominal annual operating cash flows	−23.772,237.12
Total PV redecoration costs	−8,120,080.816
Total PV hotel construction/sale	−65,870,426.64
Total PV working capital investment	−1,604,689.943
Total	99,367,434.52
Contribution per room per annum	355,382
Occupancy required to break-even (annual estimate)	280
Occupancy rate per annum	87%
NPV 100% occupancy	14,354,902

Appendix 2
Estimation of the Cost of Capital

Market value of debt		37,800,000	
Market value of equity		165,600,000	
Current price of debt		114	per 100
Interest rate (%)		12%	
Equity beta	β	0.8	
Return on market	R_m	15%	
Risk-free rate	R_f	7%	
Cost of equity (using CAPM)		13.40%	
Cost of debt			
Interest rates (%)		6.00	
		7.00	
Annual interest (%) net of tax		8.07	

Year	Cash flow	DCF 7%	DCF 6%	PV 7%	PV 6%
0	−114	1	1	−114	−114
1	8.07	0.934579439	0.943396226	7.542056075	7.613207547
2	8.07	0.873438728	0.889996440	7.048650537	7.182271271
3	8.07	0.816297877	0.839619283	6.587523867	6.775727614
4	8.07	0.762895212	0.792093663	6.156564361	6.392195862
5	8.07	0.712986179	0.747258173	5.753798468	6.030373455
6	8.07	0.666342224	0.704960540	5.377381746	5.689031561
7	8.07	0.622749742	0.665057114	5.025590417	5.367010907
8	8.07	0.582009105	0.627412371	4.696813474	5.063217837
9	8.07	0.543933743	0.591898464	4.389545303	4.776620601
10	8.07	0.508349292	0.558394777	4.102378788	4.506245850
11	8.07	0.475092796	0.526787525	3.833998867	4.251175330
12	8.07	0.444011959	0.496969364	3.583176511	4.010542764
13	8.07	0.414964448	0.468839022	3.348763094	3.783530909
13	100	0.414964448	0.468839022	41.49644479	46.88390222

TOTAL   −4.99   **4.39**

By Interpolation   6 + [(4/4+5)] × 1   6.47

Weighted Average Cost of Capital

13.40%	×	$\dfrac{165,600,000}{203,400,000}$	=	10.91%
PLUS				
6.47%	×	$\dfrac{37,800,000}{203,400,000}$	=	1.20%

| 12.11% |

Case 27

Solution to Tannam plc

Louis Murray, University College Dublin

REPORT ON ISSUES RAISED BY TANNAM PLC

Prepared by: J Milkins
Consultant

For: Gloria Knight
Finance Director
Tannam Holdings plc

1. Terms of Reference

Further to our discussions of xx/xx/xx, I present the report requested. With respect to Tannam plc, it contains an analysis and discussion on the issue of company cost of capital, together with comments on related issues. Previous diversification policies of Tannam are considered, as is the question of whether this will lead to the stated objective of reducing exposure to the risk associated with operating in a particular business sector. A separate section of the report will address the stated objective of Tom Glover, of only acquiring companies trading on a lower price earnings (P/E) ratio than Tannam itself. Numerical examples are presented to review the impact of this type of policy, and to consider the possible outcomes. A further substantial section of this report will consider the current approach towards investment appraisal, the potential difficulties associated with adapting an appraisal technique in a large diversified organisation, and the approaches that might be adapted to deal with this. A final section will offer advice on how Tannam should evaluate the current proposals, and will suggest an approach that should be adapted for any future investment proposals.

2. Recommendations

(a)   The board of Tannam should review their policy regarding diversification. It is not clear that the policy that has been pursued has in itself been beneficial.

(b)   The policy of only acquiring companies trading on a lower P/E ratio than Tannam also is questionable, and should be reconsidered. This policy may have generated a short-term improvement in share price, but the long-term benefit is very questionable.

(c)   When estimating a cost of capital or hurdle rate to apply to investment proposals, no account should be taken of the specific financial package used to finance the investment. The average re-balanced capital structure should determine cost of capital.

(d)   An individual hurdle rate for investments should be introduced for each firm in the Tannam Group. This will allow adjustments for the risk profile in each individual business.

(e)   Using appropriate beta measures for each firm, an after-tax hurdle rate will be the measure against which proposals should be evaluated. Using this measure, the recommendation is that only the following be proceeded with: New Fleet, Kenge Haulage; Warehouse Facility, Tress; New Office Building, Image Consultants; Computer Equipment, Cross Timber; Extra Storage, Laheen. The purchase of Lennox Distributors offers a highly marginal return, so after allowing for forecasting error, it may not be profitable. The recommendation therefore is that it not be purchased.

3. Issues Relating to Diversification Policy pursued by Tannam

For over ten years, Tannam has actively pursued a policy of diversification; this was motivated by a desire to reduce risk exposure to an individual business sector. As the original business had acquired a market quotation, it proved a desirable partner to other businesses seeking the opening to get access to the funding opportunities associated with a market quotation. The original decision was based on the assumption that diversification was the best means to reduce exposure to the market, or market risk as measured by beta. Although this decision would radically alter the nature of the business, and convert Tannam into a holding company, the belief was that diversification would reduce risk and cost of capital, and would therefore increase value.

Clearly, it is true that mergers and acquisitions do on occasions generate value, through either a reduction in costs, or an increase in earnings due to improved opportunities. Benefits may also however be expected, if there is an opportunity to benefit from synergies, as a result of a good fit between the businesses involved. Typically, benefits of this type will be achievable if one organisation has a particular strength in one management function, e.g. marketing, and the other has strengths in other functional areas, e.g. product or service design. In all of these cases, to achieve economic benefits, the businesses involved will need to be related to each other in some way, so that they will be able to get the benefits associated with combination. Also, the merger or acquisition can be expected to lead to an amalgamation of the businesses into a single structure, to facilitate these benefits. The research evidence on mergers and acquisitions generally is positive, as an increase in value tends to accompany an announcement of merger or acquisition. The question of whether acquiring or victim shareholders will receive this benefit is separate, and will largely depend on the state of the acquisitions market. However, as available evidence relates to an initial response on announcement, it is unclear as to whether these benefits will be sustained into the long run. This is a much more difficult research question, as many other factors will impact on longer run performance, so it will be difficult to separate out the economic impact of an earlier decision to combine two or more businesses together.

In Tannam's case, the businesses combined together to form the holding company are not related to each other. The stated objective of company policy was to achieve potential benefits through diversification. As a result, it will not be possible to secure any wealth benefits that come with combining businesses that are in some way related to each other. The expectation of management is that diversification will in itself produce benefits, through a reduction in exposure to potential poor performance in an individual business sector. In effect, by combining together unrelated companies into a single group, the risk associated with an individual business will be diversified away. Using the same logic as a fund manager who will hold shares in a range of different businesses, in order to eliminate or greatly reduce exposure to the unique risk of an individual business, the holding company will in itself become a diversified entity, also eliminating or greatly reducing exposure to individual company risk.

The benefit to a diversified business should be lower risk levels, and this should be delivered through a lower cost of capital, as investors respond by accepting lower rates of return. If this strategy does prove to be successful, lower cost of capital will result in an increase in company value[1]. An implication of this reasoning is that a single reduced cost of capital rate should be applied to all capital investments of the holding group, regardless of the business in which the investment is located. This was the approach that was adapted throughout Tannam Holdings. It is questionable however as to whether this reasoning is appropriate[2], as it requires an assumption that all businesses that form part of a holding company can be viewed as part of a diversified single entity. If they actually continue to operate as separate entities, there must be some question as to whether a net benefit will be possible. There is considerable controversy regarding this point, and it is important because the expected benefits can only come if there truly is a single diversified entity, rather than a range of unrelated businesses that happen to be owned by the same holding company. The only remaining protection to shareholders of a diversified holding company could actually be a protection against bankruptcy costs and bankruptcy related costs, in the event of failure of a firm that is a wholly owned part of the group.

4. The Policy of only Acquiring Companies that Trade on a Lower P/E Ratio

The stated policy of Tom Glover has been to pursue a policy of rapid growth of the group, through a series of acquisitions. A series of mergers and acquisitions have delivered this outcome. The only stated criteria, when considering an acquisition of a publicly quoted company has been that it is trading on a lower P/E ratio than Tannam itself. In the case of both quoted and unquoted acquisitions that have been submitted for consideration, there is no stated policy regarding a strategic fit, or a connection with existing members of the group.

The policy of only acquiring companies trading on a lower P/E ratio is undertaken to ensure that there will be no immediate negative impact on Earnings per Share. The effect is that, by only purchasing company earnings at a multiple that is relatively lower, the number of new shares that must be issued to finance the acquisition will be minimised, so that Earnings per Share will not be reduced. If a company whose shares trade on a higher earnings multiple was acquired, Earnings per Share would decline. A worked example demonstrates this point in Appendix 1. In this case, acquisition terms are such that a company acquires a company trading on a P/E of 13, when its share price is trading at only 10 times earnings.

There is however an error in this analysis, as long-term implications have not been considered. Firstly, Price/Earnings ratios provide a good indication of future potential, as investors will be prepared to pay a higher price for the earnings of a company that is considered to have better growth and development prospects. A

---

[1] Company value can be viewed as expected future earnings, discounted at company cost of capital. A reduction in cost of capital will result in a reduced discount rate, and will therefore also result in an increase in value.

[2] Please note Section 5.

decision to only consider acquiring companies that trade on a relatively lower ratio will limit Tannam to an acquisition of firms considered to have poor future growth prospects. Clearly, this could not be desirable. Secondly, the quantitative analysis on earnings per share and price/earnings assumes that, following acquisition ABC will continue to trade on a P/E ratio of 10. This may not be correct. For example, a decision to acquire XYZ, which trades on a higher P/E and is therefore well regarded by investors, may improve the prospects of ABC. This could enhance investor expectations, causing the P/E to increase above 10. As a result share price may actually increase. If for example, following the acquisition, the P/E of ABC were to increase to 11, a share price of €10.23 (*11X€0.93*) could be expected.

5. An Assessment of the Current Policy towards Investment Decisions

With the establishment of Tannam Holdings, a budgetary control system was initiated throughout the group. Discounting based appraisal methods were introduced. Before this, all appraisal decisions were evaluated just using payback period. The senior management designated after-tax internal rate of return (IRR) as the main criteria, however they also proposed that after-tax net present value (NPV) also be used as back-up criteria. Any investment proposal coming to the finance director of Tannam Holdings would be required to offer an after-tax IRR that is in excess of the after-tax cost of capital for the group.

Considering that Tannam is the holding company of a diversified group of wholly owned firms, each operates as a separate business, and has its separate financing structure of various forms of debt and equity capital. As the financing structure of the various businesses in the group does vary considerably, there are two issues that must be considered, when determining the discount rate that should be applied to the evaluation process.

(a) The balance between debt and equity capital is not the same in every firm in the Tannam Group. Also, it is likely that the form of debt capital that has been used will also vary considerably across firms in the group. Some firms will have greater concentrations of debentures or loan stock, whereas others will have greater concentrations of bank or term loans. New capital investments will be financed from various sources of either debt or equity capital that again will vary considerably across the firms in the group. The question that therefore arises is whether, when a hurdle rate is being determined for a particular proposal that will be situated in one of the firms, is it advisable to take account of how that proposal is financed? Also is it advisable to take account of the particular financing structure of the firm itself? This is a complex question, but the generally accepted solution is to assume that the holding company will tend to continuously rebalance its financial structure towards an optimal balance of debt and equity capital. This rebalancing will also take account of an optimal combination of different forms of debt capital. As a result, the specific mix of financing used for a particular proposal will be irrelevant. The fact that a large or a small proportion of a certain debt source has been used is not relevant to the proposal. It is better to view all proposals as being financed by a combination of the overall financing mix of the group.

(b)   The risk exposure of each firm in the holding group is different. Individual proposals submitted by a particular firm will have risk characteristics similar to that firm, rather than to the overall group[3]. A general overall after-tax weighted average cost of capital (WACC) value will therefore not be appropriate, as it takes no account of firm or industry specific risk characteristics. In some cases, if the firm risk profile is greater than the average profile of the group, an overall WACC will be too low, and vice versa. The recommendation therefore is that an adjustment must be made to allow for the risk profile of an individual firm in the holding group.

As a result, the cost of capital or hurdle rate that should be employed to assess a proposed investment should be determined by the following WACC formula.

$$WACC = \left(\frac{D}{V}\right) Kd \left(1 - T\right) + \left(\frac{E}{V}\right) Ke$$

Where: *WACC*: After-tax weighted average cost of capital

D:	Amount of Debt in Holding Company
E:	Amount of Equity in Holding Company
V:	Combined Value of Debt and Equity
Kd:	Average Cost of Debt
Ke:	Cost of Equity for individual firm.
T:	Company Tax rate.

Cost of Equity for an individual firm should be determined using the Capital Asset Pricing Model. The level of beta or market exposure should depend on industry type for the individual firm.

$$Ke = Rf + Bi \left(Rm - Rf\right)$$

Where:		
	Bi:	Beta or Market Risk for the industry type
	Rm:	Rate of Return on Market Index
	Rf:	Risk-free Rate of Return

6. Recommended Technique for Estimating Hurdle Rate for Each Subsidiary

As discussed in the previous section, it is highly desirable to adjust project hurdle rates for the particular risk characteristics associated with projects undertaken by

---

[3] An assumption that the investment proposal is representative of company activities is required. If not, further adjustment to account for the risk profile of the individual proposal may be required.

individual firms in the holding group. Using estimated beta values for each industry, and the formulae proposed in section 5, hurdle rates for each wholly owned subsidiary have been calculated. Calculations are presented in Appendix 2. An estimated hurdle rate for Lennox Distributors also is included, as one of the proposals under consideration is the purchase of this business. A discount rate that takes account of the risk profile of Lennox should be used, when making an evaluation of the proposal to purchase the business.

Following the estimation of appropriate hurdle rates for each subsidiary company, each proposed investment should be evaluated against a risk-adjusted rate that is appropriate for the industry type. This further adjustment will ensure more accurate decision-making. The investment proposals, their appropriate hurdle rates, and each recommendation, are listed in Appendix 3.

Appendix 1
Proposed Acquisition of Company XYZ by Holding Group ABC:
Summary Data:

	Holding Group ABC	Company XYZ
Annual Earnings	€100M	€30M
No. of Shares Outstanding	100M	50M
Earnings Per Share.	€1	€0.60
Price/Earnings	10	13
Share Price	€10.00	€7.80

Holding Group ABC makes offer for shares in Company XYZ
The terms are a share for share exchange, based on current market values.
Transfer Ratio: €7.80 / €10.00, i.e. 0.78:1.00
The number of new ABC Shares issued: $0.78 \times 50M = 39M$

Workings:
The Impact on Earnings per Share, and possibly on Share Price
Before:
E.P.S. : €100M / 100M = €1
Sh. Price : $10 \times €1 = €10$

After:
E.P.S. : €100M + €30M / 100M + 39M = €130M / 139M = €0.935
Sh. Price : $10 \times €0.935 = €9.35$

The implication is that, if an acquisition of XYZ is made on these terms, ABC will suffer a decline in Earnings per Share, and may also experience a fall in share value.

Appendix 2
Estimation of Hurdle Rates for Individual Subsidiaries in the Tannam Group

Tannam Ltd ($B = 1.9$)

$Ke = Rf + Bi\left(Rm - Rf\right)$, so

$Ke = 6 + 1.9\left(13 - 6\right) = 19.3$

$WACC = \left(\dfrac{D}{V}\right)Kd\left(1 - T\right) + \left(\dfrac{E}{V}\right)Ke$, so

$WACC = \left(0.175\right)8.5 + \left(0.035\right)11.05 + \left(0.09\right)7.65 + \left(0.14\right)10.2 + \left(0.56\right)19.3 = 14.9$

The after-tax hurdle rate is 14.9%

Spollen Properties Ltd ($B = 2.2$)

$Ke = Rf + Bi\left(Rm - Rf\right)$, so

$Ke = 6 + 2.2\left(13 - 6\right) = 21.4$

$WACC = \left(\dfrac{D}{V}\right)Kd\left(1 - T\right) + \left(\dfrac{E}{V}\right)Ke$, so

$WACC = \left(0.175\right)8.5 + \left(0.035\right)11.05 + \left(0.09\right)7.65 + \left(0.14\right)10.2 + \left(0.56\right)21.4 = 15.97$

The after-tax hurdle rate is 15.97%

CGU Distributors Ltd ($B = 0.7$)

$Ke = Rf + Bi\left(Rm - Rf\right)$, so

$Ke = 6 + 0.7\left(13 - 6\right) = 10.9$

$WACC = \left(\dfrac{D}{V}\right)Kd\left(1 - T\right) + \left(\dfrac{E}{V}\right)Ke$, so

$WACC = \left(0.175\right)8.5 + \left(0.035\right)11.05 + \left(0.09\right)7.65 + \left(0.14\right)10.2 + \left(0.56\right)10.9 = 10.09$

Fasnet Media Services Ltd ($B = 1.1$)

$Ke = Rf + Bi\left(Rm - Rf\right)$, so

$Ke = 6 + 1.1\left(13 - 6\right) = 13.7$

$WACC = \left(\dfrac{D}{V}\right)Kd\left(1 - T\right) + \left(\dfrac{E}{V}\right)Ke$, so

$WACC = \left(0.175\right)8.5 + \left(0.035\right)11.05 + \left(0.09\right)7.65 + \left(0.14\right)10.2 + \left(0.56\right)13.7 = 11.66$

Quirke Construction Ltd ($B = 1.8$)

$Ke = Rf + Bi\left(Rm - Rf\right)$, so

$Ke = 6 + 1.8\left(13 - 6\right) = 18.6$

$WACC = \left(\dfrac{D}{V}\right)Kd\left(1 - T\right) + \left(\dfrac{E}{V}\right)Ke$, so

$WACC = \left(0.175\right)8.5 + \left(0.035\right)11.05 + \left(0.09\right)7.65 + \left(0.14\right)10.2 + \left(0.56\right)18.6 = 14.4$

Kenge Haulage Ltd ($B = 1.3$)

$Ke = Rf + Bi(Rm - Rf)$, so

$Ke = 6 + 1.3(13 - 6) = 15.1$

$WACC = \left(\dfrac{D}{V}\right)Kd(1 - T) + \left(\dfrac{E}{V}\right)Ke$, so

$WACC = (0.175)8.5 + (0.035)11.05 + (0.09)7.65 + (0.14)10.2 + (0.56)15.1 = 12.44$

Tress Ltd ($B = 0.6$)

$Ke = Rf + Bi(Rm - Rf)$, so

$Ke = 6 + 0.6(13 - 6) = 10.2$

$WACC = \left(\dfrac{D}{V}\right)Kd(1 - T) + \left(\dfrac{E}{V}\right)Ke$, so

$WACC = (0.175)8.5 + (0.035)11.05 + (0.09)7.65 + (0.14)10.2 + (0.56)10.2 = 9.7$

Cross Timber Ltd ($B=0.8$)

$Ke = Rf + Bi(Rm - Rf)$, so

$Ke = 6 + 0.8(13 - 6) = 11.6$

$WACC = \left(\dfrac{D}{V}\right)Kd(1 - T) + \left(\dfrac{E}{V}\right)Ke$, so

$WACC = (0.175)8.5 + (0.035)11.05 + (0.09)7.65 + (0.14)10.2 + (0.56)11.6 = 10.48$

Image Consultants Ltd ($B = 1.7$)

$Ke = Rf + Bi(Rm - Rf)$, so

$Ke = 6 + 1.7(13 - 6) = 17.9$

$WACC = \left(\dfrac{D}{V}\right)Kd(1 - T) + \left(\dfrac{E}{V}\right)Ke$, so

$WACC = (0.175)8.5 + (0.035)11.05 + (0.09)7.65 + (0.14)10.2 + (0.56)17.9 = 14.01$

Laheen Refrigerators ($B = 1.0$)

$Ke = Rf + Bi(Rm - Rf)$, so

$Ke = 6 + 1.0(13 - 6) = 13.0$

$WACC = \left(\dfrac{D}{V}\right)Kd(1 - T) + \left(\dfrac{E}{V}\right)Ke$, so

$WACC = (0.175)8.5 + (0.035)11.05 + (0.09)7.65 + (0.14)10.2 + (0.56)13.0 = 11.27$

Lennox Distributors ($B = 0.9$)

$Ke = Rf + Bi(Rm - Rf)$, so

$Ke = 6 + 0.9(13 - 6) = 12.3$

$WACC = \left(\dfrac{D}{V}\right)Kd(1 - T) + \left(\dfrac{E}{V}\right)Ke$, so

$WACC = (0.175)8.5 + (0.035)11.05 + (0.09)7.65 + (0.14)10.2 + (0.56)12.3 = 10.87$

Appendix 3
The Investment Proposals, Hurdle Rates, and Recommendations

	Hurdle Rate (%)	IRR (%)	Invest Y or N
Improved retail premises – Tannam	14.8	17	Y
New electrical equipment – Tannam	14.8	15	Y
New fleet – Kenge Haulage	12.44	16	Y
Warehouse facility – Tress	9.7	11	Y
New office building – Image Consultants	14.01	17	Y
Computer equipment – Cross Timber	10.48	16	Y
Land purchase – Spollen Properties	15.97	15	N
Expanded storage – Laheen	11.27	14	Y
Head office building – Quirke Construction	14.4	13	N
Purchase of Lennox Distributors	10.87	12	Y*

* IRR on Lennox Distributors is only marginally above the estimated hurdle rate. As the estimation process will be subject to error, the decision to purchase this business must be highly marginal.

Case 28

Solution to Calvin plc

Peter Green, University of Ulster at Jordanstown

REPORT ON UTILISATION OF SURPLUS FUNDS

Prepared by: A. Student
Management Consultant

For: Calvin plc

1. Terms of Reference

Further to our discussions of xx/xx/xx, I present the report requested. With respect to the two main suggestions forwarded by the board of directors with regard to utilising surplus funds, that is redeeming the €20 million secured loan or increasing the dividend payment to shareholders by €20 million, given the other data you have supplied, I must advise that neither of these suggestions would appear to be desirable, when compared with the option to expand operations into the Republic of Ireland. Although I must emphasise that the calculations included in the report are based upon figures which have been supplied by the market research commissioned by your company and which I have not verified.

2. Executive Summary/Recommendations

(a)   The current cash surplus has derived from volume expansion due to an increased demand for housing. The building industry suffers from volatile fluctuations in housing demand. Hence, in future years cash shortages may be experienced, rather than the current cash surplus.

(b)   The company's gearing level in 2XX3/4 is well below the industry average (see Appendix 1). The proposed redemption of the secured loan stock may result in a reduction in interest payments over the next ten years, but if the reasons for redemption are not properly explained to the market, it may be interpreted by shareholders as a sign that the management of the company believe that future prospects are poor and this may result in a drop in share price (see section 3.3 of the report). Furthermore, if additional financing is needed within the next 10 years, which is possible given the volatile nature of the market in which the company operates, it may cost more to borrow in the future, than the current 7% payable on the loan stock.

(c)   The company's dividend payout ratio for the year 2XX3/4 was 53%, which although above the industry average (41%) is in-line with the overall UK average payout of 56%. The proposed increase for 2XX4/5 of €20 million would represent an increase to 87% (see Appendix 1). Such a significant increase may signal to shareholders, if not adequately explained, that management is unable to identify beneficial investment opportunities and may not be welcomed by some shareholders depending upon their current tax status (see section 4.2 of the report).

(d)   Despite the high transportation costs, based upon the data supplied, exporting to the Republic of Ireland is beneficial. However, an even more attractive option would appear to be the acquisition of the existing company in Dublin and the relocation of excess capacity from Belfast to Dublin, thus avoiding additional transportation costs to service the entire Republic of Ireland market. This will require the investment of more than the €20 million surplus funds, but will increase the value of the company by between €19 and €23 million. Although it must be noted that this calculation is heavily dependent upon the assumption that the operating performance in the Republic of Ireland continues at the estimated level indefinitely.

3. Issues relating to the redemption of the secured loan stock

3.1 Return to shareholders

The redemption of the loan stock will result in a reduction in interest payments of €1.4 million per year for the next ten years. As interest payments are a tax deductible expense, the net saving would be €938,000 (1,400,000 × 0.67) per year, assuming that the company has sufficient taxable profits to fully utilise tax savings. This should result in an increase in the value of the shareholders wealth of €4,707,822 (5.019 × 938,000), assuming that the required return from shareholders remains at 15% per annum and that the net saving can be invested at this rate.

3.2 Risk to shareholders

Theoretically, eliminating debt will result in a reduction of financial risk to shareholders. That is, there will be a reduction in the volatility of earnings attributable to shareholders and a decrease in the probability of liquidation and/or costs of financial distress being incurred. However, currently due to the conservative financial policy pursued by the company, the gearing level of the company is very low compared with the industry average. This implies that bankruptcy risk is not significant. The gearing of the company is at present 5%, compared with the industry average of 45%, whilst interest cover is 17.9 compared with the industry average of 6.5 (see Appendix 1).

3.3 Signalling considerations

As noted above, loan interest is a tax deductible expense and the return to shareholders is increased by this tax reduction. This is technically referred to as a 'tax shield'. This benefit will be lost if the loan is redeemed, and if not properly explained to investors, the repayment of the loan may be interpreted as a signal that there are difficult times ahead, resulting in a fall in share price.

3.4 Future interest rate

An important issue with regard to the redemption of a current fixed interest rate loan is the level of interest rates expected in the future. For example, if the loan is redeemed now at par but to borrow in the future would cost more than 7%, then redemption would probably not be worthwhile.

4. Issues relating to the proposed increase in dividends

4.1 Overview

The payment of a dividend represents a distribution of the wealth generated by a company. It is generally accepted that wealth is created by investing in assets that are worth more than they cost and financing those investments at the lowest possible cost (that is, identifying investment opportunities with a positive net present value.). As such, it is argued that dividend policy is irrelevant. However, most finance directors would appear to be of the opinion that dividend policy should be managed so that dividend payments follow a steady rate of increase over time. That is, the dividend decision is independent rather than the residue of investment and financing decisions. This positive management of dividend policy is said to increase investor confidence, though the matter is far from proven.

Due to the differential tax treatment of dividend payments and capital gains from increases in share prices, the desired level of dividend return may be different for certain classes of shareholders. For example, those individuals who pay income tax at a higher rate may prefer their return from an equity investment in the form of a capital gain, so that they can utilise their capital gains tax allowance before incurring any personal tax liability. Whereas, those individuals paying basic rate tax or no tax, may prefer their return in the form of a dividend, in order to minimise any transaction costs associated with selling their equity investment to obtain cash. In other words, tax clienteles may exist for a particular level of dividend payout.

4.2 Views of the company's shareholders

This proposal may be preferred by those shareholders who want a large immediate cash distribution and will not suffer any adverse tax consequences if it is received as a dividend. In your company's case, this may be tax-exempt institutions, such as Pension Funds who are the majority shareholders, and possibly some retired employees and current employees, who pay basic rate income tax.

4.3 Dividend signalling

The main problem with the proposed increase in dividend is that the payout ratio would increase from 55% to 87% (see Appendix 1), which is very large in comparison with both the industry average and the national average. Unless the reasons for this dramatic increase are carefully explained, this may send a negative signal to current and potential investors. Specifically, some investors may assume that the level of dividends in future years will continue to increase at the same rate, whilst others may interpret the large payment as a sign that the management of the company can not identify investment opportunities, thus questioning their competence. It is best to avoid confusion of this sort, as it can have a negative impact upon the company's share price. Companies wishing to pay large increases in cash to shareholders have historically avoided such confusion by either announcing a 'one-off' special dividend, or by making a share buy-back. The latter has the advantage of being subject to capital gains tax (for higher tax rate investors), rather than income tax, but does result in a change in the disposition of shareholdings.

5. Issues relating to expansion into the Republic of Ireland

5.1 Exporting option

Despite the high level of transportation costs, on the assumption that operations continue indefinitely in accordance with the data supplied, this option is financially viable, with a net present value of approximately €2.5 million (see Appendix 2).

5.2 Takeover option with purchase of new machinery

On the assumption that operations continue indefinitely in accordance with the data supplied, this option may be viable, provided that the purchase price is approximately €19 million. However, at the very least I would like to inspect the most recent audited accounts of the potential target firm and conduct further investigations to determine the extent to which the data supplied is reliable. Further, you should seriously consider the associated problems of integration and control with regard to the establishment of a wholly owned subsidiary in Dublin. As this is a horizontal takeover these problems may not be severe, but any financial implications should be factored into the numerical analysis.

5.3 Takeover over with transfer of machinery from Belfast

Of the possible options investigated in this report, this would appear the most desirable, based upon the data supplied. Appendix 2 provides the relevant calculations and demonstrates that this option is preferable largely as a result of the elimination of the transportation costs of finished goods between Belfast and Dublin, together with an expansion into new markets in the Republic.

As this option is a combination of the latter two, the points noted above also apply. However in addition, this will require the investment of more than the €20 million surplus funds, but will increase the value of the company by between €19 and €23 million. Given the company's current capital structure, the optimal financing policy may be to borrow any additional funds required, to take advantage of the 'tax shield' that debt provides, over a medium to long term.

5.4 Other issues

It must be noted that the analysis above is heavily dependent upon the assumption that the operating performance in the Republic of Ireland continues at the estimated level indefinitely, and on the other data supplied from the market research report, neither of which I have verified. Further analysis, should therefore be performed with regard to the reliability of this data. In particular, the analysis presented has largely focused upon return, with little or no consideration of risk. At the very least, sensitivity analysis should be performed to identify which estimates the decision to invest is most sensitive to.

Appendix 1
Dividend Payout Ratio (Assuming surplus paid as dividend)

		2XX4	2XX5
Earnings before interest and tax		25,000,000	50,000,000
Interest	$(20,000,000 \times 0.07)$	1,400,000	1,400,000
Earnings before tax		23,600,000	48,600,000
Tax @ 33 %		7,788,000	16,038,000
Earnings after tax		15,812,000	32,562,000
Dividend	$(560,000,000 \times 0.015)$	8,400,000	28,400,000
Dividend payout (%)		53.12%	87.22%
Interest cover		17.86	
Book value of debt		20,000,000	
Book value of equity		400,000,000	
Gearing (%)		5.00%	

Appendix 2
Exporting Option

		Year				
	0	1	2	3	4	5
Sales		1,000,000	2,000,000	4,000,000	8,000,000	20,000,000
Variable costs:						
Operating		700,000	1,400,000	2,800,000	5,600,000	14,000,000
Transportation		250,000	500,000	1,000,000	2,000,000	5,000,000
Legal fees	500,000					

Corporate tax rate   0.33 (Payable in current year)
Required return   0.15

Exporting Option

DCF Analysis

	0	1	2	3	4	5
			Year			
Pre-tax contribution	−500,000	50,000	100,000	200,000	400,000	1,000,000
Tax	165,000	−16,500	−33,000	−66,000	−132,000	−330,000
Post-tax contribution	−335,000	33,500	67,000	134,000	268,000	670,000
PV year 5 onwards (670,000/0.15)					4,466,666.7	
Total Net Cash Flows	−335,000	33,500	67,000	134,000	4,734,666.7	
DCF	1	0.869565	0.756144	0.657516	0.5717532	
Present Values	−335,000	29,130.43	50,661.63	88,107.18	2,707,061	

Net Present Value €2,539,960.27

Takeover Data

	0	1	2	3	4	5
			Year			
Cost of acquisition			16,000,000 to 20,000,000			
Initial working capital	8,000,000 (Not to be increased with inflation)					
New machines	4,000,000					
Transportation of Existing machinery	500,000					
Post-tax cash flows		3,000,000	5,000,000	5,000,000	5,000,000	5,000,000
Capital allowances		0.25 (Reducing balance)				

Takeover Option with Purchase of New Machinery

DCF Analysis

	0	1	2	3
		Year		
Post-tax contribution		3,000,000	5,000,000	5,000,000
Working capital	−8,000,000			
New machines	−4,000,000			
PV year 3 onwards (5,000,000/0.15)			33,333,333	
Total net cash flows	−8,335,000	3,000,000	38,333,333	
DCF	1	0.869565	0.756144	
Present values	−8,335,000	2,608,696	28,985,507	

Net Present Value   Purchase price = 16,000,000   €3,594,202.90

Purchase price = 20,000,000   −€405,797.10

Takeover Option with Transfer of Machinery

DCF Analysis

	0	1	2	3	4	5
			Year			
New ROI Market						
Sales		1,000,000	2,000,000	4,000,000	8,000,000	20,000,000
Operating costs		−700,000	−1,400,000	−2,800,000	−5,600,000	−14,000,000
Legal fees	−500,000					
Pre-tax contribution	−500,000	300,000	600,000	1,200,000	2,400,000	6,000,000
Tax	165,000	−99,000	−198,000	−396,000	−792,000	−1,980,000
Post tax contribution	−335,000	201,000	402,000	804,000	1,608,000	4,020,000
PV year 5 onwards (4,020,000/0.15)					26,800,000	
Net cash flows exporting	−335,000	201,000	402,000	804,000	28,408,000	
DCF	1	0.869565	0.756144	0.657516	0.5717532	
Present values	−335,000	174,782.6	303,969.8	528,643.1	16,242,366	

Net Present Value   €16,914,761.61

DCF Analysis

Takeover (Acquiring Target Company's Rol Market)

	Year			
	0	1	2	3
Post-tax contribution		3,000,000	5,000,000	5,000,000
Lost tax benefit on capital allowances				
Capital allowance	1,000,000	−330,000	−247,500	−185,625
	750,000			
	562,500			
Working capital	−8,000,000			
Transportation costs (existing machinery)	−500,000			
Tax on transportation costs	165,000			
Net post-tax contribution	−8,335,000	2,670,000	4,752,500	4,814,375
PV year 3 onwards (4,814,375/0.15)			32,095,833	
Total net cash flows	−8,335,000	2,670,000	36,848,333	
DCF	1	0.869565	0.756144	
Present values	−8,335,000	2,321,739	27,862,634	

Purchase price = 16,000,000   **€5,849,373.03**

Purchase price = 20,000,000   **€1,849,373.03**

Net Present Value:

Case 29

Solution to Xia Limited

John Cotter, University College Dublin

REPORT ON ISSUES FACED BY XIA LIMITED AND ITS TRADING DECISIONS

Prepared by: John Oglewski (consultant)

For: CEO of Xia Limited

1. Terms of Reference

Further to our discussions of xx/xx/xx, I present the report requested. With respect to the expansion we use three different types of analysis and discuss the associated findings. We first look at the projected cashflows supplied by Xia and value these by calculating the present values of the inflows and outflows. We also calculate the net present value and related ratios to support our findings. The numerical analysis of the cashflows in the report relates to a set of figures provided by the chief financial officer (CFO) of Xia and are taken on good faith, having not been independently verified for the purposes of this report. We also, independently, gathered macroeconomic forecasts from various sources such as the IMF and the respective countries' industrial development organisations. We have analysed this macroeconomic information in aiding the decision making process. Furthermore, we gathered, and did analysis on exchange rate data in dollars and euros. This third form of analysis on foreign exchange data uses calculations of foreign exchange exposure by looking at average changes and the level of risk in the changes. Using summary statistics we discuss the likely foreign exchange exposure facing Xia from setting up in Ireland, and comment on ways of minimising the foreign exchange exposure.

2. Recommendations

Ireland dominates Scotland as the preferred location from all available data and its associated analysis:

(a) All the net present value analysis supports choosing Ireland as the preferred location for expansion. Ireland has a higher positive net present value and associated profitability index than Scotland.

(b) These findings hold through even if the discount factor was to change (assuming that the discount factor for both Irish and Scottish investments were to remain equal).

(c) The analysis of the macroeconomic forecasts suggests choosing Ireland as the preferred location for expansion. This recommendation is driven in particular by the corporate tax rates available in Ireland for the foreseeable future.

(d) Overall the analysis of the past exchange rate changes suggests choosing Ireland as the preferred location for expansion. This recommendation is driven in particular by the volume of trade it currently does in euros compared to sterling.

(e) Our final recommendation is that Xia should consider going a step further than locating its future expansion in Ireland and that it should transfer the existing production facilities there. The main criterion for this recommendation is the fact that it would eliminate much of the exchange rate uncertainty associated with a large proportion of its trade in the eurozone.

3. Summary of issues relating to the expansion of Xia Limited

Much of the analysis of this report is based on the time value of money and converting cashflows (inflows and outflows) into present values. In Appendix 1, positive cashflows are presented in their future value form as they are given as projected future cashflows but, in contrast, negative cashflows are given as present values. We also complete analysis of macroeconomic forecasts of Ireland and Scotland's attributes in terms of location for the expansion. Our third type of analysis is the foreign exchange exposure Xia is likely to face in trading from Scotland or Ireland. In order to assess the relative merits of each location for Xia Limited we will examine the three different types of analysis separately and comment on the respective findings.

Analysis 1: Projected cashflow analysis

We use net present value and related analysis to discuss the importance of the cashflows. The current value of the outflows can be obtained directly from Appendix 1 and are £1,000m. However, projected inflows are given in the context of their future values and must be discounted by the time value of money. We use the US cost of capital as the discount factor of 5% and the timeframe of the analysis is five years. We are assuming the projected cashflows will actually evolve as forecasted. Given these assumptions and the timeframe involved, we suggest that a reasonable estimate of the present value of locating in Ireland and Scotland is given in Appendix 1. For example, the present value of the 5th year's contribution to Scotland is:

$$\$400m/(1.05)^5 = \$313.41m$$

And the present value of the 4th year's contribution to Ireland is:

$$600/(1.05)^4 = \$493.62$$

Having calculated each year's present value, we now proceed to calculate the net present value. This will allow us make a recommendation based on the projected cashflows. Thus, to obtain the net present values we need to sum the individual present values for each economy; the findings are given in Appendix 1. For example, for Scotland, we find the net present value is:

$$-1000 + 476.19 + 181.406 + 259.151 + 329.081 + 313.41 = +559.239$$

As we find that the net present value for Scotland is positive, then it is a worthwhile investment, which is very encouraging for the expansion of Xia. However, if we compare the value to that of Ireland we find Ireland's net present value is even higher (+854.745). Thus, on this basis of net present value, we would chose Ireland over Scotland.

A simple but effective way of reporting the relative superiority of Ireland over Scotland is through a profitability index. Again, we illustrate our findings for one economy and find that the profitability index of choosing Ireland is:

$$854.745/1000 = 0.854.$$

Relative to a dollar (or thousand million dollar) investment, locating in Ireland has a profit of 85.4 cent (or 854 million dollars); this shows how profitable and lucrative expanding in Ireland really is. In comparison, Scotland represents an excellent investment opportunity, but does have a lower profitability index of 0.559 so would be ranked lower than Ireland as the preferred investment location.

Another way to analyse the figures using present value approaches is to calculate the respective internal rate of return for each location. The internal rate of return is the interest rate corresponding to a zero net present value. This allows us confirm the earlier findings from the net present value analysis. Again the results for each economy are reported in Appendix 1. However to illustrate the findings for Ireland we see:

$$1000 = 300/(1 + r)^1 + 200/(1 + r)^2 + 400/(1 + r)^3 + 600/(1 + r)^4 + 700/(1 + r)^5$$

And by solving by trial and error we find r = 27%. Comparing this to the calculated IRR for Scotland we report a lower value of 24% suggesting that the rate of return on the Irish expansion is higher than that of Scotland. Again this would support the recommendation of choosing Ireland over Scotland as the preferred location for Xia's expansion.

All the analysis supports choosing Ireland as the preferred location for expansion. These findings hold through even if the discount factor was to change (assuming that the discount factor for both Irish and Scottish investments were to remain equal). However, if interest rates or the discount factor was to increase beyond 27% then both economies would have a negative net present value and neither should be chosen. If the discount factor was to increase beyond 24% but less than 27% then Scotland would have a negative net present value and Ireland would have a positive net present value and, thus, the latter only would be an attractive option.

Analysis 2: Macroeconomic Forecasts

Turning to the second type of analysis for determining the best location for Xia to expand in, we examine some macroeconomic forecasts on the respective economies. Our indications are summarised in Appendix 2. Overall the findings are very positive for both economies, as they perform well for all measures. Thus, they are both desirable destinations. However, overall we find that Ireland tends to have a more favourable set of macroeconomic forecasts, in that they dominate Scotland in more categories than *vice versa*. Also, Ireland tends to perform well in those categories that are critical to expansion.

Let us go through each of these headings and comment on the relative performance of Ireland and Scotland. First, price changes tend to be more stable in Ireland as exhibited by a lower inflation rate, although we must note that this proxy of price changes is very general and may not reflect price stability in software products and services. Second, the cost of capital is lower in Ireland and this is a very important plus for domestic firms trading there in comparison to Scotland. Given that Xia is an international firm it will source its capital in an international context so the benefit of Ireland for this factor may not a driving force in recommending that the company expands here. Nevertheless, assuming that the company does expand in Ireland and builds up good relationships with local organisations such as banks, then the lower cost of capital may be a plus when Xia comes to obtaining further capital in the future.

The next forecast is vital for the decision relating to expansion. The Profit Opportunity Rankings (POR) for Ireland is slightly higher than that of Scotland and this would indicate that Ireland offers a more attractive business climate to new enterprises. As these measures are subjective, the main finding that one should take from both rankings is that they are high and reasonably similar. If we had found low rankings for either or both economies this would have been a strong signal not to expand in the location(s). Thus both economies are attractive places for Xia to expand to. Sentiment is not (and should not be) part of any decision on expansion, but this analysis suggests that that Xia have identified two countries that would be top of any league table of countries to relocate to, with Ireland just shading Scotland on this criterion.

The next forecast, of infrastructure, is the only one that Scotland has a clear advantage over Ireland in. This factor examines the support network for a typical business, including road network and telecommunication facilities. From further analysis, it is suggested that Ireland's relative poor performance in this area is due to a relative lack of investment in this area historically compared to that of Scotland. It must be noted that this is a generic measure that does not specifically relate to any company's infrastructural needs and, as such, may or may not be relevant to Xia. Our discussions with Xia and similar companies suggest that telecommunications is an important issue but that these types of companies are not well served, given their requirements, in any economy; not even in Silicon Valley. Many software companies thus rely on privately developed telecommunication systems that build on their own expertise and avoid being totally reliant on the locally provided systems that are in place.

The quality of labour in both economies is excellent and we cannot separate the economies for this factor. Both economies have well educated workforces that fit perfectly for the high value production that Xia is involved in. However, for another vital raw material of relevance to where the company should expand we find a clear indication of the suitability of Ireland over Scotland. In the area of grants and support Ireland's industrial bodies are willing to give $22m to support Xia expanding there, in comparison to only $6 million being provided by their Scottish counterparts.

This brings us to another factor of relevance (and some might say the main factor) to help decide where Xia should expand to. We note that Ireland's corporation tax is less than half that of Scotland (10% versus 21%). Thus, for any level of profits, the net figure at the disposal of Xia will be much higher in Ireland. Given that this is a key factor (profit maximisation) for any company, the favourable tax rate in Ireland is the driving factor in recommending Ireland over Scotland. Also, it must be noted that Xia will be able to use transfer pricing between its US and Irish subsidiary (assuming Ireland is chosen) that will further enhance its net profits. Here Xia could report their profits in Ireland and thus be taxed there at the relatively low rate (10% versus 16% in the US), resulting in higher net profits.

The last two factors affecting the decision of where to expand are the measures of fiscal responsibility and of monetary stability. Scotland scores higher (just) on the first, and Ireland scores higher on the second. The main finding for these factors, however, is that both economies offer very attractive monetary and fiscal arrangements. The overall package for both economies is quite similar, although Scotland has some uncertainty associated with it due to the UK remaining outside the eurozone; we will address this issue in more detail shortly.

Thus, overall the analysis of the macroeconomic forecasts suggests choosing Ireland as the preferred location for expansion. This recommendation is driven in particular by the corporate tax rates available in Ireland for the foreseeable future.

Analysis 3: Projected exchange rate uncertainty

Turning to the third type of analysis for determining the best location for Xia to expand in, we examine six-month exchange rate changes over the past 5 years for the dollar in terms of euros, sterling and yen. These are the currencies that represent Xia's main markets, making up 80% of its current turnover. Some summary findings are given in Appendix 3. Overall, our analysis here indicates that the preferred location for Xia's expansion is Ireland.

We use summary statistics (average changes and risk of exchange rate change) to discuss the importance of exchange rate changes. Let us first look at the calculations and explain their relevance. We find that the lowest average exchange rate change $(\overline{x})$ occurs for sterling based on the following:

$$(1.8 + 1.6 + 3 + 2.3 + 2.1 + 1.7 + 2 + 3.2 + 1.2 + 1.8) = 2.07.$$

We find that the risk in exchange rate changes is lowest for the yen based on the following

$$\frac{1}{n-1} \sum_{x=1}^{n} \sqrt{(x_i - \overline{x})^2}$$

Where n is the number of six-month values (10 in this case).

Thus the risk for the yen exchange rate changes is

$$\frac{1}{9} \sqrt{\left[(2.8-3.45)^2 + \cdots + (4-3.45)^2 \right]} \quad = 0.575$$

We also report the largest (maximum) and smallest (minimum) exchange rate changes and note that sterling is associated with the smallest exchange rate change and the yen is associated with the largest rate change. Now let us interpret the figures. The dollar-sterling is the rate with the least level of uncertainty associated with it – it has a lower average value and reports the lowest minimum value. The dollar-euro has the next lowest level of uncertainty associated with it, and the dollar-yen has the highest level of uncertainty associated with it.

If Xia was deciding which market to export its products to, then the analysis suggests that exporting to the UK has lower foreign exchange exposure associated with it compared to the EU (including Ireland) and Japan. However, the issue at hand is where Xia should expand to. On this basis, if Xia chooses Ireland it would avoid higher exchange rate risk compared to choosing Scotland, because it would avoid the requirement of converting its currency from euros back to dollars. Furthermore, and the main reason for choosing Ireland over Scotland in this regard, is that the largest volume of trade that Xia has is in euros and, by locating there, they will eliminate all uncertainty associated with its euro trade. In contrast, its current volume of trade in sterling is only 25% (compared to 45% for the euro trade) and, thus, if Scotland was chosen, the amount of turnover associated with exchange rate uncertainty that would be eliminated would be smaller than if Ireland was chosen.

Thus, overall the analysis of the past exchange rate changes suggests choosing Ireland as the preferred location for expansion. This recommendation is driven in particular by the volume of trade it currently does in euros compared to sterling.

Further analysis: Expansion of Revenues

Relating to the previous analysis on the exchange rate changes we noted that Xia have a very heavy concentration of revenues being sourced from the euro-zone (and from the UK). Given that we are recommending that Xia makes its expansion in Ireland, we are now going to look at a related issue: would it be worthwhile for the company to move its production totally to Ireland at the expense of its current headquarters in Silicon Valley? However, it would maintain its headquarters and research and development facilities in Silicon Valley. Let us assume that each market is equally profitable on all considerations, with the exception of exchange rate uncertainty. In order to investigate this we gather further exchange rate data in euros and do some analysis. The values are given in Appendix 4, which details summary statistics for monthly exchange rates for the dollar, sterling and yen all in terms of euros. Results are given for a fourteen year period between 1992 and 2005, encompassing seven years before and after the introduction of the euro.

We also note that Xia's current trade is concentrated in, with descending order of importance, the EU, UK, US and Japan. In fact only 20% of its current trade is domestic (US based). Further analysis has suggested that this is due to the highly competitive nature of the US market and, in particular, due to other companies that are also based in Silicon Valley specialising in similar products. In fact, our analysis suggests that this domestic market will continue to be competitive and it may be difficult for Xia to increase its market share in the US. However, increased market share and turnover in its main markets is possible given our analysis. Thus we expect that the proportion of sales in the UK and EU will increase and that these markets represent strong growth opportunities for Xia in the future. Given this, and the fact that all markets are equally profitable we would suggest that Xia would not only expand in Ireland, but also it would actually relocate its current facilities there. It would then eliminate foreign exchange exposure for 45% of its current trade (that we project will actually increase in the future) in comparison to its current domestic trade of 20% (that we project will be constant or fall due to increasing competitive pressures).

Also we note from Appendix 4 that the uncertainty associated with trading with its second most important market, the UK, is actually lower than that of the US for the full period between 1992 and 2005. This lower level of exchange rate exposure is further enhanced in more recent times since the introduction of the euro, as the volatility of sterling-euro exchange rate changes has actually decreased on a monthly basis from 2.10% to 1.91% (in comparison, volatility in the dollar-euro has actually increased). Also, the company would be able to obtain the grants and support as a minimum noted in Appendix 2 and may actually be able to bargain for further support given that they are moving the majority of their existing staff there. Finally, by keeping its US headquarters, Xia can continue to exploit transfer pricing arrangements between the US and Ireland, while, at the same time, being able to reverse the transfer decision by keeping its intellectual capital in the US through maintaining its research and development facilities there.

Thus, our final recommendation is that Xia should consider going a step further than locating its future expansion in Ireland and that it should transfer the existing production facilities there. The main criterion for this recommendation is the fact that it would eliminate much of the exchange rate uncertainty associated with a large proportion of its trade in the Euro-zone.

Appendix I
Summary of Cash Flow Analysis for Xia Limited

	Ireland	PV(IRL)	Scotland	PV(SCT)
Year 0	−1000	−1000	−1000	−1000
Year 1	300	285.714	500	476.19
Year 2	200	181.406	200	181.406
Year 3	400	345.535	300	259.151
Year 4	600	493.621	400	329.081
Year 5	700	548.468	400	313.41
NPV		854.745	NPV	559.239
IRR		21%	IRR	18%
Profitability index		0.85475	Profitability index	0.55924

Appendix 2
Summary of Macroeconomic Forecasts for Xia Limited

	Ireland	Scotland	Winner
Inflation rates	3%	3.8%	IRL
Interest rates	3.5%	5.0%	IRL
POR	86/100	84/100	IRL
Infrastructure	81/100	93/100	SCT
Employees	91/100	91/100	−
Grants and support	$22m	$6	IRL
Taxation	10%	21%	IRL
Fiscal responsibility	96/100	97/100	SCT
Monetary stability	95/100	91/100	IRL

For each macroeconomic forecast a 'winner' is given between Ireland (IRL) and Scotland (SCT).

Appendix 3
Summary of Six-Monthly Exchange Rate Analysis for Xia

	Euro		Sterling		Yen
Mean	2.71	Mean	2.07	Mean	3.45
St. deviation	0.648845	St. deviation	0.620125	St. deviation	0.575905
Minimum	1.9	Minimum	1.2	Minimum	2.8
Maximum	4	Maximum	3.2	Maximum	4.5

The results reported deal with sample values. As well as the measure of risk (standard deviation) other summary measures of exchange rate changes are given.

Appendix 4
Summary Statistics of Monthly Exchange Rate Changes for Euro

	Minimum	Maximum	Average	Deviation
Full sample				
Dollar	−9.37	6.97	−0.09	2.86
Sterling	−4.52	10.69	−0.04	2.01
Yen	−11.23	7.89	−0.12	3.26
Pre-euro				
Dollar	−9.37	5.53	−0.20	2.82
Sterling	−4.52	10.69	−0.05	2.10
Yen	−11.23	7.89	−0.12	3.26
Post-euro				
Dollar	−5.62	6.97	0.01	2.92
Sterling	−3.93	6.46	−0.03	1.91
Yen	−7.24	5.68	−0.16	3.25

Values are given as monthly percentage changes. All currencies are quoted in euros. Deviation represents standard deviation of monthly values. The full sample is 1992–2005 inclusive with the pre-euro sample encompassing 1992–1998 and the post-euro period encompassing 1999–2005.

Case 30

Solution to Young & Co.

Maeve McCutcheon, University College Cork

CONFIDENTIAL REPORT ON THE FUTURE
DIRECTION OF YOUNG & CO

Prepared by: S Else
Consultant

For: Howard Young

Terms of Reference

This report is prepared at the request of Howard Young, managing director of Young & Co. It is based on information submitted by him and on discussions with Brad Masters, Lance Payne and David Little of that company. It contains an analysis of three options currently being considered by the company and is intended to inform discussion of those options at the forthcoming meeting of the board of directors. All calculations contained in the report are based on figures supplied by Howard Young.

Key Recommendations

- A management buyout is the best option for this company given the extent of the undervaluation of the business.
- If the buyout is to be undertaken you will need to commit €1m personally in order to ensure that you obtain control.
- Leasing the premises is unlikely to create value for this company.
- A combination of a share re-purchase and a special dividend is a good alternative to the buyout but this option does not give as much potential for gain from the company's good future growth prospects.
- You should review your company's dividend policy with a view to increasing your dividend payout ratio and avoiding financial slack.
- You should set a target level of borrowing which takes account of the tax advantages of debt.

Question 1

(a) Financial Analysis

The first step in considering the buyout recommendation is to estimate the value of the core business of the company. This type of valuation depends heavily on two key variables – the cost of capital for the core business and the estimates of growth. The detailed calculations are contained in Appendix 1.

At present the core business is not debt financed so the initial valuation is made on this basis. On the basis of the information supplied the business is most appropriately valued by separating the traditional and multimedia businesses as these are expected to follow different growth trajectories. Using the capital asset pricing model (CAPM) to estimate the cost of capital provides a cost of capital of 10% for the traditional business and a cost of capital of 12.5% for the multimedia business. The business is valued by estimating free cash flow in 2XX6 after allowing for tax payments to continue at a rate of 12.5% from 2XX6 onwards and based on a re-investment rate of 15% for both businesses. On this basis without assuming any further growth in the business beyond 2XX6 the share value is €24.29 which is close to the current market valuation.

This suggests that the current market valuation of the company does not make any allowances for future growth. If growth is projected at the rates which you suggest i.e. 2% for the traditional business and 10% for the multimedia business the value of the company is estimated at €32 .55 million or €32.55 per share. Much of the additional value comes from the multimedia business. Growth prospects increase the value of the company by €8 million of which €5million is generated in the multimedia business. Your belief in the higher share value is dependent on your belief in the ability of the multimedia business to generate this level of growth. However even if this area of the business were to grow at only 5% the business would still be worth €28 per share.

Assuming that you purchase at €28 per share and that 750,000 shares are purchased with you and the ESOT retaining your holdings, this would require an additional €11 million. This is after allowing for the €10 million released by the sale of the premises. Brad has indicated that he will advance €5 million which leaves a borrowing requirement of €6 million.

The breakdown of the financing is set out in Appendix 1. In summary as proposed by Brad the buyout would be one–third debt financed. It would seem at that level of borrowing the need for high-yield debt is questionable and that you could finance the deal at a rate lower than 9%. Even at that rate, interest payments of €540,000 per annum would be covered more than three times by earnings. You should also bear in mind that the borrowing would create a tax shelter which would add value to the company. The value in taxes saved can be estimated by multiplying the borrowing of €6million by the tax rate of 12.5%. This gives a value of €750,000.

(b) Personal impact of the buyout

A Management Buyout would have a number of significant effects on your own situation. Your shares would increase in value immediately but would be less liquid. Also you would be purchasing the company at a price considerably below what you believe it to be worth, giving you the potential for significant gains in the future which could be unlocked by a return to the market, while in private ownership you would no longer be under market scrutiny.

Your level of ownership would increase from 20% to 46% but a dispersed shareholding group would be replaced by a single large shareholder Brad with a holding of 41% and the ESOT's holding would also have increased to 11.6% giving them an effective casting vote. You should consider the merits of increasing your holding by investing an additional €1 million; this would give you effective control at 51% and would also reduce the reliance on debt.

A management buyout with your support and the support of the ESOT is likely to succeed unless a rival bidder emerges. In general the presence of the ESOT reduces the likelihood of a rival bidder being successful. In the event of a bidding war you could feel justified in paying up to €32.55 per share. In the event of a higher offer than this you should consider the merits of cashing out your holding.

Question 2

(a) Financial analysis

The lease rental of €500,000 gives a return of 2.5% on an investment of €20 million. For the lease option to make financial sense a significant capital gain is also required.

Appendix 2 shows the calculation of the NPV of a continuing €20 million investment in the Dublin property based on the assumption that the property is disposed of after year 10 and increases in value at 10% per year. This shows a modest NPV based on a these assumptions of just over €1 million. However if the property values are 6% less than anticipated the investment is no longer profitable. Even though this proposal has a positive NPV, the outcome is heavily dependent on an unreliable estimate of property values in eleven year's time. As you point out the company has little expertise in property investment. Shareholders will not benefit from diversification as we assume they are already diversified.

(b) The appropriate cost of capital

The return required on the investment in property reflects the risks of the investment, where property values are driven by speculative expectations those risks are high. The bulk of the return on property at present is based on speculative gains. The debt secured on the property increases the risk of the remainder of the property investment especially as the lenders have a first charge on the assets. For this reason the cost of the capital invested can be significantly in excess of the borrowing rate. In addition you should point out to Lance that it is the expected cost of capital which is used to discount cash flows. With the fixed rate above the variable rate it is expected that rates will rise in the future.

Question 3

You should bear in mind that investment decisions rather than financing decisions are what drive value creation. An appropriate dividend decision is one which supports the investment decisions of the company. At present the company foresees strong growth with a modest re-investment requirement of 15% so there is an argument for an ongoing increase in the regular dividend. An increase in the regular dividend will send the strongest signal to the market of the Management's perception of its future growth prospects. It appears that after the disposal of the premises and the dispersal of the proceeds this company can support both an increased level of gearing and an increased dividend payout for the foreseeable future. This would have the advantage of maintaining financial discipline as there are worrying signs that both the finance director and the employees representative are looking to create financial slack.

This will still leave the dilemma of what to do with the extra cash released from the sale of the premises. In the event of you selling the premises but not pursuing the management buyout option the options of a special dividend and a share re-purchase would both be possible vehicles for returning surplus cash to shareholders without raising expectations about the future path of dividends.

As the shares are undervalued the share re-purchase makes sense. However if shares are re-purchased you will need to ensure that the amount re-purchased does not put you into a position of having to offer for the remaining equity. The calculations in Appendix 4 show that at a buyout of above €8 million the shareholding goes above 30% at the current share price.

A special dividend would have clear tax benefits for the employees but may not be tax efficient for you or for the other shareholders. The company has not had a high payout ratio in the past and is likely to be attracting a clientele who do not favour dividends for tax reasons. It would also have the effect of leaving the current management structure unchanged. On balance given the level of undervaluation of the shares there are clear arguments in the event of sale of the premises for a share re-purchase of €8million and a special dividend of €2 per share. The employees would be rewarded with both a dividend a capital gain and a 50% increase in their level of ownership to 7.5% while you would move to 30% ownership.

Question 4

A management buyout is the best option for this company given the extent of the undervaluation of the business. At any share price up to €32.50 the buyout makes sense; however given the sensitivity of the value estimates to the projections for growth and re-investment requirements I would advise offering €28. I would also expect that borrowing rates could be pushed below the 9% currently being offered.

Maintaining the premises on the terms put forward by Lance makes no real sense for this company. You are effectively investing a sizeable amount of the company's equity in property. The NPV is positive but only on assumptions of continuing strong growth in property prices for the next ten years. This company has no expertise in property investment. There is no need for the company to be concerned about achieving diversification for shareholders we can assume that the shareholders other than yourself and the Employees are already well diversified.

A combination of a share re-purchase and a special dividend is a good alternative to the buyout but this option does not give as much potential to gain from the company's good future growth prospects and does not return control of the company to you.

The buyout should not be undertaken on the terms suggested by Brad as this would effectively give the balance of power to the employee share ownership Trust. If the buyout is to be undertaken you will need to commit €1 million personally in order to ensure that you obtain control.

Whether you go for a management buyout or a share re-purchase cum dividend I would recommend that that you review your company's ongoing dividend policy and capital structure with a view to unlocking the tax benefits of debt in the future and increasing your dividend payout ratio to reduce financial slack.

Appendix 1
Value of the company

Value of company = Value of Traditional Business + Value of Multimedia Business + unencumbered value of premises (€10m).

Calculation of costs of capital

Traditional	Re	5+(1.0)*5	10
Multimedia	Re	5+(1.5)*5	12.5

Cash Flow

2XX5   EBIT + Depreciation = 1910

Value of Traditional Business

1910 *0.90 =	1719
2XX6 estimate	1753
Tax at 12.5%	219 (Ignoring depreciation)
Cash Available	1534
Reinvest 15%	230
FCF	1304
Value with no growth	1304/0.1 = 13,040,000
Value with growth at 2%	1304.076/(0.1 − 0.2) = 16,300,950

Value of Multimedia Business

1910 *0.10	191
2XX6 estimate	210
Tax 12.5%	26 (Ignoring depreciation)
Cash Available	184
Reinvest 15%	27.57
FCF	156.24
Value with no growth	156.24/0.125 = 1,250,000
Value with growth	156.25/ (0.125 − 0.1) 6249.475

Value of business without growth
14,290,000 + 10,000,000   = 24,290,000
                                          = €24.29 per share

Value of business with growth
22,548,000 + 10,000,000   = 32,548,000
                                          = €32.55 per share

Appendix 2
Financing requirement assume €28 per share

			Ownership
Invested by Howard	200,000 * 28 =	5,600,000	46.7%
Invested by ESOT	50,000 * 28 =	1,400,000	11.7%
Invested by Brad		5,000,000	41.7%
Total		12,000,000	
Financed by debt		6,000,000	
Total		18,000,000	

Alternative scenario Howard invests an additional €1m

		Ownership
Invested by Howard	6,600,000	51%
Invested by ESOT	1,400,000	11%
Invested by Brad	5,000,000	38%
Financed by Debt	5,000,000	

Appendix 3
Valuation of Lease Option

Value of Lease in Year 11 based on eleven years growth at 10%

$20,000,000*(1.1)^{11} = 57,062,330$

T0	−20,000,000		−20,000,000
T1–T10	500,000*5.88923		2,944,616
T11	57062330*0.31728		18,104,736
		NPV	1,049,352

Change in Value

1,049,352/(0.31728)	= 3,307,337
% Change + 3,307,337/57,062,330	= 5.8%

Appendix 4

Total shares pre buyout		1,000,000
Number purchased at €24	10,000,000/24	416,666.7
Remaining number		583,333
Howard's holding	200,000	0.342857
ESOT holding	50,000	0.085714
Restrict to 30%		
Amount remaining	200,000/0.3	666,666.7
Number purchased	1,000,000 − 666,667	333,333
Cost of purchase at €24		8,000,000
ESOT holding		0.075

Case 31

Solution to the Good-to-Go Food Company

Maeve McCutcheon, University College Cork

**REPORT TO THE DIRECTORS OF THE
GOOD-TO-GO FOOD COMPANY
AN ANALYSIS OF THE BUSINESS PLAN**

Prepared by: Daisy May
The South Western Angel Network

For: Directors, Good-To-Go Food Company

Terms of Reference

The following report is based on the business plan which you submitted and your initial discussions with Sam Hall your business mentor. It contains a review of those projections and highlights some issues which need to be addressed in meeting the various targets which you have set yourselves. A suggested revised business plan is proposed which it is felt might have greater prospects of obtaining funding on acceptable terms. The report also highlights some important differences between venture capital funding and bank funding which you need to bear in mind in making financing choices. It is intended that this report will form the basis for your meeting with Sam scheduled for next week.

Key Findings

(a) The schedule of growth projected does not allow you as founders to retain control of the business.

(b) The salaries planned for the directors would raise a red flag to potential backers. Adjustments need to be considered.

(c) It is possible to achieve the level of projected growth and retain control by reviewing the roll-out in years one and two. However you will need to consider the impact that this may have on competition on the development of the franchise operation. A revised schedule is suggested which you will need to review carefully.

(d) Given the scale of funding required, the lack of tangible security and the risks of the business, venture capital funding appears more suitable than bank funding.

Question 1

(a) Financing needs

The business plan which you have presented shows the company growing rapidly and quickly becoming profitable but it requires a huge investment of cash up front. On the basis of the figures submitted you would need to obtain funding of €4 million immediately and a further €5.08 million at the end of year one – calculations are shown in Appendix 1. This is assuming that all profits are retained and no financing payments are required.

You need to consider the level of market penetration needed prior to the onset of the franchising operation as the franchising operation plays a vital role in financing future growth

(b) Financing terms

Based on the figures as they stand it is possible a venture capitalist could be persuaded to advance money on a valuation of ten times EBITDA. However you will need to present some coherent future plans beyond year six. This money would come in the form of convertible cumulative preference shares; that is, convertible into ordinary equity.

In addition to the preference dividend the VC would require conversion rights to give a 35% IRR. This means that the share of the company which they will take in year six will represent an annual growth rate of 35% on the money they advance.

Even on a relatively optimistic interpretation of these figures you would need to be prepared to trade 61% of the future value of the company in return for €9.08 million. This is assuming you receive the money in two stages with €4 million immediately and €5.08 million in one year's time. If all the funding were sought immediately the share required would rise to 71% (see calculations in Appendix 1). In addition you would need to pay a sizeable cumulative preference dividend over the period and would not be in a position to pay any ordinary dividend until year four.

You should realise that the ambitious growth projections in this schedule will be providing a hostage to fortune. The venture capitalist is likely to initially seek a seat on the board of directors. They will also tie their involvement to the project to the attainment of the targets. Thus it is likely for example that if the initial wave of roll-out is unsuccessful that they will delay or abandon the second tranche of funding. They will retain the right to replace you as directors at any stage if the company is not reaching its milestones. They will also insist that you sign a non-compete clause which will restrict you from setting up competing businesses for a period of years. They will reserve the right to be involved in the hiring of staff and may well insist on the hiring of someone with financial expertise.

Question 2

(a) Salary

A venture capitalist advancing funds to an entrepreneur will look for evidence of continuing commitment by the entrepreneur to the business. While you have shown plenty of evidence of commitment prior to the start-up of the company the manner in which you plan to take salaries out of the business would be likely to raise serious concern. Venture capitalists look for evidence that you are willing to tie your reward to future performance while your salaries as they stand are tied to growth. This gives you an incentive for rapid growth even if the machines are subsequently unprofitable. One solution here would be to tie the salaries to the roll-out of the franchise operation. If it were possible to defer salaries for a further two years you would enhance your ability to raise funding increase the value of the company at year six and reduce reliance on external funding. This would provide a valuable signal of intent to the venture capitalists.

(b) Growth

The ambitious growth projected is putting a severe strain on the ability of the company to fund growth while retaining control of the company. I have sympathy with your 'breakout' concept and would suggest that you go for the maximum installation in year one of 300 dispensers but then operate the dispensers for a two-year period in order to create space to market the franchise. Once the first dispensers are up and running you should focus on the franchise operation which would then allow you to fund any additional investment from retained earnings. Only when the franchise is fully rolled out would you set up the remaining machines.

I have completed a revised business plan (Appendix 2) which incorporates the growth trajectory and the revised salary arrangements discussed above. As you will see from this schedule the revised arrangement significantly reduce the amount of control ceded to 42.8%. Later investment i.e. year four can be funded either from retained earnings or through second stage finance.

Question 3

(a) Cost and Risk

The obvious problem with the bank's financing offer is that it is insufficient. It is difficult to raise debt finance for a company without a proven track record, and no assets to provide security. After all you haven't yet made any money and the machinery is too specialised for this purpose. While on the face of it both the bank and the venture capitalist are charging 10% there is a big difference between interest and a convertible dividend. The bank is securing its lending by personal guarantees which increases the personal risk of you as directors and of your families. The interest payments will need to be met as will the onerous repayment schedule and the loan is at variable rate adding interest rate risk. The bank is taking much less risk and charging less in consequence.

In relation to the venture capital funding you should be aware that the 10% preference dividend is additional to the conversion option so the venture capitalists have an option to take a part of the company as well as the preference dividend. This compares to the Bank whose maximum payoff in addition to interest is repayment of their principal. In return for allowing the venture capitalist to share in the upside potential of the business you are gaining a more flexible financing arrangement which allows you forego the preference dividend when needed. However you will be bound by stringent covenants as detailed in the earlier discussions. For a risky business such as this one venture capital financing is usually more suitable.

(b) Broader considerations

Venture capitalists are active investors and will expect to play a part in the management of the company. While this may have implications for your own ability to control the business especially if you fail to meet targets it does offer opportunities to tap into a broad range of skills and connections which the venture capitalists possess. The funding for your company is likely to come from investors with experience in the food business and a network of useful connections. The equity option held by the venture capitalists aligns their interests with yours and will ensure that they strive to maximise the company value. They are also skilful at exiting investments and will be motivated to arrange a trade sale or an IPO which could allow you to cash out the business. Alternatively you could buy out their holding in year six and regain ownership of the company.

Appendix I

1) Calculation of Cash Flow requirements (before financing)

	Year I	Year 2	Year 3	Year 4	Year 5	Year 6
EBITDA	920,000	3,050,000	4,760,000	6,070,000	6,670,000	7,680,000
Tax		115,000	381,250	595,000	758,750	833,750
Cash	920,000	2,935,000	4,378,750	5,475,000	5,911,250	6,846,250
Machines purchased	200	300	100	100	0	100
Investment	4,000,000	6,000,000	2,000,000	2,000,000	0	2,000,000
Prior year's cash	0	920,000	2,935,000	4,378,750	5,475,000	5,911,250
FCF	−4,000,000	−5,080,000	935,000	2,378,750	5,475,000	3,911,250

2) Calculation of share required

Based on a total cash injection of €9,080,000

At an IRR of 35 % $40000000*(1.35)^6$ = **€24,213,781**
$50800000*(1.35)^5$ = **€22,778,890**
€46,992,670

Estimated value of company in year six €76,800,000
Share of VC 61%%

3) Calculation of impact of preference dividend

FCF	−4,000,000	−5,080,000	935,000	2,378,750	5,475,000	3,911,250
Preference div	400,000	908,000	908,000	908,000	908,000	908,000
Cumulative		400,000	1,308,000	1,281,000		
Available for ordinary				189,750	4,567,000	3,003,250

Appendix 2
Revised Business Plan

1. Revised Schedule for roll-out of machines

	Year 1	Year 2	Year 3	Year 4	Year 5	Year 6
Total	300	300	600	900	1200	1500
Franchise			300	600	700	700
Own	300	300	300	300	600	800

2. Revised Earnings Forecast

Forecast Profits

	Year 1	Year 2	Year 3	Year 4	Year 5	Year 6
Gross revenue	7,200,000	7,200,000	7,200,000	7,200,000	14,400,000	19,200,000
Franchise Income	0	0	1,200,000	2,400,000	2,800,000	2,800,000
Revenue	7,200,000	7,200,000	8,400,000	9,600,000	17,200,000	22,000,000
Cost of sales	4,320,000	4,320,000	4,320,000	4,320,000	8,640,000	11,520,000
Distribution	450,000	450,000	450,000	450,000	900,000	1,200,000
Advertising	500,000	500,000	100,000	100,000	100,000	100,000
Salaries*	0	0	300,000	600,000	700,000	700,000
EBITDA	1,930,000	1,930,000	3,230,000	4,130,000	6,860,000	8,480,000
Tax		241,250	241,250	403,750	516,250	857,500
Cash	1,930,000	1,688,750	2,988,750	3,726,250	6,343,750	7,622,500
Investment**	6,000,000	0	0	0	6,000,000	4,000,000
FCF***	−6,000,000	1,930,000	1,688,750	2,988,750	−2,273,750	2,343,750

* Salaries tied to roll out of franchise.

** Roll-out based on revised schedule.

*** Covered by prior year's surplus.

3. Payment to VC

IRR of 35%

€6,000,000 * (1.35)^6 = 36,320,671

% of year six Valuation 42.8%

Case 32

Solution to Plastic Products

Derry Cotter, University College Cork

REPORT TO THE BOARD OF DIRECTORS OF PLASTIC PRODUCTS LIMITED SUBJECT: ALTERNATIVE EXPANSION ROUTES

B. Wyse
Finance Director

Contents

1. Internal expansion

Analysis of the proposed Plastech project:

(a) Payback period

(b) Accounting rate of return

(c) Weighted average cost of capital

(d) Recommendation on 'Plastech' project

(e) Sensitivity of project to level of fixed overheads

(f) Financing acquisition of machinery

2. External expansion

Evaluation of the proposed acquisition of Metal Fasteners Limited

(a) Valuation of Metal Fasteners Limited

(b) Recommendation and structuring of consideration package

(c) Evaluation of alternative methods of financing proposed acquisition

(d) Assessment of dividend policy of Plastic Products Limited

(e) Interest rate risk management

1. Internal expansion

(a) Payback period

The payback period can be computed by reference to Appendix 1. The net cash outflow at 31 July 2XX6 is €429,400. Of this amount, €424,960 is expected to be recovered by 31 July 2XX9. Therefore, the payback period is just in excess of three years.

(b) Accounting rate of return

One method of calculating the accounting rate of return is to compute the average annual accounting profit before tax, as a percentage of average investment over the lifetime of the project. This can be computed by reference to Appendix 1. The average annual profit equals ((total contribution − design costs − overheads − bad debts − discount allowed − depreciation) /4)

$$\text{Average annual profit} = \frac{(1,200,000 - 10,000 - 480,000 - 24,000 - 28,800 - 350,000)}{4}$$
$$= €76,800$$

Average investment = (Machinery cost − redundancy costs saved − scrapping costs saved − residual value of machine)/2
$$= €135,000$$

$$\text{Acc. rate of return} = \frac{76,800}{135,000} \times 100$$
$$= 57\%$$

(c) Weighted average cost of capital of Plastic Products Limited

The weighted average cost of capital (WACC) of Plastic Products Limited is 12% (see Appendix 2). This is computed using the market values of the company's existing sources of long term capital. The WACC will be used as the discount rate for the 'Plastech' project, for calculating its net present value (NPV).

(d) Recommendation

Neither the payback period nor the accounting rate of return provides a reliable basis for establishing whether the Plastech project should be accepted. Both of these methods of project appraisal fail to take the time value of money into account. It is preferable therefore to utilise a discounted cash flow method, the most reliable of which is net present value.

The net present value of the Plastech project is €67,500, as computed in Appendix 1. Therefore the project should be undertaken, as it should lead to an increase of €67,500 in the value of Plastic Products Limited.

It is assumed that the Plastech project involves the same level of risk as that of the 'average project' undertaken by Plastic Products Limited. If this is not the case, it may not be appropriate to use the Company's weighted average cost of capital to discount the project's cash flows.

(e) *Sensitivity analysis*

One method of assessing the risk of a project is sensitivity analysis. In respect of the Plastech project, an important factor is the project's sensitivity to the level of fixed overheads. This can be evaluated by calculating the present value cost of fixed overheads, and expressing this as a percentage of the project's NPV.

The PV cost of fixed overheads can be calculated as follows;

- Annual relevant fixed overheads x annuity factor for 4 years at 12%
    - = €120,000 × 3.037
    - = €364,440
- Tax effect of annual fixed overheads x annuity factor for years 2–5
    - = €120,000 × 40% × 2.712
    - = €130,176
- PV of cost of fixed overheads = €234,264 (i.e. €364,440 – €130,176)
- NPV of project = €67,500
- Sensitivity of project to fixed overheads = (67,500/234,264) × 100
    - = 28.8%

Therefore the level of fixed overheads could increase by 28.8% before the NPV of the Plastech project would be reduced to zero.

(f) *Alternative methods of financing the acquisition of the machinery*

The machinery required at 31 July 2XX6 can be acquired either by leasing or by outright purchase. The cost of these alternatives is examined in Appendix 4. As outright purchase has a lower PV cost, it is the preferred financing option.

2. External expansion

(a) *Valuation of Metal Fasteners Limited*

A detailed valuation of Metal Fasteners Limited is set out in Appendix 5:

	Earnings basis	**Assets basis**
	€	€
Value	7.5 million	2.16 million

(b) *Recommendation and consideration package*

There is a large difference in the valuation when using the two alternative bases. There is a strong case for revising the earnings valuation downwards, as the earnings for the year ended 31 December 2XX5 are significantly higher than previous years. Assuming an annual dividend of €100,000, and omitting the start-up year 2XX1, the average after tax earnings in previous years was €299,000. This could be increased to €389,000* if expected synergy benefits are included. A reasonable compromise might be to apply an equal weighting to 2XX5 earnings and to the average earnings of previous years.

A revised earnings valuation would be computed as follows;

$$[(389,000 \times .5) + (946,100 \times .5)] \times 8 = €5.34 \text{ million}$$

Average annual retained earnings in previous years = €199,000 (€596,000/3)
Add annual dividend of €100,000 + synergy benefits of €90,000
Average after tax profits in previous years + €389,000

Conclusion:

It would seem appropriate that Metal Fasteners Limited should be valued on an earnings basis, as future cash flows relate more to the firm's earnings than to its assets. The analysis above would suggest an approximate valuation of €5.3 million. This is €3.14 million in excess of the value of Metal Fasteners Limited computed on an assets basis. It should be considered therefore that Plastic Products Limited will incur a substantial loss should they be unable to operate Metal Fasteners Limited profitably after its acquisition.

Consideration package

In structuring the consideration package, Plastic Products Limited should endeavour to establish a link with the future profits of Metal Fasteners Limited. The purchase price should be at least partially dependent on profit targets being achieved. This will reduce the downside risk incurred by Plastic Products Limited, and may encourage George Simpson to retain an interest in the management of Metal Fasteners Limited, thereby ensuring that access to essential management expertise is retained.

(c) Financing the acquisition of metal Fasteners Limited

The proposed acquisition can be financed by a long term loan, or by flotation of the shares of Plastic Products Limited on the Alternative Investment Market.

• Long term loan

It seems that, at present, Plastic Products Limited does not have appropriate security to offer in respect of further loan finance. This may result in the Bank applying restrictive covenants. The Bank may establish certain financial parameters which must be achieved, e.g. times interest covered, debt: equity ratio etc. Failure to achieve these required targets could limit Plastic Products Limited's flexibility in relation to

---

* Revenue reserves at 1 January 2XX5 €596,000

its dividend policy or raising additional debt finance, and could place restraints on any further expansion. One significant advantage that would be obtained if loan finance were raised would be the related tax savings.

• *Flotation of shares on the Alternative Investment Market*

The major fear regarding a Stock Exchange flotation seems to be that the Company's shares will be under-priced, due to the use of income decreasing accounting policies by Plastic Products Limited. This would however be inconsistent with the concept of market efficiency. The semi-strong form of the efficient markets hypothesis states that share prices should reflect all publicly available information. Therefore, share prices should be determined by investors' expectations of a company's future cash flows. To the extent that accounting policy choice affects disclosed profit, but does not impact on future cash flows, it should not affect a company's share price.

It should be considered however that a Stock Market flotation will result in the existing shareholders suffering some loss of control, and in the board of directors coming under increased pressure to achieve short term performance targets. A Stock Market flotation is also not without cost, and inevitably results in a loss of privacy, as disclosure requirements of the Stock Exchange must be complied with.

(d) Assessment of the dividend policy of Plastic Products Limited

Shareholders in a company with a stock market listing expect a stable dividend, which increases gradually over time. Dividends are often perceived as a signalling mechanism, increasing dividends being a sign that management is optimistic about a firm's future earnings prospects. On the other hand, however, a decrease in a firm's dividend is often interpreted as 'bad news', and can result in a collapse in the company's share price.

Plastic Products Limited has a policy of paying an annual dividend equal to 30% of after-tax profit. By their nature, earnings are volatile, as is evident from the significant fall in Plastic Products Limited's earnings in 2XX3. A dividend policy which is based on a percentage of earnings will inevitably result in a wildly fluctuating annual dividend. This is not a suitable policy for a company with a Stock Market listing.

Should Plastic Products Limited intend to float its shares therefore, its current dividend policy will need to be reconsidered.

(e) Interest rate risk management

Should Plastic Products Limited decide to finance the acquisition of Metal Fasteners Limited by means of increased borrowings, it will need to consider its policy in relation to interest rate risk management. Presently, it is uncertain whether borrowed funds will in fact be required, as this is dependent firstly on whether Plastic Products Limited proceeds with the acquisition of Metal Fasteners Limited, and secondly on the use of debt to finance the purchase. While considering these options Plastic Products Limited may wish to protect itself against possible interest rate increases. This can be done by obtaining an interest rate option, giving Plastic Products Limited the right, but not the obligation to borrow funds at a pre-agreed rate of interest.

If raising debt finance becomes imminent, interest rate increases can be avoided by employing any of the following strategies:

- Sell interest rate futures on the London International Financial Futures Exchange (LIFFE)
- Arrange a forward rate agreement (FRA) with the company's bank. This will entitle Plastic Products Limited to borrow a specified amount of funds, for a fixed period, at a pre-agreed rate of interest.
- Once funds are in place, a fixed rate of interest can be agreed for periods of up to ten years or more. Unfortunately however, anticipated future interest rate increases will be reflected in the fixed rate.

Appendix 1

Time 31.07.	Machinery	Cap. Alls	Design costs	Contri-bution	Fixed O'Hs	Working Capital	Redun-dancy	Disc. Allowed	Bad debts	Scrap costs avoided	Taxation (excl. cap. allow-ances)	Net cash flow	PV factor @ 12%	DCF
2XX6	-400,000					-109,400	60,000			20,000		-429,400	1	-429,400
2XX7		32,000	-10,000	300,000	-120,000			-7,200	-6,000		-32,000*	156,800	0.893	140,022
2XX8		32,000		300,000	-120,000			-7,200	-6,000		-62,720	136,080	0.797	108,456
2XX9		32,000		300,000	-120,000			-7,200	-6,000		-66,720	132,080	0.712	94,041
2XX0	50,000	32,000		300,000	-120,000	109,400		-7,200	-6,000		-66,720	291,480	0.636	185,381
2XX1		12,000									-66,720	-54,720	0.567	-31,026
													NPV=	67,474

* (60,000 + 20,000) × 0.4
This represents the increased tax charge resulting from a fall in costs.

Appendix 2
Weighted average cost of capital

Source	Value €'million	% Value	% Cost	Proportionate cost
Equity	42	61.3	15.5 (note 1)	9.5%
Pref. Shares	15.7	23.0	6.7 (note 3)	1.54%
Debentures	10.8	15.7	5.6 (note 4)	0.88%
	68.5	100	WACC =	11.92%

Note 1: Cost of equity capital
Using the dividend growth model;

$$Ke = \frac{DIVI}{MVo} \times 100 + g$$

$$Ke = \frac{1.85M \times 30\% \times 1.14}{42M\ *} \times 100 + 14\% \text{ (note 2)}$$

$$= 15.5\%$$

* Net of discount and issue expenses

Note 2: Dividend growth rate
As dividends are a constant % of earnings, the dividend growth rate can be derived from the rate of earnings growth over the 4 year period 2XX1 – 2XX5

$$\text{Required PV factor} = \frac{1,100}{1,850}$$

$$= .595$$

This implies an average growth rate (using PV tables) of 14% over 4 years.

Note 3: Cost of preference shares

$$Kp = \frac{\text{Annual dividend}}{MVo \text{ (ex-div)}} \times 100$$

$$Kp = \frac{7}{104.5} \times 100$$

$$= 6.7\%$$

Note 4: Cost of Debentures

$$Kd = \frac{\text{Annual interest (net of tax)}}{MVo \text{ (ex-interest)}} \times 100$$

$$Kd = \frac{6}{108} \times 100$$

$$= 5.6\%$$

Appendix 3
Working capital

Plastic Products Limited has a choice of allowing three months credit to customers, or introducing a cash discount for payment within one month.

a) Three months credit

	€	
Debtors	145,500	(600,000 − 18,000) / 4
Finance Costs	17,460	(145,500* 12%)
Bad debts	18,000	
Total costs	35,460	

b) Discount for early payment

	€	
Debtors	89,400	[(600,000 / 12* 60%) + (600,000 − 6,000) / 4 * 40%)]
Finance Costs	10,728	(89,400 * 12%)
Bad debts	6,000	
Discounts allowed	7,200	(600,000 * 60% * 2%)
Total costs	23,928	

As total costs of the discount policy option are lower, a cash discount of 2% should be allowed for payment within one month. This will give rise to annual savings of €11,532.

Therefore, the total investment in working capital at 31 July 2XX6 will be:

	€	
Stocks	30,000	(600,000 * 50% * 10%)
Debtors	89,400	
Creditors	(10,000)	[(600,000 * 50% * 40%) /12)]
Total costs	109,400	

Appendix 4
Lease Versus Outright Purchase

The optimal financing option will be that which has the lower PV cost. This requires a comparison of the PV cost of leasing versus the PV cost of outright purchase, using the after tax cost of borrowing of 6% ($10\% \times (1 - .4)$) as the discount rate.

Leasing

PV cost of lease payments	= €130,000 × 3.673
	= €477,490
Less, PV of tax savings	= €130,000 × 40% × 3.465
	= €180,180
PV cost of leasing	= €297,310

Outright purchase

PV cost of purchase	= €400,000
Less, PV of capital allowances	= (€32,000 × 3.465) + (€12,000 × 0.747)
	= €119,844
Less PV of disposal proceeds	€50,000 × .792
	= €39,600
PV cost of outright purchase	= €240,556

Conclusion;

The machine should be financed by outright purchase.

Appendix 5
Valuation of Metal Fasteners Limited

Two alternative valuation bases are used for the valuation of Metal Fasteners Limited;

(i) Earnings Basis

An earnings valuation is computed as follows;
* Calculation of maintainable earnings of Metal Fasteners Limited
* Application of an appropriate P/E ratio to derive an imputed value for Metal Fasteners.

Calculation of maintainable earnings

	€
Profit after taxation	880,000
Less additional loan interest*	(27,500)
Add synergy benefit (after tax)	90,000
Add depreciation (€180,000 × 2%)**	3,600
	946,100

* An additional interest charge for eleven months should be levied in respect of the loan raised on 1 December 2XX5, as this will better reflect the finance costs going forward. The increased interest, on an after tax basis will be;

$$- €500,000 × 10\% × 11/12 × 60\% = €27,500$$

** Based on depreciation charge which will be avoided in 2XX6

Computation of an appropriate P/E ratio

A listed company in the metal industry has a price earnings ratio of 10 (€100m/10m). However, it may be appropriate to make adjustments to this P/E as follows;
* A premium of (say) 10% might be applied, as the valuation of Metal Fasteners Limited is in respect of a controlling interest.
* A discount of (say) 20% might be applied, to reflect the comparative lack of marketability of the shares of Metal Fasteners Limited.
* In view of its high gearing level, an additional discount of (say) 10% might be applied to the P/E ratio used in respect of Metal Fasteners Limited.

Taking the above factors into account therefore, a P/E of about 8 would seem reasonable.

Earnings' valuation

The imputed market value of Metal Fasteners Limited could be calculated as follows;

Maintainable earnings after tax × P/E ratio of similar quoted company

= €946,100 × 8

= €7.6 million, less once off rationalisation costs (after tax) of €120,000

= €7.5 million

(ii) Assets valuation

An assets valuation of Metal Fasteners Limited can be computed as follows;

	€'000
Balance sheet value of equity shareholders funds	1,476
Disposal value of premises in excess of book value	300
Increase in market value of land and buildings (1.3m − (1.1m − .18m))	380
	2,156

Case 33

Solution to Homemade Pies plc

John Cotter, University College Dublin

REPORT ON ISSUES FACED BY HOMEMADE PIES (PLC) AND THEIR EMPLOYEE PENSIONS

Prepared by: J Milkins
Consultant

For: Finance Director of Homemade Pies (plc)

1. Terms of Reference

Further to our discussions of xx/xx/xx, I present the report requested. With respect to the pension situation, we examine three different scenarios in valuing the pension fund of Homemade Pies and discuss the associated analysis. We first look at the most common valuation by calculating the present value of the assets and liabilities and the implications of the related analysis. We then measure the future value of the pension fund and comment on the various estimation issues involved and the related implications. For the third scenario, we illustrate findings for the case where we look at various different values for the inputs in scenario one and the resulting implications of changes in the inputs. We then turn our attention to the composition of Homemade Pies pension assets and comment on their risk and return attributes. Using the analysis of the company's pension assets and liabilities we discuss alternative pension schemes for the company in the future. In particular, we outline the attributes of a defined benefit scheme supported by the Pension Protection Fund (PPF) as an alternative to its current defined contribution scheme. The numerical analysis in the report relates to a set of figures provided by the finance director of Homemade Pies, are taken in good faith and have not been independently verified for the purposes of this report.

2. Recommendations

(a)   There is a (very) large pension deficit using today's prices and the company should be concerned by the contribution requirements for current employees.

(b)   This pension deficit would be difficult to eliminate and would require a very different set of assumptions than those used to do the calculations. Changing these assumptions to such an extent may not be plausible.

(c)   The company should examine and explore alternative pension schemes and compare these to the current defined contribution scheme in operation.

(d)   A defined benefit scheme, available in UK under the auspices of the PPF could offer a viable alternative to the defined contribution scheme.

(e)   Membership of the defined benefit scheme would allow the company to change its investment strategy and invest in riskier assets so as to reduce it level of pension insolvency.

(f)   The costs of joining the PPF are reasonably small and would be attractive to current employees who would receive their full pension entitlements.

3. Issues Relating to Homemade Pies (plc) and their employees pensions

Much of the analysis of this report is based on the time value of money and converting assets and liabilities into either future values or present values. In Appendix 1, assets are presented in their present value form, as they are given in current market prices, but, in contrast, liabilities are given as future values based on future contributions that must be made to current employees when they take retirement. In order to assess the attributes of the pension fund of Homemade Pies we will examine three different scenarios and comment on the respective findings. (Throughout the following scenarios, it is assumed that the employees' expected pension payments represent a future liability, when, of course, given that the scheme is a defined contribution scheme, Homemade Pies is not actually obliged to make these payments if the value of the pension fund's assets is insufficient.)

Scenario 1: current value of pension

The current value of the assets can be obtained directly from Appendix 1 and is €10 million. However, liabilities of the pension are given in the context of their future contribution values and must be discounted by the time value of money. In this case we assumed that the discount factor is the same as the Fixed Income 'returns' in Appendix 1 of 3%. The timeframe that we do our calculations is based on the number of years of the scheme and we are going to simplify the calculations by dealing with one single time period of ten years (we could also deal with other timeframes and deal with for example, an assumption that the payments made yearly over the length of the scheme would be discounted on an annual basis). We also assume that converting the assets and liabilities into cash values is equivalent and is costless, although, obviously, there are different transactions costs and liquidity issues in trading equities compared to properties etc... Given these assumptions and the timeframe involved we suggest that a reasonable estimate of the liability contributions is

$$25m/(1.03)^{10} = 25m/1.34 = €18.65m.$$

As the net value of the fund is obtained using the value of the assets less the liabilities, we find that there is a negative value of €8.65m (18.65 − 10). This represents a deficit, and if Homemade Pies was audited at the moment it would represent an insolvent pension fund (as the value of the pension contributions in today's terms is exceeded by the liabilities). The problems facing Homemade Pies plc are even clearer when you consider a ratio of fund assets over liabilities of 0.536:

$$Assets/liabilities = 10/18.65 = 0.536.$$

This ratio clearly suggests that Homemade has difficulties at present with its pension fund. Essentially, employees would only receive approximately 50% of their pension contributions or approximately €12,500 from €25,000. As Homemade Pies are currently using a defined contribution pension scheme, this must be a worry for all stakeholders of the company. These figures and analysis are based on the assumption that current market conditions prevail, but even if there were changes they would have to be very large so as to change the overall assessment that Homemade Pies has a serious pension deficiency.

Scenario 2: future value of pension

The second scenario that we will explore is the future value of the pension fund. We will take one date like the first scenario; we assume this is ten years in the future.

We also are consistent with scenario 1 in terms of the discount factor and eliminate any trading costs that may exist. In this scenario, the future value of the liabilities is available, but we need to calculate the corresponding future value of the assets of the fund. We also make the assumption that the respective growth rate of the assets correspond to the respective expected returns of the assets in Appendix 1. Thus, given the current market prices of assets in Appendix 1, the expected future value of each of the pension's assets is

$$\text{Equity} - €5m(1.20)^{10} = €30.96m$$
$$\text{Fixed income} - €3m(1.03)^{10} = €4.03m$$
$$\text{Property} - €2m(1.20)^{10} = €12.38m$$

Combining these future values, the expected future value of the portfolio of pension assets is €47.4 million. This represents an average expected value of the portfolio of the pension assets.

Now if we want to work out the value of the Homemade Pies plc pension fund, we have to make an assumption on whether the expected returns will actually happen or not. Let's first assume that these outcomes will occur. Using the same analysis as earlier on we find a positive fund value with assets exceeding liabilities by €22.4m (47.4 − 25). There is a certain amount of good news for Homemade Pies plc in these figures, especially as they will not have a pension deficit based on the assumptions underlying the calculations. Also our ratio of assets to liabilities is 1.896 (47.4/25), suggesting that there is a big cushion between pension assets and pension contributions. On this basis, the employees of Homemade Pies should receive their full pension contributions. However, they must recognise that having a surplus in the pension fund implies that they are underutilising resources to grow the firm by using this excess for some other revenue generating scheme.

Our analysis thus far is based on the assumption that the expected returns are realised. However as we can see in Appendix 1 each of the assets has an associated risk with equities being most risky with a standard deviation of 20%, followed by property with 12% and even the Fixed Income securities have some variability with a risk measure of 3%. We should incorporate these levels of uncertainty of the pension assets into our analysis and there are a number of ways of doing this. One such way is to create a portfolio and estimate the portfolio returns and the portfolio risk. On this basis the portfolio returns are the weighted average of the individual assets expected returns given the amount respectively invested. On this basis, the portfolio return is .5(0.2) + .3(0.03) and .2(0.20) = 0.149 or 14.9%. Using this we can work out the future value using the same mechanism as before $10(1+0.149)^{10} = €40.10m$.

However, there is uncertainty associated by these investments and. in a portfolio context, (assuming the asset returns are uncorrelated with one another) we can use the previous expression to get a weighted average of each asset's individual risk

$$.5(0.3) + .3(0.005) \text{ and } .2(0.12) = .1755 \text{ or } 17.55\%.$$

Allowing for this uncertainty to grow during the lifespan analysed (assuming volatility grows in proportion with time) gives a potential level of uncertainty of

$$10(1+0.1755)^{10} = €50.37m.$$

Thus, in this case the future expected value of €40.10 has a range of uncertainty of €50.37 around it, using the same assumptions that the growth effects of returns and risk are the same. Obviously our analysis in estimating the future value of Homemade Pies plc pension fund would have to incorporate both the future value of the effect of the expected returns and risk. One such way to do this is to treat the risk as the deviation from the expected value and say that our expected returns are €40.10 million, with deviation plus and minus this estimate of the portfolio's standard deviation of €50.37 million. This creates two outcomes; the positive deviation case and the negative deviation case, and if the former is analysed, then Homemade Pies plc has excess assets over liabilities by a large amount, but in the negative case the value of the assets would be zero, implying an extreme deficit.

Scenario one is a more reasonable situation and is one that analysis would commonly follow, but scenario two shows the potential impact of risk on the pension's assets and there can be two effects arising from this: either a negative or positive effect.

Scenario 3: Changing assumptions of scenario 1

There are two assumptions relating to scenario one as they affect the measurement of liabilities of Homemade Pies (plc) pension' fund. We assumed that the life span of the pension contributions would be 10 years. This would represent an average estimate of the lifespan of an employee after they retire and would be less/more for any one employee. The discount factor utilised was the same as the yield or return on the fixed income securities and is related to prevailing current market conditions. (We also assumed 100 employees that were entitled to a defined contribution scheme in Appendix 1 and this was based on the current numbers of 102 and the view of the finance director that this represented a 'steady state' going forward, so we will not comment on this further).

First, looking at the time frame of the pension fund, we need to comment on mortality rates. We know that life spans are increasing and the average lifespan of males and females can be obtained. We also know that these average life spans vary for males and females so we need additional information on the numbers of male and female employees that Handmade Pies usually have in employment. However, if the average life span of Homemade Pies employees increases (decreases), then the period over which payments will be made will increase (decrease), thereby increasing (decreasing) the future value of the pension liabilities. So, assuming an increase in life expectancies, we find that, in this case, the present value of liabilities would be even greater than that calculated in scenario 1, implying a greater pension deficit and a lower ratio of assets to liabilities. This would make the restructuring of the pension fund an even more pressing problem for Homemade Pies. In contrast, if the average lifespan of employees is reduced, the reverse will happen, and the deficit will get smaller.

Second, if we examine the discount factor, we find that if we increase its value, then the present value of the liabilities will decrease, thereby reducing the pension deficit. In contrast, if the discount rate falls, then the present value of the fund liabilities will increase, implying an even larger deficit. One final note is that predicting future interest rates is a difficult issue and a detailed discussion of this is beyond the realms of this report.

Valuation of Pension Assets:

We now turn our attention to the types of assets chosen by Homemade Pies. First, we note that there are two types of assets chosen by the company. The choice of Fixed Income securities suggests that 30% of the pension fund is put into safe assets. In the context of the CAPM, these assets would be relatively risk-free assets: this is supported by having such a low level of risk associated with this asset class. The other assets – equities and property – can be considered as risky assets, implying that they offer relatively high expected returns but are also associated with relatively high levels of risk.

To utilise the CAPM, we would create a portfolio of these risky assets based on the proportions invested in them to get the estimate of the expected returns and the expected levels of risk. So for every dollar invested, the weight for equities is 5/7 and the weight for property is 2/7, and these would affect the expected returns and risk in a similar manner as when we calculated portfolio risk and return earlier. In order to calculate the expected return according to the CAPM we are, however, missing one estimate, and this is Beta. Beta will tell us the sensitivity between movements in our portfolio of equities and property relative to some market benchmark. We can, however, comment on what the size of the Beta may entail and how this may impact upon the asset portfolio of Homemade Pies. For example, if we find a beta of 1, then we say that the portfolio of risky assets for Homemade Pies moves by the same amount as the general market. If the beta is greater than 1, we have chosen relatively risky assets compared to some market benchmark. In this case our risky portfolio should have higher return and risk levels than the market benchmark. For a beta less that 1 we find that the market is more risky, with higher returns than the chosen portfolio. Homemade Pies should be aware of the composition of their pension assets and the likely outcomes in terms of risk and returns of their chosen assets.

Analysis of alternative pension schemes:

The final issue that we want to raise in our report concerns the alternative pension schemes available to Homemade Pies. This is the key issue in our report and our analysis earlier will help us advise the company on the relative merits of the alternative schemes.

First, if the company does not change from the defined contribution scheme, they will only have to pay on the basis of the market value of the assets. In this case, if we follow the most commonly applied analysis we will examine scenario 1. As we saw in scenario 1, Homemade Pies has a very large pension deficit, with liabilities far exceeding the value of the pension fund assets. In fact, employees would only be looking to be receiving pension entitlements of approximately half of the €25,000 that they could receive if the deficit did not exist. Homemade Pies, whilst legally obliged to pay only the amount of the value of the assets, must also take into consideration other factors. Paramount to these is the reputation that Homemade Pies has developed. They are seen as a stable and successful company and problems relating to pension payments would have adverse effects on the image of the company.

Given that their success is supported by having an image of being quality producers of food products, pension problems may tarnish their image.

The main alternative for Homemade Pies (plc) is to change the type of pension being offered to a defined benefit scheme. If they do this they also have the choice of becoming a member of the PPF. Let's first comment on the defined benefit scheme. For the defined benefit scheme they would have to pay €25,000 per employee over their retirement period. In terms of public relations employees would be much more supportive of the defined benefit scheme as they will not be affected by the uncertainties of the marketplace. This payment would have to take place regardless of the level of deficit on their pension fund. Thus Homemade Pies ltd would then face the dilemma of how to deal with this situation. Again let's concentrate on the findings of scenario 1. Three options spring to mind. First, they can move funds from other parts of the company's balance sheet to eliminate the deficit. This would solve the problem but mean that Homemade Pies would be removing capital from other areas of the business and this may affect the growth possibilities of the firm going forward. Second, they could allow the deficit to continue and hope that it is reversed as time passes. Essentially this would be following a 'do nothing' strategy but given the large negative working capital for the assets and liabilities of the pension fund, it would be a very optimistic outcome that is being hoped for. Essentially we would not recommend that the company would get involved in negative net present value projects. Also given the potential changes in the determinants of the liabilities such as length of pension and discount factor, we could actually envisage the situation getting worse rather than better.

The third strategy would be to join the PPF. This would also allow for an insolvency of the fund but in this case the Government backed PPF would ensure that payments would be made to employee's up to the value of €25,000. This figure is exactly in line with the payment contributions of the current pension scheme run by Homemade Pies. Thus the potential negative publicity of having an insolvent pension scheme would be reversed once it is realised that employee's pension rights are protected. Homemade Pies could also change their investment stance and invest in more aggressive and risky assets with the hope that they will experience more positive returns so that the pension deficit is reduced. If that happens, the insolvency issue is reduced, but again if the assets perform poorly, Homemade Pies are secure in the knowledge that their employee benefits will be covered. There is a cost to membership but the maximum levy would be €125,000 (€25 million liabilities * 0.5% levy). Whilst this is not negligible it does represent a relatively small price to pay given the other alternatives that are available and the extent to which the liabilities of Homemade Pies pension exceed their assets.

Case 34

Solution to Mega Meals Limited

Paul McDonnell and Donal McKillop, Queen's University Belfast

REPORT TO MR JAMES PENNEY ON THE FUNDING AND RISK OF TWO NEW INVESTMENTS OF MEGA MEALS LIMITED

Prepared by: A Management Consultant

For: Mr James Penney

As requested, this report has been prepared in a sectionalised format. In part (a), the financing of the Birmingham plant is considered, while in part (b), a similar analysis is undertaken for the US venture.

Part (1) – Birmingham Facility

Mega Meals requires €3 million for a period of three years in order to build the facility required to fulfil its obligations with respect to its contract with Sparks and Dempster. Subject to the information provided by the company, the required analysis of the funding decision is specified below.

(a)   Fixed or Floating Rate Finance

Following an initial proposal by Mega Meals' chief accountant that this investment be funded through floating rate funds, subsequent information relating to Mega Meals' ability to borrow at a fixed rate has been provided. Your main concern with borrowing at a floating rate appears to be the risk involved, in that if a rise in interest rates occurs, the cost of servicing the debt will rise. However, one also has to consider the fact that borrowing at a fixed rate is more expensive than a current floating rate. For example, the current floating rate available for Mega Meals to borrow the sum required is 7%, compared to a fixed rate of 9%. In addition, the potential for the debt servicing payment to be *reduced* (which would occur should interest rates fall) is removed whenever fixed rate interest is chosen.

Another factor to consider when deciding whether fixed or floating-rate borrowing should be used is the business risk of the company. While paying a premium to borrow at a fixed rate certainly is a hedge against the financial risk of a rising interest rate, in another sense, it may act not as a hedge, but rather as a speculative transaction with respect to the firm's business risk. For example, if a company (say, *company x*) operates in a highly competitive market, if the other participants in the market choose to finance projects through floating rate debt (particularly if the average firm in the market is highly geared), a fall in interest rates could lead to the company being placed in an invidious position concerning its cost base. While its competitors will benefit from the fall in interest rates, *company x* will not, potentially leading to a drop in sales or profit. Of course, on the flip side, should interest rates rise, *company x* will then be in a very favourable position; however, this has to be balanced against the fact that it paid a premium for the fixed rate in the first place. Whether the benefits of the interest rate rise outweigh the cost of this premium will vary from case to case. In saying this, it would seem that this concern does not apply to Mega Meals. Given that it has negotiated a long term contract with a major customer, the company is somewhat buffered against competition. Therefore, should fixed rate financing be chosen, the potentially deleterious effect on its business risk (described above) will not be a major concern.

Another factor to consider when choosing fixed or floating rate finance is the economic outlook. If one assumes that bond markets (the price of which determines interest rates) are frictionless and efficient, then, in one sense, it doesn't matter; the fixed rate offered will be equal to the risk-adjusted market expectation of the cost of the floating rate over the duration of the loan, and it is not possible to outguess the market. On the other hand, if one doesn't believe that this market is wholly efficient, then a consideration of future interest rates may be profitable. One method of doing this is by examining the yield curve, or the relationship between interest rates and the duration of borrowings. Under the pure expectations hypothesis, future interest rates can be calculated as the rates that will be required to make the interest rates match their duration depicted on the yield curve (assuming arbitrage opportunities are minimal). If one accepts this, then the fact that the yield curve is flat may indicate that future interest rates will actually fall (predicting a slowdown in the economy). However alternative explanations for the structure of the yield curve are possible (such as the liquidity preference, market segmentation and preferred habitat theories), meaning other factors may be considered. For example, inflation has been quite stable for a long time (although it has increased over the past couple of years, while still being at an historically low level), suggesting that interest rates will remain reasonably steady (in contrast to the 1970s, a decade of fluctuating, generally high inflation and interest rates). On the other hand, some commentators suggest the housing market appears to be overheating, which may cause interest rates to rise in the medium to long term.

Having considered all of the factors listed above, particularly paying heed to the low business risk involved in the project, I can recommend that fixed rate finance be used to fund this project. This will allow budgets to be determined accurately in advance and protect against the possibility that interest rates rise by more than a couple of percent over the next three years.

(b)   Consideration of Swap Opportunities

Given that it has been recommended that the project should be financed through fixed rate borrowings, it is important to consider the potential swaps suggested by the company's chief accountant. If the company borrows the funds directly from the bank, the interest rate on the debt will be 9%. Alternatively, the company may engage in a swap transaction, either directly with Cyco Ltd or through a financial institution. The annual interest rate will be reduced to 8.5% if the direct swap is undertaken, while the rate will be 8.75% if the financial intermediary is used (See Appendix 1 for details of these calculations). Before making a recommendation as to which (if any) of these alternative options be selected, I will explain the nature of swaps, together with their relative advantages and disadvantages.

A swap is a contract for two companies to exchange cash flows in the future. The rationale for doing this is that, by engaging in the swap, both companies will be in an advantageous position compared to, for example, the interest rates they could achieve on their borrowings if the swap had not been undertaken (even allowing for commission if the swap is arranged through a financial intermediary). The primary reason why this is possible may be explained by the concept of comparative advantage.

Comparative advantage may best be explained by considering the data supplied by Mega Meals' chief accountant. Cyco is clearly a more creditworthy company than Mega Meals, as it can borrow at a lower rate in both the fixed rate market (respectively, the interest rates available on a loan of €3 million are 7% and 9%) and the floating rate market (LIBOR+1% against LIBOR+2%). This suggests that banks attach a lower degree of risk, or a lower probability of default, to Cyco. However, Cyco can borrow at a rate 2% lower than Mega Meals in the fixed-rate market, whereas its borrowing rate is 1% lower in the floating-rate market. It is the fact that these numbers are different that gives rise to the potential for an interest rate swap between these companies. Cyco is said to have a comparative advantage in the floating-rate market, while Mega Meals has a comparative advantage in the fixed-rate market. This doesn't mean that Mega Meals can borrow at a lower rate in the fixed-rate market; rather, the premium that Mega Meals pays above the rate of Cyco is lower in this market than it is in the fixed-rate market. This apparent anomaly allows for the transaction described in Appendix 1 to be structured, resulting in gains to both Mega Meals and Cyco (should Mega Meals wish to borrow at a fixed rate and Cyco at a floating rate).

You may be wondering at this point how this apparently costless opportunity can exist if bond markets are efficient. After all, one would expect these opportunities to have been arbitraged away given that swap markets have been in existence for over twenty years. The key to solving this paradox lies in the fact that the rates quoted to Cyco and Mega Meals relate to different time periods. The floating rates are six-month rates, whereas the fixed rates are for a period of three years. In the floating rate market, the lender has the opportunity to review the rate of interest charged every six months, and should the creditworthiness of either company have declined in the intervening period, it will revise the floating rate available to the company upwards. In extreme circumstances, it may refuse to roll over the loan. These factors explain the difference between the borrowing rates available to the two companies. Over the next six months, there is very little chance that either Cyco or Mega Meals will default. However, statistical analysis shows that the probability of the company with the lower credit rating (Mega Meals) defaulting over the next three years is, relatively, much larger than the probability of the company with the higher credit rating defaulting (Cyco). This explains the difference in the spreads in the two markets.

Even accounting for this fact, the calculations appear to suggest that the swap is still a better alternative than directly taking out a fixed-rate loan. However, this is conditional on Mega Meals being able to continue to borrow at the currently available floating-rate. Should the lender adjust Mega Meals credit rating downwards at any point in the next three years, the fixed rate it appears that it will pay for the duration of the loan will, in fact, rise. The 'fixed' rate loan that appears to be the outcome of the swap has actually got a floating element to it. Of course, from Cyco's perspective, it has actually locked in the spread of 1.5% above LIBOR if a direct swap is undertaken. If Mega Meals should default, however, this benefit will be lost. This demonstrates that while some swaps may appear to be an opportunity to beat the market borrowing rate, the reality is somewhat different, and other factors (not least the relative creditworthiness of the counterparties and any financial institutions involved) need to be considered before proceeding.

Should Mega Meals choose to accept either of the mooted swaps, therefore, it is important to consider the risk involved, rather than making a decision solely on which appears to be the cheapest option. Firstly, if it undertakes the swap directly with Cyco, the risk of Cyco defaulting over the period of the loan is a relevant one. Given that Cyco is more creditworthy than Mega Meals (according to the market) this may seem like a minor consideration. In addition, the value of an interest rate swap tends to remain small (relative to the size of the loan) throughout its duration, as the principal is not at risk; just the exchange of cash flows involved. Also, Mega Meals must consider that its floating-rate lender may decide to increase the six-monthly rate charged. This will depend on how likely the lender believes Mega Meals is to default on the loan. Given the fact that the company has just agreed two lucrative long term contracts, it may seem unlikely that this will occur. However, the fact that the Sparks and Dempster agreement may be cancelled after two years may give some cause for concern. Should this be the case, it is very likely that the company's lender will increase the spread above LIBOR charged on the loan, resulting in an increase in the 'fixed' rate determined by the swap.

If the alternative swap, through a financial intermediary is undertaken the same factors must be considered. However, given that this institution has an AAA credit rating, the likelihood of its default on the agreement at any stage in the next three years is negligible. This fact must be weighed up against the increased cost of the indirect transaction.

(c) Recommendations with respect to the Birmingham facility

Even though the value of the swap is negative (whether it is taken out directly (−€123,933), or through a financial institution (−€144,588) – see Appendix 1, the qualitative factors must be considered before making a final decision. Given that a large proportion of the net worth of the owners is tied up in Mega Meals, it is important that the company hedge against risk, especially given James' apparently risk-averse outlook. (If the company was owned by well-diversified individuals, this may not be the case, as individuals can hedge against risk by adjusting their own portfolio). Having decided in part (i) that the correct decision is to proceed with fixed rate finance (for the reasons given above), it appears that Mega Meals should take up one of the swaps on offer. Of course, it has been noted that, while appearing to offer fixed rate financing, there still exists a floating element to the interest rate paid after the swap occurs. Given that Mega Meals short to medium term prospects appear good, however, it seems unlikely that lenders will reduce the company's credit rating over the next three years. However, given that the interest rate achievable using a swap (of either 8.5% or 8.75%) is within half a percent of the guaranteed fixed rate available, I recommend that this facility be funded directly through a loan with the company's bank. By doing this, while market risk remains (i.e. interest rates might fall), the credit risk (that either Cyco or the financial intermediary will default on the swap) is removed.

Part (2) – US Facility

Mega Meals requires $1 million for three years in order to fund the investment in its new American venture. James is worried that adverse movements in the EUR/USD exchange rate may cause the company problems, as the returns from this investment will all be dollar-denominated, while Mega Meals is located in the euro currency area.

(a)   Methods of hedging against foreign currency risk

James is right to be concerned about the foreign exchange risk inherent in the new American contract. In effect, the investment is in dollars, making it a dollar-denominated asset (as it will not be possible to export the products made in the Massachusetts facility). If a normal, euro-denominated loan is used to fund it, this will leave the company in an unhedged position with respect to movements in the real (inflation-adjusted) EUR/USD exchange rate. Changes in the real, rather than the nominal, exchange rate are what will affect this venture because it will generate the income for this investment in the US, while it consumes in Europe. For example, if the nominal exchange rate remains the same but inflation is higher in Europe than in the US, Mega Meals will suffer a real loss, as the price they receive for their American products will not rise as much as the price of goods at home. It is unlikely that this type of situation will prevail in the long term because of purchasing power parity (PPP); in its strongest (absolute) form, PPP suggests that a given tradable good (or basket of goods) should be the same price all over the world, or, in its weaker (relative) form, changes in the price of the good in one country will be mirrored by the exchange rate adjusted equivalent change in another country. While PPP may hold in the long run, in the short to medium term deviations from it often occur. Therefore, given the fact that a large proportion of James and Peter's capital is tied up in Mega Meals, I feel that it is vitally important that this exposure is hedged.

Economic exchange rate risk (which is foreign exchange risk that depends on movements in the real rate of exchange) is hard to manage because there are so many variables that can affect it. In addition, it is necessary to have reasonably accurate forecasts about future cash flows and exchange rates in order that an off-setting position is adopted. Given that this investment is an asset with relatively well-defined cash flows, the easiest way of hedging against foreign exchange risk is to match it with a dollar-denominated liability. This is equivalent to borrowing the money in dollars, rather than euro, to fund the facility's purchase. This can be done directly in the market, or by taking out a swap (details of these alternatives are discussed below).

Other methods of hedging against this risk might be through using forward contracts, futures or options. These derivative products can be used to take a position on a future exchange rate. For example, Mega Meals is worried about the dollar weakening against the euro. It could therefore use forwards or futures to 'lock in' an exchange rate today, or, for example, take a long position in put options that will pay off if the dollar falls below a certain level against the euro. The problem with these methods is that for them to be efficacious in hedging against foreign exchange risk, the size of the cash flows they are offsetting have to be known in advanced with a reasonable degree of accuracy. In addition, use of these types of products to manage the risk of an ongoing real investment will probably require the company to adopt a number of positions with varying times to expiry. Given that Mega Meals has no experience of foreign exchange management and, apparently, no active central treasury department, it is not recommended that the company should now adopt this procedure to manage the foreign exchange risk arising from the American expansion.

From an operating perspective, this venture is protected by the fact that the American facility's cost base is in the same denomination as its revenues will be received in. This means that should the real cost of living increase in the US, its competitors in the convenience foods market will also suffer an increase in costs, assuming they source their inputs locally. On the other hand, as mentioned above, Mega Meals' owners consume in euros, whereas the returns from this project are dollar-denominated. By matching a dollar-denominated liability with this asset, this will protect the company reasonably well from adverse movements in the exchange rate. One minor problem with this is the fact that the liability is nominally-denominated whereas the investment is in a real asset, which may weaken the efficacy of the hedge if exchange rates depart drastically from PPP. Given that the investment is only for three years, and the dollar and the euro are the most actively traded liquid currencies in the world, the probability of an enormous, damaging deviation from PPP is probably very small. Notwithstanding this, it appears that the best strategy for Mega Meals is to hedge the investment using a matching liability.

(b)   Consideration of alternative matching liabilities

In Appendix 2, details of the interest rate achievable to Mega Meals by taking part in swap agreements are given. If the company borrows directly from its American lender, it will have a fixed (semi-annual) interest rate of 12% on its €1 million loan. Alternatively, if it takes part in the swap with Widgets through a financial intermediary, this interest rate will be reduced to 11.25%, a saving of 0.75%. Finally, if the swap in undertaken through the financial intermediary, the interest rate achievable is 11.35%.

Before deciding on which of these options should be selected, it is important to consider factors other than the bare numbers. One issue is whether this should be a fixed or a floating rate loan. This issue was considered above with respect to the Birmingham facility, where it was decided that fixed rate financing was a better fit for Mega Meals profile. One additional factor has to be considered in this instance however; how the choice of a fixed or a floating rate affects the efficiency of the hedge. As mentioned earlier, fixing interest payments is a hedge against the interest rate rising, but if the interest rate does rise and the real interest rate remains constant, inflation is causing the increase. Correspondingly, given a fixed real rate of interest, a falling interest rate implies a falling rate of inflation. The upshot of all of this is that if a liability is being used to match an asset, the changes in the cash flows associated with the liability should, generally, correlate as highly as possible with the changes in the cash flows attributable to the asset. It may be the case that a floating rate will better achieve this objective with respect to the new American venture. On the other hand, it may be the case that changes in the operating cash flows of the asset do not correlate well with changes in the US interest rate. In addition, the company is protected if interest rates rise in the US, while, if interest rates fall, it does have a guaranteed income from its contract with Six-Twelve, assuming it remains in business. Given that this is a state-wide concern in a relatively stable market (convenience stores), it is probably fair to assume that there is little danger of Six-Twelve folding in the next couple of years.

Overall, it may be the case that a fixed rate liability is the most appropriate choice for Mega Meals, given the discussion above. However, it would be interesting to determine whether US dollar floating rate finance could be raised, and at what rate.

The discussion will proceed under the assumption that fixed rate finance is to be used, making the decision a choice between the three options identified in the opening paragraph of this section. As with the swaps in part (1), they are possible because of the concept of comparative advantage. Mega Meals has a comparative advantage in the euro borrowing market and Widgets has a comparative advantage in the dollar market, even though Widgets can borrow at a lower fixed rate in both markets and is, therefore, more creditworthy. One criticism of the comparative advantage argument for swaps expressed in the first part of this report is that, for a company paying a floating interest rate to its banks and swapping a fixed interest rate for a floating rate with a counterparty, the overall effect of the swap is not to 'fix' the interest rate paid, as the bank may downgrade the company's creditworthiness, causing the amount of interest paid by the firm to increase. This is not an issue in this case, however, as all the cash flows are expressed in terms of fixed amounts (relating to the fixed rates of interest). On the basis of consideration of this one factor, therefore, Mega Meals should structure the deal in such a way that it pays the lowest interest rate (11.25% if the direct swap with Widgets is undertaken). Before it chooses this option, it should also consider the additional risk involved.

As mentioned above, there are two elements of a risk when a swap is undertaken; market risk and credit risk. By taking out the loan at 12%, market risk is involved (as interest rates may fall), but credit risk is totally removed. If, say, the direct swap is undertaken, it is important to consider the credit risk that Widgets will default on the agreement. Given that Widgets obviously has a lower credit rating than Mega Meals, this means that there is less credit risk than if the opposite were true. In addition, the swap currently has a slightly negative value ($-€2,631$) to Mega Meals. However, when one examines the value of the swap by decomposing it into a series of forward contracts (See Appendix 2), Mega Meals' position becomes slightly less advantageous.

What the decomposition shows is that, currently, the early cash flow exchanges all have negative values for Mega Meals, while the final exchange (including the principal) has a positive value. This means that as time goes on the value of the swap to Mega Meals is likely to increase, making the default of Widgets a cause for concern. If a swap has a negative present value at any point, the default of a counterparty is not a problem; either the company will lose its obligation (with a negative value), or the defaulting company will sell its interest in the swap to another party. On the other hand, if a counterparty defaults whenever the swap has a positive value, this value will be lost. This is more of an issue with foreign currency swaps than for interest rate swaps because the principal is exchanged at the end in two different currencies. Given these facts, and the structure of the swap agreement, it may be wise for Mega Meals to choose the swap with the financial intermediary instead. The interest rate obtainable is only 0.1% higher (and it has a lower present value of −€4,410), but the financial institution has a blue chip credit rating and is extremely unlikely to default on its obligation during the duration of the swap.

(c)   Recommendation as to the funding of the US facility

Having considered the relevant qualitative and quantitative factors, I can recommend that the US investment is funded through the foreign currency swap with the financial institution identified. This will allow the company to borrow at a fixed rate 0.65% lower than is available from Mega Meals' bank, and the fact that the liability is in dollars will hedge against the foreign exchange risk arising from the investment in the American venture.

Appendix 1
Structure of Potential Interest Rate Swaps

The diagram above shows the structure of a swap that will result in Mega Meals borrowing (currently) at a fixed rate of 8.5% (0.5% lower than the rate available from the bank on a three year loan), and Cyco borrowing at a floating rate of LIBOR + 0.5% (also 0.5% lower than the six-month floating rate available from their bank).

One method of valuing the swap to Mega Meals is to consider it as a long position in a floating rate bond and a short position in the fixed rate bond. First, the continuous compounding LIBOR rate must be determined.

$$(1.025)(1.025) = 1.050625 = e^r$$
$$r = 4.9385\%$$

(As the LIBOR zero curve is flat, the same rate will be used to discount all future payments.)

The value of the floating rate bond, Bfl, is

$$€75,000e^{-.049385*6/12} + €3,000,000\ e^{-.049385*6/12}$$
$$= €3,000,000$$

The value of the fixed rate bond, Bfix, is

$$€97,500e^{-.049385*6/12} + €97,500e^{-.049385*12/12} + €97,500e^{-.049385*18/12}$$
$$+ €97,500e^{-.049385*24/12} + €97,500e^{-.049385*30/12} + €3,097,500e^{-.049385*36/12}$$
$$= €3,123,933$$

Therefore, the value of this swap to Mega Meals is −€123,933.

If the swap with the financial institution is chosen, the structure will be as shown in the diagram below

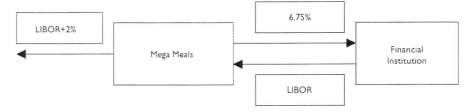

(There are no arrows to the right of the financial institution because we do not have information on the counterparty the financial institutional has identified to offset the risk created by the swap with Mega Meals.) The result of this is that Mega Meals will pay a fixed rate of 8.75% for the three year loan (assuming its six month LIBOR rate remains unchanged), a saving of 0.25% on the fixed rate available from Mega Meals lenders.

The value of this swap can be calculated in the same manner as described above. The value of the floating rate bond, Bfl, is

$$€75,000e^{-.049385*6/12} + €3,000,000\ e^{-.049385*6/12}$$
$$= €3,000,000$$

The value of the fixed rate bond, Bfix, is

$$€101,250e^{-.049385*6/12} + €101,250e^{-.049385*12/12} + €101,250e^{-.049385*18/12}$$
$$+ €101,250e^{-.049385*24/12} + €101,250e^{-.049385*30/12} + €3,101,250e^{-.049385*36/12}$$
$$= €3,144,588$$

Therefore, the value of this swap to Mega Meals is −€144,588.

Appendix 2
Structure of Potential Foreign Currency Swaps

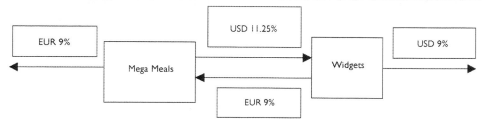

The diagram above demonstrates the structure of the foreign currency swap. The net result is that Mega Meals borrows at a rate of 11.25% in US dollars (a saving of 0.75%), while Widgets borrows at 9% in euros. This is 1.5% higher than the rate available to the company directly in the market, but whenever its dollar cash flows are taken into account (+ 2.25%); ignoring currency differences it also makes a net gain of 0.75%.

The value of this currency swap to Mega Meals may be estimated by treating the swap as a position in two bonds (as was done in Appendix 1), or as a series of forward contracts, as the swap is an agreement to exchange future cash flows. These are equivalent to forward contracts, which can be valued by assuming the forward price on the underlying asset is realised. Therefore, in order to use this method, forward exchange rates must be calculated using the interest differential. First, the continuous compounding US LIBOR rate must be determined.

$$(1.035)(1.035) = 1.071225 = e^r$$
$$r = 6.8803\%$$

This means the difference between the USD and EUR interest rates is (6.8803% − 4.9385% =) 1.9418%. The current spot rate is 1.3 USD/EUR. The forward rates are then:

6-month	$1.3e^{0.19418*0.5}$	=	1.312683 USD/EUR
1-year	$1.3e^{0.19418*1}$	=	1.32549 USD/EUR
18-month	$1.3e^{0.19418*1.5}$	=	1.338421 USD/EUR
2-year	$1.3e^{0.19418*2}$	=	1.351479 USD/EUR
30-month	$1.3e^{0.19418*2.5}$	=	1.364664 USD/EUR
3-year	$1.3e^{0.19418*3}$	=	1.377978 USD/EUR

The table below uses these forward rates, together with the cash flows involved in the swap to estimate its present value.

Time	EUR Cash flow	USD Cash flow	Forward Rate	Net Cash Flow (EUR)	PV (EUR)
0.5	34,615	−56,250	1.3127	−8,236	−8,035
1	34,615	−56,250	1.3255	−7,822	−7,445
1.5	34,615	−56,250	1.3384	−7,412	−6,883
2	34,615	−56,250	1.3515	−7,006	−6,347
2.5	34,615	−56,250	1.3647	−6,604	−5,837
3	803,846	−1,056,250	1.3780	37,325	32,185

(The continuous compounding euro interest rate (4.9385%) is used to discount the cash flows to present values.) Summing the value of the individual forward contracts underlying the swap, the total current value is −€2,631.

If the financial intermediary is used, the structure of the swap will be as shown in the diagram below.

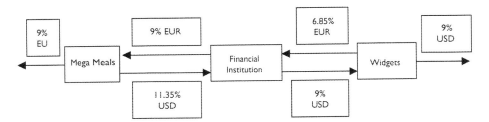

The net result is that Mega Meals pays 11.35% on its USD borrowing (a saving of 0.65% on the market rate), Widgets pays 6.85% on its EUR borrowing (also a saving of 0.65%), while the financial institution makes a net gain of 0.2% (11.35 − 9 + 6.85 − 9), ignoring currency differences.

The value of this swap to Mega Meals can also be determined by viewing it as a set of forward contracts. The result of this analysis is shown below.

Time	EUR	USD	Forward Rate	Net Cash Flow (EUR)	PV
0.5	34,615	−56,750	1.3127	−8,617	−8,407
1	34,615	−56,750	1.3255	−8,199	−7,804
1.5	34,615	−56,750	1.3384	−7,785	−7,229
2	34,615	−56,750	1.3515	−7,376	−6,682
2.5	34,615	−56,750	1.3647	−6,970	−6,160
3	803,846	−1,056,750	1.3780	36,962	31,872

Summing the present value of all the individual forward contracts gives a current value of −€4,410 to Mega Meals.

Case 35
Solution to Genero plc
Paul McDonnell and Donal McKillop, Queen's University Belfast

**REPORT TO DR MIKE O'REILLY ON THE
VARIOUS PROPOSALS RELATING TO
THE LISTING OF DERIVATIVE PRODUCTS
BASED ON THE SHARE PRICE OF
GENERO PLC**

Prepared by: A Management
Consultant

For: Mike O'Reilly

1. Introduction

In this report, a sectionalised format (as requested) has been adopted. In the next section, a general introduction to the nature of stock options, including a description of the factors that may affect their price, is provided. In the third section, the existence of upper and lower bounds on option prices is explained, together with the concept of put-call parity. These concepts are explained by making the various relevant calculations for the options proposed by Genero's bank. In the fourth section, the Black-Scholes option pricing model (BSOPM) is explained. Its assumptions and limitations are detailed, and it is used to calculate the likely price of the proposed stock options, given the data provided. In the fifth section, a method by which American options may be priced is discussed. In the sixth section, the exotic options which were queried are discussed, together with a method of determining a price for them. In the seventh section, three important option price sensitivities (delta, gamma and vega) are considered. Finally, some recommendations are contained in the seventh section.

2. Introduction to Stock Options

Options are a type of financial product whose value depends on or is derived from the value of another, underlying, asset. The price of stock options, therefore, depends on the value of an underlying stock. A call option is the right (but not the obligation) to buy an asset for a certain price, whereas a put option is the right to sell an asset for a certain price. A European option can only be exercised at the end of its life, while an American option can be exercised at any point in its life (note that this nomenclature is unrelated to the location of the option's listing, i.e. European options are available in the US and American options may be listed in European markets).

The fact that an option does not contain an obligatory component makes options quite different from other derivative products you may have heard of, such as forward contracts and futures. Purchasing an option does not commit the buyer to any future course of action should the price of the underlying security not move in his or her favour (in fact, no commitment exists even should the opposite be the case, but one may assume that if it is profitable to exercise an option, it will be exercised). In return for this privilege, however, the purchase of an option requires an upfront payment. The methods by which the quantities of such payments may be determined is the subject of the remainder of this report.

There are six factors that affect the price of a stock option. These are:

(i)   The current stock price, S_0
(ii) The strike price, K
(iii) The time to expiration, T
(iv) The volatility of the stock price, σ
(v)   The risk-free interest rate, r
(vi) The dividends expected during the life of the option

The strike price of an option is the price at which the underlying asset may be bought if a call option is held, or the price at which the underlying asset may be sold if a put option is held. This means that the payoff on exercise of a call option is equal to the difference between the stock price at that time and the strike price (as the option-holder can buy the asset at the (lower) strike price and sell it immediately at the (higher) market price. A consequence of this is that the value of call options will rise if the stock price rises and fall if the strike price rises (as if the gap is larger between the current stock price and strike price, there will be a better chance of the option's owner having a larger payoff on expiration). In contrast, the payoff to a put option on expiry is equal to the strike price less the current stock price (as the option-holder could buy the asset at the (lower) market price and sell it immediately for the (higher) strike price). This means that the current stock price and strike price have the opposite effect on the value of put options to their effect on call options; the value of a put option rises with as the current stock price falls and the strike price rises.

The next factor that affects option prices is the time to expiry of the option. If we consider two American (either put or call) options which differ only on their time to expiry, the holder of the option with the longer time to expiry has all the exercise opportunities of the short-life holder, plus more (after the short-life option has expired). This means that the longer-life option must be worth at least as much as the short-life option, or the value of the option increases with time to expiration. European put and call options are also, generally, more valuable as the time to expiry increases also. However, if we consider, say, two European call options, one with expiration date in one week and the other with expiration date one month henceforth, if the stock is going to pay a massive dividend, with the ex dividend date in three weeks time, the short-life option may be more valuable than the long-life option (as the dividend payment will reduce the payoff to the long-life option).

The volatility of an asset is the standard deviation of its continuously compounded rate of return in one year. Intuitively, this is a measure of how uncertain we are about the future price of a stock. If volatility is high, the chances of it doing very well or very poorly are increased. For a stock holder, these effects, in a sense, offset each other. For option holders, however, the downside uncertainty or risk is bounded because an option-holder's losses are limited to the cost of the option. For example, for the holder of a call option, the stock price might as well be K or zero; the payoff will be the same (zero). High-volatility stocks may be more likely to be around zero than low-volatility stocks, but they are also more likely to be greatly in excess of K, meaning a larger payoff for the holder of the call option. As the payoff structure for both put and call options is asymmetric in this fashion, their value always rises, ceteris paribus, with the volatility of the underlying stock.

The risk-free rate affects stock option prices in a slightly more subtle, less obvious fashion. As interest rates increase, the expected return required by stock investors tends to increase. In addition, the present value of any future cash flows attributable to an option decreases as the risk-free rate rises. The combination of these two effects means that the value of call options rises with the risk-free rate, while the value of put options falls as r increases. This analysis is based on none of the other factors relevant in determining stock prices changing, however. In reality, if interest rates rise, stock prices tend to fall, and vice versa. The net effect of an interest rate rise and stock price fall may be to decrease the value of a call option and increase the price of a put option. Alternatively, an interest rate fall and corresponding stock price rise may be enough to increase the value of a call option and reduce the value of a put.

Although the issue of dividends will not affect the options relating to Genero (as it doesn't currently pay dividends, nor does it plan to start at any point which may affect the value of the proposed options), their effect on option prices is simple, so I will briefly explain it for your own interest. The payment of dividends serves to reduce the price of stocks on the ex dividend date. Therefore, the value of call options is negatively related to the size of expected future dividends, while the value of put options is positively related to this factor. (For the remainder of this report, the issue of dividends will be ignored because of Genero's particular circumstances.)

The effect of the six relevant factors on the four main types of stock option is summarised in the table below.

Variable	European call	European put	American call	American put
Current stock price	+	-	+	-
Strike price	-	+	-	+
Time to expiration	?	?	+	+
Volatility	+	+	+	+
Risk-free rate	+	-	+	-
Expected future dividend payments	-	+	-	+

3. Existence of Bounds on Prices, and the Nature of Put-Call Parity

In the last section, the basic structure of the main types of stock option was explained, together with the factors that affect their price. In this section, we move on to discuss limits on the prices of these options, and another important concept in option valuation; put-call parity.

In addition to the six variables discussed above, it is appropriate at this point to introduce some additional notation:

(i) S_T is the underlying stock price on an option's maturity date

(ii) r is (now) the continuously compounded nominal risk-free rate of interest for an investment maturing in time T

(iii) C is the value of an American call option to buy one share

(iv) P is the value of an American put option to sell one share

(v) c is the value of a European call option to buy one share

(vi) p is the value of a European put option to sell one share

In the discussion below, it is assumed that there are no transaction costs, all net trading profits are subject to the same tax rate and that borrowing and lending are possible at the risk-free interest rate. While these do not correspond exactly with reality, they are reasonable approximations in a large, liquid market, whose participants will be expected to arbitrage away any such opportunities almost instantaneously.

Upper Bounds

First, it is possible to calculate upper bounds for the various options. An American or European call option gives the holder the right to buy one share of a given stock. This means that the option can never be worth more than the underlying stock, as if this were the case, an arbitrageur could buy the stock in the market and sell the call option to make a riskless profit. This implies that

$$c \leq S_0 \quad \text{and} \quad C \leq S_0$$

An American or European put option gives the holder the right to sell a share for K. this means that the value of these options can never be worth more than K; the maximum payoff to holding a put option is K, meaning it cannot be worth more than this. An American put option can be exercised at any time. Therefore

$$P \leq K$$

For a European option, a stronger bound exists for the reason that it cannot be worth more than K at expiration, which means that its price today cannot be greater than the present value of K, or

$$p \leq Ke^{-rT}$$

Lower Bounds for European Calls

It is possible to develop an expression for the lower bound of a (non-dividend paying) European call option by considering the following two portfolios:

> *Portfolio 1*: one European call option plus Ke^{-rT} in cash
> *Portfolio 2*: one share

The cash in portfolio 1 will grow to a value of K at the expiration date of the option. On this date, the call option will be worth $S_T - K$ if S_T is greater than K, or zero otherwise. This means the total value of the portfolio will be $(S_T - K + K =)$ S_T if S_T is greater than K, or K otherwise. Portfolio 2 is worth S_T at time T. Hence, portfolio 1 is always worth at least as much as portfolio 2 on the option's maturity date, and it may potentially be worth more. In the absence of arbitrage opportunities, this must also hold today, therefore

$$c + Ke^{-rT} \geq S_0$$

which implies

$$c \geq S_0 - Ke^{-rT}$$

In addition, a call option cannot have a negative value, as the worst that can happen is that it expires worthless. This means that $c \geq 0$, therefore

$$c \geq \max(S_0 - Ke^{-rT}, 0)$$

Lower bounds on European Puts

A lower bound on the value of a European put option (on a non-dividend paying stock) may be derived in a similar manner if we consider the following two portfolios:

> *Portfolio 3*: one European put option plus one share
> *Portfolio 4*: Ke^{-rT} in cash

At time T, portfolio 4 will be worth K if the cash is invested in the risk-free asset. At this point, the put option will be worth $K - S_T$ if K is less than S_T and zero otherwise. The value of the share is S_T. This means that portfolio 3, at time T, is worth

$$\max (S_T, K)$$

Given that this is always at least as large as the value of portfolio 4 at this time, it follows that it must be worth as least as much at every preceding point in time (assuming no arbitrage opportunities exist). This implies that

$$p + S_0 \geq Ke^{-rT}$$

or

$$p \geq Ke^{-rT} - S_0$$

A put option cannot have a negative value (as the worst that can happen is that it expires worthless). Therefore,

$$p \geq \max(Ke^{-rT} - S_0, 0)$$

Put-Call Parity

Having derived appropriate boundaries for the proposed European put and call options, at this juncture, it is appropriate to discuss another important condition on the relationship between the price of a European call option and a European put option. To do this, we consider two of the portfolios discussed earlier:

> *Portfolio 1*: one European call option plus Ke^{-rT} in cash
> *Portfolio 3*: one European put option plus one share

Both are worth

$$\max (S_T, K)$$

at time T, therefore both must be worth the same amount at every preceding time (assuming no arbitrage is possible) given that early exercise is not possible for either of the options. This gives rise to the condition

$$c + Ke^{-rT} = p + S_0$$

This relationship is known as put-call parity. It shows that if the price of a European call option is known the price of an equivalent put option (with the same strike price and exercise date) can be deduced from it, and vice versa.

Lower Bounds on American Options

First we will consider an American call option. We know from above that

$$c \geq S_0 - Ke^{-rT}$$

Given that the owner of an equivalent American call option has, at least, the set of exercise opportunities that the holder of the European option has, then $C \geq c$. Therefore

$$c \geq S_0 - Ke^{-rT}$$

Given that the nominal interest rate, r, must be greater than zero (else people would just hold cash), this implies

$$C > S_0 - K$$

If it were ever optimal to exercise an American call option early (on a non-dividend paying stock), then C would equal S_0 - K. Given that C is always greater than this (from the expression above), this implies that is never optimal to exercise an American call option on a non-dividend paying stock early. This can be explained intuitively as follows. If an investor (who wishes to hold the stock until the end of the option's period to expiration, at the least) holds an in-the-money American call option (that is, an option which if it were to be exercised today would have a positive payoff) with a certain time to expiration still remaining, he may be tempted to exercise the option today. However, if he waits until the expiration date, he will not have to pay the strike price until some time in the future. This is a saving, as the present value of the future payment of the strike price is less than the strike price today. In addition, there is a chance that the price of the underlying asset will fall below the strike price by the expiration date. If this happened, the investor would be happy he didn't exercise the option early. Further, if the investor does want to hold onto the stock in the long term, holding the call option acts as a form of insurance, in that the investor know he will not have to pay more than the exercise price of the option to buy the stock.

Even if the holder of an option believes the price of the underlying asset is going to fall, he is still better off selling the option rather than exercising it. The reason for this is that the option will be bought by another investor who does want to hold the asset (as there must be a demand for the asset given it has a positive price). This investor will be willing to pay more than the option's intrinsic value (which is the amount by which the current asset price exceeds the strike price) because, as we discussed earlier, the value of options increases with the time to maturity in the absence of dividends (this part of the option price, caused by a non-zero time to expiry, is known as the time value of the option).

The insight above produces the interesting result that the valuation of the American and European equivalent call options will be identical. As Genero will not pay dividends over their life, and the market has no expectation of payment either, the two types of option will have the same price, as, given that it is never optimal to exercise the American options early, they are, in effect, identical to the European options.

While this may be true for call options, it does not apply to put options. The lower bound derived for European put options is expressed in the equation

$$p \geq Ke^{-rT} - S_0$$

For an American put, the stronger condition

$$P \geq K - S_0$$

must hold, as immediate exercise is always possible. When the risk-free rate, r, is positive, it is *always* optimal to exercise an American put when $P = K - S_0$, as the option has no time value. This situation will only occur when the stock price is close to zero. At this point, there is little potential upside to the payoff of the option (as this is capped at K when $S_T = 0$), and the value of the loss in terms of receiving the payoff in the future rather than today is at least as great as the expected gain attributable to the small probability that the payoff will be larger in the future.

Application to Genero's proposed options

At this point, I will calculate the upper and lower bounds of the proposed options' prices, based on the information provided. The variables with an unchanging value used in this section are

(i) $S_0 = 11.03$ (as of July 2XX6)
(ii) $r = 0.025373156$ (See Appendix 2)

K will, of course vary, as a number of different exercise prices are proposed. The tables below give the lower and upper bounds on the value of the proposed options (which have been calculated by substituting the values of S_0, r and K directly into the formulae above).

Upper bounds for call options

	Time to expiry/ months	Strike Price/€			
		12	12.5	13	14
European Options	1	11.97465	12.4736	12.97254	
	3	11.92412	12.42096	12.9178	
	12	11.69935		12.6743	13.64924
American options	12	12		13	14

Upper bounds for put options

	Time to expiry/ months	Strike Price/€			
		12	12.5	13	14
European Options	1	11.03	11.03	11.03	
	3	11.03	11.03	11.03	
	12	11.03		11.03	11.03
American options	12	11.03		11.03	11.03

Lower bounds for call options

	Time to expiry/ months	Strike Price/€			
		12	12.5	13	14
European Options	1	0	0	0	
	3	0	0	0	
	12	0		0	0
American options	12	0		0	0

Lower bounds for put options

	Time to expiry/ months	Strike Price/€			
		12	12.5	13	14
European Options	1	0.944654	1.443598	1.942541	
	3	0.894121	1.39096	1.887798	
	12	0.669352		1.644298	2.619245
American options	12	0.97		1.97	2.97

4. Application of Black-Scholes Option Pricing Model (BSOPM)

The BSOPM was developed in the early 1970s by Robert Merton, Fisher Black and Myron Scholes. This model has revolutionised the way in which options are priced and traded, and has influenced the massive growth in derivative markets witnessed over the past twenty to thirty years.

In order to derive the formulae used to price European put and call options, a number of assumptions are necessary. These are:

1. The percentage change in the underlying stock price is normally distributed with mean $\mu \delta t$ and standard deviation $\sigma \sqrt{\delta t}$
2. It is possible to short sell securities and make full use of their proceeds
3. Transaction costs and taxes do not exist and securities are fully divisible
4. There are no dividends paid on the underlying asset during the life of the derivative
5. No arbitrage opportunities exist
6. Security trading is continuous
7. The risk-free interest rate, r, is constant and identical for all maturities.

The first assumption may seem odd, but, intuitively, all it means is that the stock has a constant expected return, and that the variability of the stock price in a short period of time is independent of the price. This type of process is known as a geometric Brownian motion (which is a type of stochastic, or quasi-random, process), and is consistent with weak form market efficiency (i.e. future changes in a stock price cannot be inferred from historical data) and the idea that investors require a constant (at any particular time) return on a stock based on its riskyness. This model conforms reasonably well with the empirical observation of stock prices.

Though the other assumptions do not exactly agree with reality (for example, transaction costs and taxes do exist, and securities markets are not constantly open), they are sufficiently close in many cases so as not to make a material difference. For example, if markets are deep and liquid enough, transaction costs are almost negligible. In addition, a number of assumptions of the model may be relaxed without affecting the validity of the Black-Scholes derivation. σ and r may be a known function of time, and the interest rate may also follow a stochastic process as well.

Given these assumptions, it is possible to derive the BSOPM by considering a portfolio that is instantaneously riskless. The reason that this is possible is that the price of the option and the stock price are both affected by the same underlying source of uncertainty, which is the movement in the stock price. In any sufficiently short period, the price of the derivative is perfectly correlated with the price of the stock. This allows a portfolio to be created such that the increase (or decrease) in the value of the stock will always exactly offset the decrease (or increase) in the value of the option position. Given that the value of the portfolio at the end of the period is known with certainty at the beginning of the period, the portfolio *must* earn the riskless rate of return in this period. To give an example, say the relationship between a small change in the share price, δs, and the resulting change in the value of a European call option, δc, is given by the relationship

$$\delta c = 0.5 \; \delta s$$

then an instantaneously riskless portfolio would consist of

1. a long position in 0.5 shares (i.e. owning 0.5 shares)
2. a short position in one call option (i.e. selling one call option)

At the end of the period δt, the value of the portfolio will be known with certainty as the changes in the value of the two elements of the portfolio will exactly counterbalance each other. One issue with this is that the relationship between δc and δs will only remain the same for a short period of time; whenever it changes it will be necessary to rebalance the portfolio. The fact that it is necessary to assume that such a portfolio may be costlessly and continuously rebalanced is one potential criticism of the BSOPM, given that everything follows from the insight that such an instantaneously riskless portfolio may be created. However, the more actively traded and deep option markets become, the closer the reality may conform with the assumption, as there will be arbitrage opportunities available to traders if such portfolios are not constantly balanced.

Following the assumptions above it is possible to derive formulae for the value of non-dividend paying European put and call options. These are (using the nomenclature from above, with the addition that σ is the annual volatility of the stock returns with continuous compounding)

$$c = S_0 N(d_1) - Ke^{-rT} N(d_2)$$

and

$$p = Ke^{-rT} N(-d_2) - S_0 N(-d_1)$$

where

$$d_1 = \frac{\ln(S_0/K) + (r + \sigma^2/2)T}{\sigma\sqrt{T}}$$

and

$$d_2 = \frac{\ln(S_0/K) + (r - \sigma^2/2)T}{\sigma\sqrt{T}} = d_1 - \sigma\sqrt{T}$$

The function $N(x)$ is the cumulative standard probability distribution function for a standardised normal variable, which is the probability that a variable with a standard normal distribution (which has a mean of zero and variance of one) will be less than x. The value of this function may be looked up in tables, or, alternatively, spreadsheet packages will provide functions that allow its value to be determined.

These equations may look complex, but in practice, it is simple to use them to determine option prices, as one simply has to substitute in the actual values for the parameters of the option. The expression $N(d_2)$ is the probability that the option will be exercised in a risk-neutral world (more of which will be discussed in the next section). The expression $S_0 N(d_1)e^{rT}$ is the expected value of a variable which takes the value S_T if S_T is greater than K and zero otherwise in a risk-neutral world. Therefore, intuitively, the expressions given for the value of put and call options above is simply the expected value of the payoff of the option on its expiration date discounted to a present value by the risk-free rate (as the expected pay-offs are calculated in a risk-neutral world).

Given that we have already ascertained that it is *never* optimal to exercise an American call option on a non-dividend paying stock early, we can also use the formula for call prices above to calculate the values of Genero's proposed American call options. As it may be optimal to exercise the American put options early, the put valuation formula cannot be used here (the standard BSOPM does not allow for the possibility that an option may be exercised in advance of its expiration date; the valuation of these options will be dealt with in the next section).

Using the formulae above, it is now possible to present a valuation for the proposed European and American call options. All the parameters required have been mentioned above, apart from the volatility of Genero's returns. This has been estimated at 15.8%, using the historic price data provided (see Appendix 1).

Estimated Price of Call Options

	Time to expiry/	Strike Price/€			
	months	12	12.5	13	14
	1	0.00748792	0.00057817	2.5748E-05	
European Options	3	0.07758299	0.02698284	0.00805072	
	12	0.43058021		0.19485961	0.07964443
American options	12	0.43058021		0.19485961	0.07964443

One interesting point clearly apparent from the table is that the value of all the one-month options is less than €0.01. The reason for this is that all the options are out-of-the-money (i.e. the current stock price is beneath the strike price), and that there is little time for the stock price to rise sufficiently such that there will be a likely payoff on the expiration date. One caveat is that these prices have been calculated using an historic volatility measure, using three years' worth of data. In reality, the market may attach a different implied volatility to Genero's stock price, as what happened to the share price three years ago may not be especially relevant to its current volatility (and the calculated volatility does seem quite low for a bioengineering stock). However, even if the market were to place a much greater volatility figure on Genero, the price of these options is so low that it is unlikely to make the options a much more valuable proposition (for instance, even if the market were to attach a volatility of 30% to Genero's shares, the price of the one-month option with an exercise price of €13 would be little over €0.01). Therefore, it may be the case that you wish to discuss with your bankers reducing the proposed exercise price of the call options, especially those with shorter periods to expiration. In this way, the intrinsic value of the options will be increased, thus raising their price.

Estimated Price of European Put Options

Time to expiry/months	Strike Price/€			
	12	12.5	13	14
1	0.95214157	1.44417573	1.9425672	
3	0.97170444	1.41794268	1.89584895	
12	1.09993265		1.83915809	2.69888895

As you can see, the estimated prices of the put options are greater than those of the equivalent call options. The reason for this is that the put options are all in-the-money (i.e., the current stock price is below the strike price), and thus have positive intrinsic value. Although these prices were calculated using the BSOPM formula for puts given above, they could also have been found by using the put-call parity relationship explained in the last section in conjunction with the calculated call prices. In fact, one may use this relationship to check the accuracy of the BSOPM workings.

5. Estimation of American Put Option Prices using a Binomial Tree Approach

In this section, the binomial tree approach to valuing options is described and subsequently used to place a value on the proposed American put options. The material in this chapter follows the approach taken by Cox, Ross and Rubinstein in a seminal 1979 paper.[1] In a binomial tree approach, we assume that at the end of each period, a stock can only have one of two possible values. This allows us to construct a riskless portfolio of a long position in a certain number of shares plus a short position in

[1] Cox, J, S. Ross and M. Rubenstein (1979), 'Option Pricing: A Simplified Approach', *Journal of Financial Economics*, 7, 229–264.

one call option. As the portfolio is riskless, we can easily calculate its present value by discounting its guaranteed future value at the risk-free rate. Once we know this, we can easily work out the value of the option as we know the current share price.

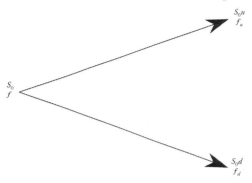

Consider the tree above. The current stock price is S_0. At the end of the period, the new stock price will either be S_0u or S_0d. The current option price is f, while its payoff if the stock price rises to S_0u will be f_u. If the stock price falls to S_0d, then the option's payoff will be f_d. If we create a portfolio of a long position in Δ shares and a short position in one call option, then the value of the portfolio at the end of the period if the share price rises will be

$$S_0u\Delta - f_u$$

If the share price falls, then the portfolio's value will be

$$S_{0d}\Delta - f_d$$

If the portfolio is riskless (i.e. its value at the end of the period is known in advance), then

$$S_0u\Delta - f_u = S_0d\Delta - f_d$$

or

$$\Delta = \frac{f_u - f_d}{S_0u - S_0d}$$

This is the ratio of the change in the option price to the change in the stock price as we move from the beginning until the end of the period. Next, we note that, given that this portfolio is riskless, its present value must be

$$(S_0u\Delta - f_u)e^{-rT}$$

while the cost of setting up the portfolio is

$$S_0\Delta - f$$

This implies that

$$(S_0u\Delta - f_u)e^{-rT} = S_0\Delta - f$$

or

$$f = S_0\Delta - (S_0u\Delta - f_u)e^{-rT}$$

Substituting for Δ and rearranging gives

$$f = e^{-rT} \left[p f_u + (1-p) f_d \right]$$

where

$$p = \frac{e^{rT} - d}{u - d}$$

These two formulae may be used to value an option if we choose values for u and d. Note that this method is independent of the probability of the stock moving up or down; the same result will be obtained no matter what this probability (which is determined by the stock's expected return) is. The reason for this is that the option is only being valued in terms of movements in the stock price. This price already incorporates all the information about the probability of future up or down movements. It is because of this fact that we are able to use the technique of risk-neutral valuation with respect to options, which I will now describe.

Though it is not necessary, it is helpful to think of the term p above as the probability of a rise in the stock price in the binomial model and $(1 - p)$ as the probability of a fall. This means that the expression

$$p f_u - (1-p) f_a$$

is the expected payoff of the option. Using this interpretation, the equation

$$f = e^{-rT} \left[p f_u + (1-p) f_d \right]$$

then means that the value of an option today is its expected payoff discounted at the risk-free rate. In addition, if p is the probability of an up-movement, then

$$E(S_T) = p S_0 u + (1-p) S_0 d$$

Substituting for p, we get

$$E(S_T) = S_0 e^{rT}$$

In other words, setting the probability of an up-movement equal to p is equivalent to assuming that the stock will grow, on average, at the risk-free rate. The value of the option can then be calculated by working out its expected payout and then discounting it at the risk-free rate. This process is known as risk-neutral valuation (mentioned in the last section), as in such a world investors require no compensation for taking on risk, meaning the expected return on all securities is just the risk-free rate. When we price an option using risk-neutral valuation, it turns out that its value is correct in the real world as well, as the value of an option is independent of the underlying asset's expected return.

Using this insight, we can use binomial trees to price options by choosing any value for u and d and calculating the risk neutral probability, p. However, in practice, we must choose these parameters so that the volatility of the stock in the model matches the volatility of the stock in reality. This is done by setting the variance of the return using the tree's parameters equal to the variance of the return based on the assumption that the stock follows the process described in assumption 1 in the last section. This gives the values

$$u = e^{\sigma \sqrt{\delta t}}$$

and

$$d = e^{-\sigma\sqrt{\delta t}} = \frac{1}{u}$$

where δt is the length of time between steps on the tree. Therefore, if we know the risk-free rate and the volatility of the stock, a binomial tree may be defined by the two equations above, plus (substituting δt for T in the equation above)

$$p = \frac{e^{r\delta t} - d}{u - d}$$

It is also possible to value put options in this way. This is done by calculating u, d and p from the volatility of the stock, risk-free rate and required time period, then calculating the discounted expected payoff of the option using the risk-neutral probabilities. In addition, it is possible to increase the number of steps in a tree indefinitely. For example, the diagram below shows an example of a two-step tree.

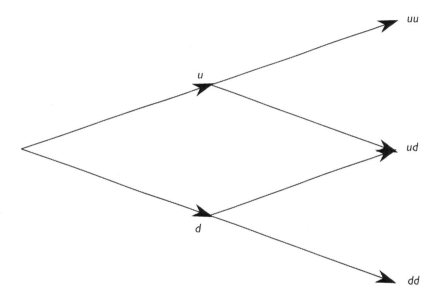

At each step, the probability of the stock price rising is p, and the probability of the stock price falling is $(1 - p)$. the tree can then be used to calculate the expected value of the payoff of the option (by finding the probability-weighted mean of the payoffs at the three right-most nodes), which can then be discounted at the risk-free rate to find the current value of the option.

By using a binomial tree, we are assuming that the time until the expiration of the option can be split up into a number of discrete time periods. Obviously, reality does not correspond to this. However, it can be shown that as δt tends to zero (or the number of steps in the tree tends to infinity), the solution for the option price obtained by using the binomial tree will converge upon the solution obtained using a continuous-time model (such as the BSOPM). This means that as the number of steps increases, the accuracy of the prices estimated using the tree will also increase (assuming the Black-Scholes assumptions above hold).

Another crucial advantage in using a binomial tree approach with respect to the pricing of American-style options is that a value for the option can be calculated at each node on the tree, by working out its discounted expected present value at that point. If we imagine the holder of an American option also has the ability to exercise the option at that point, it is also possible to calculate the payoff to exercising the option at that point. If this figure is greater than the option's expected present value, then it will be preferable for the owner to exercise the option rather than holding on to it. If this is the case, the payoff from exercise can be substituted for the present value of the option's expected payoff, while if the present value of the future payoff is higher, this substitution will occur. In this way, we can move backwards (from right to left), deciding at each point whether exercise is optimal and substituting if this so. By the time the initial node is reached, the expected value of the option at this point will be a price that reflects the American option holder's ability to exercise the option at any point up until the exercise date. By increasing the number of steps of such a procedure, the 'accuracy' of the estimated price is improved, not only for the reason mentioned above, but also because the tree will more closely replicate the investor's ability to exercise at *any* time as the number of steps increases.

Valuation of the proposed American put options

In Appendix 3, worked examples are given which demonstrate how to use the binomial tree method to value the proposed put options using four steps (i.e., assuming there are four discrete time periods within a year, at the end of each of which the option holder can choose to either exercise the option or hold it until the end of the next period). The table below shows the results from this analysis, but also demonstrates how the estimated price of the option changes with the number of steps used.

Number of	Strike Price/€		
steps used	12	13	14
2	1.23	1.97	2.97
3	1.15	1.98	2.97
4	1.19	1.97	2.97
5	1.16	1.99	2.97
10	1.17	1.99	2.97
20	1.17	1.99	2.97
50	1.17	1.99	2.97
100	1.17	1.99	2.97
500	1.17	1.99	2.97

The table demonstrates that as the number of steps in the tree increases, the estimated price of the American put options converges on a steady value (to the nearest €0.01). All of the prices above are greater than their European equivalent options' values, reflecting the fact that the holder of the American options has a greater number of exercise opportunities than his European-holding counterpart.

Finally, it is interesting to note that analysis of the American put with strike price €14 suggests that it is optimal to exercise such an option immediately. If the market were to agree with this conclusion, it doesn't make much sense to offer such a product, for the reasons given in Appendix 3 (although if the market attaches a different volatility to Genero's share price, it may not be the case that immediate exercise is optimal).

6. Exotic Options

To this point, we have discussed European and American put and call options. These are known as plain vanilla products, as they have standard, well-defined properties and are traded actively. In this section, we discuss the non-standard, or exotic, options that Genero's bank has suggested may be suitable for future listing, and outline a method by which they may be priced.

The first type of exotic option mentioned by the bank are barrier options. The value of barrier options is dependent on whether the value of the underlying asset reaches a certain level during a certain period of time. A down and in barrier option becomes active if the price of the underlying asset reaches a lower barrier at some point before the exercise date. A down and out barrier option remains active unless the stock price reaches some lower barrier before the exercise date. An up and in barrier option becomes active if an upper barrier is reached by the stock before the expiration date, and an up and out barrier option becomes inactive if the upper barrier is reached. Down and out and up and out options are collectively known as knock out options, and down and in and up and in options are collectively known as knock in options. These options may be put or call options, and may be attractive to investors interested in stocks in a volatile sector, such as bioengineering. For example, the seller of a down and out barrier option may believe that a particular stock is overpriced, or particularly volatile. If the value of the stock falls to the lower barrier, this means that the vendor's potential liability becomes zero. On the other hand, the purchaser of such a call option may find it attractive if she believes the stock price will rise, as this type of call will almost certainly be less expensive than an equivalent non-barrier option (as the two options are the same other than if the stock prices reaches the barrier, in which case the barrier option will expire worthless while the standard option remains active).

The second type of exotic option proposed is a chooser option. Chooser options give the holder the right to exercise it as a call or a put option. The date when this selection is made may be different from the exercise date, or it may be the same. This type of option may be valuable to an investor interested in the risky bioengineering sector because of its flexibility. If the asset price falls, the chooser may be exercised as a put. On the other hand, if the asset price rises, the chooser will be converted to a call option. In this way, a payoff from the option is almost guaranteed, but this is balanced against the fact that this type of option will be more expensive than its standard equivalents because of the greater opportunity set it confers upon its purchaser.

Lookback options depend on the either the maximum or minimum price of the underlying asset over the duration of the option dependent on it. The payoff from a European call lookback option is equal to the amount by which the expiration date asset price exceeds the minimum price of the asset over the period of the option and a European lookback put is equal to the amount by which the maximum price achieved by the asset exceed the expiration date asset price. For this reason, purchasing a lookback call is equivalent to 'locking in' the minimum price of the asset over the option period, while purchasing a lookback put, in effect, locks in the maximum price. Therefore, the former may be useful to someone who wishes to buy the asset, and the latter useful to a seller of the asset. For example, if someone was thinking of purchasing Genero shares as a long term investment but was concerned that its value was likely to fluctuate downwards in the short term, they could buy lookback call options, locking in the minimum price over the options' lifetime.

The final type of exotic options which have been mentioned are Asian options. Asian options are dependent on the average price of the underlying asset over the life of the option. The payoff from an average price call is the maximum of the difference between the average price and the strike price $(S_{avg} - K)$ and zero, while an average price put option has a payoff of the maximum of the strike price minus the average price $(K - S_{avg})$ and zero. An average strike call pays off the maximum of the end price and the average price $(S_{end} - S_{avg})$ and zero, and an average strike put pays off the maximum of the average price minus the end price $(S_{avg} - S_{end})$ and zero. These options may also be useful to speculators or hedgers in the bioengineering sector. For example, if a trader wished to invest in Genero but the funds to do so were not going to be available until a short period into the future, they could use average strike call options to guarantee that the price paid in the future was not any greater than the average price in the intervening period.

Although the options mentioned above may have analytical solutions, it also possible to use the Monte Carlo approach to value them. The Monte Carlo approach uses the risk-neutral valuation approach discussed in the last section. Using a computer, a large number of paths of the underlying stock price may be produced. These paths are based on the assumption that stock prices follow a geometric Brownian motion process, which was also assumed in the derivation of the BSOPM. The paths are constructed on the basis that the growth rate of the (non-dividend paying) stock is the risk free rate. The payoff to the option on the exercise date is then calculated for each of the large number of paths, and the mean of these payoffs is used as the estimate of the expected payoff. This is then discounted at the risk-free rate to a present value in order to estimate the price of the option. Of course, as the paths generated have a random element, this figure is also a random variable. However, as the number of paths increase, the standard error of the estimate will decrease such that the process converges on a single value. In practice, this convergence occurs slowly, as it can be shown that the standard error is proportional to the square root of the number of simulated stock price paths used. This means that, to halve the standard error, the number of simulations run must be quadrupled. Fortunately, there are other methods of reducing the standard error of the estimate.

To generate each step in the stock-price path (assuming geometric Brownian motion), the computer generates a random number, which corresponds to the uncertain part of the stock return. The antithetic variate technique involves calculating two estimates of the asset price for each random number generated; one calculated as normal, the other calculated by changing the sign of the random number. The reason this works is that if x is drawn from a normal distribution (which is used to create the stock path), $-x$ is equally as likely to be drawn. These pairs are use to calculate two different estimates of the option price, which are then averaged. The reason this is effective is that if one estimate is above the value that the Monte Carlo process will converge upon, the other tends to be below, and vice versa.

Another method of reducing the variance of the estimated option price using Monte Carlo is the control variate technique. The control variate technique is useful when an option without an analytical solution (say, option a) has a similar counterpart which does have an analytical solution (b). Basically, Monte Carlo estimates are obtained for the price of the two options. The difference between the analytic solution and the Monte Carlo estimate ($b_s - b_e$) is then added to the Monte Carlo estimate (a_e) of the price of the option with no analytic solution. As b_s is a constant, the variance of this new estimate will equal

$$Var(a_e - b_e) = Var(a_e) + Var(b_e) - 2Cov(a_e, b_e)$$

Therefore, the standard error of the new estimate will be smaller than the original Monte Carlo estimate if $2Cov(a_e, b_e) > Var(b_e)$. This will be the case if there is a high covariance/correlation coefficient between the Monte Carlo estimates of the two option prices. Therefore, this technique works best whenever the payoffs of the different options is most similar.

7. Option Price Sensitivities

In this section, three key option price sensitivities, which will be of interest to the holders of the options or investors in Genero, are discussed. These are delta, vega and gamma.

The delta (Δ) of an option was introduced in Section 5. It is the rate of change of the option price with respect to the change in the price of the underlying asset. It may already be apparent how important this measure is to someone who wishes to hedge a position in a stock or related option. If you recall, in the derivation of the BSOPM, it was assumed that an instantaneously riskless portfolio could be constructed, consisting of a short position in one option and a long position in a certain number of shares. This number is the delta of the option. In this way, the change in the price of the option will always be exactly offset by the change in the value of the shares, making it a riskless portfolio. Therefore, if one owns either the option or the share and wishes to hedge against the risk it will fall in value, if the delta is known it will be possible to construct a portfolio like the one described above.

For European options on non-dividend paying stocks, it is possible to calculate their deltas following the BSOPM. For such a call option (using the same nomenclature as in Section 4)

$$\Delta = N(d_1)$$

while for a put option

$$\Delta = N(d_1) - 1$$

Therefore, using delta hedging for a short position in one European call involves keeping a long position in $N(d_1)$ shares, or for a long position in a European call, a short position of $N(d_1)$ shares needs to be maintained. If a long position in European put options is held, then delta hedging requires that a long position in the underlying asset be maintained, while for a short position in put options, a short position in the asset should be maintained.

Using the formulae above, it is possible to calculate delta values for the European put and call options suggested.

Deltas of European Call Options

Time to expiry/ months	Strike Price/€			
	12	12.5	13	14
1	0.037768	0.003777	0.000207	
3	0.172016	0.071802	0.025084	
12	0.384579		0.211964	0.102355

Deltas of European Put Options

Time to expiry/months	Strike Price/€			
	12	12.5	13	14
1	-0.96223	-0.99622	-0.99979	
3	-0.82798	-0.9282	-0.97492	
12	-0.61542		-0.78804	-0.89764

(Although there are no analytical solutions for the delta (or other partial derivatives) of American options, it is possible to estimate them by using numerical methods.) By using these values, investors will be able to construct delta-hedges to protect their portfolios. When the stock price is close to the strike price of the option, the delta is much more sensitive to changes in the stock price than if the stock price is very high or very low (see below for more on this). This means that the portfolio must be rebalanced much more often in this situation in order to maintain the delta hedge.

The next key sensitivity we will consider is gamma (Γ). The gamma of an option is the rate of change of its delta with respect to the change in the underlying stock price. This is equivalent to the second partial derivative of the option price with respect to stock price. When gamma is small, delta changes slowly, and the adjustments required to keep a portfolio delta neutral (i.e., such that the change in the value of the options will exactly offset the change in the value of the underlying asset) will be quite infrequent. This occurs when the stock price is relatively high or low, described above. On the other hand, when gamma is high, delta will be very sensitive to movements in the stock price, implying a necessity to rebalance the portfolio much more often in order to maintain delta neutrality. Gamma is at its highest when the stock price equals the strike price of the option.

Gamma may also be used to balance a portfolio that may include Genero's shares. By comparing the gamma of such a delta-neutral portfolio (i.e. the second partial derivative of the portfolio value with respect to Genero's share price) with the gamma of an option which depends on the Genero share price, it is possible to introduce a number of options to the portfolio such that the gamma of the new portfolio is zero. (Of course, by doing this, the delta of the portfolio will depart from zero; this can be corrected by adjusting the quantity of Genero shares in the portfolio). The delta of this new portfolio will be much less sensitive to movements in Genero's stock price, reducing the frequency of rebalancing required to maintain delta neutrality.

For a European call or put option on a non-dividend paying stock, following the BSOPM, it is possible to show that

$$\Gamma = \frac{N'(d_1)}{S_0 \sigma \sqrt{T}}$$

where

$$N'(d_1) = \frac{1}{\sqrt{2\pi}} e^{-d_1^2/2}$$

The tables below show the values for gamma calculated for the proposed European options.

Gammas of European Put and Call Options

Time to expiry/	Strike Price/€			
months	12	12.5	13	14
1	0.163319	0.022347	0.001557	
3	0.292347	0.156987	0.067202	
12	0.219073		0.16613	0.102334

As gamma is the same for equivalent put and call options, only one table is necessary. As expected, as the exercise price of the option gets further away from the current stock price of €11.03, the gamma declines.

The final price sensitivity we will describe is vega (ϒ). Vega is the rate of change of a derivative (or portfolio of derivatives) with respect to the change in the volatility of the underlying asset. If vega is high, the derivative will be very sensitive to changes in the volatility in the underlying stock price, while if vega is low it will be relatively insensitive with respect to this factor. By comparing the vega of a portfolio with the vega of a derivative of a stock contained in the portfolio, it is possible to rebalance the portfolio such that it is vega-neutral; that is, the value of the portfolio will be insensitive to changes in the volatility of the underlying share price. However, a vega-neutral portfolio is generally not gamma-neutral (unless two or more traded derivatives dependent on the underlying asset are used). This means that the decision whether to use an option for vega or gamma hedging depends on the relative variability of the underlying asset's volatility (the greater this is, the more attractive vega-hedging becomes) and the frequency which the portfolio is going to be rebalanced (with gamma-hedging becoming more appropriate as the period between adjustments is increased).

Following, the BSOPM, it is also possible to calculate the vega for European put or call options. For non-dividend paying stocks

$$\Upsilon = S_0 \sqrt{T} N'(d_1)$$

Calculating vega from the BSOPM (which assumes the underlying volatility is constant) may seem odd, but the results from using this are very similar to the figures obtained from models which do not assume constant volatility; hence, we will produce the calculated vegas for our proposed European options below.

Vegas of European Put and Call Options

Time to expiry/	Strike Price/€			
months	12	12.5	13	14
1	0.002618	0.000358	2.5E-05	
3	0.014062	0.007551	0.003232	
12	0.042149		0.031963	0.019689

Similarly to gamma, vega increases with the underlying stock price up until the strike price, and then decreases. This pattern is, again, evident on consideration of the table above.

8. Recommendations

This report has provided an overview of stock options, some methods of calculating their value and a discussion of how their value may vary upon changes in the value of the variables that determine them. This analysis was applied to the options proposed by your bank. It is suggested that the listing of options dependent on Genero is a good thing, as it may attract investors to the company as they will be able to hedge their position using some of the strategies mentioned above. However, it appears that the American put option with strike price €14 should be exercised immediately. Therefore, it is recommended that this option is not listed. In addition, as Genero neither pays dividends nor plans to in the short-to-medium term, there is little point in listing both the American and European call options suggested. This may change in the future when the company begins to pay dividends, but there is currently no value in providing two such products. Finally, the addition of exotic options based on Genero may well be a worthwhile development in the future, as it will allow traders to tailor their strategies more precisely than if only vanilla options are available. However, given that both hedging and speculative strategies are possibilities with the plain options, I concur with the bank in their recommendation that the listing of the proposed exotic options be deferred until some point in the future.

Appendix 1
Calculation of Genero's Historic Volatility

One of the parameters required to estimate the price of options is the volatility of the underlying asset. The volatility of an asset is the standard deviation of its continuously compounded rate of return in one year. Often when an option has a market price, its volatility can be estimated using the BSOPM, as all of the other parameters in the model are known (this is known as the implied volatility). However, if one wishes to estimate the price of a stock option using the BSOPM, then, of course, it is necessary to have some estimate of the volatility of the stock price. In the question, we are given historic price data for Genero. This can be used to estimate its volatility.

In order to calculate the volatility of Genero's returns with the material provided, first the continuously compounded return for each monthly interval is calculated. Notationally,

$$u_i = \ln\left(\frac{S_i}{S_{i-1}}\right)$$

where u_i is the return in period i, S_i is the stock price at the end of the period and S_{i-1} is the stock price at the beginning of the period. Next, the standard deviation of the u_i's is calculated. This is used to estimate the volatility of the asset's returns through the formula

$$\hat{\sigma} = \frac{s}{\sqrt{\tau}}$$

where $\hat{\sigma}$ is the estimated volatility, s is the standard deviation of the u_i's and τ is the period between stock price observations in years. The table below shows how the sequence of u_i's are calculated.

Appendix 1
Historic Data Relating to Genero's Share Price, the Market Index, and the One-Month Euro Treasury Bill Rate

Date	Genero Share Price/€	Market Index	1 month T-Bill rate
Aug-03	2.57	3546	2.61
Sep-03	2.63	3477	2.45
Oct-03	2.91	3982	2.48
Nov-03	3.35	4952	2.44
Dec-03	3.34	4614	2.41
Jan-04	3.56	4887	2.40
Feb-04	3.84	5336	2.52
Mar-04	4.27	6184	2.50
Apr-04	4.52	6492	2.58
May-04	4.85	6976	2.52
Jun-04	5.11	7253	2.56
Jul-04	5.22	7092	2.55
Aug-04	5.50	7370	2.57
Sep-04	5.78	7614	2.64
Oct-04	5.82	7236	2.65

Date	Genero Share Price/€	Market Index	1 month T-Bill rate
Nov-04	5.82	6778	2.68
Dec-04	5.86	6420	2.73
Jan-05	5.89	6087	2.71
Feb-05	5.64	5212	2.68
Mar-05	6.02	5567	2.71
Apr-05	6.62	6307	2.69
May-05	6.82	6265	2.67
Jun-05	7.10	6363	2.68
Jul-05	7.66	6930	2.64
Aug-05	7.93	6951	2.64
Sep-05	8.17	6903	2.64
Oct-05	8.37	6796	2.59
Nov-05	8.03	5860	2.61
Dec-05	8.30	5849	2.63
Jan-06	8.84	6213	2.62
Feb-06	8.40	5260	2.58
Mar-06	9.52	6318	2.57
Apr-06	9.12	5432	2.55
May-06	9.81	5887	2.55
Jun-06	10.45	6251	2.56
Jul-06	11.03	6522	2.54

Next, the standard deviation of the monthly returns is calculated using the formula

$$s = \sqrt{\left(\frac{1}{n-1} \sum (u_i - \bar{u})^2 \right)}$$

where n is the total number of price observations. This gives a figure of 0.045651 for s. The final step in estimating the volatility is to divide s by $\sqrt{\tau}$. As one month is a twelfth of a year, $\tau = 0.083333$, $\sqrt{\tau} = 0.288675$, making the estimated volatility for Genero's returns, $\hat{\sigma}$, 0.045651/0.288675 = 0.158141, or 15.8%.

Appendix 2
Calculation of Continuously Compounded Annual Risk-Free Rate

In the information given, the current (July 2XX6) one-month Treasury bill interest rate is 2.54%. The calculation below shows how we find r, the annual risk-free rate with continuous compounding

0.0254/12 = 0.00211667 (monthly interest)
$(1.00211667)^{12}$ = 1.25697795 (compounded annual return)
ln(1.25697795) = 0.025373156 (annual interest with continuous compounding)

This means that r = 0.02537, or 2.537%. Given that the term structure is flat, this value of r can be used when calculating the value of any stock option, irrespective of its time to expiry.

Appendix 3
Calculation of the Value of the Proposed
American Put Options using Binomial Trees

Using the method described in Section 5, this appendix shows the trees used to estimate the present value of the proposed American options. Four-step trees are used, though if the number of steps were to be increased, the accuracy of the estimates would increase for the reasons discussed in section 5. The parameters used to construct the tree are:

(i) $\sigma = 0.158141$

(ii) $S_0 = 11.03$

(iii) $\delta t = 0.25$

(iv) $T = 1$

(v) $r = 0.02537$

The values of these variables imply that

$$u = e^{\sigma\sqrt{\delta t}} = 1.08228$$

$$d = e^{-\sigma\sqrt{\delta t}} = 0.923975$$

$$p = \frac{e^{r\delta t} - d}{u - d} = 0.52044$$

With these parameters, we can then construct the tree that will allow the value of the put option to be estimated.

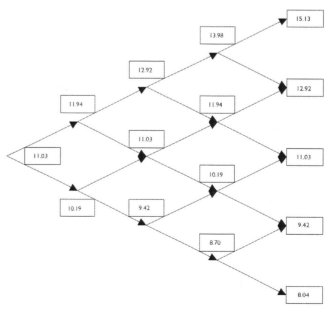

Figure 1

The tree depicted above shows the stock price path for Genero over the next year in a risk-neutral world. This can then be used as a basis for calculating, at each node, both the payoff from immediate exercise (on top) and the present value of the expected future payoff (below).

The larger of these (emphasised throughout in bold) is then used to calculated the present value of the expected future payoff at the node to the left, where the process is repeated until the initial node (representing the present time) is reached.

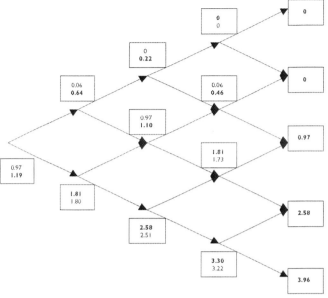

Figure 2

Thus this tree gives a current value of €1.19 for this option, as the present value of the expected future payoff of the option is greater at the initial node than the payoff from immediate exercise.

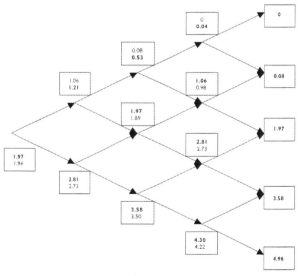

Figure 3

For this option, the estimated value is €1.97. Interestingly, this value is realised by exercising the option immediately, as its payoff now is greater than the present value of its future payoff if left unexercised. If investors believed this to be the case in practice, it would make little sense to trade this particular option, as no-one would buy them (as the real selling price will be slightly higher than its immediate payoff because of the vendor's selling costs).

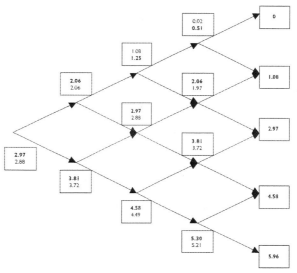

Figure 4

The option value this time is estimated to be €2.97, with immediate exercise also the optimal strategy.

A SURVEY OF GRAPHS

A SURVEY OF GRAPHS

by

W. A. SCANES, B.Sc.(LONDON), A.M.I.E.E., M.I.E.T.

Headmaster, Whitehawk County Secondary
School for Boys

ALLMAN & SON, LONDON

First published in 1967 by Allman & Son Ltd
50 Grafton Way, Fitzroy Square, London W1

MADE AND PRINTED IN GREAT BRITAIN
BY RICHARD CLAY (THE CHAUCER PRESS), LTD.,
BUNGAY, SUFFOLK

CONTENTS

PREFACE

IN our present age the use of graphs and of pictorial representation of facts and figures is increasingly apparent not only in science and engineering but also in commercial and publicity work. Even in our newspapers and on our television screens we see aspects of these subjects graphically presented to us and hence it is necessary for every secondary school student to have a working knowledge of graphical representation as a background to their general education. Furthermore, the great development of industry and its alliance with teaching and engineering, mathematics and science today make it imperative that students should have more than a "working knowledge" of graphs if they are to make any real progress in such careers as involve these subjects.

Last, but not least, is my desire to change a conception in some minds that graphs are an integral part of mathematics alone. That may, to a certain extent, be true, but a graph is a tool which can be used not only in mathematics but in almost every subject on a school timetable. Hence questions and problems given in this book cover history, geography (commercial and industrial), domestic science, sports and pastimes as well as engineering, mathematics and all branches of science. It must, however, be emphasized that these are intended to indicate some of the aspects of graphical representation, but make no attempt to cover all and every application. The scope of this book would, therefore, be of value to all types of secondary schools—modern, technical and grammar—comprehensive schools, technical and commercial evening classes as well as forming a useful reference book on graphs for all teachers of mathematics.

In conclusion, I should like to express my appreciation of the generous permission of:

(a) Mr. Shakeshaft of the Cavendish Laboratory of Cambridge for the use of his research data in the paragraphs relating to Sputnik 1.

(b) To Mr. E. Pawley (Head of B.B.C. Engineering Services Group) and the editor of *I.E.E. Proceedings* for permission to reproduce the two graphs on "V.H.F. Population Coverage" and "Growth of Broadcasting Receiving Licences".

(c) To Mr. J. P. Van den Bergh for permission to use food statistics published in *Progress*, the Unilever quarterly.

(d) To the Blaidell Publishing Company of New York, a division of Ginn and Company, for permission to reprint their notes on the history of graphs from *The History of Mathematics*, Vols. I and II by David Eugene Smith.

(e) To Mr. E. Piper of the Brighton College of Technology for assistance and advice in preparing the manuscripts.

W. A. SCANES

1

INTRODUCTION

Cartesian Co-ordinates

RENÉ DESCARTES, who wrote on mathematics and physics, was born at La Haye in Touraine on March 31, 1596, and died at Stockholm on December 11, 1650.

He combined algebra and geometry in that branch of mathematics known as analytical geometry; he also expounded and illustrated the general methods of solving equations up to the fourth degree and believed that his method could go beyond.

The method of graphical representation he developed is known as the Cartesian System. A similar system is found in many modern atlases and maps used by motorists and in the Grid System as applied to military map reading.

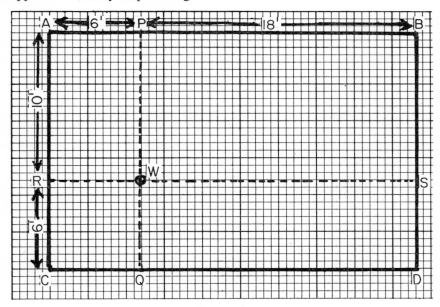

FIGURE 1

Plotting and Position

If *ABCD* represents a room (drawn to scale) and we wish to describe the position of any object in it, such as a wastepaper basket (*W*) it is not sufficient to say it is 6 ft. away from the wall *AC* and/or 18 ft. away from *BD* because the basket may be at any point along the line *PQ*.

Similarly, to describe it as being 6 ft. from wall *CD* and/or 10 ft. from wall *AB* would only result in a realization of the fact that it could be anywhere along the line *RS*.

But if we combine both these items of reference and say that the basket is 10 ft. from corner *A* along *AC* and 6 ft. from it, we position it exactly.

9

Hence the construction of a graph, which after all is only a pictorial representation of mathematical facts, is based on measurements from two basic lines known as the "axes". The point of intersection O is known as the "origin" whilst the two lines *AB* and *CD* are known, for algebraic convenience, as the *X* and *Y* axes respectively. (Note "axes" is the plural of "axis".)

Positive and Negative Numbers

Again for convenience, in algebra the position *OB* is known as the positive part and *OA* as the negative part of the *X* axis. Similarly *OC* is the positive part and *OD* is the negative part of the *Y* axis. All measurements are made from the point of origin "*O*" along all four portions of the

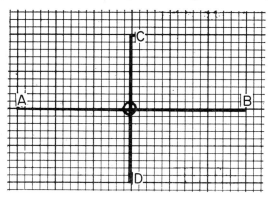

FIGURE 2

axes: hence our diagram becomes, with a suitable scale marked along it, as shown. Now if we wish to indicate the position of the point *P* (which is 4 units distant from the origin along the *X* axis and 6 units from the origin along the *Y* axis) we place the *X* value before the *Y* value as in the diagram.

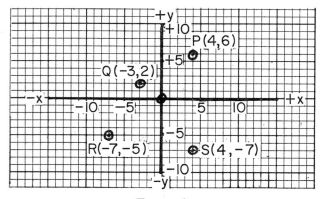

FIGURE 3

Similarly, *Q* is indicated by the figures (−3, 2) *R* by (−7, −5) and *S* by (4, −7).

The "*X*" distance (which is the first figure of the pair) is called the *X*-ordinate or abscissa whilst the "*Y*" distance (*i.e.*, the second figure of the pair) is the *Y*-ordinate; the two figures being known as the "co-ordinates" of the point under consideration. This, briefly, is the Cartesian System of plotting the position of points with reference to a given origin.

EXERCISES

1. By marking suitable scales along two axes indicate the position of points P (3, 5), Q (−3, 5), R (0, −4), S (−6, 0) and T (−2, −6).

2. Find the distance between the points (−3, 6) and (2, −6).
   Answer: 13

3. Plot the points A (3, 2) and B (−3, −2). Join them with a straight line and state at what point this line cuts the two axes.
   Answer: The origin
On the same graph join the points C (−2, 1) and D (0, −2) by a straight line. What do you notice about these two lines?
   Answer: They are at right angles
Plot the point E (2, −5). What do you notice about this point?
   Answer: It lies on the line CD
Plot the point F (4, 1). Join CF. What do you notice about the line CF?
   Answer: It is parallel to the X axis
Plot the point G (−2, −5). Join CG. What do you notice here?
   Answer: The line CG is parallel to the Y axis and at right angles to the line CF. The points C and G are the same distance apart as C and F
What are the co-ordinates of the point H which would make the figure $CFGH$ a square?
   Answer: (4, −5)

4. Plot the following points: A (−4, 7), B (−1, 7), C (−4, 2); and D (6, 2), E (−4, −1), F (6, −1), G (−4, −5) and H (−1, −5).
Join A, C, E and G. What do you notice about these four points?
   Answer: All four lie on the same straight line
Join CD and EF. What can you say about these two lines?
   Answer: They are parallel to each other and at right angles to the first line AG
Join B to H and state any observations you can now make.
   Answer: BH is parallel to AG and at right angles to both CD and GF
The lines CD and EF cut the line BH in points J and K respectively. Write down the co-ordinates of these points.
   Answer: $J = (−1, 2)$ *and* $K = (−1, −1)$
What is the shape of the figure $CJKE$?
   Answer: A square
What is the length of the following lines: AC, JD, EF and EG?
   Answer: 5, 7, 10 *and* 4 *units respectively*
What is the area of $JDFK$?
   Answer: 21 *square units*
Which is the greater distance, B to D, or H to F? (N.B. Measure against *either* the X or Y scales for comparison.)
   Answer: B to D
Join A to H. What are the co-ordinates of the point where it cuts the line EKF?
   Answer: (−2, −1)
Join AD. At what point does it cut the Y axis?
   Answer: (0, 5)

5. The point A (4, 5) is joined to the point B (-3, -6) by a straight line. Write down the co-ordinates of its mid point C.

    Answer: ($\frac{1}{2}$, $-\frac{1}{2}$)

6. The point D (-3, 3) is joined to the point E (3, -6) by a straight line. The point F is situated $\frac{1}{3}$ of the way along the line from E. Write down the co-ordinates of the point F.

    Answer: (1, -3)

Addition and Subtraction

We can use either the X or Y axis to indicate graphically the processes of addition and subtraction. Thus, if we wish to find the answer to the simple problem of $+8$ -4 -2 $+7$ $+1$ -5 -9 we can draw the axis with a suitable scale as shown in Figure 4.

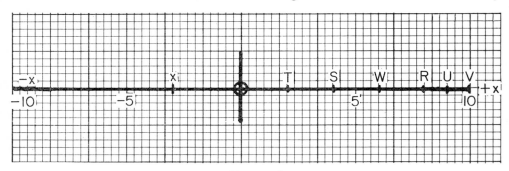

FIGURE 4

    It is fairly obvious from previous remarks that quite a good rule automatically develops, *viz:* "A change of sign is a change of direction." If we start from the origin to indicate positive numbers we move to the right, whilst to indicate negative numbers we move to the left.

    Now, back to our problem. Start from O and indicate a point R ($+8$) units away as shown. To indicate -4 we must move 4 units in the opposite direction, arriving at point S. Now move to position T which is -2 units away from S; then U which is $+7$ units from T; next V which is $+1$ from U; then W which is -5 from V and finally X which is -9 from W. We finish at the position $X = -4$ showing that the result of:

$$+8 -4 -2 +7 +1 -5 -9 = -4$$

EXERCISES

    Graphically obtain the results of:

1. 6 $+2$ -3 $+1$ -5 $+9$ -7
    Answer: $+3$

2. 3 -4 $+7$ -8 $+5$ $+2$ -9
    Answer: -4

3. -2 -1 $+5$ $+6$ -4 $+1$ -3
    Answer: $+2$

4. 5 $+4$ -7 $+3$ -8 -6
    Answer: -9

2

COLUMN GRAPHS

(Histograms or Bar Graphs)

Scales

IN the paragraph on "Plotting and Position" it was stated that "a graph is only a pictorial representation of mathematical facts". One of the simplest methods of portraying certain facts is by means of a "column graph" (Fig. 5).

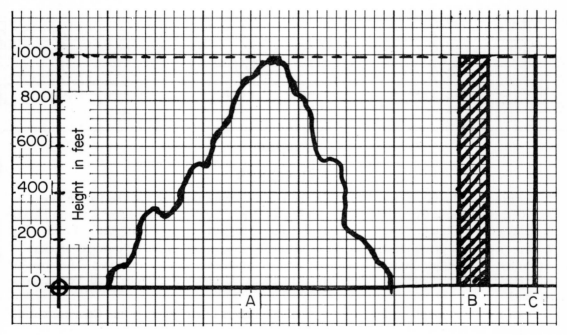

FIGURE 5

For example, the height of a hill 1,000 ft. high could be represented by a drawing such as at *A* with a suitable scale beside it to indicate its height; but it could equally have been represented with more economy of space by a simple column as at *B* (or even by a simple line as at *C*).

To take this further, suppose we wish to indicate graphically that the height of Mt. Everest is (approximately) 29,000 ft.; Mt. Kinchinjunga (also in the Himalayas) is 28,000 ft.; Mt. Logan in the Yukon is 20,000 ft.; Mt. Chas. Louis in New Guinea is 18,000 ft. and Mt. Kenya is 17,000 ft., we can construct the graph shown in Figure 6 (taking, for example, a scale of 1 in. = 10,000 ft.).

13

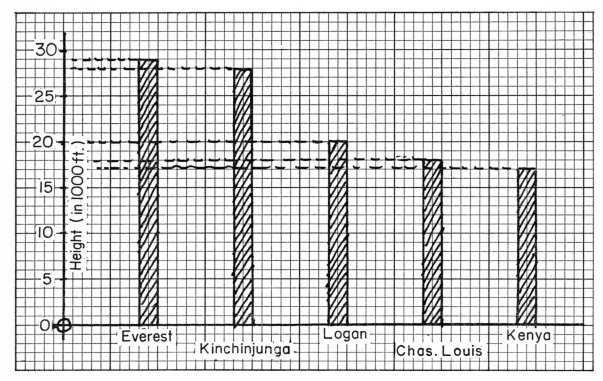

FIGURE 6

EXERCISES

1. Construct a column graph to show that the greatest depth (approx.) of the Pacific Ocean is 35,000 ft., the Atlantic Ocean is 30,000 ft., the Indian Ocean 23,000 ft. and the Arctic Ocean 18,000 ft. (Hint—draw columns downwards from base line to suggest depths utilizing the $+X$ and $-Y$.)

2. Draw a column graph illustrating the approximate populations of the following countries:
Argentina 20 millions; Bolivia 4 millions; Brazil 60 millions; Chile 7 millions; Colombia 13 millions; Ecuador $3\frac{1}{2}$ millions; Paraguay $1\frac{1}{2}$ millions; Uruguay 3 millions; and Venezuela 6 millions.

3. Draw a column graph to illustrate the relative numbers of emigrants to the Commonwealth countries from the United Kingdom in 1956.
Canada 43,400; Australia 32,400; New Zealand 11,500; S. Africa 4,900; E. and W. Africa 4,600; Central African Federation 5,200; India and Pakistan 3,100; Malaya 5,100; British West Indies and Bermuda 2,400; other Commonwealth countries 4,200.

4. By means of a column graph illustrate the approximate population (in millions) of the following conurbations, *i.e.*, continuous urban areas:
London $8\frac{1}{2}$; Berlin $3\frac{1}{2}$; Paris 4; Moscow 5; Tokyo 6; Cairo $2\frac{1}{2}$; Sydney $1\frac{1}{2}$; New York 10; Buenos Aires $4\frac{1}{2}$.

5. Construct a column graph showing the number of farm animals in the United Kingdom in 1954 (numbers in 100,000s):
Cattle 107; Sheep 229; Pigs $62\frac{1}{2}$; Poultry $836\frac{1}{2}$; Horses 3.

6. Construct a column graph to show the United Kingdom's exports of iron and steel products in 1954 (in thousand tons) to the following countries:
Australia 332; New Zealand 199; Canada 177; British West Africa 102; Netherlands 102; British East Africa 97; India 95; Pakistan 68; Denmark 83; Sweden 82; Norway 81; Finland 74.

7. Graphically illustrate the relative emissive powers of these surfaces when kept at 120°C:
Lamp Black 100; White Lead 100; Paper 98; Polished Platinum 10; Copper foil 5; Polished Silver 2.

8. Construct a column graph to illustrate the longevity of the following animals:
Tortoise 150 years; Elephant 70 years; Horse 62 years; Rhinoceros 47 years; Dog 34 years; Gorilla 26 years; Lion 25 years; Goat 17 years; Cow 17 years; Rat 4 years; Mouse 1 year.

9. Compare also in a similar way the length of life of birds, *viz*:
Cockatoo 90 years; Pelican 52 years; Eagle 46 years; Ostrich 40 years; Pigeon 35 years; Owl 27 years; Swan 25 years; Sparrow 14 years; Rook 9 years.

10. Compare by a column graph the speeds on land of the following animals:
Cheetah 70 m.p.h.; Jack Rabbit 45 m.p.h.; Racehorse 43 m.p.h.; Porcupine 2 m.p.h.; Greyhound 37 m.p.h.; Wolf 36 m.p.h.; Hare 35 m.p.h.; Pig 11 m.p.h.; Kangaroo 30 m.p.h.; Common Rabbit 25 m.p.h.; Dog 20 m.p.h.; Elephant (charging) $24\frac{1}{2}$ m.p.h.

11. Compare by a column graph the speeds of the following fish in water:
Swordfish 60 m.p.h.; Tunny 44 m.p.h.; Flying Fish 35 m.p.h.; Pike $20\frac{1}{2}$ m.p.h.; Salmon 25 m.p.h.; Trout 23 m.p.h.; Minnow 8 m.p.h.; Carp $7\frac{1}{2}$ m.p.h.; Sperm Whale 20 m.p.h.; Perch 10 m.p.h.; Stickleback $6\frac{3}{4}$ m.p.h.; Chub 5 m.p.h.; Octopus 4 m.p.h.; Eel $7\frac{1}{2}$ m.p.h.; Shrimp $\frac{1}{2}$ m.p.h.

12. Graphically compare the speeds of the following birds in the air:
Golden Eagle 100 m.p.h.; Golden Plover 70 m.p.h.; Falcon 62 m.p.h.; Mallard 60 m.p.h.; Lapwing 50 m.p.h.; Rook 45 m.p.h.; Kestrel 43 m.p.h.; Pigeon 39 m.p.h.; Gull 31 m.p.h.; Sparrow Hawk 25 m.p.h.; Woodcock 13 m.p.h.; Goldfinch 18 m.p.h.

13. Draw a column graph to illustrate the comparative approximate atomic weights of the following substances (Metals):
Aluminium 27; Calcium 40; Chromium 52; Copper $63\frac{1}{2}$; Gold 197; Lead $207\frac{1}{4}$; Manganese 55; Mercury $200\frac{1}{2}$; Nickel $58\frac{1}{2}$; Platinum $195\frac{1}{4}$; Silver $107\frac{3}{4}$; Tin $118\frac{3}{4}$; Zinc $65\frac{1}{3}$.

14. The speed of sound in feet per second for these materials is as follows: Air 1,090; Water 4,758; CO_2 850; Coal gas 1,680; Hydrogen 4,160; Oak 14,000; Mahogany 14,500; Deal 16,250; Brass 12,000; Glass 16,500; Pitch pine 1,250. Illustrate these facts by means of a column graph.

15. Construct three column graphs to illustrate the comparative specific gravities of the following solids, liquids and gases:

(a) *Solids* (Water = 1)
Ice 0·92; Ordinary brick 1·5; Chalk 2·5; Wood charcoal 0·33; Coke 1·00; Flint 2·6; Glass 2·7; Granite 2·95; Plaster of Paris 2·27; Porcelain 2·35; Sand 1·9; Tar 0·94.

(b) *Liquids* (Water = 1)
Sulphuric Acid 1·84; Nitric Acid 1·22; Milk 1·03; Hydrochloric Acid 1·20; Linseed Oil 0·94; Olive Oil 0·91; Petrol 0·89; Alcohol 0·79.

(c) *Gases* (Air = 1)
Chlorine 2·44; Carbon dioxide 1·53; Oxygen 1·11; Hydrogen 0·07; Ammonia 0·59; Coal gas 0·44; Nitrogen 0·97.

16. Construct a column graph showing the comparison in the England Test Match batting averages against the West Indies team in 1957 from the following data of runs:
Graveney 118; May 97·8; Trueman 89; Cowdrey 72·5; Richardson 58·7; Sheppard 54; Evans 50·25; Close 29·66; Lock 12·33; Statham 10; Laker 9; Smith 8·33; Bailey 1·66; Loader 0·5.
(N.B. Owing to the wide range of figures mm. graph paper may be more convenient on which to work.)

17. Graphically compare the velocity of sound in the following solids (in 1,000s mm./sec.) by means of a column graph:
Aluminium 510; Copper 397; Gold 208; Nickel 497; Wrought Iron 500; Cast Iron 430; Silver 264; Tin 249; Zinc 368; Brass 365.

18. Construct a column graph to illustrate the tenacity (in lbs. per sq. in.) of the following timbers:
Teak 15,000; Lancewood 20,000; English Oak 15,000; Ash 17,700; Pitch Pine 12,000; Beech 17,000; Elm 14,000; Larch 11,000; Red Pine 10,500.

19. Graphically compare the tensile strengths (in tons per sq. in.) of the following metals and alloys:
Manganese steel 38; Aluminium bronze 25; Phosphor bronze $15\frac{1}{2}$; Cast iron 15; Copper wire 25; Cast copper 10; Gun metal 12; Brass 10; Zinc 3; Tin 2; Cast lead 1·5; Wrought aluminium 14·7; Annealed aluminium 6·0.

20. Graphically compare the relative values of spring materials when made into cylindrical spiral springs:
Cast steel hardened 809; Cast steel unhardened 136; Mild steel hardened 128; Mild steel unhardened 32; Phosphor bronze hardened 20; Wrought iron unhardened 19; Brass hardened 4; Gun metal unhardened 2·3.

21. By means of a column graph compare the wave lengths (in ten-millionths of a millimetre) of the colours of the spectrum:
Red 6,708; Orange 6,104; Yellow 5,893; Green 5,173; (Strontium) Blue 4,607; (Calcium) Blue 4,227; Violet 4,046.

22. Graphically compare the specific heats of the following substances:
Brickwork 0·192; Chalk 0·215; Anthracite coal 0·201; Glass 0·190; Ice 0·504; Sulphur 0·203; Wood 0·550.

23. Draw a column graph to illustrate the melting points (°C) of these metals:
Aluminium 657°; Copper 1,084°; Gold 1,065°; Iron 1,505°; Lead 327°; Manganese 1,207°; Nickel 1,451°; Osmium 2,500°; Platinum 1,755°; Silver 961°; Tin 232°; Zinc 419°.

24. Draw a column graph to illustrate the comparative heat conductivity of the following metals, taking silver = 1000:
Silver 1,000; Gold 981; Copper 845; Mercury 677; Aluminium 665; Zinc 641; Wrought iron 436; Tin 422; Steel 397; Platinum 380; Cast iron 359; Lead 287; Antimony 215; Bismuth 61.

25. By means of a column graph illustrate the latent heats of fusion of the following substances:
Ice 80; Nitrate of sodium 63; Nitrate of potassium 47; Paraffin wax 35; Zinc 28; Silver 21; Tin 14; Sulphur 9·4; Lead 5·5; Mercury 3.

26. Construct a column graph to show the world production of natural rubber during 1954 from the following details (data given in thousand tons):
Indonesia 739; Malay 584; Siam 117; Ceylon 94; Vietnam and Cambodia 78; Sarawak 23; Brazil 22; India 21.

27. Draw a column graph to show the trade in 1955 of our greatest seaports from the following facts (given in £ millions):

London 2,410; Liverpool 1,517$\frac{3}{4}$; Hull 375; Manchester (and Runcorn) 365$\frac{1}{4}$; Glasgow 302; Southampton 301$\frac{1}{2}$; Bristol 185; Swansea 124$\frac{1}{2}$; Tyneside 111; Dover 75$\frac{1}{2}$; (N.B. Airports 179$\frac{1}{3}$).

28. Construct a column graph to show the comparative expenditure in Colonial Development (by territories) during 1955–1956 from the following data:

South Africa £4·6 million; Pacific £5·2 million; Mediterranean £6·8 million; Central Africa £9·9 million; (General) £12·3 million; Hong Kong and Borneo £13·5 million; West Indian and America £29·5 million; East Africa £32·4 million; West Africa £47·2 million.

29. Construct a column graph as above to show the colonial expenditure (by subjects) from the following data:

Electricity and Power £0·4 million; Miscellaneous £2·3 million; Forestry, Fisheries and Industrial £4·1 million; Irrigation, land and drainage £7·4 million; Other transport than road £6·5 million; Water and sanitation £14·2 million; Social welfare and housing £9·2 million; Research £14·7 million; Administration, Surveys and Training, etc., £14·3 million; Medical and Health, Education £18·5 million; Roads £20·9 million; Agriculture and Veterinary £19·7 million; Education £29·2 million.

30. Draw a graph to show the comparative heights of these mountains:

Ben Nevis 4,406; Elbruz 18,526; Mont Blanc 15,781; Stalin Peak 24,590; Everest 29,002; Kilimanjaro 19,321; Mt. Cook 12,349; Aconcagua 22,835; McKinley 20,270.

31. Graphically illustrate the coal resources (1956) in millions of metric tons of these countries:

U.S.A. 479·1; U.S.S.R. 429·6; U.K. 225·6; Japan 46·6; W. Germany 134·4; Poland 95·1; China 94·0; France 55·1; India 40·1; Czechoslovakia 62·8.

32. By using a column graph show the reigning periods of the English monarchs in the House of Hanover from the following data:

George I 13 years; George II 33 years; George III 59 years; George IV 10 years; William IV 7 years; Victoria 63 years.

33. Construct a column graph showing the calories per ounce of the following meat foods:

Corned beef 69; Bacon 128; Fresh beef 89; Ox liver 40; Mutton 94; Pork sausage 82; Shepherd's pie 41.

34. Construct a column graph showing the calories per ounce of the following vegetables:

Baked beans 25; Haricot beans 71; Cabbage 7; Carrot 6; Cauliflower 6; Green peas 17; Dried peas 84; Spinach 6; Tomato 4; Fresh potato 21; Turnip 5.

35. Construct a column graph showing the calories per ounce of these foods:

Butter 211; Cheese 117; Egg 45; Dried milk 135; Cooking fat (lard) 253; Margarine 218; Whole milk 17; Condensed milk 89.

36. By means of a graphical construction illustrate the following air distances (in miles) from London, England:

Berlin 579; Buenos Aires 6,916; Cairo 2,181; Calcutta 4,947; Capetown 6,012; Caracas 4,660; Chicago 3,950; Mexico City 5,550; Montreal 3,282; Moscow 1,555; New York 3,458; New Orleans 4,674; Paris 213; Rio de Janeiro 5,766; Hong Kong 5,982; Honolulu 7,228; Istanbul 1,552; Stockholm 890; Tokyo 5,940; Sydney 10,564; Washington 3,663.

B

37. Use a column graph construction to compare and contrast the population density per square mile of the following areas;
Asia 139·1; Africa 18·7; Australia 3; North America 25·7; Europe 215·1; Oceanea 19·5; South America 18·3; U.S.S.R. 23·3; (The World 46·0).

38. By column graph illustrate the figures given below for the industrial production indices for Western Europe in 1956 (1953 = 100):
Austria 138; France 133; Luxembourg 126; Netherlands 124; Belgium 122; Greece 145; Germany (Fed. Rep.) 139; Norway 122; Denmark 111; Ireland 102; U.K. 112; Sweden 114.

39. Construct a column graph to compare the percentage germination of the following seeds:
Beans 90; Beetroot 70; Cabbage 80; Carrot 55; Celery 50; Leek 60; Onions 75; Parsley 50; Pea 80; Spinach 68; Turnip 75; Lettuce 88.

40. Graphically illustrate the germination periods of the following seeds under average conditions:
Cereals 3 days; Mustard $1\frac{1}{2}$ days; Turnips 2 days; Peas 3 days; Beans 4 days; Cucumber 7 days; Carrots 6 days; Marrow 6 days.

41. On a second graph illustrate also the time the above seeds take to appear above the ground:
Cereals 12 days; Mustard 4 days; Turnips 6 days; Peas 10 days; Beans 16 days; Cucumber 42 days; Carrots 38 days; Marrow 15 days.

42. Graphically compare the approximate maximum heights of these common trees:
Indian Cedar 150 ft.; Scotch Pine 100 ft.; Ash 80 ft.; London Plane 70 ft.; Alder 60 ft.; Yew 50 ft.; Hazel 40 ft.; Laburnum 30 ft.; Hawthorn 20 ft.; Blackthorn 10 ft.

43. Make a graphical record of the weights of the following fertilizers per bushel:
Bone meal 56 lb.; Ground chalk 100 lb.; Phosphate of potash 82 lb.; Phosphate of lime 92 lb.; Peat 76 lb.; Sulphate of ammonia 57 lb.; Phosphate of soda 68 lb.; Sulphate of potash 120 lb.; Sulphate of soda 72 lb.; Superphosphate 62 lb.

44. By means of a column graph illustrate the following approximate periods of gestation and incubation (in days):
Ass 360; Bear 210; Cat 60; Chicken 21; Cow 280; Dog 63; Duck 28; Elephant 628; Ewe 151; Goat 150; Hippopotamus 240; Kangaroo 39; Lioness 108; Mare 336; Monkey 164; Mouse 25; Pigeon 18; Rabbit 31; Rat 22; Sow 115; Squirrel 32; Vixen 55; Whale 320; Wolf 63; Woman 270.

45. By means of a column graph illustrate the following boiling points (°C) of substances under normal pressure conditions:
Nitrous oxide −88°C; Ammonia −$33\frac{1}{2}$°C; Ether 35°C; Chloroform 60°C; Alcohol 78°C; Water 100°C; Benzene 80°C; Turpentine oil 159°C; Linseed oil 316°C; Sulphuric acid 325°C; Mercury 357°C.
(N.B. To show negative columns the vertical scale line can be carried down below the horizontal axis and the columns are therefore indicated in reverse.)

46. Graphically illustrate the following common and important temperatures in two separate graphs:
The Sun 5,500°C (approx.); Electric arc 3,500°C; Oxy-hydrogen flame 2,800°C; Bessemer furnace 2,230°C; Platinum melts 1,715°C; Iron melts 1,500°C; Copper melts 1,080°C.
Water freezes −39°C; Mixture of salt and ice −17°C; Mercury freezes −39°C; Record natural lowest temperature −$61\frac{1}{2}$°C; Oxygen liquefies −183°C; Hydrogen liquefies −253°C; Helium liquefies −$268\frac{1}{2}$°C; Absolute zero −273°C.
(See note after Question No. 45.)

47. Graphically illustrate the comparative expansions of the following solids. (Figures in ten-millionths per °C as coefficients of linear expansion):

Invar steel 9; Quartz 17; Glass 86; Platinum 89; Cast iron 110; Steel 120; Copper 170; Brass 190; Silver 190; Lead 280; Tin 230; Ice 400; Oak 500; Sulphur 600.

48. Graphically illustrate the comparative expansions of the following liquids. (Figures in millionths per °C as mean coefficients of real expansion.)

Mercury 181; Water 193; Glycerine 530; Aniline 910; Petroleum 990; Turpentine 1,050; Alcohol 1,080; Chloroform 1,400.

49. Illustrate graphically the latent heats of vaporization of the following substances at boiling point under normal pressure:

Water 540; Sulphur 362; Alcohol 202; Ether 90; Oil of Turpentine 74; Liquid air 55.

50. Printing type is classified in sizes on a point system (72 points = 1 inch). The names of the type with their sizes under the point system are as follows:

Pearl 5; Ruby $5\frac{1}{2}$; Nonpareil 6; Minion 7; Brevier 8; Bourgeois 9; Long Primer 10; Small Pica 11; Pica 12; English 14; Great Primer 18.

Construct a column graph to illustrate these sizes.

51. By means of a column graph compare and contrast the death rates for the following European countries in 1956. (Rate = number of deaths per 1,000 population.)

Austria 12·3; Belgium 12·6; Finland 9·0; France 12·4; Italy 10·3; West Germany 11·0; Luxemburg 12·5; Netherlands 7·8; Norway 8·5; Portugal 12·0; Spain 9·9; Sweden 9·6; Switzerland 10·2; United Kingdom 11·7.

52. Draw a column graph to illustrate the principal religions of the world from the following very rough approximation of the number of its followers (in millions):

Christian 820; Roman Catholics 484; Eastern Orthodox 129; Protestant 207; Jewish 12; Moslem 416; Shinto 30; Taoist 50; Confucian 300; Buddhist 150; Hindu 319; Primitive 121; Others or none 406.

53. Using two column graphs compare and contrast the distances of the following planets from the sun (in millions of miles approx.).

(a) Mercury 35; Venus 67; Earth 93; Mars 142; Jupiter 484.

(b) Saturn 887; Uranus 1784; Neptune 2795; Pluto 3675.

54. Draw a column graph to illustrate the relationship of the English mile compared with other European measures from the following table. (English mile = 1·0):

English Geog. Mile 1·153; Dutch Ure 3·458; French Km. 0·621; Norwegian Mile 7·021; German Geog. Mile 4·610; Swedish Mile 6·664; Russian Verst 0·663; Danish Mile 4·682; Austrian Mile 4·714; Swiss Stunde 2·987.

55. The approximate weights of common U.K. coinage (in grains) is as follows:

Crown $436\frac{1}{3}$; Half-crown 218; Florin $174\frac{1}{2}$; Shilling $87\frac{1}{4}$; Sixpence $43\frac{2}{3}$; Threepence 105; Penny 146; Halfpenny $87\frac{1}{2}$; Farthing $43\frac{3}{4}$.

Graphically compare their weights using the column system.

56. The following figures give the weight (in lb./head) of certain fresh fruit and vegetables consumed in this country in 1963. Construct a graph (column) to compare these statistics:

Edible pulses 9·2; Fresh fruit (other than citrus) 53·4; Fruit juices (natural strength) 3·3; Fresh tomatoes 13·1; Cabbage and greens 27·4; Leafy salads 4·2; Fresh legumes 16·0; Carrots 11·5; Other fresh vegetables 27·4.

(Note that the consumption of potatoes—not included above—during the same year was 227·6 lb./head.)

Double Column Graphs

If only two (or three) items are to be compared and contrasted, it is sometimes more convenient to use double (or triple) columns side by side on the same format, *e.g.*, if we wish to compare the consumption of oats products with that of breakfast cereals in the United Kingdom from the following data, a double column graph is sufficient (Fig. 7).

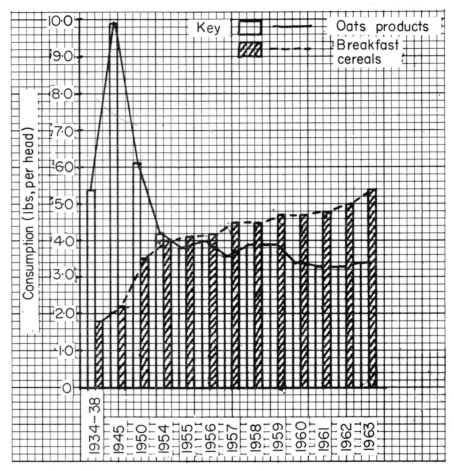

FIGURE 7

Year	1934–38	1945	1950	1954	1955	1956	1957	1958	1959	1960	1961	1962	1963
Oats Products: (lb./head)	5·4	9·9	6·1	4·2	3·8	4·0	3·6	3·9	3·9	3·4	3·3	3·3	3·4
Breakfast cereals: (lb./head)	1·8	2·2	3·5	4·0	4·1	4·2	4·5	4·5	4·7	4·7	4·8	5·0	5·4

(Note that by joining the tops of their respective columns these two products could be compared statistically equally well by means of two line graphs.)

EXERCISES

1. (**a**) By means of a column graph graphically illustrate the following rates of exchange in relation to sterling:

Australian pound 1·25 to £; Canadian dollar 2·672 to £; Ceylon rupee 13·31 to £; Egyptian pound 0·975 to £; Hongkong dollar 16·134 to £; Indian rupee 13·33 to £; Malayan dollar 8·59 to £; Netherlands guilder 10·674 to £; New Zealand pound 1·07 to £; U.S.A. dollar 2·796 to £.

(**b**) Obtain the current rates from a daily newspaper and compare the data by means of a double column graph.

2. (**a**) The following figures show the consumption of meat in the United Kingdom during the year 1963 in lb./head per annum. Illustrate these by means of a column graph:

Beef 53·2; Mutton and lamb 23·4; Pork 21·9; Bacon and ham 25·2; Canned meat (imported) 7·5; Poultry meat 14·9; Game and rabbit 0·5.

(**b**) By means of a second column graph (this may be drawn separately or on the same diagram by a second column adjacent to that of the previous graph) compare this consumption with the figures given for 1934–1938 *viz*:

Beef 54·9; Mutton and lamb 25·2; Pork 10·6; Bacon and ham 28·1; Canned meat (imported) 3·1; Poultry meat 5·1; Game and rabbit 3·7.

3. (**a**) Illustrate by means of a column graph how the consumption per head of coffee in the United Kingdom has risen from 1934 to 1963:

Year	1934–38	1945	1950	1954	1955	1956	1957	1958	1959	1960	1961	1962	1963
Consumption: (lb./head)	0·7	1·2	1·5	1·3	1·3	1·5	1·6	1·7	1·9	2·0	2·1	2·7	2·9

(**b**) By means of a column graph compare the previous figures of the consumption of coffee with that of tea during the same years, utilizing the following data:

Year	1934–38	1945	1950	1954	1955	1956	1957	1958	1959	1960	1961	1962	1963
Consumption: (lb./head)	9·3	8·2	8·5	9·7	9·3	10·1	9·8	9·9	9·7	9·3	9·9	9·4	9·5

4. Compare and contrast by means of a double column graph the consumption of butter and margarine (in lb./head) in the United Kingdom during the following years:

Year	1934–38	1945	1950	1954	1955	1956	1957	1958	1959	1960	1961	1962	1963
Butter (lb./head)	24·7	8·5	16·9	14·1	14·7	15·5	17·3	20·0	18·5	18·3	19·7	20·3	19·3
Margarine: (lb./head)	8·7	17·1	17·0	18·3	17·9	17·1	15·5	13·7	14·8	15·0	13·3	13·1	13·5

Multiple Column Graphs

The method of column representation can be further developed to show various classes of groups of statistics, under different headings, *e.g.*, take the following table of statistics and construct, first of all, a column graph showing the figures of the last column (Total).

Country	Cattle (in millions)	Sheep (in millions)	Pigs (in millions)	Total (in millions)
India	148	0	0	148
U.S.A.	94½	31	48½	174
U.S.S.R.	63	112½	47½	223
France	17	0	7	24
Australia	15½	127	0	142½
S. Africa	11½	36	0	47½
U.K.	10½	23	6	39½

If we now apply a "key" as is commonly done in atlases, we can sub-divide each column representing the numbers of each country's livestock to show the various groups of animals (Fig. 8).

Any statistics suitable for column graphs may, however, be represented in a form which is

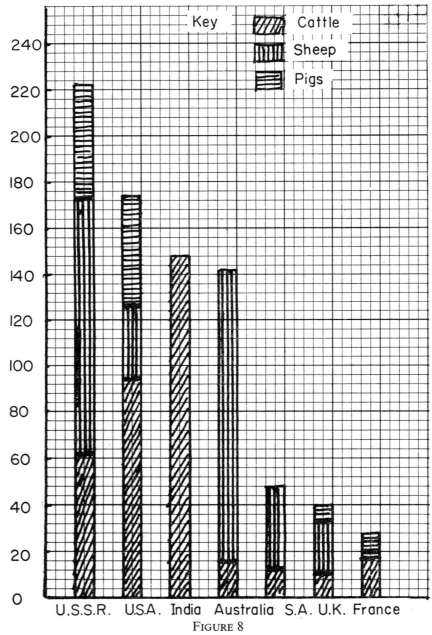

FIGURE 8

sometimes known as compound bar graphs (or charts). In this form of representation all the bars are of equal length but the types of shading represent the ratio, proportion or percentage of the various component parts (Fig. 9).

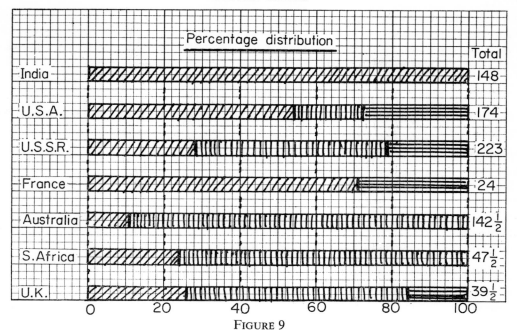

FIGURE 9

Yet again these percentages may be shown by proportional sectors of a circle and hence are known as sector graphs (circular diagrams, "pie" graphs, "cake" charts, etc.). Four of the above countries are illustrated below as examples of this type of graphical representation, using the same key shading (Fig. 10).

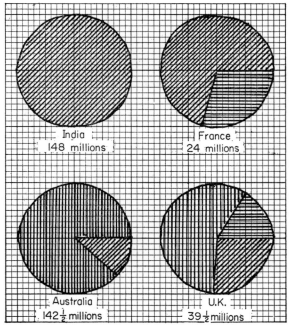

FIGURE 10

Other more elementary forms of proportional representation are known as pictographs, ideographs, etc. These are simply pictures repeated as pictorial elements to show by the numbers of elements, the numbers of the items under consideration; in the example shown, pictures of sheep, cows and pigs would be used.

EXERCISES

1. Construct a multiple column graph to illustrate the following statistics. (Hint: Construct the total column first.) Shipbuilding, gross tonnage launched, in thousand tons (approx.):

Country	1956	1955	1938	Total
Japan	1,650	800	450	
U.K.	1,400	1,550	1,000	
Germany	1,000	900	450	
Sweden	500	500	150	
Netherlands	450	400	250	
Italy	350	200	100	
France	300	350	50	
U.S.A.	300	300	200	
Norway	150	150	50	
Denmark	100	150	150	

2. The following table gives the number of accidents to school children from the ages of 5 to 15 (Juniors 5–10, Seniors 11–15) in a certain seaside town, during a twelve-month period of observation—January to December.

Month	1	2	3	4	5	6	7	8	9	10	11	12
Total number of accidents	2	4	5	12	10	7	8	11	12	8	5	3
Males	1	4	4	10	6	7	4	7	10	7	4	2
Females	1	0	1	2	4	0	4	4	2	1	1	1
Juniors	2	4	4	4	5	2	4	7	5	7	0	1
Seniors	0	0	1	8	5	5	4	4	7	1	5	2

Construct two column graphs showing the totals for each month sub-divided into: (1) Males and Females; (2) Seniors and Juniors.

(a) In which months did the greatest number of accidents occur? Can you suggest a possible reason?

(b) Why are there more accidents for Males than Females?

(c) Why are there slightly more Juniors involved throughout the year than Seniors? Suggest reason.

(d) Why should many more Seniors be injured from April to September than in other months?

3. By means of a multiple column graph illustrate the percentages of various constituents in certain foodstuffs.

Food	(a) Water	(b) Protein	(c) Carbo-hydrate	(d) Fat	(e) Mineral Salts
Butter	15	1	—	82	2
Egg yolk	48	16	—	33	3
Apple	82	2	14	1	1

Food	(a) Water	(b) Protein	(c) Carbo-hydrate	(d) Fat	(e) Mineral Salts
Banana	68	3	23	3	3
Cabbage	93	1	3	1	2
Carrot	87	1	10	1	1
Beef (steak)	53	14	—	29	4
Orange	77	1	20	1	1
Lettuce	94	1	1	1	3

4. Construct a multiple column graph illustrating the United Kingdom's production of motor vehicles (in thousands):

Year	Private cars	Public service	Goods vehicles	Total
1935	338	5	81	424
1951	476	11	248	735
1952	448	9	234	691
1953	595	7	233	835
1954	769	8	262	1,039

5. Using a multiple column graph illustrate the distribution of the non-white population in the U.S.A. (omitting Negroes) from the following table (population in thousands):

	Indian	Japanese	Chinese	Others
1910	266	72	$71\frac{1}{2}$	3
1920	244	111	62	$9\frac{1}{2}$
1930	332	139	75	51
1940	334	127	$77\frac{1}{2}$	$50\frac{1}{2}$
1950	343	142	$117\frac{1}{2}$	110

6. By means of a multiple column graph illustrate the numbers of cattle, sheep and pigs in 1953–1954 (in million head) from the following table:

Country	Cattle	Sheep	Pigs
India (1951)	148	—	—
U.S.A.	$94\frac{1}{2}$	31	$48\frac{1}{2}$
U.S.S.R.	63	$112\frac{1}{2}$	$47\frac{1}{2}$
Brazil	$57\frac{1}{2}$	—	—
Argentine (1952/53)	45	$55\frac{1}{2}$	—
France	17	—	7
Australia	$15\frac{1}{2}$	127	—
S. Africa (1952/53)	$11\frac{1}{2}$	36	—
West Germany	$11\frac{1}{2}$	—	$12\frac{1}{2}$
U.K.	$10\frac{1}{2}$	23	6

Double Scale Column Graphs

It is sometimes convenient to utilize both vertical axes to carry two separate scales in a double column graph as in Figure 11. Here the L.H. vertical scale carries the % population coverage (plain columns) whilst the R.H. vertical scale carries the "number of transmitting stations"

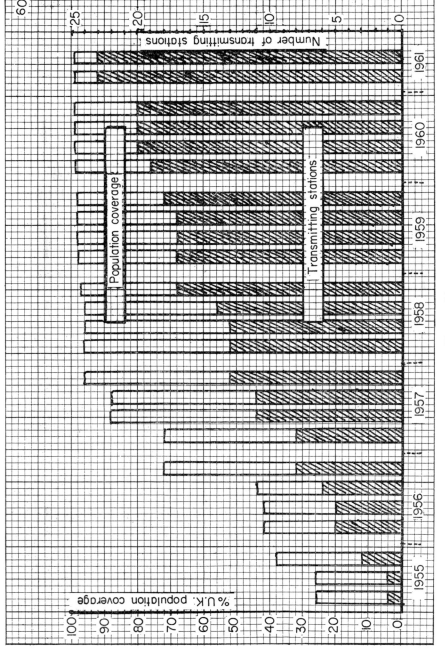

FIGURE 11

(shaded columns), thus enabling the two graphs to be compared in one pictorial format as well as saving time in duplicating the columns and horizontal scale of years (Fig. 11).

Horizontal and Vertical Representation

An artist, in painting a picture, is very well aware of the power of suggestion and as graphs are "mathematical pictures" it is quite easy to appreciate that the same can apply, and like any good picture a graph should effectively convey the essential information. For instance, in making a

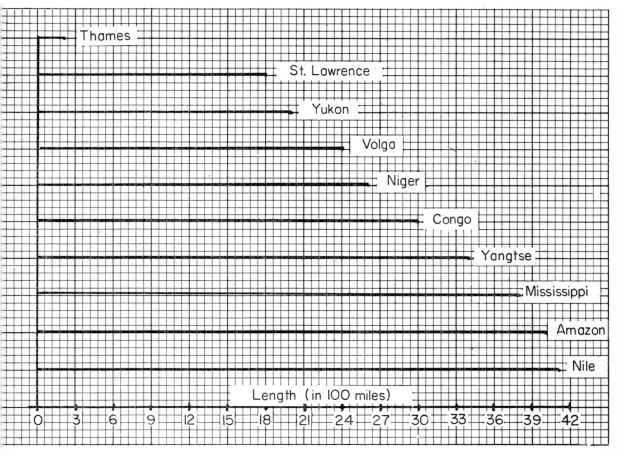

FIGURE 12

column graph of the heights of mountains or trees, etc., a vertical column conveys the idea more forcibly, but if we wish to illustrate the lengths of various rivers (in miles), e.g., Nile 4,160; Amazon 4,050; Mississippi 3,710; Yangtse 3,400; Congo 3,000; Niger 2,600; Volga 2,400; Yukon 2,000; St. Lawrence 1,800; Thames 210; it will be seen that a horizontal lay-out is more effective (Fig. 12).

If a topic does not lend itself particularly to either of these methods of representation, then it is a matter of free choice and one method can be as effective as the other provided it shows the facts clearly and simply.

EXERCISES

1. Construct a horizontal column graph to illustrate the lengths of the following rivers (in miles approx.):

Colorado 2,000; Danube 1,720; Euphrates 1,700; Indus 1,700; Murray 1,609; Severn 220.

2. Construct a horizontal column graph to show the comparative lengths of the following famous bridges (in ft. approx.):

Lower Zambesi 11,300; Tay 10,300; Montreal (Victoria Jubilee) 5,300; Golden Gate 6,200; Forth 8,300; Quebec 3,200; Sydney Harbour 4,100; Brooklyn 3,400.

	Speed m.p.h.	*Thinking distance (ft.)*	*Braking distance (ft.)*	*Total or overall stopping distance (ft.)*
3.	10	10	5	15
	20	20	20	40
	30	30	45	75
	40	40	80	120
	50	50	125	175

The above is a table showing what proper brakes can do on good, dry, level surfaces.
(N.B. "Thinking Distance" = Distance travelled before driver reacts.

"Braking Distance" = Distance travelled after driver applies brakes.)
Construct a multiple column graph horizontally to show both factors "Thinking Distance" and "Braking Distance" at the various speeds.

4. Graphically illustrate the comparative lengths of the following rivers (in miles):

Shannon 230; Volga 2,400; Danube 1,725; Yenisel 3,300; Yangtse 3,400; Nile 4,160; Murray-Darling 1,900; Amazon 4,050; Mississippi 3,710.

5. Draw a horizontal column graph to illustrate and compare the lengths of some of the great ship canals of the world from the following facts (in miles):

Amsterdam $16\frac{1}{2}$; Elbe 41; Gota 115; Kiel 61; Manchester $35\frac{1}{2}$; Panama $50\frac{1}{2}$; Princess Juliana (Holland) 20; Suez 100; Welland $26\frac{3}{4}$.

3

STATISTICAL GRAPHS

Line Graphs

In the first paragraph on column graphs it was shown that the height of a mountain could be represented by (*a*) a scale against a picture, (*b*) a column or (*c*) a plain straight line.

Hence a number of mountains (*A–F*) instead of being shown as vertical columns could be compared in height by vertical lines, thus saving time and labour (Fig. 13).

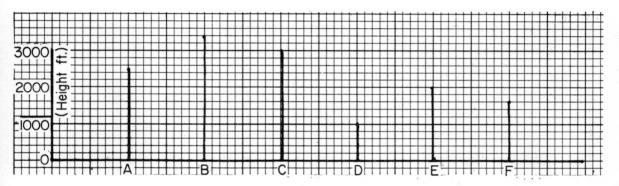

FIGURE 13

Now we know from our studies in geometry that "a point indicates the extremities of lines". Hence, since these vertical lines are all based on the horizontal axis we can simplify our diagram still further by just indicating the *top* of each column by a point (Fig. 14).

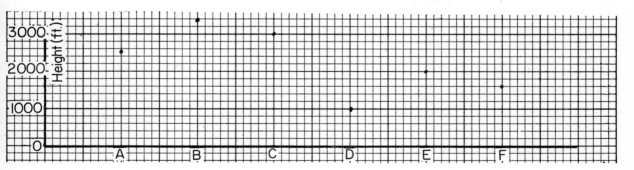

FIGURE 14

If we join up these points we obtain a "line graph" and again it simplifies matters if we place our first point A on the vertical scale column (Fig. 15).

(*Cf*. Previous notes on column graphs, *et seq*.)

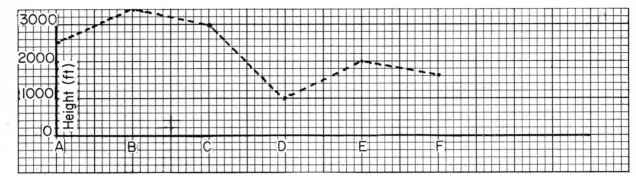

FIGURE 15

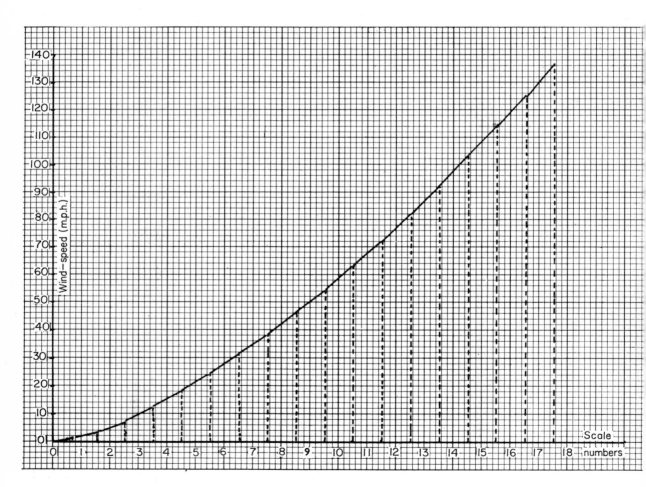

FIGURE 16

It is interesting to see the possibilities of combining types of graphs (*e.g.*, column and line) in the following representation of the Beaufort Scale of wind force.

Scale No.	Wind force	Wind speed (m.p.h.)
0	Calm	1
1	Light air	1–3
2	Slight breeze	4–7
3	Gentle breeze	8–12
4	Moderate breeze	13–18
5	Fresh breeze	19–24
6	Strong breeze	25–31
7	High wind	32–38
8	Gale	39–46
9	Strong gale	47–54
10	Whole gale	55–63
11	Storm	64–72
12	Hurricane	73–82
13		83–92
14		93–103
15		104–114
16		115–125
17		126–136

The columns representing the scale numbers are not drawn square at the top; the left-hand side of each column representing in length the minimum speed, and the right-hand side the maximum speed. The tops of the columns hence join up, forming a "curve" similar to that obtained in a statistical graph. However, the whole gives a good pictorial representation of the factors appertaining to the Beaufort Scale of Wind Force in a clear diagrammatic form (Fig. 16).

EXERCISES

1. Construct two line graphs on the same axes to compare the annual temperature variations of Dunedin (New Zealand) with Cloncurry (Queensland):

Month	Jan.	Feb.	Mar.	Apr.	May	June	July	Aug.	Sept.	Oct.	Nov.	Dec.
Cloncurry	87	85	83	78	71	64	61	67	72	83	85	88
Dunedin	58	58	55	52	47	44	42	44	48	51	53	56

Give reasons why one record is consistently higher than the other.

2. Construct two line graphs on the same axes to compare the rainfall of Wellington (New Zealand) with that of Wilcannia (N.S.W.) from the following data:

Month	Jan.	Feb.	Mar.	Apr.	May	June	July	Aug.	Sept.	Oct.	Nov.	Dec.
Wellington	3·3	3·1	3·3	3·9	4·7	4·8	5·6	4·5	4·0	4·1	3·5	3·2
Wilcannia	1·0	0·8	1·1	0·7	1·0	1·1	0·6	0·8	0·7	0·9	0·7	0·8

Give reasons why one place should be so much wetter than the other.

3. Draw a line graph to illustrate the fastest Atlantic passages by sea from the following data:

Year	1862	1869	1882	1889	1894	1909	1934	1935	1936	1937	1938	1952
Time	9 days	8 days	7 days	6 days	5½ days	4 days 10 hrs	4 days 6 hrs	4 days 3 hrs	4 days	3 days 23 hrs	3 days 21 hrs	3 days 10 hrs

4. By means of a line graph illustrate the post-war production of coal (in million tons) in the United Kingdom comparing this with 1938:

Year	1938	1945	1946	1947	1948	1949	1950	1951	1952	1953	1954
Weight:	227	184	190	197	209	215	216	223	226	224	224

5. By means of a line graph show the following figures of employment of labour in America (in millions of persons):

Year	1929	1932	1941	1943	1945	1950	1953	1956	1957
Number:	46·7	37·9	50·4	54·5	52·8	60·0	61·9	65·3	63·5

6. By means of a line graph illustrate the growth of the world's population from the following data.

Year	1650	1750	1800	1850	1900	1920	1930	1940	1950
Population (millions)	470	694	919	1,091	1,571	1,834	2,008	2,216	2,406

7. Compare and contrast graphically by drawing two line graphs on the same axes the maximum temperatures (°F) at London (Croydon) for December 1956 and June 1957 from the following data:

Day	1	3	5	7	9	11	13	15	17	19	21	23	25	27	29	30
Dec. 1956	47	53	52	52	46	51	48	53	53	41	38	38	34	36	47	49
June 1957	74	78	61	66	68	61	69	80	83	66	71	65	62	80	92	88

8. On the same graph axes draw three separate line graphs to illustrate the comparative costs of the Local Health Authority Services in (a) England and Wales; (b) Scotland; (c) Northern Ireland, from the figures given (in £ millions) in the following table:

Year ending	(a)	(b)	(c)
1949	$179\frac{1}{4}$	$22\frac{1}{3}$	$5\frac{2}{3}$
1950	$305\frac{1}{4}$	40	$8\frac{1}{3}$
1951	$336\frac{1}{2}$	$40\frac{1}{4}$	$9\frac{1}{2}$
1952	$348\frac{1}{2}$	$43\frac{1}{2}$	10
1953	384	$47\frac{1}{2}$	11
1954	368	$46\frac{1}{2}$	11
1955	389	50	$11\frac{3}{4}$
1957*	471	58	$14\frac{3}{4}$
1958*	$490\frac{1}{2}$	$59\frac{1}{2}$	$15\frac{1}{2}$

(N.B. * Estimated costs.)

As these figures show a wide range of costs it will be found more convenient to use mm. graph paper for this exercise.

9. On the same graph area draw three line graphs to show the relationships between the live births, marriages and deaths in the United Kingdom. (Figure are given in rate per 1,000.)

Year	1938	1951	1952	1953	1954	1955	1956
Live births	15·5	15·8	15·7	15·9	15·6	15·8	16·1
Marriages	17·2	16·4	15·9	15·6	15·5	16·1	15·9
Deaths	11·8	12·6	11·4	11·4	11·5	11·6	11·7

What effect will these factors have on the population of the country?

10. From the following data construct a graph to illustrate the U.K. post-war building progress:

Year	1946	1947	1948	1949	1950	1951	1952	1953	1954	1955	1956
Houses and flats (1,000s)	$52\frac{1}{2}$	$127\frac{1}{2}$	$206\frac{1}{2}$	172	$172\frac{1}{3}$	172	209	280	309	$283\frac{1}{3}$	$268\frac{3}{4}$

11. On the same graph draw two line graphs to compare the approximate budget receipts and estimates (in £ millions) in the United Kingdom:

Year	1947	1948	1949	1950	1951	1952	1953	1954	1955	1956
Receipts	$1,155\frac{1}{2}$	$1,194\frac{1}{2}$	$1,360\frac{1}{2}$	$1,436\frac{3}{4}$	$1,414\frac{1}{4}$	$1,682\frac{1}{4}$	$1,751\frac{1}{4}$	$1,716\frac{1}{4}$	1,874	$1,945\frac{1}{2}$
Estimates	1,111	1,086	1,309	1,490	1,388	$1,624\frac{3}{4}$	$1,804\frac{1}{4}$	$1,782\frac{1}{4}$	1,800	$1,874\frac{1}{2}$

12. On the same area draw three line graphs to show the average earnings of manual wage-earners in the United Kingdom during the past 20 years:

Year	1938	1946	1947	1948	1949	1950	1951	1952	1953	1954	1955	1956
Men	69/–	120/9	128/1	137/11	142/8	150/5	166/–	178/6	189/2	204/5	222/11	237/11
Women	32/6	65/3	69/7	74/6	78/9	82/7	90/1	96/4	102/5	108/2	115/5	123/2
All	53/3	101/–	108/2	117/4	121/9	128/–	141/1	151/11	160/1	171/9	187/2	200/8

13. The following table gives the number of working tinners in the Devon stannaries as recorded by the Stannary authorities in the Pipe Rolls during the latter half of the 13th century:

Year	1243	1288	1289	1290	1291	1292	1293	1294	1295	1296	1297	1298	1299	1300	1301
Number	149	300	308	323	450	457	453	334	258	199	218	346	415	436	440

Draw a line graph to illustrate the fluctuations of employment during this period.

14. The following table shows the average numbers of registered unemployed in the United Kingdom from 1942 to 1956:

Year	1942	1943	1944	1945	1946	1947	1948	1949	1950	1951	1952	1953	1954	1955	1956
Total (1,000s) approx.	139	99	$89\frac{1}{2}$	157	406	$510\frac{1}{2}$	338	338	341	$281\frac{1}{2}$	$462\frac{1}{2}$	380	$317\frac{3}{4}$	$264\frac{1}{2}$	287

Graphically illustrate the variations shown during this period.

15. By means of a line graph show the decrease in mortality in the U.S.A. since the beginning of the century:

Year	1900	1910	1920	1930	1940	1950	1956
Rate (per 1,000 pop.)	17·2	14·7	13·0	11·3	10·8	9·6	9·4

16. The following figures record the percentage of unemployed in the U.S.A. from 1942 to 1956:

Year	1942	1943	1944	1946	1947	1948	1949	1950	1951	1952	1953	1954	1955	1956
%	4·7	1·9	1·2	3·9	3·6	3·4	5·5	5·0	3·0	2·7	2·5	5·0	4·0	3·8

By means of a line graph illustrate the fluctuations noted.

17. Illustrate the percentages of the total working population of women in America above the ages of 10 from the following table:

Year	1870	1880	1890	1900	1910	1920	1930	1940	1950
%	14·8	15·2	17·2	18·3	19·9	20·4	22·0	24·3	27·5

C

18. Compare and contrast by drawing two line graphs for males and females on the same area the percentages of population married in America from 1890 to 1956 in the age group 14–19 years:

Year	1890	1900	1910	1920	1930	1940	1950	1956
Male	0·4	0·9	1·0	1·8	1·5	1·5	2·9	2·4
Female	8·0	9·4	9·7	10·8	10·9	10·0	14·4	15·0

19. The fall of temperature along two rods, one of copper and another of iron, is recorded when both are exposed at one end to a constant temperature:

Distance (in cm.) from heated end	10	20	30	40	50	60	70	80	90	100
Temp. of Copper rod (°F)	137	96	79	60	48	39	32	27	25	23
Temp. of Iron rod (°F)	128	48	32	22	18	16	15	14·8	14·5	14·5

By drawing the two graphs on the same area compare the fall in temperature along the two rods.

20. The following table gives facts relating to the world's records in the 1,500 metres race (to nearest second):

Year	1912	1926	1933	1943	1944	1954	1957
Time (min./sec.)	3·56	3·51	3·49	3·45	3·43	3·42	3·38

Draw the line graph showing these facts and also on the same area construct the line for the mile race for comparison from the following data (again to the nearest second):

Year	1913	1923	1931	1942	1943	1945	1954	1957
Time (min./sec.)	4·14	4·10	4·09	4·04	4·02	4·01	3·58	3·57

21. Plot the following data of the population statistics of the U.S.A. by means of a line graph. Note the rise and fall of the population in relation to the following historical events, etc.

1850–1860   Famine in Ireland and unrest in Germany.
1870–1880   High birth rate after the Civil War.
1900   Expanding industry attracts 112 million immigrants.
1920   First World War—immigration and birth rate decline, also "flu epidemic".
1920–1930   Post-war prosperity.
1940   Depression period coupled with lowest birth rate.
1950   A rising birth rate and immigration, gain 19 millions.
1950–1960   An unprecedented prosperity with larger families and effect of medical research on longevity, etc., gain 29 millions.

Year	1790	1800	1810	1820	1830	1840	1850	1860	1870
Population (millions)	4	5	8	10	13	16	23	31	39

Year	1880	1890	1900	1910	1920	1930	1940	1950	1960
Population (millions)	50	62	75	92	106	122	131	150	179

22. Construct a graph from the following table showing the world's records in the pole vault:

Year	1912	1922	1925	1927	1935	1937	1940	1942	1957
Height (ft. in.)	13·2¼	13·6	13·10½	14·0	14·5	14·11	15·1	15·7¾	15·9¾

On the same graph area by means of a second line show the world's records in the high jump, labelling each graph line separately:

Year	1912	1924	1934	1941	1953	1957
Height (ft. in.)	6·7	6·8¼	6·9	6·11	6·11½	7·1

23. Graphically show the production of war planes in America from 1940 to 1945 from the following figures by a line graph:

Year	1940	1941	1942	1943	1944	1945
Total	6,019	19,433	47,836	85,898	96,318	47,714

24. The following table gives the U.S.A. records in ski-jumping:

Year	1887	1904	1907	1910	1916	1919	1932	1937	1939	1942	1949	1951
Distance (ft.)	37	82	112	140	192½	214	224	244·4	257	289	297	316

Illustrate these statistics by a line graph.

25. Record graphically the following statistics of the Indianapolis Motor Speedway times in this 500-mile race:

Year	1911	1914	1922	1925	1932	1937	1950	1953	1954	1956
Average speed (in m.p.h.)	74·6	82·47	94·48	101·13	104·144	113·58	124	128·74	130·84	128·49

26. Show graphically the improvement in motor boat speeds from the following statistics relating to the Gold Cup Winners in the U.S.A.:

Year	1904	1909	1912	1913	1917	1920	1927	1932	1933	1939	1946	1951	1955
Best heat (m.p.h.)	23·6	32·9	44·5	50·49	56·5	70·0	50·9	59·2	60·86	67·05	70·88	91·76	100·95

27. Draw a line graph to show the increase of television in the homes of America since 1946, from the following figures:

Year	1946	1947	1948	1949	1950	1951	1952	1953	1955	1956
Number (in 1,000s)	8	250	1,000	4,000	10,400	15,500	21,000	26,000	34,000	37,000

28. Draw a line graph to illustrate the road casualties in Great Britain in the following years:

Year	1949	1950	1951	1952	1953	1954	1955	1956
Total (1,000s)	176¾	201½	216½	208	226¾	238¼	268	268

29. Draw a line graph to illustrate the advance in airplane records over a measured straight course:

Year	1923	1924	1932	1933	1934	1935	1937	1939	1945	1946	1947	1948	1952	1953	1955	1956
Speed	266½	278½	294	305	314	352	379	469	606	615¾	651	671	698½	755	822¼	1,132

30. By means of a line graph illustrate the following altitude records for aircraft:

Year	1927	1929	1930	1932	1933	1934	1936	1937	1938	1948	1953	1955
Altitude (ft.)	38,419	41,795	43,166	43,976	44,819	47,352	49,944	53,937	56,046	59,445	63,668	65,889

31. Illustrate by a line graph the times for the 100 m. run in the Olympic Games since 1896:

Year	1896	1900	1904	1906	1908	1912	1920	1924	1928	1932	1936	1948	1952	1956
Time (sec.)	12	10·8	11	11·2	10·8	10·8	10·8	10·6	10·8	10·3	10·3	10·3	10·4	10·5

Also illustrate on the same graph the 400 m. race from the following:

Year	1896	1900	1904	1906	1908	1912	1920	1924	1928	1932	1936	1948	1952	1956
Time (sec.)	54·2	49·4	49·2	53·2	50·0	48·2	49·6	47·6	47·8	46·2	46·5	46·2	45·9	46·7

32. The following data records the losses by fire in the United Kingdom in 1956 and 1955:

Month	Jan.	Feb.	Mar.	Apl.	May	June	July	Aug.	Sept.	Oct.	Nov.	Dec.
1956 loss (in £1,000)	2,025	2,681	2,873	2,963	2,545	1,608	1,824	1,391	2,918	1,579	2,429	2,676
1955 loss (in £1,000)	1,855	2,191	5,166	2,144	1,605	3,373	1,386	1,516	2,874	1,374	2,659	1,552

Draw two line graphs on the same area showing these losses, dating each line separately.

33. (a) On the same graph area illustrate the times of sunrise and sunset in London (G.M.T.) from the following table:

Date (1958)	Jan. 5	Feb. 2	Mar. 2	Apl. 6	May 4	June 1	July 6	Aug. 3	Sept. 7	Oct. 5	Nov. 2	Dec. 7
Sunrise (a.m.)	8·05	7·37	6·44	5·26	4·28	3·49	3·51	4·26	5·21	6·06	6·54	7·50
Sunset (p.m.)	4·06	4·51	5·42	6·40	7·27	8·07	8·18	7·45	6·34	5·30	4·32	3·52

(b) Using the data given in the previous question, by means of a column graph compare the lengths of each of the twelve days chosen during the year 1958.

34. Two wires were subjected to tensile loading and the following results were obtained:

Load (lb.)	0	5	10	15	20	25
Extensions (in.) A	0	0·02	0·04	0·06	0·10	0·21
Extensions (in.) B	0	0·015	0·03	0·045	0·06	0·075

Draw the two graphs on the same area. What difference do you note and how do you account for them?

35. Growth of the production of aluminium in the world (in thousand metric tons). Illustrate variations by a line graph:

Year	1934	1936	1938	1940	1942	1950	1951	1952	1953
Production	160	340	540	710	1,320	1,310	1,600	1,810	2,190

36. The number of births per 1,000 population in the U.S.A. are given below. Illustrate by a line graph:

1945	1946	1947	1948	1949	1950
19·5	23·3	25·8	24·2	23·9	23·6

1951	1952	1953	1954	1955	1956
24·5	24·7	24·6	24·9	24·6	24·9

37. The number of people visiting an exhibition on each day of the week is as follows. Show variations by both line and column graphs:

	Monday	Tuesday	Wednesday	Thursday	Friday	Saturday
Number	4,300	3,550	3,750	4,900	4,600	5,400

38. Construct a line graph showing the variations during these years of the average change of Rateable Value per £ on the rates in the United Kingdom.

Year ending	1943	1944	1945	1946	1947	1948	1949	1950	1951	1952	1953	1954	1955	1956
Rate	12/7	12/10	12/11	13/10	15/1	17/4	16/11	17/3	17/6	18/10	19/7	21/7	22/1	22/3

39 (a) From 1934 to 1963 the consumption of shell eggs in the United Kingdom was as follows:

Year	1934–38	1945	1950	1954	1955	1956	1957	1958	1959	1960	1961	1962	1963
Consumption (lb./head)	25·9	17·0	28·2	28·4	27·0	27·3	28·9	29·7	30·5	31·1	31·3	31·2	31·1

Show these statistical variations over the period by means of a line graph.

(b) The consumption of fish during these same years (in lb. per head) was as follows:

1934–38	1945	1950	1954	1955	1956	1957	1958	1959	1960	1961	1962	1963
26·2	24·7	21·7	20·8	21·3	22·4	21·8	22·7	22·0	21·4	20·3	21·5	20·2

By means of a second line graph compare and contrast these figures concerning our food supplies.

40. By drawing two line graphs compare the consumption of cream and cheese in this country during the following years:

Year		1954	1955	1956	1957	1958	1959	1960	1961	1962	1963
Consumption (lb./head.)	Cream	0·5	0·7	0·7	0·8	1·0	1·2	1·4	1·7	1·9	2·2
	Cheese	9·4	9·0	9·3	10·0	9·9	9·3	9·8	10·2	10·3	10·3

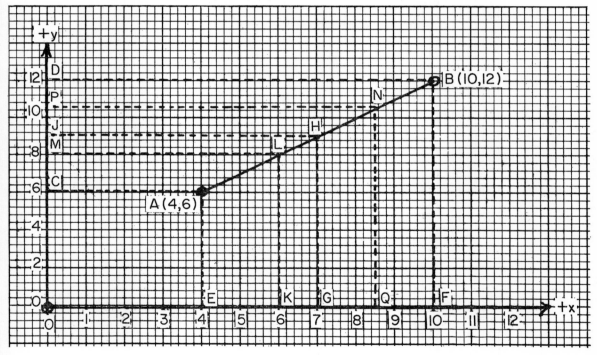

FIGURE 17

Ratio and Proportion

If we plot the two points *A* (4, 6) and *B* (10, 12) as above (Fig. 17) and join them with a straight line *AB* then any proportionate division of this line will be automatically evaluated on the axes. Hence, if *G* is the mid point of *E* and *F* (the X-ordinates of *A* and *B*) and if we follow up to the line *AB*, meeting at *H*, and travel across to the *Y* axis we shall arrive at the point *J* which will be seen to be mid-way also between the Y-ordinates of *A* and *B*.

Similarly if we move say one-third of the way from E to F (point K), follow up to the graph line AB (point L) and move over to the Y axis we shall arrive at the point M which is seen to be one-third of the way from C to D.

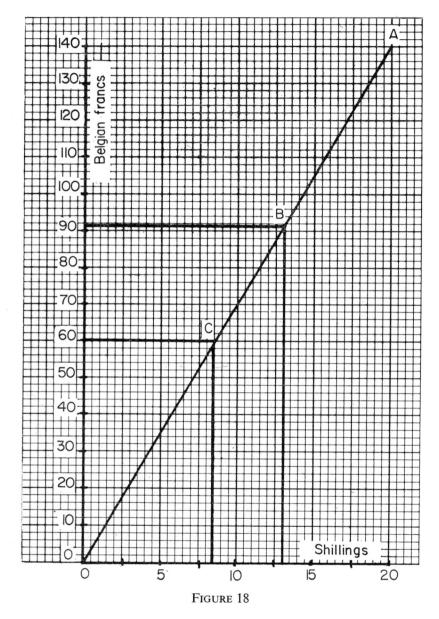

FIGURE 18

It follows, too, that if we move say three-quarters of the way along AB from A by projecting on to the two axes we obtain points P and Q, both of which are three-quarters of the way along CD and EF respectively.

(N.B. Geometric method of sub-dividing a straight line.)

Ready Reckoners

This simple process of interpolation can be used in obtaining facts by a quicker method than by arithmetic (but not necessarily with the same accuracy). For instance, suppose that we know the rate of exchange between Belgium and England is at the rate of 140 B. francs to £1; then by constructing a graph with suitable scales we can plot the point *A* linking the scales 140 B. fr. = 20*s*. and join the origin *O*, because 0 fr. = 0*s*. (Fig. 18).

This line constitutes a ready reckoner table, *e.g.*, if we wish to find the English equivalent of 60 B. fr., from the value 60 on the B.-fr. axis we strike a line horizontally to *OA* and from the point of contact *C* drop down to the shillings axis, arriving at a value about 8·5, *i.e.*, 8*s*. 6*d*. approximately, thence we can arrive at the estimation that 60 B. fr. are approximately equal to 8*s*. 6*d*. in English money.

Conversely, if we wish to convert 13*s*. to Belgian currency, from the value 13 on the shillings axis we draw a line vertically to meet our conversion line *OA* in the point *B*, then projecting horizontally to the vertical axis we arrive at the point 91, thus showing the relationship of 13*s*. to 91 B. fr.

To take another example: suppose a shopkeeper desires to add 17% to the cost price of his articles in order to arrive at a reasonable selling price, *i.e.*, an article costing 100 would be sold for 117 whatever currency the figures represent (shillings, pence, dollars or cents). A graph is constructed and the conversion line *OA* is drawn (Fig. 19).

Using the graph as before, we can estimate that an article costing 30 would sell at 35 approximately and conversely an article selling at 80 had cost about 68½.

(N.B. Greater accuracy can be obtained by using mm. graph paper instead of $\frac{1}{10}$ in. or $\frac{1}{8}$ in.)

Plotting a Straight Line—Method of Averages

In experimental graphs where it is necessary to construct a straight line through a number of obtained points and find its equation this method may be used (Fig. 20).

Suppose that the co-ordinates of twelve such points obtained are as follows:

(0·2, 1·8)   (0·6, 2·8)   (1·8, 3·8)   (2·4, 5·4)   (4·0, 6·0)   (4·2, 7·4)
(5·2, 7·6)   (5·8, 8·2)   (6·0, 9·2)   (7·0, 9·6)   (7·6, 10·8)   (9·0, 11·6)

These are plotted in the usual way as shown (Fig. 20). The next stage is to divide the points into arbitrary groups, *e.g.*, the first six and the last six and their ordinates are averaged as follows:

	Group 1			Group 2	
	x	*y*		*x*	*y*
	0·2	1·8		5·2	7·6
	0·6	2·8		5·8	8·2
	1·8	3·8		6·0	9·2
	2·4	5·4		7·0	9·6
	4·0	6·0		7·6	10·8
	4·2	7·4		9·0	11·6
Total	13·2	27·2	Total	40·6	57·0
Average	2·2	4·53	Average	6·77	9·5

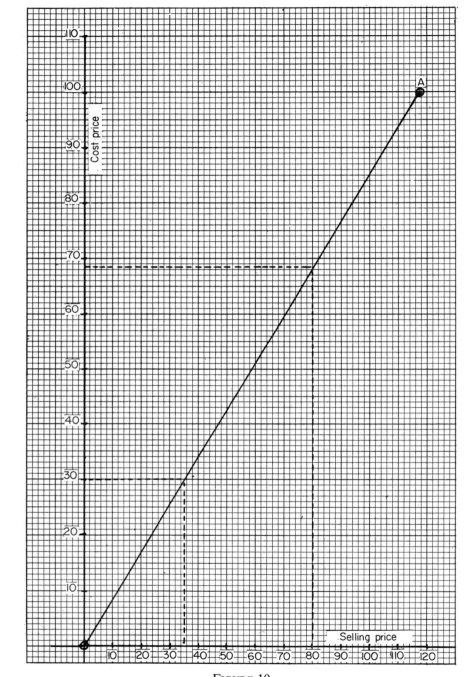

FIGURE 19

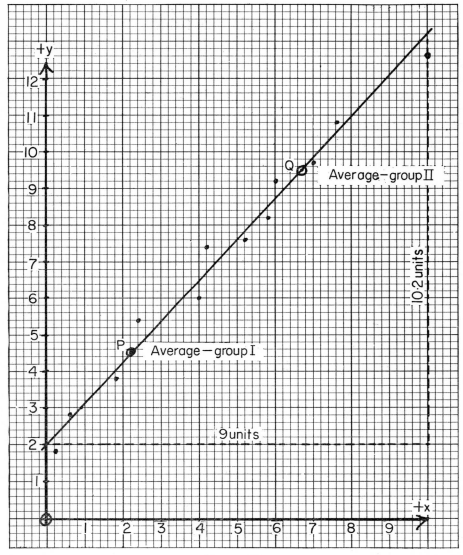

FIGURE 20

The two average points P (2·2, 4·53) and Q (6·77, 9·5) are then plotted and joined by a straight line as shown, the equation is then obtained from the general form $y = ax + b$ where a is the gradient of the line 10·2/9 and b is the point where it cuts the y axis, *i.e.*, 2.

Hence the equation of the line is

$$y = ax + b$$

$$= \frac{10·2}{9} x + b$$

$$= \frac{10·2x}{9} + 2$$

$$\text{or } 9y = 10·2x + 18$$

Double Scale Line Graphs

As has been seen in the section on "Column Graphs", it is a useful procedure when necessity demands to utilize a double vertical scale to show two factors.

In line graphs a similar problem arises when it is necessary to graph a range of data which would not be practically useful on a small sheet unless the data were divided into two groups (or more).

To take a simple example let us consider the data given in the following table concerning the weights of square mild steel bars:

Size	$\frac{1}{4}$ in.	$\frac{3}{8}$ in.	$\frac{1}{2}$ in.	$\frac{5}{8}$ in.	$\frac{11}{16}$ in.		
Wt./lb. per ft.	0·213	0·478	0·850	1·33	1·61		
Size	$\frac{3}{4}$ in.	1 in.	$1\frac{1}{4}$ in.	$1\frac{1}{2}$ in.	$1\frac{3}{4}$ in.	2 in.	$2\frac{1}{4}$ in.
Wt./lb. per ft.	2·60	3·40	5·31	7·65	10·41	13·60	17·21

If we tried to bring all these facts into a single graph for bars up to 20 ft. in length, with normal procedure the scale would have to be such that the first three sets of data would result in lines so close to the base line that they would be of no value graphically. On the other hand, if we increased the scale to overcome this difficulty we would find that the data of the last three or four bars would have to be omitted. It can, of course, be solved by taking the first group and constructing a graph on a fairly large scale, and taking the second group on a much smaller scale, but we should have, therefore, two separate graphs to cover one set of data.

It is a simple matter, however, to produce a compromise which in effect is the same as adding the second graph in a condensed form to the top of the first graph as shown in the diagram (Fig. 21).

Here $\frac{1}{10}$ in. represents 1 lb. weight up to 50 lbs. and above that $\frac{1}{10}$ in. represents 10 lb. weight.

To construct the graph up to the $\frac{11}{16}$-in. bar for a 20 ft. length is straightforward, but for the larger size bars it is necessary to work on a shorter length to form the lower portion of the graph, e.g., for a $1\frac{1}{2}$-in. square bar take the weight of a 6 ft. length (i.e., 45·90 lb.) and then from the point where it reaches the 50-lb. axis draw the line to the final figure for a 20 ft. length (i.e., 153 lb.) as indicated on the right-hand vertical axis. By this method a readable graph can be obtained in a single format for all the bars.

EXERCISES

1. A house agent charges 5% commission on the first £500 of the selling price of a property and $2\frac{1}{2}$% on any further amounts. Taking 1 in. = £100 selling price on the vertical axis up to £500 and $\frac{1}{10}$ in. = £100 selling price beyond £500, construct a graph up to a selling price of £4,000. On the horizontal axis use 1 in. = £20 commission charged up to £120.

From your graph estimate:

(a) The commission charged on a property worth £2,700.
   Answer: £80

(b) The selling price of a property on which £60 commission is charged.
   Answer: £1,900

2. A carrier charges 3 fr. for taking a parcel of 5 kgm. (or *pro rata* up to 5 kgm.). Above this weight he charges 1 fr. for 10 kgm. and *pro rata*. By taking 1 in. = 1 kgm. (up to 5 kgm.) and

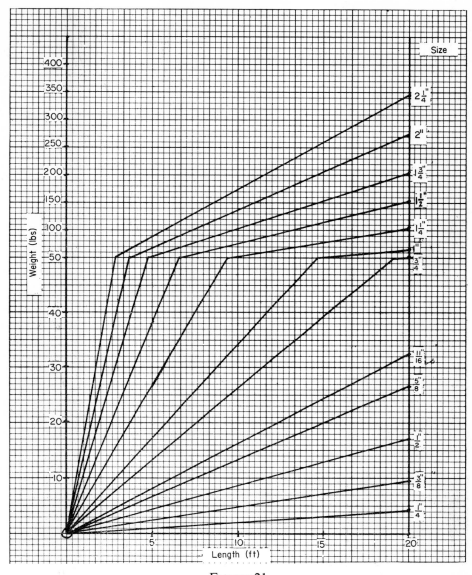

Size

FIGURE 21

1 in. = 10 kgm. beyond this weight on your vertical axis construct a scale up to 35 kgm. On the horizontal axis use a scale of 1 in. = 1 fr.

From your graph estimate:

(a) The weight carried for $2\frac{1}{2}$ fr.
  Answer: 4·167 or $4\frac{1}{6}$ kgm.
(b) What would be the charges on a package weighing 22 kgm.?
  Answer: 4·70 fr.
(c) What would be the charges on a package weighing 33 kgm.?
  Answer: 5·80 fr.

3. A courier, carrying confidential documents, charges for personal services over and above expenses incurred, 6*d.* a mile up to 100 miles; beyond this distance he charges 2*d.* a mile.

Taking the vertical axis to represent distance on a scale of 1 in. = 20 miles up to 100 miles, and 1 in. = 100 miles beyond; also a scale of 1 in. = £1 for personal charges on the horizontal axis construct a graph for journeys up to 450 miles.

From the graph estimate:

(a) The charge for a 340-mile journey.

    Answer: £4 10s.

(b) What would be his journey for a charge of £5?

    Answer: 400 miles

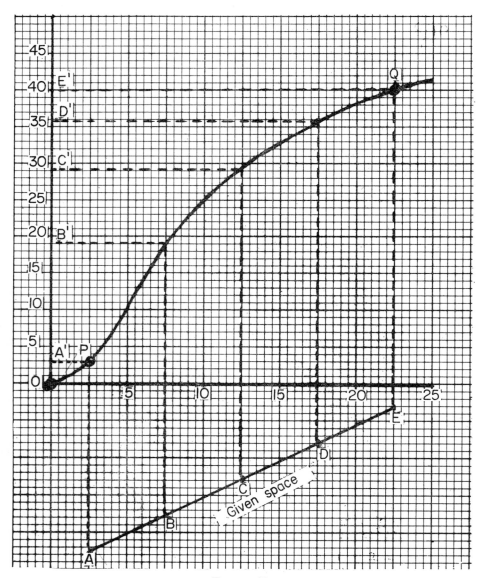

FIGURE 22

Change of Format

Often in engineering some odd length has to be sub-divided into parts, thus a part of a curve PQ (Fig. 22) is to be transferred to a given space (Fig. 23).

By marking off any convenient lengths in the given space and laying the length across the points P, Q, we can obtain the corresponding readings on the vertical axis, e.g., value A' for point A in the given space, value B' for point B, and so on.

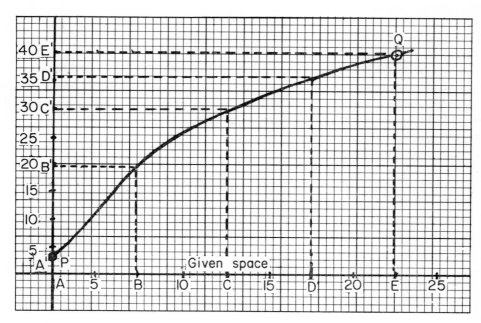

FIGURE 23

Hence by erecting a vertical scale in the given area and utilizing the values (A', B', C', D' and E') obtained from the points A, B, C, D and E, in the given space we can form the curve PQ as required.

EXERCISES

1. A certain chemical costs £5 for $\frac{1}{2}$ ton. Graphically obtain:

(a) The cost of 7 cwt.
   Answer: £3 10s.

(b) The cost of 4·4 cwt.
   Answer: £2 4s.

(c) How much chemical could be purchased for £4 2s.?
   Answer: 8·2 cwt.

Check your results arithmetically.
Use 1 in. = £1 on the horizontal axis and $\frac{1}{2}$ in. = 1 cwt. on the vertical axis.

2. A man earns £700 per annum. Graphically estimate:

(a) How long he would take to earn £140.
Answer: 2·4 months

(b) How much would he earn in 7·2 months?
Answer: £420

Use $\frac{1}{2}$ in. $= 1$ month on the horizontal axis and 1 in. $= £100$ on the vertical axis.

3. If 48 articles cost £2 4s. graphically estimate:

(a) How many articles can be purchased for 16s. 6d.?
Answer: 18

(b) What would be the cost of 37 articles (to nearest 3d.)?
Answer: 34s.

Take 1 in. $= 10s.$ on the horizontal axis and 1 in. $= 10$ articles on the vertical axis.

4. A passenger travelling by rail was charged £1 5s. for a 150-mile journey (second class). Construct a graph showing the cost up to 150 miles. Use mm. graph paper, taking a horizontal scale of 1 cm. $= 20d.$, and a vertical scale of 1 cm. $= 10$ miles.

From your graph find:

(a) The cost of travelling 103 miles?
Answer: 17s. 2d.

(b) What distance could be covered for a cost of one guinea?
Answer: 126 miles

5. Given that 3 in. equals $76\frac{1}{4}$ mm. approximately, graphically obtain the equivalents of:

(a) 62 mm.
Answer: 2·437 in.; $2\frac{7}{16}$ in.

(b) $1\frac{1}{2}$ in.
Answer: 38 mm.

Take $\frac{1}{10}$ in. $= \frac{1}{16}$ in. (*i.e.*, 16 squares on the graph paper to 1 in.) and $\frac{1}{10}$ in. $= 1$ mm. on your scales.

6. Given that a pressure of 71 lb./sq. in. is equal to 5 kgm./sq. cm. graphically estimate the values of:

(a) 3 kgm./sq. cm. in lb./sq. in.
Answer: $42\frac{1}{2}$

(b) 64 lb./sq. in. in kgm./sq. cm.
Answer: 4·5

Take 1 in. $= 1$ kgm./sq. cm. and 1 in. $= 10$ lb./sq. in.

7. The weight (W) of cast iron pipes $\frac{1}{4}$ in. thick in lb./lineal ft. are given below for certain bores (B) in inches:

W (lb.)	3·06	5·53	7·98	10·44	15·34	20·22
B (in.)	1	2	3	4	6	8

Construct a graph and from it estimate:

(a) The weight of a pipe with a 5-in. bore per foot.
Answer: $12\frac{3}{4}$ lb./ft

(b) The bore of a pipe weighing 17·8 lb./foot.
Answer: 7-in. bore

(Rule an average straight line.)

8. The following figures relate to the stock sizes of tin foil:

Gauge number	4	6	8	10	12	15	20
Sq. ft./lb.	20	30	40	50	60	75	100

Estimate the gauge number of tin foil having 25 sq. ft./lb. and the number of sq. ft./lb. for 18-gauge foil.
(Rule an average straight line through the points plotted.)
  Answers: No. 5; 90 sq. ft./lb.

9. The relationship between the draught power (in inches of water) and the height of a boiler chimney (in feet above the firegrate) are given below:

Height (ft.)	10	30	60	90	120	150
Draught power (in. of water)	0·07	0·22	0·44	0·66	0·88	1·10

Graphically determine the height of the chimney which produces a draught power of 0·26 inches and the draught power of a chimney 109 ft. high.
(Rule an average straight line.)
  Answers: 36 ft.; 0·80 in.

10. The percentage efficiency of an air compressor at various altitudes above sea level are given below:

Altitude (ft.)	0	2,000	4,000	6,000	8,000	10,000
Efficiency (%)	100	94	88	82·8	77·5	72·7

Estimate the efficiency at an altitude of 3,000 ft. and the height at which 80% efficiency is obtained.
(Rule an average straight line.)
  Answers: 91%; 7,200 ft.

11. The correction figures for the glass scale of a barometer at a certain pressure for various temperatures are as follows:

Temp. (°C.)	2	10	14	22	34
Correction (mm.)	0·24	1·21	1·69	2·66	4·10

Graphically estimate the correction for 18°C and 30°C by ruling a straight line through the plotted points.
  Answers: 2·18 mm.; 3·62 mm.

12. The table below gives the focus required for different size pictures at various distances from the screen with a 6-in. lantern objective:

Distance (ft.)	10	13	15	25	35	50
Diameter of picture (ft./in.)	5′	6′ 6″	7′ 6″	12′ 6″	17′ 6″	25′

Graphically estimate the distance required to obtain a picture 15 ft. in diameter.
  Answer: 30 ft.
What diameter picture is produced by the lantern being placed at 11 ft. from the screen?
  Answer: 5 ft. 6 in.

13. In an experiment to test Ohm's Law the following results were obtained:

E (volts)	0·1	0·3	0·5	0·7	0·9	1·1	1·3	1·5
I (amps)	0·09	0·27	0·47	0·63	0·81	0·99	1·17	1·35

(a) Draw the average straight line through these points and taking any pair of values from the graph estimate R (the constant) in the law $E = IR$.
Answer: 1·1
(b) What voltage is given when a current of 0·72 amp is flowing?
Answer: 0·8 volts
(c) What current flows under a voltage of 1·4?
Answer: 1·26 amp

14. The resistance R (ohms) of a wire was determined at various temperatures t °C.

R (ohms)	0·29	0·3	0·31	0·32	0·33	0·34
t °C	13	22·5	35	44	55	67

(a) Graphically determine the temperature when the resistance is 0·35 ohms (by ruling an average straight line).
Answer: 78°C
(b) Find the resistance of the wire at 0°C.
Answer: 0·278 ohms

15. The following table gives the barometric pressure (in mm.) at various heights above sea level (in metres).

Altitude	0	100	200	300	400	500	600	700	800	900
Pressure	760	751	742	733	724	716	707	699	690	682

Rule an average straight line and from your graph determine the barometric pressure at an altitude of 360 m. and the height at which the pressure is 712 mm. of mercury.
Answers: 728 mm.; 540 m.

16. The variations of temperature with altitude above sea level (in thousands of feet) is given in the following table:

Altitude	0	2	4	6	8	10	14	16	18	25	30
Temp. °F	59·0	51·8	44·8	37·5	30·4	23·3	9·2	1·9	−5·2	−30	−47

Rule an average straight line through the points and from your graph line estimate the temperature at a height of 12,000 ft. and the height at which the temperature is −12°F.
Answers: 16°F; about 20,000 ft.

17. The variation of the weight of 1 cubic foot of air with temperature is as follows:

Temp. °F	0	60	90	120	150
Weight (lb.)	0·086	0·076	0·072	0·0685	0·065

Draw the average straight line graph and from it estimate the weight of air per cubic foot when at a temperature of 50°F, and the temperature which will cause air to weigh 0·675 lb./cu. ft.
Answers: 0·0775 lb./cu. ft.; 130°F

18. The following table gives the volume of free air corresponding to 1 cu. ft. of air at given pressure (in lb.):

Pressure (lb.)	0	10	20	30	40	50	60
Vol. (cu. ft.)	1	1·68	2·36	3·04	3·72	4·40	5·08

Estimate the pressure necessary to compress 4 cu. ft. of air to 1 cu. ft., and the volume of free air which occupies 1 cu. ft. under pressure of 15 lb.
(Rule an average straight line.)
  Answers: 44·5 lb.; 2·0 cu. ft.

19. A certain Building Society offers the following terms of mortgage to its borrowers at 5% interest rate per £100:

Number of years	5	10	15	20	25
Repayments per month	38s. 6d.	21s. 7d.	16s. 1d.	13s. 5d.	11s. 10d.

Construct a graph and from it estimate the rate of repayment per £100 for a period of 12 years.
  Answer: 19s.
Also how many years would cover repayments at a rate per £100 of 14s. 6d. per month?
  Answer: 17½ years

20. The price of a certain cheese is £6 for 45 lb. Construct a graph showing the price of any quantity up to 45 lb., and from your graph find:

(a) The cost of 12 lb.
  Answer: 32s.
(b) The weight of cheese to be bought for £3 4s.
  Answer: 24 lb.

21. A cubic foot of water (1,728 cu. in.) weighs 62·3 lb. Construct a conversion graph and from it determine:

(a) The volume of 30 lb. of water.
  Answer: 830 cu. in.
(b) The weight of 1,500 cu. in. of water.
  Answer: 54 lb.

22. A gallon of water weighs 10 lb. What is the volume of this weight of water?
  Answer: 277 cu. in. approx.
(N.B. Use 1 cm. = 100 cu. in., and 1 cm. = 5 lb. on your scales.)

23. Given that 50 kgm. equal 1 cwt. approximately, graphically estimate:
(a) 20 kgm. in lb.
  Answer: 45 lb. approx.
(b) 94 lb. in kgm.
  Answer: 42 kgm. approx.

24. Given that 100 litres equal 22 gallons, graphically estimate:
(a) The number of litres in 57 gallons.
  Answer: 260 litres
(b) The number of gallons in 182 litres.
  Answer: 40 gallons
  D

25. Two lifting machines are tested with various loads (L lb.) and the effort required (F lb.) noted as follows:

Load	0	25	50	75	100	125	150	175	200
F_1	3	5	$6\frac{1}{2}$	$8\frac{1}{2}$	10	$11\frac{1}{2}$	14	15	$16\frac{1}{2}$
F_2	5	$7\frac{1}{2}$	10	13	16	18	21	$23\frac{1}{2}$	$25\frac{1}{2}$

Plot the points given above for both machines and by drawing two *average* straight lines through them estimate:

(a) The effort required by machine 1 to lift 120 lb.
   Answer: about $11\frac{1}{4}$ lb.
(b) The effort required by machine 2 to lift 120 lb.
   Answer: about $17\frac{1}{2}$ lb.
(c) Compare the effort required of these two machines in lifting this load. Which is the more efficient?
   Answer: $11\frac{1}{4} : 17\frac{1}{2}$, i.e., $9 : 14$. The first machine has therefore about 55% advantage.

26. Given that 200 Norwegian Kroner are equal in value to 145 Swedish Kroner, by means of a graph estimate the exchange value of:

(a) 60 Norwegian Kr.
   Answer: 43·5 Swedish Kr.
(b) 59 Swedish Kr.
   Answer: 80 Norwegian Kr.

27. The boiling points of water on the Fahrenheit and Reaumer scales are 212° and 80° respectively, whilst the freezing points of water are 32° and 0° respectively. By means of a graph estimate the conversion values of 86°F, 140°F, and 68°R.
   Answers: 24°R; 48°R; and 186°F

28. Given that 33 knots = 38 m.p.h., draw a conversion graph to show this relationship and from it estimate:

(a) How many m.p.h. are equivalent to 12 knots?
   Answer: 13·8 m.p.h.
(b) How many knots are equivalent to 23 m.p.h.?
   Answer: 20 knots

29. The following table gives the length (L) of a spring, in inches, when weights (W) in pounds are suspended on it:

W (lb.)	10	20	30	40	50
L (in.)	16	16·8	17·5	18·3	18·9

On plotting these points it will be seen that they all lie approximately on a straight line which should be drawn as near as possible to obtain an average result (Hooke's Law: Force $\propto$ Extension).

(a) Estimate the length of the spring when no weights are attached.
   Answer: 15·22 in.
(b) What would be the length of the spring with a load of 25 lb.?
   Answer: 17·18 in.
(c) What weight would stretch the spring to a length of $17\frac{1}{2}$ in.?
   Answer: About $42\frac{1}{2}$ lb.

30. An experiment is carried out to determine the variation of pressure of a column of water on different piston areas, the results being as follows:

Pressure (lb.)	10	18	25	37	50	70
Piston Area (sq. in.)	0·8	1·5	2·0	3·0	4·0	5·6

Taking 1 in. = 1 sq. in. of piston area as graph base, and 1 in. = 10 lb. pressure on the vertical axis, construct the best straight line through the plotted points, and from your graph estimate:

(a) What is the pressure when the area of the piston is 25 sq. in.?
Answer: 31 lb.
What is the area on which the column will exert a pressure of 60 lb.?
Answer: 4·8 sq. in.

31. A factory is illuminated by a number of lamps of equal power, and records of running costs show the following figures:

Number of lamps	100	200	270	380	450	580
Cost per hour (in pence)	24	48	66	90	108	138

Construct a graph by drawing the best straight line through the plotted points, taking 1 in. = 100 lamps as base, and 1 in. = 30d. on the vertical axis. From your graph estimate:

(a) The cost per hour of illuminating the factory with 350 lamps.
Answer: 7s. per hour

(b) How many lamps could be utilized for running costs of 10s. per hour?
Answer: 500 lamps

32. An experiment is conducted to investigate how a spiral changes in length when different weights are attached to the end, the recorded results being as follows:

Weight applied (in gm.)	11	25	39	50	59	68
Length of spiral (in cm.)	11	25	33	39	45	50

Plot these points and by drawing the best straight line through them find:

(a) The length of the spiral when no weight is attached.
Answer: 10 cm.

(b) Length of the spiral when the load is 34 gm.
Answer: 30 cm.

(c) The load necessary to stretch the spiral by 30 cm.
Answer: 51 gm.

33. A record is made of the time taken by an excavating machine to cut a certain channel, the results being as follows:

Length cut (in ft.)	12	24	38	50	66	80
Time (hours)	1·0	2·0	3·2	4·1	5·5	6·5

Taking 1 in. = 1 hour on the base and 1 in. = 10 ft. on the vertical axis, draw the average straight line through the plotted points and from your graph estimate:

(a) Length of trench cut by the machine in 5·1 hours.
Answer: 62 ft.

(b) The time required to dig 18 ft. of channel.
Answer: 1·5 hours

34. A voltmeter and ammeter on a certain test gave the following pairs of corresponding readings:

Volts	36	52	72	86	104	126
Amperes	0·25	0·8	1·4	1·9	2·45	3·15

Construct a graph showing the relationship of the readings given by drawing the best possible straight line through the plotted points and from it estimate:

(a) The reading of the voltmeter when the ammeter records 2 amps.
    Answer: 90 volts
(b) The reading of the ammeter when the voltmeter shows 82 volts.
    Answer: 1·75 amps

35. Records were taken as follows, of the number of articles made by a certain automatic machine:

No. of articles	100	180	270	360	480
Time of production (in min.)	3	5·2	8·0	10·4	14

By constructing the best line graph through the points plotted, estimate:

(a) The number of articles produced in 7 min.
    Answer: 240 articles
(b) How long the machine would take to produce 300 articles.
    Answer: 8·8 min.

36. A landscape gardener gave a customer the following figures as a guide to the cost of levelling and grassing a lawn:

Area (sq. ft.)	50	125	200	250	300
Cost (shillings)	16	38	62	78	94

Using 1 in. = 50 sq. ft. on your base, and 1 in. = 20*s.* cost on the vertical axis, construct a graph by drawing the best straight line and from it estimate:

(a) The cost of laying a lawn of 160 sq. ft.
    Answer: 50s.
(b) What area of lawn could be put down for 70*s.*?
    Answer: 225 sq. ft.

37. Given that 110 Spanish pesetas are equal in value to £1, construct a graph and from it find the values of 7*s.*, 9*s.* and 13*s.* in Spanish currency.
    Answers: 38 ptas.; 49 ptas.; 71 ptas.
Also ascertain the English equivalent of 20 ptas.; 45 ptas., and 85 ptas.
    Answers: 3s. 7½d.; 8s. 2d.; 15s. 5½d.

38. Given that 14½ Swedish Kr. equal £1, and 80 Portuguese escudos also equal £1, construct a graph giving the conversion of kroner to escudos and vice versa.
From your graph find approximately:

(a) How many Swedish Kr. are equal in value to 60 escudos?
    Answer: 10·90 Kr.
(b) What is the value in Portuguese currency of 5½ kroner?
    Answer: 30·3 escudos

39. Given that the freezing points of water on the Centigrade and Fahrenheit scales of temperature are 0° and 32° whilst the boiling points are 100° and 212° respectively, construct a conversion
graph showing the relationship between the two scales.
(Hint. Plot the two points representing the boiling and freezing points by their respective pairs
of figures and join by a straight line, *i.e.*, 0°C = 32°F, and 100°C = 212°F.)
From the graph read off in Fahrenheit: 10°C; 35°C; 84°C.
    Answers: 50°F; 95°F; 183°F
Read off in Centigrade: 85°F; 140°F; 185°F.
    Answers: 29½°C; 60°C; 85°C

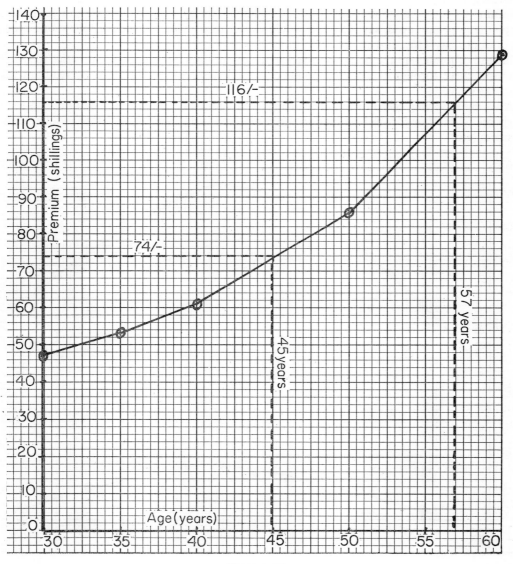

FIGURE 24

Interpolation

This principle can be utilized in estimating facts by *interpolation* from known data to arrive at suggested or approximate answers. For instance, if the insurance premiums for Whole Life Assurance with a certain company are listed as follows:

Age	30	35	40	50	60
Premiums (in shillings)	47	53	61	86	129

By constructing the graph we can proportionately estimate the premium required for intermediate ages (Fig. 24).

Joining up the points obtained from the tabulated data by straight lines we can see from the graph that a person aged, say, 45 years would expect to pay 74s. for such a policy, one aged 57 years would pay 116s. and so on.

Instead of joining up the points by a series of straight lines it is a common practice to sketch a freehand curve through the plotted points and estimates are then obtained by readings taken from the curve.

Also, by following the directional tendency of a curve an estimate may be obtained for the purposes of back or forward estimation when required, *e.g.*, forecasting future requirements in business, etc.

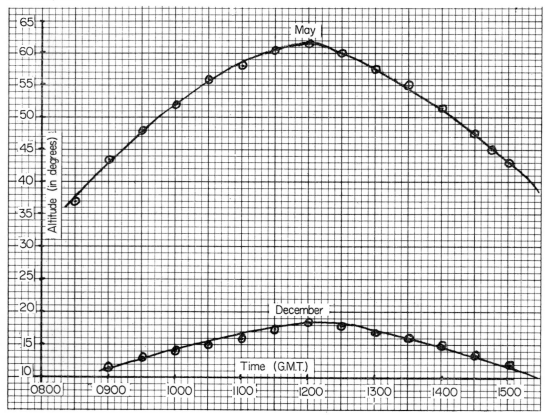

FIGURE 25

Experimental Data

Statistical graph forms are used by research workers in tabulating the date of their experiments and by skilful interpretation of the picture that evolves, important laws can be deduced. Such graphs often facilitate a better appreciation of observed phenomena.

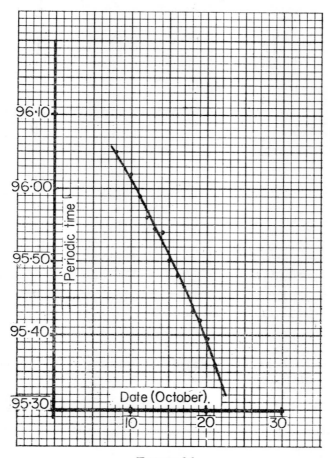

FIGURE 26

To take a simple example, a group of schoolboys note the altitude (angle above the horizon) of the sun by means of a theodolite at various intervals during the day in May and December. Their results are as follows (Fig 25):

December

Time (G.M.T.)	9.0	9.30	10.0	10.30	11.0	11.30	Noon	12.30	1.0	1.30	2.0	2.30	3.0
Angle (°)	$11\frac{1}{2}$	13	14	15	16	$17\frac{1}{2}$	$18\frac{1}{2}$	18	17	16	15	$13\frac{1}{2}$	12

May

Time (G.M.T.)	8.30	9.0	9.30	10.0	10.30	11.0	11.30	Noon	12.30	1.0	1.30	2.0	2.30	2.45	3.0
Angle (°)	37	$43\frac{1}{2}$	48	52	56	58	$60\frac{1}{2}$	$61\frac{1}{2}$	60	$57\frac{1}{2}$	55	$51\frac{1}{2}$	$47\frac{1}{2}$	45	43

On plotting the points it will be seen that they all lie approximately on two curves but owing to personal and experimental errors the curves are not perfectly defined. Hence, it is necessary to sketch the curves which *on the average* fit the data. Results too high would show themselves as points above the line whilst those too low would be placed below the line. The resultant curves, therefore, show quite clearly the altitude of the sun in winter compared with that in early summer.

To take another example: Early on Saturday October 5, 1957, the news of the first Russian satellite reached the Cavendish Laboratory, Cambridge. As the satellite had been launched the previous evening it was decided to make observations of its track (Fig. 26).

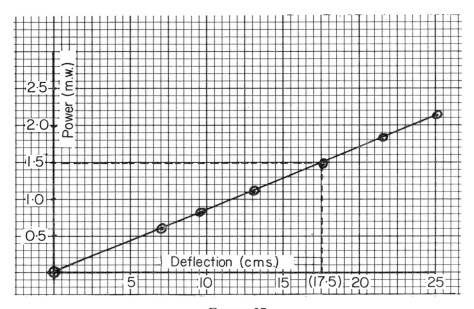

FIGURE 27

Amongst these observations were included measurements of its "period", *i.e.*, its time of rotation around the earth; a simple analysis of the data being as follows:

Date—

October	8	10	11	12	13	14	15	16	17	18	19	20	21	22
Periodic time (min./sec.)	96.05	96.02	95.59	95.56	95.54½	95.54	95.50	95.48	95.46½	95.43	95.42	95.39½	95.36	95.33

On sketching an *average line* as above it will be seen that a curvature in the graph is detectable showing that the satellite is getting down to regions of greater density resulting in a greater "drag" on its speed.

From such a curve it was found that the *average* decrease in period was about 2 sec. per day which corresponded to a change in the semi-major axis of its orbit of about 3·5 km. per day.

To take a final example, in this case an electrical instrument after manufacture is being calibrated by noting the deflection (in cms.) produced by a galvanometer when various powers (in mWs.) are applied to it, the data being as follows (Fig. 27):

Deflection (cm.)	0	7	9½	13	17½	21½	24
Power (mW.)	0	0·6	0·8	1·1	1·45	1·8	2·05

In this case all the points very closely approximate to a straight line, hence the *average* line can be drawn by a ruler and a reliable calibration "curve" obtained.

This calibration graph is, of course, attached to the apparatus and given to the purchaser for his use in conjunction with the instrument after leaving the factory.

Furthermore, from this graph in particular, being a straight line, a constant can be found by which deflection can be converted into milliwatts. It looks as though the constant is

$$\frac{17\cdot5}{1\cdot5} = 11\cdot667, \text{ thus } 11\cdot667 \times \text{galvo. deflection} = \text{milliwatts.}$$

EXERCISES

1. Construct a graph showing the cost of production of pig meat from the following table:

Live weight (lb.)	140	160	180	200	220	240	260	280
Cost, Dead wt. (£)	2·11	2·04	1·97	1·93	1·89	1·87	1·84	1·83

Join the points by straight lines and from the graph estimate the cost of production of pig meat from a live pig weighing 210 lb.

Answer: £1·91

2. A baby is weighed every six months and the following records are kept:

Age in months	0	6	12	18	24	30	36	42	48
Weight in lb.	6·5	15·7	20·8	24·7	27·6	30·0	34·0	38·2	41·4

Construct a graph and from it estimate:

(a) The baby's weight at the age of $3\frac{3}{4}$ years.

Answer: 39·8 lb.

(b) The baby's age when it weighed 32 lb.

Answer: 33 months

3. A boy's height is measured each birthday and the following records are kept. Construct a graph to represent these facts and from it estimate the boy's height at the age of 11 years, and at 17 years:

Age	10	12	13	14	15	16	18	19	20	21
Height (in.)	52	54	58	$59\frac{1}{2}$	60	62	$67\frac{1}{4}$	$69\frac{1}{2}$	70	70

Answers: 53 in. at 11 years; $64\frac{5}{8}$ in. at 17 years

4. The charge for inland letters and packets (1959) was as follows:

"Up to 1 oz. 3*d.*; 2 oz. $4\frac{1}{2}d$.; each additional 2 oz. or part $1\frac{1}{2}d$."

Construct a graph showing these values using 1 cm. = 1 oz. on the horizontal axis and 1 cm. = 1*d.* on the vertical scale. From the graph estimate:

(a) The cost of a 10 oz. parcel.

Answer: $10\frac{1}{2}d$.

(b) What weight package could be carried for 1*s.*?

Answer: $\frac{3}{4}$ lb. maximum

5. The record of a boy's age and height are given in the following table:

Age (years)	4	5	6	7	8	12	13	14
Height (in.)	37	40	43	46	47	55	57	59

By sketching an average curve through these points estimate his height at the age of 9, 10 and 11 years. (Take $\frac{1}{10}$ in. = 1 in. in height and $\frac{1}{2}$ in. = 1 year in age.)

Answers: 50 in. at 9; 52 in. at 10; $53\frac{3}{4}$ in. at 11

6. The following table gives the census figures of the United Kingdom (to the nearest million). Construct a graph showing these figures and from it estimate the population in 1941 when a census was not taken:

Year	1801	1811	1821	1831	1841	1851	1861	1871	1881	1891	1901	1911	1921	1931	1951
Population (millions)	9	10	12	14	16	18	20	23	26	29	33	36	38	40	44

Answer: 42 millions

By taking the data from 1891 and 1901 and by plotting on a larger scale (*e.g.* 1 in. = 1 million and $\frac{1}{2}$ in. = 1 year) join the two points by a straight line. Estimate from your graph line the population of the country in 1893.

Answer: 29,800,000

In what year did the population number 31,800,000 approximately?

Answer: 1898

7. It was noted that the seed of beet germinated in 22 days at a temperature of 40°F; in 9 days at 50°F; in $3\frac{3}{4}$ days at 60°F and in $3\frac{1}{2}$ days at 66°F. Plot these points and join in a smooth curve taking 2 in. = 10°F and 2 in. = 10 days on your scales. From your graph estimate:

(a) The temperature required to germinate beet seed in 5 days.

Answer: About $57\frac{1}{4}°F$

(b) How long it would take the seed to germinate at 45°F.

Answer: About $13\frac{3}{4}$ *days*

8. The table below sets out the effective rate of income tax for a single person and all earned income.

Income (£)	200	250	300	350	400	600	700	800	1000	1250
Effective rate	2d.	6d.	$11\frac{1}{2}d.$	1s. $4\frac{1}{2}d.$	1s. 8d.	2s. $8\frac{1}{2}d.$	3s. $2\frac{1}{2}d.$	3s. $7\frac{1}{2}d.$	4s. $2\frac{1}{2}d.$	4s. $8\frac{1}{2}d.$

Sketch an even curve through the plotted points and from your graph estimate:

(a) The effective rate on an income of £500.

Answer: About 2s. 3d.

(b) What income group shows an effective rate of 4s.?

Answer: About £900

9. By drawing two line graphs on the same area compare the expectation of life for boy and girl babies in England and Wales from the following figures:

Year	Boys	Girls
1871	40·4 years	43·5 years
1901	45·9 years	49·8 years
1911	51·5 years	55·4 years
1931	58·7 years	62·9 years
1951	65·84 years	70·88 years
1954	67·58 years	73·05 years

By joining the points obtained by straight lines, estimate from your graph the expectation of life for boy and girl babies in 1941.

Answer: 62·27 years and 66·89 years respectively

10. Construct a graph showing the number of notified cases of diphtheria during the following years:

Year	1938	1943	1944	1945	1946	1948	1949	1950	1951	1952	1953
Number (1,000s)	65	$34\frac{1}{2}$	$23\frac{1}{4}$	$18\frac{1}{2}$	12	$3\frac{1}{2}$	2	1	$\frac{3}{4}$	$\frac{1}{2}$	$\frac{1}{3}$

Taking $\frac{1}{2}$ in. = 10,000 cases and $\frac{1}{2}$ in. = 1 year (from 1938–1953) sketch an average curve and estimate the number of cases notified in 1942 and 1947.

Answer: Actually 46,281 and 5,609 respectively. Estimate 37,000 and 7,500 respectively.

11. Construct a graph line showing the infant mortality rate in England and Wales (*i.e.*, the number of infants who die under one year of age out of every 1,000 babies born alive) during the following years:

Year	1904	1914	1924	1934	1944
Number	145	105	75	59	46

By drawing an average curve through the plotted points and extending it to 1954 try to estimate the mortality rate for 1954, should the trend in death rate continue at the previous rates.

Answer: Estimate about 35. (Actually deaths in 1951 were 29; in 1952, 28, and in 1953, 27)

12. The record of a girl's age and weight are as follows:

Age (years)	4	5	6	8	9	11	12	14
Weight (lb.)	36	39	$41\frac{3}{4}$	52	$55\frac{1}{2}$	68	$76\frac{1}{2}$	$96\frac{3}{4}$

By sketching an average curve through the plotted points estimate the girl's weight at the ages of 7, 10 and 13 years respectively.

Answer: Actually $47\frac{1}{2}$, 62 and 87 lb. Estimated 47, $61\frac{3}{4}$ and $85\frac{1}{2}$ lb.

13. The following table gives the time in minutes for development of a negative for various temperatures of the developer:

Temp. (°F)	40	48	56	64	72	80
Time (min.)	42	33	26	20	15	11

Draw a graph on a temperature base and from it find the correct development time, to the nearest minute, when the developer is at 69°F, also the temperature to the nearest degree, which gives a developing time of half an hour.

Answer: Time 17 min. Temperature 51°F

14. The following table indicates the boiling points (°C) of water at various barometric heights (in mm. of mercury):

Barometric height	680	690	700	710	720	730	740	750	760	770	780
Boiling point	96·91	97·32	97·71	98·11	98·49	98·88	99·25	99·63	100·0	100·37	100·73

Graphically estimate the boiling point of water under a pressure of 726 mm., and the barometric height when water boils at 99·4°C.

Answer: 98·7°C. 744 mm.

15. The temperatures of a volume of air at a certain pressure are varied and the respective temperatures and volumes recorded as follows:

Temperature (°C)	0	10	20	30	40	50	60	70	80
Volume	36	37	38·6	40	41·2	42·6	44·2	45·4	46·8

Plot the points drawing an average graph line and hence obtain the temperature of the air when its volume was 43, also the volume at a temperature of 16°C.

Answers: 52°; 38

16. A certain volume of air is kept constant whilst its pressure is increased by raising the temperature, the following results being obtained:

Temperature (°C)	0	21	32	54	75	100
Pressure (mm. of mercury)	760	818	849	910	968	1,038

What conclusion can you make from a study of the graph form?

17. The following table gives the exposure suitable for various distances of the lens of an enlarger from the printing paper:

Distance (in.)	6	16	24	32	43
Exposure (sec.)	2	14	32	56	104

Draw a graph on a distance base, and from it find what exposure is needed for a distance of 1 ft., also what distance is being used when the correct exposure is 86 sec.

Answers: 8 sec.; 39 in.

18. The correct exposures for a camera for various lens aperture numbers for a particular object are as follows:

Aperture number	4	16	26	37	43
Exposure (seconds)	1	12	32	70	100

By constructing a graph on an aperture base, find the exposure necessary for aperture number 40, also the aperture which requires an exposure of 20 sec.

Answers: Exposure 82 sec. Aperture No. 21

19. A fishing tackle catalogue quotes the following figures for gut substitute:

Size	1	2	3	4	5	6	8	10	14	16	18	20
Breaking strain wet (in lb.)	1	2	3	4½	6	8	14	25	54	68	83	100

(a) What is the breaking strain of No. 7 gut substitute?
(b) What minimum size tackle would be needed to safely land a 36 lb. fish?

Answers: (a) 10 lb. (b) No. 12 with 40 lb. breaking strain

20. The following table gives the sizes of steel swivels for fishing, with their lifting ability (in lb.):

Size	3/0	2/0	1/0	1	3	4	6	8	9	10
Lift (lb.)	150	135	120	107	82	70	49	30	23	18

Graphically determine the lift of a No. 2 swivel and what is the smallest size of swivel which would safely lift the 36 lb. fish mentioned in the previous question?

Answers: 94½ lb. A No. 7 swivel with lift of 40 lb.

21. The comparative volumes of a certain mass of water are estimated at various temperatures under normal conditions:

Temp. (°C)	0	1	3	5	6	8	10
Volumes	1·000130	1·000072	1·000008	1·000008	1·000030	1·000116	1·000260

Represent these facts in a graph and find the temperature at which water will obtain its maximum density. (As all data re volume is 1 + it is very convenient to plot only the 4th, 5th and 6th decimal places, *i.e.*, ranging 130, 72, 8, 8, 30, 116 and 260.

Answer: 4°C

Estimate the volumes at 7°C and 2½°C.

Answers: 1·00007 and 1·00002

22. The following table relates the density of water to its temperature under normal pressure conditions:

Density	0·999	0·999	0·998	0·995	0·992	0·988	0·983	0·978	0·972	0·965	0·958
Temp. (°C)	0	10	20	30	40	50	60	70	80	90	100

Sketch the graph as evenly as possible and from it estimate the density of water at 85°C and the temperature at which water has a density of 0·980.
    Answers: 0·969; 65°C

23. The following table gives the time at which the sun crosses the meridian at Greenwich, on different dates:

Date	March 15	March 27	April 8	April 22	May 1	May 15
Time (hr.)	12·09	12·05$\frac{1}{2}$	12·02	11·58	11·56	11·55

Draw a graph on a date base and hence find the time of the sun's crossing of the meridian on March 22, also the date on which the crossing occurs at 12·00 hours exactly.
    Answers: Transit at 12·07 hours; Date: April 15

24. This table gives the length in hours of the longest day at various latitudes:

Latitude	0°	13°	34°	50°	60°	65°
Day	12	12$\frac{3}{4}$	14$\frac{1}{4}$	16	18$\frac{1}{2}$	21

Draw a graph using latitude as base. From it find the length of the longest day at latitude 56°, also the latitude where the longest day is 13$\frac{1}{2}$ hr.
    Answers: Length of day, 17$\frac{1}{4}$ hr.; Latitude 24°

25. (a) The following tables give the areas of certain polygons when the side in each case is 1. Plot the points indicated, join with a smooth curve, and from your graph complete the missing values.

No. of sides	3	4	5	6	7	8	9	10	11	12
Area	0·4	1	1·7	?	?	4·8	?	7·7	?	11·2

    Answers: 2·6, 3·6, 6·2 and 9·35

(b) The following tables give the areas and circumferences of certain circles. Plot the given data, join with a smooth curve, and estimate the circumference of circles whose areas are 2, 15 and 26:

Circumference	3$\frac{1}{2}$	6	10	13	16	20
Area	1	3	8	13$\frac{1}{2}$	20	32

    Answers: 5, 13$\frac{3}{4}$ and 18

26. The angles between two adjacent sides of various regular polygons are as follows:

No. of sides	3	4	5	6	8	10	12
Angle°	60	90	108	120	135	144	150

Plot the graph joining up the points in a smooth curve and estimate from your graph the angles between the adjacent sides of (a) a heptagon (7 sides); (b) a nonagon (9 sides) and (c) unodecagon (11 sides).
    Answers: (a) 128$\frac{4}{7}$°; (b) 140°; (c) 147$\frac{3}{11}$°

27. The following table gives the Birmingham Wire Gauge numbers with their diameters in inches:

No.	0	5	10	15	20	30	36
Diameter	0·340	0·220	0·134	0·072	0·035	0·012	0·004

Plot the values, sketch a smooth curve and estimate:

(a) The diameter of a No. 8 wire.
  Answer: 0·165 *in.*
(b) The gauge number of a wire whose diameter is 0·020 in.
  Answer: No. 25 *B.W.G.*

28. The following data concerns Whitworth Standard Screw Threads for bolts (D = diameter in in.; N = number of threads per in.):

D	0·25	0·5	0·75	1·0	1·5	2·0	2·5
N	20	12	10	8	6	4·5	4·0

Sketch an average curve and from it estimate:

(a) The diameter of a bolt with 14 threads per inch.
  Answer: 0·4 in.
(b) The number of threads per inch on a bolt 1·75 in. in diameter.
  Answer: 5·0

29. The gauge number (No.) and threads per inch (T.P.I.) of certain B.A. apparatus screws are as follows:

No.	25	23	20	17	14	10	6	2	0
T.P.I.	362·8	282·2	211·6	149·4	110·4	72·6	47·9	31·4	25·4

By sketching an approximate curve estimate the number of threads per inch on a No. 16 bolt, and the gauge number of a bolt with 255 T.P.I.
  Answers: About 135; *No.* 22 *B.A.*

30. The weights (W) of steel rods per foot are as follows with various diameters (D):

D (in.)	0·5	1·0	1·5	2·0	2·5	3·0
W (lb.)	0·65	2·7	6·0	10·7	16·8	24·0

Estimate from your graph the weight per ft. of rods $1\frac{1}{4}$ in.; $2\frac{1}{4}$ in. and $2\frac{3}{4}$ in. in diameter.
  Answers: 4·5 *lb.;* 13·66 *lb.;* 20 *lb.*

31. Steel shafts of varying diameters (D) transmitted the following horse power (P) when revolving at 50 r.p.m.

D (in.)	1·5	2·0	2·5	3·0	4·0	5·0
P (h.p.)	3·3	8·0	15·6	27·0	64	125

Plot the points, join by a smooth curve, and estimate:

(a) The horse power a $4\frac{1}{2}$ in. shaft would transmit.
  Answer: 95 *h.p.*
(b) What diameter shaft would be required to transmit 43 h.p.?
  Answer: $3\frac{1}{2}$ *in.*

32. A cotton driving rope 1 in. in diameter when tested at certain speeds transmitted the following horse power:

Speed (ft./min.)	2,500	3,000	3,500	4,000	4,500	5,000	5,500
H.P.	11·8	12·3	13·6	14·5	15·0	15·0	14·5

Graphically determine:

(a) The maximum horse power which could be transmitted with this driving rope.
(b) The speed necessary to obtain the maximum h.p. transmission.
(c) The horse power transmitted at 3,800 ft./min.
(d) The speed necessary to transmit 12 h.p.
   Answers: (a) 15·1 h.p.; (b) 4,750 ft./min.; (c) 14·2 h.p. and (d) 2,800 ft./min.

33. The following is a table of the diameter of wires fusing at various current strengths:

Current (amps)	1	2	3	4	5
Diameter (in.)	0·0026	0·0041	0·0054	0·0065	0·0076

Draw a graph and from it determine the diameter of a wire which will fuse at 3·4 amps; also the current which will fuse a wire of diameter 0·0046 in.
   Answers: 0·00585 in.; 2·35 amps

34. Engine

revs./min.	1,500	2,000	2,500	3,000	3,500	4,000	4,500
Pumping losses lb./sq. in.	2·0	2·3	2·9	4·0	5·4	6·9	8·6

Draw a graph of these data using engine revs. as base. Find the pumping losses at 2,700 revs./min., also the speed which gives a loss of 6·2 lb./sq. in.
   Answers: 3·3 lb./sq. in.; 3,800 revs./min.

35. Engine

revs./min.	1,500	2,000	2,500	3,000	3,500	4,000	4,500
Friction losses lb./sq. in.	7·7	8·6	10·0	11·4	13·1	15·1	17·3

Draw a graph of these data using engine revs. as base. Find the friction loss at 2,300 revs./min., also the speed which gives a friction loss of 14·2 lb./sq. in.
   Answers: 9·4 lb./sq. in.; 3,800 revs./min.

36.

Air Temp. (°Abs.)	276	268	258	248	238	228
Engine efficiency %	79·2	67·5	54·8	44·2	35·3	28·0

Using temperature as a base, draw a graph of these data and from it find the efficiency at a temperature of 265° Abs., also the temperature at which the efficiency is 40%.
   Answers: 63%; 243½° Abs.

37.

Diameter of cylinder (in.)	1	2	3	4	5
Permissible load (tons)	16	63	141	251	393

The above table gives the permissible loads for certain cylindrical metal shafts. Draw a graph using diameter as base. From it read the diameter needed to carry a load of 200 tons; also, the load carried by a cylindrical metal shaft of diameter 2·5 in.
   Answers: 3·55 in.; 100 tons

38. This is a table of errors of an airspeed indicator at varying speeds:

True speed (m.p.h.)	100	150	200	350	300	350
Error (m.p.h.)	−15·0	−4·0	+2·5	+6·0	+8·5	+9·0

Positive values mean the indicator reads too high, negative values, too low.

(a) At what speed is the indicator correct?
     Answer: 178 *m.p.h.*
(b) What is the reading of the indicator when true speed is 130 m.p.h. and when it is 330 m.p.h.?
     Answers: 122 *m.p.h. and* 338·8 *m.p.h.*

39. If an aeroplane is flying at a certain speed the angle at which it should bank for a turn (with given radius) is given below:

Radius of turn (ft.)	350	450	550	600	700	812
Angle of bank	70°	65°	$60\frac{1}{4}°$	$58\frac{1}{4}°$	54°	50°

Using radius as a base, draw the graph and find from it:

(a) The angle of bank for a turn of radius 200 ft.;
(b) The radius of a turn if it is banked at 63°.
(Suggested scales 1 in. = 100 ft. radius of turn and 2 in. = 10° bank.)
     Answers: $77\frac{1}{2}°$ *and* 490 *ft.*

40. The following table gives the efficiency of an aeroplane engine at various altitudes:

Height above sea level (ft.)	0	2,000	4,000	6,000	8,000	10,000
Relative efficiency	1·000	0·930	0·857	0·792	0·732	0·675

Graphically determine the height at which the efficiency is 0·890 and the efficiency at 7,000 ft. using height as base.
     Answers: 3,100 *ft.;* 0·7625

41. For a certain aeroplane the possible rates of climbing for various speeds are shown in the following table:

Rate of climb (ft./min.)	374	437	511	493	397	242
Speed (ft./sec.)	65	70	80	90	100	110

Sketch the curve as carefully as possible and from it estimate the maximum rate of climb and the speed necessary for this.
     Answers: 517 *ft./min.;* $83\frac{1}{4}$ *ft./sec.*

42. From trials made with the engine of a ship the following data were obtained:

Speed (knots)	2	4	6	8	10	12
Coal consumption (tons/day)	5·5	11·5	19·5	28	41	59

Graphically estimate:

(a) The coal consumption for a speed of 5 knots.
     Answer: $15\frac{1}{4}$ *tons per day*
(b) The speed for a consumption of 37·5 tons per day.
     Answer: $9\frac{1}{2}$ *knots*

43. In the following table the angle of attack and the lift coefficient of a certain aircraft are connected by these values:

Angle of attack	0°	1°	2°	3°	4°	5°	7°
Lift coefficient	0·288	0·359	0·418	0·468	0·508	0·541	0·550

Draw a graph using the angle of attack as base. From it find the lift coefficient corresponding to an angle of 2·6° and the angle of attack giving a lift coefficient of 0·520.
Answers: 0·448; 4·3°

44. This is a table of engine efficiency at various speeds of revolutions:

Revs./min.	240	360	480	600	720	840	960
% efficiency	23·0	31·2	37·8	42·0	42·4	39·5	34·5

Using revolutions as base, find the speed which gives the greatest efficiency, also the efficiency at this speed.
Answers: 670 revs./min.; 43%

45. The power output of a certain aero-engine, without boost, depends on the height above sea-level. This is a table of output at different heights, expressed as a percentage of sea level output:

Height (ft.)	0	10,000	20,000	30,000	40,000	50,000	60,000
Output (%)	100	77·5	58·9	42·3	29·0	18·0	8·0

Draw a graph with height as base and from it find at what height the output is 70%; also find the output at 35,000 ft.
Answers: 14,000 ft.; 36%

46. To allow for the effect of altitude on an airspeed indicator, the readings can be multiplied by a correction factor. Values of this factor are given for different heights in the table below:

Height (ft.)	0	10,000	20,000	30,000	40,000	50,000	60,000
Correction factor	1·00	1·16	1·37	1·63	2·02	2·57	3·34

Draw a graph, using height as base, and from it find the value of the correction factor at 24,000 ft.; also the height at which the correction factor has the value of 2·40.
Answers: 1·46; 47,000 ft.

47. The pitches in millimetres of B.A. screws are listed below with their gauge numbers:

No.	0	2	5	9	13	16	18	22
Pitch mm.	1·0	0·81	0·59	0·39	0·25	0·19	0·15	0·10

Graphically determine the pitch of a No. 6 B.A. screw and the gauge number of a screw with pitch 0·28 mm.
Answers: 0·53 mm.; No. 12 B.A.

48. The safe loads which can be carried by tubular struts of different lengths are given below:

Load (lb.)	6,000	5,400	4,700	3,000	2,000	1,300	920
Length (in.)	3·0	10·0	15·0	22·1	27·0	37·0	50·0

Draw a graph using length as base, and find how long the strut is that will just carry 4,000 lb.; also, the permissible load on a strut 32 in. long.
Answers: 18·5 in.; 1,550 lb.

E

49. The cylinder head temperatures for various percentages of Benzole in the fuel supplied to an engine are as follows:

Benzole (%)	0	10	20	30	40	50	60
Temp. (°F)	690	670	640	560	490	475	470

Draw a graph using % Benzole as base and from it read the cylinder head temperature for fuel 35% Benzole, also the % Benzole which gives a temperature of 610°F.
Answers: $517\frac{1}{2}$°*F; 25%*

50. The combustion chamber temperatures of an engine for various proportions of Tetra-ethyl lead in cc. per gallon of fuel are given below:

Tetra-ethyl lead (cc.)	0·4	0·6	0·8	1·0	1·2	1·4
Temperature °C	414	396	379	365	353	344

Draw a graph with fuel mixture as base and estimate the temperature corresponding to 0·72 cc.; also, the proportion which will give a temperature of 360°C.
Answers: 385°C; 1·075 cc.

51. Corresponding values of the performance (*D* miles per gallon) and the speed (*V* m.p.h.) for a particular motor-cycle engine are given in this table:

V (m.p.h.)	0	10	20	30	40	50	60
D (m.p.h.)	0	35	52	62	62	59	56

Draw a graph using speed as base, and so find the most economical running speed, and the mileage per gallon at this speed.
Answers: Speed $34\frac{1}{2}$ *m.p.h.; consumption* $63\frac{1}{4}$ *m.p.g.*

52. This table gives the thermal efficiency of a particular engine for different compression ratios:

Compression ratio	4·0	4·5	5·5	6·5	7·5	8·0
Efficiency %	29·0	31·2	34·6	37·3	39·6	40·0

Draw a graph using compression ratio as base and from it find the thermal efficiency corresponding to a compression ratio of 5·0; also, the compression ratio for an efficiency of 36%.
Answers: 32·9%; ratio of 6·0

53. The following table gives the values of the Brake Horse Power developed by an engine (expressed as a percentage of the maximum obtainable) for different values of the air–petrol ratio of fuel supplied. Draw a graph using air–petrol as base and hence find the ratio giving maximum Brake Horse Power, also the percentage horse power obtained for a ratio of 18:

Ratio	10	$12\frac{3}{4}$	15	17	$18\frac{3}{4}$	20
% Power	94	99	98	90	79	70

Answers: $13\frac{3}{4}$*; 84%. (N.B. Graph must touch* 100%.)

54. Experiments with a speed indicator show that the pressure set up depends on the speed as in the following table:

Speed (m.p.h.)	40	50	60	70	80
Pressure (mm. of mercury)	20·0	31·3	45·1	61·4	80·2

Draw a graph on a speed base and hence determine the pressure developed at 75 m.p.h., and the speed corresponding to a pressure of 38 mm. of mercury.
Answers: 71 mm.; 55 m.p.h.

55. This table gives the load (in lb.) which can be supported by steel wires of different Standard Wire Gauges:

S.W.G.	13	14	16	18	20	22	24
Load (lb.)	1,260	1,080	720	410	230	140	80

Draw a graph using gauge as base. From it find:

(a) The load carried by a 21-gauge wire.
Answer: 180 lb.
(b) The gauge of a wire which will just carry 900 lb.
Answer: 15 S.W.G.

56. This table gives the weight in lb./sq. ft. of aluminium sheet of different thicknesses, in Standard Gauge numbers:

Gauge No.	16	18	20	22	24	26
Weight (lb./sq. ft.)	0·89	0·67	0·49	0·38	0·31	0·25

Draw a graph using gauge numbers as base and from it find:

(a) The wt./sq. ft. of 17 gauge sheet.
Answer: 0·775 lb.
(b) The gauge which weighs 0·345 lb./sq. ft.
Answer: 23 S.W.G.

57. The following table gives the maker's recommendations for the smallest advisable pulley diameters for a certain $\frac{3}{4}$-in. rope when moving at various rope velocities:

Diameter (in.)	13	15	19	24	28
Velocities (ft./min.)	2,000	3,000	4,000	5,000	6,000

Using velocity as base, estimate the pulley diameter for a speed of 3,400 ft./min. and the speed permissible for a pulley of diameter 27 in.
Answers: $16\frac{1}{2}$ in.; 5,700 ft./min.

58. On test, certain iron crane chains gave the following safe loads according to their diameters:

Diameter (in.)	$\frac{5}{16}$	$\frac{1}{2}$	$\frac{13}{16}$	$\frac{15}{16}$	1	$1\frac{1}{2}$	2
Safe load (tons)	$\frac{1}{2}$	$1\frac{1}{2}$	4	$5\frac{1}{4}$	6	$13\frac{1}{2}$	24

Graphically estimate the safe load for a chain of $1\frac{3}{16}$ in. diameter and the diameter of the chain which could safely lift a load of 17 tons.
Answers: $8\frac{1}{2}$ tons; $1\frac{11}{16}$ in.

59. The following table shows the quantity (Q) of steam per hour (in thousands of lb.) according to the various lifts (L) of the valve (in.).

L	0	0·2	0·4	0·8	1·2	1·5
Q	0	60	120	160	188	200

Find how much the valve must be opened to pass 180,000 lb. of steam per hour and how much is passed when the valve is opened 0·3 in.
Answers: 1·09 in.; 100,000 lb. per hour

60. The coefficient of friction was determined for various air compressors with different pipe diameters, the results being as follows:

Diameter (in.)	1	2	3	4	7	10	12
Coefficient of friction	0·012	0·0075	0·006	0·005	0·004	0·0036	0·0035

Estimate the frictional coefficient in a pipe $1\frac{1}{2}$ in. in diameter and the diameter of a pipe which would give a coefficient of 0·0042.

Answers: 0·009; 6 *in.*

61. The following table gives the percentage elongation (E) of a sample of rubber cord for different values of the load (L lb.) applied to it:

L (lb.)	0	49	75	84	100	125	190	285
E (%)	0	25	50	75	100	125	145	155

Draw a graph with load as base and from it find the elongation for a load of 150 lb., also the load to produce an elongation of 60%.

Answers: 135%; 80 *lb.*

62. The water vapour pressure at certain temperatures is recorded as follows:

Temperature (°C)	0	10	20	30	40	50
Pressure (mm. of mercury)	4·6	9·2	17·4	31·5	54·9	92·0

(a) At what temperature is the pressure 40 mm. of mercury?

Answer: 34°C

(b) What is the vapour pressure at 24°C?

Answer: 22 mm. of mercury

63. The variations in the tension of a sonometer string which is varied in length to keep constant pitch is recorded below:

Tension (lb.)	4	6	8	10	12	14	16	18	20
Length (cm.)	30	36	41·6	46	49·8	54·5	58·5	62	66

What relationship can you suggest from a study of this graph?

64. The following table records the time of oscillation and the length of a simple pendulum.

Length (cm.)	4	9	16	25	36	49	64	81	100
Time (sec.)	0·4	0·6	0·8	1·0	1·2	1·4	1·6	1·8	2·0

Draw on the same area for comparison the two graphs showing:

(a) The relationship of length and time.
(b) The relationship of length and (time)².
What conclusions can you deduce from these graphs?

65. The following is a table of the diameter of wire needed to carry different electric currents in safety:

Current (amps)	1	2	3	4	5
Diameter (in.)	0·021	0·034	0·044	0·053	0·062

Draw a graph and from it determine the diameter of a wire which will carry 2·6 amps and also the current which can be carried by a wire of diameter 0·048 in.

Answers: 0·040 *in.*; 3·45 *amps*

66. This table gives the lifting power of an electric magnet for different currents:

Current (amps)	0	1·1	1·8	2·5	3·1	4·0	5·0
Lift (lb. wt.)	0	50	210	400	500	530	530

What is the lift for a current of 2·8 amps and what current will lift 260 lb. wt.?

Answers: 460 lb. wt.; 2·00 amps

67. A sonometer wire is tuned to certain notes by weights tensioning it. On test the following results were obtained with some tuning forks:

Fork	C	D	E	F	G	A	B	C
No. of vibrations (per sec.)	256	288	320	341	384	426	480	512
Tension (kgm.)	3·6	4·6	—	6·5	8·1	10·3	—	14·8

Graphically estimate the tension required to tune the wire to the notes E and B the frequencies of which are given above.

Answers: 5·7 kgm.; 13 kgm.

68. This table gives the noise output in decibels of a loudspeaker unit for different settings of the control. Draw a graph and find output at setting 23, also the setting required for 40 decibels output.

Settings	0	9	20	30	40	50
Output	12	35	49	56	60	62

Answers: 53 decibels; setting 12

69. An adjustable resistance on test gave the following corresponding figures of current and resistance:

Resistance (Amps)	1·0	2·0	3·3	4·0	5·0	10·0
Current (Ohms)	145	31	12	9	6·5	1·5

Graphically estimate the resistance when a current of 2·6 amps is flowing, also the current passed by a resistance of 8 ohms.

Answers: 18 ohms; 4·4 amps

70. An induction coil on test showed the following data for spark gap voltages under normal conditions:

Gap between points (in.)	1	2	3	4	6	8
Pressure (kv.)	30	50	65	77	102	125

Graphically determine the pressure on a 5-in. spark gap and the gap necessary for 150 kv. discharge.

Answers: 90 kv.; 10·2-in. gap

71. The following table gives the approximate resistances (in ohms per 1,000 yd.) for copper wire 100% conductivity in various gauges (standard wire gauge).

S.W.G.	12	14	18	20	22	24	26	30
Resistance	2·9	4·8	13·5	24·1	39·8	64·6	99·5	203

Graphically find the resistance per 1,000 yd. of 16 S.W.G. wire and the gauge of wire which would give about 150 ohms resistance per 1,000 yd.

Answers: 7·6 ohms; 28 S.W.G.

72. A length of 12 S.W.G. nichrome wire is stretched horizontally in free air and heated by passing varying currents. The temperature and currents recorded are

Temperature (°C)	100	200	500	700	1,000
Current (amps)	12·5	22·5	45	57·5	75·5

Find the temperature produced by a current of 40 amps, also the current necessary to heat the wire to 800°C.

Answers: 430°C: 64 amps

73. The following table gives the current in milliamps flowing through a thermionic valve for various values of the plate voltage.

Voltage	−8	0	+10	+20	+29	+38	+50	+60
Current	0·0	2·0	8·6	23·5	40·0	51·0	55·0	56·5

Draw a graph using voltage as base.

(a) What current is produced by a voltage of 34 volts?

Answer: 47 m.amps

(b) What voltage will produce a current of 15 m.amps?

Answer: 14·6

74. This table gives the value of the Magnetic Variation in London (Regents Park) on various dates (all values are West of True North).

Year	1665	1715	1765	1800	1850	1900	1935
Variation	1½°	11½°	20°	24°	23°	16½°	11°

Draw a graph to show Variation, using date as base. Hence find the Variation, correct to nearest half degree in 1790; also the years in which the magnetic variation was 15°.

Answers: (a) 23°; (b) 1736 and 1911

75. The resistance of a resistance thermometer is measured in ohms at various temperatures and recorded as follows:

Temp. (°C)	14·5	30·0	47·5	63	100
Resistance (ohms)	6·8	7·2	7·6	7·9	8·5

Plot these points, sketching an average calibration curve for the instrument and from it estimate:

(a) The resistance of the thermometer at 40°C.

Answer: 7·44 ohms

(b) The temperature at which the resistance is 8·1 ohms.

Answer: 75°C

76. The following figures relate to the results of a night vision test on a particular airman, the sensitivity recovered after different periods in the dark being expressed as a percentage of his full night sensitivity.

Time (min.)	0	5	10	15	20	25	30
Sensitivity (%)	10	46	70	84	90	94	96

Draw a graph, using time as base and hence find the percentage sensitivity after 23 min. in the dark, also the time needed to recover 58% sensitivity.

Answers: 93%; 7 min.

77. The average lumen output of a single coil gas-filled electric lamp throughout its life compared with its wattage when used on a 230 volt supply is as follows:

Watts	40	100	300	500	750	1,000	1,500
Lumen output	360	1,200	4,400	7,900	12,700	17,800	28,400

From your graph estimate the lumen output of a 1,200 watt lamp and the wattage of a lamp giving 10,000 lumens output.

Answers: 22,000 lumens; 600 watts

78. An 80 watt single lamp fitting when tested at various heights above the working plane gave the following figures for mean illumination in foot-candles:

Height (ft.)	2	3	4	5
Illumination (foot-candles)	70	40	25	15

Plot the curve and by extending its direction try to estimate the illumination of this particular lamp when at a distance of 1 ft. above the working plane; also at what distance would it produce a mean illumination of 32 foot candles?

Answers: 120 foot candles; $3\frac{1}{2}$ ft.

79. The proportion of carbon dioxide in the exhaust gases of an engine for various ratios of the air to petrol used are given below:

Air–Petrol ratio	9	10	11	12	13	14
% CO_2	6·7	8·2	9·6	11·1	12·5	13·5

Find graphically what % of carbon dioxide is produced by an air–petrol ratio of 10·6; also the air–petrol ratio which will produce 12% CO_2 in the exhaust.

Answers: 9·0%; 12·6

80. In the table below S = number of grams of anhydrous ammonium chloride which when dissolved in 100 gm. of water make a saturated solution at the temperature stated:

S (gm.)	29·4	33·3	37·2	45·8	55·2	65·6	77·3
Temp. (°C)	0	10	20	40	60	80	100

Graphically estimate the value of S for a temperature of 15°C and what temperature is necessary to saturate a solution of 100 gm. of water and 50 gm. of ammonium chloride.

Answers: 35·25 gm.; 50°C

81. At a curve on a railway line the outer rail must be raised above the level of the inner. The following table gives the necessary elevation (H in.) for various values of the radius of the curve (R yd.):

R (yd.)	1,000	2,000	3,000	4,000	5,000
H (in.)	6	3	2	1·5	1·2

Draw a graph using R as base and find the elevation necessary for a radius of 3,500 yd.; also the radius for which 4 in. elevation would be sufficient.

Answers: 1·72 in.; 1,550 yd.

82. The velocities (V) of discharge of water (in ft./sec.) due to different heads (H) (in ft.) are given below:

H (ft.)	0	2	10	20	30	40	50	60	70	80	90
V (ft./sec.)	0	11	25	36	44	51	57	62	67	72	76

Estimate the head of water required to give a velocity flow of 40 ft./sec., and the velocity produced by a head of 66 ft. of water.

Answers: 25 ft.; 65 ft./sec.

83. The following figures relate the head of water (in ft.) to the equivalent pressure in lb./sq. in.

Head (ft.)	0	5	10	19	27	33	45	50
Pressure (lb./sq. in.)	0	2·16	4·33	8·22	11·69	14·29	19·49	21·65

Estimate the pressure equivalent to a head of 15 ft. and the head of water corresponding to a pressure of 16 lb./sq. in.
　　Answers: 6·46 lb./sq. in.; 37 ft.

84. Draw a graph to illustrate the total value of books produced in the United Kingdom during the following years:

Year	1945	1946	1947	1948	1949	1950	1951	1952	1953	1954	1955	1956
Value (£ million)	22	27	$30\frac{1}{4}$	$33\frac{1}{4}$	$34\frac{1}{4}$	37	$41\frac{1}{2}$	$42\frac{3}{4}$	45	$46\frac{1}{4}$	$49\frac{1}{2}$	$56\frac{2}{3}$

By taking the figures of the last four years and sketching an average curve to show the upward trend of production try to estimate the value for 1957.
　　Answer: About £65 million

85. The following is a table of the atmospheric pressure in millibars at various heights above sea level in England:

Height (in km.)	0	1	2	3	4	5	6
Pressure (mbs.)	1,014	900	795	699	615	538	469

Draw a graph and from it find the pressure at a height of 3·5 km., also the height at which the pressure is 770 millibars.
　　Answers: 650 mbs.; 2·2 km.

86. The following table indicates the count of cut steel nails per lb. according to their lengths (in.).

Length (in.)	6	5	$4\frac{1}{2}$	$3\frac{1}{2}$	3	2	$1\frac{1}{2}$	$1\frac{1}{4}$	1
Number/lb.	9	14	19	35	55	150	280	390	620

Graphically estimate the number/lb. for 4-in. and $2\frac{1}{2}$-in. nails.
　　Answers: 25; 90

87. The force exerted by gravity (*g*) is used as the unit to measure the time taken to escape in a rocket from the pull of the earth and obtain a final velocity of 7 miles/sec. The various accelerations and "time of escape" are as follows:

Acceleration	3g	4g	5g	6g	7g	8g	9g	10g
Duration (min./sec.)	9·31	6·21	4·45	3·48	3·10	2·40	2·20	2·06

Show this relationship in graphical form and obtain the approximate escape time for an acceleration of $5\frac{1}{2}g$, also what accelerating force is required for a duration of 5 min. 50 sec.?
　　Answers: 4 min. 12 sec.; 4·3g

88. This is a portion of a table of lighting up times. Draw a graph using date as base and from it find the lighting up time to the nearest minute on January 18. Also the date when the lighting up time was 5 p.m.

Date	Jan. 1	Jan. 8	Jan. 15	Jan. 22	Feb. 5	Feb. 12
Time	4.5 p.m.	4.16 p.m.	4.28 p.m.	4.43 p.m.	5.14 p.m.	5.31 p.m.

Answers: 4.34 p.m.; January 30

89. Construct a graph of the squares of the natural numbers from 0 to 10 (*i.e.*, $y = x^2$). From your graph determine:

(a) $\sqrt{21}$

Answer: 4·6 *approx.*

(b) $\sqrt{42}$

Answer: 6·5 *approx.*

(c) $\sqrt{74}$

Answer: 8·6 *approx.*

90. Draw a graph showing the cubes of all the whole numbers from 0 to 6 (*i.e.*, $y = x^3$). From your graph determine:

(a) $\sqrt[3]{59}$

Answer: 3·9 *approx.*

(b) $\sqrt[3]{80}$

Answer: 4·3 *approx.*

(c) $\sqrt[3]{150}$

Answer: 5·3 *approx.*

91. The areas of circular fields (in acres) are related to their radii (in yd.) as follows:

Area (acres)	1	2	3	4	5	6
Radius (yd.)	39·2	55	68	78·5	87·7	96·2

Draw the graph and from it estimate:

(a) The area of a field whose radius is 72 yd.

Answer: 3·37 *acres*

(b) The radius of a field whose area is $2\frac{3}{4}$ acres.

Answer: 64 yd.

92. The areas of square fields (in acres) are related to their sides (in yd.) as follows:

Area (acres)	1	2	3	4	5	6
Side (yd.)	69·6	98·4	120·5	139·2	155·6	170·4

Graphically estimate:

(a) The length of the side of a field whose area is $3\frac{1}{2}$ acres.

Answer: 130 yd.

(b) The area of a field having a side of 110 yd.

Answer: $2\frac{1}{2}$ *acres*

93. This table gives corresponding values of two quantities "*R*" and "*S*":

$R =$ 0·33	0·41	0·51	0·61	0·69	0·75	0·83	0·90
$S =$ 6·9	7·8	8·3	8·1	7·5	6·7	5·5	4·4

From your graph estimate:

(a) Value of S when $R = 0.44$.

Answer: $S = 8.0$

(b) Value of R when $S = 6.4$.

Answer: $R = 0.775$

(c) Maximum value of S.

Answer: 8·325

(d) Value of R for S maximum.

Answer: 0·53

94. The table below gives corresponding values of "R" and "A":

R	-4.5	3.5	18.2	27.0	27.0	18.3	6.3
A	-1	0	2	4	6	8	10

Graphically estimate the maximum value of R and the value of A corresponding to this, using A as base.
    Answers: R max. $= 28\frac{1}{2}$; $A = 5$
Find also the value of A which makes R equal to zero.
    Answer: $-\frac{1}{2}$

95. The following table gives corresponding values of radians and degrees (circular measure):

Degrees	$10°$	$20°$	$30°$	$40°$	$45°$
Radians	0.175	0.35	0.52	0.70	0.78

From your graph estimate the number of degrees corresponding to 0·25 radians, and the number of radians in 37°.
    Answers: $14\frac{1}{2}°$; 0·646 radians

96. This table gives the time taken by a carrier to pass along pneumatic tubes of various lengths:

Lengths (yd.)	0	700	1,400	2,200	2,700	3,700
Time (min./sec.)	0	0·30	1·20	2·50	3·50	6·00

Graphically determine:

(a) The time taken to pass along a tube 3,400 yd. long.
    Answer: 5·21
(b) The length of the tube which would be traversed in 55 sec.
    Answer: 1,100 yd.

97. This is a table giving the weight per mile of steel wire of different diameters:

Weight (cwt./mile)	21	56	114	223	348	502	669
Diameter (mm.)	1	1·6	2·3	3·3	4·1	4·9	5·6

Draw a graph using diameter as base and read off the diameter of wire weighing 20 tons per mile; also the weight per mile of wire 3·0 mm. in diameter.
    Answer: 4·375 mm.; 190 cwt. (or $9\frac{1}{2}$ tons)

98. The following figures are given for excess tyre wear at various speeds:

Speed (m.p.h.)	30	40	50	60	70
Rubber wasted (%)	0	24	41	57	70

Draw a graph with speed as base and hence find the speed which produces a wastage of 50%; also the waste at 44 m.p.h.
    Answers: 55·3 m.p.h.; 31·25%

99. In an attempt to intercept an enemy aircraft flying at 14,000 ft., an aircraft took off at 13.00 hours. The altitude at regular 10-min. intervals take-off was recorded as 9,400 ft., 16,300 ft., 21,500 ft., 24,300 ft. and 25,100 ft.
Draw a graph on a time base and find the height at 13.35 hours; also the time at which the height of the enemy aircraft was attained.
    Answers: 23,200 ft.; 13.16$\frac{1}{4}$ hr.

100. In an experiment to verify Snell's Law $\left(\dfrac{\text{Sin } i}{\text{Sin } r} = \mu\right)$ for the refraction of light the following results were obtained:

Incident angle ($i°$)	10	20	30	40	50	60
Refracted angle ($r°$)	$6\frac{1}{2}$	13	19	25	31	35

Draw a graph of sin i and sin r and from it find a value for μ

N.B. Suggested method: Plot sin i on y axis and sin r on x axis; draw *average* straight line between the points. Then by taking any point on the line

$$\mu = \frac{\sin i}{\sin r} = \frac{\text{value of } y \text{ ordinate}}{\text{value of } x \text{ ordinate}} \text{ (average)}$$

Answer: 1·5

101. This is a table of pressure exerted by varying winds:

Wind speed (m.p.h.)	15	21	27	37	50	59
Pressure (lb./sq. ft.)	0·7	1·3	2·3	4·6	7·9	10·5

Draw a graph and from it find the wind pressure at 45 m.p.h., also the speed of wind which gives a pressure of 4 lb./sq. ft.

Answers: $6\frac{1}{2}$ lb./sq. ft.; $34\frac{3}{4}$ m.p.h.

102. This table gives the range in feet of the jet from a fire engine for different angles of elevation of the jet.

Angles (°)	22	25	35	40	50	60	70
Range (ft.)	77	92	$112\frac{1}{2}$	118	118	102	80

Draw a graph with angle as base. What is the maximum range of the jet and what angles give a range of 98 ft.?

Answers: Maximum range $120\frac{1}{2}$ ft.; angles 27·23° and 61·9°

103. The following table gives the height above ground of a shell for various distances from the gun which fired it.

Distance (yd.)	100	200	300	500	700	800	900
Height (yd.)	4·9	9·1	12·8	17·4	16·7	13·7	8·3

Draw a graph using distance as base and from it find the maximum height reached; also the distances where the height of the shell is 10 yd.

Answers: 18·05 yd.; 225 yd. and 870 yd.

104. In determining the melting point of naphthalene the following temperatures and times were recorded:

Time (min./sec.)	1·0	2·0	3·0	4·0	5·0	6·0	7·0	8·0	9·0	10·0	11·0	12·0
Temp. (°F)	91·5	88·2	85·3	82·8	80·3	79·2	79·2	79·2	79·0	78·7	78·3	77·6

From your graph estimate the melting point of the substance which occurs where a "step" is formed in the curve. (Draw your graph on a time base.)

Answer: 79·2°F

105. The dew point ($t°C$) and the mass of water (m) in grammes contained in 1 cu. m. of air are related as follows:

Temp. ($t°C$)	0	5	10	15	20	25	30
m (gm.)	4·9	6·8	9·4	12·8	17·2	22·9	30·1

From your graph estimate the value of m when $t = 7°C$, and the value of t when $m = 14·5$ gm/cu. metre.

Answers: 7·7 gm./cu. m.; 17°C

106. In an experiment on water vapour pressure at different temperatures the following results were recorded:

Temp. °C		60	50	40	30	20	10	0
Max. vapour pressure (in mm. of mercury)		149	92	55	31	17	9	5

(a) When is the increase of vapour pressure most marked?
   Answer: At higher temperature ranges
(b) When least marked?
   Answer: At lower temperature ranges
(c) Estimate the vapour pressure at 35°C.
   Answer: 41½ mm.
(d) At what temperature is the maximum vapour pressure 130 mm.?
   Answer: 56¾°C

107. The atomic weights and specific heats of various elements are as follows:

Element:	Li	Na	Mg	K	Mn	Fe	Ag	Pt	Au	Hg	Pb
A. wt.	7	23	24	39	55	56	108	195	196	200	206·4
S. ht.	0·94	0·29	0·245	0·166	0·122	0·112	0·057	0·032	0·032	0·032	0·031

Graphing specific heats on the X axis and atomic weights on the Y axis, sketch a smooth average curve and comment on any relationship you can infer from these factors.
   Answer: As A. wt. increases, S. ht. decreases

108. The temperature in the film-gate of a photographic slide projector was read at intervals, whilst the machine was running, and the following data obtained:

Time (min.)	0	0·5	1·0	1·5	2·0	3·0	4·0	5·0	7·0	9·0	11·0	13·0	15·0
Temp. (°F)	70	110	114	124	130	135	138	140	142	144	146	148	150

Sketch a smooth curve and from your graph estimate what the temperature in the gate would be after (a) 2½ min.; (b) 12 min.
   Answers: (a) 133°F; (b) 147°F
If it is damaging to a film to keep it in a gate above 145°F how long would it take to reach this temperature?
   Answer: 10 min.

Time and Distance Problems

If a pedestrian is walking at a *steady* 3½ m.p.h., we know from this fact that the distance covered can be tabulated as follows:

Distance (miles)	0	3½	7	10½	14	17½	21	24½	28	} etc.
Time (hr.)	0	1	2	3	4	5	6	7	8	

If we now construct a graph from this data it will be found to be a perfectly straight line (Fig. 28).

By developing this we can utilize a graphical construction to solve simple problems involving the factors of time and distance.

Example: A pedestrian walks from A to B at 4 m.p.h. At the same time a cyclist rides from B to A at 10 m.p.h. If A and B are 50 miles apart, when and where do they pass each other? (See Fig. 29.)

Mark off on one side (*e.g.*, horizontal) a distance scale of miles and indicate the two towns *A* and *B*, 50 miles apart. Erect on the other side (vertical) a suitable time scale in hours.

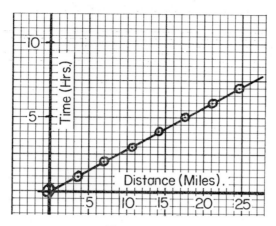

FIGURE 28

Now the pedestrian will take $12\frac{1}{2}$ hours ($=\frac{50}{4}$) to walk the distance from *A* to *B* and the cyclist 5 hours ($=\frac{50}{10}$) to cover the journey from *B* to *A*.

Hence starting from *A* (the assumed origin) we obtain the point *C* as the position of the

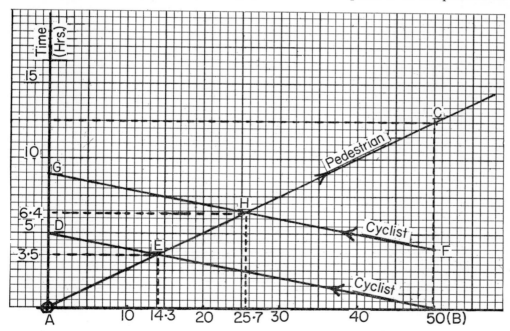

FIGURE 29

pedestrian who reaches *B* $12\frac{1}{2}$ hours later. Conversely the cyclist starting from *B* is shown arriving above the point *A* 5 hours later, *i.e.*, at D.

(N.B. It is always wise to indicate the graph lines by arrows and descriptions.)

We now see that the two graph lines cross at the point E where the cyclist and pedestrian pass each other. This point indicates a time of 3·5 hours approximately and a distance of 14·3 miles approximately from A, thus solving the problem in a very simple manner.

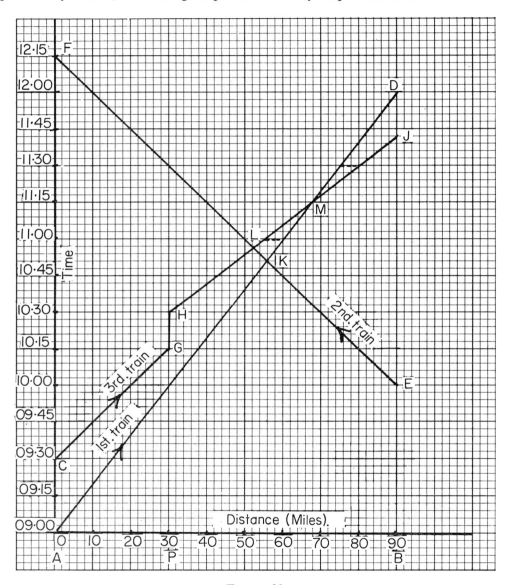

FIGURE 30

If we vary our problem by letting the cyclist leave B 4 hours *after* the pedestrian leaves A, then the starting point of the cyclist is shown by the point F and his finishing point by G. The time of meeting each other is now given by the point H indicating 25·7 miles from A and 6·4 hours approximately after the pedestrian started.

This type of problem can be extended to find out other data.

Example: Two stations *A* and *B* are 90 miles apart with a railway halt *P* situated 30 miles from *A* between them. A train leaves *A* at 9 a.m. travelling non-stop to *B* at 30 m.p.h. A second train leaves *B* at 10 a.m. travelling non-stop to *A* at 40 m.p.h., whilst a third train leaves *A* at 9.30 a.m. travelling to *B* at 40 m.p.h., waiting for 15 min. at *P* then proceeding to *B* at 50 m.p.h.

Construct the Time/Distance graph of the trains. (See Fig. 30.)

First, construct the time and distance axes using suitable scales as before, marking the position also of the halt *P*. Now, if the first train starts from *A* at 9 a.m. it will reach *B* at noon, *i.e.*, point *D*, hence its graph line *AD* is easily constructed. The point *E* indicates the second train leaving *B* at 10 a.m. and will obviously reach *A* at 12.15 p.m. (90 miles at 40 m.p.h.) *i.e.*, point *F*. By joining *EF* the graph line of the second train is determined.

The starting point of the third train is given by *C* and as it will take $\frac{3}{4}$ hour to reach halt *P* (30 miles at 40 m.p.h.) its arrival at the halt is indicated by the point *G* (on the time of 10.15 a.m.). To show the waiting time of 15 min. a vertical line is drawn from *G* to *H* indicating a forward movement of *time* (vertical axis) of $\frac{1}{4}$ hour, but no forward movement of distance (horizontal axis). This train, we are told, travels at a steady 50 m.p.h. (*i.e.*, 25 miles in $\frac{1}{2}$ hour); hence by positioning a point 25 miles to the right of *P* and $\frac{1}{2}$ hour upwards in time, we can construct the final position *HJ* of the graph representing the journey of the third train.

It is quite clear that the points *L*, *K* and *M* represent the places where the trains either meet (*L* and *K*) or overtake (*M*) each other, times and distances being read off from the axes. We also find that the third train reaches *B* (point *J*) at about 11.42 a.m., *i.e.*, 18 min. before the first train.

Again, suppose we wish to know when the first train is 5 miles away from the third train; it is obvious that *two* such occasions occur, *i.e.*, when the third train is catching up the first and again when it has passed the meeting point *M*. To find these times graphically take a piece of paper and on one of its straight edges mark off a distance equal to 5 miles from the horizontal distance axis. Then, by moving the paper between the two lines representing the first and third trains (keeping the piece of paper horizontal) find the two places, *e.g.*, at 11 a.m. and 11.30 a.m. (indicated by dotted lines on the diagram).

EXERCISES

1. A man sets out to walk 20 miles from one town to another. After 2 hours walking at $3\frac{1}{2}$ m.p.h. he rests for $\frac{1}{2}$ hour and then completes the journey at 3 m.p.h. If he starts at mid-day show graphically that he arrives at his destination at 6.50 p.m.
How far is he from his starting point at 4 p.m.?
Answer: $11\frac{1}{2}$ *miles*
At what time has he completed half his journey?
Answer: 3.30 *p.m.*

2. At 9 a.m. a man starts to walk to a town 10 miles away travelling at 3 m.p.h. At 11 a.m. a friend follows him on a cycle at 12 m.p.h. When and where does he catch up with the pedestrian?
Answer: 8 *miles from starting point at* 11.40 *a.m.*

3. A motorist starts from *A* to travel to *B* which is 60 miles away, at 30 m.p.h. An hour later another motorist leaves *B* to travel to *A* at 40 m.p.h. If the first motorist started at 2 p.m., when and where do they pass each other?
Answer: 43 *miles from A at* 3.26 *p.m.*

4. A cyclist starts from *A* and rides steadily towards *B*, 60 miles away, at 12 m.p.h. Two hours later a motorist leaves *B* for *A*, travelling at 36 m.p.h. When and where does the motorist meet the cyclist?

Answer: $2\frac{3}{4}$ hours after the cyclist started at a point 33 miles from A

5. A motor car starts off at a uniform rate of 15 m.p.h., and half an hour later a second car starts from the same point at the uniform rate of 20 m.p.h. When and where does the second car overtake the first?

Answer: 2 hours after the first car began; 30 miles from the start

6. A cyclist leaves *P* at 9 a.m. and rides at 8 m.p.h. to *Q*, 30 miles away. A motorist leaves *X* at 9.30 a.m. taking the same route to *Q* at 24 m.p.h. when he waits for 10 min. before returning to *P*. When and where does he pass the cyclist?

Answer: At 9.45 a.m., 6 miles from P, and at 11.24 a.m. when 19 miles from P

7. A man (*A*) making a journey, travels for 3 hours at 18 m.p.h., stops for 1 hour, then travels for 2 hours at 15 m.p.h. He again stops for 1 hour and then completes his journey by walking for 4 hours at the rate of 4 m.p.h.

A second man (*B*) starts 4 hours later and follows him at a uniform rate of 20 m.p.h. Find when and where the second man passes the first.

Answer: 90 miles from starting point after had been travelling for 8·5 hours

8. *A* and *B* are two towns 60 miles apart. A cyclist leaves *A* at noon to travel to *B* at 12 m.p.h., but at 1.30 p.m. receives a puncture which delays him for half an hour. To make up time he speeds up to 15 m.p.h. for 2 hours and then completes the journey at 12 m.p.h.

A motorist leaves *B* at noon also travelling to *A* at 36 m.p.h. At 1 p.m. he stops for lunch for 1 hour, continuing his journey at 24 m.p.h.

(a) When and where does he pass the cyclist?
  Answer: $20\frac{1}{4}$ miles from A, at $2.09\frac{1}{4}$ p.m.
(b) At what time before meeting are they 20 miles apart?
  Answer: 12.50 p.m.
(c) At what time after meeting are they 20 miles apart and what are their positions at the time?
  Answer: At $2.40\frac{1}{4}$ p.m. when the cyclist is 28 miles from A, and the motorist 8 miles from A
(d) How far apart are they at 2.45 p.m.?
  Answer: $23\frac{1}{4}$ miles

9. A motorist leaves London at 9 a.m. to travel to Brighton via Crawley, a distance of 54 miles. A cyclist leaves Crawley, which is 23 miles from Brighton, at the same time to take the same road at 12 m.p.h., whilst the motorist travels at 36 m.p.h. When and where on the route does the motorist pass the cyclist?

Answer: Approximately $7\frac{1}{4}$ miles from Brighton at 10.18 a.m.

10. A man leaves home at noon to catch a bus at a halt 420 yd. distant, reaching it at 12.07 p.m. At first he walked at $52\frac{1}{2}$ yd./min. until reaching the village church when, noticing the time, he speeded up to 70 yd./min. At what time did he pass the church and how far from the bus halt was he then?

Answers: 12.04 p.m.; 210 yd., i.e., he was half-way to the bus halt

11. An object moving at a steady speed is observed to be 30 ft. from a fixed point after five seconds travel, whilst 10 sec. later it was 50 ft. What was its distance from the fixed point when timing commenced?

Answer: 20 ft.

12. *A* and *B* are two stations, 70 miles apart, with two halts *C* and *D*, 20 miles and 40 miles respectively from *A*. A train leaves *A* for *B* at 10 a.m. travelling at 30 m.p.h. non-stop. A second train leaves *B* for *A* at 11 a.m. at 25 m.p.h., staying at halt *D* for $\frac{1}{4}$ hour and then going on to *A* at 30 m.p.h. When and where do these two trains pass each other?

Answer: $51\frac{9}{11}$ miles from A at $11.43\frac{7}{11}$ a.m.

A third train leaves *A* at 11 a.m. travelling at 40 m.p.h., calling at halt *C* for 30 min., and is required to pass the second train on a loop line 35 miles from *A*. At what speed must it travel from *C* to *D* to enable this to be done?

Answer: 24·3 m.p.h.

This third train stays 12 min. at halt *D*, travelling on to *B* at 25 m.p.h. What is the time of arrival at its destination?

Answer: $2.13\frac{1}{3}$ p.m.

Estimate also the arrival times of the other two trains at their respective destinations.

Answer: First train 12.20 p.m., Second train 1.47 p.m.

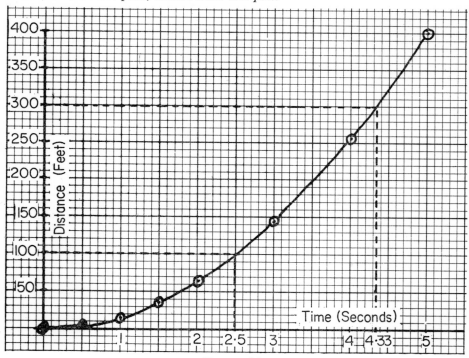

FIGURE 31

Non-Linear Velocity

It may of course happen that an object does not travel at a steady rate at any moment during its path—such as a stone falling under gravity. In such cases the graph will not be a straight line but, in the case of the falling stone, a curve.

By tabulating the distance fallen after regular intervals, *e.g.*,

Distance (in ft.)	0	4	16	36	64	144	256	400
Time (in sec.)	0	$\frac{1}{2}$	1	$1\frac{1}{2}$	2	3	4	5

we can plot the graph of a body moving under constant acceleration; in this case, gravity; using the formula $S = 16t^2$ where S = distance fallen in feet and t = time taken in seconds (Fig. 31),

F

and by the interpolation we can estimate intermediate distances and times. For instance, from the graph we can see that it would take 4·33 sec. for a stone to fall 300 ft. and that it would fall 100 ft. in 2½ sec.

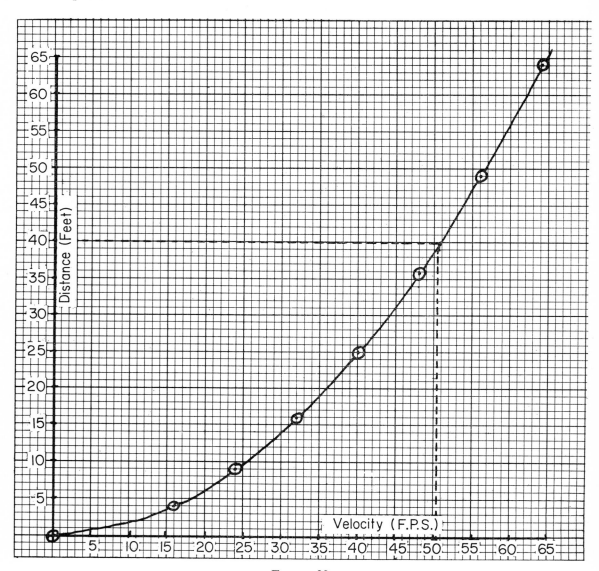

FIGURE 32

Hence we see that in any given time we can find the distance fallen. By utilizing another formula $V^2 = 64S$ (where V = velocity in ft./sec. and S = distance in ft.) we can construct another graph based on distance and velocity *viz:*

Distance (ft.)	0	4	9	16	25	36	49	64
Velocity (ft./sec.)	0	16	24	32	40	48	56	64

Example: A stone is dropped from a window 40 ft. from the ground; how long does it take to fall and what is its velocity on impact?

From the previous graph we find that to fall 40 ft. the stone would take about 1·58 sec. and from the latter graph it would strike the ground at approximately 50·6 ft./sec. (Fig. 32). (N.B. 88 ft./sec. = 60 m.p.h.)

EXERCISES

1. Using the formula $S = 16t^2$ find the distance fallen by a stone in: 0, $\frac{1}{2}$, $\frac{3}{4}$, 1, $1\frac{1}{4}$, $1\frac{1}{2}$, $1\frac{3}{4}$, 2, $2\frac{1}{2}$, 3, $3\frac{1}{2}$, 4, $4\frac{1}{2}$, 5 and $5\frac{1}{2}$ sec.
Construct the graph using 2 cm. = 1 sec. on the horizontal axis and 1 cm. = 30 ft. on the vertical axis, and from it determine:

(a) How long would it take a stone to fall from the top of the world's longest natural bridge—the Landscape Arch in Utah—which is 100 ft. in height and 291 ft. in span?
Answer: $2\frac{1}{2}$ *sec.*

(b) The time taken for a stone to fall from the roof of the largest known underground chamber in the world—the "Big Room" of the Carlsbad Caverns in New Mexico—which is 4,000 ft. long, 300 ft. high and 625 ft. wide?
Answer: 4·33 *sec.*

(c) The time taken for a stone to fall from the top of the world's largest living thing—at present the Californian Redwood Tree in the National Park of California—which is 272 ft. tall?
Answer: 4·12 *sec.*

(d) How long would the stone take to fall from the top of the tallest tree of all time, believed to be the Baron Tree, a eucalyptus tree in Australia, which in 1868 was reckoned to be 464 ft. high?
Answer: 5·4 *sec.*

2. From the above graph estimate how far a stone would fall in:

(a) 3·4 sec.
Answer: 185 ft.

(b) 1·8 sec.
Answer: 52 ft.

3. Construct a graph from the formula $V^2 = 64s$, for a body falling from rest, where V = velocity in ft./sec., and S is the distance fallen (as in previous graph) in ft.

From your graph estimate the height from which a stone fell if it hit the ground at 30 m.p.h., and how long it took to fall.
Answers: 30·25 *ft.;* 1·37 *sec.*

4. The position of a stone falling from rest is given by the formula $S = 16t^2$ where S = space traversed (ft.) and t = time taken (sec.).

Draw a graph to show the distances fallen in the first 5 sec. and from it determine how far a stone would fall in $1\frac{1}{2}$ sec., also how long it would take to fall 78 ft.
Answers: 36 *ft.;* 2·21 *sec.*

4

ALGEBRAIC GRAPHS OF THE FIRST DEGREE

THE STRAIGHT LINE

Graphs through the Origin

IN algebra first degree equations are those in which none of the two variables is squared or cubed, etc. To take a simple example $y = x$. Now if we construct a graph from a table based on this equation we shall see it is a perfectly straight line, *AB*, passing through the origin (Fig. 33).

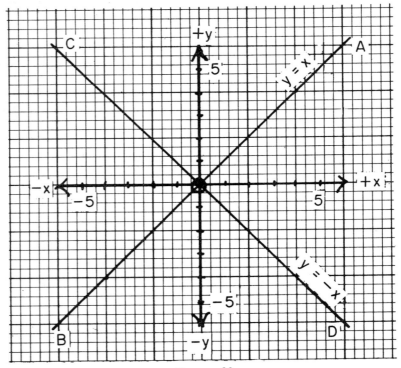

FIGURE 33

$x =$	-4	-3	-2	-1	0	$+1$	$+2$	$+3$	$+4$
$y =$	-4	-3	-2	-1	0	$+1$	$+2$	$+3$	$+4$

If we construct a graph from the equation $y = -x$

$x =$	-4	-3	-2	-1	0	$+1$	$+2$	$+3$	$+4$
$y =$	$+4$	$+3$	$+2$	$+1$	0	-1	-2	-3	-4

84

we find that the graph line *CD* swings to the opposite slope. (N.B. a change of sign is a change of direction.) The graph is still a straight line passing through the origin.

Now let us add, or subtract, a constant term to the *x* terms in the equation and see what effect it has on the graph, *e.g.*, by plotting the graphs of:

$y = 4x$; $y = 4x + 3$; $y = 4x - 5$ (Fig. 34).

x	-4	0	$+2$	$+4$
$4x$	-16	0	$+8$	$+16$
$+3$	$+3$	$+3$	$+3$	$+3$
y	-13	$+3$	$+11$	$+19$

$y = 4x + 3$

x	-4	0	$+2$	$+4$
$4x$	-16	0	$+8$	$+16$
-5	-5	-5	-5	-5
y	-21	-5	$+3$	$+11$

$y = 4x - 5$

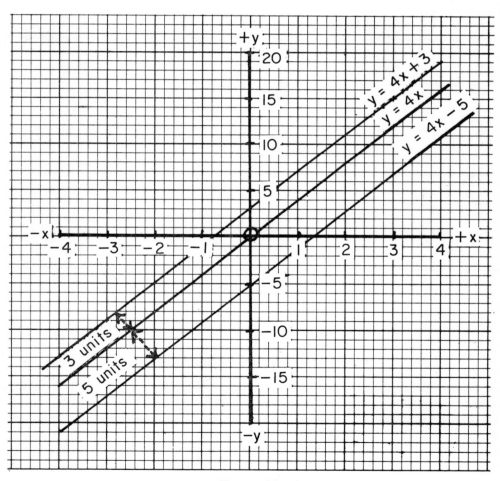

FIGURE 34

The effect is quite obvious; by *adding* a constant to the equation we *raise* the graph by the value of that constant and conversely by *subtracting* a constant we *lower* the graph by that value. In neither case do we alter the slope or gradient of the graph, the lines $y = 4x + 3$ and $y = 4x - 5$ being parallel to the line $y = 4x$ (if we draw it in for comparison).

Hence we see that the *slope* of the graph is quite independent of the *constant term* in the equation and, as we shall see later, only depends on the *ratio* of one variable to the other.

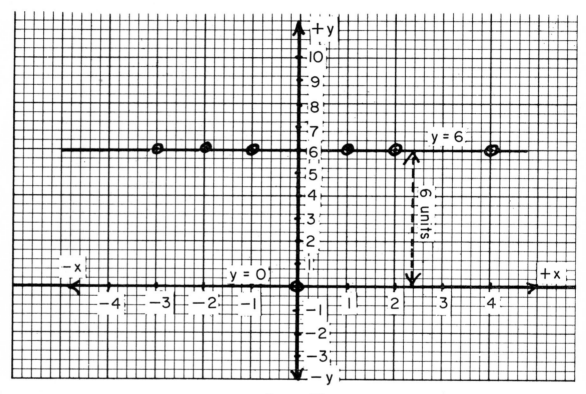

FIGURE 35

Lines Parallel to the Axes

If we remove one of the *variables* from an equation of the first degree we shall obtain a line parallel to one of the axes according to which variable we remove, *e.g.*, taking the equation $y = 6$ (Fig. 35) we obtain:

x	-3	-2	-1	0	$+2$	$+4$
y	6	6	6	6	6	6

Whilst the equation $y = -8$ (Fig. 36) produces:

x	-4	-2	0	$+1$	$+3$	$+5$
y	-8	-8	-8	-8	-8	-8

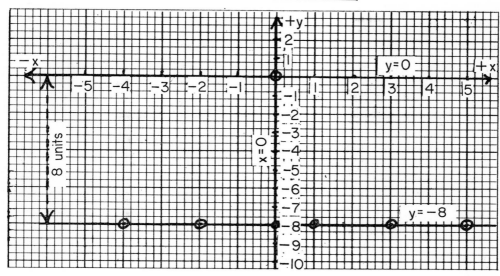

FIGURE 36

Similarly, the lines $x = +4$ and $x = -2$ result in the graphs shown below (Fig. 37):

From these experimental graphs, we can see that the x axis has for its equation $y = 0$ and the y axis has the equation $x = 0$.

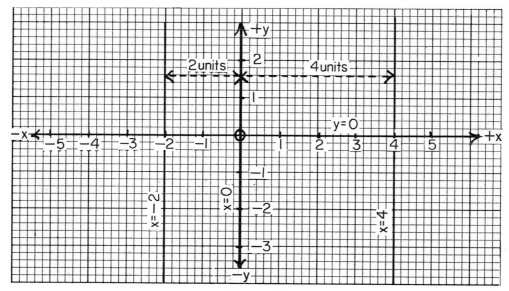

FIGURE 37

Let us increase the coefficient of the x term in the equation and plot the graphs of $y = 2x$, $y = 3x$, $y = 4x$, $y = 5x$ (Fig. 38).

x	-4	-3	-2	-1	0	$+1$	$+2$	$+3$	$+4$
$y = 2x$	-8	-6	-4	-2	0	$+2$	$+4$	$+6$	$+8$
$y = 3x$	-12	-9	-6	-3	0	$+3$	$+6$	$+9$	$+12$
$y = 4x$	-16	-12	-8	-4	0	$+4$	$+8$	$+12$	$+16$
$y = 5x$	-20	-15	-10	-5	0	$+5$	$+10$	$+15$	$+20$

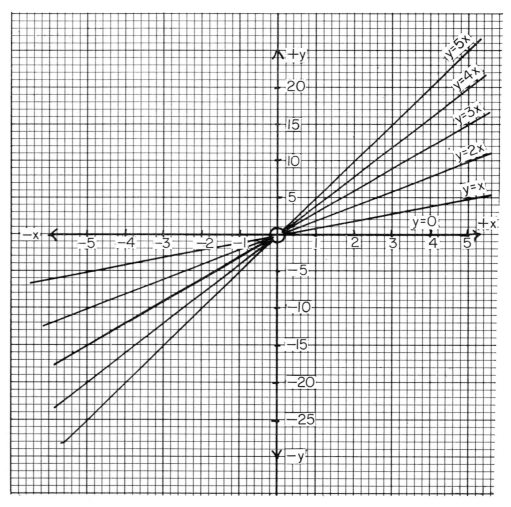

FIGURE 38

From the results (plotted on the same sheet) we see that the result of *increasing* the x coefficient is to steepen the slope, or gradient of the graph.

Conversely, it is easy to see that if we *increase* the y variable we shall flatten the gradient of the graph, *e.g.*, $2y = x$; $3y = x$; $4y = x$ and $5y = x$.

In other words, as we increase the coefficient of x, so the angle with the x axis is increased, and conversely as we increase the coefficient of y then the angle with the y axis is increased; this is demonstrated in the following diagram also.

For if $2y = x$ then $y = \frac{1}{2}x$ and if $3y = x$ then $y = \frac{1}{3}x$, etc., resulting in (Fig. 39):

x	-4	-2	0	$+3$	$+5$
$y = \frac{1}{2}x$	-2	-1	0	$+1\frac{1}{2}$	$+2\frac{1}{2}$
$y = \frac{1}{3}x$	$-1\frac{1}{3}$	$-\frac{2}{3}$	0	$+1$	$+1\frac{2}{3}$
$y = \frac{1}{4}x$	-1	$-\frac{1}{2}$	0	$+\frac{3}{4}$	$+1\frac{1}{4}$
$y = \frac{1}{5}x$	$-\frac{4}{5}$	$-\frac{2}{5}$	0	$+\frac{3}{5}$	$+1$

FIGURE 39

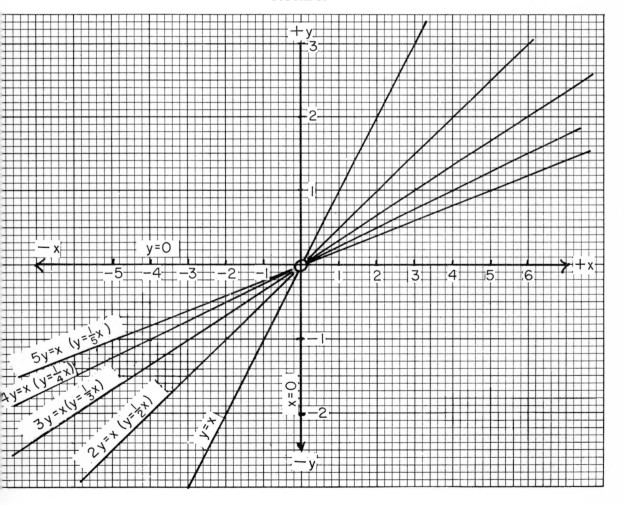

EXERCISES

1. Draw the graph of $3x - 4y = 9$.

(a) At what point does this line cut the x axis?
Answer: $x = 3$

(b) At what point does this line cut the y axis?
Answer: $y = -2\frac{1}{4}$

(c) If $x = -5$ what is the corresponding value of y?
Answer: $y = -6$

(d) If $x = +4$ what is the corresponding value of y?
Answer: $y = +\frac{3}{4}$

(e) For what values of x does the graph show positive values of y?
Answer: Above $x = +3$

2. Draw the graphs of $3x + 2y = 22$ and $2x + 3y = 23$ on the same area.

(a) At what point do they intersect?
Answers: 4, 5

(b) Read from your graph lines the corresponding values of x when $y = 3$.
Answer: $5\frac{1}{3}$ and 7

(c) What are the corresponding values of y when $x = 3$?
Answer: $5\frac{2}{3}$ and $6\frac{1}{2}$

3. Draw the graphs of:

(a) $6y - 5x = 30$
(b) $6y = 30 - 5x$
(c) $6y = 7x + 42$
(d) $6y = 42 - 7x$ on the same area.

   (i) What are the co-ordinates of the point of intersection of lines **(a)** and **(b)**?
Answer: 0, 5
   (ii) What are the co-ordinates of the point of intersection of lines **(c)** and **(d)**?
Answer: 0, −7
   (iii) What sort of triangle is formed by lines **(a)** and **(b)** with the x axis?
Answer: Isosceles
   (iv) Calculate the area of this triangle.
Answer: 30 sq. units
   (v) Calculate the area of the triangle formed by lines **(a)** and **(c)** with the y axis.
Answer: 36 sq. units

4. By drawing the graphs of $y = 3x + 4$ and $y = 3x - 5$ show that they both cut the x and y axes at the same angle and are therefore parallel.

5. Draw the graphs of $x + y = 3$ and $x - y = 3$ on the same area utilizing the same scale on both axes. Show by measurement with a protractor that these two lines are at right angles to each other, and state the co-ordinates of the point of intersection.
   Answer: 3, 0
   At what angles do they cross the y axis?
   Answer: 45° (or 135°)

Solutions of First Degree Equations (General)

The solution of an equation (in x and y) is the value of x which gives $y = 0$. Hence in the equation $y = 4x - 5$ we find the solution algebraically by writing it in the form: $0 = 4x - 5$, *i.e.*, $5 = 4x$, or $x = 1\frac{1}{4}$.

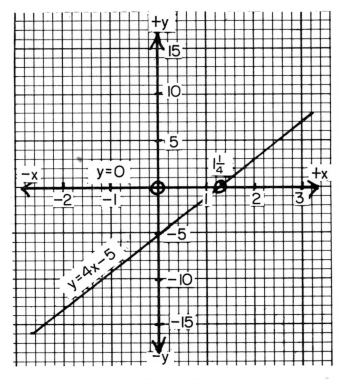

FIGURE 40

If we construct the graph (Fig. 40) from the equation $y = 4x - 5$ we see that this value of x is indicated by the point where the graph line cuts the x axis, *i.e.*, where the y ordinate is zero and also where the graph cuts the line which has for its equation $y = 0$.

$y = 4x - 5$

x	-3	-1	0	$+2$	$+4$
$4x$	-12	-4	0	$+8$	$+16$
-5	-5	-5	-5	-5	-5
y	-17	-9	-5	$+3$	$+11$

Note that the scale used on the two axes does not in any way affect the result obtained.

In the equation $y = 4x - 5$ "y" is sometimes described as a *function* of x and is therefore written $f(x) = 4x - 5$, in which case the value of $f(x) = 0$ gives the solution of the equation, x being known as the *variable* of the function. It is usual to equate the function to y, the value of

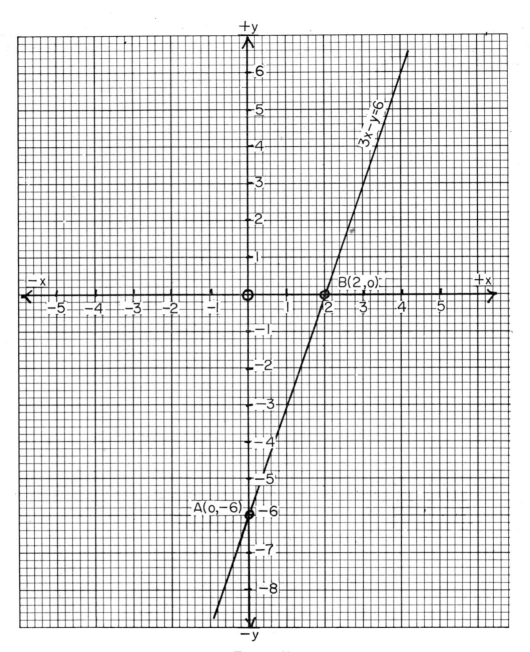

FIGURE 41

which is known when that of x is given. For this reason x is spoken of as the *independent variable* of the function, y as the *dependent variable*.

A quantity which does not contain the variable and whose value therefore does not depend upon that of the variable is called a *constant*, a self-explanatory term we have already used.

In the equation $y = 4x - 5$, -5 is the constant, since whatever value we assign to x the value of -5 remains unaltered. The 4 is the multiplier, or coefficient of x.

Intercept Method

We have already seen that the graphs of the first degree all constitute straight lines. Now the minimum number of points required to define the position of a straight line is two, so that, *providing we are accurate in our calculations*, we need only ascertain two points to form our graph from a first degree equation.

The simplest way is obviously to find the two points where the graph line cuts both the x and the y axes, *i.e.*, where the graph intersects with the line whose equations are $x = 0$ and $y = 0$.

Hence by substituting the values of $x = 0$ and $y = 0$ in the equation we can obtain the required points of intersection with the axes.

Example: In $3x - y = 6$ (Fig. 41).
　　(i) Putting $x = 0$ we obtain $-y = 6$ or $y = -6$
　　(ii) Similarly, putting $y = 0$ we get $3x = 6$ or $x = 2$.

The first point A $(0, -6)$ and the second point B $(2, 0)$ define the line $3x - y = 6$, the two portions of the axes OA and OB being known as the intercepts.

Any third point can now be found as a check against any possible error.

The solution of the equation (*i.e.*, where $y = 0$) is, of course, given by the value $x = 2$ already determined.

EXERCISES

1. (a) Find graphically where the line $3x - 4y = 9$ cuts the x axis.
　　Answer: $x = 3$
(b) Where does it cut the y axis?
　　Answer: $y = -2\frac{1}{4}$
(c) Read from your graph the value of y when $x = -3$.
　　Answer: $y = -4\frac{1}{2}$
(d) What value of x will make $y = -6$?
　　Answer: -5

2. Draw the graph of $-2\frac{1}{2}x + 3y = 10$.

(a) At what point does it cross the x axis?
　　Answer: At $x = 4$
(b) Where does it cut the y axis?
　　Answer: At $y = 3\frac{1}{3}$
(c) What is the value of x when $y = 8$?
　　Answer: $-5\cdot6$
(d) What is the value of y when $x = 7$?
　　Answer: $-2\cdot5$

3. Plot the graph of $2y = 5 - 3x$

(a) State the co-ordinates of the points at which it cuts the two axes.
   Answer: $(0, 2\frac{1}{2})$ *and* $(1\frac{2}{3}, 0)$
(b) What value of x will make $y = 4$?
   Answer: $x = -1$
(c) What value of y will make $x = 4$?
   Answer: $y = -3\frac{1}{2}$

4. Solve the equations $y = 2x + 3$ and $7x = 2y + 3$
   Answer: $x = 3; y = 9$

5. Plot the points (5, 10) (−5, 10) (−10, 5) (+10, +5) (−10, −5) (−5, −10) (5, −10) and (10, −5). Join them with straight lines and write down the equations of the four lines parallel to the axes.
   Answer: $y = 10, y = -10, x = 10, x = -10$
Calculate the area of the figure drawn.
   Answer: 350 *sq. units*

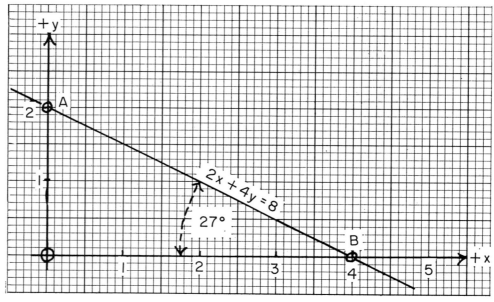

FIGURE 42

Gradient of a Graph

Let us draw the graph of $2x + 4y = 8$ (Fig. 42) by the intercept method.
Putting $x = 0$ we get $4y = 8$ or $y = 2$, and
Putting $y = 0$ we get $2x = 8$ or $x = 4$
   Knowing that $OA = 2$ units in length and OB is 4 units long from the elementary definition of the tangent in trigonometry, the tangent of the angle OBA is given by $\frac{2}{4}(=\frac{1}{2})$ and from our tangent tables we can ascertain that the angle is about 27°, which can be actually checked by means of a protractor, *provided* that the scales used on both the axes were the same; if the scales

used were different then this angle cannot be verified practically except by making a correction for the ratio of the two scales.

If we change the form of our equations $2x + 4y = 8$ to $4y = 8 - 2x$ or $y = 2 - \frac{2}{4}x$ we see that this fraction obtained by the trigonometrical use of the tangent is shown in the coefficient of x and this will happen in every case.

Note that the minus sign before the x coefficient is easily explained by the fact that in trigonometry angles are always measured in a counter-clockwise direction and the sign of the tangent value varies with the quadrant in which the line occurs, being minus in the 2nd and 4th and positive in the 1st and 3rd.

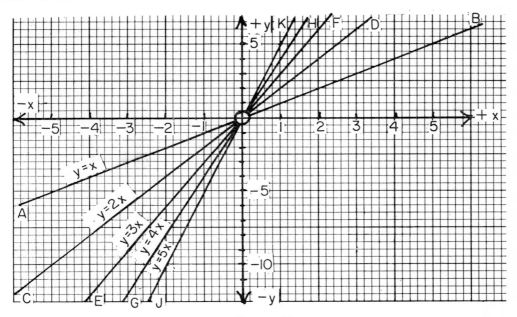

FIGURE 43

From this it is clear that the coefficient of x in the equation is the tangent of the angle made with the axis of x when in the form $y = mx + c$. The tangent of the angle is spoken of as the *slope* (or *gradient*) of the line. Notice that, in each case, the coefficient of y is unity and, as a general rule, if the equation is written in the form of $y = mx + c$ then m represents the slope (c being a constant which does not alter the slope as we have already seen).

Example: Draw the graph of $y = 2x$, $y = 3x$, $y = 4x$ and $y = 5x$ using the same scales on both axes (Fig. 43).

By completing the following table we can verify the tangent form of the equation $y = mx$.

Line	Equation of line	Tangent from "m"	Angle from tables	Angle by measurement
AB	$y = 1x$	1	45°	
CD	$y = 2x$	2	64° approx	
EF	$y = 3x$	3	72° approx	
GH	$y = 4x$	4	76° approx	
JK	$y = 5x$	5	$78\frac{1}{2}$°	

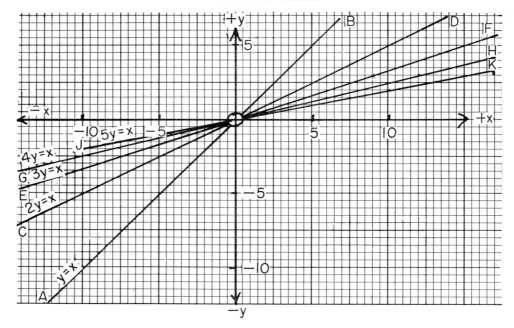

FIGURE 44

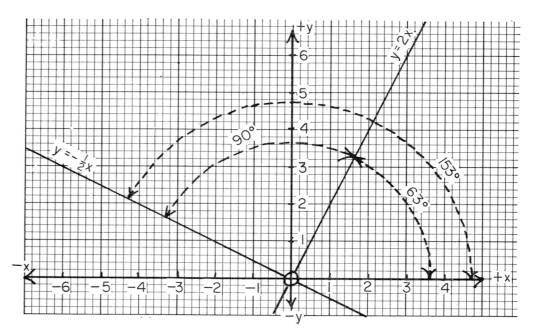

FIGURE 45

By repeating this experiment with the equations $y = x$, $2y = x$, $3y = x$, $4y = x$ and $5y = x$ we can confirm the tangent form here also, *e.g.*, Figure 44 opposite.

Line	Equation of line	Tangent from "m"	Angle from tables	Angle by measurement
AB	$1y = x$	1	$45°$	
CD	$2y = x$	$\frac{1}{2}$ $(=0\cdot5)$	$25°$ approx.	
EF	$3y = x$	$\frac{1}{3}$ $(=0\cdot33)$	$18\frac{1}{2}°$ approx.	
GH	$4y = x$	$\frac{1}{4}$ $(=0\cdot25)$	$14°$ approx.	
JK	$5y = x$	$\frac{1}{5}$ $(=0\cdot2)$	$11\frac{1}{2}°$ approx.	

If we plot the graphs of the following pairs of equations:

> (a) $y = x$ and $y = -x$
>
> (b) $y = 2x$ and $y = -\frac{1}{2}x$
>
> (c) $y = 3x$ and $y = -\frac{1}{3}x$
>
> (d) $y = 4x$ and $y = -\frac{1}{4}x$, etc.,

on the same area *with the same scale on both axes* we shall see that every pair of graphs forms two straight lines at right angles.

Example: $y = 2x$ and $y = -\frac{1}{2}x$ (Fig. 45).

By trigonometry the gradients are 2 and $-\frac{1}{2}$ respectively, giving the angles of slope as $63°$ and $153°$ nearly (check by protractor).

From the general form $y = mx + c$ in the first case $m_1 = 2$ and in the second $m_2 = -\frac{1}{2}$, hence $m_1 m_2 = -1$.

This is the condition for a pair of lines to be perpendicular to each other and can be seen from an inspection of the two equations when they are arranged in the general form.

Example: $y = 4x + 3$ and $x + 4y = 8$

$$\therefore m_1 = 4 \qquad \qquad i.e., 4y = 8 - x$$

$$y = 2 - \frac{1}{4}x$$

$$\text{and} \qquad \therefore m_2 = -\frac{1}{4}$$

Hence $m_1 m_2 = (4) \times (-\frac{1}{4}) = -1$ $\therefore$ these two lines are at right angles (Fig. 46).

G

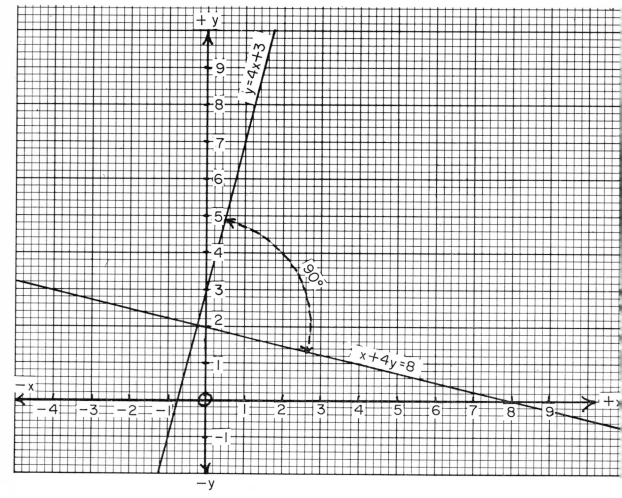

FIGURE 46

EXERCISES

1. Draw the graphs of $y = x + 7$ and $y = 7 - x$. What kind of triangle do they form with the x axis?

Answer: Isosceles

Can you say anything about the two sides and state why this should be so?

Answer: Right angles to each other. Because $m_1 m_2 = -1$.

2. Using the same scales on both axes plot the following graphs on the same area:
$x + y = 1; \ y - x = 1; \ -y - x = 1; \ x - y = 1.$

(a) What figure is produced?

Answer: A square

(b) Measure the length of its side against either scale by means of dividers or compasses.

Answer: 1·4 units

(c) Calculate its area.
  Answer: 2·0 *sq. in.*

3. Using the same scales on both axes plot these lines on the same area:
$y = 12; y = -5; x = 8$; and $x = -14$

(a) What figure is formed?
  Answer: A rectangle
(b) Find its area.
  Answer: 374 *sq. units*

4. Show graphically that the point (10, 13) lies on the line $y = x + 3$.

5. Show graphically that the point (−6, −6) lies between the two lines:
$y = x + 3$ and $y = 2x + 3$.

6. Find the area of the triangle enclosed by the lines:
$y = x + 3; y = 2x + 3$; and $x = 10$
  Answer: 50 *sq. units*

7. Solve the equations $x + 2y = 5$ and $2x - 3y = 6$
  Answer: $x = 3\frac{6}{7}; y = \frac{4}{7}$

8. By drawing on the same area show that the following graph lines have a common point of intersection and state its co-ordinates.
$3x + 2y - 5 = 0; y = 4 - 2x; 4x = 2 - 5y$
  Answer: (3, −2)

9. Find the gradient of the line which passes through the point (2, 3) and cuts the x axis at the point (4, 0). Ascertain also its equation.
  Answer: Gradient $= -1\frac{1}{2}$
  $(m = -1\frac{1}{2})$ $3x + 2y = 12$

10. Draw the following graphs on the same area, using the same scales on both axes and obtain by means of a protractor the approximate angle at which they cut the x axis.
(a) $y = 3x + 7$.
  Answer: $71\frac{1}{2}°$ *(or* $108\frac{1}{2}°$*)*
(b) $2y + 5x = 8$.
  Answer: $68°$ *(or* $112°$*)*
(c) $3x - 5y = 10$.
  Answer: $31°$ *(or* $149°$*)*
Check your results by calculation.

11. Draw the graphs of a, b and c, using equal scales on both axes.
(a) $y = 3x + 7$
(b) $3x - 5y = 10$
(c) $4x = 2 - 5y$
Measure with a protractor the internal angles of the triangle so formed, to the nearest $\frac{1}{2}°$.
  Answers: $70°$; $69\frac{1}{2}°$; $40\frac{1}{2}°$
Check your results by calculation.
What angles are formed by the intersection of the line $4x = 2 - 5y$ with the x axis?
  Answers: $38\frac{1}{2}°$ and $141\frac{1}{2}°$

12. Draw the graph of $y = 2x - 2$ and construct the straight line which is perpendicular to it, passing through the point $(-2, 4)$ giving its equation and gradient.

Answer: $2y = 6 - x$; Gradient $= -\frac{1}{2}$ ($m = -\frac{1}{2}$)

13. Show graphically that certain values of x and y which satisfy $x + 2y - 1 = 0$ and $y = 3x - 2$ also satisfy $2x = 1 + 3y$.

Answer: Lines are concurrent at $(\frac{5}{7}, \frac{1}{7})$

14. In an experiment to verify Newton's Law of Cooling the following values were obtained where R is the rate of cooling (°C per min.) and T is the temperature in excess of the surroundings.

T	82·3	64·3	47·0	33·5	26·0
R	1·82	1·37	1·03	0·69	0·53

By plotting the graph test the above results to see if they fit Newton's Law that $R = KT$ where K is a constant.

15. An experiment on a screw-jack produced the following values of load w (lb.) and effort p (lb.):

w (lb.)	50	100	175	200	250
p (lb.)	10	16	25	28	34

(a) Determine the relationship between p and w in the form $p = aw + b$ (where a and b are constants) from the plotted graphs.

Answer: $p = 0·12w + 4$

(b) Find the value of p when $w = 125$

Answer: $p = 19$ *lb.*

Confirm by calculation from answer (a).

(c) What load can be raised with an effort of 40 lb.?

Answer: 300 lb.

Confirm by calculation from answer (a).

16. In a test on a pulley block tackle the following results of loads L (lb.) and effort E (lb.) were obtained.

L	0	14	28	42	56	70
E	3·5	7	11	15	19	24

(a) Find the law of the machine from the graph line (draw an average straight line) in the form $E = aL + b$ where a and b are constants.

Answer: $E = 0·29L + 3$

(b) When $L = 40$ find from your graph the value of E and check by the formula in (a).

Answer: $14\frac{3}{4}$ *lb.*

(c) Find L when $E = 10$ lb. and check by calculation as before.

Answer: $23\frac{3}{4}$ *lb.*

17. A train travelling at V m.p.h. can be stopped in a distance of 5 yd. From the data given plot values of $\frac{S}{V}$ against V, and show that the results fit an equation of the form $\frac{S}{V} = PV + Q$ where P and Q are constants.

V m.p.h.	25	30	40	45	60
S yards	75	105	180	225	390

Graphically obtain values for both P and Q.

Answer: $P = 0·1$ *and* $Q = +\frac{1}{2}$

18. In a factory it is found that when 100 articles are made the cost of production works out at 9s. 9d. each; when 300 are produced the cost falls to 8s. 3d. each, but when 50 are produced they cost 10s. $1\frac{1}{2}d.$ each.

It was thought that the costs of production (P) were related to the number of articles (N) by the formula $P = aN + b$, where a and b are constants.

(a) Ascertain if this is so, and give reasons.

(b) Find from your graph the values of a and b.

> *Answer: a* $= -0.09$
> $b = 126$

(c) Find the value of P when $N = 150$.

> *Answer:* 9s. $4\frac{1}{2}d.$

(d) Find the value of N when $P = 8s.\ 7\frac{1}{2}d.$

> *Answer:* 250

Simultaneous Equations

We have already seen that an equation containing first powers of two variables is a straight line which can obviously be extended indefinitely in either direction.

Its variables therefore can have an infinite number of variations in the pairs of values since the line is composed of an infinite number of points, no two of which are in the same position; in such a case the equation is said to be indeterminate.

If, however, we have two such equations we shall obtain two straight lines which may *possibly* intersect (*i.e.*, if they are not parallel) and whilst each equation *separately* has a limitless number of pairs of values for its variables, there is clearly but one pair of values in common, *viz.*, the values of x and y corresponding to the point of intersection, if this should be the case.

These values satisfy the two equations because the point of intersection is the only point which lies on *both* graphs; such equations are said to be solved *simultaneously*.

Example: Solve simultaneously the two equations

$$(a)\ 3x + y = 11 \quad \text{and} \quad (b)\ x - 2y = 6$$

(a) If $x = 0$	then	$y = 11$
If $y = 0$	then	$3x = 11$ or $x = 3\frac{2}{3}$
(b) If $x = 0$	then	$-2y = 6$ or $y = -3$
If $y = 0$	then	$x = 6$

The graphs (Fig. 47) intersect on point A $(4, -1)$ and this pair of values ($x = 4$, $y = -1$) satisfies the two equations simultaneously.

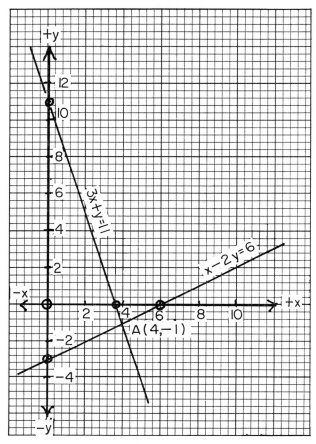

FIGURE 47

If the two lines do not intersect exactly on a convenient spot it may be necessary, in order to obtain a more accurate reading, to make a fresh drawing on a larger scale.

Example: Solve the equations $x + 2y = 5$ and $2x - 3y = 6$ simultaneously (Fig. 48).

(a) $x + 2y = 5$ or $y = \frac{1}{2}(5 - x)$

x	$+1$	$+9$	$+5$
$5 - x$	$+4$	-4	0
y	$+2$	-2	0

(b) $2x - 3y = 6$ or $y = \frac{1}{3}(2x - 6)$

x	-3	$+3$	$+1$
$2x - 6$	-12	0	-4
y	-4	0	$-1\frac{1}{3}$

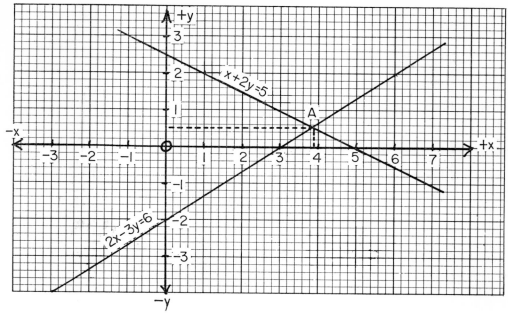

FIGURE 48

In this case the point of intersection A gives a value of x between 3·8 and 3·9, whilst the value of y obviously lies between 0·5 and 0·6; hence it is necessary to draw the graph on a far larger scale if we are to obtain a more accurate result.

Summary

Different forms of equation of a straight line:

(a) $\dfrac{y - y_1}{x - x_1} = \dfrac{y - y_2}{x - x_2}$ Two-point Form

(b) $\dfrac{x}{a} + \dfrac{y}{b} = 1$ Intercept Form

(c) $y - y_1 = m(x - x_1)$ Slope-Point Form

(d) $y = mx + b$ or $y = (\tan A)x + b$ Slope-Intercept Form

(e) $x \cos \theta + y \sin \theta = p$ Normal Form

(f) $Ax + By + C = 0$ General Form

Angles between two straight lines

(a) $\tan \theta = \dfrac{m_1 - m_2}{1 + m_1 \cdot m_2}$ angle between two lines of slope m_1 and m_2.

(b) $m_1 = m_2$ when lines are parallel.

(c) $m_1 = -\dfrac{1}{m_2}$

     or   when lines are perpendicular.

    $m_1 m_2 = -1$

EXERCISES

1. Solve the following simultaneous equations:

$2x + 3y = 17$ and $3x + 4y = 24$
    Answer: $x = 4$ and $y = 3$

2. Solve simultaneously the equations:

$y = \dfrac{x}{2} + 1\frac{1}{2}$ and $y = \dfrac{4x + 5}{4}$
    Answer: $x = \frac{1}{2}$ and $y = 1\frac{3}{4}$

3. Solve the following pairs of equations graphically and check your results by calculation in each case:

(a) $x + y = 12$ and $x - y = 4$.
    Answer: $x = 8$ and $y = 4$
(b) $x - y = 7$ and $x + y = 0$.
    Answer: $x = 3\frac{1}{2}$ and $y = -3\frac{1}{2}$
(c) $3y - 6 = x$ and $x - y = 0$.
    Answer: $x = 3$ and $y = 3$
(d) $x + y = 0$ and $3y - 6 = x$
    Answer: $x = -1\frac{1}{2}$ and $y = 1\frac{1}{2}$

4. Construct the line joining the points $(2, 5)$ and $(-4, -6)$.

(a) Find the equation of this line.
    Answer: $6y = 11x + 8$
(b) At what point does it cross the Y axis?
    Answer: $Y = 1\frac{1}{3}$
(c) Where does this line intersect with the line $3x - 2y = 4$?
    Answer: $(2, 5)$

5. Show that the line $4y = 60 - 3x$ passes through the point of intersection of the line $4y = 3x + 60$ and $2y = 30 - 3x$. State the co-ordinates of this common point.
    Answer: $(0, 15)$

5

ALGEBRAIC GRAPHS
OF THE SECOND DEGREE

THE PARABOLA

Minimum and Maximum Values

Example: Construct the graph of the function x^2, *i.e.*, let $y = x^2$ (Fig. 49).

x	-4	-3	-2	-1	0	$+1$	$+2$	$+3$	$+4$
$y = x^2$	16	9	4	1	0	1	4	9	16

On plotting these points we find that they do not lie on a straight line, and therefore it will be necessary to draw a smooth curve through the points given in the table. Owing to the big variation between the values of x and those of y, we must use two quite different scales on the axes in order to make the graph as large as possible, thus ensuring the greatest accuracy of our results.

We see from an examination of the values in the table that no part of the graph lies below the x axis, since no value less than 0 for y can be obtained.

Again from the graph (and the table) we see that the curve is perfectly symmetrical about the y axis, which, in this case, is also known as the axis of symmetry, or the axis of the *parabola*, the name given to this particular mathematical curve.

A further examination of the data and graph shows that the value of y, and therefore of x^2, as we move along the curve from A towards B in the diagram continually diminishes until the point O is reached when its value is zero and then increases indefinitely from O to B and onwards.

The value of x^2 at this point O is known as the *minimum value* and the point O is a turning point of the curve.

If we draw the graph of $y = -x^2$ (Fig. 50) however, we should obtain an inverted parabola, *viz.*:

x	-4	-3	-2	-1	0	$+1$	$+2$	$+3$	$+4$
$y = -x^2$	-16	-9	-4	-1	0	-1	-4	-9	-16

In this case the curve will turn at a *maximum value* and thus we see that a maximum or minimum value of a function corresponds with a turning point of the graph.

This parabolic curve is one which is frequently met in ordinary life, *e.g.*, the path of a ball thrown into the air, the trajectory of a bullet or shell, the design of reflectors in cars and

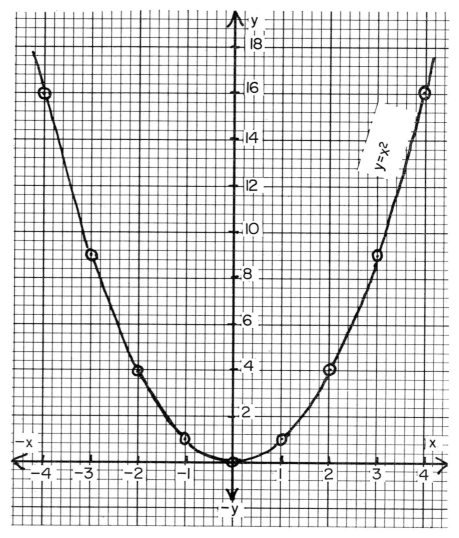

FIGURE 49

searchlights, etc. However, it differs slightly in form from two other mathematical curves, *e.g.*, half an ellipse or the catenary, which is the form taken up by suspending a heavy chain or rope from both ends. The paths of heavenly bodies are generally ellipses, but comets may take a path which can very closely approximate to a parabola.

For comparison it is useful to draw on the same graph the parabolas obtained from the equations $y = x^2$; $y = 2x^2$; $y = 3x^2$; $y = 4x^2$; $y = 5x^2$, etc. (Fig. 51).

On studying these curves it will be at once discovered that the effect of increasing the coefficient of x^2 is to narrow the form of the curve.

Conversely, if we draw the curves $y = x^2$; $y = \frac{1}{2}x^2$; $y = \frac{1}{3}x^2$; $y = \frac{1}{4}x^2$, etc., we should see that the curves increase in width (Fig. 52).

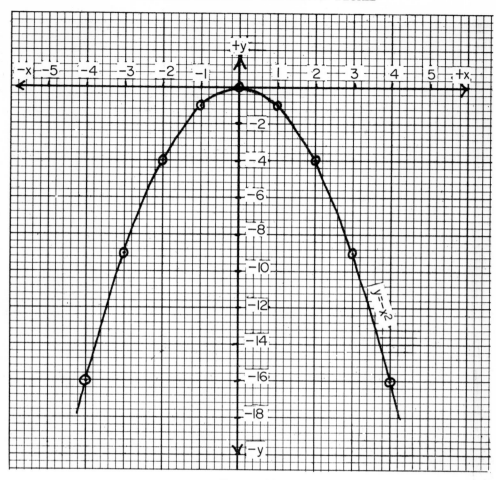

FIGURE 50

Now by constructing the graph of $y = (x + 2)^2$, which is itself a perfect square, we shall see points of similarity as well as of difference.

x	-14	-13	-2	-1	0	$+1$	$+2$	$+3$	$+4$
$x + 2$	-2	-1	0	1	2	3	4	5	6
$y = (x + 2)^2$	4	1	0	1	4	9	16	25	36

From an examination of the value of y in this table it is obvious that the curve is symmetrical about the point $x = -2$ and touches the x axis at this point also ($y = 0$). (Fig. 53.)

Hence it will be seen that whenever a function is a perfect square, the graph is of parabolic form, touching the x axis for only one value of x.

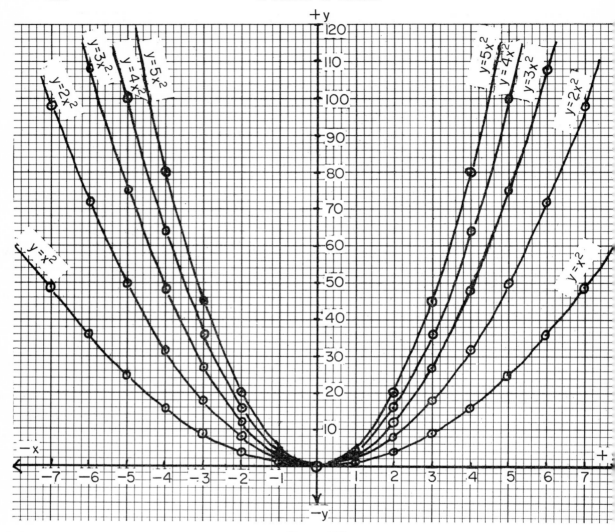

FIGURE 51

If, however, the function is not a perfect square, *e.g.*, $y = x^2 + 3$ the graph will not touch the x axis, but may rise above or fall below it.

x	-4	-3	-2	-1	0	$+1$	$+2$	$+3$	$+4$
x^2	16	9	4	1	0	1	4	9	16
$y = x^2 + 3$	19	12	7	4	3	4	7	12	19

From a study of this table and the graph it will be seen that the effect of the constant term $+3$ to the equation of $y = x^2$ has merely been to *raise* the $y = x^2$ graph vertically by 3 units, *viz.* Figure 54, below.

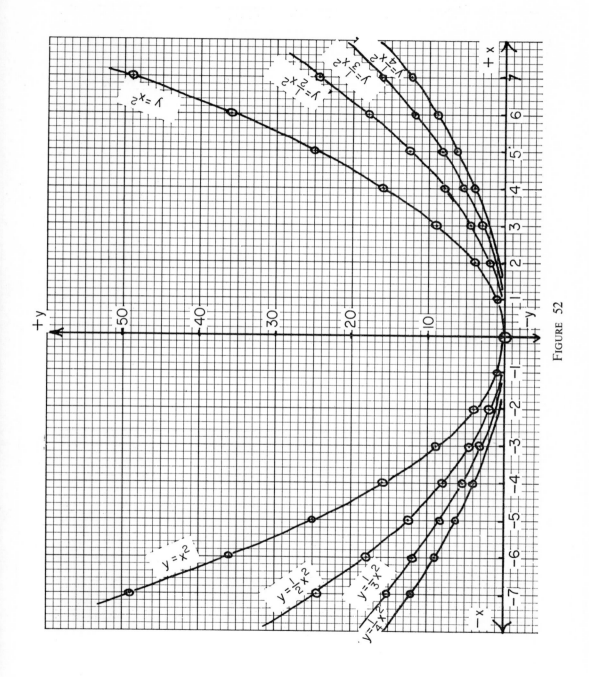

FIGURE 52

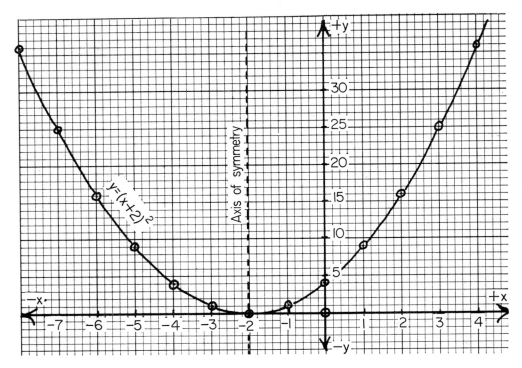

FIGURE 53

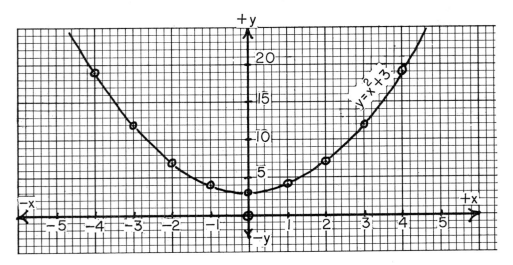

FIGURE 54

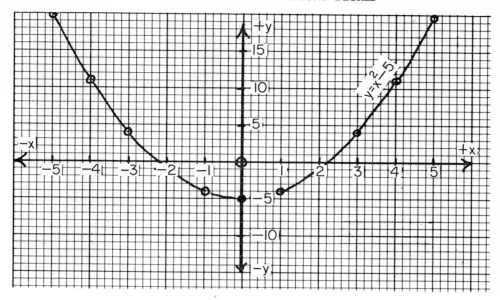

FIGURE 55

Conversely the graph of $y = x^2 - 5$ is the $y = x^2$ curve *dropped* 5 units (Fig. 55).

It is important to note, however, that raising or lowering the parabola by a fixed number of units does not make a series of parallel lines as occurred with equations of the first degree which were straight lines (Fig. 56).

To take the experiment a stage further let us add a first degree term to the function, *e.g.*, $y = x^2 + x - 2$ (Fig. 57).

x	0	1	2	3	4	$-\frac{1}{2}$	-1	-2	-3	-4	-5
x^2	0	1	4	9	16	$\frac{1}{4}$	1	4	9	16	25
$+x$	0	1	2	12	4	$-\frac{1}{2}$	-1	-2	-3	-4	-5
-2	-2	-2	-2	-2	-2	-2	-2	-2	-2	-2	-2
y	-2	0	4	10	18	$-2\frac{1}{4}$	-2	0	4	10	18

We see that the x axis is not tangential to the curve in this case because the function $x^2 + x - 2$ does not constitute a perfect square.

The constant term (-2) is now indicated by the point where the graph cuts the y axis whilst the axis of symmetry of the parabola has moved to the *left* of the y axis, in fact to the point $x = -\frac{1}{2}$.

Conversely, if the first degree term of the function had a *minus* sign instead of a plus sign before it, we should see that the axis of symmetry would move to the right.

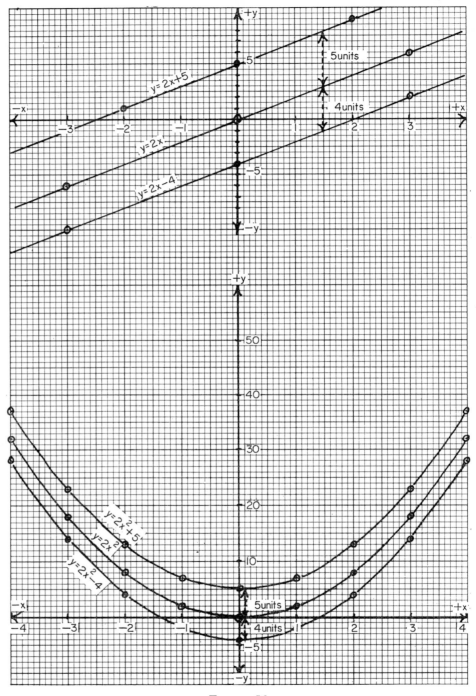

FIGURE 56

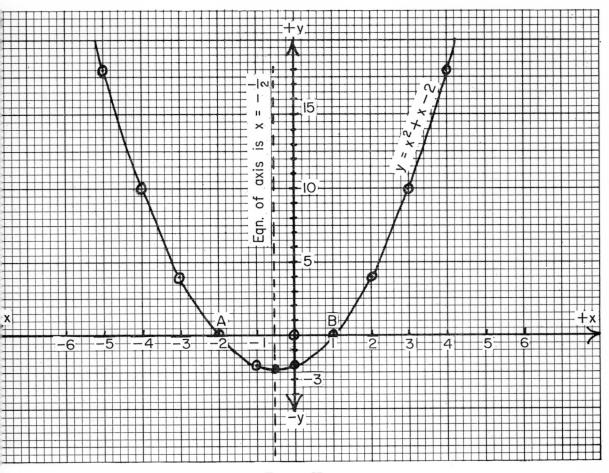

FIGURE 57

These points relating to the graph of the general equation $y = ax^2 + bx + c$ can therefore be briefly summarized thus:

(a) In *general* functions of the 2nd degree form parabolas.

(b) If the function constitutes a perfect square the x axis becomes a tangent to the curve.

(c) If the values of y and x^2 have the same sign then the parabola is upright (minimum value) but if the signs are different then the parabola becomes inverted (maximum value).

(d) The addition of the constant term alone has the effect of raising or lowering the parabola according to the sign. If a first degree term is present in the function then the constant term indicates the point where the curve cuts the y axis ($x = 0$).

(e) The effect of adding a first degree term to the equation is to move the axis of symmetry off the y axis. To the left if the first degree term is positive and to the right if it is negative— provided the parabola is "upright"; the movement would, of course, be reversed with respect to an "inverted" parabola. (A change of sign in the equation results in a change of direction in the shift of the axis.)

H

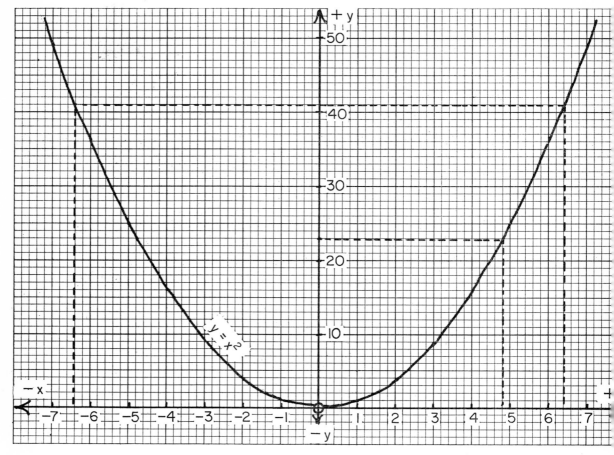

FIGURE 58

Square Roots—Parabolic Graph

If we draw the graph of $y = x^2$ we produce a "ready reckoner" for squares and square roots within the compass of the scales chosen. For instance, in the graph above if we wish to find the value of $(4\cdot8)^2$ we take $4\cdot8$ on the x axis, strike the curve and read off the intercept on the y axis, obtaining the value of 23, *i.e.* $(4\cdot8)^2 = 23$ approximately.

Conversely, if we wish to determine $\sqrt{41}$ by drawing a horizontal line at $y = 41$, we strike the curve, reading off the value of $-6\cdot4$ and $+6\cdot4$ on the x axis; in other words $\sqrt{41} = \pm6\cdot4$ approximately.

The choice of scales and size of the area involved will give the requisite accuracy and scope required.

Solution of Quadratic Equations

First method

Referring to the previous graph of $y = x^2 + x - 2$ (Fig. 57) the solution is given by $y = 0$, *i.e.*, $f(x) = 0$, hence the values are indicated by the points A and B $x = -2$ and $x = +1$ where the parabola cuts the x axis, in other words where it intersects with the straight line $y = 0$.

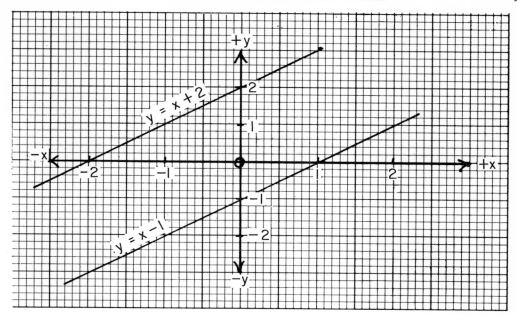

FIGURE 59

Second method

If, however, the equation can be factorized, *e.g.*, $x^2 + x - 2 = (x - 1)(x + 2)$, instead of drawing the parabola $y = x^2 + x - 2$ we can draw the two straight lines from $y = x - 1$ and $y = x + 2$ obtained from the two factors. These two lines will be seen to give the same points of intersection with the x axis as in the previous method.

Using the intercept method:

$$y = x - 1 \quad \text{If } x = 0 \; y = -1 \quad \text{and} \quad y = 0 \; x = +1$$
$$y = x + 2 \quad \text{If } x = 0 \; y = +2 \quad \text{and} \quad y = 0 \; x = -2$$

Third method

To solve the equation $y = x^2 + x - 2$ means finding the value of x when $y = 0$; *i.e.*, when $0 = x^2 + x - 2$ or $2 - x = x^2$.

If we draw the graphs of the two functions $y = 2 - x$ and $y = x^2$ we shall see that the points of intersection of the straight line $y = 2 - x$ and the parabola $y = x^2$ again give us the same values ($x = +1$ and -2) for the solution of the equation.

Equal Roots

Example: Draw the four graphs of $y = x^2 + 6x + 12$; $y = x^2 + 6x + 9$; $y = x^2 + 6x + 6$ and $y = x^2 + 6x + 3$ (Fig. 61).

The solutions of the equation $0 = x^2 + 6x + 3$ are given by the values of x as indicated by the points $A = -5{\cdot}45$ and $B = -0{\cdot}55$. Similarly, the solutions of the equation $0 = x^2 + 6x + 6$ are given by $C = -4{\cdot}73$ and $D = -1{\cdot}27$.

As we have seen before, if we increase the value of the constant term in the equation the effect is to raise the parabola by the value of the increase, in this case 3 units.

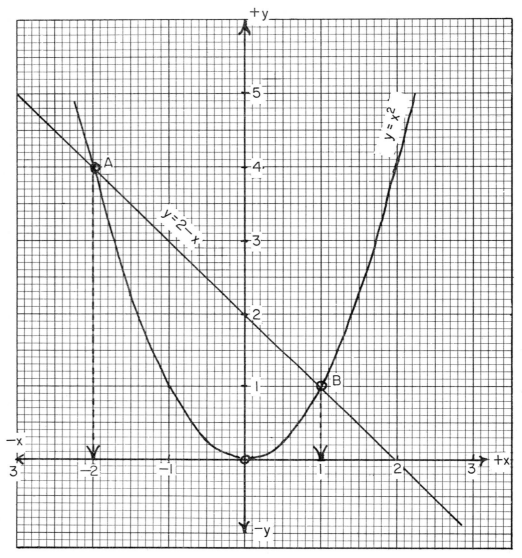

FIGURE 60

As a result, the two solutions C and D of the second graph approach towards each other on the x axis as compared with A and B. If, however, we increase the constant term by yet another 3 units to the equation $y = x^2 + 6x + 9$ we shall lift the parabola further still, and the two points of solution will again approach closer together. In fact, they will coincide, the points E and F being on the same value of $x = -3$.

We can write the equation $x^2 + 6x + 9 = 0$ in the form $(x + 3)(x + 3) = 0$. Hence the function $x^2 + 6x + 9$ comprises a perfect square which we know results in the x axis becoming a tangent to the parabola, the point of contact $x = -3$ being the solution to the equation $y = x + 3$, and as *two* such factors occur in $x^2 + 6x + 9$ this explains the coincidence of the *two* points E and F on the *one* value of $x = -3$.

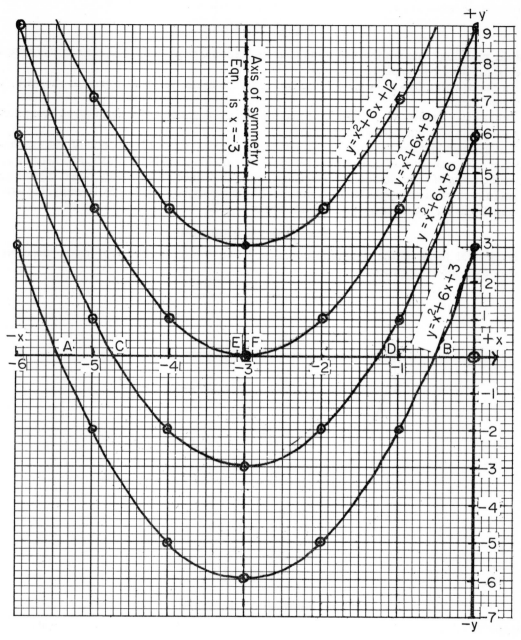

FIGURE 61

To sum up, therefore, if the graph touches the x axis only in *one* point then that point indicates *two* roots of equal value since the equation still constitutes a perfect square.

Imaginary Roots

In the previous examples the two roots of the equation $0 = x^2 + 6x + 3$ are *real and unequal*, being indicated by the points A and B.

In the equation $0 = x^2 + 6x + 6$ the two roots are again *real and unequal*, as shown by the points C and D.

In the equation $0 = x^2 + 6x + 9$ the two roots of the equation are *real and equal*, being shown by the point of contact (EF) on the x axis.

Let us again increase the equation by 3 units, *i.e.*, to $x^2 + 6x + 12 = 0$, and lift the graph still further. We now find, of course, that the graph line no longer cuts the x axis, and hence we say that the roots of the equation are *imaginary*. Note that since we have only varied the constant term in each of these graphs we have not moved the parabola $y = x^2 + 6x$ laterally, the axis of symmetry in every case being given by the line $x = -3$.

The General Equation

The general form of the quadratic equation $y = ax^2 + bx + c$ has for its solution when $ax^2 + bx + c = 0$ the roots

$$x = \frac{-b \pm \sqrt{b^2 - 4ac}}{2a}$$

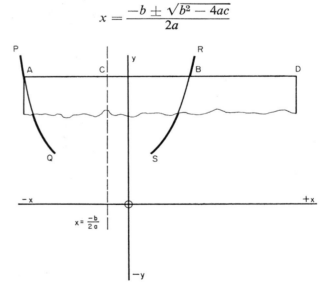

FIGURE 62

Equation of the Axis

Now if it is desired to check the equation of the axis, which is the first part of the general equation, *viz.*: $x = \dfrac{-b}{2a}$, after plotting the graph in the normal way the position of the axis can be determined *practically* by taking several distances across the parabola and determining their central points. This may very conveniently be done by marking off the distance AB on the straight edge of a piece of paper and folding in the centre C to give the middle, as in Figure 62.

Let PQ and RS be the sides of the parabola, $ACBD$ being the straight edge of a piece of paper. The point B is marked when the corner A is on the curve PQ; A is then folded over on to B, the centre established and the point C determined. Do this four or five times at intervals between PQ and RS—then construct the position of the axis by drawing the best straight line obtained by plotting C. This line should therefore check with the values of $x = \dfrac{-b}{2a}$ from the general equation.

The turning point of the parabola can then be accurately plotted from this practical determination of the point C.

The Discriminant

The latter portion of the general equation $\pm\sqrt{b^2 - 4ac}$ will check the actual position of the graph from the values of a, b and c in the given equation.

(a) If the graph cuts the X axis in two places, the roots are real and unequal, therefore $b^2 - 4ac$ is of positive value.

(b) If the graph just touches the X axis, the roots are real and equal; $b^2 - 4ac$ is then *zero*.

(c) If the graph does not cut or touch the X axis, the roots are imaginary and $b^2 - 4ac$ will be found to be *negative* in value.

Solution of Similar Equations

Example: $y = x^2 + x - 2$, as before (Fig. 63).

As we have already seen, the solutions of the equation $0 = x^2 + x - 2$ are given by the values of x where $y = 0$, *i.e.*, by the intersection of the parabola $y = x^2 + x - 2$ with the straight line $y = 0$, which is of course the X axis, giving the values $+1$ and -2 at the points A and B respectively.

Now we can use this graph to solve a similar equation, *e.g.*, $y = x^2 + x - 1$ without drawing a separate curve, for $x^2 + x - 1$ can be written as $x^2 + x - 2 + 1$ and if $x^2 + x - 1 = 0$ then $-1 = x^2 + x - 2$.

Hence, it can be seen that if the solution of $x^2 + x - 2$ is given when $y = 0$, then the solution of $x^2 + x - 1 = 0$ is given when $y = -1$ and the intersection of the curve with this line at points E and F give values of $x = +0.6$ and -1.6 approximately.

Similarly the solution of: $\qquad 0 = x^2 + x - 3$

$$\text{or} \quad +1 = x^2 + x - 2$$

is given by the intersection of the curve with $y = +1$ giving values $x = +1.3$ and -2.3 approximately.

To take this development a stage further we can use the curve of $y = x^2 + x - 2$ to solve $0 = x^2 + 2x - 6$, for $x^2 + 2x - 6$ may be written as $(x^2 + x - 2) + x - 4$.

Hence to solve $x^2 + 2x - 6$ we put $y = 0$

i.e., $\qquad\qquad\qquad 0 = x^2 + 2x - 6$

$$\text{or} \quad 0 = (x^2 + x - 2) + x - 4$$

$$\text{or} \quad 4 - x = x^2 + x - 2.$$

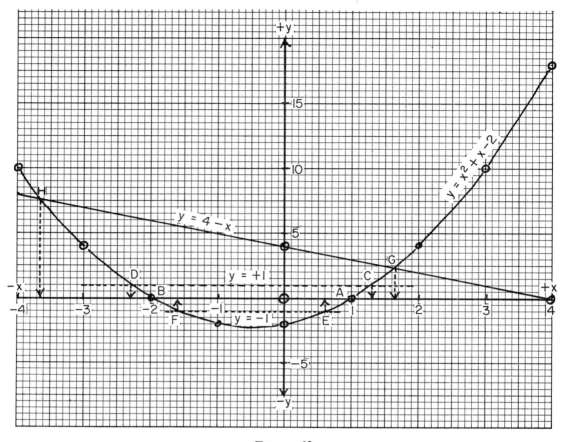

FIGURE 63

By drawing the line $y = 4 - x$ therefore and noting the intersection with the curve $x^2 + x - 2$ we can obtain the solution of $x^2 + 2x - 6 = 0$.

By following this procedure the points G and H give approximate values of x as $+1 \cdot 65$ and $-3 \cdot 65$ (Fig. 64).

Change of Variable (Linearization)

In the process of plotting experimental results in a straight line it is a simple procedure to draw the "best" straight line and from this line obtain the equation connecting the variables under consideration. If, however, the points do not approximate to a straight line but to a curve, then the relationship between the variables cannot be directly determined. In such cases it is often desirable to distort the scales and to produce a straight line where the relationship can be established, and then from the known distortion factor the desired result may be obtained. This process is called "linearization".

For example, let us consider the equation $y = 2x^2 + 2x - 1$ which in the normal procedure is plotted as the parabola shown in figure 65.

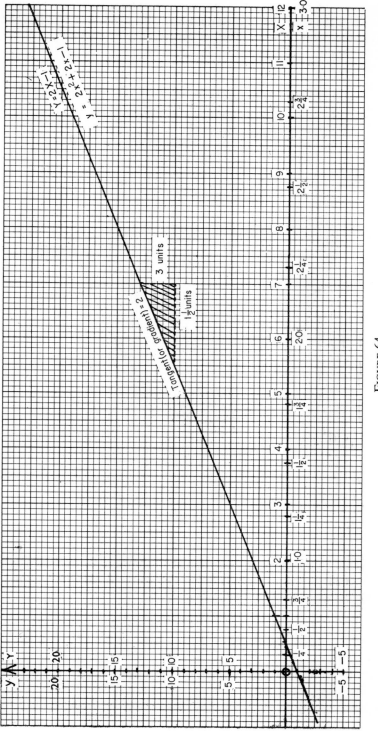

FIGURE 64

If now we take this equation and by substituting $Y = y$ and $X = x^2 + x$ we obtain the equation $Y = 2X - 1$ which is the equation of a straight line with a gradient of 2 (*i.e.*, tan.) and cutting the vertical axis at the point $(0, -1)$. This, of course, may be constructed also by plotting two points, *e.g.*, $(0, -1)$ and $(12, 23)$ as shown in figure 64.

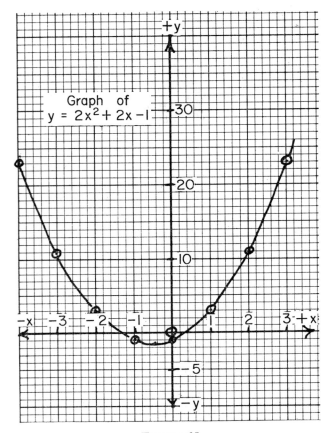

Graph of
$y = 2x^2 + 2x - 1$

FIGURE 65

As we have taken $Y = y$ there is no distortion at all shown in the vertical axis scale which may be drawn as before. Distortion, however, does occur in the X axis but we can form the x-scale from the relationship we have taken that $X = x^2 + x$.

x	$\frac{1}{4}$	$\frac{1}{2}$	$\frac{3}{4}$	1	$1\frac{1}{4}$	$1\frac{1}{2}$	$1\frac{3}{4}$	2	$2\frac{1}{4}$	$2\frac{1}{2}$	$2\frac{3}{4}$	3
X	0·3	0·75	1·3	2·0	2·8	3·75	4·8	6·0	7·3	8·75	10·3	12

From this data therefore it is easy to mark off the x scale underneath the regular X scale as shown above. Readings from the X and Y scales are, of course, related to the equation $Y = 2X - 1$ whilst those from the x and y scales are fixed by the equation $y = 2x^2 + 2x - 1$.

EXERCISES

1. Draw the graph of $y = x^2 + x - 56$ and state the co-ordinates of the points at which it cuts the X axis.

Answer: $(7, 0)$ *and* $(-8, 0)$

2. In the case of the following parabolas, state:

(a) Whether they have a maximum or a minimum value.
(b) The maximum (or minimum) value.
(c) The point where they cut the Y axis.
(d) The points, if any, where they cut the X axis.
(e) The equation of the axis of symmetry.

(i) $y = (x + 3)(x + 5)$
Answers: (a) Minimum, (b) -1, (c) $(0, 15)$, (d) $(-3, 0)$ and $(-5, 0)$, (e) $x = -4$
(ii) $y = x^2 - 2x$
Answers: (a) Minimum, (b) -1, (c) Origin $(0, 0)$, (d) Origin and $(2, 0)$, (e) $x = +1$
(iii) $y = 3 - 4x - 4x^2$
Answers: (a) Maximum, (b) $+4$, (c) $(0, 3)$, (d) $(-1\frac{1}{2}, 0)$ and $(\frac{1}{2}, 0)$, (e) $x = -\frac{1}{2}$
(iv) $y + 2x^2 = 8x$
Answers: (a) Maximum, (b) 8, (c) Origin $(0, 0)$, (d) Origin $(0, 0)$ and $(4, 0)$, (e) $x = +2$
(v) $4y = 8x + x^2$
Answers: (a) Minimum, (b) -4, (c) Origin $(0, 0)$, (d) $(-8, 0)$ and $(0, 0)$, (e) $x = -4$
(vi) $y = 4x^2 - 5(2x - 1)$
Answers: (a) Minimum, (b) $-1\frac{1}{4}$, (c) $(0, 5)$, (d) $(0.7, 0)$ and $(1.8, 0)$ approx., (e) $x = 1\frac{1}{4}$

3. Show by plotting the graph of $y = (x + 2)^2$ that the X axis is a tangent to the parabola at its turning point and give the co-ordinates of its point of contact.

Answer: $(-2, 0)$

What is the equation of the axis?

Answer: $x = -2$

4. Show graphically that the roots of the equation $y = (x + 2)(x - 3)$ are -2 and 3.

(a) What is the equation of its axis?
Answer: $x = \frac{1}{2}$
(b) Has the function a maximum or a minimum value?
Answer: Minimum
(c) Write down the co-ordinates of its turning point.
Answer: $x = 0.5$ *and* $y = -6.25$

5. (a) Find graphically the solution of the equation $x^2 - 2x - 5 = 0$.
Answer: $x = -1.45$ *and* 3.45
(b) Write down the equation of its axis.
Answer: $x = 1$
(c) For what positive values of x is the function negative?
Answer: Between the values $x = 0$ *and* 3.45
(d) Has the function a maximum or minimum value?
Answer: Minimum

(e) What is the equation of the straight line which with the parabola $y = x^2$ would give the same solution?

    Answer: $y = 2x + 5$

(f) What is the equation of the line which with the parabola $y = x^2 - 2x$ would give the same solution?

    Answer: $y = 5$

6. Show graphically that the equation $y = x^2 + 6x + 9$ is a perfect square.

(a) What is the equation of its axis?

    Answer: $x = -3$

(b) By drawing the line $y = 4$ on the same area obtain the roots to the equation $y = x^2 + 6x + 5$.

    Answer: $x = -1$ and -5

7. (a) Solve the equation $2x^2 = 5(2 + x - y)$ for x when $y = 0$.

    Answer: $x = -1 \cdot 32$ and $+3 \cdot 82$

(b) Has the function a minimum or a maximum value?

    Answer: Maximum

(c) What are the co-ordinates of its turning point?

    Answer: $(1 \cdot 25, 2 \cdot 625)$

(d) When the values of x lie between 1 and 3 is the function positive or negative?

    Answer: Positive

(e) Write down the equation of the tangent at its turning point.

    Answer: $y = 2 \cdot 625$

8. Draw the graph of $2y = (x - 3)(x + 1)$ and use it to solve the equation $(x + 1)(x - 3) = 2$, and that of $(x - 3)(x + 1) + 5 = 0$.

    Answers: $-1 \cdot 4$ and $3 \cdot 3$; no solution

What is the minimum value of the function $2y = (x - 3)(x + 1)$?

    Answer: $y = -2$

For what value of x does this occur?

    Answer: $x = 1$

9. (a) Show graphically that the two straight lines $y = 2x + 3$ and $y = x + 6$ cut the X axis at the same points as the parabola $y = 2x^2 + 15x + 18$.

(b) What are the other points of intersection of the lines $y = 2x + 3$ and $y = x + 6$ with the parabola?

    Answer: $(-1, -5)$ and $(-5, -7)$

(c) What are the co-ordinates of the point of intersection of the two straight lines?

    Answer: $(3, 9)$

(d) What are the solutions to the equation $2x^2 + 15x + 18 = 0$?

    Answer: $-1\frac{1}{2}$ and -6

10. Find graphically the maximum value of y in the equation $y = 16(x - 1)(4 - x)$.

    Answer: 36

What are its roots if $y = 0$?

    Answer: $x = 1$ and 4

  1. By writing the equation $0 = 3x^2 - 10x + 3$ in the form $3x^2 = 10x - 3$, and by drawing the graphs of $y = 3x^2$ and $y = 10x - 3$, find the roots of the equation $3x^2 - 10x + 3 = 0$.

    Answer: $x = 3$ and $\frac{1}{3}$

12. By writing the equation $0 = x^2 + 4x - 1$ in the form $x^2 + 4x = 1$, and by drawing the graphs of $y = x^2 + 4x$ and $y = 1$, solve the equation.

Answer: $x = -4\cdot2$ and $0\cdot2$ approx.

13. Draw the graph of the function x^2 and use it to solve the equations:

(a) $x^2 - 2x - 10 = 0$.

Answer: $4\cdot32$ and $-2\cdot32$

(b) $2x^2 - 5x - 3$.

Answer: $3\cdot0$ and $-0\cdot5$

14. Use the graph of $3y = (x - 2)(3 - x)$ to obtain the roots of the equation $x^2 - 5x + 3 = 0$.

Answer: $4\cdot3$ and $0\cdot7$

15. Find the maximum value of y in the equation $10y = 17 + 18x - 6x^2$.

Answer: $\dfrac{30\cdot5}{10} = 3\cdot05$

16. Obtain graphically the values of y which make the equation $y^2 - 2y - 9$ equal to zero. Find also the minimum value of the function.

Answers: $4\cdot16$ and $2\cdot16;$ -10

17. Draw the graph of $y = 5 + 4x - 2x^2$.

(a) Has the curve a maximum or minimum point?

Answer: Maximum

(b) What are the co-ordinates of the turning point?

Answer: $(1, 7)$

(c) What is the equation of the tangent at the turning point?

Answer: $y = 7$

18. Solve simultaneously the equations $x - y = 4$ and $2x^2 - 4 = 2x + y$.

Answer: $x = 0$ and $1\cdot5$, $y = -4$ and $-2\cdot5$

Find the maximum value of the equation $y = \frac{1}{2}(1 - x)(2x + 7)$.

Answer: $5\cdot06$

19. Graphically demonstrate that the equation $y = 2x^2 - 5x + 3$ is always positive except when the values of x lie between 1 and $1\frac{1}{2}$.

20. Show graphically how to divide a line 12 in. long so that the sum of the squares on the two parts shall be the least possible.

Answer: 6 in. and 6 in. Minimum value $= 72$

21. Show graphically how to divide a line 12 in. long so that the rectangle contained by the two parts shall be the greatest possible.

Answer: 6 in. and 6 in. Maximum value $= 36$

22. Draw the graph of $5y = x^2 - 2x + 2$ from $x = -3$ to $+3$.

(a) What are the roots of the equation, if any?

Answer: No roots

(b) Use the graph to solve the equation $x^2 - 2x + \frac{1}{2} = 0$.

Answer: $x = 1\cdot7$ and $0\cdot29$

On the same graph plot the line $4x + 15y = 4$.

(a) What values of x will satisfy both these equations?

Answer: $x = -1\cdot3$ and $+2$

(b) What equation can be solved by both these values?

Answer: $10x^2 - 7x - 26 = 0$

23. Draw graph of $y = \sqrt{x}$ from $x = 0$ to 100. Read off from your graph:

(a) $\sqrt{24}$.

  Answer: 4·9

(b) $\sqrt{48}$.

  Answer: 6·9

(c) $\sqrt{59}$.

  Answer: 7·7

(d) $\sqrt{88}$.

  Answer: 9·4

By drawing the line $y = 6 - \dfrac{x}{10}$ on the same graph, solve the equation $6 - \dfrac{x}{10} = \sqrt{x}$.

  Answer: $x = 18$

THE CIRCLE

Circle Centred on the Origin

If we draw any circle of radius r and centre on the origin, then any point P on the circumference whose co-ordinates are (x, y) can be shown by Pythagoras' Theorem (as applied to the triangle *OPM*) to have the relationship $x^2 + y^2 = r^2$.

This then is the general equation of a circle with its centre on the origin, *provided that the scales are the same on both axes.*

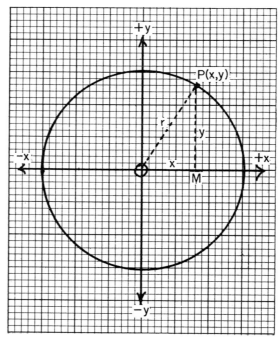

FIGURE 66

Example: Graph $x^2 + y^2 = 16$ (Fig. 67), *i.e.,* $y^2 = 16 - x^2$

x	0	± 1	± 2	± 3	± 4
y	± 4	$\pm\sqrt{15}$	$\pm\sqrt{12}$	$\pm\sqrt{7}$	0

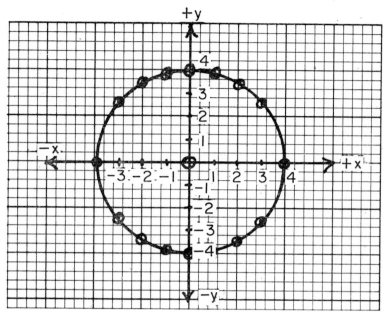

FIGURE 67

Circles Not Centred on the Origin

By plotting the graph of the equation $x^2 + y^2 - 4x = 0$ or $y^2 = 4x - x^2$

x	0	$+1$	$+2$	$+3$	$+4$
$4x$	0	$+4$	$+8$	$+12$	$+16$
$-x^2$	0	-1	-4	-9	-16
y^2	0	$+3$	$+4$	$+3$	0
y	0	$\pm\sqrt{3}$	± 2	$\pm\sqrt{3}$	0

we see that the graph resolves itself into a circle with its centre at the point P (2, 0) and radius 2 units (Fig. 68).

Since the equation may be written in the form $(x^2 - 4x + 4) + y^2 = 4$, or

$$(x - 2)^2 + y^2 = 4$$

Putting X for $x - 2$ and Y for y, we have: $X^2 + Y^2 = 4.$

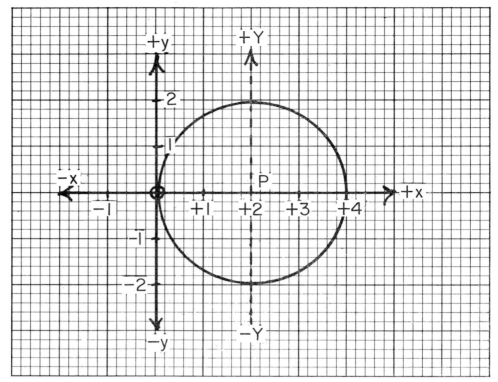

FIGURE 68

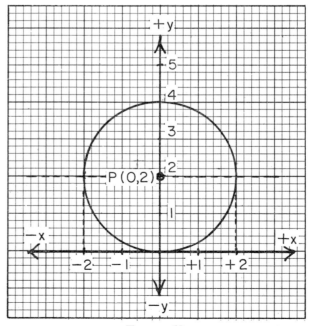

FIGURE 69

We have thus taken a new origin P (the point $(2, 0)$) and a new axis parallel to the original axis, the X axis remaining in the same position.

Again by plotting the graph of the equation $x^2 + y^2 - 4y = 0$ it will be obvious that the only change will be in the transfer of the point P to the Y axis since the term $-4x$ in the first equation now becomes $-4y$.

By writing the equation in the form

$$x^2 + (y^2 - 4y + 4) = 4$$

or

$$x^2 + (y - 2)^2 = 4$$

i.e.,

$$X^2 + Y^2 = 4 \text{ where } Y = (y - 2)$$

we shall confirm this variation of the graph (Fig. 69).

Hence we see that by introducing a first degree term in x or y to the general equation $x^2 + y^2 = r^2$, the only effect is to shift the origin to another point on the X or Y axis.

Following this logically, it will be seen that by introducing first degree terms in x and y to the general equation the centre of the circle will be moved both ways, i.e., it will move off the original axes entirely.

EXERCISES

1. Construct the graph of $x^2 + y^2 = 16$.

(a) At what points on the X axis does this graph intersect with the line $y = -3$?
Answer: $x = \pm 2 \cdot 64$

(b) At what points on the Y axis does it intersect with the line $x = -2$?
Answer: $y = \pm 3 \cdot 46$

(c) At what points on the X axis does it intersect with the line $y = x + 2$?
Answer: $x = -3 \cdot 64$ and $1 \cdot 64$

(d) Find the X-ordinates of the points of intersection of this circle with the parabola $y = x^2 - 3$.
Answer: $x = \pm 2 \cdot 55$

(e) Join the points $P(-3, 2)$ and $Q(2, -3)$ by a straight line and write down the co-ordinates of the points of intersection of this straight line with the above.
Answer: $(3 \cdot 25, 2 \cdot 26)$ and $(-2 \cdot 26, -3 \cdot 25)$

2. With the point $R(3, 4)$ as centre, construct a circle of radius 2 units. Write down the equation of the circle.
Answer: $(x - 3)^2 + (y - 4)^2 = 4$ (or $x^2 + y^2 - 6x - 8y + 21 = 0$)

(a) What is the equation of the lines parallel to the X axis and tangential to the circle?
Answer: $y = 6$ and $y = 2$

(b) What is the equation of the line parallel to the Y axis through the centre of the circle?
Answer: $x = 3$

(c) From the point $P(1, 1)$ lines are drawn tangential to the circle. Write down the co-ordinates of their points of contact.
Answer: $(1, 4)$ and $(3 \cdot 8, 2 \cdot 2)$

(d) Construct the graph of $xy = 10$ from $x = 1$ to $x = 6$. What are the co-ordinates of its points of intersection with the circle?
Answer: $(1 \cdot 78, 5 \cdot 58)$ and $(4 \cdot 2, 2 \cdot 4)$

I

3. Solve graphically the following simultaneous equations:

(a) $x^2 + y^2 = 25$
   $x - 5 = 2y$
   Answer: $(-3, -4)$ $(5, 0)$

(b) $x^2 + y^2 = 9$
   $y = -2$
   Answer: $(-2 \cdot 24, -2)$ $(2 \cdot 24, -2)$

(c) $x^2 + y^2 = 36$
   $y = 5 - x$
   Answer: $(5 \cdot 9, -0 \cdot 9)$ $(-0 \cdot 9, 5 \cdot 9)$

(d) $(x + 1)^2 + (y + 2)^2 = 16$
   $x = y + 4$
   Answer: $(2 \cdot 9, -1 \cdot 1)$ $(-1 \cdot 9, -5 \cdot 9)$

(e) $(x - 2)^2 + (y - 3)^2 = 9$
   $y = 3$
   Answer: $(-1, 3)$ $(5, 3)$

(f) $(x + 1)^2 + (y + 2)^2 = 16$
   $xy = 5$
   Answer: $(-4 \cdot 85, -1 \cdot 0)$ $(-0 \cdot 85, -5 \cdot 59)$

(g) $x^2 + y^2 = 16$
   $y = x^2$
   Answer: $(1 \cdot 9, 3 \cdot 5)$ $(-1 \cdot 9, 3 \cdot 5)$

(h) $x^2 + y^2 = 4$
   $y = x^2 - 4$
   Answer: $(\pm 2, 0)$ $(\pm 1 \cdot 75, -1)$

(i) $(x - 1)^2 + y^2 = 4$
   $x = 0$
   Answer: $(0, 1 \cdot 73)$ $(0, -1 \cdot 73)$

4. Find the equation of the circle which passes through the following three points: A $(3, 2)$ B $(-2, 4)$ and C $(-1, -3)$.
   Answer: $(x + 0 \cdot 42)^2 + (y - 0 \cdot 62)^2 = (3 \cdot 66)^2$

5. (a) What is the equation of the circle which has the following lines as tangents?
(i) $y = 6$; (ii) $x = -4$; (iii) $y = -4$.
   Answer: $(x - 1)^2 + (y - 1)^2 = 25$

(b) Construct the tangents to the circle at the points on its circumference where $x = -3$. What are the co-ordinates of the point of contact?
   Answer: $(-3, 4)$ *and* $(-3, -2)$

(c) What are the co-ordinates of the point of intersection of these two tangents?
   Answer: $(-5 \cdot 2, 1 \cdot 0)$

(d) What is the equation of the line joining this point of intersection of the tangents with the centre of the circle?
   Answer: $y = 1$

(e) What are the points of intersection of the circle with the line $x = 5$?
   Answer: $(5, 4)$ *and* $(5, -2)$

(Hint: The use of mm. graph paper might be preferable, using 1 cm. $= 1$ unit on both axes, as also in the following question.)

6. Two points P (2, 4) and Q (−4, −2) lie on the circumference of a circle whose radius is 6 units. Find:

(a) The co-ordinates of its centre.
Answer: (2, −2)

(b) The equation of the circle.
Answer: $(x − 2)^2 + (y + 2)^2 = 36$

(c) The equation of the tangents at the point where $x = 2$.
Answer: $x = −8$ *and* $x = 4$

Example: Draw the curve of the equation $x^2 + y^2 − 4x + 2y + 1 = 0$. Rearranging this we have:

$$(x^2 − 4x + 4) + (y^2 + 2y + 1) = 4$$
$$(x − 2)^2 + (y + 1)^2 = 4$$

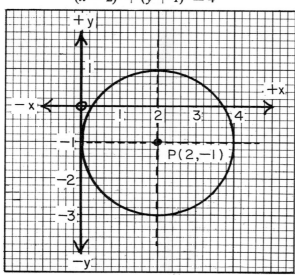

FIGURE 70

Writing X for $(x − 2)$ and Y for $(y + 1)$ we again have the general form $X^2 + Y^2 = 4$ which is a circle radius 2 units and having its centre at the point (2, −1) (Fig. 70). Graphically we have:

X	0	+1	+2	+3	+4
$4x$	0	+4	+8	+12	+16
x^2	0	+1	+4	+9	+16
$\sqrt{4x − x^2}$	0	$\sqrt{3}$	$\sqrt{4} = 2$	$\sqrt{3}$	0
y	−1	0·73 or −2·73	1 or −3	0·73 or −2·73	−1

since $x^2 + y^2 − 4x + 2y + 1 = 0$ gives
$$y^2 + 2y + 1 = 4x − x^2$$
i.e. $$y + 1 = \sqrt{4x − x^2}$$
or $$y = −1 + \sqrt{4x − x^2}$$

THE ELLIPSE

Referring again to general equation $\frac{x^2}{a^2} + \frac{y^2}{b^2} = 1$, and comparing it with this example $\frac{x^2}{16} + \frac{y^2}{9} = 1$,

we see that $a^2 = 16$ (or $a = \pm 4$) and
$$b^2 = 9 \ (\text{or } b = \pm 3).$$

The values ± 4 and ± 3 are indicated in the graph itself (Fig. 71) by the lengths of the intercepts on the X and Y axes respectively, *i.e.*, $OB = a$ and $OC = b$.

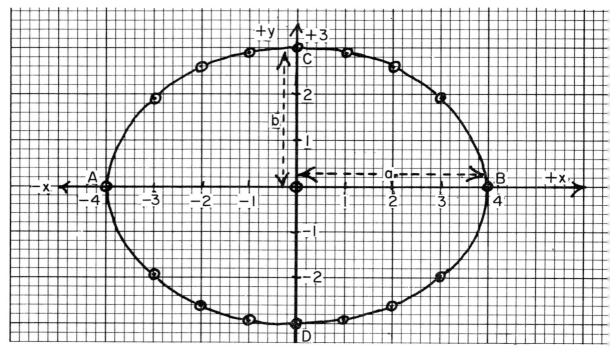

FIGURE 71

The general form of the equation in this case is:

$$\frac{x^2}{a^2} + \frac{y^2}{b^2} = 1 \text{ where } a \text{ and } b \text{ are constants.}$$

Example: Plot the graph of the equation $\frac{x^2}{16} + \frac{y^2}{9} = 1$.

Writing y in terms of x, we have:

$$\frac{y^2}{9} = 1 - \frac{x^2}{16}$$

or
$$\frac{y}{3} = \pm \frac{\sqrt{16 - x^2}}{4}$$

or
$$y = \pm \tfrac{3}{4}\sqrt{16 - x^2}$$

As in the case of the circle we see that the graph is symmetrical about the axes of X and Y since, for every value of x, there are two values of y, equal in magnitude and opposite in sign.

x	-4	-3	-2	-1	0	$+1$	$+2$	$+3$	$+4$
x^2	16	9	4	1	0	1	4	9	16
$16 - x^2$	0	7	12	15	16	15	12	7	0
$\sqrt{16 - x^2}$	0	$\pm 2{\cdot}646$	$\pm 3{\cdot}464$	$\pm 3{\cdot}873$	± 4	$\pm 3{\cdot}873$	$\pm 3{\cdot}464$	$\pm 2{\cdot}646$	0
y	0	$\pm 1{\cdot}98$	$\pm 2{\cdot}59$	$\pm 2{\cdot}9$	± 3	$\pm 2{\cdot}9$	$\pm 2{\cdot}59$	$\pm 1{\cdot}98$	0

The curve is known as an "ellipse", the lengths across the X axis being known as the "major axis" and that along the Y axis as the "minor axis".

6

ALGEBRAIC GRAPHS OF THE THIRD DEGREE—CUBIC GRAPHS

THIS form of graph is obtained from equations of the third degree, *e.g.*, $y = x^3$ or $y^3 = x$, etc., and generally take the form of an *S* curve.

Example: Plot the graph of $y = x^3$ (Fig. 72).

x	0	± 1	± 2	± 3	± 4	± 5
y	0	± 1	± 8	± 27	± 64	± 125

If we draw on the same area the graph of $y = 2x^3$

x	0	± 1	± 2	± 3	± 4
y	0	± 2	± 16	± 54	± 128

We shall note that a similar effect results as when the graphs of $y = x^2$ and $y = 2x^2$ were previously compared, *viz.*: that an *increase* in the coefficient of x^3 results in a narrowing of the curve as a whole. Conversely, a decrease in the coefficient of x^3 (or an increase in that of y^3) would result in a widening of the graph.

Again, the graph of $y^3 = x$ would be a similar shape, but on the other side of the axis of symmetry (Fig. 73).

Cube Roots

In constructing the graph of a quadratic function which could be factorized (second method) we saw that we could obtain the two roots more easily by drawing the two straight lines representing each factor.

In the same way we can obtain the roots of a cubic equation by drawing the *S* curve *or*, if it can be factorized, by drawing the separate graphs of each of the three factors.

Example: $y = x^3 + 4x^2 + x - 6$ (Fig. 74).

x	-1	-2	-3	-4	0	$+1$
x^3	-1	-8	-27	-64	0	1
$+4x^2$	4	$+16$	36	$+64$	0	4
$+x$	-1	-2	-3	-4	0	1
-6	-6	-6	-6	-6	-6	-6
y	-4	0	0	-10	-6	0

By constructing the *S* curve we see that the roots of the equation are $x = -3, -2$ and $+1$. As this equation factorizes into $y = (x - 1)(x + 2)(x + 3)$ if we draw the three straight lines

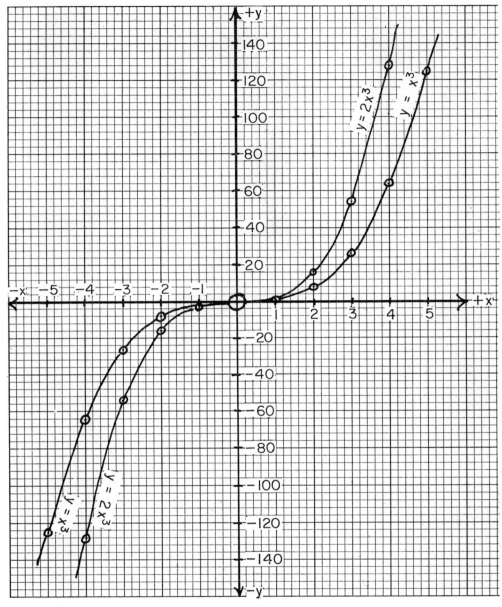

FIGURE 72

represented by $y = x - 1$, $y = x + 2$ and $y = x + 3$ we shall see that these three lines cut the X axis at the same three points, thereby giving the same three roots as solutions to the equation.

Again referring to the third method of obtaining the roots of a quadratic equation by equating two expressions (parabola and straight line) we can easily see that a parallel method can be adopted with a cubic equation.

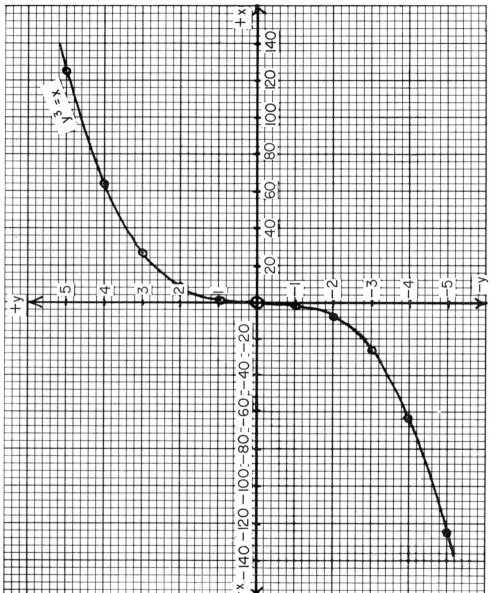

FIGURE 73

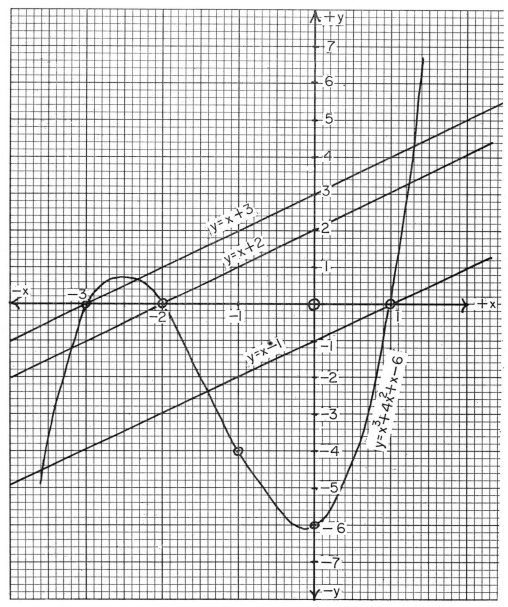

FIGURE 74

Example: To solve $0 = 2x^3 - 10x - 6$ using the graph $y = 2x^3 - 10x - 6$, put $y = 0$, *i.e.*,

$0 = 2x^3 - 10x - 6$

or $\dfrac{10x + 6}{2} = x^3$ (or $5x + 3 = x^3$)

Hence by plotting the S curve $y = x^3$ and the straight line $y = \dfrac{10x + 6}{2}$ the three points of intersection so obtained will give the three roots (A, B and C) for the required solution (Fig. 75).

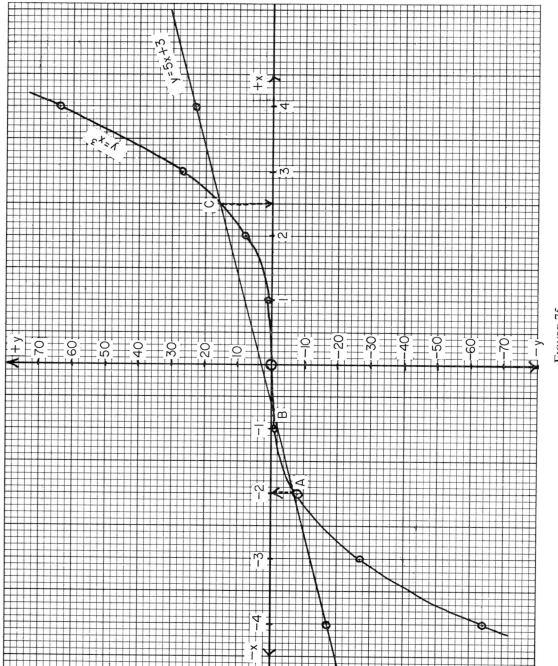

FIGURE 75

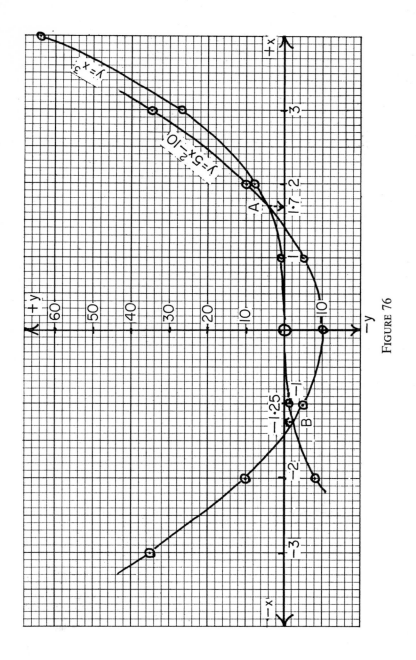

FIGURE 76

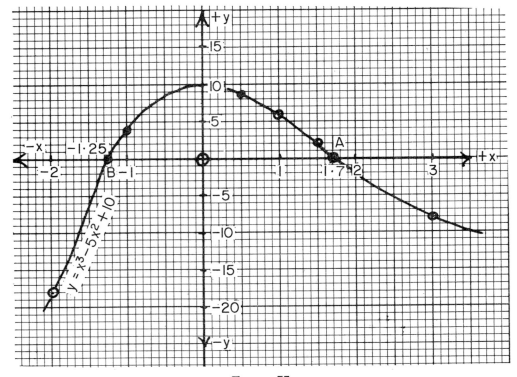

FIGURE 77

If the function cannot easily be factorized then, in general, this is the quickest way of solving a cubic equation.

Example: Solve the equation $y = x^3 - 5x^2 + 10$

If $y = 0$ then $x^3 - 5x^2 - 10$ (see Tables 1 and 2 which follow).

Thus we see that either by drawing the S curve or by equating two component functions we shall obtain identical solutions in both cases.

TABLE 1

x	$+1$	$+2$	$+3$	0	-1	-2	-3
$5x^2$	$+5$	$+20$	$+45$	0	$+5$	$+20$	$+45$
-10	-10	-10	-10	-10	-10	-10	-10
y	-5	$+10$	$+35$	-10	-5	$+10$	$+35$

TABLE 2

x	$+1$	$+2$	$+3$	0	-1	-2	$+\frac{1}{2}$	$+1\frac{1}{2}$
x^3	$+1$	$+8$	$+27$	0	-1	-8	$+\frac{1}{8}$	$+3\frac{7}{8}$
$-5x^2$	-5	-20	-45	0	-5	-20	$-1\frac{1}{4}$	$-11\frac{1}{4}$
$+10$	$+10$	$+10$	$+10$	$+10$	$+10$	$+10$	$+10$	$+10$
y	$+6$	-2	-8	$+10$	$+4$	-18	$+8\frac{7}{8}$	$+2\frac{1}{8}$

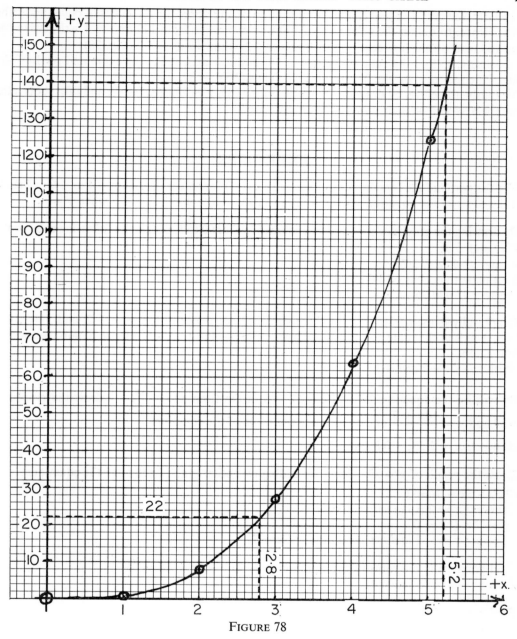

FIGURE 78

Point of Inflexion

The point of inflexion of a cubic curve is the point mid-way between the maximum turning point and minimum turning point, and is therefore easily found by obtaining the co-ordinates of these turning points and finding their average values.

We have already seen with the equations of the first and second degree that their graphs can be utilized as Ready Reckoners as well as for obtaining approximate squares and square roots.

Similarly, the graph of $y = x^3$ can be utilized to obtain approximate values of cubes and cube roots. Hence, to obtain the cube root of 140 we draw a line from 140 on the Y axis, strike the curve and read off the intercept on the X axis at 5·2—thus $\sqrt[3]{140} = 5\cdot2$ (Fig. 78).

Conversely, to find the cube of 2·8, from 2·8 on the X axis, strike the curve and read off the value of the intercept on the Y axis, viz., 22. Thus $(2\cdot8)^3 = 22$.

Obviously, therefore, by drawing the graphs of $y = x^4$, $y = x^5$, etc., fourth and fifth roots, etc., of numbers as well as their powers can be estimated.

EXERCISES

1. Plot the graph of the function $(x - 2)(x + 3)(x - 5)$ for values of x from -4 to $+6$ and show that the roots of the equation $y = (x - 2)(x + 3)(x - 5)$ are -3, 2 and 5 when $y = 0$.

2. By drawing the graphs of $y = x^3$ using values of x from 0 to 5, obtain the following cube roots:
$\sqrt[3]{47}$ and $\sqrt[3]{51}$
   Answer: 3·60 and 3·7
and estimate the cubes of 4·6 and 3·3.
   Answer: 97 and 36

3. Graphically demonstrate that the three straight lines $y = x - 1$, $y = x + 2$, and $y = x + 3$ cut the X axis at the same points as the curve $y = x^3 + 4x^2 + x - 6$. Hence obtain the roots of this function.
   Answer: -3, -2 and $+1$

4. By writing the equation $2x^3 - 10x - 7 = 0$ in the form $x^3 = \dfrac{10x + 7}{2}$ draw the graphs of $y = x^3$ and $y = \dfrac{10x + 7}{2}$ and so estimate the roots of the equation.
   Answers: $x = 2\cdot55$; $-0\cdot8$ and $-1\cdot72$

5. Draw the graph of $y = x^3$. Hence by adding two other graph lines solve the equations:
(a) $2x^3 - 5x - 6 = 0$.
   Answer: $x = 2$ is the only real root
(b) $x^3 - 3x + 2 = 0$.
   Answer: $x = -2$ and two equal roots of $x = 1$

6. Find graphically the roots of the equation $x^3 - 4x^2 - 5x + 14 = 0$.
   Answer: -2; 1·59 and 4·41

7. Find graphically the roots of the equation $x^3 = 3x$.
   Answer: 0, $-1\cdot732$ and $+1\cdot732$

8. Find the roots of $x^3 + 2 = 2x^2 + 3$.
   Answer: -1, $+1$, $+2$

9. A sheet of tin 12 in. square is cut to form a box by removing equal squares from each corner and bending up. Graphically estimate the size of the box to obtain the maximum cubic capacity.
   Answer: 8 in. square base $\times$ 2 in. high, i.e., 128 cu. in. maximum value

10. Draw the graph of $y = x^3 - 4x + 1$ from $x = -2\frac{1}{2}$ to $+2\frac{1}{2}$.

(a) What is the maximum value of the function?
   Answer: 4·1 *approx.*

(b) What value of x will produce its minimum value?
   Answer: 1·16

(c) Find its point of inflexion.
   Answer: (0, 1)

11. By drawing the separate graphs of $y = x^3$ and $y = 5x^2 - 10$ solve the equation $x^2 - 5x^2 + 10 = 0$.

   Answer: $x = -1·25$ *and* 1·7

   Check your results by plotting the curve $y = x^3 - 5x^2 + 10$ on the same area and find its maximum value.
   Answer: $y = 10$

12. Draw the graph of $y = \frac{1}{2}x(x + 1)(x - 2)$ from $x = -2$ to $+3$ and find the roots of this equation.

   Answer: $x = -1, 0$ *and* $+2$
   By drawing the line $y = -\frac{1}{2}$ on the same area find the values of x at the points of intersection.
   Answer: $x = -1·25$, $x = 0·5$ *and* 1·75
   What equation is solved by these points?
   Answer: $\frac{1}{2}x(x + 1)(x - 2) = -\frac{1}{2}$; *or* $x(x + 1)(x - 2) = -1$; *or* $x^3 - x^2 - 2x = -1$; *or* $x^3 - x^2 - 2x + 1 = 0$

13. Show graphically that the roots of the equation:
$y = 8(x - 1)(x - 3)(x - 4)$ are the same as those obtained by the intersections of the line $y = 8(x - 4)$ and the parabola $y = (x - 1)(x - 3)$ with the X axis.

14. Show graphically that the graph of $y = x^3 + 4x^2 + x - 6$ cuts the X axis at the same points as the lines $y = x - 1$, $y = x + 2$, and $y = x + 3$.

15. By taking a scale of $\frac{1}{2}$ in. to 1 unit on the Y axis and 1 in. on the X axis, plot the graph of $y = x^3 - 4x + 1$.

(a) At what point does this curve cut the X axis?
   Answer: (0, 1)

(b) What are the co-ordinates of its turning point?
   Answer: Maximum is $(-1·15, 4·1)$ *and minimum is* $(1·154, -2·1)$

(c) What are the co-ordinates of its point of inflexion?
   Answer: (0, 1)

(d) What is the least value of y for positive values of x?
   Answer: $-2·15$

(e) What is the greatest value of y for negative values of x?
   Answer: 4·1

(f) Find the roots of the equation.
   Answer: 1·86, 0·26, *and* $-2·12$

7

RECIPROCAL GRAPHS

MATHEMATICALLY $\frac{1}{4}$ is known as the reciprocal of 4, and 4 is the reciprocal of $\frac{1}{4}$; similarly $\frac{2}{3}$ is the reciprocal of $1\frac{1}{2}$ and $1\frac{1}{2}$ is the reciprocal of $\frac{2}{3}$.

In algebra $\frac{1}{x}$ is hence the reciprocal of x, and $\frac{1}{x^2}$ that of x^2.

The graph of $y = x$ is, as we have seen, a straight line but the reciprocal graph of $y = \frac{1}{x}$ is by no means so (Fig. 79).

x	0	$\pm\frac{1}{6}$	$\pm\frac{1}{5}$	$\pm\frac{1}{4}$	$\pm\frac{1}{3}$	$\pm\frac{1}{2}$	0	±1	±2	±3	±4	±5	±6	∞
$y = \frac{1}{x}$	∞	±6	±5	±4	±3	±2	0	±1	$\pm\frac{1}{2}$	$\pm\frac{1}{3}$	$\pm\frac{1}{4}$	$\pm\frac{1}{5}$	$\pm\frac{1}{6}$	0

The Hyperbola

The graph therefore develops as two curves in the 1st and 3rd quadrants and is known as a "hyperbola". Many simple problems can produce curves of this type.

Example: If a man walks at 4 m.p.h., a cyclist travels at 10 m.p.h., a motorist at 40 m.p.h., a horse and cart at 6 m.p.h., draw a graph to show the times taken to cover a journey of 100 miles.

Speed (m.p.h.)	4	6	10	40
Time (hours)	25	$16\frac{2}{3}$	10	$2\frac{1}{2}$

Taking the speeds as given we see that the respective times taken for the journey are as tabulated above. Plotting these factors on a graphical basis produces the hyperbolic curve because the formula $T = \frac{D}{S}$ where T is time, S is speed and D is distance (a constant). Speed therefore is a reciprocal function of time (Fig. 80).

In the example above the constant term in the equation was the distance ($= 100$); in other words $T = \frac{100}{S}$.

(Note that since $xy = $ constant, by taking any points (P and Q) on the curve the rectangles formed by the ordinates to the axes are of equal area, *e.g.*, point P gives a square $10 \times 10 = 100$, whilst point Q gives a rectangle $20 \times 5 = 100$.)

To see the effect of altering the value of the constant in the equation let us draw, for example, the graphs of $xy = 1 \left(\text{or } y = \frac{1}{x} \right)$, $y = \frac{6}{x}$ (or $xy = 6$) and $x = \frac{9}{y}$ (or $xy = 9$), on the same axes, these equations being obviously of the same forms, *viz.*: $xy = 1$, $xy = 6$, $xy = 9$ or $y = \frac{1}{x}$, $y = \frac{6}{x}$, $y = \frac{9}{x}$.

144

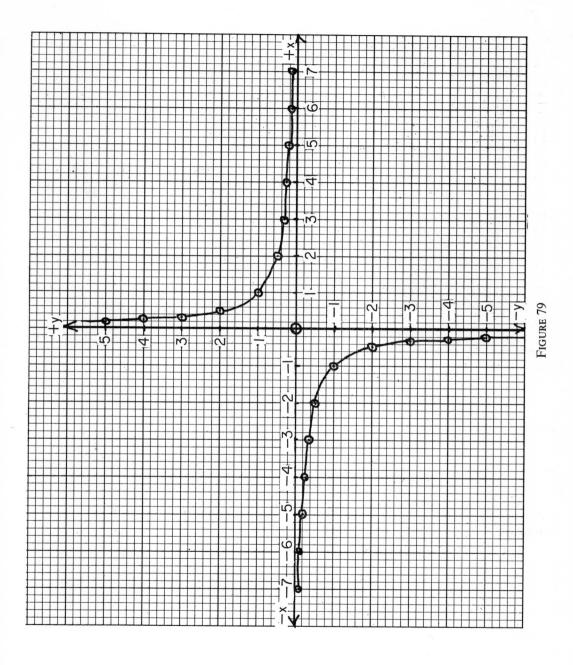

FIGURE 79

K

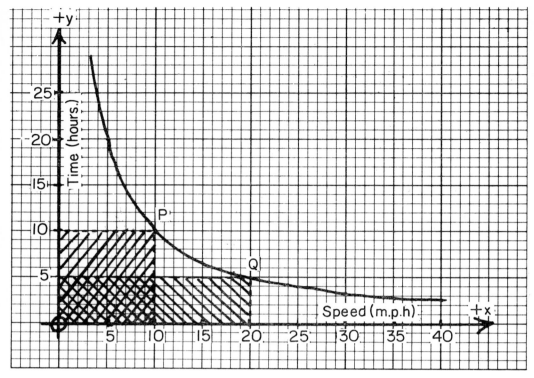

FIGURE 80

First: $xy = 1$ or $y = \dfrac{1}{x}$

x	±1	±2	±3	±4	$\pm0{\cdot}5$	$\pm0{\cdot}2$
y	±1	$\pm0{\cdot}5$	$\pm0{\cdot}33$	$\pm0{\cdot}25$	±2	±5

Secondly: $y = \dfrac{6}{x}$ or $xy = 6$

x	±1	±2	±3	±4	±5	±6	$\pm1{\cdot}5$
y	±6	±3	±2	$\pm1{\cdot}5$	$\pm1{\cdot}2$	±1	±4

Thirdly: $y = \dfrac{9}{x}$ or $xy = 9$

x	±1	±2	±3	±4	±6
y	±9	$\pm4{\cdot}5$	±3	$\pm2{\cdot}25$	$\pm1{\cdot}5$

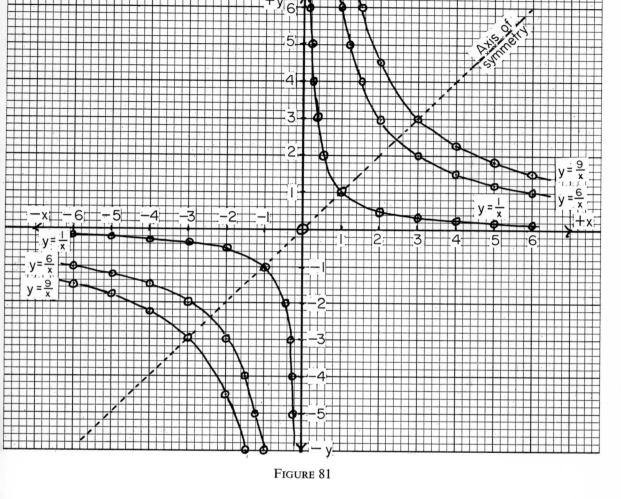

FIGURE 81

We thus see that as the constant term increases in proportion, $y = \dfrac{1}{x}$, $y = \dfrac{6}{x}$ and $y = \dfrac{9}{x}$, the respective curves become flatter in comparison, all pairs of curves being symmetrical about the origin (Fig. 81).

This symmetry can be utilized to draw the second branch from the data of the first (*AB*) (Fig. 82).

Draw a line from point *B* through *O* and produce it to point *C*, making *BO* = *OC*. Similarly, draw *AO* and produce it to *D* making *AO* = *OD*.

Now choose any point *E* on the curve *AB*, join *EO* and produce to *F*, making *EO* = *OF*. Repeat for as many points as necessary to produce a good "mirror image" *CD* of *AB*.

The curve *CD* is hence the other branch of the complete hyperbola of which *AB* was the first part.

The axis of symmetry is, of course, either of the graph lines $y = \pm x$, whilst the origin may be taken as a "centre of symmetry".

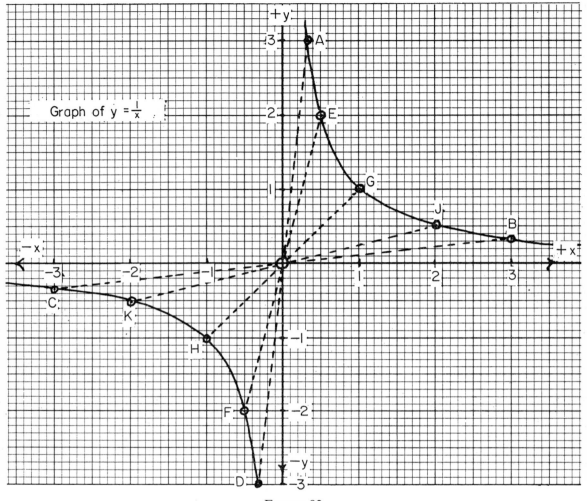

FIGURE 82

A further interesting experiment is to see the effect of introducing a constant term in the y or x portions of the equation and compare resultant graphs.

Example: Draw on the same graph area the graphs of (a) $y = \dfrac{144}{x}$ and (b) $y = \dfrac{144}{x - 10}$.

Data (a) $y = \dfrac{144}{x}$ (Fig. 83).

x	± 6	± 8	± 12	± 18	± 24	± 30	± 36
y	± 24	± 18	± 12	± 8	± 6	$\pm 4 \cdot 8$	± 4

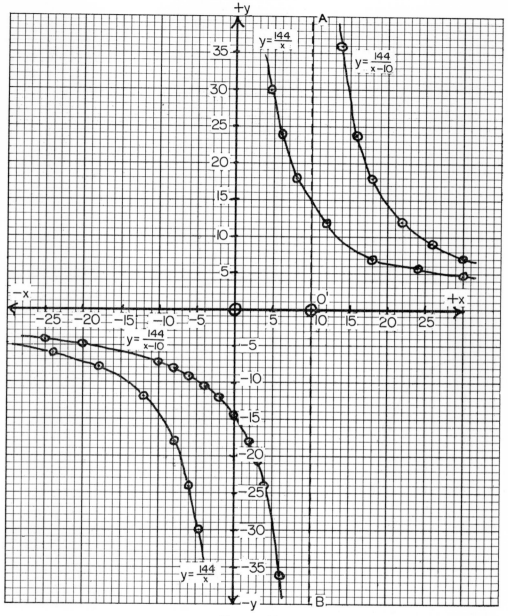

FIGURE 83

(b) $y = \dfrac{144}{x - 10}$

x	+6	+4	+3	+2	0	−2	−4	−6	−8
$x - 10$	−4	−6	−7	−8	−10	−12	−14	−16	−18
y	−36	−24	−20·6	−18	−14·4	−12	−10·3	−9	−8

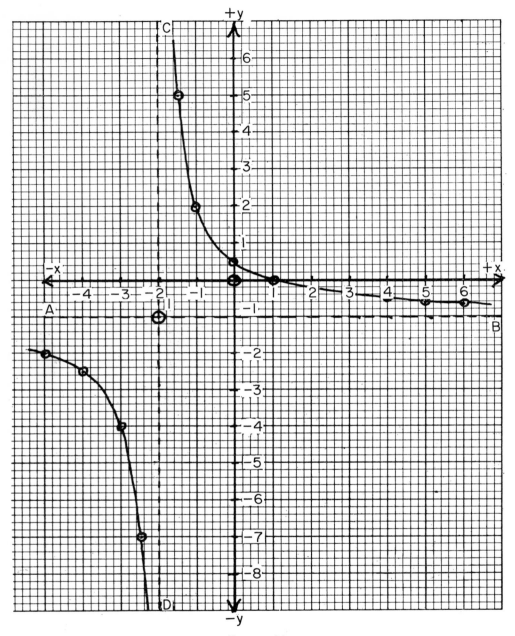

FIGURE 84

x	-10	$+18$	$+22$	$+26$	$+30$	$+16$	$+14$	-20	-25
$x-10$	-20	$+8$	$+12$	$+16$	$+20$	$+6$	$+4$	-30	-35
y	$-7\cdot2$	$+18$	$+12$	$+9$	$+7\cdot2$	$+24$	$+26$	$-4\cdot8$	$-4\cdot1$

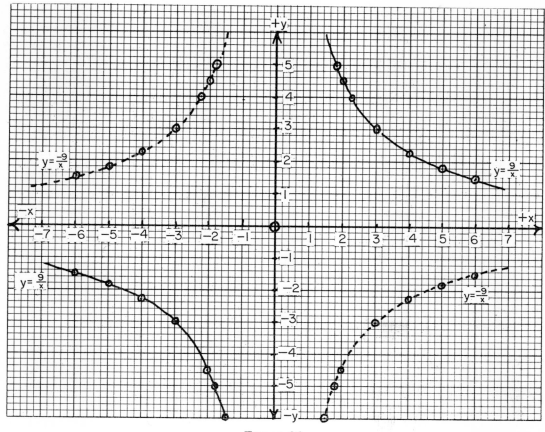

FIGURE 85

The first graph $\left(y = \dfrac{144}{x}\right)$ occupies its normal position with respect to the two axes which are known as the "asymptotes" to the hyperbola, but the graph of $y = \dfrac{144}{x - 10}$ has moved to such a position that its two branches are now symmetrical about the X axis and a new "Y axis", the line $AO'B$. These two lines are therefore the asymptotes to the second hyperbola.

As these pairs of asymptotes are at right angles, the graphs are known as "rectangular hyperbolas"; in more difficult problems the asymptotes are not at right angles but cross each other obliquely, thus producing an "oblique hyperbola".

Example: Draw the graph of $y = \dfrac{1 - x}{2 + x}$ (Fig. 84).

x	-5	-4	-3	$-2 \cdot 5$	-2	$-1 \cdot 5$	-1	0	$+1$	$+2$	$+3$	$+4$	$+5$	$+6$
$1 - x$	6	5	4	$3 \cdot 5$	3	$2 \cdot 5$	2	1	0	-1	-2	-3	-4	-5
$2 + x$	-3	-2	-1	$-0 \cdot 5$	0	$0 \cdot 5$	$+1$	$+2$	$+3$	$+4$	$+5$	$+6$	$+7$	$+8$
y	-2	$-2\frac{1}{2}$	-4	-7	∞	$+5$	$+2$	$+0 \cdot 5$	0	$-0 \cdot 25$	$-0 \cdot 4$	$-0 \cdot 5$	$-0 \cdot 6$	$-0 \cdot 625$

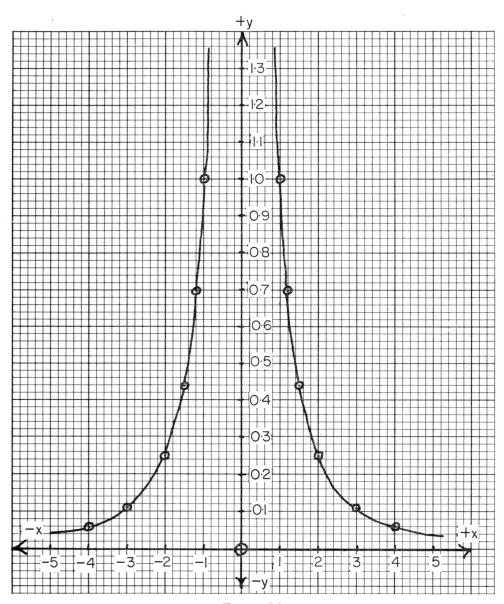

FIGURE 86

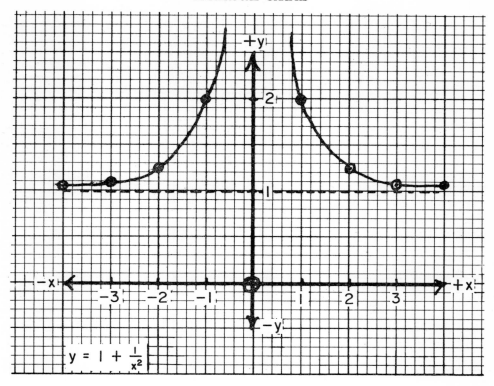

FIGURE 87

We see therefore that the asymptotes to the two branches of the resultant hyperbola are the dotted lines *AB* and *CD* intersecting at the centre of symmetry *O'*.

Now for a final experiment make one of the variables different in sign to the other, *i.e.*, compare the graphs of $y = \dfrac{9}{x}$ and $y = \dfrac{9}{-x}$ $\left(\text{or } y = \dfrac{-9}{x} \text{ or } -y = \dfrac{9}{x} \right)$. We shall see that the effect is to obtain another hyperbola of two branches but in the opposite pair of quadrants (Fig. 85).

This change of sign has resulted therefore in a change-over of the quadrants (*cf.*, "A change of sign is a change of direction").

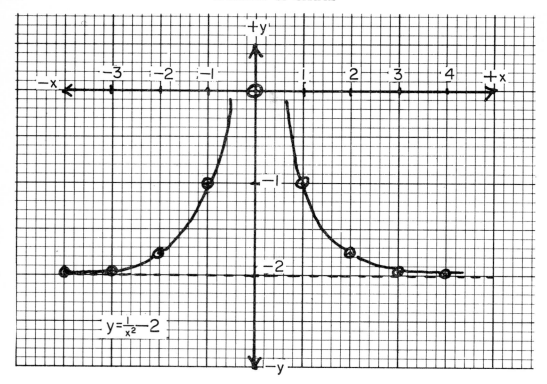

$$y = \frac{1}{x^2} - 2$$

FIGURE 88

Truncus

A reciprocal curve of the second degree, *e.g.*, $y = \frac{1}{x^2}$ produces a symmetrical graph of a different pattern, known as the "truncus" from its obvious resemblance to the trunk of a tree (Fig. 86).

x	±4	±3	±2	$\pm1\frac{1}{2}$	$\pm1\cdot2$	±1	0
x^2	16	9	4	2·25	1·44	1	0
$y = \frac{1}{x^2}$	0·06	0·11	0·25	0·44	0·7	1	∞

The addition or subtraction of a constant term to the reciprocal merely results in a raising or lowering of the truncus just as we saw was the effect in a graph of the first degree, *i.e.*, a straight line (Figs. 87 and 88).

8

COMBINATION GRAPHS

FOND grandparents frequently trace resemblances of the parents in the grandchild—this may be so, but in the graphing of an equation formed of known shapes it certainly is the case.

For instance, if we draw the graph of $y = x + \frac{1}{x^2}$ we know already that the graph of $y = x$ is a straight line passing through the origin with a gradient of 1. Also, that the graph of $y = \frac{1}{x^2}$ is the truncus previously described.

If now we draw the combination graph of straight line plus truncus the result is extremely interesting in revealing the characteristics of both "parents" (Fig. 89).

x	$+4$	$+3$	$+2$	$+1$	0	-1	-2	-3	-4
$\frac{1}{x^2}$	0·06	0·11	0·15	1	∞	1	0·25	0·11	0·06
$y = x + \frac{1}{x^2}$	4·06	3·11	2·25	2	∞	0	$-1·75$	$-2·89$	$-3·94$

In the diagram above the graphs of $y = x$ and $y = \frac{1}{x^2}$ are shown dotted, whilst the combination of both is shown with a solid line. Hence it will be seen that the usual truncus—which was originally asymptotic to both the X and Y axes—is now distorted and is now asymptotic to the line $y = x$ and the Y axis.

This combination graph, of course, could be obtained by drawing the graphs of $y = x$ and $y = \frac{1}{x^2}$ (shown dotted) and then adding ordinates to obtain the final curve.

Therefore remembering the basic graphs will enable us to form any combination, *e.g.*:

(a) All graphs of the first degree are straight lines except the reciprocal form $y = \frac{1}{x}$ which is a hyperbola: the constant term merely moving the graph up or down as the case may be.

(b) All graphs of the second degree are parabolas (if only one variable is squared) or circles and ellipses (if both variables are squared) except again the reciprocal form which is a truncus; the first degree terms move the graph sideways whilst the constant term again functions by moving the graph vertically.

(c) All graphs of the third degree take the well-known S curve; second and first degree terms only accentuate the bend of the curve by introducing a more pronounced kink in the line producing a maximum and a minimum turning point.

155

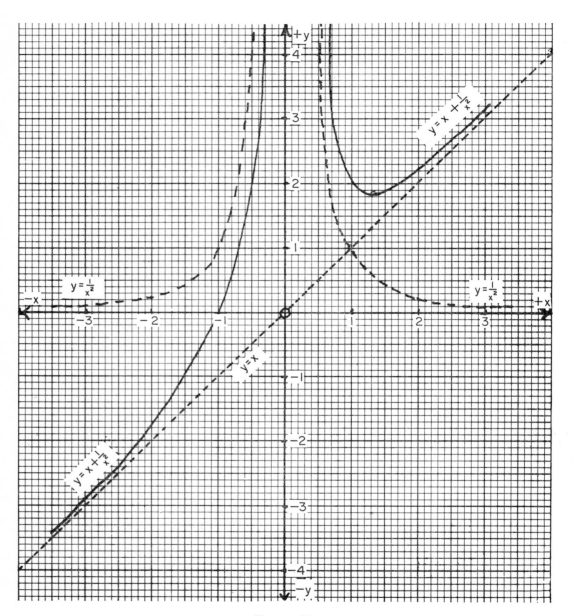

FIGURE 89

EXERCISES

1. Draw the graphs of $y = x^3 + 3x^2$ and $y = 4 + \dfrac{5}{x}$ and determine the values of x which satisfy the equation $x^3 + 3x^2 - 4x - 5 = 0$.
  Answer: 1·57, −0·84, −3·73

2. Draw the graphs of $y = 3 + 4x - 4x^2$ and $xy = 1$ from $x = -1$ to $x = 3$. Name the X ordinates of the points of intersection.
  Answer: −0·7, 0·27, 1·35

3. Boyle's Law states that Pressure × Volume of a gas is constant for constant temperature, hence for given volumes of pressure (P) and volume (V) we have:

if	$P = 200$	100	$66\frac{2}{3}$	50	40	$33\frac{1}{3}$	25
	$V = 0.5$	1·0	1·5	2	$2\frac{1}{2}$	3·0	4·0

By plotting these values on a graph show that the expansion of a gas with pressure follows the form of a hyperbola ($xy =$ constant) since $PV =$ Constant.

4. Draw the graph of $y = x^3 + x^2 + x$ from $x = -2$ to $+2$ and find the co-ordinates of the point of inflexion.
  Answer: (−0·3, −0·26)

5. Draw the graph of $y = x^3 + x^2 + 1$ from $x = -2$ to $+2$.
(a) Find the co-ordinates of the maximum turning point.
  Answer: (−0·066, 1·15)
(b) Find the co-ordinates of the minimum turning point.
  Answer: (0, 1)
(c) Find the co-ordinates of the point of inflexion.
  Answer: (−0·33, 1·08)

6. Draw the graph of $y = x^3 + x + 1$ from $x = -3$ to $+2$ and find the co-ordinates of the point of inflexion.
  Answer: (0, 1)
Also, solve the equation.
  Answer: −0·7

7. Draw the graph of $y = x^3 + x^2 + \dfrac{1}{x}$ from $x = -2$ to $+2$ and find the co-ordinates of its turning points.
  Answer: Maximum at (−1, −1); *minimum at* (0·6, 2·2)

8. Draw the graph of $y = x^3 + x + \dfrac{1}{x}$ from $x = -2$ to $+2$ and find the co-ordinates of its turning points.
  Answer: Maximum at (−0·7, −2·5); *minimum at* (0·7, 2·5)

9. Draw the graph of $y = x^3 + x^2 + \dfrac{1}{x^2}$ from $x = -2$ to $+2$. Solve the equation and find the co-ordinates of its turning point.
  Answer: $x = -1.3$ and (0·8, 2·7)

10. Draw the graph of $y = x^3 + \dfrac{1}{x} + 1$ from $x = -2$ to $+2$ and find the co-ordinates of its turning points.
  Answer: Maximum turning point at (−0·8, −0·8); *minimum turning point at* (0·8, 2·8)

11. Draw the graph of $x^2 + x + \dfrac{1}{x}$ from $x = -3$ to $+2$.

Find the co-ordinates of its turning point and point of inflexion.

Answer: Minimum turning point at (0·7, 2·6); point of inflexion at (−1, −1)

12. Draw the graph of $y = x^2 + \dfrac{1}{x} + 1$ from $x = -2$ to $+2$.

(a) Solve the equation.

Answer: x = −0·6

(b) Find whether it has a maximum and/or minimum turning point and its co-ordinates.

Answer: Minimum at (0·8, 2·9)

13. Draw the graph of $x^3 + \dfrac{1}{x^2} + 1$ from $x = -3$ to $+3$.

(a) Solve the equation.

Answer: x = −1·2

(b) Find the co-ordinates of its turning point and state whether it is a maximum and/or minimum.

Answer: Minimum at (0·9, 3)

14. Draw the graph of $x^2 + \dfrac{1}{x^2} + x$ from $x = -3$ to $+3$ and find the co-ordinates of its turning

points, stating whether they are maximum or minimum value.

Answer: Both minimum at (0·9, 2·9) and (−1·2, 0·9)

15. Solve the equation $y = x^3 + \dfrac{1}{x^2}$ by drawing its graph from $x = -2$ to $+2$.

Answer: x = −1

16. (a) Draw the graph of $x^2 + x = y$, and hence find the roots of the equation.

Answer: x = 0 and −1

(b) What is the equation of its axis of symmetry?

Answer: $x = -\frac{1}{2}$

(c) What are the co-ordinates of its turning point?

Answer: Minimum at $(-\frac{1}{2}, -\frac{3}{4})$

17. Draw the graph of $y = x^3 + \dfrac{1}{x} + \dfrac{1}{x^2}$ from $x = -3$ to $+3$.

(a) Has it a maximum or minimum value?

Answer: Minimum

(b) What are its co-ordinates?

Answer: (1, 3)

(c) Solve the equation.

Answer: x = −0·8 approx.

18. Graph the equation $y = x^2 + x + 1$ from $x = -3$ to $+2$.

(a) Find the roots of the equation, if any.

Answer: No roots

(b) Find its maximum or minimum value.

Answer: Minimum $\frac{3}{4}$

(c) What value of x will produce this value?

Answer: $x = -\frac{1}{2}$

(d) What is the equation of its axis of symmetry?

Answer: $x = -\frac{1}{2}$

19. Graph the curve $y = x^2 + \dfrac{1}{x}$ by the method of adding the ordinates of the curves $y = x^2$ and $y = \dfrac{1}{x}$ from $x = -3$ to $+3$.

(a) Find the roots of the equation, if any.
    Answer: x = -1

(b) What are the co-ordinates of its turning point?
    Answer: Minimum at (0·8, 1·9)

20. Graph the curve $y = x + \dfrac{1}{x}$ by adding the ordinates of $y = x$ and $y = \dfrac{1}{x}$ and show that it can have no values of y between -2 and $+2$.

21. Solve simultaneously the two equations $y = \frac{3}{4}x$ and $y = \dfrac{3x^2}{x^2 + 2}$.
(N.B. Plot the curve for $x = -1$ to $+4$.)
    Answer: x = 0, 0·6 and 3·4

22. Plot the graphs of (a) $y = x + \dfrac{9}{x}$ from $x = -7$ to $+7$; (b) $y = \frac{3}{8}(x^2 - 25)$.

What value of x will satisfy both equations?
    Answer: x = -3, -1·17 and 6·83

23. Solve the equations $\dfrac{2x^2 - 3}{x + 8} = \frac{2}{5}$ and $2x^2 - x - 11 = 0$ by drawing the graph of $y = \dfrac{2x^2 - 3}{x + 8}$ from $x = -3$ to $+3$.
    Answer: 1·86 and -1·66; 2·6 and -2·1

24. Plot the graph of $y = \dfrac{1 - x}{2 + x}$ from $x = -5$ to $+3$, and use it to solve the equations:

(a) $\dfrac{1 - x}{2 + x} = -5$.
    Answer: x = -2·75

(b) $\dfrac{1 - x}{2 + x} = 2x$.
    Answer: x = 0·2 and -2·7

25. Plot the graph of $y = x^3 + x^2$ from $x = -2$ to $+2$.

(a) What are the co-ordinates of its maximum turning point?
    Answer: (-0·7, 0·2)

(b) What are the co-ordinates of its minimum turning point?
    Answer: (0, 0)

(c) What are the co-ordinates of its point of inflexion?
    Answer: (-0·35, 0·1)

26. Plot the graph of $y = x + \dfrac{1}{x} + \dfrac{1}{x^2}$ from $x = -4$ to $+4$.

(a) Solve the equation.
    Answer: -0·6 approx.

(b) What is the equation of its asymptote?
    Answer: y = x

(c) What is the minimum value of the function for positive values of x?
    Answer: 2·6 when x = 1·5 approx.

27. Plot the graph of $y = x^2 + \dfrac{1}{x^2} + 1$ from $+3$ to -3.

(a) What is the minimum value of the function for negative values of x?
Answer: $y = 3$
(b) What is the minimum value of the function for positive values of x?
Answer: $y = 3$
(c) What are the co-ordinates of its turning points?
Answer: $(-1, 3)$ and $(+1, 3)$

28. (a) Determine graphically whether the function $x^2 + \dfrac{1}{x} + \dfrac{1}{x^2}$ has minimum or maximum values.
Answer: Two minimum values
(b) What are these values?
Answer: $-0\cdot8$ and $2\cdot9$

29. (a) Show that the graph of $y = x + 1 + \dfrac{1}{x}$ cannot lie between the lines $y = 3$ and $y = -1$.
(b) Find the equation of its asymptote.
Answer: $y = x + 1$
(c) What are the co-ordinates of its turning points?
Answer: Minimum at $(1, 3)$ and maximum at $(-1, -1)$

30. Plot the graph $y = x + \dfrac{1}{x} + \dfrac{1}{x^2}$ from $x = -3$ to $+3$.

(a) Has it a maximum or minimum turning point?
Answer: Minimum
(b) What are its co-ordinates?
Answer: $(1\cdot26, 2\cdot9)$
(c) Find the root(s) of the equation.
Answer: $x = -1\cdot5$

9

AREAS BY GRAPHICAL METHODS

Counting Squares

AREAS may easily be determined by the above method by counting the whole squares and averaging the broken ones. Hence, portions of squares greater than a half of one are balanced by those which are less than half.

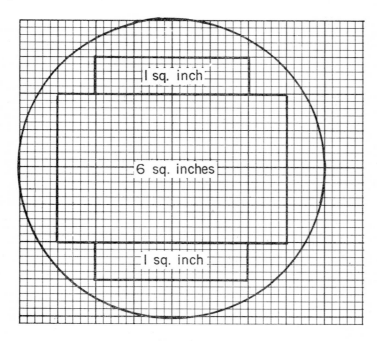

FIGURE 90

Simpson's Rule

To find the area enclosed by a curve, divide it into an *even* number of parts by an *odd* number of equidistant ordinates including the first and the last. Number the ordinates in order, then the area will be the sum of the first and the last ordinates, plus twice the sum of the other *odd* ordinates, plus four times the sum of the other *even* ordinates, the total being multiplied by one third the distance between one ordinate and the next.

L   161

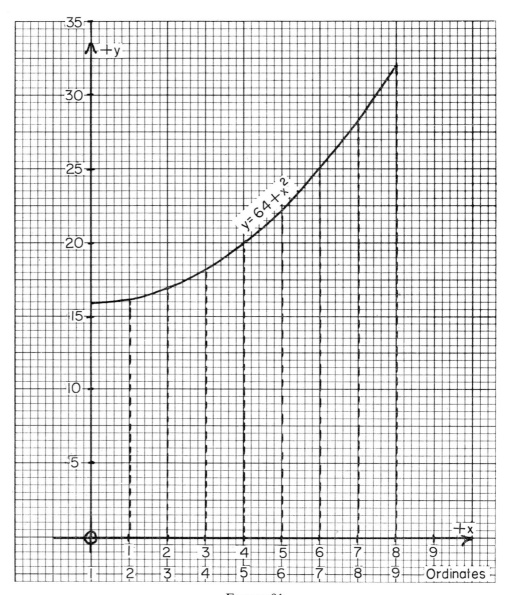

FIGURE 91

Example: Draw the graphs of $4y = 64 + x^2$ from $x = 0$ to $x = 8$ (Fig. 91). Use Simpson's Rule to determine the area bounded by the curve, the X axis and the ordinates at $x = 0$ and $x = 8$.

x	0	1	2	3	4	5	6	7	8
64	64	64	64	64	64	64	64	64	64
$+x^2$	0	1	4	9	16	25	36	49	64
y	16	$16\frac{1}{4}$	17	$18\frac{1}{4}$	20	$22\frac{1}{4}$	25	$28\frac{1}{4}$	32

Construct 9 ordinates from the above values of x.

$\therefore$ ordinate	1	2	3	4	5	6	7	8	9
height	16	$16\frac{1}{4}$	17	$18\frac{1}{4}$	20	$22\frac{1}{4}$	25	$28\frac{1}{4}$	32

Hence area $= \frac{1}{3}[(16 + 32) + 2(17 + 20 + 25) + 4(16\frac{1}{4} + 18\frac{1}{4} + 22\frac{1}{4} + 28\frac{1}{4})]$

$\qquad = \frac{1}{3}(512)$

$\qquad = 170 \cdot 66$ square units.

10

TRIGONOMETRICAL GRAPHS

IN constructing the graphs of the simple trigonometrical functions, e.g., sin, cos and tan we must bear in mind the fact that the signs of each change according to the quadrant of the circle in which they occur, viz:

Quadrants	1st	2nd	3rd	4th
Positive	sin, cos, tan	sin	tan	cos
Negative	—	cos, tan	sin, cos	sin, tan

The reciprocals of the sin, cos and tan (cosec, sec and cot) are, of course, positive or negative in the same quadrants as the original functions.

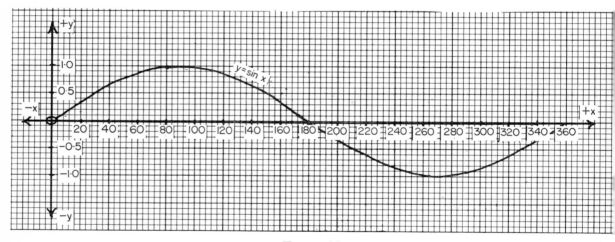

FIGURE 92

Using the trigonometrical tables we can tabulate the data for the graph of $y = \sin x$, viz.:

$x°$	0	10	20	30	40	50	60	70	80	90
$y = \sin x$	0	0·1736	0·3420	0·5000	0·6428	0·7660	0·8660	0·9397	0·9848	1·0000

and hence we can complete all four quadrants of the graph (Fig. 92).

Similarly, by remembering that $\sin x = \cos (90 - x)$, the graph of cos x may be obtained from that of sin x

$$e.g. \quad \cos \ 0° = \sin 90°$$
$$\cos 30° = \sin 60°$$
$$\cos 60° = \sin 30°$$

The graphs of sin x and cos x are, therefore, of the same shape, but that of cos x reaches its maxima and minima midway between those of sin x, viz., Figure 93.

164

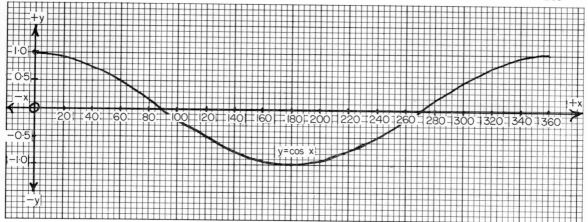

FIGURE 93

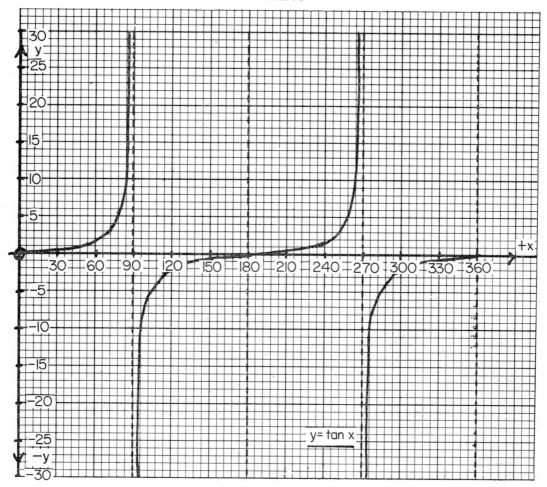

FIGURE 94

If the graph is continued to the left beyond 0° it shows that cos $(-x) = \cos x$, e.g., cos $(-30°)$ = cos 30°.

To enable us to draw the graph of the function $y = \tan x$ from the trigonometrical table we tabulate:

$x°$	0	10	20	30	40	50	60	70	80	87	90
$y = \tan x$	0	0·1763	0·3640	0·5774	0·8391	1·19	1·73	2·75	5·67	19·08	∞

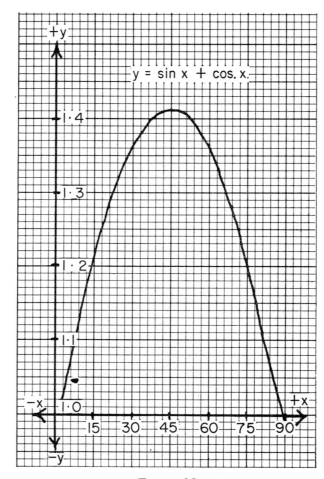

FIGURE 95

Then, correcting for the sign of the tangent in the succeeding quadrants and remembering that $\tan x = \tan [x + n(180)]$ where n is any integer positive or negative, we can draw the complete graph (Fig. 94).

The combination of two trigonometrical functions in any equation do not prevent any difficulty, viz., Figure 95.

Example 1: Draw the graph of $y = \sin x + \cos x$ from 0° to 90°.

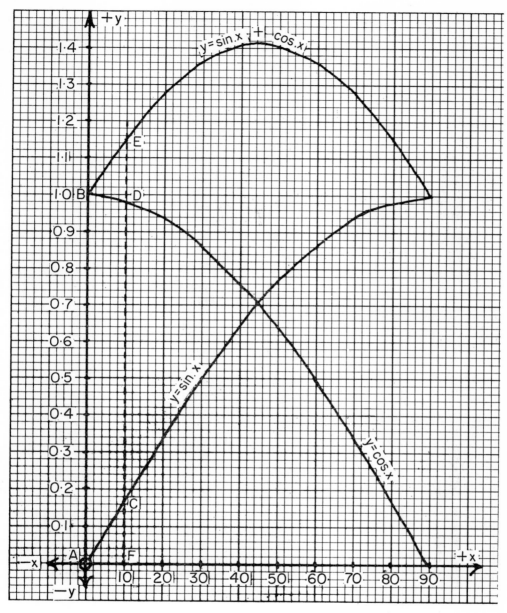

FIGURE 96

x°	0	10	20	30	40	45	50	60	70	80	90
sin x	0	0·1736	0·3420	0·5000	0·6428	0·7071	0·7660	0·8660	0·9397	0·9848	1
cos x	1	0·9848	0·9397	0·8660	0·7660	0·7071	0·6428	0·5000	0·3420	0·1736	0
y	1	1·1584	1·2817	1·3660	1·4088	1·4142	1·4088	1·3660	1·2817	1·1584	1

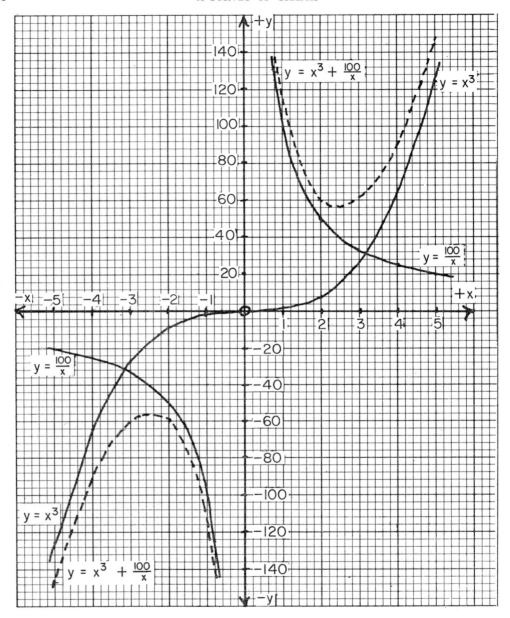

FIGURE 97

It is interesting to note that this graph can easily be obtained from the two graphs $y = \sin x$ and $y = \cos x$ by adding the ordinates (Fig. 96). (See following paragraphs on "Addition of Ordinates".)

The ordinate AB represents $\cos 0° (= 1)$ whilst $\sin 0° = 0$, hence the sum of the two ordinates becomes $0 + 1 = 1$. (Hence B not only represents $\cos 0°$ but also $\cos 0° + \sin 0°$.) Similarly CF represents $\sin 10°$ and DF represents $\cos 10°$, therefore if we add the length CF—by stepping

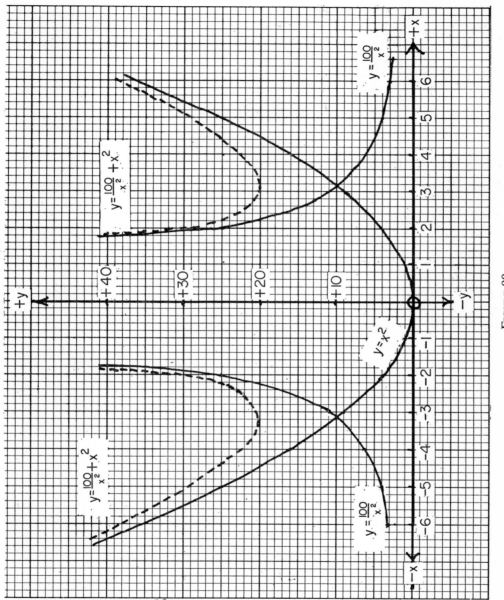

FIGURE 98

upwards with a pair of dividers—to the point E, *i.e.*, making $DE = CF$ then FE represents $CF + DF$, *i.e.*, $\sin 10° + \cos 10°$. By repeating this process at $10°$ intervals the graph of $y = \sin x + \cos x$ can be plotted.

Example 2: $y = x^3 + \dfrac{100}{x}$ (Fig. 97)

Example 3: $y = x^2 + \dfrac{100}{x^2}$ (Fig. 9)8

EXERCISES

Trigonometrical Graphs

Draw the graphs of: (from $x = 0°$ to $x = 360°$)

(a) $\sin (x - 30°)$.
(b) $\cos (x + 30°)$.
(c) $5 \sin x + 10 \cos x$.
(d) $10 \cos x - 5 \sin x$.
(e) $\sin 3x$.
(f) $\cos (3x + 30°)$.
(g) $2 \sin x + \sin 2x$.
(h) $3 \cos x + \cos 3x$.
(j) $\sin 2x - 2 \sin (x - 10°)$.
(k) $4 \tan x + 3 \sin x$.

11
ADDITION OF ORDINATES

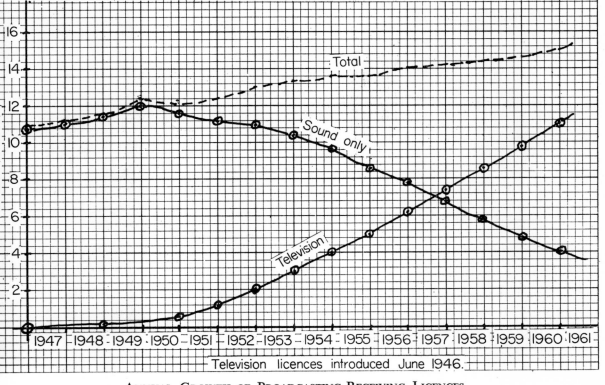

ANNUAL GROWTH OF BROADCASTING RECEIVING LICENCES

FIGURE 99

THE above is a simple example of addition of ordinates where the two curves "Television" and "Sound only" are added to form the "TOTAL" curve. This could, of course, be simply done by adding the statistical figures together to plot the "TOTAL" curve, but it can be done otherwise by taking the vertical ordinates at various points along the "Television" curve, *e.g.*, by means of a pair of dividers, and adding the respective distances to the "Sound only" ordinates to obtain the final curve.

Curves Drawn From the Addition of Ordinates

Referring back to the paragraphs on the curves of trigonometrical functions, it was shown that by *adding* the ordinates of $y = \sin x$ and $y = \cos x$ together, the graph of $y = \sin x + \cos x$ could be constructed. Similarly by subtracting ordinates the graphs of $y = \sin x - \cos x$ (or $y = \cos x - \sin x$) can be formed.

171

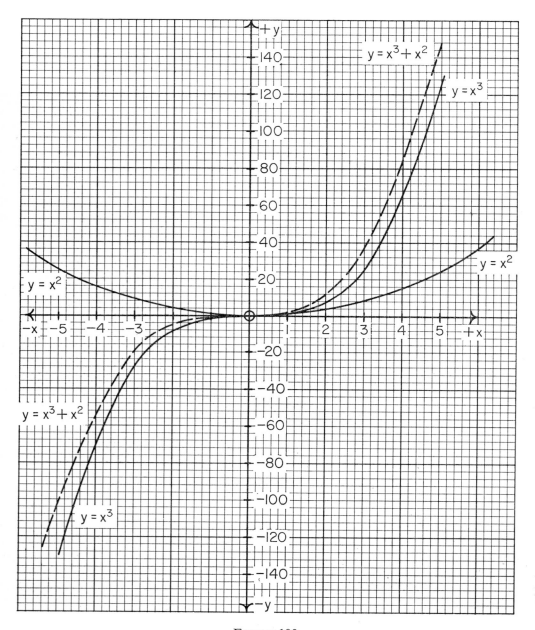

FIGURE 100

This method of adding or subtracting ordinates can be used to draw combinations of any curve.

Example: $y = x^2 + x^3$ (Fig. 100)

EXERCISES

Plot the following graphs, taking the values of x from -3 to $+3$, using 1 in. on the X axis. The scale on the Y axis will vary according to needs.

No.	Equation	Method suggested
1	$y = x^2 + x$	Add ordinates of $y = x^2$ to $y = x$
2	$y = x^2 - x$	Subtract ordinates of $y = x$ from $y = x^2$
3	$y = x^3 + x^2$	Add the ordinates of $y = x^3$ to $y = x^2$
4	$y = x^3 - x^2$	Subtract the ordinates of $y = x^2$ from $y = x^3$
5	$y = x^3 + 10x$	Add the ordinates of $y = x^3$ to $y = 10x$
6	$y = x^3 - 12x$	Subtract the ordinates of $y = 12x$ from $y = x^3$
7	$y = x^2 + \dfrac{1}{x}$	Add the ordinates of $y = \dfrac{1}{x}$ to $y = x^2$
8	$y = x^3 + \dfrac{12}{x}$	Add the ordinates of $y = x^3$ to $y = \dfrac{12}{x}$
9	$y = x^3 - \dfrac{10}{x}$	Subtract the ordinates of $y = \dfrac{10}{x}$ from $y = x^3$
10	$y = 2x^3 + \dfrac{4}{x^2}$	Add the ordinates of $y = 2x^3$ to $y = \dfrac{4}{x^2}$
11	$y = x^3 - \dfrac{4}{x^2}$	Subtract the ordinates of $y = \dfrac{4}{x^2}$ from $y = x^3$
12	$y = x^3 - x + 3$	Subtract the ordinates of $y = x - 3$ from $y = x^3$
13	$y = x^3 + 15$	Add the ordinates of $y = x^3$ to $y = 15$
14	$y = \dfrac{30}{x^2} + x + 40$	Add the ordinates of $y = \dfrac{30}{x^2}$ to $y = x + 40$
15	$y = \dfrac{4}{x} + 2$	Add the ordinates of $y = \dfrac{4}{x}$ to $y = 2$
16	$y = \dfrac{2}{x} + \dfrac{3}{x^2}$	Add the ordinates of $y = \dfrac{2}{x}$ to $y = \dfrac{3}{x^2}$
17	$y = \dfrac{2}{x} - \dfrac{3}{x^2}$	Subtract the ordinates of $y = \dfrac{3}{x^2}$ from $y = \dfrac{2}{x}$
18	$y = x + 1 + \dfrac{2}{x}$	Add the ordinates of $y = x + 1$ to $y = \dfrac{2}{x}$
19	$y = x + 5 + \dfrac{10}{x^2}$	Add the ordinates of $y = x + 5$ to $y = \dfrac{10}{x^2}$
20	$y = 2x^2 - 2 - \dfrac{3}{x}$	Subtract the ordinates of $y = \dfrac{3}{x}$ from $y = 2x^2 - 2$

12

LOGARITHMIC GRAPHS

FROM the general mathematical relationship that

$$y = a^x, \text{ e.g., } 9 = 3^2$$

we have that the number is equal to base $^{\log}$, in other words, 9 is the number, 3 the base and 2 the log, or, the logarithm of 9 to the base 3 is 2. In the parallel algebraic relationship, therefore, we have that the logarithm of y to the base a is x. By giving different values to a and x we can thus construct a series of graphs, as above, showing the effect of altering the base of the logarithms.

In general, books of logarithms are to the base 10 and when this graph is inserted on the diagram it will be seen that as we raise the base number the effect on the graphs becomes progressively smaller for, as may be seen, raising the base from 6 to 10 has caused these graphs to be closer together than when the base was raised from 4 to 5.

Data   Base $= 1$, *i.e.*, $y = 1^x$

Log	(x)	0	1	2	3
Number	(y)	1	1	1	1

Base $= 2$, *i.e.*, $y = 2^x$

Log	(x)	0	1	2	3
Number	(y)	1	2	4	8

Base $= 3$, *i.e.*, $y = 3^x$

Log	(x)	0	1	2	3
Number	(y)	1	3	9	27

Base $= 4$, *i.e.*, $y = 4^x$

Log	(x)	0	1	2	3
Number	(y)	1	4	16	64

Base $= 5$, *i.e.*, $y = 5^x$

Log	(x)	0	1	2	3
Number	(y)	1	5	25	125

Base $= 6$, *i.e.*, $y = 6^x$

Log	(x)	0	1	2	3
Number	(y)	1	6	36	216

Base $= 10$, *i.e.*, $y = 10^x$

Log	(x)	0	0·30	0·60	0·78	0·90	1	1·15	1·3	1·4	1·48	1·58
Number	(y)	1	2	4	6	8	10	14	20	26	30	38

(N.B. This table is, of course, compiled from a normal set of logarithms of numbers.)

EXERCISES

1. During a chemical change the following results were noted:

Temp. (°C)	1	2	5	10	18	23	30
Time (min.)	22·5	22·54	22·6	22·67	22·78	22·84	22·90

Show that the above results can be related to the equation

$$T = P + Q \log (t + 19) \text{ where } T = \text{time}$$

$$t = \text{temperature}$$

$$P \text{ and } Q \text{ are constants.}$$

174

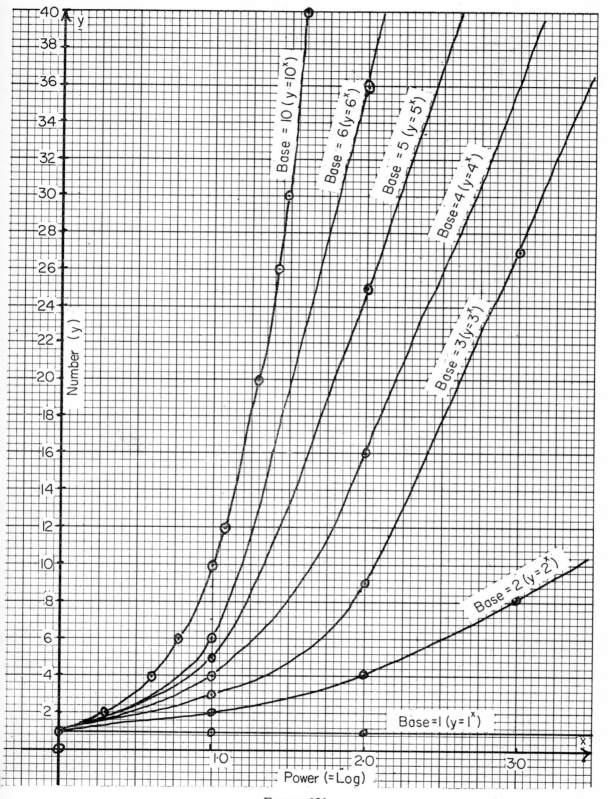

FIGURE 101

Hence graphically obtain approximate values for both constants P and Q by ruling an average straight line.

Answer: P = 21·2; Q = 1

2. Draw the graph of $y = 10^x$ from $x = -0·2$ to $x = 1$, taking 5 in. = 1 unit on the X axis and $\frac{1}{2}$ in. = 1 unit on the Y axis.

(a) If the line $y = 9 - 3x$ is drawn on the graph, what equation is solved by the point of intersection? Find this value.

Answer: (i) $10^x = 9 - 3x$ *or* $10^x + 3x - 9 = 0$; *(ii)* 0·8175

(b) Use the graph of $y = 10^x$ to solve the equation $10^x = 9x$.

Answer: x = 0·15 and 0·92

(c) Plot the points P (0, 1) and Q (0·7, 5) and join them with a straight line. What equation is solved by the intersection of this line with the curve $y = 10^x$?

Answer: $10^x = 5\frac{5}{7}x + 1$

(d) Solve simultaneously the equations:

$y = 9x$ *and* $y = 9 - 3x$

Answer: x = 0·75 and y = 6·75 approx.

13

POLAR CO-ORDINATES

THIS system is not so widely used as others, but in certain aspects, *e.g.*, engineering, etc., in which angles are involved, it has great advantages over the Cartesian system.

In this method, instead of the X and Y axes, we have a base line (or initial line) OX and one of the radial lines (*e.g.*, 30°) the "pole", corresponding to the origin in Cartesian co-ordinates (Fig. 102).

If we are plotting, for example, the graph of $r = \sin \theta$, we mark off a suitable scale on the OX axis; a line at 30° to OX from the pole is drawn and the value 0·5, the value of sin 30° is marked off on this radial line, this point (r, θ) represents by its length from the pole the value of sin 30°, *i.e.*, 0·5 according to the scale. If this process is carried out for other values at intervals of 10° the complete graph of $r = \sin \theta$ may be obtained by joining up the points, in this case it is a circle of radius = 0·5.

The angle is known as the "argument" and the radius r as the "modulus". This angle may be expressed in degrees or radians (Figs. 103 and 104).

To take a practical example, imagine a radio transmitter (T) is placed at the pole and the signal strengths are measured at a given distance, *e.g.*, 50 miles. By accepting the strengths received as a decimal fraction of that transmitted, a polar diagram can be constructed as above. If the engineers decide that any reception lower than 0·4 of that at the transmitter is "unsatisfactory reception", by striking a circle radius 0·4 we can see that the shaded portion of our graph is a picture of the area where reception must be improved for the benefit of listeners in that area, such as by special aerial design to overcome the effect on signal strength by hills, tall buildings, factories, etc., which may be the cause of reducing strength in that direction.

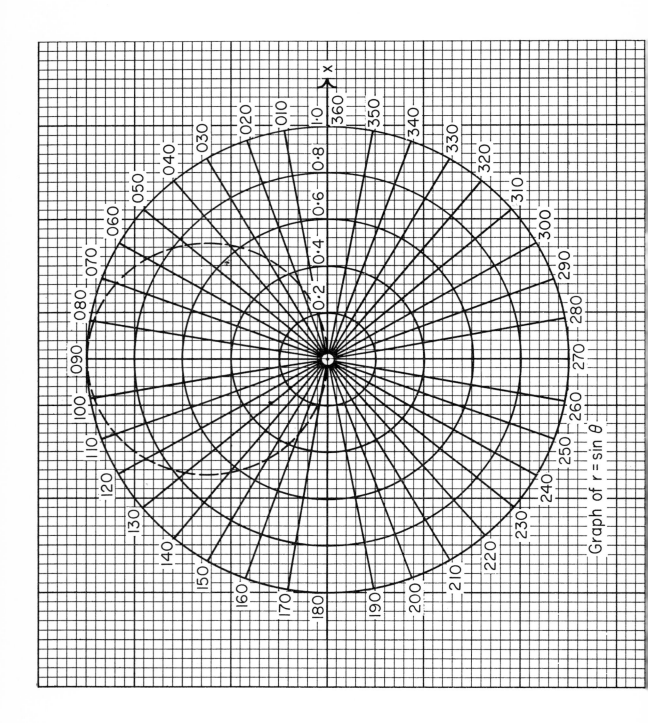

Graph of $r = \sin \theta$

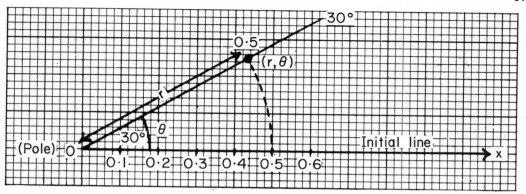

FIGURE 103

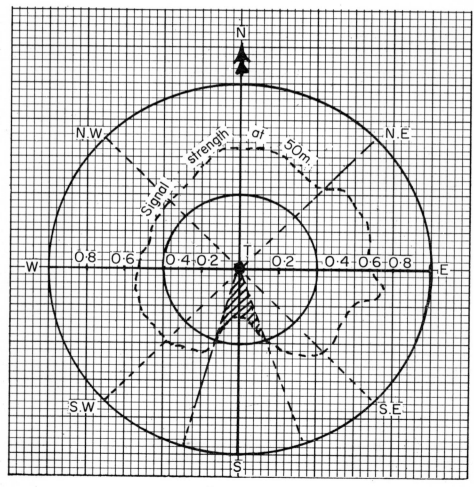

FIGURE 104

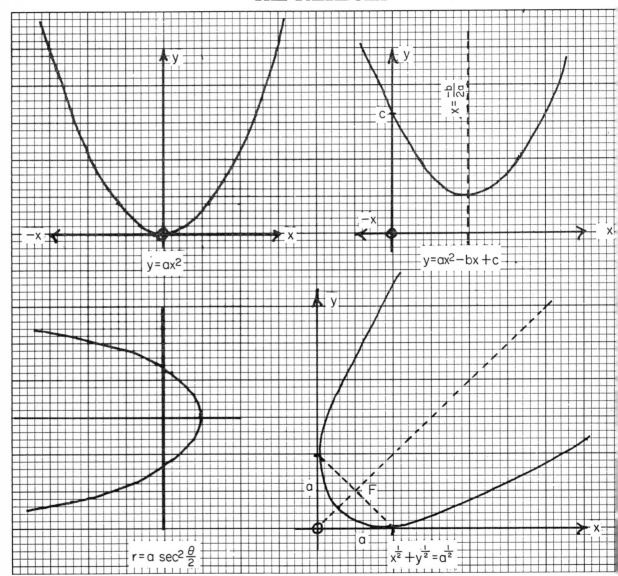

FIGURE 105

A PARABOLA is one of the conic sections and is formed by cutting a cone parallel to a sloping edge. F is the focus of the parabola. The conic sections which Proclus ($c.$ 460 B.C.) says were considered by him were probably the "Menaechmian Triads" of Eratosthenes ($c.$ 230 B.C.). It is said that he obtained them by cutting cones by planes perpendicular to an element—the parabola from a right-angled cone, the hyperbola from an obtuse-angled cone, and the ellipse from an acute-angled cone.

Archimedes (287–212 B.C.) succeeded in squaring a parabola, that is, in proving that the area of a parabolic segment is $\frac{4}{3}$ of the triangle with the same base and vertex, or $\frac{2}{3}$ of the circumscribed parallelogram (*c.* 225 B.C.).

THE HYPERBOLA

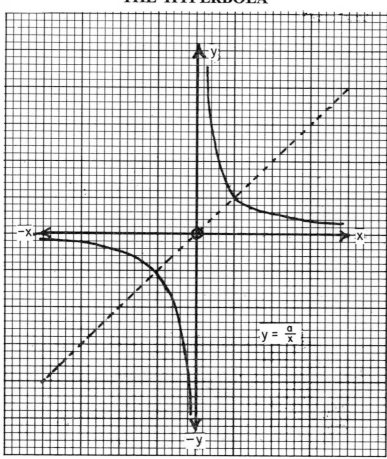

FIGURE 106

This curve, like that of the parabola, is a conic section (see notes on the parabola), and is obtained by passing a plane through a cone, parallel to its vertical axis, *i.e.*, the generator of the cone.

In the case above $\left(y = \dfrac{a}{x}\right)$ the curve is known as a rectangular hyperbola since the two asymptotes (*viz.*, the *X* and *Y* axis) are at right angles to each other. If the two asymptotes are not at right angles then the curve is known as an oblique hyperbola. The form $xy = a^2$ is attributed to Menaechmus (*c.* 350 B.C.).

The fact that the area of the hyperbola $xy = 1$ found by Gregoire de Saint-Vincent (1647) is related to logarithms was recognized by Fermat (1608–1665), and Nicolaus Mercator (1620–1687), one of Denmark's greatest mathematicians, made use of the principle in his calculations of these functions.

THE CUBICAL PARABOLA

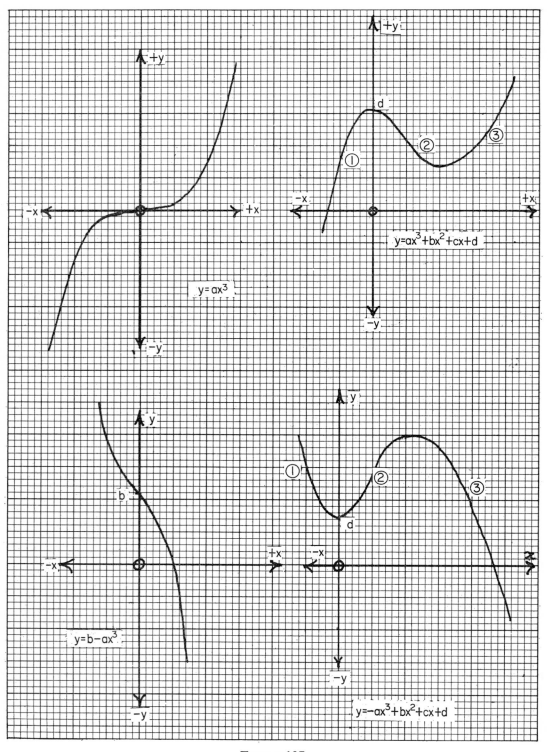

FIGURE 107

For some values of coefficients (*e.g.*, $y = b - ax^3$) the curve may be seen as above, etc., but in general the number of "legs" of the graph will be equal to the highest power of "x" in the equation —hence in the cubic equation we have three "legs" as shown in the above example on the right. The number of "legs" may be less than the highest power for certain coefficients but can never be greater.

THE SEMI-CUBICAL PARABOLA
(Neile's Parabola)

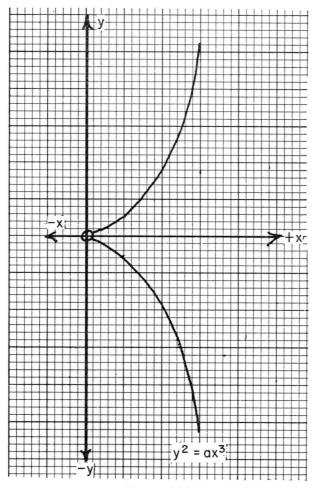

FIGURE 108

William Neile discovered the curve in 1657 and it was later studied by Fermat and Wallis (1659).

THE CYCLOID

Ordinary Case—Vertex at Origin

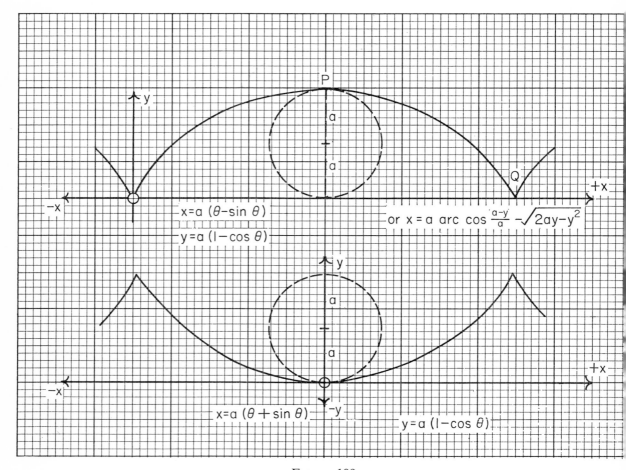

$$x = a\,(\theta - \sin\theta)$$
$$y = a\,(1 - \cos\theta)$$

$$\text{or } x = a \text{ arc } \cos\frac{a-y}{a} - \sqrt{2ay - y^2}$$

$$x = a\,(\theta + \sin\theta)$$
$$y = a\,(1 - \cos\theta)$$

FIGURE 109

At one time this curve was known as the Brachistochrome (the curve of quickest descent) and was first studied by Charles de Bonelles (1501), then by Galileo (1597). It is the locus of a point on the circumference of a circle which rolls without sliding along a straight line. It was later studied by Mersenne (1628) and Roberval (1634); Pascal (1659) called it the roulette, completely solved the problem of its curvature and found the centre of gravity of a segment cut off by a line parallel to the base.

As the equation in Cartesian co-ordinates is very complicated, the form shown in polar co-ordinates is more easily utilized. The length of the curve OPQ is eight times the radius of the generating circle (in this case $= 8a$), whilst the area between the curve OPQ and the straight line is three times the area of the generating circle—this latter factor being established by Roberval in 1634.

The name cycloid is not only linked with that of the Brachistochrome but also with the tauto-chrome; the relationships being studied by Leibnitz, Newton, Christopher Wren, Pierre Fermat and Bernoulli.

THE CATENARY

(Fr. = *chainette*)

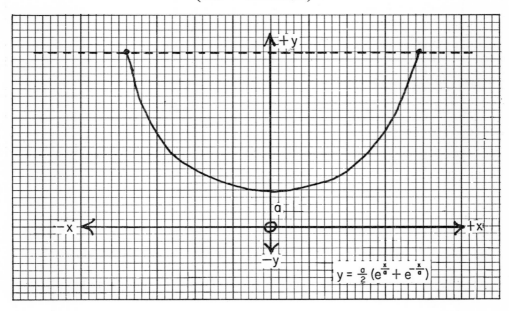

$$y = \frac{a}{2}\left(e^{\frac{x}{a}} + e^{-\frac{x}{a}}\right)$$

FIGURE 110

This is the shape adopted by a heavy cord or chain with its extremities fixed on the same horizontal level.

The name of the curve (catenaria) and the discovery of the equation and its properties are due to Leibnitz in the 17th century (*c.* 1682).

LOGARITHMIC CURVES

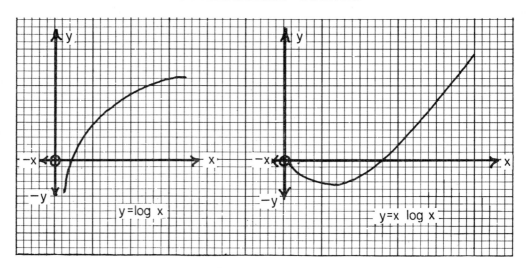

FIGURE 111

LOGARITHMIC OR EQUIANGULAR SPIRAL

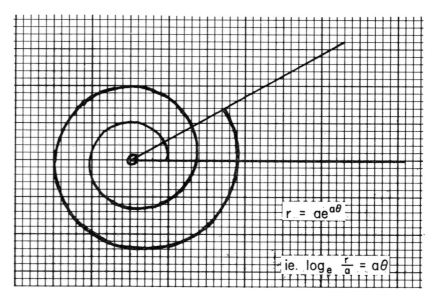

FIGURE 112

Studied by Bernoulli (1692) who spoke of it as a "spira mirabilis". It is still to be seen, in rude form, upon his tomb in Basle.

EXPONENTIAL CURVE AND PROBABILITY CURVE

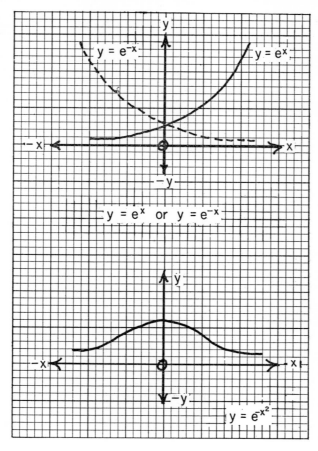

FIGURE 113

(N.B. As e is a constant, these curves may be obtained by putting any constant value in its place

i.e.,
$$y = a^x (\text{or } a^{-x}))$$

SPIRALS

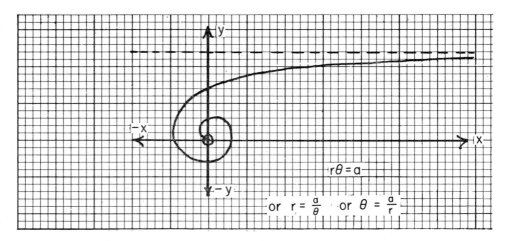

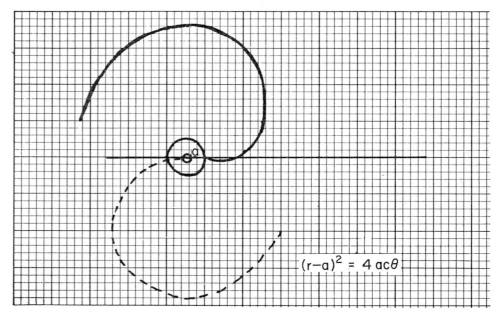

FIGURE 114

The Parabolic Spiral

$$(r - a)^2 = 4ac\theta$$

The Hyperbolic or Reciprocal Spiral

$$r\theta = a$$

$$\text{or} \quad r = \frac{a}{\theta} \quad \text{or} \quad \theta = \frac{a}{r}$$

THE LITUUS

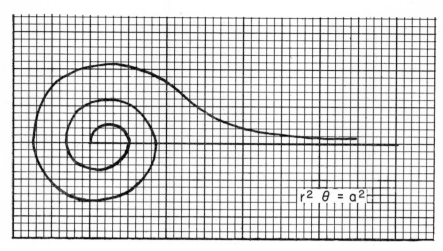

FIGURE 115

The word given to this curve comes from the Latin and means a crosier or crooked staff. Here the angle θ is in radians.

The curve was first studied in 1722 by the English mathematician Roger Cotes, who died at the early age of 45.

THE SPIRAL OF ARCHIMEDES

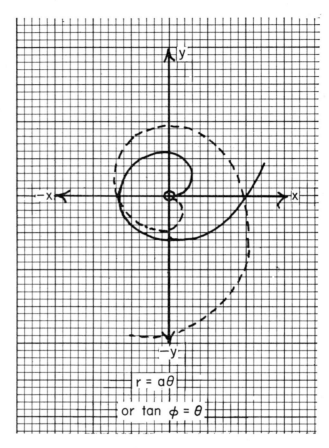

FIGURE 116

Archimedes (c. 225 B.C.) invented this spiral by imagining a hollow tube to rotate uniformly about one end whilst at the same time a particle moves uniformly along the tube. He gave it the name of "Helix" after it had been already studied by his friend Conon of Samos, who may have invented it, as he was influenced by his observations of the coiled basketry work of the Egyptians.

Conon is mentioned by Apollonius (c. 225 B.C.) as having studied the number of points of intersection of two conics.

LEMNISCATES AND ROSES

The Two-Leaved Rose Lemniscate

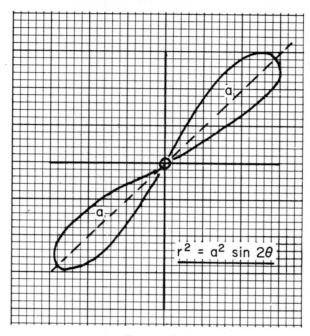

$$r^2 = a^2 \sin 2\theta$$

FIGURE 117

A lemniscate is the technical term given to a curve like the figure "8". This curve was first mentioned by Jacques Bernoulli (1694). Its principal properties were discovered by Fagnans (1750); and its analytical theory by Euler (1751–1752).

The general lemniscate has for its equation:

$$(x^2 + y^2)^2 = 2a^2(x^2 - y^2) + b^4 - a^4$$

and is also known as Cassini's Oval, after Giovanni Domenico (Jean Dominique) Cassini, who described it in 1680.

The Lemniscate of Bernoulli or the Hyperbolic Lemniscate

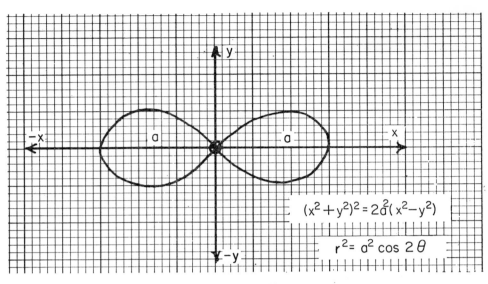

FIGURE 118

This, as mentioned above, was studied by Bernoulli in 1694 and has for its general equation:

$$(x^2 + y^2)^2 = 2a^2(x^2 - y^2)$$

Three-Leaved Roses

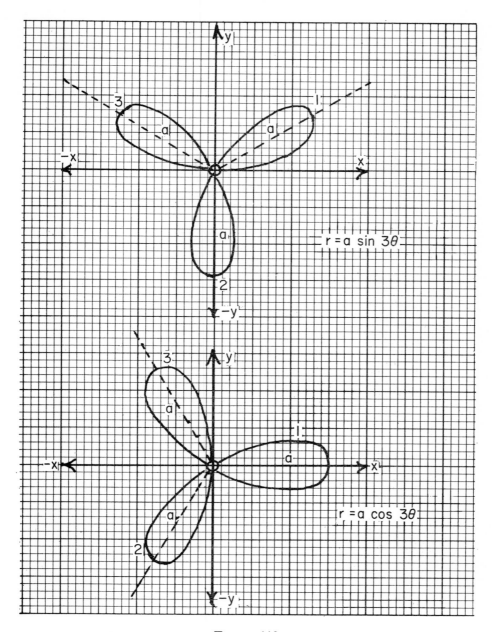

FIGURE 119

N

Four-Leaved Roses

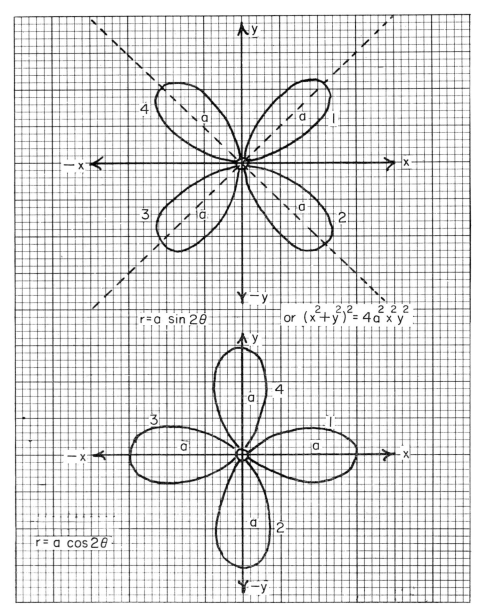

$$r = a \sin 2\theta \qquad \text{or} \qquad (x^2+y^2)^2 = 4a^2 x^2 y^2$$

$$r = a \cos 2\theta$$

FIGURE 120

The Roseate Curve, Rosace or Rhodonea—the latter being due to Guido Grandi (1713)—are the names given to the curve whose general polar equation is:

$$r = a \cos m\,\theta, \text{ or } r = a \sin m\,\theta$$

(see the eight-leaved rose opposite, figure 121).

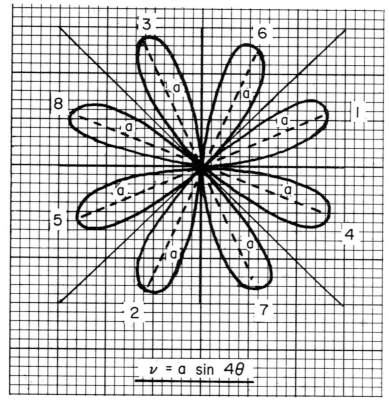

$$\nu = a \sin 4\theta$$

FIGURE 121

THE CONCHOID OF NICOMEDES
(*c.* 180 B.C.)

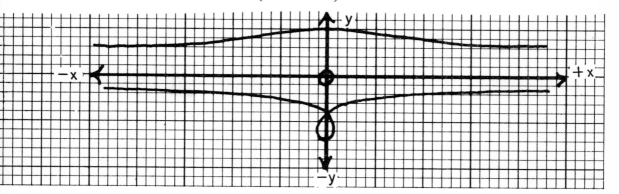

FIGURE 122

$$x^2y^2 = (y + a)^2(b^2 - y^2) \text{ or } (x - a)^2(x^2 + y^2) - b^2x^2 = 0$$

$$r = a \operatorname{cosec} \theta + b \text{ or } r = \frac{a}{\cos \theta} + b$$

This curve known as the "shell-shaped" or "mussel-shaped" curve was invented by him in the study of the trisection of an angle.

The Cartesian equation is:

$$(x - a)^2(x^2 + y^2) - b^2x^2 = 0$$

and the polar equation is:

$$r = \frac{a}{\cos \theta} + b$$

THE FOLIUM OF DESCARTES

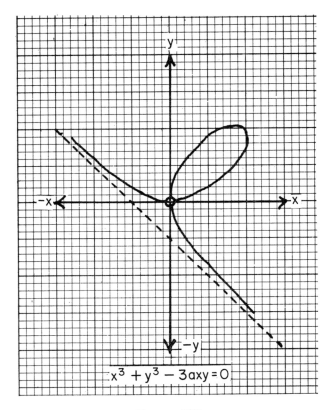

$$x^3 + y^3 - 3axy = 0$$

FIGURE 123

Named after Rene Descartes, a philosopher who was born at La Haye in Touraine. His mathematical contributions included the introduction of Cartesian Co-ordinates and the method of undetermined coefficients (1596–1650).

Roberval mistakenly named it "fleur de jasmin" in determining the tangent to this curve. It is also known as the "noeud de ruban".

THE TRACTRIX

(*Tractoria*)

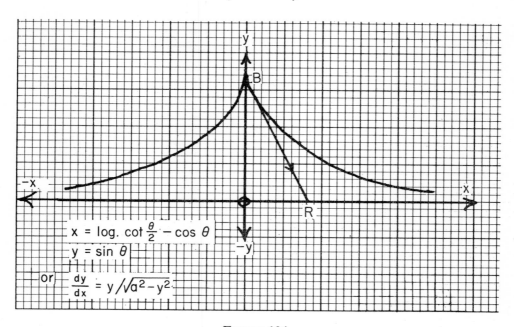

$$x = \log. \cot \frac{\theta}{2} - \cos \theta$$

$$y = \sin \theta$$

or $\dfrac{dy}{dx} = y / \sqrt{a^2 - y^2}$

FIGURE 124

The name is derived from the Latin meaning "to drag" and refers to the fact that the curve would be formed by the weight if a heavy weight hanging from a cord *BO* is moved so that the end of the cord *O* moves along the straight line *OX*. At any instant, therefore, the cord is a tangent to the curve as well as being of constant length, the *X* axis being an asymptote to the curve. This was first studied by Huygens in 1692.

THE CARDIOID

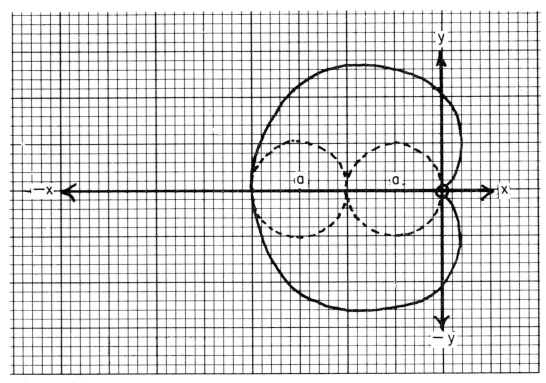

FIGURE 125

The Greek name is given to this curve because of its heart-like shape. Geometrically it can be drawn by plotting the path of a point on the circumference of one circle which is rolling, without sliding, round another fixed circle of equal radius. Hence in moving once round the fixed circle the moving circle makes two revolutions. This curve was first studied by the Dutchman Koersma in 1689.

THE CISSOID OF DIOCLES

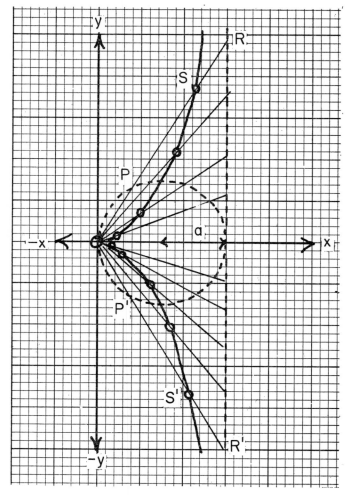

FIGURE 126

In this curve the constant term a is the radius of the generating circle and if any line is drawn from O to the asymptote to the curve (*i.e.*, the tangent to the circle) and the distance RS is made equal to the chord OP, then the curve can be drawn geometrically.

The area between the asymptote and the curve is three times that of the generating circle.

The word "cissoid" comes from the Greek and means "ivy-like". The curve is said to have been invented by Diocles (*c.* 180 B.C.) to solve the problem of duplicating a cube, or finding how to construct a cube double the volume of another cube.

THE COCKED HAT

(Fr. = *bicorne*)

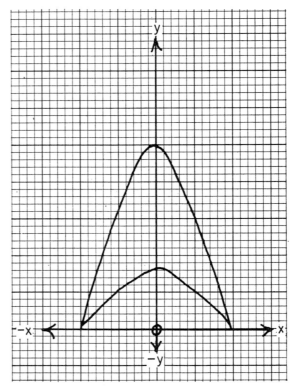

FIGURE 127

In its expanded form the equation is:

$$x^4 - 2x^2 + 4x^2y + x^2y^2 - 4y + 3y^2 + 1 = 0$$

or:

$$x^2 + \left(\frac{a^2x^2}{y} - 2a\right)^2 - a^2 = 0$$

It was first given this name in the *Educational Times* in 1896, the modern name being due to Sylvester.

THE LIMAÇON
(A Snail)

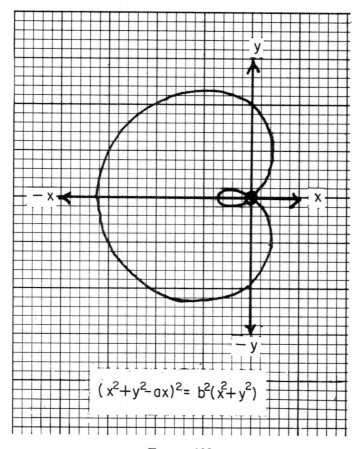

$$(x^2 + y^2 - ax)^2 = b^2(x^2 + y^2)$$

FIGURE 128

Called by the French "conchoide du cercle"; its general equation being:

$$(x^2 + y^2 - ax)^2 = b^2(x^2 + y^2)$$

Roberval called it the Limaçon of Pascal as Etienne Pascal had discovered it. German writers describe it as "Paschal'sche Schnecke".

THE STROPHOID

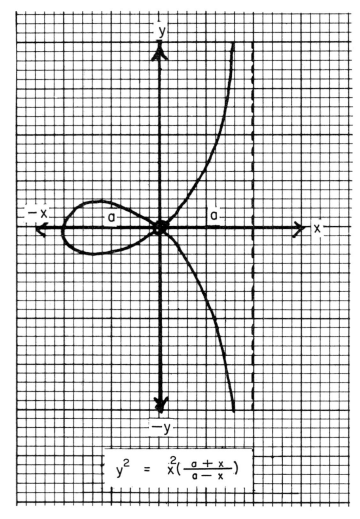

$$y^2 = x^2\left(\frac{a+x}{a-x}\right)$$

FIGURE 129

The name was proposed by Montucci (1846). Lehmus in 1842 proposed the name "kukemaeide" or "cucumber seed"—other names have also been used.

The curve has been studied by Barrow, Jean Bernoulli, Agnesi (1748), James Booth (1858) and others.

THE WITCH OF AGNESI

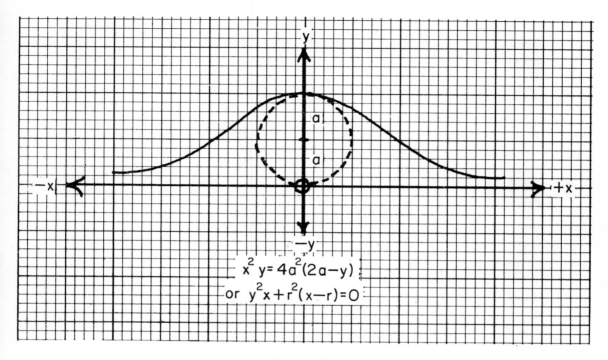

$$x^2 y = 4a^2(2a - y)$$
$$\text{or } y^2 x + r^2(x - r) = 0$$

FIGURE 130

This curve is sometimes known as the "Cubique d'Agnesi" or "Agnesienne" as it was discovered by Maria Agnesi in 1748, who occupied for a time the chair of mathematics in the University of Bologna.

THE COCHLIOID

$r = \dfrac{a \sin \theta}{\theta}$ is a spiral curve studied by Perk (1700) and due to Neuberg, a Belgian geometer. The name originated in 1884 with two recent writers Bentham and Falkenburg.

THE CONCHOID OF DE SLUZE

This was first constructed by René de Sluze (1662) and is a cubic curve

$$a(r \cos \theta - a) = k^2 \cos^2 \theta$$

or:

$$a(x - a)(x^2 + y^2) - k^2 x^2 = 0$$

THE CURVE OF PURSUIT

(Fr. *courbe du chien*)

The name "ligne de poursuite" is apparently due to Pierre Bourguer (1732) although the curve had been noticed by Leonardo da Vinci.

THE DEVIL'S CURVE

(Fr. *courbe du diable*)

The general equation of this is $y^4 - x^4 + ay^2 + bx^2 = 0$, the polar equation being

$$r = 2a\sqrt{\frac{25 - 24\tan^2\theta}{1 - \tan^2\theta}}$$

from the particular equation

$$y^4 - x^4 - 96a^2y^2 + 100a^2x^2 = 0$$

It was studied by Cramer (1750) and Lacroix (1810).

THE ELASTIC CURVE

(Fr. *courbe élastique*)

This was first studied by Jacques Bernoulli (1703), the differential equation being:

$$dy = \frac{x^2dx}{\sqrt{a^4 - x^4}}$$

THE EPICYCLOID

The epicycloid is a curve traced by a point on a circle which rolls on the convex side of a given circle. Its equation is $(x^2 + y^2 - a^2) = 4a[(x - a)^2 + y^2]$ and has been studied by Hipparchus (*c.* 140 B.C.), Albrecht Dürer (1525) who described it for the first time in a printed work, Désargues (1635), Lahire (1694) and Euler (1781).

THE HYPOCYCLOID OF FOUR CUSPS

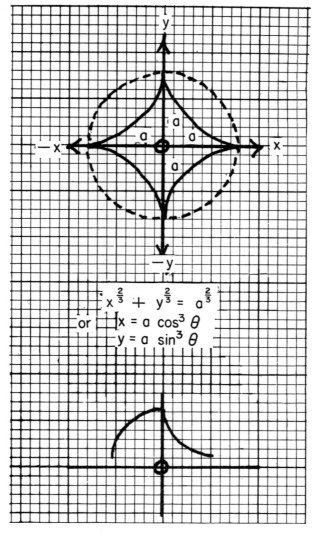

$$x^{\frac{2}{3}} + y^{\frac{2}{3}} = a^{\frac{2}{3}}$$

or

$$x = a \cos^3 \theta$$
$$y = a \sin^3 \theta$$

FIGURE 131

A hypocycloid curve is that produced by the locus of a point on the circumference of a circle which is rolled around *inside* a larger circle, *e.g.*, the shape of the sides of the teeth of a watch pinion.

THE EVOLUTE OF ELLIPSE

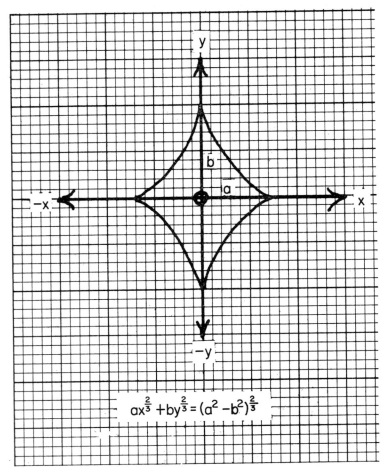

FIGURE 132

The locus of the centres of curvature of a given curve is called the evolute of that curve. An approximate construction of the evolute of a curve can be made by estimating (from the shape of the curve) the lengths of the radii of curvature at different points on the curve and then drawing them in and drawing the locus of the centres of curvature.

AN INVOLUTE CURVE

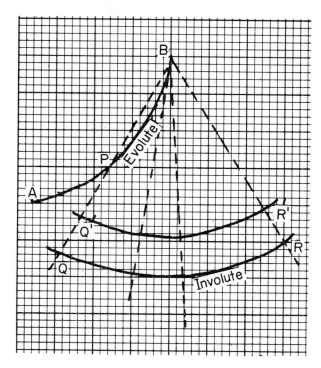

FIGURE 133

If a round flexible ruler be bent in the form of the evolute curve AB and if a string with one end fastened at B be wrapped around the ruler, it is clear that when the string is unwound and kept taut the free end will describe the curve QR. Hence the name involute. The curve QR is said to be the involute of AB. Obviously any point on the string will describe an involute so that a given curve has an infinite number of involutes but only one evolute. The involutes (*e.g.*, QR and $Q'R'$) are called parallel curves since the distance between any two of them measured along their common normals is constant.

PEARLS

A name given by Pascal and de Sluze to the curves whose equation is

$$p + q - ry^r = x^p (a - x)^q$$

or in particular

$$a^2y = x^2(a - x)$$

De Sluze suggested them to Huygens (1658) who studied them carefully.

THE SERPENTINE CURVE

A name proposed by Newton for the curve of

$$y = \frac{abx}{a^2 + x^2}$$

THE SPIRAL OF FERMAT

$r^2 = \theta$ is a curve first proposed by Fermat to Mersenne in 1636.